Th   **ss:**

©Hans-Christian Andersen, Caroline Barras, Helen M Douglas, Nigel Evans, Gill Forster, David Grant, Ken Harrop, David Holding, Janice McMillan, Bridget Major, Stephen Mason, Amanda Miller, Graham Mowl, Julia Sharpley, Richard Sharpley, Alain Young 2002

ISBN 1 901888 23 1

First published 2002
  Reprinted 2004

Cover Design Tim Murphy Creative Solutions

Published in Great Britain by
Business Education Publishers Limited
The Teleport
Doxford International
Sunderland
SR3 3XD

Tel: 0191 5252410
Fax: 0191 5201815

British Cataloguing-in-Publications Data
A catalogue record for this book is available from the British Library

Printed in Great Britain by The Alden Group, Oxford.

Preface

Over the last twenty years or so, tourism has undergone enormous changes and development. As an activity participated in by millions of people, it has continued to grow both in scale and spread – the absolute volume of international tourist arrivals continues to grow year on year (and is forecast to do so for the foreseeable future) – whilst the number of countries both generating and attracting tourists also continues to grow. Indeed, few, if any, countries are not now international tourist destinations. At the same time, the tourism industry has also changed beyond all recognition both in terms of its structure and operations. The integration of operations and businesses, whether through acquisition or the formation of alliances, has resulted in truly global industry, whilst the manner in which businesses operate has been influenced or has had to respond to political, technological and legislative change. Moreover, new challenges continually emerge – at the time of writing, for example, the combined effects of the foot and mouth crisis throughout 2001 and the terrorist attacks in the USA on September 11th 2001 have resulted in enormous problems for the UK tourism industry as a whole.

The study of tourism has also changed remarkably since the early 1980s. Not only is it now widely offered as a university degree course at both undergraduate and postgraduate levels, as well as in sixth forms and further education colleges, but the level of knowledge and understanding of tourism from a variety of disciplinary backgrounds has also increased remarkably. Consequentially, the last ten years have witnessed nothing less than an explosion in the number of tourism text books available, as well as the introduction of a large number of tourism academic journals. To a great extent, this expansion in the tourism literature has been characterised by increasing focus and specialisation. That is, many new books address specific issues or topics from either a sectoral, tourist activity or destinational point of view, whilst tourism journals are firmly rooted within a particular discipline, such as economics, marketing or cultural studies.

This is not to say that more generalist books or journals are no longer being produced. However, there are few, if any books available to the student of tourism that are, in effect, course texts which recognise the fact that tourism is most commonly taught and studied within a business context. For example, over half of the undergraduate courses at British universities are located within business schools and most, if not all, such courses, particularly in the first year, combine general business modules with tourism specific ones. At the same time, few tourism courses ignore the tourism industry or the more general role of tourism as an economic sector – that is, as a global business.

This book aims to fulfil this need. Its overall focus is upon tourism as a business, a business which is made up of a diverse array of different sectors, such as airlines, tour operators and accommodation providers, which all face some issues and challenges that are both unique to each sector but others that are common to all businesses and organisations within tourism. Thus, it introduces the reader to the structure and operations of the tourism industry, but also addresses a variety of broader issues that influence all tourism businesses, such as legislative requirements, financial management, economics, human resource issues and marketing, and that are commonly included in tourism courses. Indeed, this book is based on the longstanding BA(Hons) Travel and Tourism Management degree programme at the University of Northumbria and the chapters are written by colleagues who contribute to the teaching of that course.

Given the diversity of topics covered, albeit within the context of the tourism business, each chapter is intended to be more of a guide to the main themes, issues, concepts and challenges relevant to its subject rather than an in-depth and detailed analysis. Therefore, each chapter includes suggested further reading and students are encouraged to explore particular issues in more depth by reading more specialised literature, including those sources referred to in each chapter. Additionally, each chapter also provides suggested discussion topics which draw on the principal themes covered.

As with any book of this nature, thanks are due to a variety of individuals who have, in one way or another, contributed to it. In particular, however, I would firstly like to thank Business Education Publishers, in particular Andrea Murphy and Moira Page, for their support and help in this project. Secondly, my sincere thanks must go to all my colleagues at the University of Northumbria who have produced chapters for this book – the concept and the content depended on your contributions and, literally, the book could not have been written without you.

Richard Sharpley
Centre for Travel and Tourism, University of Northumbria

Contributors

Dr. Hans-Christian Andersen is Senior Lecturer in Travel and Tourism Management, University of Northumbria.

Caroline Barras, formerly Lecturer in Tourism at Newcastle College, is Groups Product Manager at DFDS.

Helen Douglas is Principal Lecturer in Human Resources, University of Northumbria.

Nigel Evans is Principal Lecturer in Travel and Tourism Management, University of Northumbria.

Professor David Grant is Director of the Travel Law Centre, University of Northumbria.

Gill Forster is Senior Lecturer in Human Resources, University of Northumbria.

Dr. Ken Harrop is Principal Lecturer in Politics, University of Northumbria.

David Holding is Senior Lecturer in Transport, University of Northumbria.

Bridget Major is Senior Lecturer in Travel and Tourism Management, University of Northumbria.

Stephen Mason is Senior Partner at Mason Bond, Solicitors, Leeds.

Dr. Janice McMillan is Senior Lecturer in Politics, University of Northumbria.

Amanda Miller, formerly at the University of Northumbria, is Lecturer in Tourism at Manchester Metropolitan University.

Graham Mowl is Senior Lecturer in Geography, University of Northumbria.

Julia Sharpley is Senior Lecturer in Travel and Tourism Management, University of Northumbria.

Dr. Richard Sharpley is Reader, Travel and Tourism Management, University of Northumbria.

Alain Young is Senior Lecturer in Travel and Tourism Management, University of Northumbria.

Table of Contents

List of Figures

List of Tables

Chapter 17

Section 1

An Introduction to Travel and Tourism

The focus of this book is the tourism business. That is, it is principally concerned with introducing and exploring the operations, planning and management of those businesses and organisations that directly supply, or support the provision of, the tourism 'product' or tourist experiences. In doing so, two broad perspectives are adopted. Firstly, it considers the tourism industry from the point of view of the specific sectors that comprise it and, secondly, it addresses the broader framework and planning/management issues common to all sectors of the industry.

However, the tourism business can only be fully understood in the context of the market that it is supplying – tourism and tourists. Therefore, as both a logical and essential starting point, this section of the book introduces the reader to the modern, global phenomenon of tourism. The first chapter defines tourism and demonstrates the scale and value of tourism as both a social and economic activity before going on to explore the role and importance of the tourism business within the overall tourism system. Subsequent chapters then broadly consider the demand for tourism in terms of its historical growth and 'democratisation' as a modern-day, mass activity, the present state of world tourism with respect to major markets, destinations and tourist flows and, finally, the nature and characteristics of tourism demand at the level of the individual tourist. Thus, this first section provides the foundation and the framework the rest of the book.

Tourism: Definitions and Concepts

Richard Sharpley

Learning objectives

This chapter introduces a variety of concepts and definitions, providing a foundational framework for the study of tourism. It enables the reader to:

- *appreciate the nature and scope of tourism*

- *define, both technically and conceptually, the meaning of tourism*

- *explain the importance of tourism as a business*

- *define and identify the constituent elements of the tourism system*

Introduction

Tourism is frequently and justifiably described as a major phenomenon of modern times. The number of international tourist arrivals has grown spectacularly, from just 25 million in 1950 to over 664 million by the end of the last century, representing an annual growth rate of 7 percent (WTO 2000). Receipts from international tourism have also increased remarkably – in 1950, international tourism generated US$2.1 billion, a figure which had risen to US$455 billion by 1999. At the same time, tourism has also spread dramatically, to the extent that few, if any, countries are not now tourism destinations. In 1950, just 15 countries accounted for almost all international arrivals but, by 1999, more than 70 countries attracted over one million arrivals, whilst even remote areas, such as Antarctica, now attract significant numbers of tourists each year.

However, these figures alone do not define what tourism is all about; despite its scale, scope and value and its global presence, tourism still means different things to different people. To many, of course, tourism is synonymous with holiday-taking, a time to escape and relax, whilst for those who work in the multitude of businesses that enable others to be tourists, it is their job and livelihood. Equally, people who live in destination areas may view tourism as a necessary evil to be endured whilst, at the national level, many governments consider tourism to be a vital element of economic and social development policies. Inevitably then, definitions of tourism and tourists abound.

The purpose of this introductory chapter, therefore, is to explore the meaning and scope of tourism as an essential foundation to the subsequent chapters in this book. In so doing, it will highlight the fact that tourism is essentially a social activity which involves millions of individuals travelling either within their own country or overseas. At the same time, however, tourism is big business. That is, most destinations do not welcome tourists for philanthropic reasons. Rather, tourism is developed primarily for its potential contribution, through tourists' expenditure, to local and national economies whilst, in both destinations and tourism generating countries, a vast and diverse array of organisations and businesses enable and facilitate people's participation in tourism.

In short, the driving force behind the development and promotion of tourism is economic gain through the profitable satisfaction of tourists' needs. It is, therefore, logical that the study of tourism should focus, as this book does, on tourism as a business. The first question to ask, however, is why study tourism in the first place?

Why study tourism?

Tourism has been the subject of academic interest for well over fifty years, although it is only more recently that it has been offered as a specific course of study. As a relatively new subject area it suffers a number of weaknesses, such as a lack of definitional consensus or formal theoretical underpinning enjoyed by other, more traditional disciplines (see Cooper *et al* 1998: 3), yet there is no denying its popularity amongst students. At the same time, as academics from a variety of disciplinary backgrounds increasingly contribute to knowledge and understanding of tourism, the subject is gaining increasing academic credibility. Nevertheless, the reason for studying tourism remains the subject of intense debate.

On the one hand, it can be argued that the study of tourism is primarily vocational; that is, it prepares students for careers in travel and tourism. To an extent, this is indeed the case, as significant numbers of tourism students subsequently secure jobs within the industry. On the other hand, there is also a variety of reasons why tourism is deserving of academic study in its own right:

- It is a major social phenomenon, the largest peacetime movement of people within and between countries that the world has known. The study of tourism provides an understanding of the nature of this movement, what drives it, and its consequences.

- Tourism has significant economic, environmental, social and cultural consequences for destination areas and communities. Whilst a recognition of these consequences contributes to the more effective management of tourism, it also contextualises the role of tourism in broader social and economic change and development at the national and international level.

- Tourism is often claimed to be the world's largest industry. Although its identity as an 'industry' is debatable (see below), there is no doubting the significant contribution tourism makes to the global economy and its interdependence with other economic sectors.

- Tourism provides a focus for an enormous variety of issues, whether environmental, political, social, economic, legal, or cultural, and is relevant to the challenges of planning and development, effective business management, and governance. In other words, tourism is, in a sense, woven into the fabric of national and global economic, political and social systems and, therefore, provides a valid basis for the study of those systems.

More generally, of course, as tourism has become increasingly 'democratised', or available to the masses (see Chapter 2), it has become part of most people's lives. Therefore, it could also be argued that an activity of such prevalence, as well as the industry that supports and enables it, is deserving of academic study.

Definitions of tourism

Such has been the growth and spread of tourism over the last fifty years that it is now 'so widespread and ubiquitous... that there are scarcely people left in the world who would not recognise a tourist immediately' (Cohen 1974). However, recognising someone as a tourist and defining who or what a tourist, or tourism, is are different matters and, given the rather abstract nature of the concept of tourism (Burns and Holden 1995), it is not surprising that there are varying and numerous definitions.

As a starting point, Chambers English Dictionary (1988) refers to tourism as 'the activities of tourists and those who cater for them', a tourist being someone who simply 'makes a tour... a sightseeing traveller or a sportsman'. More usefully, perhaps, the Oxford Concise Dictionary (2000) suggests that tourism is:

> *the organisation and operation of (especially foreign) holidays... as a commercial enterprise*

whilst a tourist is defined as:

> *a person making a visit or tour as a holiday; a traveller, especially abroad.*

In both cases, a distinction is made between the tourist as, implicitly, someone on holiday, and tourism as the process or industry that enables people to be tourists. However, neither fully embraces the true scope and meaning of tourism as either a social activity or a business, whilst the specificity of the definitions leaves many questions unanswered. For example, tourism implicitly involves travel (although it can be argued that 'armchair travel' – that is, watching travel programmes on television or reading a travel book – is a legitimate form of tourism), but how far does a person have to travel to be a tourist? Does travel have to be international, and for how long? Is a traveller always a tourist? Does tourism always necessarily require the involvement of commercial organisations?

As we shall see shortly, a number of definitions have been proposed that attempt to address these and other questions. However, the dictionary definitions cited above undoubtedly reflect the most widely held (though not necessarily accurate) perception that tourism is, essentially, the process or activity of holiday-making. Therefore, an initial way of exploring what tourism involves is to consider it in the context of one of the most commonly used tools employed by the tourism industry, namely, the ubiquitous tourist brochure.

The significance of the brochure

Despite the advent of e.commerce and increasing popularity of the Internet (see Chapter 18), the tourist brochure remains the primary means through which tour operators sell holidays. At the same time, browsing through brochures is often an essential part of a tourist's holiday purchasing process; indeed, as discussed in Chapter 4, planning or anticipating the holiday is all part of the overall tourism experience. However, the brochure is more than a medium through which holidays are bought and sold, for it is indicative of the breadth and scope of tourism, particularly as a subject of study. Not only does it embrace the role of the tourist, epitomising what many consider to be the social activity of tourism, but it also points to the scale and complexity of the business of tourism. The contribution of the brochure to the understanding of tourism is summarised in Figure 1.1.

Figure 1.1: *Brochures and the meaning of tourism*

Significance	Relevance to the understanding of tourism
Travel	Brochures signify travel, usually overseas and usually by air, to places that are distant, different or exotic. Thus, tourism involves physical movement to a new place, bringing tourists into contact with people from different societies and cultures.
Escape/relaxation	Typically, the pictures in brochures imply that tourism enables people to escape, relax and have fun in destinations where the sun is always shining. Thus, tourism also involves mental/psychological movement to new places.
Expenditure	Tourism is an expenditure driven activity, as signified by prices quoted in brochures. Tourists often pay significant sums of money in the pursuit of tourism experiences; their expenditure contributes to the global economic value of tourism.
International	Most brochures sell holidays in a variety of countries, signifying that tourism is an international/global activity and business. It also points to the challenge of selling a product (a holiday) that is consumed in another country.
Sectoral	Brochures highlight the different elements of a package holiday – accommodation, transport (flights and transfers), entertainment, activities, refreshment, insurance, and so on. In short, tourism involves a diverse array of businesses which collectively produce the holiday.
Promotion	Brochures attempt to sell holidays profitably whilst satisfying the needs and perceptions of tourists. Thus, from the industry perspective, tourism is a commercial activity driven primarily by the need make a profit.
Legislation	The brochure content is regulated by law; both the operator and the tourist are bound by the contract made between them and, thus, tourism is a highly regulated business/activity.
Environment	Brochures display pristine environments, and the success of tourism is dependent on maintaining an attractive environment for tourists. Thus, tourism is an ecological phenomenon in that it impacts upon and interacts with its environment.

Typically, brochures suggest that tourists are motivated by the desire to escape on holiday to places, usually by air, where they can unwind and relax, and that there is a complex, multi-faceted industry which can satisfy their needs. However, whilst this is undoubtedly one aspect of tourism, it is not the only one. In other words, the 'tourism' epitomised by the tourist brochure exacerbates a number of myths about tourism which contribute, according to Cooper *et al* (1998: 2), to its unrealistic 'glamorous' image. In particular:

- Although it is international tourism that has the higher profile, domestic tourism (people travelling in their own country) is more predominant. It has been estimated that, globally, the total number of domestic tourism trips is between six to ten times greater than the number of international trips.

- Although air travel is more 'glamorous', the great majority of tourist trips involve surface travel, particularly by car.

- Although staying away is frequently an integral element of a tourism experience, in many countries day trips account for a significant proportion of trips and spending. In the UK, for example, day visits generated £38 billion in 1999, almost 60 percent of the total of £64 billion earned from all tourism that year.

- Although tourism is synonymous with leisure travel, many forms of tourism, such as business, are non-leisure related.

Already, then, tourism is evidently a much broader concept than is initially apparent. Nevertheless, a variety of definitions have attempted to embrace both the 'technical' aspects of tourism and it essence or meaning as a social activity.

Tourism: technical vs. conceptual definitions

There are two main groups or classifications of tourism definitions, often referred to as *technical* and *conceptual* definitions (Burkhart and Medlik 1981: 41-43).

(a) Technical definitions

Technical definitions attempt to identify different categories of tourist (and non-tourists) and different tourism activities, principally for statistical or legislative purposes. In other words, they are primarily designed to set the criteria by which tourism activity can be measured and recorded. The first such definition, proposed by a group of statisticians at the League of Nations in 1937, defined a tourist simply as someone who travels for 24 hours or more outside their normal country of residence. This definition included those travelling on business in addition to travel for pleasure, health or other reasons, and also introduced the concept of the 'excursionist' as someone who stayed in a country for less than 24 hours (for example, someone on a cruise holiday). Domestic tourists, however, were not included in the definition.

A similar definition, though utilising the more general term 'visitor', was suggested in 1963 by the International Union of Official Travel Organisations (IUOTO), the precursor to the World Tourism Organisations (WTO). It states that a visitor is:

> *any person visiting a country other than that in which he has his usual place of residence, for any reason other than following an occupation remunerated from within the country visited.*

Within this definition, visitors are sub-categorised as either tourists, who stay overnight, or excursionists on day visits. Again, however, domestic tourism is overlooked, an omission which the Tourism Society in the UK attempted to rectify in its definition of tourism:

> *Tourism is the temporary short-term movement of people to destinations outside the places where they normally live and work, and their activities during their stay at these destinations; it includes movement for all purposes, as well as day visits or excursions.*

Although including domestic tourism, this definition is still problematic inasmuch as not only does it include virtually any activity as tourism as long as it includes travel, but also the home environment and the necessary distance to travel to qualify as a tourist are not clarified. Nevertheless, it does demonstrate how broad a definition must be in order to cover all aspects of tourism.

In an attempt to provide set criteria in order to standardise the statistical measurement of tourism (the premise being that global tourism can only be measured accurately if all countries work to identical parameters), the WTO has published recommendations for the collection of technical data on tourism (WTO/UNSTAT 1994). These set out a variety of conditions, including:

- Minimum and maximum lengths of stay – one night and one year respectively (with the exception of day visitors/excursionists)

- Distance from the normal home environment – 160 km

- Purpose of visit categories. Most commonly, these include holidays, business, visiting friends and relatives (VFR) and 'other', although more specific purposes are also identified (see Figure 1.2)

Importantly, it demonstrates that tourism embraces a much wider set of activities and purposes than the more traditional perception of tourism as a leisure activity allows for.

Figure 1.2: *Technical definition of a tourist*

To be included in tourism statistics		Not to be included in tourism statistics
Category	Purpose	Category
Tourists:	Holidays	Border workers
non-residents	business	Transit passengers
nationals resident abroad	health	Nomads
crew members	study	Refugees
	meetings/missions	Members of armed forces
Excursionists:	VFR	Diplomats
cruise passengers	religion	Temporary immigrants
day visitors	sport	Permanent immigrants
crews	others	

Source: adapted from WTO (1994)

(b) Conceptual definitions

In contrast to technical, measurement-based definitions, conceptual definitions attempt to convey the meaning of tourism from the point of view of the individual tourist. That is, they attempt to address the role or function of tourism as a particular element of social life. Thus, it has been suggested that a tourist is a 'temporarily leisured person who voluntarily visits a place for the purpose of experiencing a change' (Smith 1989:1). Similarly, Graburn (1983) proposes that tourism 'involves for the participants a separation from normal 'instrumental' life and the business of making a living, and offers entry into another kind of moral state in which mental, expressive and cultural needs come to the fore'. In both cases, the emphasis is very much placed on tourism as a leisure activity, in particular one which acts as a contrast or safety valve to the pressure of normal, everyday working life. This, of course, excludes many of the non-leisure purposes of tourism referred to in Figure 1.2 but is, perhaps, more in accordance with popularly held perceptions of tourism.

It is evident, then, that it is difficult, if not impossible, to propose a single, all-embracing definition of tourism. Essentially, it is a social activity, in that it involves the voluntary movement of people, with the following characteristics:

- It is normally considered a leisure activity, although for statistical purposes some forms of non-leisure travel, such as pilgrimage, or business travel are also recognised forms of tourism.

- It normally occurs outside the usual place of residence and work; that is, it is associated with a change of location and escape from the routine or ordinary.

- it is a short-term activity or condition; the intention is always to return home.

- it is socially patterned. That is, participation in tourism and the choice of holiday or trip is influenced by a tourist's socio-cultural and demographic characteristics, including age, wealth, education, and gender.

Nevertheless, as already suggested, tourism as a social activity could not occur on the international scale that it does today without the support of the so-called tourism industry. Indeed, just as the dictionary definitions of tourism cited earlier in this chapter refer to tourism as the commercial organisation and operation of holidays, it is important to view the industry as an integral element of the modern phenomenon of tourism. In other words, tourism is as much about the businesses and organisations that facilitate tourism as it is about the activities of tourists themselves and, therefore the study of tourism should embrace both 'the study of man [sic] away from his usual habitat [and] of the industry which responds to his needs' (Jafari 1997). Therefore, having looked at definitions of tourism as a social activity, the following section considers tourism from an industry/business point of view.

The business of tourism

As pointed out earlier, tourism is big business; in fact, many would claim that tourism is the world's biggest business or industry. As we consider shortly, it is not perhaps appropriate to describe it as an 'industry' in its own right but, nevertheless, there is no doubting the global economic importance. International tourism receipts alone (that is, the total spending by tourists on overseas visits) amounted to US$455 billion in 1999 and, if current forecasts prove to be correct, that figure could rise to US$2 trillion by 2020 (WTO 1998). If international fare receipts (receipts related to passenger transport of residents of other countries) are added to the value of tourism receipts, then international tourism in 1999 was an export market worth some US$532 billion. (International tourism is an export, in that a country sells its 'product' to overseas customers in return for foreign exchange earnings. Uniquely, however, tourism is not physically exported – instead, tourists 'consume' the product – tourism services – in the country where it is produced.)

As Table 1.1 shows, in 1999 international tourism was the world's most valuable export category, generating US$7 billion more than the second highest export category, namely, automotive products.

Table 1.1: *Worldwide export earnings 1998*

		US$ billion	%
	Total worldwide exports: goods and services	6,738	100.0
1	Tourism: International tourism receipts	441	6.5
	International fare receipts	91	1.3
	Total tourism:	*532*	*7.9*
2	Automotive products	525	7.8
3	Chemicals	503	7.5
4	Food	443	6.6
5	Computers/office equipment	399	5.9
6	Fuels	344	5.1
7	Textiles/clothing	331	4.9
8	Telecommunications equipment	283	4.2

Source: adapted from WTO (2000)

However, international tourism is, of course, only part of the picture. If the value of all domestic tourism that occurs globally is added, then it has been estimated that tourism as a whole generates a staggering US$ 4,000 million, a figure which, according to the World Travel and Tourism Council (WTTC), could reach US$7,500 million by 2006. This would represent 11.4 percent of global GDP. At the same time, it has been suggested that, by then, over 380 million people will directly and indirectly depend on tourism for employment.

Of course, such vast figures are, at best, only estimates – given the scale and diversity of tourism, the paucity of accurate statistics in many countries and the difficulty in defining what businesses actually contribute to tourism, it is unlikely that the true value of tourism worldwide could ever be calculated. Nevertheless, even at the national level the economic importance of tourism is evident. In the UK, for example, tourism makes a significant contribution to the national economy (see Table 1.2).

The value of the global tourism business is, therefore indisputable; the nature or structure of the business is, however, less clear. In other words, the myriad of businesses and organisations that collectively provide tourist services and enable people to participate in tourism is often referred to as the tourism industry, but the extent to which this is a valid description is debatable.

Table 1.2: *Contribution of tourism to the UK economy*

Total revenue from tourism	£64 billion
(of which: foreign exchange earnings)	*£12.5 billion*
Tourism: contribution to GDP	4%
Tourism: contribution to employment	7% of workforce
Tourism: tax contribution to economy	£1.5 billion

Tourism: an industry?

An industry is normally considered to be a single, clearly identifiable economic activity with particular production methods, recognisable chains of supply and specific products or outputs. Thus, for example, the oil industry embraces exploration, drilling, refining and the production of oil products, some of which are sold as end products, such as petrol, and others which are supplied as inputs to other industries. Similarly, the automobile industry is in the business of designing, manufacturing and selling cars, and is comprised of car manufactures, such as Ford and General Motors, and the multitude of smaller businesses that supply products or parts to them.

In the case of tourism, the inputs, products, methods of production and chains of supply are much less clear (see Mill and Morrison 1998: 1-8). For a start, there is no single, definable tourism 'product'. Tourists 'consume' a tourism experience, the nature of which is as much dependent on the activities of tourists themselves as it is on the tourism 'industry' – in many cases, such as when driving to visit friends or relatives, tourists may not require any products or services provided by the industry. Secondly, tourist services are supplied by an enormous variety of businesses and organisations, many of which, such as airlines or accommodation, are industries in their own right. Thirdly, although some businesses, such as tour operating or travel retailing, are quite evidently directly involved in tourism, the relationship between other businesses or organisations and tourism is less clear. For example, financial institutions provide foreign currency services and insurance companies provide travel insurance, yet neither could be described as tourism businesses. Similarly, a publishing company may produce travel guides, but it would normally be considered to be in the publishing industry, not the tourism industry. In short, the boundary between tourism and non-tourism businesses is often blurred. Fourthly, a number of other organisations in the public sector, from locally run information centres to national tourism bodies, also play a role in the production of tourism, though often on a non-commercial basis. Finally, there is no single management structure within tourism. Unlike traditional industries where, for example, the management of a car manufacturer has overall control, there is no distinct chain of command in tourism and frequently the power lies not with 'producers', such as airlines or hotels, but with intermediaries, such as tour operators.

The organisations which collectively supply tourism, and the relationship between them, is considered in more detail in Section 2 of this book. The important point here, however, is that although it is easy and convenient to refer to the tourism 'industry', in reality it cannot be described as such. Instead, it is best thought of as a production system, the structure and nature of which may vary in different contexts according to the differing relationship between its different elements. Moreover, to further complicate matters, this tourism production system is itself a constituent part of a broader system. That is, the production system (or tourism business) is but one element of a wider set of inter-related structures and processes that collectively have been referred to as the tourism system, a concept which, as the final section of this chapter now discusses, provides a useful framework for the study of tourism as a whole.

Tourism as a system

As has become evident throughout this chapter, tourism is a complex, multi-dimensional phenomenon that is difficult, if not impossible, to define. It is certainly a social phenomenon, in that tourism is manifested in the movement of millions of individuals, both within their own countries and internationally, for a variety of purposes. However, that movement of people would not, for the most part, occur without the services provided by the 'industry', or tourism production system. Together, tourists (the demand side of tourism) and the production system (the supply side of tourism) combine into what has been described as a 'functioning tourism system' (Gunn 1994), an interdependent and dynamic system where, ideally, demand is balanced by supply.

This functioning tourism system has, according to Leiper (1979), three geographical elements:

Tourism generating regions: the regions which stimulates tourism, and where much of the tourism production system (especially tour operators and travel retailers) is located.

(i)   Tourism destination regions: the regions which attract tourists, which experience the consequences of tourism, and where primary elements of the production system (hotels, attractions, facilities) are located.

(ii)   Transit route region: this is both a temporal region (the short time spent travelling between home and the destination) and places visited *en route*.

(iii) There are clear inter-dependencies throughout this functioning system. For example, tourism businesses in the destination are dependent upon generating region-based companies (tour operators, travel agencies, airlines) for a supply of customers; equally, tour operators require an adequate supply of hotels in the destination, tourists require appropriate attractions and facilities, generally, destinations must be able to satisfy the needs of tourists, needs which are created or influenced by their own, home environment.

More importantly, perhaps, this core tourism system is also subject to a variety of external factors which determines how it functions (Figure 1.3).

Figure 1.3: *Tourism as a system*

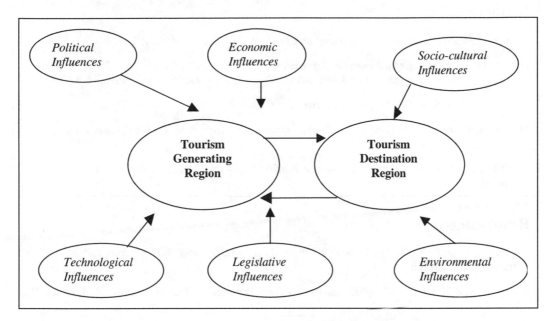

These external factors not only add to the complexity of planning and managing tourism as a phenomenon that is related to national and international economic, political and socio-cultural structures, but also point to the enormous range of approaches to the study and understanding of tourism. Indeed, tourism is, perhaps, best defined as a social and economic phenomenon that cannot be divorced from the world within which it occurs.

Conclusion

In attempting to define and conceptualise tourism, this chapter has demonstrated the breadth and complexity of the phenomenon as a subject of study. Not only is tourism an activity participated in by millions of people every year, but it is supported and facilitated by an enormous and diverse industry, or production system. At the same time, tourism is both influenced by, and impacts upon, the environments within which it occurs. Nevertheless, the fundamental feature of tourism is that it is, in a broad sense, a global business; without the 'industry', people could not become tourists and, for most destinations, the *raison d'être* of developing tourism is its expected economic benefits. Therefore, this book focuses primarily upon the business of tourism as, arguably, the linchpin of the global phenomenon of tourism.

Discussion questions

1.   *Why is it difficult, if not impossible, to accurately define tourism?*

2.   *How valid is the claim that tourism is the world's largest industry?*

3.   *What are the advantages of considering tourism, on the global scale, as a system?*

Further reading

Cooper, C. et al (1998), *Tourism: Principles and Practice, 2nd Edition*, Harlow: Longman – *Chapter 1.*

Gilbert, D. (1990), Conceptual issues in the meaning of tourism, in C. Cooper (ed.*) Progress in Tourism, Recreation and Hospitality Management, Volume 2*, London: Bellhaven Press: 4-27.

Holloway, J. C. (1998), *The Business of Tourism, 5th Edition*, Harlow: Longman – *Chapter 1.*

Mill, R. and Morrison, A. (1998), *The Tourism system: An Introductory Text*, Dubuque, Iowa: Kendall/Hunt Publishing.

WTO/UNSTAT (1994), *Recommendations on Tourism Statistics*, Madrid: World Tourism Organisation.

References

Burkhart, A. and Medlik, S. (1981), *Tourism: Past, Present and Future, 2nd Edition*, Oxford: Butterworth Heinemann.

Burns, P. and Holden, A. (1995), *Tourism: A New Perspective*, Hemel Hempstead: Prentice Hall International.

Cohen, E. (1974), Who is a tourist? A conceptual clarification, *Sociological Review* 22(4): 527-555.

Cooper, C., Fletcher, J., Gilbert, D., Shepherd, R. and Wanhill, S. (1998), *Tourism: Principles and Practice, 2nd Edition*, Harlow: Longman.

Graburn, N. (1983), The anthropology of tourism, *Annals of Tourism Research* 10(1): 9-33.

Jafari, J. (1997), Editors page, *Annals of Tourism Research* 5(1): 8.

Gunn, C. (1994), *Tourism Planning: Basics, Concepts, Cases, 3rd Edition*, London: Taylor & Francis.

Leiper, N. (1979), The framework of tourism, *Annals of Tourism Research* 6(1): 390-407.

Mill, R. and Morrison, A. (1998), *The Tourism System: An Introductory Text*, Dubuque, Iowa: Kendall/Hunt Publishing.

Smith, V. (ed.) (1989), *Hosts and Guests: The Anthropology of Tourism, 2nd Edition*, Philadelphia: University of Pennsylvania Press.

WTO (1998), *Tourism – 2020 Vision: Influences, Directional Flows and Key Influences*, Madrid: World Tourism Organisation.

WTO (2000), *Tourism Highlights 2000, 2nd Edition*, Madrid: World Tourism Organisation

WTO/UNSTAT (1994), *Recommendations on Tourism Statistics*, Madrid: World Tourism Organisation.

2

A History of Tourism

Richard Sharpley

Learning objectives

This chapter traces the history of tourism from earliest times through to the emergence of mass tourism in the twentieth century. Having read this chapter, the reader will be able to:

- *identify the main periods and transformations in the evolution of tourism*

- *understand the relevance of past trends in tourism to the growth of modern, mass tourism*

- *highlight and explain the principal factors that have facilitated the growth of tourism*

Introduction

It is generally accepted that the roots of modern, mass tourism lie in the social and economic changes that occurred during the nineteenth and twentieth centuries. Certainly, technological innovation provided the means for faster, safer, more reliable and cheaper travel, whilst increasing levels of personal income and greater amounts of free time meant that more people could participate in tourism. At the same time, changes in the way people lived and worked, resulting in particular from rapid industrialisation and urbanisation during the 1800s, created the need or desire to go on holiday. Thus, it is not surprising that tourism is often considered a phenomenon of modern times.

Tourism is also generally regarded as a European and, more specifically, a British 'invention'. That is, it is often claimed that Britain played a dominant role in the evolution of tourism with, for example, the emergence of resort-based tourism (in spa towns and at the seaside) setting the patterns of tourism, whilst technological advances combined with the entrepreneurial talents of travel 'organisers', in particular Thomas Cook, enabled increasing numbers of people to become tourists.

However, both of these perceptions are largely incorrect. Although it is only relatively recently that tourism, especially international tourism, has become an activity that the majority of people (at least in the wealthier developed countries) can enjoy, people have been able to travel for as long as there have been the means to do so. The first sea-going ships were designed and built some 5000 years ago and people have been 'tourists', travelling for education, pleasure or spiritual fulfilment, for as long as they have been physically able to travel from one place to another. Nor, of course, was Britain the only country that was instrumental in the evolution of tourism. Many other countries and societies, in both modern and ancient times, have contributed to the emergence of tourism, although it is probably the history of tourism in Europe that is best documented in the literature (see, for example, Towner 1996).

Nevertheless, a British perspective on the evolution of tourism provides a basis for understanding how and why tourism has, in general, become the global phenomenon that it is today. More specifically, it also demonstrates how tourism has become increasingly 'democratised' – that is, available to and enjoyed by the masses – in a pattern that is being repeated to this day in other parts of the world. Therefore, this chapter focuses on the contribution of Britain to the evolution of tourism, highlighting specific periods and influences that provided the foundation for modern-day tourism. First, however, it introduces the subject by looking briefly at early forms of tourism.

Tourism in ancient times

From the earliest times, two factors inhibited the growth of tourism, namely, the difficulty or danger of travelling and, for the majority, a lack of money. Typically, travel by ship was the safest and most convenient mode of transport and was primarily motivated by either trade or warfare – opportunities to travel for pleasure were extremely rare. Nevertheless, the ancient Greeks enjoyed tourism of a sort, through primarily for religious or sporting purposes or for consulting oracles. For example, the oracle at Delphi drew people from far and wide to seek advice on various matters whilst the Pythian Games, also at Delphi, were a popular event. However, it was Olympia, home of the Olympic Games, that was probably one of the most popular destinations of the time. The first Games were held in 776BC and, thereafter, attracted thousands of visitors from home and abroad to witness the sports and other events which gave the Games their deep religious significance. Indeed, tourism to the ancient Greeks was not leisure, but 'a trip in accordance with tradition and ritual. The man who travelled tightened his links rather than liberated himself from his social background' (Sigaux 1966: 10).

Tourism and the Romans

It was the Romans who first overcame one of the major hurdles to the development of tourism by developing a road network across the Empire. This not only allowed for the rapid movement of troops and administrative personnel but also increased the opportunity for private individuals to travel. By the first century AD, it was possible to travel along paved roads all the way from Hadrian's Wall in the north to the southern edge of the Empire in Africa, with travellers being able to break their journeys at staging posts, or hotels, along the route. However, travel remained primarily for the purpose of trade or military service, with only wealthier Romans able to travel internationally for pleasure.

In contrast to the philosophy of the Ancient Greeks, tourism for the Romans became a form of leisure and escape. For those who could afford it, 'second home ownership' became a way of avoiding the summer heat of Rome, whilst the building of the road network led to the development of a number of resorts along the Bay of Naples. Through a process that was to be repeated around the Mediterranean some 2000 years later, small fishing villages were transformed into bustling seaside resorts where excessive drinking, loud parties and nude bathing were commonplace. Thus, whereas previously tourism had been for the purpose of trade, health or religion, the Romans introduced the concept of tourism as a means of escape pleasure and self-indulgence, a form of tourism that disappeared with the decline of the Roman Empire during the fifth century AD and which would not reappear until the twentieth century. In fact, the tourism as a leisure activity was to disappear for almost a thousand years, although other forms of travel and tourism were to emerge in the intervening period.

Tourism in the Middle Ages

Following the collapse of the Roman Empire, travel became more difficult and hazardous and, generally, few people had the means, opportunity or desire to travel. As a result, tourism, such as it existed at this time, was limited to local fairs, festivals and religious holidays (or 'holy days', from which the word holiday is derived), with longer journeys usually being for the purpose of trade.

Nevertheless, one popular form of 'voluntary' travel during this period was pilgrimage. 'In its purest form, pilgrimage was a voluntary journey to worship at some holy shrine, and the journey itself was expected to be hard and fraught with difficulties, as a form of penance' (Jubb 1986: 3). Although such journeys had been undertaken since the third century, during the Middle Ages increasing numbers of people set out on pilgrimages, mostly on foot, usually to one of the three most popular destinations of Jerusalem, Rome and Santiago de Compostella in north west Spain. By 1300, for example, an estimated 300,000 pilgrims visited Rome each year although shorter, domestic trips were also popular, such as English pilgrimages to Canterbury or Winchester. Interestingly, the trip to Santiago de Compostella is once again a popular walking route, though principally as a long distance walk rather than a journey of spiritual significance.

Tourism between 1600 and 1800

Whereas the earlier periods are of interest in their own right, the seventeenth and eighteenth centuries are of more importance in the historical development of modern tourism. Although they preceded the modernisation and industrialisation of society, it was during this period that the pattern of tourism development through to the present time was established. In particular, it was then that the democratisation of tourism began, a process that has culminated with the mass participation in tourism that we know today.

Fuelling this process were a variety of factors that were, and remain, essential for tourism to flourish. In other words, tourism, 'in any age, can only operate within a broader environment which embraces a number of important cultural, social, geographical, economic, political and economic conditions' (Towner 1994: 7). Figure 2.1 summarises these tourism 'enabling factors' which, as will become evident, have underpinned the democratisation of tourism.

Figure 2.1: *Tourism's enabling factors*

• *adequate leisure time*	– long enough blocks of time at suitable periods
• *sufficient money*	– sufficient 'disposable' income
• *need or motivation*	– the desire or need to participate in tourism
• *freedom of movement*	– political and personal freedom to travel
• *necessary infrastructure*	– tourism infrastructure: means and modes of travel, accommodation, etc.

In the seventeenth century, of course, few if any of these factors had come to the fore. Nevertheless, two forms of tourism were prevalent during this period, both of which were influential in changing both the style and meaning of tourism. These two forms of tourism were:

- The Grand Tour
- Spa Tourism

The Grand Tour

By the late 1500s and early 1600s, the religious conviction that had motivated the pilgrimages of the Middle Ages was being replaced by more secular approach to travel, in particular travel for the purpose of education, self-improvement and, to a lesser extent, pleasure. More specifically, by the start of the seventeenth century it had become customary for the English aristocracy to send their sons, once they had graduated from university, on a tour of Europe. Usually accompanied by a tutor, the young aristocrat would undertake a 'Grand Tour' for a period of anything up to three or four years, visiting major cities, enrolling on courses at universities and learning not only academic subjects and languages but also social refinements. In a sense, Europe become a large 'finishing school' for young Englishmen, preparing them for careers as diplomats or in government. By the mid-1700s, an estimated 20,000 such 'Grand Tourists' were abroad at any one time, travelling through France, Switzerland and Germany, with the northern Italian cities of Turin, Verona and Venice featuring in most tours.

The Grand Tour is described in detail elsewhere (Towner 1985). However, the important point here is that, over time, the characteristics of both the Grand Tour and those who undertook it changed. In particular, a greater number of tourists started to tour on the Continent, but their trips tended to be shorter both in distance and duration and the focus of the trip became pleasure rather than education. At the same time, the tourists themselves came increasingly from the professional middle classes rather than the aristocracy. In short, the Grand Tour became popularised and, in a sense, moved 'downmarket' as tourists began to gain a reputation for showing little or no interest in the people, language or culture of the countries through which they passed.

By the late 1700s, then, the Grand Tour had been abandoned by the aristocrats who, setting a trend that has been repeated throughout the history of tourism, sought more socially exclusive resorts or destinations elsewhere (only, as we shall see, to once again be 'invaded' by the masses). The meaning or purpose of tourism had also changed from a cultural to a leisure activity; proactive learning and discourse had been replaced with passive sightseeing.

In particular, and reflecting the emergence of the romantic movement, nature, landscape and scenic beauty became the object of the tourists' gaze in a process perhaps best epitomised by the popularity of the English Lake District. Inspired by writers, artists and poets, such as William Wordsworth, increasing numbers of visitors visited the Lake District from the 1750s onwards to gaze upon the landscape that represented the romantic antithesis to the rapid urbanisation and industrialisation of eighteenth and nineteenth century Britain. Thus, by the late 1700s, travelling for pleasure or escape had emerged as an element of the tourism experience although still only a relatively small proportion of the population could actually participate in tourism.

Spa Tourism

At the same time that the Grand Tour was becoming a popular form of touring amongst the aristocracy, the spa towns of England and Europe were once again becoming popular destinations for the first time since their heyday in Roman times. In fact, spa tourism at this time represented the first example of resort based tourism and, similar to the development of seaside resorts a century or so later, the renewed interest in the spas was initially based on the perceived health benefits of 'taking the waters'. Bath, in particular, became internationally renowned, largely as a result of a book published by William Turner in 1562 which drew attention to the alleged medicinal properties of its waters. However, a large number of other spas were established across England (see Figure 2.2), whilst the fashion also spread into Europe with spas in France, Germany and Italy being redeveloped to cater for increasing demand.

Figure 2.2: *Spa Towns in England and Wales*

It was not long, however, before the spas resorts were transformed from health resorts into social centres as medicinal considerations became subordinated to 'seeing and being seen'. In other words, visiting spas became an annual event on the social calendars of the upper classes, with Bath reaching the height of its popularity by the beginning of the eighteenth century. As more and more facilities were provided to entertain visitors they became, in effect, holiday resorts disguised as health centres and, perhaps inevitably, they also began to attract increasing numbers of visitors from the expanding middle classes wishing to emulate the traditional clientele of the spas. Gradually, their social exclusivity began to suffer and, as retailers, innkeepers and a variety of other trades moved in to satisfy the needs of visitors, the spa resorts were being transformed into residential and commercial centres. Indeed, by the late 1700s their popularity had diminished significantly and tourists turned their attention to the new seaside resorts that, by the early 1800s, were becoming important tourist destinations.

Tourism in the 1800s

The nineteenth century is, undoubtedly, the most important period in the history of tourism. At the beginning of the century, tourism remained an activity enjoyed by a relatively small, privileged proportion of the population. For example, it is estimated that about 40,000 English citizens were either living or travelling in Europe at that time yet, by 1840, some 100,000 people were crossing the English Channel each year, a figure which had risen to one million by the start of the twentieth century (Young 1973). This rapid growth in tourism resulted from a number of influences, including:

- Technological advances, particularly the introduction and rapid development of the railway network;

- Increases in personal income, combined with greater amounts of free time;

- Social transformations that created the motivation for tourism;

- The foundation of the tourism industry.

Thus, although the greatest growth in tourism, manifested in the emergence of mass, international tourism, was to occur during the second half of the twentieth century, the foundations for such growth were laid during the nineteenth century. Of particular importance was the development of seaside resorts as the first step towards mass participation in tourism.

British seaside resorts

With the declining popularity of the spas during the late 1700s, the attention of tourists turned towards coastal resorts. Like the spas, the initial impetus was provided by the medical profession which extolled the supposed recuperative powers of seawater; a paper published by Dr. Richard Russell in 1753 described the alleged benefits of both bathing in and even drinking seawater and, in order to practice what he preached, he moved to Brighthelmstone (Brighton) on the south coast. By the turn of the century, Brighton had replaced Bath as the fashionable leisure centre outside London, its popularity boosted by a visit the resort by the Prince Regent in 1783, and the town expanded rapidly. Similarly, a number of northern coastal resorts, such as Blackpool, Southport and Scarborough, also grew in popularity, whilst resorts on the Kent coast, such as Margate, played host to increasing numbers of visitors from London.

Again like the spas, it was initially the upper classes that were attracted to the seaside resorts. Blackpool, for example, was described in the Blackburn Mail in 1795 as:

> *the first watering place in the Kingdom, whether we consider the salubrity of the air, the beauty of the scenery, the excellence of the accommodation or the agreeable company of which it is the general resort.*

This exclusivity was based on the initial health motivations for visiting the resorts – the experience was anything but pleasurable, with visits frequently made during the winter months! – and also on the difficulty of travelling there. Even at the beginning of the nineteenth century, the trip from London to Brighton could take two days and the cost of the journey was beyond the means of most people. However, by the latter part of the century many resorts had become, in effect mass tourism destinations.

The rise (and subsequent fall) of the seaside resorts is discussed at length in the literature (see, for example, Shaw and Williams 1997; Walton 1983, 2000; Walvin 1978). However, it is important to consider here the factors that gave rise to their popularity as tourist destinations and which, more generally, contributed to the growth and democratisation of tourism.

(a) Transport technology

Although it was rail transport that as to be a defining factor, the Kent resorts along the Thames estuary were attracting an ever-widening range of social groups by the early 1800s, primarily as a result of the introduction of steamboat services. Sailing cargo ships had already carried passengers to resorts such as Margate but, by 1830, paddle steamers were carrying Londoners to the seaside in their thousands. In fact the icons of British seaside resorts – their piers – were originally built for landing passengers rather than as places of entertainment.

Nevertheless, the evolution of the railways was to be as instrumental in the growth of tourism in the 1800s as was international air transport in the 1990s. The first rail journey took place between Liverpool and Manchester in 1829 (travelling at an average speed of 16 mph). By 1836 there were 700 miles of track in England and by 1848 this had expanded to over 5000 miles. The number of passengers using the railways also increased dramatically; by 1847, 51 million rail journeys were being made annually and the cost of rail travel fell rapidly. Thus, for the first time, cheap, safe and relatively fast transport (essential ingredients of the tourism product) were available. As a consequence, the seaside resorts expanded rapidly, with some, such as Rhyll in north Wales, owing their existence entirely to the building of the railways. It is also suggested that the social tone of resorts was, to an extent, dictated by when the railways reached the resorts and the distance from the main industrial centres. However, the development of the seaside resorts was a complex process and their degree of exclusivity cannot be explained by the expansion of the railways alone (Walton 2000). At the same time, it was not only the seaside that became popular – by the 1880s, rural areas such as the Lake District were also attracting significant numbers of tourists.

(b) Social conditions

At the beginning of the nineteenth century, Britain was still largely a pre-industrial, rural society. About 80 percent of the population lived and worked in the countryside and their leisure was determined primarily by custom and the agricultural calendar. By the end of the century, it was in the burgeoning industrial towns and cities that 80 percent of people lived as the country passed experienced the Industrial Revolution. This rapid industrialisation and urbanisation of society created a number of condition for tourism to thrive.

In terms of wealth, average income per head quadrupled over the course of the century and so, although poverty remained widespread (mass participation in tourism amongst the working classes would not occur until the twentieth century), some working people were able to accumulate savings to pay for holidays. Indeed, some employers established savings clubs to encourage their workers to save for holidays. More time also became available for leisure. The working week/day was shortened during the 1800s and, for the first time, the Bank Holiday Act in 1871 provided workers with official holidays. Paid holidays would not be legally sanctioned until the 1930s but, nevertheless, the more enlightened employers offered their workers regular, official (though unpaid) holidays in order to improve productivity. Thus, 'wakes weeks', when factories, mills or even entire towns closed for a week's holiday, became commonplace in the industrial north.

Social conditions in the new industrial cities also created the desire to escape. Not only did increasing numbers of people take advantage of the travel opportunities offered by rail travel but cycling and rambling clubs were also formed, and the concept of the holiday camp emerged, as leisure became an important or essential element of social life.

Interestingly, whilst tourism within Britain was rapidly expanding during the nineteenth century, the upper classes, once again 'evicted' from their leisure spaces (the seaside resorts) by the arrival of the masses, sought exclusivity overseas. International rail services, such as the Orient Express, offered luxurious travel across Europe whilst the Mediterranean resorts along the French Côte d'Azur became popular amongst European aristocracy. For example, Queen Victoria and the Russian Czar both visited Cannes in the 1890s and, in real terms, the French Riviera was five times more expensive then than it was during the 1960s. This growth in international tourism was in no small measure aided by the emergence of an identifiable tourism industry, with Thomas Cook in particular playing a central role.

Thomas Cook

Although not the first to organise tourism commercially – Sir Roland Hill is accredited with 'inventing' excursion trains – it was Thomas Cook who was the first to fully exploit the opportunities offered by the new travel infrastructure. Indeed, it was Cook who, in effect, revolutionised tourism by transforming it from the preserve of the privileged into an international industry and, in the process, creating the package tour as one of the most popular forms of tourism. His success lay not only in his organisational abilities but, perhaps more importantly, also in his recognition that people simply did not know how to be tourists – they needed to be organised.

Thomas Cook's first organised trip was in 1841 when he took 570 travellers on a short, 11 mile journey from Leicester to Loughborough to attend a temperance meeting. Following its success, other trip were organised, motivated more by Cook's altruism than the desire for commercial success) and soon he was running regular excursions. From 1848, tours were made in Scotland with up to 5000 tourists each season using Cook's services and, in the same year, he took a group to Belvoir Castle. Although he first contemplated overseas tours in 1850, it was not until 1855 that his first overseas tour set off. This, however, ended in Calais owing to resistance from the French railway authorities!

Despite this initial setback, Cook's overseas tours became more successful and travelled further afield. His first tour to America was undertaken in 1866 and, once his son John Mason Cook (hence the initials of the present-day tour operator JMC) had joined him, the business went from strength to strength. Indeed, in some parts of the world, the company began to wield enormous power – for example, it controlled all passenger steamers on the River Nile from 1880 onwards and enjoyed a virtual monopoly on all tourism to and from India. In 1872, the first Cook's Circular Notes, forerunners to the modern traveller's cheque, were also issued. These were similar to the letters of credit used by travellers during the previous century but were much more flexible, being exchangeable at any bank or hotel involved in the scheme. That same year, Cook's first round-the-world tour was also organised.

Thomas Cook was not, of course, alone in organising tourism during the nineteenth century. Other now famous names also established tourism businesses, such as Sir Henry Lunn, who was organising skiing holidays in Switzerland by the 1880s, as well as a number of companies, including the Co-operative Holiday Association, that embraced educational and social aims in providing holiday opportunities. Collectively, they brought international tourism within the reach of the masses, removing the much of the mystique of overseas travel and providing standards and services that were affordable to a greater proportion of the population. Thus, by the late 1800s, the scene had been set for the dramatic expansion and democratisation of tourism in the twentieth century.

Tourism in the Twentieth Century

In the early 1900s, the development of tourism continued along the course that had been set during the previous century. The upper classes spent the summers in the south of France (it was on the Riviera during the 1920s that sunbathing first became fashionable) and increasing numbers of tourists travelled overseas. Yet, for the majority of British people, tourism was primarily domestic (at the seaside) and would remain so until the 1960s and 1970s. Nevertheless, international tourism in general was on the increase. Large numbers of Americans crossed the Atlantic and, prior to the outbreak of the First World War, up to 150,000 American tourists visited Europe each year. Travel was becoming increasingly comfortable and easy, no passports were required in Europe and, consequently, many countries were becoming increasingly reliant on tourism as a source of income.

During the first half of the twentieth century, then, the pattern of tourism remained relatively unchanged, although ever increasing numbers of people were able to enjoy the benefits of tourism. Not surprisingly, the same three factors of time, income and technology were most influential. Certainly, levels of disposable income continued to increase but, from the late 1930s onwards, the amount of time available for holidays, in the form of holidays with pay, increased significantly for the majority of the population. At the same time, other factors influenced holiday activity:

- Holidays with Pay: in the 1920s, some 17 percent of workers benefited from holidays with pay, though usually at the discretion of their employers. However, following the 1938 Holidays with Pay Act, paid holidays became available to most workers. By 1969, 97 percent of workers enjoyed two week paid holiday; by 1988, 99 percent enjoyed four weeks.

- Car ownership: in 1919, there were 109,000 cars on the road in Britain, a figure which had risen to 2 million by the outbreak of the Second World War. Thus, although international travel was beyond the means of most people, many were no longer dependent on public transport. Motoring became a popular form of leisure, opening up newer destinations and leading to the eventual decline in the railways.

- Holiday camps: holiday camps had existed since the late 1890s and, by 1939, over one and a half million people in Britain spent their holidays under canvas and in camps of all kinds (Ward and Hardy 1986). However, the 'holiday camp' is, perhaps, most widely associated with Billy Butlin who, after opening up his first camp in Skegness in 1936, went on to build a holiday business that remained popular through to the 1960s. By 1948, it was estimated that one in twenty holiday makers stayed at a Butlin's camp each year and, generally, holiday camps were important inasmuch as they established the concept of mass, organised holidays for people to whom paid holidays and free time were a relatively novel experience. As a result, people were prepared to take advantage of the revolution that was to occur in tourism from the 1960s, manifested in the emergence of international mass tourism.

The development of mass tourism

The last forty years or so have, without a doubt, been the most significant in the history of tourism. The foundations of modern tourism were undoubtedly built in the preceding century, whilst the pattern of tourism development, whereby the fashion or trend is set by the upper classes or élite, only to be emulated by the middle classes, has been in evidence since the Grand Tour and continues to this day. For example, once exclusive destinations, such as the Caribbean, are now included in package tour brochures and cruising, again a previously up-market activity, has also been packaged.

However, recent decades have not only witnessed not only the explosion of mass international tourism in terms of numbers of tourists, but also its transformation from a luxury enjoyed by a privileged minority into an activity enjoyed by a large majority of the population (at least in the wealthier, industrialised countries). That is, it has become an accepted, or even expected, part of people's lives, a necessity rather than a luxury, a mass social activity that many consider their right to enjoy. In short, tourism has, since the 1960s, become democratised.

This remarkable and rapid growth in tourism has resulted from the same three factors that have enabled the development of tourism throughout history. Working hours continue to fall, though not to the same extent in different countries. Europeans, for example, tend to have longer paid holidays than Americans, although on average the British work longer hours than their colleagues on the Continent. More flexible working practices have also contributed to greater amounts of time available for leisure activities whilst many people now retire early. Collectively, these trends have resulted in not only more people taking holidays but also, and more importantly, individuals taking more holidays. Thus, although the proportion of people in the UK taking holidays (of 4 days or more) has remained unchanged for three decades, the number taking two or more holidays a year has rose from 15 percent to 25 percent of the population between 1971 and 1998 (ONT 2001).

Similarly, income has increased significantly, allowing people to take advantage of the free time that has become more available and to spend a greater proportion on tourism. Between

1950 and 1980, for example, real wages for men doubled and, between 1971 and 1999, the amount spent by British tourists abroad increased sixfold in real terms (ONT 2001).

However, the most significant influence on the emergence of mass international tourism has been advances in air transport technology which, in turn, has underpinned the development of a sophisticated tourism industry. Following the end of the Second World War, large numbers of surplus aircraft became available. This, combined with the introduction of jet airliners in the 1950s, set the scene for the rapid expansion of commercial air transport in general and charter air travel in particular (see Holloway 1998: 32-35). As the large airlines bought new jets, smaller charter companies could buy cheap, second-hand aircraft to fly tourists to their holiday destinations and, taking advantage of economies of scale, the cost of international air travel fell dramatically. Subsequent advances in air transport, including the introduction of wide-bodied jets and the latest generation of efficient airliners, have continued to make air travel relatively cheaper, thus encouraging the continuing expansion of international travel.

The first person to operate a charter holiday flight was Vladimir Raitz who, in 1950, organised a trial trip to Corsica. He went on to build his business under the name of Horizon Holidays (later to be bought out by Thomson Holidays) and, following his lead, a large number of tour operators were established both in Britain and abroad. Since then, the package tourism industry has become increasingly sophisticated and diversified, whilst the scale of operations has increased enormously.

The structure of the tourism industry in general and tourism distribution, including tour operating, in particular are discussed in more detail in Chapters 5 and 6. The important point here, however, is that the emergence of a complex and sophisticated tourism production system has been a dominant factor in the growth of mass tourism. In other words, although the same factors throughout history (time/money/technology) have enabled more and more people to participate in tourism, the driving force that has created the modern global phenomenon of international tourism has been the development of the tourism industry and its related sectors, as well as changes in the demand for tourism. These are summarised in Figure 2.3.

Figure 2.3: *Factors influencing the development of international tourism*

Transport	Technological improvement:	- wide bodied jets
		- more efficient aircraft
		- alternative (e.g.: high speed trains)
	diversification:	- charter operations
		- 'no-frills' flights
Accommodation	Innovation in accommodation services:	- time share/club share
		- self-catering
		- all-inclusives
Emergence of travel operators	Tour operating & travel retailing:	- large operators providing the 'complete' experience
		- image of safety, reliability
		- widespread network of retailers
	Scale of operations:	- economies of scale/the package providing competitive prices
Integration	Vertical and horizontal integration:	- improved quality
		- economies of scale
Development of support services	Banks/currency:	- increasing ease of obtaining currency
	Insurance:	- variety of insurance and insurance providers
	Information:	- Travel/safety information (the Internet)
	Health:	- Improved health services
Public sector involvement	Government policies:	- positive policies to develop tourism
	Consumer protection:	- regulation (e.g. EU Package Travel Directive)
	National/local organisations:	- services for tourists
Changing demand	Holidays:	- demands for new destinations, experiences etc.
	International business:	- growth in global business related travel
	VFR markets:	- new VFR markets related to global migration patterns

Conclusion

In a sense, Figure 2.3 represents the agenda for the remainder of this book. In other words, we are concerned here primarily with the business of tourism, the system of tourism production that enables millions of people to participate in tourism and which, as this chapter has suggested, has been a major influence in the emergence of tourism as a modern, world-wide phenomenon.

More generally, however, the history of tourism has been characterised by two trends which, to this day, remain evident in the evolution of tourism. Firstly, tourism has followed a pattern of democratisation, also known as the aristocratic model of tourism development, whereby the fashion has been set by the élite who are then emulated by the masses. This is, of course, inevitable in many forms of consumption. However, it has been a particular feature of tourism and continues to this day – the first space tourist who bought a 'holiday' on the international space station in 2001 is evidence of this.

Secondly, a variety of enabling factors have, throughout time, underpinned the growth and democratisation of tourism. In particular, technological innovation, increases in time and wealth and, latterly, the emergence of the tourism industry have all been major influences. Nevertheless, this remains only part of the story. Tourism would not have become the mass phenomenon that it is today, so it is important to consider the factors that influence the demand for tourism. This is the subject of the following two chapters.

Discussion questions

1. *To what extent has the development of the travel and tourism industry been a vital factor in the growth of international mass tourism?*

2. *Is it likely that 'old' forms of tourism and travel, such as spa tourism, will become popular again?*

3. *What does the history of tourism tell us about possible future developments and trends in tourism?*

Further reading

Brendon, P. (1991), *Thomas Cook: 150 Years of Popular Tourism*, London: Secker & Warburg.

Holloway, J. C. (1998), *The Business of Tourism, 5th Edition*, Harlow: Longman – *Chapters 2 and 3*.

Inglis, F. (2000), *The Delicious History of the Holiday*, London: Routledge.

Pimlott, J. (1947), *The Englishman's Holiday*, London: Faber & Faber.

Towner, J. (1996), *An Historical Geography of Recreation and Tourism in the Western World 1540-1940*, Chichester: John Wiley & Sons.

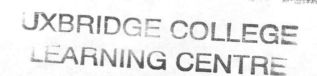

References

Holloway, J. C. (1998), *The Business of Tourism, 5th Edition*, Harlow: Longman.

Jebb, M. (1986), *Walkers*, London: Constable.

ONT (2001), *Social Trends 31*, London: Office for National Statistics.

Shaw, G. and Williams, A. (1977), *The Rise and Fall of British Coastal Resorts: Cultural and Economic Perspectives*, London: Mansell Publishing.

Sigaux, G. (1966), *History of Tourism*, London: Leisure Arts Ltd.

Towner, J. (1985), The Grand Tour: a key phase in the history of tourism, *Annals of Tourism Research* 12(3): 297-333.

Towner, J. (1994), The history and development of tourism, in P. Callaghan, P. Long and M. Robinson (eds.) *Travel & Tourism, 2nd Edition*, Sunderland: Business Education Publishers: 7-23.

Towner, J. (1996), *An Historical Geography of Recreation and Tourism in the Western World 1540-1940*, Chichester: John Wiley & Sons.

Walton, J. (1983), *The English Seaside Resort: A Social History, 1750-1914*, Leicester: Leicester University Press.

Walton, J. (2000), *The British Seaside: Holidays and resorts in the twentieth century*, Manchester: Manchester University Press.

Walvin, J, (1978), *Beside the Seaside*, London: Allen Lane.

Young, G. (1973), *Tourism: Blessing or Blight?*, Harmondsworth: Penguin.

3

The State of World Tourism

Julia Sharpley

Learning objectives

This chapter introduces tourism from a global perspective, enabling the reader to:

- *appreciate the global importance of tourism (economically, socially and environmentally)*

- *outline the main barriers to global tourism development*

- *explain the principal limitations of tourism statistics and data*

- *understand the main patterns of tourism growth and flows worldwide*

Introduction

Tourism today is a global issue. Not only have international tourism arrivals more than doubled since 1983, but also the number of destinations drawn into the so called 'pleasure periphery' (Turner and Ash 1975) has grown to the extent that there are few countries or regions worldwide which could claim to be outside the international tourism system. At the same time, many issues relating to tourism, including its role in development, its social, political and environmental consequences and its alleged position as the world's largest industry, deserve consideration at the global level. However, with the exception of figures relating to the overall volume and value of tourism, many global issues are all too frequently overlooked.

The purpose of this chapter, therefore is to assess the present state of world tourism. This will include not only a statistical analysis of current trends and flows in international tourism, but will also, firstly, address the question: why adopt a global perspective on tourism?

A global perspective on tourism?

It is inevitable, perhaps, that most tourism issues are viewed primarily at a national or local level. This stems largely from the competitive nature of national and international tourism; although tourism is described as a global activity, most countries are in competition with all other countries for a share of the world tourism market. Similarly, at the national level, regions compete for their share of domestic and incoming tourism. Therefore, national and local governments or tourism organisations work primarily in the national and regional interest.

Nevertheless, there are many aspects of tourism which transcend national and regional boundaries. In other words, whilst tourism is undoubtedly a significant worldwide economic activity, there are also other aspects or issues which can, or should, be considered on a global basis. For example, sex tourism or tourism-related prostitution has, in the past, been viewed as a problem for particular destinations. However, solutions to the problem can only be found at the international level, as evidenced by the fact that some tourism generating countries, including the UK and Australia, now prosecute their nationals found guilty of such activities whilst on holiday overseas. Similarly, the challenge of sustainable tourism, by definition, demands a global perspective, as do many other inter-related issues.

Generally, however, global issues related to tourism can be addressed under three broad headings:

- Tourism and world economic development

- Tourism and the world environment

- Tourism, international understanding and peace

It is with these issues that this first section is concerned.

Tourism and world economic development

It has long been recognised that international tourism can be used as a developmental tool. Indeed, the primary reason for developing tourism is its potential for bringing about social and economic development. It is not surprising, therefore, that 'many of the world's countries now regard tourism as an important and integral aspect of their development strategies' (Jenkins 1991: 62).

The developmental role of tourism is normally associated with the economic benefits that accrue from international tourism, such as foreign exchange earnings, employment opportunities, income generation, and direct and indirect contributions to government revenues. Moreover, tourism, as a specific economic activity, is frequently favoured over other activities as a development tool for a number of reasons:

- Tourism is, historically, and continues to be, a growth industry.

- Much of the investment in international tourism comes from the richer, developed countries.

- International tourism is a source of hard currencies.

- Tourism is typically a labour intensive sector.

- Normally tourism does not face trade or quota restrictions.

- Many attractions (e.g. climate, culture, environment) already exist and are, in a sense, 'free'.

- Tourism encourages the expansion of other sectors of the local economy.

However, despite the apparent ease with which tourism should be developed and bring economic benefits to destination areas and, indeed, despite the continuing growth in arrivals and tourist expenditure as demonstrated by international tourism statistics, in reality the full developmental potential of tourism is rarely realised. For example, many destinations, such as The Gambia, retain a relatively small proportion of the income generated by international tourism (see Sharpley and Sharpley 1996). This suggests that the state of world tourism in terms of development may not be as healthy as the figures might indicate. Moreover, there are a number of other key characteristics and influences not generally highlighted in statistical analyses of international tourism which shape tourism's role and potential as a tool of economic development. Many of these influences relate, quite simply, to the nature of tourism and the nature of the tourism industry at a global level. These are considered below.

The nature of travel and tourism

International travel and tourism, by its very nature, necessitates the movement of individuals across national boundaries (a movement which in 1999 totalled some 664 million international arrivals). By implication, therefore, if international tourism is to achieve its full developmental potential this movement of people must be made as easy as possible. However, like any other international trade, there exists a number of barriers or impediments which may negatively influence the international flow of tourists. In a general sense, these can be social, economic and physical conditions in both generating and host countries which influence travel. For example, Ascher (1984) has observed that factors deterring tourism to particular destinations include 'poor transportation and communications, work stoppages, inferior health and sanitary conditions, unpleasant food, overcrowding, and inadequate hotel and travel facilities'.

More specifically, there are a variety of other barriers to which may restrict international tourism (Figure 3.1):

Figure 3.1: *Barriers to international tourism*

i. Government intervention:	• visa restrictions
	• entry/exit quotas
	• currency restrictions
	• travel/departure tax
	• direct tourism policy
	• bi-lateral agreements
	• travel advice
	• local equity requirements
ii. Political instability:	• military regimes
	• coups d'état
	• terrorism
	• fundamentalism
iii. Conflict:	• wars/war zones
iv. Crime:	• mugging/theft
	• violent crime
v. Natural disasters:	• earthquakes/hurricanes
	• famine
	• illness

Whilst a number of these barriers to international tourism, such as natural disasters, are uncontrollable, many others can be addressed or overcome through international agreement or co-operation. Such agreement may be bi-lateral, that is, between two countries, or multi-lateral, where a number of nation states agree to certain mutual rights and obligations. For example, while visa agreements can represent a significant barrier to tourism development, particularly where numbers are restricted or where visa charges act as a disincentive to travel, the removal of such barriers is possible through international co-operation. There are many forms of international agreement which are beyond the scope of this chapter. However, the important point here is that efforts must be made at a global level to facilitate and encourage freedom of movement to encourage the development of tourism. It is no coincidence that this is the prime purpose of organisations such as the World Tourism Organisation (WTO) and the World Travel and Tourism Council (WTTC).

Furthermore, as an international service industry, tourism is also subject to the General Agreement on Trade in Services (GATS) – an offshoot of the wide-ranging General Agreement on Tariffs and Trade (GATT). GATS operates on the principle that free market forces are the most effective way of giving customers worldwide the best choice of service products at the best prices. The purpose of GATS in relation to tourism is, therefore, to put in place a system which will progressively eliminate barriers to tourism growth, such as restrictions on the ability of tourism companies to employ foreign personnel, establish management contracts and effect international money transfers and payments (for a fuller discussion of the effect of GATS and tourism, see WTO 1994). This is, perhaps, a sign that at last there is worldwide recognition of the value of tourism and that efforts must be made to continue to facilitate its appropriate development. However, it has also been recognised that GATS may have certain detrimental effects. That is, the process of liberalisation which GATS has set in motion may well enable western-owned, multinational companies to increase their power and influence in countries where tourism is currently under-developed (see below).

The state of world tourism today is not, however, just characterised by the extent to which nation states can lower political barriers. It also relates to the flow of tourism, globally. Tourism as an activity is dominated by the richer developed Western economies and the economic benefits of tourism mainly stay within these areas.

The nature of tourist flows

A further important characteristic of tourism in relation to its developmental potential is the pattern of international tourism flows. The most obvious trend has been the dramatic growth in international tourist arrivals which, since 1950, has increased by a factor of twenty four, with a corresponding increase in international tourism receipts. At the same time, tourism has also spread; in 1950, just 15 countries accounted for almost all international arrivals but, by 1999, the top 15 receiving countries saw their share decrease to less than two-thirds whilst more than 70 countries attracted over one million arrivals. Nevertheless, not all tourist destinations have benefited from tourism's growth. According to Shaw and Williams (1994: 23) international tourism flows display three distinctive patterns:

- *Polarity:* international tourism is still largely dominated by the industrial world with the major tourism flows being either between the more developed countries or from developed countries to lesser developed countries. Thus, it has been pointed out that, 'the industrialised countries receive 56 percent of international tourism receipts, while low-income countries (including India and China) receive just 1.5 percent of receipts' (Vellas and Bécherel 1995: 19). Therefore, although the East Asia and Pacific region has, in recent years, become an increasingly significant source of international tourists, the benefits of international tourism remain highly polarised.

- *Regionalisation:* international tourism is highly regionalised. In other words, the most significant flows of international tourists occur within well-defined regions, in particular within Europe. Other important regions include North America, with major flows between Canada and the United States and between the United States and the Caribbean, and the Japan and East Asia region.

- *European dominance:* the third major characteristic of international tourism is that it is largely concentrated within Europe. Indeed, in the early 1960s, Europe's share of world tourism represented over 70 percent of world arrivals. This has since fallen, although a number of Eastern European countries have recently experienced rapid growth in arrival numbers.

These statistics and flows are analysed in greater detail in the latter half of this chapter. However, the important point here is that by looking at tourism statistics globally, significant discrepancies in arrivals, visitor spending and hence developmental potential, become evident. In particular, the economic benefits generated by tourism are predominantly shared between the industrialised countries – in 1997, developing countries collectively received just 30.5 percent of international tourism receipts – although it is likely that, in future years, the East Asian region including China will play a more dominant role in international tourism flows.

The nature of the industry

A particular feature of the tourism industry is that it is diverse, fragmented and multi-sectoral. That is, it comprises a large number of predominantly small, private organisations in sectors as diverse as accommodation, retail, entertainment and transport. However, the major players within the industry are large multinational corporations such as airlines, hotel chains and tour operators, and it is no coincidence that the majority of these are based in the major tourism-generating countries. For example, the United States remains the world's largest generator of international tourism and 8 out of 10 top hotel chains are American.

This feature has major implications for tourism development because these organisations are able to influence styles of tourism, levels of investment and tourist flows. In some cases, this may lead to destinations becoming dependent on the continued support of overseas organisations, particularly where there is heavy reliance on one major generating market. In Cyprus, for example, up to 50 percent of tourists come from the UK and it could be argued that it is the influence of some UK tour operators which has led to the current state of tourism development on the island. What this means is that, although tourism appears to be a powerful vehicle for global development, not only does much of the influence come from the major tourism generating countries, but also much of the earnings from tourist activity remain with, or are repatriated to, those countries.

A further characteristic of tourism in the context of global economic development is that tourism, perhaps more than any other economic activity, can lead to serious social and environmental consequences for destination areas. In many cases, these negative impacts may outweigh the economic benefits of tourism. This suggests that, as discussed in the next section, the environmental aspects of tourism must also be considered on a global basis.

However, to conclude this section, tourism and world economic development can be looked at from different points of view but, given the general process of worldwide economic development, no country today – developed or developing – can view their economy, or any aspect of it, in isolation from the rest of the world. All nation-states are now part of an interdependent global village where increasing emphasis is being placed on international, as opposed to domestic, production and consumption and where an industry's growth potential is assessed within the context of a global marketplace. Tourism is no exception to this process of globalisation.

Tourism and world environment

Reflecting the dramatic growth in tourism during the latter half of the twentieth century, in particular the emergence of international mass tourism, there has been an ever-increasing concern for its effect on the environment. It is now generally recognised that any tourism development has to take into account not only economic benefits of tourism but also its environmental and social consequences. Equally the study of tourism would not be complete without an understanding of the socio-cultural and environmental aspects of tourism (see Chapters 11 and 20).

Although most tourism textbooks address the topic, the point to be emphasised here is that the environmental aspects of tourism development must be considered on a global basis. This is not to say that sustainable environmentally-friendly approaches to the planning and management of tourism at the micro, destinational level are not important. On the contrary, appropriate forms of tourism development must start at the local level and there have been many examples from the 1970s onwards, where a sustainable approach to tourism has been successfully put into practice (see Eber 1992; Inskeep and Kallenberger 1992; Harrison and Husbands 1996).

However, as important as these local initiatives are, tourism is a global phenomenon; therefore, environmentally appropriate planning must also be global. To do otherwise would be to simply shift the so-called problem of tourism (normally associated with mass tourism) from one destination to another. In other words, where a destination adopts strict environmental policies for tourism development, such as restricting numbers or promoting niche-type tourism products (e.g. eco-tourism), it is likely that the tourism industry or tourists may switch their allegiance to less restrictive or expensive destinations.

In general, it has been recognised that environmental issues can only be addressed on the global stage. For example, the Earth Summit at Rio de Janeiro in 1992 represented a significant step towards global policies for the environment, although more recent events have demonstrated that there are many difficulties to be overcome before this will be achieved. Nevertheless, truly sustainable tourism will only occur if an holistic global approach is adopted and nowhere is the much-used adage 'think global, act local' more relevant than in the context of tourism (but, see Sharpley 2000).

Tourism, international understanding and world peace

A number of international bodies have suggested that tourism has the potential to contribute to international understanding and world peace (see Var et al 1994). For example, not only does the WTO consider its fundamental role to be to 'develop tourism in order to contribute to economic expansion, international understanding, peace and prosperity', but also, in

1980, it went as far as to proclaim tourism as 'a vital force for world peace' (WTO 1980). Similarly, a number of commentators support the idea that, as a worldwide social activity that brings different societies and cultures together, tourism should foster greater international harmony and understanding.

However, this potential role of tourism has been the subject of some debate. Furthermore, other general assumptions about the extent of the relationship between tourism, international understanding and world peace have also been called into question. Three points in particular deserve consideration:

Tourism and international understanding

Var *et al* (1998) consider that there are two related aspects of tourism which contribute to world peace: 'the promotion of cultural exchange as a means of breaking down the barriers between individuals or people of different nations...[and]...the development of greater understanding between individuals or people of different nations resulting from this exchange'. In other words, it is the contribution which tourism can make to the attainment of international understanding which will promote and safeguard peace. A number of specific schemes, such as student exchange programmes, have been specially designed in recognition of this.

However, international understanding takes place at a number of different levels, including political, individual and corporate, and is by no means an inevitable outcome of the development of tourism in general. Indeed, it could be argued that due to both the nature of the current tourism system, which is dominated by western generating markets, and the differing personal motivations for international travel, tourism can serve merely to underline existing divisions and prejudices between diverse cultural and ethnic groups. As Ap and Var (1990) observe, there is little evidence to suggest that tourism generates international understanding or strong inter-cultural relationships, it being more likely reinforce stereotypic images between peoples of different nations. This supports the findings of a number of other studies, for example Milman *et al* (1990) and Pizam *et al* (1991).

However, it is still possible that 'tourism, properly designed and developed, can help bridge the psychological and cultural distances that separate people of diverse races, colours, religions, and stages of social and economic development' (D' Amore 1988). Although empirical research to date has established only tenuous evidence of tourism's role as a contributor to world peace, any improvement in the state of international understanding as a result of tourism is clearly to be encouraged and, therefore, further research as to how this may be achieved would be desirable.

Tourism as peace-broker

Perhaps the most ambitious perspective that we might take regarding the power of tourism to promote peace is the hypothesis that tourism can help to resolve existing conflicts and prejudices between unfriendly nations. Pizam (1996) attempted to test this theory by interviewing first-time tourists before and after visits to one of four destinations: Israelis visiting Egypt, Americans visiting the USSR, Greeks travelling to Turkey and Turks travelling to Greece. It was found that tourism did not contribute to positive attitudinal changes nor to perceived reduction of ethnic and nationality differences. In fact, most of the opinion changes which took place were in a negative direction. However, Pizam concludes that part of the reason for this was the fact that the tourist experiences of all four groups comprised escorted bus tours with little opportunity for meaningful interaction with local people.

Clearly, many forms of tourism, however benign, cannot support the claim of organisations, such as the WTO, that tourism is an effective means of achieving global peace and harmony. Exceptions to this might be, for example, where tourists engage in cultural exchange programmes or where individuals travel with the specific purpose of meeting with and developing an understanding of local people and cultures. However, these meetings generally take place only a small scale. Therefore, it is important to work towards developing a deeper understanding of tourist-host relationships and the potential for tourism as a broker of peace worldwide.

Peace as a pre-condition for tourism

In addition to addressing the role of tourism as a means of achieving greater worldwide peace and harmony, it is also important here to consider the tourism-peace relationship from the opposite viewpoint. That is, it is necessary to assess the extent to which peace (i.e. peaceful conditions in destination areas) is a pre-condition for successful tourism development. Reference has already been made to the fact that political upheaval or conflict represents a barrier to tourism development and events, such as the war in former Yugoslavia, the 1991 Gulf Conflict and the massacre of international tourists at Luxor in Egypt in 1997, serve to highlight the fragility of tourism as an international industry and its dependence on world peace (see Ryan 1991). Much is often made of flight cancellations, the exodus of tour operators and the effects on the tourism-dependent regions affected. However, scant attention is given to the ability of the international tourism industry to cope with continuing or recent conflict and political tensions in destination areas or to its ability to recover from these setbacks. For example, despite evidence of on-going conflict or attacks against tourists in a number of destinations, tourism has proved to be remarkably resilient. Sri Lanka is one such destination.

Peace in itself is a difficult concept to define and this makes its relationship with tourism all the more difficult to analyse. Does it mean absence of war, absence of conflict or, more generally a safe environment for tourism? Can, for example, a country with a poor record of human rights be said to be 'at peace'? Again, Sri Lanka is a good example of an area that has experienced internal conflict and whose tourism industry has fluctuated with events, but survived. Moreover, some tourists have been known to positively seek conflict as part of the 'travel' experience – there is even a guide for travellers to 'The World's Most Dangerous Places' (Pelton 1997) – or are willing to travel through 'risky' regions. Nevertheless, whatever definition of peace is used, the evidence suggests that, for the most part, countries will only attract significant numbers of tourists where, firstly an aura of peace is evident and second, where tourists perceive that they will not personally be at risk. Thus, the degree to which individual countries or regions may be considered peaceful is an important element in assessing the state of world tourism.

Features of global tourism

Having outlined various issues relating to the analysis of the state of world tourism at the global level, this second section of the chapter now considers current trends and flows in international tourism. Two points should be emphasised here. Firstly, any statistical analysis

of tourism should be undertaken within
we shall now consider, all tourism stati

Tourism statistics

The need for tourism statistics on
recognised. Statistics not only provid
tourism, but also they provide a
marketing strategies.

In short, it is statistical data tha
development of tourism.

One of the roles of the WTO is t
basis. For example, according to
some $455 billion which, as we
international tourism (WTO 2000
is so impressive, but the fact tha
(Cooper *et al* 1993: 57). In other wo
measure; not only is the collection of reliable and accur...
with difficulties owing to the complex nature of the tourism industry, o.
countries do not have the facilities, or are unwilling to commit scarce resources to in-depth
data collection. Therefore prior to examining international tourism statistics in more detail, it
is important to outline why such statistics should be used with care. There are two broad
areas of concern:

Definitions

A pre-requisite to any form of data collection is the need to set the parameters for the
research – it is impossible to measure or count things before it is known who, or what, is to
be counted. In other words, it is necessary to define different types of tourists, their activities
and relevant measurement criteria (e.g. length of stay, purpose of trip, etc.) prior to any
attempt to collect information. Unfortunately, however, although attempts have been made
by the WTO and other organisations to produce universally acceptable definitions of tourism
(see Chapter 1), not all countries adhere to them. Moreover, there is still considerable
confusion surrounding tourism definitions. For example, different destinations may or may
not include business travellers and day visitors in their tourist arrival statistics and generally,
what should, in theory, be a simple process is, in practice, rather complex.

The important point is, in order to be effective statistical parameters, definitions must be
simple, understandable and perhaps most important, universally applicable. Unfortunately,
however, 'a review of any of the statistics published by the UN/WTO points up the
innumerable footnotes to the data indicating national variations, differences in data collection
methodology and significant diversity in terminology standards' (Theobald 1998: 11).

Measurement techniques

The measurement of tourism can be broadly divided into the collection of statistics relating
both volume and value. Volume statistics include, for example, arrivals figures and/or the
number of nights a tourist spends in the destination, whilst value statistics are used to show
the level of tourists' expenditure during their visit. The latter usually includes any payments

for transport components owned by
tourism statistics include both measu
different data collection methods
meaningful.

These different collection m

- counting total ar
- sample surve
- accommo

In each of th
double-cou
countries
accom
acc

the host (destination) country and, typically, most
res. However, problems frequently emerge as a result of
in different destinations, thereby making comparisons less

ethods include:

ivals and/or departures at frontiers;

ys of arrivals/departures; and

dation records.

ese cases, certain difficulties may arise. For example, there is a danger of
ating the same visitor at border crossings, particularly in the case of landlocked
used as a route to and from the final destination. Statistics based on
modation records may also be inaccurate, especially where only registered
mmodation returns are used and, therefore visits to friends or relatives or non-registered
ccommodation are not counted. There are also inherent dangers in sample surveys, mainly
relating to the size or selection of the samples.

Despite these problems, it is trends and changes rather than absolute values which are of
most importance. Therefore, although statistical data may not always be accurate, they are
often the best available estimates and they do provide a useful source of information
regarding trends and changes in demand and a basis for marketing, planning and forecasting.

The growth of international tourism

The growth in international tourism has been a major phenomenon of the latter half of the
twentieth century. Since 1950, international tourist arrivals have increased from 25 million
to over 625 million by 1998, with the preliminary 1999 figure totalling 664 million (see
Table 3.1). This represents an overall growth factor of 24, whilst average annual growth has
been between four and eight percent. This suggests that international tourism has been, and
remains, reasonably resilient to external factors, although a number of significant world
events have temporarily halted its growth. In particular:

- *Conflict in the Middle East and Vietnam in the late 1960s.* These conflicts had a
  significant effect on the economies of major generating countries and were a
  contributing factor in the brief downturn in worldwide tourism growth in this period.

Table 3.1: *International Tourist Arrivals and Receipts, 1950-1998*

Year	Arrivals (000s)	Receipts (US$mn)	Year	Arrivals (000s)	Receipts (US$mn)
1950	25,282	2,100	1991	463,951	277,568
1960	69,320	6,867	1992	503,356	315,103
1965	112,863	11,604	1993	519,045	324,090
1970	165,787	17,900	1994	550,471	353,998
1975	222,290	40,702	1995	565,495	405,110
1980	285,997	105,320	1996	596,524	435,594
1985	327,188	118,084	1997	610,763	435,981
1990	458,229	268,928	1998	625,236	444,741

Source: adapted from WTO (1999)

- *The oil crises of 1973/4 and 1976.* The increase in the price of fuel and subsequent rise in transport costs brought about by the oil crises led to an inevitable fall in demand for international travel.

- *The economic recessions of the early 1980s and 1990s.* Widespread unemployment and an overall fall in disposable incomes in many countries affected people's propensity to travel. Moreover, in the early 1990s, the recession in the world's main economies was accompanied by the effects of the Gulf War in 1991 which led to an additional fall in demand for international travel.

Despite these setbacks, the figures reveal a continuing upward trend in international tourist arrivals. Moreover, as Table 3.1 also shows, the absolute value of world tourism in terms of receipts has also increased annually, as has tourism's contribution to the world's economy.

However, although the figures for tourism on a global scale are dramatic, growth has not been equitable. That is, not all parts of the world have experienced similar growth rates. Therefore it is necessary to consider who the major generators and receivers of tourism are before looking at trends and flows on a more regional basis.

Profile of international tourism

As mentioned earlier in this chapter, although tourism is significant to a large number of countries it is, in fact, dominated by relatively few. As Table 3.2 shows, about half of all international arrivals can be accounted for by ten nations, with the top fifteen attracting over 62 percent of global arrivals in 1999.

Table 3.2: *World's top 15 tourism destinations*

Rank				International Tourist Arrivals (million)			% change	Market share
1997	1998	1999	Country	1997	1998	1999	1998/9	1999
1	1	1	France	67.3	70.0	73.0	4.3	11.0
3	2	2	Spain	43.3	47.4	51.8	9.2	7.8
2	3	3	USA	47.8	46.4	48.5	4.5	7.3
4	4	4	Italy	34.1	34.9	36.1	3.3	5.4
6	6	5	China	23.8	25.1	27.0	7.9	4.1
5	5	6	UK	25.5	25.7	25.7	0.0	3.9
9	8	7	Canada	17.6	18.9	19.6	3.7	2.9
8	7	8	Mexico	19.4	19.8	19.2	-2.9	2.9
14	13	9	Russian Fed	15.4	15.8	18.5	17.0	2.8
7	9	10	Poland	18.8	18.8	18.0	-4.4	2.7
12	10	11	Austria	16.6	17.4	17.5	0.7	2.6
13	11	12	Germany	15.8	16.5	17.1	3.7	2.6
10	12	13	Czech Rep.	16.8	16.3	16.0	-1.8	2.4
11	14	14	Hungary	17.2	15.0	12.9	-13.8	1.9
17	15	15	Greece	10.1	10.9	12.0	9.9	1.8

Source: adapted from WTO (1999; 2000)

A similar story is evident in terms of tourism receipts (Table 3.3). The USA earns the most from tourism, over double the second placed country, whilst almost 55 percent of the world's receipts from tourism are earned by the top ten countries.

Table 3.3: *World's top 15 tourism earners*

Rank	Country	International Tourism Receipts (US$ billions)		% Change	Market Share
		1998	1999	1998/99	1999
1	USA	71.3	74.4	4.5	16.4
2	Spain	29.7	32.9	10.7	7.2
3	France	29.9	31.7	5.9	7.0
4	Italy	29.9	28.4	-5.1	6.2
5	UK	21.0	21.0	0.0	4.6
6	Germany	16.4	16.8	2.4	3.7
7	China	12.6	14.1	11.9	3.1
8	Austria	11.2	11.1	-0.9	2.4
9	Canada	9.4	10.0	6.7	2.2
10	Greece	6.2	8.8	41.6	1.9
11	Russian Fed.	6.5	7.8	19.4	1.7
12	Mexico	7.9	7.6	-3.9	1.7
13	Australia	7.3	7.5	2.6	1.7
14	Switzerland	7.8	7.4	-5.9	1.6
15	China/HK	7.1	7.2	1.8	1.6

Source: WTO (2000)

Moreover, of the ten most popular destinations for international tourism, five (United States, France, Italy, Austria and UK) are also ranked within the ten largest tourism generators (Table 3.4).

Table 3.4: *World's top 15 tourism generators*

Rank	Country	International Tourism Expenditure (US$ bn)		% Change	Market Share
		1998	1999	1998/99	1998
1	US	56.1	60.1	7.1	14.8
2	Germany	46.9	48.2	2.6	12.4
3	Japan	28.8	32.8	13.8	7.6
4	UK	32.3	-		8.5
5	France	17.8	17.7	-0.3	4.7
6	Italy	17.7	16.9	-4.2	4.7
7	Netherlands	11.0	11.4	3.6	2.9
8	Canada	10.8	11.3	5.0	2.8
9	China	9.2	-		2.4
10	Austria	9.5	9.2	-3.3	2.5
11	Belgium/Lux	8.8	-		2.3
12	Sweden	7.7	7.6	-2.1	2.0
13	Russian Fed.	8.3	7.4	-10.2	2.2
14	Switzerland	7.1	7.0	-1.8	1.9
15	Austria	5.4	5.8	7.5	1.4

Source: WTO(2000)

This pattern and concentration of world tourism has remained largely unchanged for a number of years although, more recently, this established shape of world tourism has begun to change. For example in recent years, Japan has been fast overtaking some European countries in generating tourism, the reason for this being both its rapid increase in wealth and also the increasing desire of the Japanese to travel overseas. Indeed, the Japanese government has been positively encouraging outbound travel among its population in an attempt to redress, to some extent, the country's large trade surplus with the rest of the world.

Other countries which have shown a significant growth in international tourism expenditure since 1980 include Taiwan, Korea, Singapore and Thailand, all of which have shown an average annual growth rate of between 17 and 21 percent during this period. This can be compared with the average growth rate of six to eight percent for a number of the traditionally dominant tourism generators, such as Germany, UK and France, and, despite the downturn in many Asian economies during the late 1990s, this trend is likely to continue.

Nevertheless, it is worth noting that the increasing significance of countries such as Japan, Taiwan and Singapore is based on tourism spending - the WTO has found that 'expenditure' is a more reliable measure of outbound tourism than aggregated departure statistics. In other words, the growing prominence of these countries stems not necessarily from the absolute numbers travelling but from the average spend per tourist on each trip. Table 3.5 shows the fifteen countries which produce the highest expenditure per trip.

Table 3.5: *Top ten countries with highest expenditure per trip abroad 1996*

Rank	Country	Av. expenditure per trip abroad (US$)
1	Venezuela	4,405
2	Thailand	2,260
3	Japan	2,218
4	Macau	2,014
5	Brazil	1,979
6	Australia	1,948
7	Singapore	1,857
8	Belgium	1,752
9	Iceland	1,631
10	Slovakia	1,581
11	Republic of Korea	1,497
12	Mauritius	1,491
13	Papua New Guinea	1,480
14	Bermuda	1,480
15	Norway	1,461

Source: WTO (1988)

Interestingly, neither the major European generating countries nor the United States feature in the top twenty in this league table, whilst the greatest spenders per trip, with the exception of Japan, are not normally considered to be major tourism generators. To illustrate this point, Venezuelans, for example, spent an average of $4,405 per trip in 1996 (latest available figures) while German travellers spent, on average, $657 per trip. However, Venezuela was responsible for roughly 511,000 international departures in 1996 as compared with around 77 million from Germany. Consequently, not only must statistics generally be treated with some caution, but care must also be taken in judging the relative importance of different markets on a worldwide scale.

However, it is not only changing markets for tourism which are responsible for influencing trends in global tourism flows. Although the world's four most popular destinations remained the same in 1998 as in 1980 (i.e. France, United States, Spain and Italy), many emerging destinations are gaining an ever-increasing share of international arrivals. China, Hong Kong, Turkey, South Africa, Indonesia and Thailand have, amongst others, experienced significant average annual growth rates in arrivals of between 12 and 15 percent since 1980.

In terms of earnings from tourism, these countries have also experienced significant rates of increase. For example, Hong Kong has broken into the top fifteen of tourism earners in the world, while China, Singapore, Thailand and Indonesia as well as Australia and Poland, have all moved into the top twenty tourism earning destinations since 1980.

It is apparent, then, that while the major worldwide economies continue to dominate global tourism, this traditional position is now being challenged. Moreover, it is also evident that there are large differences in the geographical distribution of arrival and receipts and that a definite regional pattern of growth and stagnation is emerging. Therefore, it is important to consider global tourism from a regional perspective in order to:

- identify major inter-regional and intra-regional tourist flows

- assess regional growth potential

- illustrate the regional nature of international tourist flows

Regional trends in global tourism

For analytical purposes, the WTO has divided the world into six regions: Europe, The Americas, Middle East, South Asia, East Asia and Pacific, and Africa. Broadly speaking, it is the East Asia Pacific region which has experienced the most significant growth in terms of its share of international tourist arrivals over the last decade, whilst most other regions, although continuing to attract greater numbers of tourists, have seen their share of world tourism decline. More specifically, each region has faced particular challenges and opportunities. These are outlined below.

Europe

As Table 3.6 illustrates, Europe receives the greatest proportion of international tourism each year - three times as many as its nearest 'rival', the Americas.

Europe's dominant position results from a number of factors. The region:

- is made up of a large number of small, geographically close nation states;

- is densely populated, with relatively high disposable incomes and a high priority placed on foreign holidays, particularly within France, Germany and the UK;

- has established communication networks and a large tourism industry and infrastructure; and

- is climatically, geographically and culturally diverse.

Table 3.6: *International tourism arrivals and receipts by region, 1998*

Region	Tourist arrivals (million)	% share of world arrivals	Tourism receipts (US$Bn)	% share of world receipts
Europe	383.8	60.3	232.5	52.7
Americas	119.9	18.8	118.0	26.8
East Asia Pacific	87.4	13.7	67.8	15.4
Africa	24.9	3.9	9.8	2.2
Middle East	15.3	2.4	8.6	1.9
South Asia	5.2	0.8	4.3	1.0
World	636.6	100	441.0	100

Source: adapted from WTO (2000)

With the exception of 1980, 1981 and 1991, international tourist arrivals in Europe have grown every year and, since 1970, have more than tripled from 113 million visits in 1970 to over 383 million in 1998. However, despite the growing number of arrivals in the region, Europe's share of world tourism is gradually declining. There are a number of inter-related reasons for this:

- increasing competition from 'new' destinations outside Europe;

- the growing propensity for Europeans to travel to other areas of the world for holiday/business purposes;

- the perception that many European tourism destinations are expensive in comparison with destinations elsewhere;

- the growing maturity of the tourist market in Europe and the tourism industry; and

- the downturn in some generating economies, particularly Germany.

The main problem facing tourism in Europe in recent years has been a lack of world competitiveness, exacerbated by the over-reliance on tourists from within the region. For example, although in 1991, over 80 percent of international tourism in Europe was generated internally, this proportion had fallen by 1995. During the same period, the proportion of travellers from the European region arriving in South Asia, Africa and the Middle East increased by 6 to 8 percent. Should this trend continue, it is most likely that those hardest hit would be western and southern European countries, such as France Spain and Italy, which have traditionally accounted for the largest percentage of both arrivals and receipts in the region.

Europe's proportion of world earnings from tourism has also declined correspondingly, although the figures have tended to fluctuate. For example, in 1990, Europe's share of international receipts was 54.4 percent, reached a low point at 50 percent in 1993, but has recovered to around 52 percent in the late 1990s. However, the general trend is downwards, a fact which is even more concerning given that tourism is an increasingly important sector in the economies of Europe. In 1995, earnings from tourism represented 8.7 percent of the region's export earnings, compared with 6.4 percent in 1985.

The Americas

The Americas region, which includes North, Central and South America as well as the Caribbean is, after Europe, the second most important tourism-receiving region of the world. In 1998, it accounted for 18.8 percent of international tourist arrivals and almost 27 percent of world tourism receipts. However, the extent of tourism within this region is much greater than the figures would suggest. Whilst the United States, Canada, Mexico and Brazil receive the majority of international arrivals in the area, they also have highly developed domestic tourism industries, a fact that is not accounted for in the WTO statistics.

The main tourist flows in the Americas come from within the region; 74 percent of arrivals are generated internally - half of these come from the United States and Canada - followed by European arrivals (14.6 percent). Despite the dominance of the internal market, arrivals from both Europe and East Asia Pacific (EAP) are increasing, particularly from the UK and Japan. The reason for this can be attributed, in part, to the competitively priced nature of the tourism product in the region. Not surprisingly, the US attracts both the highest number of arrivals in the region (39 percent) and the greatest proportion of receipts (63 percent). Indeed, the US tops the list of the world's highest tourism earners. However, the Caribbean accounts for a surprisingly large proportion of international tourism in the region - 13.1 percent of arrivals and 12.7 percent of receipts. Conversely, despite their large populations and geographical size, both South and Central America attract a relatively low proportion of international tourists (12.6 percent and 3.3 percent respectively in 1999). This is largely because of economic and political difficulties.

Africa

In contrast to the Americas and despite its geographical size, the African region enjoys a relatively low proportion of international tourism. In 1998, the region accounted for just 3.9 percent of all international arrivals and 2.2 percent of receipts. These low figures can be explained by a number of factors, including:

- there are many developing countries in the region lacking tourism infrastructure, investment and tourism development policies;

- many countries have suffered severe political and economic difficulties; and

- intra-African tourism remains under-developed; in 1995, only 42 percent of arrivals were from within the region, compared with almost 35 percent from Europe alone.

Of the European arrivals, the highest number come from France, followed by Germany and the UK, the pattern of tourist flows undoubtedly being influenced by historical colonial ties. For example, the majority of international tourist arrivals in The Gambia are from Britain, whilst the former French colony of Senegal attracts almost exclusively French tourists. Arrivals from the Americas remain low, partially as a result of a lack of international air routes.

Despite the overall low number of arrivals in the region, some individual countries have successfully exploited their tourism potential. For example, both Tunisia and Morocco have become popular destinations, making use of their proximity to the major European markets. Tunisia is the region's second most popular destination with over 4.7 million arrivals in 1998, followed by Morocco which attracted 3.2 million tourists in the same year. However, as a result of its more settled political climate, South Africa has rapidly increased its share of arrivals and is now the highest tourism earner and attracts the greatest number of international tourists within the region. In 1998, South Africa accounted for 27.8 percent of receipts and 23.4 percent of arrivals in the region.

Other countries have also begun to develop tourism industries including Zimbabwe, Mauritius, Namibia and Tanzania, but still twenty African countries still receive fewer than 100,000 visitors a year and thirteen of these attract less than 50,000. Nevertheless, the region possesses a great deal of potential for further tourism development and tourism is becoming an increasingly important part of the region's economy. For example, the contribution of tourism to Africa's export earnings increased from 4.9 percent in 1985 to 8 percent in 1995. However, for this to continue, significant levels of investment in tourism infrastructure and promotion, combined with a more stable political and economic environment, will be required.

The Middle East

Between 1994 and 1996, tourist arrivals in the Middle East grew more quickly than in any other region and, in 1999, achieved the world's fastest growth rate of 16 percent. Such a growth rate is surprising, particularly since the Gulf War in 1991 seriously impacted upon tourism in the area. However, as early as 1992, tourist arrivals had surpassed pre-Gulf War levels and, by 1996, total arrivals in the region had increased by 70 percent since 1990. Similarly, the region's share of world tourism arrivals has grown every year since 1991, although it remains low at just 2.7 percent.

The main destinations within the Middle East are Saudi Arabia with over 3.3 million arrivals in 1998, followed by Egypt (3.2 million) and Dubai (2.2 million). More generally, tourist flows to the region tend to be erratic, primarily as a result of political events and upheavals. For example, the massacre of tourists at Luxor in Egypt in 1997 had a significant impact on arrivals (although provisional 1999 figures point to a remarkable recovery, the country attracting almost 4.5 million visitors), whilst the tourism industries in many other countries suffer from the region's tendency towards political instability. Nevertheless, tourism does remain surprisingly resilient; this can be explained, in part, by the region's unique cultural and religious attractions.

South Asia

This region comprises those countries encircling and including the Indian sub-continent, such as Pakistan, Bangladesh, Nepal and Sri Lanka, and accounts for the smallest share of world tourism arrivals. Moreover, only 23 percent of international arrivals are generated within the region, partially as a result of the under-developed transport infrastructure and partly as a result of political tensions between countries in the region. The largest proportion (over 45 percent) of international arrivals come from Europe, with the UK representing the single largest generating country, although the Americas is an increasingly important market for the region.

Just under two thirds of all international arrivals in the region are shared by India and Pakistan. Indeed, India is the main destination with 45 percent of arrivals and 68 percent of receipts in 1998. However, a number of other countries, including Nepal, Sri Lanka and the Maldives, are all highly dependent on tourism. Nevertheless, tourism remains very under-developed in many parts of South Asia. Military conflict, political upheavals and human rights issues have discouraged tourism in countries such as Afghanistan, Myanmar (Burma) and Iran, and, whilst arrivals in general are increasing annually, the area has not matched the remarkable growth of the neighbouring East Asia Pacific region.

East Asia/Pacific

Of all the regions identified by the WTO, the EAP area has experienced the most significant and sustained growth. Between 1990 and 1997, international arrivals increased by 70 percent, from 53 million to 90 million. During the same period, receipts from tourism have more than doubled.

This remarkable growth was, until the financial crisis in the late 1990s, fuelled by the increasing strength of the economies in the EAP region. As a result, intra-regional tourism has been very strong; in 1995, almost 80 percent of international arrivals were generated from within the region. Japan, South Korea and Taiwan, in particular, have contributed to this trend. Conversely, Europe supplied just 12 percent. At the same time, many of these countries have been developing and investing heavily in their tourism industries. Thailand, Malaysia, South Korea, Hong Kong, Singapore and Indonesia have all undertaken development and promotional programmes. Therefore, international tourism in the region has benefited from both the growth in business-related tourism and more traditional types of tourism.

The main destinations in the region are China, Hong Kong, Malaysia, Thailand, Singapore and Indonesia, all of which have shown significant growth in tourist arrivals and receipts in the last fifteen years; they also achieved significant growth in 1999 following the region's economic turmoil in 1997/1998. However, new destinations, such as Vietnam and Cambodia, are also developing their tourism industries with some success, whilst Australia is also becoming more popular. Arrivals there rose from less than one million in 1980 to over 7.3 million in 1998, partially because of increased charter flights from Europe. At the same time, tourism to the tiny island states of Polynesia, Melanesia and Micronesia is also increasing, despite their geographical isolation. The attraction of these destinations lies in their quality tourism image and their proximity to New Zealand and Australia.

However the future growth prospects for the region are uncertain. The economic crisis of 1997 indicated a lack of economic stability and, although arrivals figures as a whole have bounced back (partly because of the devaluation of many South East Asian currencies, making the countries relatively cheap to visit), longer-term growth remains less certain.

Conclusion

This chapter started by emphasising the need for a global perspective on tourism. In doing so, it highlighted three particular areas of concern, namely, the role of tourism in global economic development, the need for a global approach to the environmental impacts of tourism, and the potential contribution of tourism to world peace. In each case, the adoption of a broad perspective identifies the actual state of world tourism, revealing ways in which tourism is, to a greater or lesser extent, achieving its 'ideal' objectives.

The statistical analysis in the latter half of this chapter reinforces many of these issues. In particular:

- The continuing domination of Europe and North America is evidence of the imbalance in world tourism flows and, hence, inequitable development potential of tourism. This pattern of world tourism is beginning to change, however, as a result of the emergence of new generating/receiving countries and changing patterns of demand in the more traditional markets.

- The growth in international tourism is dependent on economic growth; it is no coincidence that the region which has experienced the most significant growth in the share of world tourist arrivals has been the EAP.

- Conversely there are areas of the world where tourism growth has been restricted by either poor economic conditions, an unfavourable political climate, or a combination of both. Many African nations fall into this category.

- The continuing, albeit slowing, growth in world tourism, combined with the rapid development of 'new' mass tourism destinations has implications for the global environment.

Discussion questions

1. *To what extent can international tourism really contribute to world peace through the attainment of international understanding?*

2. *Explain now and why the traditional dominance of the world's major tourism generators and destinations is mow being challenged.*

3. *Why is tourism widely used as a vehicle of economic and social development?*

Further reading

Boniface, B. and Cooper, C. (2001), *Worldwide Destinations: The Geography of Travel and Tourism*, Oxford: Butterworth Heinemann.

Lockwood, A. and Medlik, S.(eds.) (2000), *Tourism and Hospitality in the 21st Century*, Oxford: Butterworth Heinemann.

Sharpley, R. and Telfer, D. (2002), Tourism and Development: Concepts and Issues, Clevedon: Channel View Publications

Theobald, W. (1998), *Global Tourism: The Next Decade, 2nd Edition*, Oxford: Butterworth Heinemann.

References

Ascher, B. (1984), Obstacles to international travel and tourism, *Journal of Travel Research* 22(3): 2-15.

Ap, J. and Var, T. (1990), Does tourism promote world peace?, *Tourism Management* 11(3): 267-273.

Cooper, C., Fletcher, J., Gilbert, D. and Wanhill, S. (1993), *Tourism: Principles and Practice*, London: Pitman Publishing.

D'Amore, L. (1988), Tourism - a vital force for peace, *Annals of Tourism Research* 15(2): 269-271.

Eber, S. (1992), *Beyond The Green Horizon: Principles for Sustainable Tourism*, Godalming: WWF.

Harrison, L. and Husbands, W. (eds.) (1996), *Practising Responsible Tourism: International Case Studies in Tourism Planning, Policy and Development*, Chichester: John Wiley & Sons.

Inskeep, I and Kallenberger, M. (1992), *An Integrated Approach to Resort Development: Six Case Studies*, Madrid: World Tourism Organisation.

Milman, A., Reichel, A. and Pizam, A. (1990), The impact of tourism on ethnic attitudes: the Israeli-Egyptian case, *Journal of Travel Research* 29(2): 45-49.

Pelton, R. (1997), *Fieldings: The World's Most Dangerous Places*, Fieldings Worldwide.

Pizam, A. (1996), Does tourism promote peace and understanding between unfriendly nations? in Pizam, A. and Mansfield, Y. (eds.) *Tourism, Crime and International Security Issues*, Wiley, Chichester.

Pizam, A., Milman, A. and Jafari, J. (1991), Influence of tourism on attitudes: US students visiting USSR, *Tourism Management* 12(1): 47-54.

Ryan, C. (1991), Tourism, terrorism and violence: the risks of wider world travel, *Conflict Studies 244*, RISCT: London.

Sharpley, R. (2000), Tourism and sustainable development: exploring the theoretical divide, *Journal of Sustainable Tourism* 8(1): 1-19.

Sharpley, R. and Sharpley, J. (1996), Tourism in West Africa: the Gambian experience, in Badger, P. Barnett, L. Corbyn and J. Keefe (eds.), *Trading Places: Tourism as Trade*, Wimbledon: Tourism Concern: 27-33.

Shaw, G. and Williams, A. (1994), *Critical Issues in Tourism: A Geographical Perspective*, Oxford: Blackwell.

Theobald, W. (1998), The context, meaning and scope of Tourism, in W. Theobald (ed.), *Global Tourism: The Next Decade, 2nd Edition*, Oxford: Butterworth Heinemann: 3-21.

Turner, L. and Ash, J. (1975), *The Golden Hordes; International Tourism and the Pleasure Periphery*, London: Constable.

Var, T., Ap, J., Van Doren, C. (1998), Tourism and world peace, in Theobold, W. (ed.) *Global Tourism: The Next Decade, 2nd Edition*, Butterworth-Heinemann, Oxford: 44-57.

Vellas, F. and Bécherel, L. (1995), *International Tourism: an Economic Perspective*, Basingstoke: Macmillan.

WTO (1994), *Tourism and the General Agreement on Trade in Services (GATS)*, Madrid: World Tourism Organisation.

WTO (1999), *Yearbook of Tourism Statistics 1996, 52nd Edition, Vols I and II*, Madrid: World Tourism Organisation.

WTO (2000), *Tourism Highlights 2000, 2nd Edition*, Madrid: World Tourism Organisation.

4

The Demand for Tourism

Richard Sharpley

Learning objectives

This chapter introduces the tourism demand process and, in particular, highlights the forces and influences that determine the outcome of tourist-consumer decision making. It enables the reader to:

- *understand the structure and flow of the tourism demand process*

- *appreciate the importance of motivation in tourism demand*

- *identify the factors that influence and shape the decision-making process*

- *appreciate the influence of consumer culture on the demand for tourism*

Introduction

The preceding two chapters have, in effect, been primarily concerned with the demand for tourism. Chapter 2 outlined the historical growth of tourism and its transformation (or democratisation) from an activity enjoyed by a privileged minority into a mass social phenomenon. In so doing, it identified a number of enabling factors, such as increases in free time and personal income, technological advances and the emergence of a sophisticated travel industry, that have facilitated the growth of mass, international tourism. Chapter 3 then looked at tourism from a global perspective, focusing in particular on the characteristics of major international tourist flows and trends and changes in those flows. Thus, both chapters have described how tourism has grown (i.e. how the demand for tourism has increased) and the volume and direction of present tourism flows (i.e. the current demand for tourism, or the number of people who participate in tourism and where they go).

Importantly, however, neither chapter has fully explored *why* it is that tourism has become such a widespread leisure activity, particularly in developed, western nations. That is, although a variety of conditions must be in evidence for people to be able to participate in tourism (and for particular countries or destinations to be attractive to tourists), these do not alone explain why it is that people decide to 'consume' tourism, as opposed to other products or services, or what form that tourism will take. To put it another way, even though most people may have the ability to be tourists, it does not follow that they will all do so or, indeed, seek similar tourist experiences.

For example, roughly 60 percent of the adult British population take a holiday (defined as four or more nights away) each year; conversely, 40 percent do not take a holiday, a proportion that has remained the same for almost twenty years. Thus, the growth in tourism in the UK (domestic and outbound) is primarily accounted for not by more people participating in tourism, but by existing tourists taking additional holidays. At the same time, of course, the market for tourism is neither uniform nor homogenous. Different tourists seek an enormous variety of different tourism experiences, and are influenced or motivated to do so by an equally diverse variety of factors. Thus, for tourism businesses to be able to market their products effectively, to identify and target specific markets or segments and to satisfy their needs (see Chapter 18), some understanding of the complex and dynamic nature of the demand for tourism is necessary.

Therefore, purpose of this chapter is to explore the demand for tourism at the level of the individual tourist. In particular, it focuses upon:

- the tourism demand process

- tourist motivation

- factors that pattern or influence the nature of tourism demand

- transformations in tourism demand

What is demand?

Tourism demand can be defined in a number of ways. Most commonly, it refers to the actual, measurable participation in tourism as a whole, or specific types of tourism, and it is presented in the form of statistical data. It is referred to as expressed, effective or actual demand. Thus, the actual demand for international tourism to the UK is roughly 25 million visitors, this being the annual number of overseas visitors who have visited the UK in recent years. In addition to expressed, actual demand, however, there are three other categories of demand:

- *Suppressed demand*: there may be significant numbers of tourists who wish to visit the UK, but are unable to do because of time constraints, a lack of money, or some other factor that prevents then from fulfilling their wish. Thus, their demand is suppressed until such time that their circumstances allow them to become part of the actual demand for tourism to the UK.

- *Latent demand*: in addition to suppressed demand, there are undoubtedly tourists who would visit the UK but do not because of a lack of knowledge or a lack of awareness of the means and opportunities for visiting the country. Latent demand may also exist if potential tourists feel that the services or products but they desire are not currently provided by the tourism industry.

- *No demand:* there will always be those who do not wish to travel, who will never demand tourism.

For travel and tourism businesses, therefore, the challenge is to maintain and increase their share of actual demand at the same time as converting latent demand to actual demand. Similarly, the aim of national tourist organisations is, primarily, to satisfy latent demand. It is also evident that, globally, the total demand for tourism (expressed plus suppressed plus latent) is significantly higher than actual demand, the main growth opportunities being in those countries and regions where, currently, demand is suppressed (see Chapter 3).

The tourism demand process

The demand for tourism, as for most products or services, is far more complex than is immediately evident. That is, the apparently simple process of deciding to go on a holiday and then purchasing one is influenced at every stage by a variety of tangible and intangible factors, from the obvious and measurable constraints of time and money to the more subjective individual needs of the tourist. Thus, although the desire to travel can be seen as the result of having 'itchy feet', or the 'travel bug' – a condition referred to by Michael Palin in his book 'Around the World in 80 Days' as *dromomania* – in reality, such is the diversity of influences that determine the demand for tourism that explaining why people travel is a difficult, if not impossible, task. Indeed, it has been observed that most tourists themselves are unable to identify what motivates them into going on holiday (Krippendorf 1987) whilst, within tourism studies, there is no common theory or understanding of the tourism demand process (Jafari 1987). Nevertheless, for travel and tourism businesses to be able to plan, develop and market their products effectively to satisfy the needs of tourists, then it is necessary to understand the nature of the tourism demand process.

As a starting point, it is important to note three related points. Firstly, many tourism texts refer simply to 'tourist motivation' when considering the demand for tourism. However, 'the term tourism demand should not be equated with tourism motivation. Tourism demand is the outcome of tourists' motivation' (Pearce 1992: 113) and is, in fact, only the first step in the demand process. Secondly, the tourism demand process is not a one-off event in people's lives. That is, although the actual holiday may only last one or two weeks, the overall experience, including anticipating the holiday, selecting and purchasing it, and remembering it afterwards, may represent a continual, cyclical process in people's lives, with previous experiences influencing the nature of subsequent holiday decisions (see Figure 4.1).

Figure 4.1: *The tourism demand cycle*

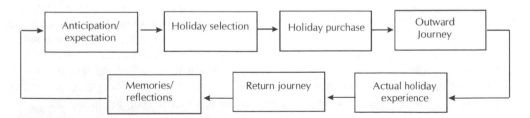

In this model, each element is an important part of the overall demand process, with certain aspects, such as anticipating or dreaming about the holiday, being as exciting and satisfying (if not more so!) than the holiday itself.

Finally, the demand for tourism should not be viewed in isolation from other demand processes or from the broader socio-cultural setting within which it occurs. Not only does tourism 'compete' with other products and services for a share of an individual's usually finite disposable income, but also a number of factors, such as values, tastes, fashion and 'consumer culture', influence behaviour. As Solomon observes, 'consumption choices simply cannot be understood without considering the cultural context in which they are made' (Solomon 1994: 536).

Collectively, these points suggest that the demand for tourism is highly complex. It is related to both personal preferences and constraints and external socio-cultural influences, as well as being dynamic and evolving in line with the tourist's own experience and expectations. A number of authors have attempted to develop models of this complex process (see Goodall 1991 and, more generally, Cooper *et al* 1998 – Chapter 3), some of which are simple, unidirectional linear models, whilst others are more sophisticated. All, however, follow the basic premise that, once they have decided to purchase a holiday, tourists go through a process of acquiring information, deciding what holiday would best satisfy their needs and, subsequently, evaluating the extent to which those needs were met. Moreover, each stage in this process is shaped by a variety of personal and external factors. Figure 4.2 summarises this tourism demand process.

Figure 4.2: *The tourism demand process*

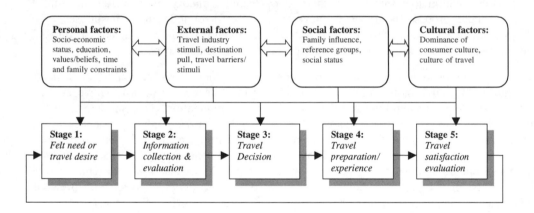

Inevitably, perhaps, this model over-simplifies the tourism demand process, although it does highlight the principal elements of consumer decision-making. Thus, prior to any purchase decision, the consumer (tourist) must feel or recognise a need which may be satisfied by the consumption of a particular product or service. The choice of product/service selected is then determined both by personal and external social factors and by the choice on offer (i.e. the attraction of different destinations and the way in which it is sold or packaged), as well as the experience of previous holidays. At the same time, however, the entire process is influenced by broader cultural factors, in particular the role of consumption in society.

These elements of the tourism demand process are usefully summarised by Gilbert (1991: 79), as follows:

(a)   *Energisers of demand*: These are the various forces, including motivation, that act as a trigger setting off the tourism demand process.

(b) *Filterers of demand*: these are all the factors, such as time, income and demographic characteristics, that constrain choice or 'filter out' inappropriate products.

(c) *Affectors of demand*: the actual choice of holiday will be affected by the attributes and image of different destinations.

(d) *Roles:* the role of the tourist as a consumer (who is making the decision and 'how' they consume) will also determine the final choice of holiday.

Of course, any attempt to explain the overall tourism demand process is fraught with difficulty, particularly as most consumers are unlikely to follow, whether consciously or unconsciously, a logical decision-making process. For example, many holidays are undoubtedly bought as last-minute, impulse purchases whilst, more generally, going on holiday (buying on trust, experiencing unusual environments, and so on) is hardly rational behaviour. Indeed, the annual mass rush for the sun has been likened to the behaviour of lemmings (Emery 1981)! Nevertheless, it is important to appreciate specific influences on the decision-making process, and it is with these that the following sections are concerned.

Tourist motivation

Motivation is the most important yet, at the same time, most complex elements of tourism demand. Certainly, without motivation there would be no demand for tourism: 'the importance of motivation in tourism is quite obvious. It acts as a trigger that sets off all events in travel' (Parrinello 1993). In other words, it is motivation that provides the link between a need and action to satisfy that need; it is motivation that translates a need into goal-orientated consumer behaviour. However, much less clear is how needs emerge in the first place and how the satisfaction of those needs can be related to tourism in particular. For example, there are those who argue that motivation is purely a psychological concept and, therefore, that tourism demand is the result of intrinsic, psychological needs, such as relaxation, love and affection, and so on (hence the common reference to Maslow's 'hierarchy of needs' in many tourism texts).

Conversely, there can be no doubt that the motivation for tourism is also socially determined. That is, it is society that, in one way or another, creates the need within people to travel, to participate in tourism. For example, society 'expects' people to take a summer holiday and, in a sense, tourism is 'social therapy, a safety valve keeping the everyday world in good working order' (Krippendorf 1986). Undoubtedly, for most people it is the need to escape, from work, from the 'rules' of society or whatever, that provides the primary motivation to go on holiday, whilst a variety of socially-determined factors also influence the type of holiday people take. These are considered in more detail in Chapter 20.

It is not surprising, therefore, that the literature on tourist motivation encompasses a broad spectrum of ideas and approaches. By way of summary, Dann (1981) identifies seven different perspectives on motivation that have been adopted:

(a) *Travel as a response to what is lacking yet desired*. The motivation for travel lies in the desire to experience something new or different. People become tourists because their own physical and cultural environment cannot fulfil this need.

(b)   *Destinational pull in response to motivational push*. This approach highlights the importance of push factors in tourist motivation (see below). Such factors may be determined by the tourist's home environment or by an individual's own psychological needs.

(c)   *Motivation as fantasy*. Tourists may be motivated by the perceived opportunity to indulge in forms of behaviour that would not normally be 'allowed' in their usual home/work environment.

(d)   *Motivation as classified purpose*. In contrast to push factors, this approach views the purpose of a trip as the primary motivating factor.

(e)   *Motivational typologies*. Typologies of tourists are often used as models of tourist motivation. However, they may be more accurately seen as factors that influence the nature of tourist behaviour rather than a primary force behind the initial need to consume tourism.

(f)   *Motivation and tourist experiences*. This approach suggests that tourist motivation is largely determined by the expected experience in relation to the home environment, in particular by the promise of authenticity (again, see Chapter 20).

(g)   *Motivation as auto-definition and meaning*. The ways in which tourists define and respond to situations, rather than simply describing their behaviour, is seen by some as one way of explaining tourist motivation.

It is neither possible nor appropriate here to review all of these (see, for example, Sharpley 1999). Nevertheless, certain points which more fully explain the role and nature of tourist motivation deserve emphasis.

Push versus pull factors

In order to clarify the importance and position of motivation in the tourism demand process, a distinction must be made between what are called 'pull' and 'push' factors. Pull factors refer to all the knowledge, information, images and perceptions that an individual has of a particular holiday or destination. These 'destination-specific attributes' (Goodall 1991: 59) include tangible factors, such as accommodation facilities, beaches, entertainment facilities, the prospect of good weather, and so on, whilst more subjective factors include how fashionable the resort is.

Conversely, push factors influence, or push, the individual into wanting a holiday in the first place. These 'person-specific motivations' are the needs that push an individual into wanting a holiday or trip of a particular type, or a holiday as opposed to another product or service. Thus, only when a need or push has been recognised do pull factors come into play; push factors motivate the individual to buy a holiday, whereas pull factors determine which holiday or destination is chosen to best satisfy the individual's needs.

The distinction between push and pull factors is of fundamental importance to understanding the role of motivation within the demand for tourism. For example, the choice of a beach holiday might be explained by the 'pull' of the climate and the likelihood of getting a suntan. However, the true motivation may well result from the need to be seen with a suntan; the push is to get a suntan that can be shown off when the tourist returns home. Similarly, the motivation to visit exotic destinations may not be the desire to see a particular place, but the opportunity to say that you have been there (reinforced by the opportunity to send the ubiquitous post card or to take holiday photos to show at home!). In short, 'the key to understanding tourist motivation is to see vacation travel as a satisfier of needs and wants' (Mill and Morrison 1985: 4). The task then is to consider what creates these needs.

Intrinsic versus extrinsic motivation

Although a number of different approaches are evident in the literature, there are two distinct perspectives which are of particular use and which, for the most part, embrace much of the existing theory and knowledge of tourist motivation. At the same time, they also recognise the traditional dichotomy between motivation as a psychological or a sociological concept.

i. Intrinsic motivation

The basis of intrinsic motivation is that all individuals possess a variety of unique personal needs, the satisfaction of which has long been considered the primary arousal factor in all motivated, goal-oriented behaviour, including tourism. Therefore, the understanding of human motivation is, from an intrinsic motivational perspective, dependent upon what those needs are and how they can be fulfilled or satisfied.

One of the best known and most widely referred to theory of motivation is, of course, Maslow's hierarchy of needs (see Chapter 13 for more detail). Maslow originally proposed five classes of needs, from basic physiological needs through to self-actualisation, each of which must be satisfied before the individual is motivated by the next level in the hierarchy. Given its simplicity, Maslow's model has been adapted to different contexts, including tourism, in order to explain human behaviour. For example, a similar framework of tourist motivation was developed by Pearce and Caltabiano (1983), who suggest that hierarchical needs, ranging from biological (rest and recuperation), through relationship and special interest needs to self-actualisation, can be used to explain tourist behaviour.

More simply and generally, intrinsic psychological needs have been collectively referred to as 'ego-enhancement' motivational factors (Dann 1977), which suggest that people are motivated to participate in tourism in the expectation of intrinsic psychological rewards. In other words, people are motivated to travel or to go on holiday to have their ego or confidence boosted, to personally and psychologically gain from tourism and to feel better about themselves. This may be achieved whilst travelling (for example, by staying at an hotel that provides levels of service or luxury not normally experienced during the tourist's day-to-day life at home) or on return (as before, the opportunity to show off the suntan). A number of other psychological motivations have also been listed by Krippendorf (1987), who includes compensation and social integration, escape, communication, broadening the mind, self-determination, self-realisation, and happiness as intrinsic needs that may form the basis of tourist motivation.

ii. Extrinsic motivation

In contrast to intrinsic motivation, extrinsic motivational factors are those forces and pressures which emanate from an individual's social and cultural environment and which may, to a lesser or greater extent, influence that individual's needs and motivations. In a general sense, this may simply be 'society' as a whole. That is, for most people, tourism represents the opportunity to escape from the pressures, strain or even boredom of everyday life, to unwind and relax or to seek excitement and new experiences. Indeed, it is probably true to say that tourism has become an essential ingredient in an individual's life cycle in modern society – in order to survive modern life and society, an individual must, periodically, escape from it. In this sense, modern tourism has achieved the status of a new religion; it is a kind of sacred journey which provides physical and spiritual refreshment.

More specifically, however, both the need or desire to go on holiday, and the nature of the experience sought, may be directly influenced by external (as opposed to intrinsic, psychological) factors which become translated into needs within the individual. These are discussed in more detail in Chapter 20, but are summarised in Figure 4.3.

Figure 4.3: *Extrinsic motivational factors*

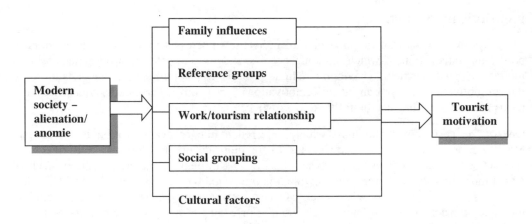

Inevitably, not all of these extrinsic factors will influence an individual tourist. Indeed, if it were actually possible to accurately ascertain the factors and influences that determine an individual's motivation to participate in tourism (an unlikely event given the fact that most tourists do not recognise – or are not prepared to admit – what actually motivates them), it is likely that there are as many forms of tourist motivation as there are tourists. Nevertheless, it is safe to suggest that, for the most part, tourists are motivated by a combination 'escape' and 'ego-enhancement' needs and, therefore, the challenge facing the tourism industry is to recognise and satisfy these needs with products and experiences that are attractive to tourists.

Factors that pattern or influence the nature of tourism demand

According to the model of the tourism demand process (Figure 4.2), once an individual is motivated to purchase a holiday or trip (i.e. the tourism demand process has been 'energised'), he or she then goes through a process of collecting information, from brochures, travel agents, advertisements, guide books, word of mouth and personal experience before making a travel decision. That decision is, partly, based on the extent to which a particular trip, holiday or destination satisfies the individual's needs (for example, a skiing holiday for someone who seeks a healthy lifestyle), but also partly according to constraints or factors which limit or shape the eventual choice. These are the 'filterers' and 'affectors' referred to earlier and are, in effect, a set of both tangible or measurable factors and subjective, psychographic factors. (The latter category includes the tourist's attitudes, values and beliefs which, perhaps inevitably, also impact upon motivations, but for the sake of simplicity we shall consider them here separately from motivation.) Thus, although a skiing holiday has been identified as the ideal holiday, the actual destination, length and time of holiday and other variables will be subject to a number of factors.

Tangible demand factors

In the previous chapters, a number of tourism 'enabling' factors were identified which, since the mid-1800s, have contributed to the emergence and democratisation of tourism. Principally, these factors can be grouped under the headings of 'time', 'money' and 'technology', increases or advances in which have been the driving force behind the historical growth in tourism. At the same time, the development of a sophisticated travel and tourism industry, greater public sector support, changes in the structure of the tour operating industry (see Chapter 5), improvements in information and ancillary services, such as insurance, and innovation in product design have all, all the 'macro' level, contributed to the expansion of tourism.

Some, if not all, of these have also had an impact on tourism demand at the individual, micro level and it is important to consider these and other factors that act as filters and affectors in the tourism demand process.

Mobility

As a prerequisite to tourism (which by implication involves travel), an individual must benefit from mobility. In one sense, this means having the freedom to travel, something that the populations of the industrialised, western world have long enjoyed – subject to visa restrictions in destination countries – but which those in many other countries have only recently begun to enjoy. At the same time, however, mobility may be taken more literally as the physical ability to travel. Thus, in the UK domestic market, car ownership is a significant influence on mobility whilst, more generally, the extent to which facilities are provided for those with disabilities has a significant impact on tourism demand.

Employment and income

As already noted, the nature of an individual's work may be related to the desired type of holiday experience. However, as tourism is an expensive activity that requires a certain level of income before participation is possible, employment plays a more fundamental role in the demand for tourism. More simply stated, with the exception of certain groups, such as those with independent means or retired people on private or occupational pensions, it is usually necessary for at least one family member to be in employment to pay for a holiday.

However, simply having a job and income does not guarantee the ability to participate in tourism. Although it is safe to assume that, as income rises, so too does the demand for tourism, it is vital to consider tourism as an item of expenditure on the household budget. In other words, although some level of gross income is necessary before a holiday can be afforded, tourism is usually a discretionary, or non-essential, form of expenditure. All households have certain outgoings that cannot be avoided – the mortgage or rent, income and local tax, expenditure on food, clothing, transport, and so on – and only when these have been paid can some (or all!) of the remaining, discretionary income be spent on tourism. At the same time, all households have different discretionary income levels. A 'double-income-no-kids' household may have significant sums of money to spend on tourism compared with a young family; conversely, they may have committed themselves to very high mortgage before having children and therefore have little spare cash for holidays.

This suggests that the effect of income on tourism demand must be considered at the individual level although, when average levels of discretionary income fall, such as during a recession or when interest rates are high, it has been found that it is the amount spent on a holiday, rather than the number of holidays, that decreases. This suggests, in turn, that tourism is becoming an essential (i.e. non-discretionary) element of household expenditure.

In addition to discretionary income levels, it is important to note two other economic factors that influence the demand for tourism:

(a) **Absolute cost of tourism.** The ability to pay for a holiday is dependent on not only levels of income, but also the 'real' cost of the holiday. Thus, if holidays become cheaper in real terms, then it is likely that overall demand will increase or that the demand will shift to more exotic/luxurious types of holiday or destination. Certainly, the average price of package holidays out of the UK fell during the early 1990s, contributing to the growth in international tourism, whilst the inclusion of cruising in package holiday brochures significantly increased demand for a once exclusive form of holiday.

(b) **Relative costs.** As a result of exchange rate fluctuations and local economic conditions in the destination, the demand for particular destinations can rise and fall. In the mid-1990s, for example, the French franc was relatively strong against sterling and, as a consequence, the number of British visitors to France fell dramatically. Conversely, the strong pound over the last two years has made many countries much more affordable to British tourists, particularly those which have devalued their own currencies.

Paid holiday entitlement

Related to employment and income, the amount of paid holiday that an individual enjoys is also a major determinant of tourism demand. Since the Holidays with Pay Act was passed in Britain in 1938, ever-increasing numbers of employees have benefited from greater amounts of paid holiday time. For example, by 1969, 97 percent of all full-time manual workers in Britain received two weeks paid holiday; by 1988, 99 percent received four weeks, with many of those in the professions enjoying even longer paid holidays. Thus, paid holiday entitlement has inevitably had a positive impact on the demand for tourism, in particular permitting additional holidays to the traditional two-week summer break, although more flexible work practices, such as 'flexi-time', have also enabled people to take more short-break holidays.

Of course, not all countries enjoy the same levels of paid holidays. It tends to be more generous in developed countries, although the USA is less generous than many European countries. Much also depends upon the number of public or 'bank' holidays which are more numerous in some countries than others, whilst the availability of paid holidays does not always guarantee that all employees take full advantage of their entitlement. Equally, not all paid time off will be spent on holiday, suggesting that, overall, there is not an entirely clear relationship between the levels of paid holiday and the demand for tourism.

Education

Typically, a positive relationship exists between levels of education attainment and the propensity to travel (Cooper *et al* 1998: 43), although it is probably fairer to suggest that it is not participation in tourism itself, but the *type* of tourism demanded, that varies according to education. Therefore, it is likely that the more educated tourist is more likely to seek out new destinations, new experiences and, perhaps, view tourism itself as an education.

Demographic factors

Inevitably, the demand for tourism is affected by a variety of demographic variables, including age, stage in the family life cycle, race and gender. Thus, parents with young children are constrained by destination choice and by time if the children are at school, whilst older people (or 'empty-nesters') enjoy more flexibility, particularly if they are retired and can travel at times to suit themselves. Race is also an important variable. Increasingly, international tourist flows follow historical patterns of migration, with a significant demand for tourism between, for example, Britain and the Indian subcontinent or Australia/New Zealand and Britain, whilst some forms of tourism are entirely determined by race/culture, such as the annual pilgrimage to Mecca. Gender is, generally, a less significant determinant of tourism demand although women travellers may be discouraged from visiting certain countries as a result of local cultural or religious practices.

Values, attitudes and beliefs

As suggested above, all stages of the tourism demand process are influenced by a potentially large variety of factors which determine not only the comparison of alternatives and choice of holiday, but also the actual and evaluated holiday experience. In particular, these factors include demographic variables: 'it is commonly believed that tourist behaviour [is] affected, if not determined, by the tourist's age, sex, marital status, education, disposable income, place of origin and other similar factors' (Pizam and Calantone 1987). However, although such factors are useful for segmenting markets and as a basic predictor of how particular groups may consume tourism, they reveal little about *why* tourists behave in particular ways.

As a result, it is increasingly recognised that so-called psychographic or life-style variables, which include values, attitudes, opinions and interests, are more important influences in the tourism decision-making process. In other words, although certain descriptive variables, such as demographic characteristics, may limit or affect the eventual holiday choice, the entire decision-making process is framed and guided by values, attitudes or beliefs upon which the individual bases most, if not all, forms of behaviour and decisions.

The most powerful of these influences are, according to Rokeach (1973), values. Whereas an attitude refers to the application of a number of beliefs to a specific situation or object, a value 'refers to a single belief of a very specific kind' (Rokeach 1973: 18). In other words, values are concerned with acceptable or appropriate forms of behaviour or end-states that an individual aspires to and, thus, govern that individual's interests, attitudes, consumption behaviour and other activities that define a lifestyle.

According to Rokeach, not only do individuals carry these beliefs or values that determine their modes of behaviour, but they also organise them into a value system. This represents a continuum of the relative importance of the different values they hold, which then guides behaviour and decision-making according to different situations. Thus, an individual who embraces 'pleasure' as a higher value and 'environmental concern' as a lower value may normally buy environmentally friendly products except in the case of a holiday, where pleasure will be the dominant desired end-state. Rokeach himself devised a 'value survey' of 18 'instrumental' and 'terminal' values, which includes values such as 'pleasure', 'freedom', 'exciting life' and 'self-respect', all of which of direct relevance to tourism as well as reflecting the two primary motivational factors of escape/avoidance and self-reward/ego-enhancement. Indeed, many of Rokeach's terminal values are likely to be dominant in the tourism decision-making process (see Figure 4.4)

Figure 4.4: *Rokeach's terminal values*

A comfortable life	Inner harmony
An exciting life	Mature love
A sense of accomplishment	National security
A world at peace	Pleasure
A world of beauty	Salvation
Equality	Self-respect
Family security	Self-recognition
Freedom	True friendship
Happiness	Wisdom

Source: Rokeach (1973: 359-40)

A more simple version of a value scale for segmenting consumer behaviour is the Values and Lifestyle Scale (VALS) that divides American consumers into nine lifestyles or types under four categories based upon their self-images, aspirations, values and beliefs (Figure 4.5)

Figure 4.5: *VALS categories*

Need Driven Groups:	**Outer Directed Groups:**
Survivor lifestyle Sustainer lifestyle	Belongers lifestyle Emulator lifestyle Achiever lifestyle
Inner Directed Groups:	**Outer/inner Directed Groups:**
I-am-me lifestyle Experiential lifestyle Societally-conscious lifestyle Self-directed lifestyle	Integrated lifestyle

Here, there are evident links between these groups and sub-groups of consumer types and different forms of tourist behaviour, suggesting that the VALS scale represents a useful predictor of tourism demand. For example, inner directed, societally-conscious consumers are, perhaps, likely to favour 'appropriate' forms of tourism, such as eco-tourism, whilst outer-directed groups are more likely to choose holidays or trips that offer the opportunity for status enhancement.

Surprisingly, perhaps, few empirical studies have been made into the influence of values on tourism demand in particular (see Sharpley 1999: 171). Those that have been undertaken have demonstrated that values are indeed related to holiday or destination choice criteria and different forms of actual behaviour. At the same time, however, they suggest that values alone are not a sufficient criterion for predicting behaviour. Not only does the importance place on specific values vary according to context but, within tourism, there is a greater likelihood of value conflict. That is, values of socially acceptable behaviour may, for example, conflict with hedonistic-type values. Thus, the importance of values to the study of tourism demand lies in their contribution – as one of a number of factors – to a greater understanding of how and why tourists make particular consumption decisions, rather than underpinning the entire process.

Consumer culture and tourism

For the most part, research into the tourism demand process in general, and tourist motivation in particular, has been highly tourism-centric. That is, attention has been largely focused on the actual tourism decision-making process and the factors, at the level of the individual, that influence that process. Conversely, until recently, less importance has been placed on exploring the significance and meaning of tourism as a form of consumption in general, and the ways in which the consumption or styles of tourism may be influenced by cultural transformations and developments in the tourist's home environment in particular.

To put it another way, it is certainly important to understand the process that tourists go through in purchasing a holiday and to appreciate the factors that shape or direct that process. However, to focus specifically on the needs and wants of individuals and how tourism may satisfy those needs and wants is to overlook the broader cultural forces that influence not only tourism, but all forms of consumer behaviour. Tourism is but one of innumerable forms of consumption in a world where people's lives are increasingly defined by their consumption habits; that is, people consume, or buy, products and services not only for utilitarian need satisfaction, but also to give 'meaning' to their social existence. Tourism is no exception and, therefore, it is important to understand the role of this 'consumer culture' in general on the consumption of tourism in particular.

What is 'consumer culture'?

Consumer culture may be defined as the character, significance and role of the consumption of commodities, services and experiences within modern societies. Its existence as a cultural phenomenon implies that consumption, as a social activity, has become culturally significant. More simply stated, the emergence of a dominant consumer culture reflects a shift in power from the producer to the consumer. Whereas throughout the twentieth century, up to the early 1970s, the consumer was obliged to accept what was produced by manufacturers (indeed, the success of mass production as pioneered by Henry Ford – hence the term 'Fordist' production – was dependent on willing mass consumption), more recent years have witnessed the emergence of 'consumer power', with producers having to respond to frequent changes in taste and fashion.

In part, this has come about as a result of changes in the social and economic system in post-industrial societies that have enabled the practice of consumption to assume a leading role in people's lives. These changes include:

- the large, widely-available and ever-increasing range of consumer goods and services;

- the popularity of 'leisure shopping';

- the emergence of consumer groups and consumer legislation;

- pervasive advertising; and

- widely available credit facilities.

Collectively, these factors have provided the consumer with enormous choice and, hence, power (Lury 1996).

However, it is not only the practice of consumption that has underpinned the emergence of consumer culture. It has long been recognised that commodities, whether goods or services, have a meaning or significance beyond the basic economic exchange or use value. Therefore, when people buy things, not only do they buy commodities that fulfil a particular function, but also they acquire things which create or shape their social life. In short, people consume products and services not only for their basic use, but also to say something about themselves. The obvious example is, of course, the car which, fundamentally, is a convenient means of travelling from one place to another. However, the car is also, arguably, one of the most powerful status symbols of modern times.

Collectively, the practice and significance of consumption can be thought of as 'the active ideology that the meaning of life is to be found in buying things and pre-packed experiences' (Bocock 1993: 50). That is, people add meaning to or embellish their day to day existence through consumption of goods and services, and tourism is no exception to this process. In other words, tourism has long had a significance beyond its 'utilitarian' value of providing rest, relaxation, escape, education, and so on, with people choosing different modes of transport, types of holidays or destinations for other reasons. Most typically, people consume tourism as a means of classification or self-identity creation, to classify themselves in relation to other people and to establish social status. As one commentator has observed, 'while travel has remained an expression of taste since the eighteenth century, it has never been so widely used as at present' (Munt 1994). Thus, people may choose to holiday at an all-inclusive resort in the Caribbean, such as Sandals, in order to feel exclusive, or to have a holiday in Agia Napa in Cyprus to be part of the 'club scene'.

The implication for the travel and tourism industry is that, increasingly, it is having to develop more specialised, niche products to satisfy the demands of tourists who are no longer satisfies with the standard 'off-the-shelf' package holiday. Thus, eco-tourism holidays, all-inclusives, fly-cruise holidays, more distant or exotic destinations and more individualistic holidays (albeit within the framework of the traditional package of flights, transfers and accommodation) are becoming more widely available, offering the aura of status or luxury though at a relatively affordable price. In other words, although tourists are undoubtedly motivated by the desire to escape, rest, relax and have fun, their consumption of tourism experiences is framed by a cultural dimension of which the industry is becoming increasingly aware.

Changes in demand: shift to the new tourist?

As evidence, perhaps, of the influence of consumer culture on the demand for tourism, there is little doubt that tourists are becoming more discerning, more quality and value conscious, more individualistic and, generally, more experienced in the practice of consuming tourism. In other words, it would appear that tourists are increasingly rejecting the standardised package for holidays or tourism experiences that do not conform with the image of a mass produced / consumed (and, by implication, down-market) product.

Certainly, changes in the demand for tourism over the last decade tend to support this view. In general, tour operators and other tourism businesses are having to develop more specialised products for niche markets. Mention has already been made of the introduction of 'package-cruises' by major tour operators in the early 1990s (see also Chapter 7), but other notable trends include:

- an increasing demand for activity-based holidays;

- significant growth in the 'eco-tourism' market – this is considered by many to be the fastest growing sector of international tourism;

- an expansion of the long-haul holiday/package market;

- the increasing popularity of theme parks and holiday parks;

- a consequential relative drift from traditional sun-sea-sand holidays to cutural tourism, urban and rural tourism;

- growth in the short-break market;

- a relatively greater incidence of independent, as opposed to organised (packaged) holidays.

This list is, of course, by no means exhaustive. The important point here, however, is that some would claim that these changes in the demand for tourism are themselves evidence of the emergence of the 'new' tourist. For example, Poon (1993) suggests that 'old', mass tourism, characterised by mass produced, mass marketed and standardised holidays, were consumed by inexperienced, 'sun-lusting', unadventurous tourists. Conversely, she argues that the new tourist is, for example, more flexible, more experienced, has more special interests, is environmentally sensitive, is more independent and seeks variety, adventure and quality. Similarly, others suggest that tourists are becoming 'greener', that they are demanding holidays that are more environmentally appropriate (the growth in demand for eco-tourism usually being cited in support of this argument). This latter point is certainly open to debate although, as argued elsewhere, there is little evidence to suggest that tourists do in fact take environmental factors into consideration when buying a holiday (Sharpley 1999; Swarbrooke and Horner 1999). Indeed, with reference to the previous section on consumer culture, it has been suggested that eco-tourism (which tends to be exclusive and expensive and usually occurs in more exotic destinations) should actually be called 'ego-tourism' (Wheeller 1992)!

Whether or not the new, 'good' tourist exists, two points should be emphasised. Firstly, the package tour remains highly popular, suggesting that significant numbers of tourists are satisfied with the convenience, safety and value of the traditional package holiday. Secondly, however, there is no doubt that people have become more experienced tourists. They are less willing to accept poor quality or service and poor value for money, they understand their legal rights as consumers (see Chapter 15), and they increasingly seek more individualistic holidays, albeit within the framework of the package. Thus, tour operators are becoming obliged to focus more on quality, service, diversity whilst, at the same time, maintaining the relatively low prices that underpin the success of the tour operating business (see Chapter 5). Whether this can be achieved through greater efficiency or, as is more likely, through increases in the average price of holidays remains to be seen.

Conclusion

This chapter has considered the tourism demand process, focusing in particular on the variety of influences and forces that determine why and how people 'consume' tourism. Emphasising the fact that motivation does not equate with demand – the demand for tourism is, in effect, the outcome of tourist motivation – it has demonstrated that there are no simple answers to the question 'why do people participate in tourism?'. Indeed, such is the variety of influences, both tangible or measurable, such as income or time, and socio-cultural, that each tourist goes through a unique, personal demand process. Nevertheless, it is vital that tourist businesses understand and appreciate this variety of influences on tourism demand in order to be able to continue to satisfy the changing needs of tourists.

Discussion questions

1. Why is it important for tour operators and other tourism businesses to understand the tourism demand process?

2. Consider the extent to which tourists are primarily motivated by the desire to 'escape'.

3. How relevant are an individual's values to the tourism decision-making process?

4. In what ways, and to what extent, have tour operators been obliged to respond to the influence of consumer culture in tourism?

Further reading

Cooper, C., Fletcher, J., Gilbert, D., Shepherd, R. and Wanhill, S. (1998), *Tourism: Principles and Practice, 2nd Edition*, Harlow: Longman – Part One.

Ryan, C. (1991), *Recreational Tourism: A Social Science Perspective*, London: Routledge.

Sharpley, R. (1999), *Tourism, Tourists & Society, 2nd Edition*, Huntingdon: Elm Publications.

Swarbrooke, J. and Horner, S. (1999), *Consumer Behaviour in Tourism*, Oxford: Butterworth Heinemann.

References

Bocock, R. (1993), *Consumption*, London: Routledge.

Cooper, C., Fletcher, J., Gilbert, D., Shepherd, R. and Wanhill, S. (1998*), Tourism: Principles and Practice, 2nd Edition*, Harlow: Longman.

Dann, G. (1977), Anomie, ego-enhancement and tourism, *Annals of Tourism Research* 4(4): 184-194.

Dann, G. (1981), Tourist motivation: an appraisal, *Annals of Tourism Research* 8(2): 187-219.

Emery, F. (1981), Alternative futures in tourism, *International Journal of Tourism Management* 2(1): 241-255.

Gilbert, D. (1991), An examination of the consumer behaviour process related to tourism, in C. Cooper (ed.) *Progress in Tourism, Recreation and Hospitality Management, Volume III*, London: Bellhaven Press: 78-105.

Goodall, B. (1991), Understanding holiday choice, in C. Cooper (ed.) *Progress in Tourism, Recreation and Hospitality Management, Volume III*, London: Bellhaven Press: 58-77.

Jafari, J. (1987), Tourism models: the sociocultural aspects, *Tourism Management* 8(2): 152-159.

Krippendorf, J. (1987), *The Holiday Makers*, Oxford: Heinemann.

Lury, C. (1996), *Consumer Culture*, Cambridge: Polity Press.

Mill, R. and Morrison, A. (1985) *The Tourism System*, New Jersey: Prentice Hall International.

Munt. I. (1994), The 'other' postmodern tourism: culture, travel and the new middle classes, *Theory, Culture and Society* 11(3): 101-123.

Parrinello, G. (1993), Motivation and anticipation in post-industrial tourism, *Annals of Tourism Research* 20(2): 233-249.

Pearce, P. (1992), Fundamentals of tourist motivation, in D. Pearce and R. Butler (eds.) *Tourism Research: Critiques and Challenges*, London: Routledge: 113-134.

Pearce, P. and Caltabiano, M. (1983), Inferring travel motivation from travellers' experiences, *Journal of Travel Research* 22: 16-20.

Pizam, A. and Calantone, R. (1987), Beyond psychographics – values as determinants of tourist behaviour, *International Journal of Hospitality Management* 6(3): 177-181.

Rokeach, M. (1973), *The Nature of Human Values*, New York: The Free Press.

Sharpley, R. (1999), *Tourism, Tourists & Society, 2nd Edition*, Huntingdon: Elm Publications.

Solomon, M. (1994), *Consumer Behaviour: Buying, Having and Being, 2nd Edition*, Needham Heights, Mass.: Allyn and Bacon.

Wheeller, B. (1992), Eco or ego tourism: new wave tourism, *ETB Insights, Vol III*, London: English Tourist Board: D41-44.

Section 2

The Tourism Industry

As suggested in Chapter 1 of this book, the term 'tourism industry' is rather misleading. That is, the numerous and diverse businesses and organisations that collectively supply the tourism 'product' cannot be described as an industry in the traditional sense of the word – most sectors are industries in their own right, some are only indirectly involved in tourism and others play a more supportive role. Thus, it is, perhaps, more accurate to describe this overall network of organisations as the tourism production system.

Nevertheless, as the diagram below demonstrates, this production system comprises three broad areas – the core producers/suppliers of tourism, private sector supporting businesses, and public sector or governmental organisations. All play an essential role in the overall supply of tourist experiences, but the central, core group of producers represent what is usually referred to as the tourism industry.

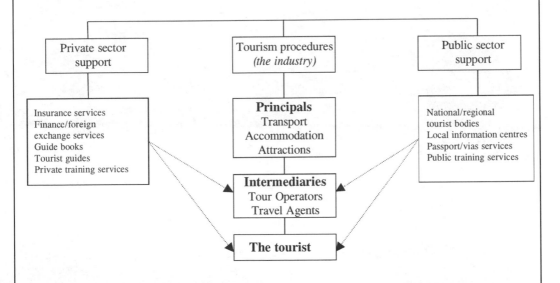

This section of the book introduces the separate elements of the tourism industry (the tourism producers), their operation and role within the production system and the opportunities and challenges facing the individual sectors.

5

Tour Operations

Julia Sharpley

Learning objectives

This chapter explores the development, structure and functions of the tour operating sector. On completion of this chapter, the reader should be able to:

- *explain the structure of the tour operating industry*

- *understand the role and implications of integration within the sector*

- *appreciate the different functions and activities of tour operators and constraints on those activities*

- *discuss the main challenges facing the tour operating sector*

Introduction

Since the early 1950s, when Vladimir Raitz established Horizon Holidays and offered what is considered to be the first charter flight-based package holiday (Yale 1995: 38), tour operators have played a dominant role in the production and distribution of tourism. Not only have they made a significant contribution to the growth and democratisation of international mass tourism (see Chapter 2), but also they have come to occupy a strategically dominant position within the international tourism industry. Indeed, as Ioannides (1998: 139) suggests, tour operators act as 'gatekeepers' to the industry, being able to exert 'enormous influence over the geography of origin-destination tourist flows and, ultimately, the fortunes of individual destinations'.

At the same time, and despite the more recent growth in demand for independent holidays, inclusive tours/package holidays remain as popular as ever. Thus, although inclusive tours represent a declining proportion of total overseas holidays taken by British tourists (Table 5.1), the total number of overseas holidays continues to grow, as does the number of inclusive tour holidays, albeit at a slower rate. In fact, an estimated 17 million inclusive tours were taken by the British in 1999, only slightly below the record 17.4 million in 1998; of these, 13.7 million, or 81 percent, were holidays by air (Mintel 2000). The number of licensed tour operators also continues to grow; in the UK, for example, there are now in excess of 1400 Air Travel Organisers License (ATOL) holders. However, the majority of these are small, specialist companies and it is the large, international operators that are best known and which, over the last decade, have achieved a dominant position within the industry.

Table 5.1: *Independent/inclusive overseas holidays taken by British tourists (millions)*

	1986	1990	1995	1997	1986 – 97 % change
Total overseas holidays	17.5	20.5	26.0	26.5	+51
Of which:					
independent holidays	6.5	9.0	11.0	11.5	+77
inclusive tour holidays	11.0	11.5	15.0	15.0	+36
Inclusive tours as % of total	62.8	56.1	57.7	56.6	

Source: adapted from Pender (2001: 7)

The purpose of this chapter is to explore the structure and activities of the tour operating sector. In particular, it focuses upon:

- The role of the tour operator in the production and distribution of tourism.

- The structure of the industry and the benefits of integration.

- The planning and creation of a package holiday.

- The importance of consumer protection.

- Quality management in tour operating.

Firstly, however, it is important to define what is meant by the term 'tour operating'.

Tour operations: a definition

Perhaps the best way of explaining the nature and scope of tour operating is to define the product of tour operating – that is, the inclusive tour or package holiday.

The package holiday

According to Section 2(1) of the EU's Package Travel, Package Holidays and Package Tours Regulations 1992 (see also Chapter 15), a package holiday is legally defined as:

'the pre-arranged combination of at least two of the following components when sold or offered for sale at an inclusive price and when the service covers a period of more than 24 hours or includes overnight accommodation:

(a) transport

(b) accommodation

(c) other tourist services not ancillary to transport or accommodation and accounting for a significant proportion of the package.'

Thus, although package holidays are, perhaps, most commonly thought of in terms of charter flights to summer sun destinations, there is in fact an enormous variety of types of package holiday. Package holidays by air, for example, can be subdivided into travel by scheduled carrier (known as ITX) and travel by charter flight (ITC).

For simplicity, different types of package tour can be characterised by:

- *Mode of transport*: in addition to air inclusive tours, the transport element of a package holiday may involve travel by ship (ferry, cruise liner, hovercraft, chartered yacht, etc.), rail, coach (travel to or around the destination) or hired car or bicycle. Some packages can also be characterised by the holidaymaker providing their own transport such as walking, cycling and domestic self-drive holidays.

- *Mode of accommodation*: the accommodation element of a package may be a room in an hotel, guest house or other serviced accommodation (Chapter 8), a self-catering apartment or villa, a tent or caravan, or may even be combined with the transport element, such as a cabin on a cruise ship.

- *Services provided*: a package may include only the basic flight, transfer and, say self-catering accommodation. At the other extreme, it may be 'all-inclusive', where all meals, drinks and, perhaps, activities and entertainment are provided.

- *International vs. domestic*: although most usually associated with outgoing international tourism (for example, UK tourists taking holidays overseas), an important sector of the market is incoming inclusive tours, organised by either overseas operators or operators based within the UK. At the same time, package holidays are also sold to the domestic market, typically based on coach travel or self-drive.

- *Length of holiday*: the length of a package holiday may vary from a short-break of between one and three nights away to longer holidays (i.e. four or more nights away). Typically, this is the 7, 10 or 14 night holiday, although some tour operators offer extended winter-sun holidays for the retired market.

- *Distance to destination*: The majority of package holidays are taken within Europe – 90 percent of inclusive tours from the UK are to Europe, with Spain accounting for over 30 percent of the market (Mintel 2000) – and are, therefore, to 'short haul' destinations (normally considered to be up to four hours flying time). However, long haul destinations, including North America, the Caribbean, the Far East and Australia, are becoming increasingly popular.

Overall, then, the package holiday is a much broader concept than is immediately apparent. Indeed, even a six-month overland trip through, for example, South America, which would include return flights, transport in trucks and/or local transport, and basic accommodation and food is, in fact, a package holiday. Adventure tour operators offering these types of holiday are, however, unlikely to refer to them as such – ironically, they are usually referred to as 'independent travel'!

It is also evident that a package holiday need not necessarily include air travel. However, the majority of inclusive tours are by air and therefore, it is with these operators that this chapter is principally concerned.

The tour operator

Following on from the above definition of an inclusive tour/package holiday, a tour operator (or what the EU Package Travel regulations refer to as a 'tour organiser') is clearly an individual or organisation who buys the various components of the package (usually in bulk), combines them to produce the package holiday, and then sells it to the customer either directly or through a travel agent. This implies, of course, that a travel agent who assembles a holiday for an individual customer can also take on the role of a tour operator.

In a sense, therefore, a tour operator is a wholesaler, occupying an intermediary position in the chain of distribution between producers (principals) and the retailers, although some would argue that, by assembling a variety of products into a single, new product, tour operators themselves are producers. In practice, this intermediary role reflects the activities of the majority of smaller operators (see also Chapter 6); however, as we shall see shortly, the larger tour operators own both certain elements of production, such as airlines and hotels, and retailers (travel agencies), reinforcing their role as 'gatekeepers' referred to above.

The role of tour operators

Tour operators exist and are, by and large, successful because they fulfil an important function within the tourism industry. In other words, tour operators are needed by both principals and customers and, undoubtedly, they remain in business by satisfying the needs of these two groups.

The needs of principals

The attraction of tour operators to tourism producers or principals, specifically airlines, hotels and ground operators (for example, local coach operators or tour organisers in the destination) is their ability to reach customers and their access to distribution channels to sell their products. In other words, tour operators are able to provide principals with business which they might not otherwise be able to attract. For example, many hotels in tourism destinations are smaller, independent businesses which possess neither the necessary resources for marketing nor the reputation to attract customers. Thus, tour operators provide an essential link between destination accommodation providers and the major tourism generating markets. Through bulk purchasing, they are also able to provide, subject to certain conditions, a guaranteed level of business for hotels over particular periods, such as the summer season. Similarly, for airlines, particularly scheduled flights which must operate irrespective of the number of seats booked, tour operators play an important role in filling seats which may otherwise go unsold (Holloway 1998: 192-194).

In both cases, the ability of tour operators to provide a guaranteed level of sales through their marketing power, their access to large numbers of potential customers and their brand image, enables principals to cover their high levels of fixed costs and to plan more effectively in what is, traditionally, a volatile and uncertain business where demand and supply are rarely in balance.

The needs of customers

Although the advent of the Internet has allowed tourists to assemble their own package more easily and quickly (see Chapter 19), tour operators still offer a number of significant benefits to customers:

- *Price*: as a result of bulk purchasing and their dominant position in the chain of distribution, tour operators can usually negotiate prices that are much lower than those which an individual tourist could secure. Although the 'no-frills' airlines, such as EasyJet, have significantly reduced the cost of flights to many destinations, package holidays are still a cheap way to enjoy overseas holidays.

- *Convenience*: by combining all the elements of the holiday into a single package (and then selling it through the brochure), tour operators make it much easier for tourists, who normally do not have the necessary expertise, knowledge, time or access to principals, to purchase holidays. Indeed, the convenience of 'one-stop' holiday shopping has probably been, along with price, one of the most important factors in the development of mass, package tourism.

- *Reliability*: travel and tourism, particularly overseas travel, inevitably involves an element of risk and uncertainty for the tourist. In other words, by travelling from an environment (their home) with which they are familiar to one (the destination) with which they are not – they may not speak the local language, be familiar with local customs, and so on – they are putting themselves at risk. At the same time, as the tourism product can be 'pre-tested', they may be unsure about the quality of the experience that they are paying for. Conversely, the tour operator, through the package holiday, provides an element of reliability and quality, as well as an aura of safety, to the potential tourist. In short, the package holiday is relatively safe and predictable although, in practice, the quality and service promised in the brochure may not always be provided. In such circumstances, the tour operator also offers:

- *Consumer protection*: since the introduction of the Package Travel Regulations in 1992 (see Chapter 15 for more detail), tour operators are liable for all aspects of the holidays which they assemble and sell. Therefore, in buying an inclusive tour from a tour operator, tourists enjoy rights and a degree of protection that would not be available to them if they were holidaying independently.

If the importance of tour operators to both principals and consumers was to diminish, then they would be in danger of disintermediation. That is, if tourists were increasingly able to deal directly with airlines and hotels at a reasonable cost and if principals were able to attract a sufficient customer base of their own, thereby reducing their often total dependence on intermediaries, then tour operators would, in effect, be overlooked in the chain of distribution. However, there is no evidence to suggest that this is likely to occur to any great extent in the near future.

The structure of the tour operating sector

The tour operating sector of the UK travel industry is currently dominated by four major tour operators – Airtours plc, Thomson Travel Group, Thomas Cook and First Choice Holidays plc – who between them control around 60 percent of the market for package holidays. However, as already noted, there are over 1400 'air' operators alone who require a license (ATOL) from the Civil Aviation Authority (CAA) and, although this figure also includes licenses provided to 'flight-only' operators, the CAA figures probably provide the best guide to the proliferation of smaller tour operators in the UK. At the same time, there are, of course, many other types of tour operators, including outgoing/incoming international operators and domestic operators, which utilise other forms of transport. As a result, it is impossible to estimate accurately the total number of tour operators in the UK. Here, we are concerned primarily with air tour operations.

The current structure of the tour operating sector is characterised by:

- An élite group of about 10 vertically integrated tour operators which collectively account for 70 percent of the air holiday market. This group includes the 'big four', along with other well-known companies, such as Unijet Travel and Virgin Holidays.

- A central group of established, medium sized operators which enjoy strong a strong, niche market presence. These carry between 100,000 and 300,000 passengers a year. As discussed shortly, however, in recent years, a number of these have come under the ownership of the majors – for example, Direct Holidays is now part of the Airtours group.

- A very large number of small, specialised operators, carrying up to 100,000 (but usually fewer) passengers, which focus on particular markets or destinations.

Table 5.2 lists the top 20 ATOL carriers in the UK in 2000.

Table 5.2: *Top 20 ATOL tour operators[i] in the UK, 2000*

Operator	Passengers carried	Operator	Passengers carried
Thomson Holidays	4,172, 570	Gold Medal Travel Group	369,680
Airtours	3,106,646	Direct Holidays	303,297
JMC Holidays	2,915,009	British Airways Holidays	287,302
First Choice Holidays	1,895,469	Kuoni Travel	261,136
Unijet Travel	917,800	Specialist Holidays	257,960
Avro	601,808	Lotus International	211,433
Trailfinders	592,827	Libra Holidays	199,460
Virgin Holidays	394,339	Travel 2	176,104
Thomas Cook Retail	287,145	Kosmar Villa Holidays	161,483
Cosmosair	374,681	Panorama Holidays Group	146,851

Source: ATOL (2001a)

[i.] It is important to note that an ATOL is awarded to individual tour operators, not to the parent company. Thus, for example, Airtours are licensed separately from Direct Holidays and Panorama, although all are part of the Airtours group.

Two principal factors have led to the present structure. Firstly, recent years have witnessed increasing concentration (or horizontal integration) within the sector, with the larger companies increasing their market share by purchasing smaller operators. Secondly, the sector has also been characterised by vertical integration, with the larger tour operators owning and/or controlling their own airline and travel agencies.

Over the two decades, this process of horizontal and vertical integration has led to significant transformations in the structure and ownership of the tour operating sector. Not only have some companies been able to grow into large, multi-national corporations (Airtours, for example, started off as a small travel agent in the north-west of England, Pendle Travel, which first set up tour operating division in 1980), but some of the largest of the UK operators have themselves been taken over by overseas groups – the Thomson Travel Group, for example, is now owned by the German company Preussag AG, the world's largest tourism group.

At the same time, it has also resulted in a number of spectacular failures, the first being the collapse of Court Line/Clarksons Holidays in 1974 which stranded 50,000 tourists abroad. Similarly, International Leisure Group (ILG), the owners of the then second largest tour operator in the UK, Intasun, collapsed in 1991. Usually, such failures result from one or more of the following factors:

- Over-rapid growth based upon excessive borrowing to finance expansion.

- Insufficient profit resulting from price cutting to maintain market share.

- External factors, such as fuel prices rises or political instability.

For example, the terrorist attacks in the USA on September 11th 2001 and the subsequent drop in demand (by December 2001, an estimated one million UK tourists had cancelled or re-arranged their overseas travel plans, whilst summer 2002 bookings remained 50 percent down on the previous year) are expected to lead to a number of operator failures.

The changing structure of the tour operating sector over the last decade is outlined by Holloway (1998: 199-200), whilst Figure 5.1 details the most recent patterns of ownership with respect to the four major UK tour operating groups.

Figure 5.1: *The four major UK tour operators: who owns what*

	Tour operations	Retail Operations	Cruise Operations	Airline Operations
Airtours plc	Airtours Holidays Panorama Bridge Travel Service Cresta Holidays Eurosites Tradewinds Worldwide Jetset Europe Leger Holidays Holidays for Less (Aspro) Direct Holidays Manos	Going Places (729 outlets) Travel World (138 outlets) Late Escapes Go Direct Flightdeck Holidayline	Airtours Sun Cruises The Carnival Corporation	Airtours International
Thomson Travel Group	Thomson Holidays Portland Direct Skytours Club Freestyle Just Port Philip Group	Lunn Poly (794 outlets) Callers Pegasus (34 outlets) Sibbald Travel (12 outlets)	Thomson Cruises	Britannia Airways

Thomson Travel Group	Austravel Budget Travel Thomson Breakaway Thomson Ski, Lakes & Mountains Crystal Holidays Jetsave Jersey Travel Service Tropical Places Greyhound Intrenational American Holidays Something Special Hols. Spanish Harbour Hols. Magic Travel Group SimplyTravel Headwater Holidays	The Travel House (61 outlets) Team Lincoln Budget Travel Manchester Flights Thomson preferred agents – aligned independents (2,500 outlets)		
Thomas Cook	JMC Thomas Cook Holidays Neilson Club 18-30 Time Off Style Holidays Sunworld Ireland Skiers World British Airways Holidays (50:50 venture)	Thomas Cook shops (700 outlets) Thomas Cook Plus (6 travel warehouses) Thomas Cook Direct ARTAC Worldchoice partnership (800 outlets)	None	JMC Airlines
First Choice Holidays plc	First Choice Holidays Eclipse 2wentys Sovereign First Choice Ski, Lakes & Mountains Unijet Flexi Conference & Incentives Flexiski Skibound Ski Partners Travelbound Schools Abroad Sunquest Hayes and Jarvis Meon Group Sunsail Crown Holidays Falcon (Ireland) JWT (Ireland)	Travel Choice and Travel Choice Express (200 outlets) Travel Choice Direct Bakers Dolphin (78 outlets) holiday Hypermarkets (32 outlets) Hays Travel (partner – 23 outlets) Holiday Express (partner – 22 outlets)	First Choice Cruises Alliance with Royal Caribbean International from summer 2002	Air 2000 Viking Aviation (seat broker)

As is evident from Figure 5.1, each of the four major tour operators are highly integrated organisations, each owning a significant number of tour operating companies/brands, retail outlets, and an airline. Not shown here, however, is the wider extent of their activities. Airtours, for example, has a significant interest in tour operations in Scandinavia, America and Germany, whilst Thomsons, as well as owning overseas operations in the Nordic region, also controls a number of specialist holiday companies including Crystal Ski, Austravel, Breakaway (short and city break holidays) and Headwater Holidays (adventure holidays) which come under the banner of its Specialist Holiday Group. Until relatively recently, Thomson was also a major player in domestic tourism in the UK with its Holiday Cottages Group which has now been sold.

Whilst the actual structure of the tour operating sector is of interest (and, of course, dynamic), of greater importance in the context of this chapter is the reason why this concentration and integration has occurred within the industry. Therefore, the following section explores the factors that have brought about the present patterns of ownership and control.

Tour operating: integration

The benefits of both horizontal and vertical integration can be explained from two perspectives. Firstly, and in a practical sense, integration provides a number of benefits to tour operating businesses, as follows:

Horizontal integration (i.e. across one level of the chain of distribution) provides a tour operator with:

- economies of scale (bulk purchasing, marketing economies, etc.)

- increased market share

- the opportunity to strengthen through expansion

- the opportunity to strengthen through diversification (new products)

Vertical integration (i.e. linking with organisations at different levels in the chain of distribution) provides a tour operator with:

- economies of scale

- continuation of supply – tour operators depend upon a supply of hotel beds and airline seats

- the ability to control quality – given their liability under the Package Travel Regulations, it has become increasingly important for operators to control the quality of all elements of the package

- control over distribution (retailing) and merchandising – it is more likely that an operators products will be sold if it owns its own retailing operation.

Secondly, integration can be explained more broadly as a means of surviving and growing within a highly competitive and dynamic industry such as tourism.

Integration as a competitive strategy (see Dale 2000)

According to Porter (1980), there are five major forces within the competitive environment which any organisation must be aware of and react to in order to survive (see Figure 5.2).

According to this model, the most challenging competitive conditions occur when new entrants are likely, when buyers and suppliers are able to exercise control over the market place and when there are many substitutes. To a great extent, this reflects the potential characteristic of tour operating industry and, therefore, Porter's model can usefully explain both horizontal and vertical integration as a logical response to competition within tour operating.

Figure 5.2: *Porter's five forces model*

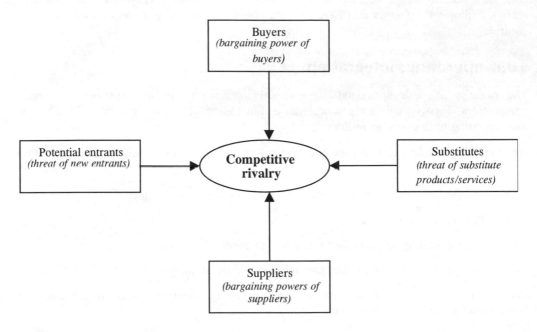

i. New entrants

Tour operating has, traditionally, been an easy industry to enter; that is, there are relatively few barriers to entry. Not only does it require little capital, but there is easy access to suppliers and retailers, whilst there is little chance of retaliation as the industry is comprised mainly of hundreds of other small businesses. Therefore, for existing companies to survive and make a profit in the face of the threat of new entrants, companies need to either grow or specialise; a quick way to achieve this is, of course, by acquiring other companies (i.e. horizontal integration).

ii. Buyer power

Tour organisers and travel retailers can be viewed as 'buyers' within the chain of distribution, each with the potential to exert a powerful influence on their suppliers. Tour organisers 'buy' the required elements of their package holiday (accommodation, flights, ground handing etc.) from principals and depending on their 'buying power' can exercise considerable control over them. At the same time, however, retailers can also exercise power over tour organisers in their role as buyers. Although holiday products are not bought and sold in the same way as tangible goods, the larger of the national and regional holiday retail chains, such as Lunn Poly and Going Places, are, given their access to a wide customer base, able to exert power over tour operators through their selection of which holiday companies products to sell. This retailer power can be reinforced in the following situations where:

- there are too many tour operators trying to place their products with too few retailers

- they have a brand that is stronger than that of the smaller operators

- backward integration with a tour operator can increase the power of an agency over non-integrated operators.

This power is often manifested in higher commissions being demanded to 'stock' a particular tour operators holidays, or in the directional selling (the favouring through, for example, the racking of brochures) of a particular operator's products. Thus, in order to compete, tour operators must either secure distribution channels – that is, integrate vertically downwards – or seek alternative distribution methods. For example, First Choice have, in recent years, sought to expand their retail operations (see Figure 5.1 above), whilst Airtours bought Direct Holidays in 1998 in order reach the customer directly.

Of course, as mentioned, many tour operators themselves enjoy buyer power over the principals, particularly when they are larger and can choose from a large number of suppliers. This is most often the situation faced by destination accommodation providers who cannot hope to have a stronger brand than, or better access their generating markets than, the tour operators who buy from them. Nonetheless, it is possible for very well-established, high quality hotels to achieve such a good reputation in popular resorts that it can pick and choose between potential buyers. This is known as supplier power (see below).

iii. Supplier power

The suppliers, such as airlines, hotels and ground handlers, have power over tour operators when:

- there are few or just one large supplier

- the supplier enjoys strong brand recognition amongst potential tourists

- the supplier integrates forward with another operator

- tour operators are insignificant to the supplier's overall business.

This supplier power is particularly evident in the case of airlines and their relationship with non-integrated operators. They might supply them with the least desirable seats or flight times or, given the fact that seats on aeroplanes tend to be less plentiful than hotel beds, not supply them at all. Indeed, as the industry has become more integrated, independent operators have found it increasingly difficult to secure seats on airlines owned by other tour operators.

Hotels may also have power over tour operators, particularly the larger hotel groups in popular resorts. In response, tour operators can integrate backwards, buying their own airline, hotels and, in some cases, ground handling operations, in order to guarantee both the supply and the quality of these elements of the package holiday. Alternatively, smaller tour operators may seek alternative sources of supply, such as new destinations, or grow (through horizontal integration) to gain more buying power.

Tour operators can also wield considerable supplier power over travel agents in deciding whether or not to distribute their holiday offering through them. Many tourists would, for example, expect to be able to buy a well-recognised brand such as Thomson or Airtours from their agent and would take their business elsewhere if they could not.

iv. The threat of substitute products

Within tourism, an enormous variety of substitutes exist for any one tour operators products. These can include, for example:

- Domestic holidays for overseas holidays.

- Skiing holidays for summer sun holidays.

- Short breaks for one long holiday.

- Activity holidays for beach holidays.

- All-inclusive holidays for self-catering.

- One destination/country for another.

A particular challenge for tour operators is where independent travel becomes a substitute for the package holiday, rendering the tour operator's product obsolete. More usually, however, the main problem facing tour operators is that their products can be easily substituted. Not only are there many other companies offering similar products, but tourists are increasingly seeking new or different types of holidays or more exclusive, up-market experiences.

In order to survive, integration is once again a key strategy. That is, many operators have diversified, through integration, into 'substitute' areas in order to keep their customers. Thomsons, for example, offer a wide range of specialist expertise through those companies they have acquired which now form their Specialist Holiday Group, First Choice satisfy the demand for more exclusive holidays through their acquisition of Hayes and Jarvis, whilst Bridge Travel has given Airtours a foothold in the city-break market. Additionally, operators are adding more benefits or quality to their existing offerings, something that is likely to occur more frequently as opportunities for strategically beneficial integration diminish. It is also worth noting that non-holiday products can also substitute for a holiday purchase, making it especially important that holiday companies improve on the personal benefits to be gained from a holiday and deliver them.

v. Competitive rivalry

Finally, competitive rivalry is most likely to occur when:

- Competitors are the same size.

- There are high fixed costs and, thus, there is a high level of competition to cover these costs.

- Markets are undifferentiated – most companies sell the same products to the same customers.

- In order to gain competitive advantage, extra capacity must be bought in large quantities.

These characteristics largely reflect the current structure of the (integrated) tour operating industry. As a result, the large operators compete aggressively for market share and, certainly in recent years, their focus has been upon growth through integration and pricing strategies. However, as there are now fewer opportunities for large scale integration, particularly in the British, if not the European context, following the blocking of Airtours' bid for First Choice, it is likely that other strategies, such as the development of quality, will come to the fore.

Tour operations

As we have already seen, there is an enormous variety of tour operators, ranging from the large, integrated, multinational organisations, such as the Thomson Travel Group, to small, specialist companies with, perhaps, up to six core staff. As a result, the way in which tour operations function will also vary enormously according to a number of factors, such as the type and scale of operation, destinations offered and the season of travel. Thus, for example, a small company offering up-market, long-haul winter-sun holidays faces a different set of challenges compared with a large company operating in the highly competitive, short-haul summer sun market.

Nevertheless, most tour operators follow a largely similar process in the planning and construction of a package holiday. In other words, for a particular package holiday to be commercially viable, a tour operator is likely to follow a pattern of steps or stages from initially considering an idea through to the actual sale of the holiday. Prior to embarking on this process, however, a tour operator should consider its overall business objectives and strategy.

Tour operations: objectives and strategy

As in any business, it is essential that the planning and development of a new product does not occur in isolation from the major business objectives and the strategic direction of the company. That is, decisions regarding product development, such as the creation of a new package holiday, should meet the longer-term objectives of the company and the strategies designed to achieve those objectives.

The principal short-term objective of most tour operators is, of course, to make money and stay in business, thereby fulfilling their obligations to shareholders, employees, banks, customers and other stakeholders. However, other business objectives may vary according to the characteristics of different companies and their managers. For example, a smaller operator may focus upon becoming a specialist, niche market supplier, whilst the objective of larger operators may be to consolidate or increase market share. At the same time, all operators will have longer-term and inter-related objectives, such as market positioning, desired profit levels, or the scope and scale of the business.

Whatever the overall objectives of a tour operator, its strategy is likely to be directed towards a combination of two related elements:

Profit: all companies seek to make a profit. However, if an operator wishes to earn higher profits, not only will it need to manage its finances effectively (see Chapter 16), but its strategy will focus on reducing costs and achieving higher margins on each holiday that it sells.

Market share: if an operator seeks to increase its market share, the challenge is to increase the number of holidays it sells; that is, it will seek to increase its capacity. Capacity estimations are one of the most vital decisions in tour operating. Each year, an operator's ATOL is renewed according to projected numbers of tourists but, perhaps more importantly, the extent to which capacity targets are met determines the profit levels of a company. The reason for this is that, in order to increase capacity and, hence, market share, a tour operator must increase the number of beds and aircraft seats that it agrees to 'buy' from principals. However, it is almost impossible to predict the numbers of holidays which will be sold – unforeseen events or the activities of competitor operators may reduce expected demand – and, frequently, operators suffer from over-capacity. That is, they often have unsold holidays, meaning that they have to operate yield management systems to set late, discounted prices which will attract customers but which, at the same time, minimise potential losses. Not surprisingly, therefore, increases in market share are usually achieved at the cost of reduced profit levels.

The trade-off between profit margins and market share is illustrated by the example of Airtours. In 2000, the company raised its capacity by 15 percent in the UK market, whilst in other markets, particularly Germany, it had severe over-capacity – in fact, the German operator Fti, wholly owned by Airtours, lost some £100 million in 2000. Therefore, Airtours' strategy for 2001 was to consolidate its position and increase margins rather than seek market growth, with a 30 percent reduction in capacity (800,000 passengers) in its German operation.

To summarise, then, the initial decision to develop a new package holiday must be guided by the tour operator's overall business strategy, with the most appropriate type of package being selected to meet the company's objectives. Once this decision has been made, a set of key stages must be followed, determined to a great extent by the 'calendar' of tour operating.

Tour operations: creating the package

Depending upon the nature of a particular package holiday, the planning and creation of a package holiday through to its sales may take anything from nine months to three years. Within this period, however, a number of key activities must be undertaken including research, capacity planning, finance and administration, sales and marketing and tour management. Although a detailed consideration of these is beyond the scope of this chapter (see Yale 1995; Cooper *et al.* 1998: 257-268; Holloway 1998: 209-223), they can be summarised within the context of a 'typical' tour operating calendar for a 'summer sun' product.

Year 1: (*August to December*)

Prior to developing a product, *research* must be undertaken to determine choices of destinations, types of holidays, prices, capacity, and so on. Usually, such research will include:

- a review of the company's performance and objectives (see previous section)

- market trends and growth – changes in demand, tourist flows, etc.

- existing products and competitive supply – the activities of competitors; are there any gaps in the market?

- destination research – essentially, a feasibility study to determine ease of access, extent of existing tourism infrastructure and services, and the local legal and political climate.

Once answers have been found to these questions, the tour operator can then devise a marketing strategy that balances the objectives of the company with the product development opportunities revealed by the research.

Year 2

The second year of the calendar embraces what is, in effect, the creation of the package. Four fundamental activities are undertaken at this stage:

Capacity planning

In line with company objectives and strategy, target capacity figures must be planned which, in turn, determine the characteristics of the package according to type, size and frequency of operation. Once the specifications of the package have been set, the operator then negotiates with principals (hotels and airlines) in a process known as contracting.

Accommodation may be contracted in one of two ways:

1. **allocation** – beds are contracted on a sale or return basis, with any unsold rooms being returned to the hotelier with between 2 to four weeks notice. The advantage of allocation is that the risk is transferred from the operator to the principal. For example, following the 11th September terrorist attacks on the United States, many tour operators quickly sought to drop allocation bookings to long-haul destinations around the world. The disadvantage of allocation bookings is that hoteliers will often make contracts with a number of operators in order to cover themselves. This sometimes leads to double booking, when operators find that the rooms they have contracted are occupied by another operator's clients.

2. **commitment** – the operator pays a non-returnable deposit on rooms whether they are sold or not (and the hotelier may not offer the beds to another operator). Such contracts may be based on a cheaper rate then allocation, but are more risky. Therefore, the operator must be relatively certain of selling its holidays.

Contracting aircraft seats is a crucial activity. Not only is about 40 percent of the final holiday price is paid for the aircraft seat, meaning that unsold seats may result in significant losses, but also, for many destinations, aircraft seats are less plentiful than hotel beds. Thus, for popular destinations, it may be difficult for smaller operators to acquire the seats they require.

Aircraft seats are contracted in a number of ways. As already noted, the larger operators have their own airline and will focus on maximising the use of the aircraft (see Chapter 7). They may also sell blocks of seats to other operators. For the majority of other operators who do not enjoy this benefit, seats can be contracted either on scheduled flights (ITX) or on charter flights (ITC). ITX flights are usually more expensive and are, therefore, most commonly used by specialist, niche operators. ITC seats are cheaper, and can be booked in a variety of ways depending on the nature of the operation.

- a block of seats on a flight
- the whole plane for a specific flight (whole plane charter)
- an aircraft for the whole season (time charter)
- with air crew (wet lease) and without (dry lease)

Financial planning

The high street prices for mainstream package holidays are usually estimated between eight months and twelve months before the holiday is actually taken, based on current and forecasted exchange rates, inflation and fuel prices. Thus, operators are subject to a variety of risks. These financial risks also include insurance costs (raised following the terrorist attacks in the USA on September 11th 2001), destination and UK taxes, and so on. Therefore, as discussed in detail in Chapter 16, effective financial management is an essential requirement. Moreover, the actions of competitors, available supply to particular destinations, market demand and will all need to be taken into account. Therefore, in reality, prices can change at the latest possible moment before launch. Thus, all brochure details are often printed well in advance, with the exception of pricing panels which are overprinted later. Depending upon the take up of sales, alternative pricing strategies may need to be employed (see Chapter 18), subsequent edition brochures may be printed and/or systems of 'flexible pricing' may be adopted. Here, customers are invited to enquire as to the latest discount available on particular holidays. (Perhaps the most extreme form of price flexibility is the Internet holiday auction).

Sales and Marketing

The most popular means of selling package holidays remains the brochure. Brochure production usually starts a number a number of months before launch date and can only occur once the previous stages of the package creation process have been undertaken (although, as noted below, operators may re-negotiate contracts with suppliers for subsequent editions of brochures). Both the timing of the brochure launch and its distribution are crucial. Larger operators selling mainstream holidays will seek maximum exposure by distributing brochures widely (particularly through their own retail chain), and will try to beat their competitors to the launch. In recent years, this has resulted in brochures being launched ever earlier (sometimes summer-sun brochures have been launched during the Spring of the previous year!), with discounting schemes designed to attract the early booker. Conversely, specialist operators usually have a more limited distribution, thereby reducing costs and conveying a sense of exclusivity (see Cooper *et al.* 1998: 262).

At the same time sales reservation systems must be made ready to take bookings, and sales promotions and advertising to the trade and to the public will need to be timed to coincide with the brochure/product launch. Moreover, as bookings are generated and competitors' brochures are launched, it may be necessary for an operator to re-negotiate with suppliers if it finds that its products are more expensive – tour operators are now able, with the appropriate computer software, to calculate what their competitors have paid for the different elements of the package.

Hence the marketing role is not confined to brochure production and promotion alone. It is central to the whole process of product development and planning. It involves research and communication across all departments from the initial exploratory research stage through interim performance and sales measurement to the monitoring of customer feedback and competitor performance. All of this information will be used to determine future development of the product.

Administration

During the second year, a number of administrative activities are undertaken. These include:

- recruiting and training reservation staff
- setting up the reservations systems
- recruiting resort staff
- processing initial bookings.

Year 3

A number of activities occur during the third stage of the tour operation calendar, broadly reflecting the patterns of the holiday season. Throughout the main season, for example, sales will be monitored, capacity will be adjusted where possible and yield management systems will be implemented to maximise sales of holidays. Indeed, many operators will review sales figures daily and will sell off excess capacity at a discount. More specifically, the following destination management activities will occur:

- holiday management – tourists are met, transferred to resort and welcomed.

- brochure accuracy reports – representatives will assess the accuracy of the details presented in the brochures with respect to, for example, the facilities available, as well as more specific quality/safety aspects, such as the depth of the pool, fire exits, and so on.

- customer care – representatives attend to the needs of tourists, sort out problems, accompany local tours when appropriate, and so on.

- account payments to suppliers – the operator will pay the principals, usually by an agreed date.

Monitoring quality – most operators distribute customer questionnaires in order to determine the performance of the representatives and the customers satisfaction with the various elements of the package. The results of these feed into the planning process for the following year. At the same time, tour operators must respond to any correspondence or complaints received from customers once they have returned from their holidays. Indeed, as the next section shows, customer care/protection has become an increasingly important element of tour operating.

Inevitably, the tour operating process is more complex than presented here. Moreover, it is a continual process of research, planning, product development, review and monitoring so that, in reality, no clear boundaries exist, in a temporal sense, between the different activities and functions. Nevertheless, the tour operating calendar as outlined here can be summarised as below in Figure 5.3.

Figure 5.3: *A typical tour operating 'calendar'*

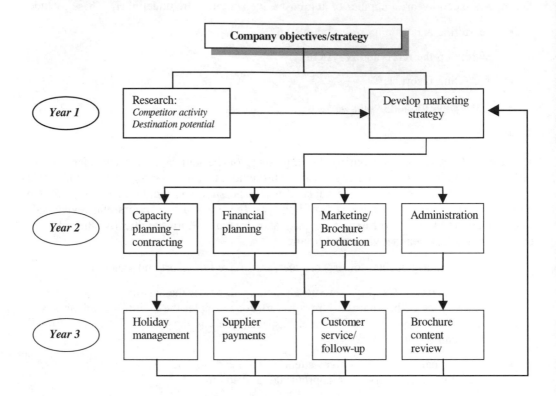

Tour operating: consumer protection

There are two reasons why consumer protection is of importance in the context of tour operating. Firstly, holidays are normally bought on trust. That is, tourists spend usually significant sums of money on a product that cannot be tried out or even viewed before purchase. At the same time, of course, package holidays are a combination of different elements, some of which are provided by local businesses in the destination, and as a result, it may be difficult for the operator to ensure consistent quality. Therefore, it is inevitable that holidays do not always meet with tourists expectations or do not match up with what is promised in the brochure. In other words, the nature and complexity of the package holiday are such that tourists often do not receive what they have paid for or, more precisely, what they believe they have paid for.

Secondly, less frequently but more seriously, tour operators go out of business. Although major business failures, such as the collapse of Court Line/Clarksons in 1974 and ILG in 1991, are relatively rare, a significant number of operators fail each year. In fact, between January 1986 and March 2001, 303 licensed operators failed, leaving a total of 181,814 tourists stranded overseas and well over a million people unable to take the holidays they had paid for (ATOL 2001b).

Thus, tourists require two forms of protection:

- protection designed to ensure that (a) tour operators provide the scope and standards of service as described in the brochure and (b), should they fail to do, mechanisms for gaining redress or compensation; and

- protection against tour operator failure that either (a) provides for repatriation or continuation of the holiday should the company fail while a tourist is overseas or (b) provides refunds for holidays paid for but not yet taken.

To a great extent, both forms of protection are provided for in the form of regulations that restrict the activities of tour operators or define their liability for the degree and quality of services provided. In terms of consumer law – that is, legal measures that seek to protect and assert the rights of consumers – tour operators have become subject to an increasingly complex array of both UK and EU legislation designed to shift the emphasis from the tradition of *caveat emptor* (buyer beware) to producer liability. Perhaps the most important element of this is the European Package Travel Directive, which has provided the principal legal framework for tour operators within Europe since 1990 (this is enshrined in UK law via the Package Travel, Package Holidays and Package Tours Regulations 1992 which are considered in detail in Chapter 15). Not only do the Regulations set out in detail what an operator may or may not do, but they also make the operator liable for any problems with any part of the package contracted out to other suppliers. As a result, tour operators have become obliged to focus on improving the quality and reliability of their products (see below), whilst it has become easier for the travelling public to assert their rights (of which they are becoming increasingly aware) as consumers.

Protection against tour operator failure

Following the collapse of Fiesta Tours in 1964, stranding some 5,000 tourists abroad, it became evident that some form of protection against the financial failure of tour operators was necessary. In response, the following year the Association of British Travel Agents (ABTA) established a 'common fund' based on 50 percent of its membership subscriptions in order to reimburse or repatriate tourists affected by any future failure. ABTA fully expected the government to introduce legislation to regulate tour operators but, when this did not occur, it established 'Operation Stabiliser'. This controversial scheme meant that ABTA tour operators could only sell their packages through ABTA travel agents and vice versa, whilst tourists would only be protected if they had bought their holiday from an ABTA agency (see Yale 1995: Chapter 10).

Operation Stabiliser was removed in 1993 as a result of the Package Travel Regulations which, amongst other things, require all travel organisers to be 'bonded'; that is, to have sufficient funds or security to refund customers or cover the cost of repatriation in the event of financial failure. This regulation extended to *all* packages (which come within the definition of a package as set out in regulation 2(1) of the Package Travel Regulations) a system first introduced in the UK by the Civil Aviation Authority (CAA) in 1972, which required all tour operators using charter flights or block-booked scheduled seats to apply for an Air Transport Organisers Licence (ATOL).

The ATOL system is still the principal statutory consumer protection scheme applied to air travel. Under the Civil Aviation (Air Travel Organisers Licensing) Regulations 1995, anyone – other than airlines themselves – selling either air inclusive packages or air seats must apply for and receive an ATOL. Failure to do so is a criminal offence with a fine of up to £5000 and two years in prison. The purpose of the ATOL system is to protect the customer against the failure of tour operators by refunding those who have paid but not yet travelled or by repatriating those stranded abroad.

Businesses that are required to apply for an ATOL include package tour operators, group and conference travel organisers, seat consolidators and many travel agents. Protection through ATOL is assured as far as possible because:

- All those applying for an ATOL must undergo stringent financial health checks – an ATOL is granted for only 12 months.

- Before being granted an ATOL, all travel organisers must arrange a bond with a recommended insurance company which is sufficient to reimburse or pay for the repatriation of customers in the event of the company failing. Under the Package Travel Regulations, this bond should amount to 25 percent of a company's annual turnover although for companies that are members of an approved body, such as ABTA, this can be limited to 10 percent.

- If an insolvent company's bond is insufficient to cover the cost of claims, the shortfall is made up from the Air Travel Trust Fund. Set up in the 1970s and originally funded by a 2 percent levy on holidays, the Fund is administered by the CAA and, although it is in significant deficit, it is guaranteed by government. Since 1986, roughly one third of all failures have drawn on the Fund which has paid out a total of £42 million.

As a legal requirement for air travel organisers, the ATOL system protects up to 28 million passengers from losing money or being stranded abroad, and more details about the system and the different types of ATOL can be found on its web site (www.atol.org.uk). There are some exceptions – most notably, airlines do not require an ATOL and, therefore, a traveller who buys a ticket on a scheduled flight direct from the airline is not covered. However, for those on package holidays, ATOL is an effective system which, in combination with consumer legislation, provides tourists with significant degree of protection. Conversely, tour operators are having to function in an increasingly regulated environment, particularly with respect to consumer legislation, and, as we now consider, this is one of the reasons why operators are increasingly focusing on the quality of the products they provide.

Quality management in tour operating

Having long enjoyed a dominant position within the international tourism system, tour operators now face a number of challenges to the future success of their business.

- *Competition:* the tour operating sector has become increasingly competitive. Not only are the smaller, specialist operators threatening to erode the market share of the 'big players', but that market share remains largely based on price, undermining the longer-term drive for increased margins.

- *Sophisticated tourists:* people have become more experienced as consumers of tourism products and now seek a variety of benefits other than a low price in the holidays they purchase. In particular, non-price factors, such as quality of services provided, have become more important - indeed, as early as the 1970s it was predicted that price competition would become subordinate to quality competition.

- *Consumerism:* in most industries, increasing attention is being paid to the rights of consumers and tourism is no exception. Recent years have witnessed a dramatic growth in media interest in the quality of tourism, with numerous newspaper articles and television programmes, for example, highlighting 'tourism disasters' and the ways in which tourists can claim compensation.

- *Legislation*: linked to consumerism, the increasingly regulated environment described above has resulted in tour operators paying out large amounts in compensation to dissatisfied tourists each year. According to a recent survey (Holiday Which? 2001), the most common reason for being unhappy with a tour operator was the service provided by holiday representatives, while in previous surveys, hotel quality has been rated the most disappointing aspect.

Collectively, these factors have led to a new awareness of the need for quality within the tour operating sector. Not only are large sums of money paid out, perhaps needlessly, each year compensating tourists for poor quality, but also quality has emerged as a minimum requirement for market entry and an important means of gaining competitive advantage. However, it has been suggested that the majority of problems and challenges facing tour operators *can* be addressed by management (Gilbert and Joshi 1992).

There is, then, little doubt that the implementation of quality management systems is, in theory, both desirable and necessary in the context of tourism. However, two questions must be addressed:

- how, in general, can quality management be achieved in a service industry?

- how applicable are quality management models to the specific challenges of the tourism industry?

Approaches to quality management

As Hope and Mühlemann (1998) point out, all service industries possess a number of characteristics that complicate the management process. These characteristics are widely referred to in the tourism literature (see also Chapter 18), and represent challenges for quality management:

Simultaneity: as the delivery and consumption of a service occur simultaneously, there is little or no chance for problems to be sorted out without the customer being aware. Therefore the challenge is in providing effective damage-limitation and recovery.

Heterogeneity: no two customers or service providers are the same; therefore, a standard, agreed level of quality is difficult to attain.

Intangibility: performance measurement, a key element of quality management, is difficult

Perishability: a particular service cannot be stored if unsold by a particular date. This can produce a pressured selling environment which can lead to a mismatch of customers and products.

The management of quality in tourism is further complicated by the fact that the tourism system covers three separate regions – the generating region, the transit route, and the destination – each of which requires appropriate service delivery. Nevertheless, a number of models have been proposed that are potentially applicable to tourism (see Gilbert and Joshi 1992; Hope and Mühlemann 1998 for more detail), the most useful of which are summarised as follows:

(a) Gronroos (1982, cited in Gilbert and Joshi 1992) argues that consumers' image of service quality is determined by the extent of the gap between the service they expect and the service which they perceive that they get. This image is created by a combination of technical quality or 'hard factors' (such as the quality of the meal the customer receives, the bed they sleep in, etc.) and functional quality or 'soft factors' (that is how the service is transferred to the customer). Thus, it is suggested that quality, as perceived by the customer, can be improved by focusing on elements of functional quality, such as the behaviour, attitudes or appearance of staff, as well as attempting to influence customer expectations.

(b) Similarly, Parasuraman *et al.* (1985) suggest that service quality is represented overall by the gap between expected and perceived service and that four 'sub gaps' contribute to this:

(i)   the gap between expected service and the management's expectations of customer expectations; more simply, a failure on the part of management to understand what customers expect.

(ii) the gap between management perceptions of customer expectations and the service quality specifications – the setting of low or inappropriate standards.

(iii) the gap between service quality specifications and service delivery; that is, poor employee performance.

(iv) the gap between service delivery and external communications to customers. In other words, and as frequently occurs in tourism, inconsistencies exist between the quality image portrayed in promotional literature and the actual service provided.

Thus, researching and addressing these gaps can provide the foundation for developing quality orientated strategies that work towards greater 'fit' between expectations and actual experiences.

(c) A broader approach is provided by the concept of Total Quality Management (TQM). TQM is 'a management philosophy embracing all activities through which the needs and expectations of the customer and the community, and the objectives of the organisation are satisfied in the most efficient and cost-effective way by maximising the potential of all employees in a continuing drive for improvement' (Hope and Mühlemann 1998). At the centre of TQM are key 'processes' which link the supplier with the customer, and the quality/efficiency of these processes can be influenced by the use of appropriate systems, tools and teamworking.

According to Hope and Mühlemann (1998), the factor that links all models of quality management, and that is of particular importance to an international service industry such as tourism, is people. That is, the success of any quality initiative is dependent upon the ability of staff to respond and adapt to demands for increased quality in the delivery of services. Thus, human resource issues, including staff selection, training and empowerment, as well as the implementation of appropriate rewards schemes, are fundamental to the management of quality.

Quality in tour operating?

The final question to consider is the extent to which quality management is a viable objective in tour operating. In other words, although the need for quality is evident in order to address the challenges of competition, consumerism and legal considerations, the extent to which the tour operating sector can respond to this need is less certain.

On the one hand, there is no doubt that human resource policies can be tailored towards recruiting, training, and empowering staff, whilst performance-related rewards schemes may provide a useful incentive – much depends, however, on the overall company culture and management philosophy.

On the other hand, a number of factors potentially militate against the successful implementation of quality management. The characteristics of services referred to above represent an initial hurdle, as does the international nature of tour operations. More specifically:

- The external environment at the destination influences tourists' perceptions of quality. This may include the behaviour of other tourists, the standard of attractions and facilities or even the general local ambience.

- Despite increasing integration within the sector, parts of the package are not directly owned by operators. As a result, operators have less control than is necessary to manage quality, with limited influence, for example, over the employment policies of hotels.

- As with all services, the human element of tourism is subjective. That is, different people have different perceptions of quality, whilst the nature of work within tour operating, particularly at the destination, suggests that consistent quality is difficult to achieve. For example, tour reps often tend to be younger, seasonally employed individuals with relatively little training. As a result, they may have little loyalty or commitment to the company and to a philosophy of quality.

More generally, tourism is about dreams – it could be argued that rarely, if ever, are tourists' expectations fully satisfied. Nevertheless, there is little doubt that, as tourists become more experienced, more discerning and more demanding, tour operators will have to pay greater attention to the issue of quality. However, this is only likely to be achieved at the cost of more expensive holidays.

Discussion questions

1. *Why do many tour operators enjoy a dominant position within the tourism chain of distribution?*

2. *How can Porter's 'five forces' help to explain the widespread vertical and horizontal integration within the travel and tourism industry?*

3. *Visit the ATOL web site (www.atol.org.uk) and, having done so, explain the role of the Civil Aviation Authority in providing consumer protection for tourists. .*

4. *Why is it necessary for tour operators to focus on quality management and what challenges do they face in improving the quality of their products?*

Further reading

Dale, C. (2000), The UK tour-operating industry: a competitive analysis, *Journal of Vacation Marketing* 6(4): 357-367.

Holloway, J. C. (1998), *The Business of Tourism, 5th Edition*, Harlow: Longman – *Chapter 12*.

Laws, E. (1997), *Managing Packaged Tourism*, London: International Thomson Business Press.

Pender, L. (2001), *Travel Trade and Transport: An Introduction*, London: Continuum.

Yale, P. (1995), *The Business of Tour Operations*, Harlow, Longman.

References

ATOL (2001a), *ATOL Business*, Issue 18 (August), London: CAA.

ATOL (2001b), *A brief history of consumer protection for customers of air travel organisers*, www.atol.org.uk/atol/student/history12.htm.

Cooper, C., Fletcher, J., Gilbert, D., Shepherd, R. and Wanhill, S. (1998), *Tourism: Principles and Practice, 2nd Edition*, Harlow: Longman.

Dale, C. (2000), The UK tour-operating industry: a competitive analysis, *Journal of Vacation Marketing* 6(4): 357-367.

Gilbert, D. and Joshi, I. (1992), Quality management and the tourism and hospitality industry, in C. Cooper and A. Lockwood (eds.) *Progress in Tourism, Recreation and Hospitality Management, Volume 4*, London: Bellhaven Press.

Holloway, J. C. (1998), *The Business of Tourism, 5th Edition*, Harlow: Longman.

Hope, C. and Mühlemann, A. (1998), Total quality, human resource management and tourism, *Tourism Economics* 4(4): 367-386.

Ioannides, D. (1998), Tour operators: the gatekeepers of tourism, in D. Ioannides and K. Debbage (eds) *The Economic Geography of the Tourist Industry: A Supply-side Analysis*, London: Routledge: 139-158.

Mintel (2000), *Inclusive Tours*, London: Mintel International Group Limited.

Parasuraman, A., Zeithaml, V. and Berry, L. (1985), A conceptual model service quality and its implications for future research, *Journal of Marketing* 49(4): 41-50.

Pender, L. (2001), *Travel Trade and Transport: An Introduction*, London: Continuum.

Porter, M. (1980), *Competitive Strategy: Techniques for Analysing Industries and Competitors*, New York: The Free Press.

Yale, P. (1995), *The Business of Tour Operations*, Harlow, Longman.

6

Tourism Distribution

Amanda Miller

Learning objectives

Distribution is a key feature of the travel and tourism industry and by the end of this chapter you should be able to:

- *understand the concept of distribution*
- *identify and explain the channels of distribution*
- *understand the role of intermediaries*
- *realise the importance of Information Technology to distribution*

Introduction

This chapter is concerned with the means and mechanisms used by organisations within the travel and tourism industry to distribute their products. Distribution is a fundamental concern for the industry as, quite simply, the tourism product needs to be made available to, and be purchased by, consumers (tourists). Owing to its very nature, consumers need to be able to access the tourism product at multiple points of sale away from the places of service production. Unlike manufacturing, the product cannot be physically transported to the consumer and, therefore, distribution within travel and tourism is concerned with the provision of customer access to the product rather than physical transportation of goods.

The principal focus of this chapter will be on the role of distribution in enticing customers to destinations and making the product accessible. However, it must nevertheless be remembered that distribution also refers to physical location or locational analysis. Locational analysis is used to determine the best sites for the distribution of facilities, such as hotels and resorts, and the identification of such sites is becoming increasingly important as the continued growth of tourism has led to intensive competition for prime sites. It is also of crucial importance to the small-to-medium tourism enterprises that constitute the bulk of the travel and tourism industry. For these small businesses, locational analysis can determine the size of their service production and also their main sales point (Pender 1999).

What is distribution?

Distribution is the means by which the product is made available and accessible to customers. It involves getting sufficient and appropriate information to the right people at the right time and at the right place in order to allow purchase decisions to be made, and providing the mechanism whereby consumers can make and pay for purchases. The distribution system needs to be efficient, positive and dynamic. In the tourism industry context, distribution can be defined as 'an operating structure, system or linkage of various combinations of travel organisations through which a producer of travel products describes and confirms travel arrangements to the buyer' (McIntosh 1995).

Distribution in the wider picture

Within marketing, distribution is synonymous with one of the classic four 'Ps' of the marketing mix – 'Place' (see also Chapter 18). It plays a key role in the success of the other elements in the marketing mix and, importantly, distribution choices have implications and ramifications for the other elements of the marketing mix, as distribution does not exist in isolation. If, for example, travel agents are used as a means of distributing the tourism product, it might well have cost implications and lead to increases in prices. These travel agents have to be serviced with brochures to ensure that they are aware of the products available – i.e. promotion. If brochure supplies were not kept up to date, consumers entering travel agents in response to advertising campaigns may be persuaded to book alternative holidays. Thus, as with all elements of the marketing mix, there is a need for flexibility and fluidity. There is a need to adapt to changing consumer patterns, expanding markets, maturing products, entering of new competition and new and innovative distribution channels emerge (Kotler *et al.* 1996).

Characteristics of the tourism product

The unique characteristics of tourism also need to be considered when examining distribution. These characteristics are:

Intangibility

This as a key feature that separates the tourism product (and other services) from virtually all other forms of retailing as the product cannot be seen or touched prior to purchase. This not only heightens the role of information in representing the product, but also it can pose particular difficulties for those whose job it is to market tourism. Furthermore, the purchase of a package tour has been described as 'a speculative investment' (Holloway 1995). Thus, it also involves a high degree of trust on the part of the purchaser, particularly because holidays are likely to be one of the most expensive purchases made in the year. Within the distribution process, the brochure takes on a crucial role as it is one means of illustrating the holiday and making it 'real' to the consumer.

Perishability

If the service is not sold, then the business can never be recovered as an empty room or train seat cannot be put into storage for later consumption. Unsold revenue is lost and, therefore, effective and efficient communication of such information is vital so that loads and yields are maximised and losses minimised. There is a need to be able to provide last minute distribution of unsold products as services cannot be stored for future sale. Within the UK travel and tourism industry, the late booking market has also evolved through developments in information technology, such as call centres and, of course, the Internet (see Chapter 19).

Dynamism

Tourism destinations are usually in a constant process of change as they grow, develop and adjust to the market. In this sense, the tourism product is always an unfinished product as it is always responding and adjusting to planning and marketing imperatives and opportunities. The use of communication and information technology allows for such changes and is having a considerable impact on the methods of distribution available. This characteristic also impacts upon the location of tourism services within resorts and destinations.

Heterogeneity

It is difficult for suppliers to provide the same standard or level of service at every consumption occasion, as standards and quality vary over time and under different circumstances. As almost all services provided to tourists have to be delivered at the time and place at which they are produced, one consequence is that the quality of the social interaction between the provider of the service and the consumer is part of the 'product' being purchased by tourists. If certain aspects of the social interaction are unsatisfactory, then what is purchased is, in effect, a different service product. At the same time, tourists tend to have high expectations of what they should receive, since 'going away' is an event endowed with particular significance. For distribution, this can place an increasing importance on the service provided by the elements of the distribution channel – the suppliers, travel agents and tour operators.

Inseparability

This refers to the overlap between the production and performance of the service and its consumption. It means there is an inseparability in buyer's minds, as those who provide the service are the service, and buyers are often unable to judge the quality of a service prior to purchase. Such services cannot be produced anywhere; they have to be produced and consumed in very particular places and so part of what is consumed is, in effect, the place in which the service producer is located. Consumers will see buying the product as part of the overall experience, although the purchase of a holiday from a travel agent has no direct relevance to the service provided by a tour operator.

These characteristics of the tourism product highlight the crucial role of the distribution function in tourism. When a tour operator, such as Thomson, have an unsold package holiday they may well decide to have the holiday advertised as a late booking via a travel agency chain such as Lunn Poly, as once the departure date has gone the holiday is lost as it is perishable. Equally, the inseparability of the product places further emphasis on the importance of the travel agent as the consumer sees them as the face of the holiday and it is, therefore, crucial they retain good communications with the tour operator. In the example of Thomsons and Lunn Poly, as they are integrated and part of the same group, it may well be easier to retain such links of communication.

The special characteristics of the tourism product also mean that the distribution of tourism is different to that of manufactured goods. In manufacturing, goods are transported to the consumer whilst, in tourism, it is the consumer that is transported to the product. This difference is extremely important as it means that information assumes a vital role, with subsequent implications for the method of distribution. Indeed, consumers are unable to physically inspect the product/service and are, therefore, forced to rely on information about the product. In turn, suppliers not only provide the product but also provide information on price, quantity, times (arrival and departure), quality, supplements, conditions of purchase and booking procedures.

Channels of distribution

Distribution channels are the sequence of firms or organisations involved in the moving of the service from the 'producer' to consumer (Cowell 1991). They vary according to size and types of organisation, and larger principals (i.e. those producers at the top of the chain – in tourism, this includes airlines, hotels, and so on) tend to use more than one form of distribution channel. The travel and tourism distribution process can be visualised as a model (see Figure 6.1):

Figure 6.1: *Channels of distribution within travel and tourism industry*

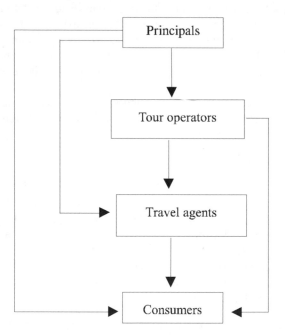

There are a number of routes that can be taken through the distribution model to ensure the tourism product reaches the consumer. The principals, such as the transport and accommodation providers, can choose to sell direct to the consumers or go via an intermediary – tour operator and/or travel agent – whilst tour operators have two options of selling direct or selling through travel agents. (Of course, extensive vertical integration within the travel and tourism industry, as described in the previous chapter, means that tour operators are now often principals, as well as owning distribution businesses – travel agencies – further down the chain). With domestic tourism, it is common for tourists to purchase directly because they usually have good product knowledge and ready access to telephones to make reservations.

The distribution channel in tourism creates the link between the producers of tourism services and their customers, with tour operators frequently playing a pivotal role in distributing and channelling international tourism products to the consumer. Indeed, since tourism products are experimental and consumed on site, tour operators are an integral link in the distribution system (Mill *et al*. 1992). The relationship is one of reliance and need throughout the channels of distribution to ensure the consumer is purchasing the product required. Principals rely on tour operators to supply them with tourists and to honour contractual obligations – a tour operator, for example, may well be committed to filling all of a hotels rooms during the peak summer season. It is important, therefore, that the tour operator is able to fulfil this as otherwise the hotelier might have unfulfilled capacity and so lose revenue.

Equally, consumers rely on the tour operator to package and distribute the package holiday so that they do not need to do so themselves. They rely on the tour operator to provide accurate and sufficient information about the holiday to facilitate an informed purchase, so that when the tourist arrives at the destination their expectations are realised.

The traditional package holiday involves the principals selling to the tour operator who combines the elements of the holiday (transport and accommodation) into a package to be sold to consumers via travel agents or direct. If selling via a travel agent, the information regarding the package holiday is passed onto the travel agent to enable the product to be purchased, but travel agents themselves do not hold any stock. In principle, they merely facilitate information dissemination and ensure that the consumers' needs are addressed by the particular holiday being booked.

The tourist industry and market is diversified and fragmented and, perhaps inevitably, the different market segments and principals involved influence the nature of different channels of distribution. In recognition of this, Bottomley Renshaw (1997) has adopted a sector approach to distribution and proposes separate models of distribution for airline travel, surface transport, accommodation and inclusive tours. As an example, Figure 6.2 shows the possible channels of distribution open to an hotel chain. Additionally, the changing needs and perceptions of consumers (see Chapter 4) has also had significant impact on distribution.

Distribution choices

According to Holloway (1995), the three most important factors which influence distribution choice are cost, control and level of service, whilst Lumsdon (1997) further identifies the nature of the market, resources commitment and competitor activity as influencing channel choices. Additionally, the market coverage required, the costs involved of distribution, the effectiveness of generating sales for motivation and image channels, the characteristics of the destination and tourism service and economic concentration all need to be considered when an organisation is choosing the most appropriate distribution strategy for it products.

The importance of making the right distribution choices cannot be overstated and, undoubtedly, an effective distribution strategy can be a competitive weapon. This can be clearly seen with First Choice which, following its UK expansion and distribution strategy from 1998 to 2000, became a fully vertically integrated travel group. It increased its competitiveness through buying into travel agents and, most notably, acquired full control of Holiday Hypermarkets in May 2000. Holiday Hypermarkets had been a joint venture between West Co-operative Society, United Norwest Co-operative Society and First Choice.

First Choice Holiday Hypermarkets now 'holds the number one position in the growing town travel retailing sector with 33 sites across the UK, as at June 2001' (First Choice 2001).

Figure 6.2: *Chain of distribution in the accommodation sector*

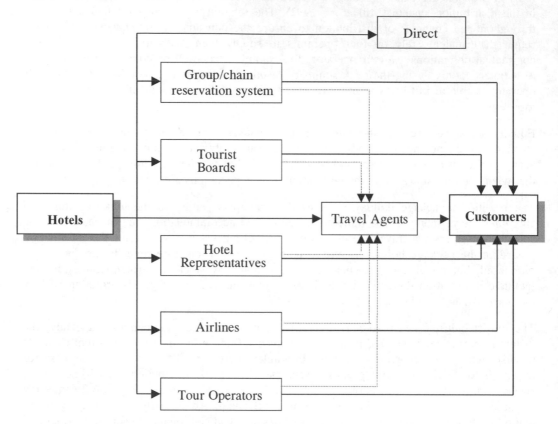

Channel decisions must be based on an analysis of the market, the product, the producer and competitive factors, with the overriding decision being where, when and how consumers choose to buy the good or service. Within this, the dynamic nature of distribution strategies and, hence, the need for reassessment must be acknowledged; that is, it is important to determine what services consumers in various target segments desire and, by determining what channels are most appropriate or productive, to consider whether a new strategy is needed. Following First Choice's strategy from 1998 to 2000 of acquiring a presence in the retail travel agent sector, their stated aim is to now to 'further develop distribution capabilities and increase the percentage of sales via direct routes to market' (First Choice 2001). Thus, along with a significant number of tour operators, First Choice see the potential of electronically distributing travel products, be it via the Internet or digital television, for example.

In formulating a distribution strategy, there is a need to take into account the degree of intensity required. This can be intensive, exclusive, or selective (Holloway 1995).

Intensive approach

This involves the use of many outlets to distribute the product. It can, therefore, incur considerable costs in terms of print runs for brochures and level of support and is, perhaps, best suited to the general, mass market type holiday. So, in theory, a basic package holiday to Ibiza could be sold via all travel agents in the UK. Conversely, it is unlikely to be appropriate for more specialised, niche market products, such as the booking of luxury self-catering accommodation and exclusive package holidays as offered by BA Holidays and Kuoni. Generally, however, an intensive approach is increasingly less likely with tour operators and travel agents becoming integrated, as there is a greater tendency for tour operators to favour aligned travel agents and visa versa.

Selective distribution

Here, the supplier selects a limited range of outlets and employs minimum criteria to be met by them. These criteria might include travel agents meeting financial guarantees, minimum staffing qualifications and minimum turnover, or it may involve the use of travel agents which are owned by or linked to tour operators. Airtours UK Leisure Group, which includes Airtours Holidays, Aspro, Panorama, Direct and Manos Holidays, are distributed via Airtours plc retail network, which encompasses Going Places and Travelworld on the high street, and the Holidayline telephone distribution business (integration is further discussed below). Targeting can also be done via specialist tour operators, such as Sunvil, which focuses on a limited number of destinations where their travel products are either sold direct or via their own retail travel agents. Not only can targeting can be done via the type of holiday on offer, be it luxury and exclusive, but it can also be done by age range and customer type. For example, Saga Holidays focus their direct marketing activities on people aged 50 and over (although an accompanying spouse or partner may be aged 40 or over). These particular types of products are specific to customer type and may be favoured by a number of specialist independent travel agents.

Exclusive distribution

Exclusive distribution is rare in travel and tourism, but occurs when a supplier grants exclusive rights to an agent to sell its products. It can sometimes occur with destinations or tourism offerings that offer themselves to an exclusive set of customers, such as island resorts or hotel complexes. This is the case with Sandals, which is a collection of ten all-inclusive resorts, which are purely for couples, whilst private island resorts such as Guana Island (www.guana.com) and Musha Cay (www.mushacay.com) offer highly exclusive destinations.

Whilst these decisions concern the extent of the distribution strategy, as, for example, whether to use multiple chains of travel agents or a selective number of independent travel agents, there are other ways of expanding distribution. Integration and co-operative distribution systems can lead to the opening up of new and more extensive distribution channels.

Integration

Significant features of the UK travel and tourism retail industry in recent years have been both the 'march of the multiples' and vertical/horizontal integration. The 'multiples', that is, the large national and regional chains of travel agents (such as Lunn Poly and Going Places) enjoy, as a result of their size, great negotiating power which enables them to control terms and lay down expectations and wants to principals. At the same time, however, bias can also result from vertical integration, as the retail outlets might favour the tour operator they are linked with by racking brochures in prominent positions and promoting their holidays more strongly to customers when face to face selling. This situation can be further complicated by horizontal integration, as with Thomson's ownership of Lunn Poly and Callers Pegasus, the latter formerly being an independent chain of retail travel agents in the north east of England.

Co-operative distribution systems

Co-operative distribution systems include franchises and consortia. Franchises are an arrangement whereby a business grants an organisation the right to use their name and market its product in exchange for a fee. The franchisee benefits from the right to an established brand name and centralised marketing support whilst franchisers benefit from a rapid expansion of sties and a central fund. Within the travel and tourism industry, Holiday Inns are the oft-cited example of successful franchising operation (see also Chapter 8). Consortia involve organisations uniting for marketing purposes whilst they retain their independence. This can result in joint brochures being produced, or access to central reservation systems, whilst for travel agency consortia a significant benefit is the negotiation of higher rates of commission for group members.

Worldchoice, formerly ARTAC, and Advantage Travel Centres are examples of travel agency consortia, and represent the largest networks of independent travel agents in Europe. Membership of Worldchoice leads to certain benefits, such as the offering of an overbranded Lakes and Mountains brochure produced with Airtours, increased negotiating power in setting commissions from tour operators, and private health care and motor insurance for agents. Advantage Travel Centres have developed a sophisticated web site that offers consumers online booking, holiday search facility and links to other consortium members, with the option for consumers to deal directly through a local travel agent by searching the online database. In America, the Virtuoso travel agency consortium provides marketing, sales, technology support, and exclusive services and products to leading independent luxury and adventure travel agencies.

Direct sale versus intermediaries

In making distribution channel choices, one simple yet important question must be addressed – that is, whether to sell direct or via intermediaries. The tourism product lends itself to direct selling. The product cannot be seen, touched or physically inspected before purchase, which means that the consumer is, essentially, dependent on information. This information can just as easily be obtained directly from a supplier as through a third party and, nowadays, tour operators are increasingly combining direct sale operations with those brands which are sold via travel agents. Airtours, for example, own their own travel agent, Going Places, a web site booking facility (mytravelco) and a direct sell tour operator, Direct Holidays.

In the promotion of products sold direct, there are associated price advantages to the consumer from buying direct whilst tour operators benefit from not having to pay commission to travel agents. Travel agents are sensitive regarding the publication of direct telephone numbers within tour operator brochures, which are available via the travel agency network, and the offering of cheaper prices when booking direct. One such instance was when First Choice was accused by a travel agent of offering a special discount to a client booking direct, as it makes it very difficult for agents to compete when tour operators undercut them (Richardson 2000). Direct Holidays, in their advertising campaign which clearly refers to cutting out the middleman (i.e. travel agents) to cut the costs, have annoyed travel agents to the extent that they requested that ABTA suspend Direct Holidays membership (Travel Trade Gazette 2001).

Direct sell: costs and benefits

For direct sell, the fixed costs that are incurred are higher, such as the initial investment in infrastructure and information technology. There are also issues of concern for tour operators choosing direct sell, such as how to make late availability known to potential customers. Travel agents offer an easy and viable means of advertising last minute offers as seen with advertisements in the windows of high street travel agents. If a tour operator found there was excess availability on a package holiday, it would be expensive to mailshot customers from their database. Technological developments have also facilitated the growth of call centres and travel agents, such as Freedom Direct, have exploited Teletext as an alternative means of advertising last minute special offers, allowing customers to then book the holiday via their call centres.

Conversely, for tour operators selecting direct sell, costs might be reduced in terms of brochure production, as there would not be the need to gear the brochure runs to supplying intermediaries and the numbers needed would be more in line with consumer demand. Direct sell operations also, of course, place the control over sales in the hands of the product providers, thus helping to induce brand loyalty since the company is advertising itself direct to the consumer. With greater control of the system, this can lead to greater responsiveness to the needs of the consumer and the current selling position, with additional sales opportunities through relationship marketing and increased profit levels through the elimination of the travel agent's commission. For the customer also, buying direct from the producer can lead to greater control as they are dealing directly with the company packaging the product. There can also be time savings and greater accuracy, as the customer is communicating with the knowledgeable tour operator rather than a travel agent who might not be familiar with that particular product. For consumers, it could also be assumed that they gain from lower prices as there is no commission payable to a travel agent, although research undertaken by Holiday Which found that only one direct sell operator, Eclipse, was actually cheaper than a high street agent for a comparable holiday (Mintel 2000). However, as discussed below, the 'traditional' travel agent still offers advantages over direct forms of retailing.

Categories of companies that sell direct include those that sell direct exclusively, those that sell both direct and via a travel agent, travel agents selling direct and credit card companies selling direct. In addition, direct selling offers new opportunities to established operations, which handle the business of third parties. For example, Thomas Cook Direct runs the newly formed First Direct Travel which was launched by the phone banking service First Direct and an established operator also handles the Barclays Travel Shop Direct (Mintel 1998).

Direct sell affords a greater degree of control and some principals, such as airlines, are by nature geared to it. Airlines are selling a simple, singular product and they have successfully exploited the opportunity afforded by the Internet with the use of e-ticketing and have cut commissions to travel agents so making it less profitable for airline tickets to be sold by travel agents. Some operators have turned to direct sell following dissatisfaction with the level of service travel agents have offered them. For a large number of smaller and independent tour operators, the issue of racking and difficulties of getting a prominent position in travel agents mean they resort to direct sale as the easiest option.

Intermediaries: costs and benefits

Intermediaries – travel agents, tour operators, tour retailers, specialist brokers, business agents and tour wholesalers – can provide a practical solution to the problems of distribution as they allow for a variety of economies. The tour operator can focus on the delivery of an appropriate package without the worry and hassle of selling it to consumers as an experienced intermediary can do this for them. If there is under capacity, they can simply turn to the intermediaries to sell the package as a last minute special offer and, in using intermediaries, they can take advantage of the relationships the intermediaries have developed with their customers.

At the same time, however, the use of intermediaries can result in the incurring of extra costs, such as commission payments and higher costs of brochure production, and less control and difficulties with the level of service. Nevertheless, the distribution sector of tourism is much stronger, and travel intermediaries have far greater power to influence and direct consumer demand, compared to their counterparts in other industries. Unlike other products that flow from producer to consumer, tourists flow to the product. This inverted distribution system relies on intermediaries to perform much more than simple delivery services with, for example, travel agents being seen as the 'reassuring human face' of the travel industry.

Thus, the changing structure of the tourism industry and the development of new technology has undoubtedly led to difficulties for travel agents. Airlines have, for example, been cutting commissions and attempting to cut out the middleman by selling direct and effectively using call centres and the Internet to do so. This is especially the case for the 'no-frills' airlines such as Ryanair and Easyjet, whilst many tour operators are developing direct sell operations, as in the case with Airtours and their purchase of Direct Holidays. Similarly, Thomas Cook has Thomas Cook Direct, First Choice has Eclipse and Thomson has Portland Direct. Although these operations tend to only sell a selection of the holidays featured in the main brochures, to their parent companies and where the same holidays do feature there is often a different in the prices offered (Mintel 2000). Nevertheless, although some would claim that the days of the travel agent (in particular the independent, as opposed to chain, agency) are numbered, the travel agent, as the following section suggests, will continue to play an important role in travel distribution.

The role of the travel agent

Although it is not within the scope of this chapter to be able to enter into a full discussion on the role of travel agent (see Bottomley Renshaw 1997), travel agents are a key intermediary and, as such, deserve some attention. Travel agents are distinctive from other types of retailers as they carry no stock and so bear little financial risk, never purchase products but act on behalf of consumers, and receive commission on sales from their 'suppliers' (i.e. from the principals upon whose behalf they act as agents). This means that the contract of sale is not between the customer and the travel agent, but between the customer and the principal. Travel agents can also emphasise products which earn higher commissions, whilst the issue of racking is another contentious area allowing for favouritism. There can be extreme problems in getting brochures racked by the travel agents, and there are also costs such as servicing the agent, commissions, overrides and other incentives and information technology. The wide variety of products available in travel agents also require extensive knowledge and skill. Therefore, the level of service can be variable as the average travel agent cannot know everything and anything about all products on sale.

The role of the travel agent is dependent on the products sold, the customers, the degree of specialisation of the agency, the demand within the area and the levels of commission offered. It must also be noted that the role of the travel agent has developed differently in different counties, as in America, for example, they have developed a role as packager of holidays. The discussion here, however, is mainly concerned with the situation as it is in the UK.

There are about 7000 travel agents in the UK, including leisure and holiday agents and business agencies (Mintel 2000). Leisure and holiday agents can either be general agencies or specialist agencies. General agencies sell all types of products from Inclusive Tours to coach tickets and airline tickets but, by dealing with such a wide range of products, associated problems can arise. The focus tends to be on low cost and low revenue business, such as coach tickets, whilst the staff can fail to develop specialist knowledge as they have to know about everything and anything. As a result, some travel agents specialise in particular types of holidays, such as those to long haul destinations (for example Austravel), student travel (for example STA Travel) or flight only (for example, Trailfinders and Flightbookers).

High street travel agents do not tend to specialise in business travel, although they do provide flights to business clients, mainly daily return fares within the UK or to mainstream Europe. Conversely, business agencies sell to commercial clients and not the general public. The UK business travel market is significant, valued at around £10.5 billion in 1998 (Mintel 2000). It is also a highly lucrative market, with hotel groups and airlines relying on revenue that is generated from this target audience, although the success of the low-cost/no-frills airlines such as Ryanair, Easyjet, Go and Buzz, as well as the opportunity for businesses to save on travel costs by booking direct, is a threat to the continued success of business agencies. Other areas of concern for business travel agencies include commission cuts, passenger service charge and the introduction of management fees. Major business agencies include American Express, Business Travel International UK, Hogg Robinson, Carlson Wagonlit and Rosenbluth. Medium sized players in the UK market include Britannic Travel, Portland Travel, Seaforth Travel and The Travel Company.

Organisation of the travel agency sector

The travel agency sector in the UK can be crudely divided into multiples and independents and a dominant feature since the 1980s, as with the tour operator sector, has been increasing concentration and consolidation. This phenomenon has been referred to as the 'march of the multiples'. The multiples travel agencies are usually integrated with tour operators and around a third are owned by the top three high street chains (Mintel 2000). Indeed, in 1999, the top four travel companies (Thomson, Airtours, Thomas Cook and First Choice) accounted for around 70 percent of the retail travel agency market by volume. Renshaw (1998) identifies how the increase in power and weight for companies' means they can control terms and lay down expectations and wants to principals. Bias can also result from vertical integration, as the retail outlets might favour the tour operator they are linked with. This is referred to directional selling, as travel companies sell their own inclusive tours through their own travel agents in preference to other alternatives. Mintel (2000) research has shown this is common practice (Mintel 2000), despite it being the subject of a Monopolies and Mergers Commission investigation in the UK. The 1997 investigation cleared the integrated operators of anti-competitive practices and, since then, the degree of vertical integration has increased substantially (Mintel 2000). A succession of takeovers and mergers occurred and the major companies now own a wide portfolio of tour operators, airlines and, significantly, travel agents.

Not surprisingly, independent travel agents, such as Bath Travel, Althams Travel Services, Dawson & Sanderson, and Phoenix Travel, claim that directional selling is against the public interest because consumers are not given a real choice of product or price. Similarly, the Campaign for Real Travel Agents claims the multiples are just becoming distribution points for the major tour operators (Mintel 2000). Certainly, it is increasingly difficult for the independent sector to remain competitive and, as a result, the number of such agencies is constantly falling (Mintel 2000). Those that remain have realised that, unless they specialise in niche products (such as cruises and golf packages), their future will remain threatened.

A further challenge to independent travel agents is the emergence of online specialist travel agents, whilst the major multiples have also started to offer their own in-house online offers. Mintel (2000) research has shown that direct sales, especially through specialist online agents, is growing all the time as consumers become more confident at travelling 'unpackaged' and the prices represent better value for money. Thus, it is estimated that direct sales will grow from 22 percent in 1997 to 30 percent of total online sales in 2002 (Poon 2001). For small independents, however, the costs of setting up this new technology are very high and it may be difficult to raise the necessary finance. At the same time, the profits are low and, consequently, independents are being challenged by the domination of the multiples and the new online specialist travel agents.

Moreover, a further feature of distribution concerning travel agents is the trend towards disintermediation. Disintermediation is the term used to describe the process whereby the ability of principals in the tourism distribution chain to use information technology to communicate with consumers in their homes or in other public places may, ultimately, cut out the travel agent. However, in order to completely eliminate travel agents, a number of obstacles, encompassing social, economic and political, as well as technological, factors would need to be surmounted (Bennett 1995). Indeed, it can be argued that travel agents will continue to have an important role in reducing the complexity of the communication network, as they are experienced in finding out information from the increased information available (van Heijden 1996). Moreover, Bennett (1995) emphasises the importance of the travel agent as the reassuring human face of the travel industry, as consumers often seek advice which only the travel agent can provides. Travel agents can also provide the choice and help in the comparing of different companies' products. In short, the personal service travel agents provide is an invaluable part of their role and, were they to be removed from the distribution process, it could lead to a reduction in communication rates, consumer resistance to new technology, and the bias of technology owners and developments excluding other competitors. Therefore, although Inkpen (1998) argues that the Internet will lead to disintermediation as an increasing number of sophisticated sites offer on-line booking of accommodation and events, travel agents will not necessarily be marginalised by the threat of the Internet. They will, however, need to embrace it.

The importance of information technology

Within the travel and tourism industry, technological developments have had a significant impact on distribution as the industry attempts to meet the demands of discerning customers who have increasingly diverse profiles. The nature of the tourism product (intangible, perishable, volatile, heterogeneous) is particularly suited to the adoption of information technology because of the dependence on the supply and exchange of information throughout the production and distribution chain. Within this distribution chain, computers have come to play an increasingly strategic and dominant role.

The dynamic nature of the tourism product is such that a mechanism is required to transmit information about products between the different sectors in the chain of distribution. Indeed, without such a mechanism, the travel and tourism industry's operational efficiency would be severely restricted. At the same time, competition between suppliers further heightens the need for efficient, reliable and accurate information regarding the products and their availability. As a result, the means of conveying information in and around the chain of production and distribution becomes virtually as important as the information itself. Therefore, it is not, perhaps, surprising that information technology is proving to be all-pervasive within the travel and tourism industry – certainly, travel agents, tour operators, airlines and hotels are all heavy users of information technology, to the extent that Poon (1988) refers to it as a 'total information system'.

Developments in information technology have undoubtedly had significant impacts on distribution, although there are disparities in the introduction of and level of development in different countries. For example, destination marketing systems have met with success in Canada, yet this is not the case in the UK or in Switzerland (see Alford (2000) for further details). Similarly, the development of Computer Reservation Systems (CRS) has been particularly advantageous in the USA where, because of the geographical size of the country, they have become widely used for the booking of both domestic and outbound holidays. With domestic holidays, Americans are more likely to travel via air and so use travel agents to book flights and accommodation. Conversely, in the UK, customers are more likely to book domestic holidays direct as they tend to use their own transport and are sufficiently confidant to book their own accommodation. Other technological developments have also become more established in some countries than elsewhere, such as multi-media kiosks which provide destination specific information at the destination and, sometimes, incorporate a booking facility. In the USA, these are located in a variety of venues, including state welcome centres, hotel lobbies and tourist attractions.

Despite these national variations, information technology has undoubtedly had a significant impact on distribution, in particular in the context of outbound tourism, with the development of Computer Reservation Systems (CRS) playing a particularly important role. The initiative for CRS initially came from international airlines which needed a means of selling their tickets electronically and automated seat reservations and procedures. The focus of the CRS was, therefore, on selling airline tickets. Conversely, in the UK a sophisticated leisure market had developed providing packages holidays for which the CRS was not an effective means of distribution. Therefore, tour operators in the UK developed videotext systems in order to sell their package holidays electronically. CRSs have now evolved from being airline focused to being complete global distribution systems (GDS), and now sell a range of travel products in addition to airline tickets. Over the last five years, though, new technological developments, specifically the Internet, have threatened the dominance of such distribution systems.

Existing Tourism Information Distribution Systems

The impact of information technology on distribution has been significant and there are a number of existing tourism information distribution systems. Although the increasing use of the Internet is an important part of this process, the implications of the Internet for travel and tourism organisations is discussed in more detail in Chapter 19.

Computer reservation systems (CRSs) and global distribution systems (GDSs)

Over the last 40 years, CRSs have emerged as the dominant technology in the travel and tourism industry, controlling the sale and distribution of a wide array of travel related services. CRS enables information to be distributed and reservations to be processed in an efficient manner and, in many markets, such as in flight only and business travel, it has become an essential business tool (Lindsay 1992). Essentially, CRS is a database that enables a tourism organisation to manage its inventory and make it accessible to its distribution channel partners. Subscribers are provided with up-to-date information on airfares and services and can book, change and cancel reservations, and issue tickets. The rapid growth of both tourism demand and supply in recent decades has demonstrated the need for these advanced computer systems.

The impetus for the development of the CRS came from the airlines in the United States. In the early 1960s, American Airlines saw the need to develop a system which automated seat reservations and the procedures of airlines. As a result, SABRE (Semi-Automated Business Resource Environment) was then developed and introduced. To be successful, it had to:

- be a continuously operated, real-time, inquiry response system so agents could get an immediate answer to queries;

- have a large, geographically dispersed data communications network that connected all users of the reservation system to the central site (Sheldon 1997).

By the mid-1970s, not only had most other airlines followed American Airlines example (see Table 6.1 below), but also there was the increasing occurrence of direct travel agency access into these systems via a dedicated terminal located at the agency itself. CRSs were developed as businesses in their own right and became extremely profitable as revenues were obtained through imposing a small charge per booking and from payments by travel agents for the right to access the system (Archdale 1991). Initially, the systems sought to manage only reservations and passenger tracking functions and provided few support features. Today, however, CRSs have evolved into GDSs as they do so much more than sell airline tickets and automate procedures. They support window functions and multi-tasking, allowing travel agents to book flights, hotels, cars and look up other information such as visa requirements, currency conversion rates, and current weather conditions.

In short, CRSs have evolved into complete travel information systems and, as such, are GDSs (Poon 1993); they have multiple carrier affiliations and they all provide important electronic distribution channels for a variety of travel products. Moreover, GDSs are increasingly adapting business to include Web based products and services. The Internet reservation systems that are evolving are not necessarily a threat to GDSs as they can offer added value with services, such as theatre and restaurant bookings. Indeed, it seems inevitable that existing computer reservation systems and global distribution systems will become integrated with the Internet. At the same time, the continuing development of these communication techniques will inevitably mean that organisations involved in processing and distributing vast quantities of information will move to the Internet to facilitate these activities.

Table 6.1: *Global Distribution Systems*

Name	Developed by:	Key UK customers (1999) include:
Amadeus	Air France, Lufthansa, Iberia and Sabena	Lunn Poly, Flightbookers, Travel 2/4
Galileo	British Airways, KLM, Swissair, Austrian, Aer Lingus, Air Portugal, Olympic	BTI Hogg Robinson, Carlson Wagonlit, Portland, Gold Medal, Trailfinders, Airtours Group, Seaforths
Sabre	American Airlines	Amex, STA Travel, P&O, The Travel Co. MSW Group, Travelforce, Carlson Wagonlit, Bakers Dolphin, Phoenix
Worldspan	Delta, Northwest, TWA	Thomas Cook, Going Places, TMPL Group, Co-op Travelcare, Globepost, Crystal Holidays, Lotus Leisure, Global Travel Group, Scotway Group, Microsoft Expedia

Source: adapted from Mintel (2000)

The problems associated with CRSs

i. Inherent bias in CRSs

From the outset, airlines saw CRSs as their own property and, as a result, there were legitimate concerns that CRSs would be biased as, in theory, the schedules of the owning airline appeared before that of the competition. At the same time, airlines that were not involved in the development of a CRS found they were expected to pay a higher fee for having a presence on the CRS. The income from these fees were then used to offer incentives to the travel agencies to ensure they booked flights with CRS owner airlines rather than the airline that was simply paying for use of the system. Revenue management systems also monitored sales and calculated fares that gave CRS owners a competitive advantage in the marketplace.

Over time, however, this inherent bias has largely been eradicated through codes of conduct implemented in US and Europe, although systems still give the airlines control over the distribution of the travel product in the US and have been used to protect and increase market share. Although rules have succeeded in eliminating display bias, incremental revenues continue to be obtained through architectural bias and from the relationship between vendor airlines and travel agencies that foster travel agency loyalty to the vendor airline (Poon 1993).

ii. Insufficient scope of services

With regard to product presentation, the offers are almost exclusively limited to the owner airlines and, as a result, other service providers only have a very limited reservation rate or are not displayed at all. Fare quoting is still a complicated and confusing process, and price transparency or even price negotiations are not supported by the systems (Schulz 1997). CRS owners have also been slow to extend functions into the leisure market and this, in turn, prompted the development of videotext technologies to fulfil the need.

iii. High distribution costs

The high costs of using CRSs mean that many providers, such as small to medium tourism enterprises (for example owner run hotels), avoid using the system. For smaller agencies, Internet reservation systems can be a more cost effective means of distribution as they offer a wide range of products, but are based on less restrictive contracts than CRSs and can be used as the sole source of booking for an agency.

iv. CRSs discrimination against other tourism enterprises

CRSs are expensive, difficult to install and maintain, and do not automatically provide hotels, airlines and other suppliers with an automatic increase in business unless they are used to their full potential. Many commercial factors inhibit non-air vendors from automating their inventories and from using electronic distribution services. Principally, these factors relate to cost, control of inventory and conflict with existing business practices. For the hotel provider, an entry on a CRS can lead to problems of commission payments, different languages and totally different standards and codes (Lindsay 1992).

Viewdata

In the UK and in Europe, agency systems' development has taken a different route from the US experience, with Viewdata and videotext systems playing a major role, particularly for the leisure market (Tracey 1989).

The role of the tour operator is considerably greater in Europe than in the USA, as in Europe tour operators played an important role in the development and introduction of computerised bookings of tour packages themselves (Poon 1988). Within the UK, Thomson has been active in the development of technology since the early 1980s and provides a good example of the role of UK tour operators in automating the distribution of holidays. Thomson and Olympic Holidays were amongst the first operators to launch viewdata systems in the early 1980s (Bottomley Renshaw 1998). In the UK, most packaged holidays can only be accessed through on-line viewdata terminals developed and provided by the major tour operators. This is because UK tour operators have invested in the development of their own viewdata technology while other suppliers have become partners or co-hosts in airline CRS and still others chose not to automate – using conventional telephone calls as the main vehicle for bookings. In 1998, Thomson Holidays, a leading UK travel organisation, began to move its Viewdata system on to the Internet. The company will use the 'net to receive 'incoming requests from travel agents' Web browsers and then links up to the existing applications on Thomson's IBM mainframes'.

Destination marketing systems (DMS)

Destination Marketing Systems can encompass both reservations and information and can operate at national, regional and local levels (Bennett 1995). Destination marketing systems can also be referred to as destination databases (DD), destination management systems (DMS), travel information systems (TIS), and destination information systems (DIS) (Bennett 1996).

A DMS can have up to three components:

- Product database - of attractions, accommodation, travel information etc.;

- Customer database - of those using, or those who have used, the database;

- Booking and reservation system (Baker *et al*. 1996).

DMS can incorporate any number of the following features:

- product database;

- client database;

- marketing facilities;

- information retrieval;

- reservations;

- distribution.

The focus of the DMS may vary from pre-trip to post-arrival information, reservations and product databases. DMSs fill a large gap left by the GDS in the electronic distribution of destination information, as CRSs tend to favour large chain companies with high prices whilst DMSs include all types of travel products – large or small (Sheldon 1997). The trend away from packaged travel has created a demand for easily accessible information on destinations, particularly on small and medium sized enterprises which DMSs can respond to and meet the need for (Vlitos-Rowe 1992). DMS tend to be destination specific and are, as such, a restricted form of distribution.

DMSs have met with varying degrees of success and failure. The funding and level of public and private sector support given to these systems have led to difficulties and insurmountable obstacles. Swissline, in Switzerland, never emerged from the planning stage due to a lack of public and private support, whilst Hi-Line in Scotland was implemented in a region where there was insufficient volume of business and without public tourist organisation support (Sussmann 1994). DMSs can be divided into non-commercial and commercial models, where the former are supported by public funds, are an instrument of economic development and more prevalent. Speculation would suggest a brighter future for fully commercial DMS (Baker *et al*. 1996), and small to medium tourism enterprises and national tourism organisations are increasingly looking to such systems as the way forward. This is the case in Germany, Austria and Switzerland where Tiscover AG (a pioneering company in the development of destination management systems in Europe) had provided systems to leading national and regional tourism organisations.

Video Conferencing

The integration of the Personal Computer and the Internet will see an increase in the use of video conferencing. For a relatively small investment in additional equipment, organisations can arrange meetings without having to travel to a specific location. On the one hand, a tourism organisation can benefit from the efficiencies that might result but, on the other hand, this may mean that the need for business travel declines.

Kiosks

In the early 1990s, kiosks were seen as a possible way forward for the distribution of tourism information, especially to the tourists seeking information about, or at, destinations. Self service multi-media kiosks have enormous potential in terms of dissemination of information and reservation purposes. Kiosks are a means of distributing information in a particularly user friendly way because they tend to use a 'touch screen' interface. People who are intimidated by 'technology' might find using a kiosk more intuitive and less threatening than a computer terminal. Kiosks are currently used by both the private and public sector to promote tourism and provide tourist information. They can be sited in tourist areas like railway stations, airports or city streets and have the advantage of being available 24 hours a day, 365 days a year. It seems likely that kiosks will be more tightly integrated with the Internet and designed to take advantages of Internet technology in the coming years.

Home Shopping

The growth of non-terrestrial television and digital television, coupled with a relaxation of government controls in this sector, will mean that home shopping will increase in the next few years. The arrival of interactive digital TV in the UK has opened up a major new front for competition among global distribution systems, as all four GDS companies see the Internet as providing a focus for advances in travel technology (Mintel 2000). By becoming the booking engine behind the Internet companies, GDSs believe they will gain massively increased exposure through interactive TV. Worldspan has links with Microsoft in the US, UK and Europe as the booking engine behind Expedia; Sabre has Travelocity in the US and UK; Amadeus has Compuserve in the UK (Mintel 2000). The takeover of Expedia, a major Internet travel agency in 2001, by American media group, USA Network, reflects the increasing importance placed on home shopping. USA Network believes that 'using a website in conjunction with an interactive TV channel would put Expedia at the head of the pack when interactive digital TV takes off in Europe (Travel Trade Gazette 2001).

This is important for the tourism marketer, as it will allow tourism organisations to find another way to communicate with their customers. Currently, many TV providers and manufacturers are working on ways to integrate TV technology with the Internet. This will mean that consumers will not have to own a personal computer to access the 'net. This has enormous implications for e-commerce and home shopping. The Internet will no longer be the preserve of the technologically advanced, who are currently a distinct but relatively small market segment, but will be accessible to anyone with a TV – which, of course, is most people.

Conclusion

Distribution is a vital component of the travel and tourism industry and it has become the primary area for seeking competitive advantage in both cost reduction and service improvement. The advantages afforded by the increasing use of information technology means that the inherent problems of the tourism product – its perishability, intangibility, heterogeneity and inseparability – can be diminished and controlled.

This chapter has shown how distribution of the tourism product primarily concerns information as consumers need to be able to access the tourism product at multiple points of sale away from the places of service production and this involves information being passed down the distribution channels. Developments in information technology are having significant impact on distribution choices being made. Direct sale is becoming ever more popular whilst it has been argued that travel agents position may well be under threat. The later chapter on e-commerce will open up the whole area of distribution even further.

Discussion questions

1. *Discuss the importance of information to the distribution process?*

2. *What are the advantages and disadvantages of using intermediaries rather than direct sale?*

3. *Discuss the impact of information technology on distribution.*

Further reading

Alford, P, (2000), *E-business in the Travel Industry*, London: Travel & Tourism Intelligence.

Bottomley Renshaw, M. (1997), *The Travel Agent, 2nd Edition*, Sunderland: Business Education Publishers.

Middleton, V. (2001), *Marketing in Travel and Tourism, 3rd Edition*, Oxford: Butterworth Heinemann.

Poon, A. (2001), Travel distribution: the future of travel agents, *Travel and Tourism Analyst*, No.3: 57-80.

Sheldon, P. (1997), *Tourism Information Technology*, Wallingford: CAB International

References

Alford, P. (2000), *E-business in the Travel Industry*, London: Travel & Tourism Intelligence.

Archdale, G, (1991), Computer reservation systems - the international scene, *ETB Insights, Volume 3*, English Tourist Board: D15-19.

Archdale, G. (1992), Computer reservation systems, Part 2, *ETB Insights, Volume 3*, London: English Tourist Board: D21-25.

Baker, M., Hayzelden, C. and Sussman, S. (1996), Can destination management systems provide competitive advantage? A discussion of the factors affecting their survival and success of destination management systems, *Progress in Tourism and Hospitality Research* 2(1):1-13.

Bennett, M. (1995), The consumer marketing revolution: the impact of IT on tourism, *Journal of Vacation Marketing*, 1(5): 376-382.

Bennett, M. (1996), The marketing mix: tourism distribution, in A. Seaton and M. Bennett (eds) *Marketing Tourism Products: Concepts, Issues, Cases*, London: International Thomson Business Press.

Bottomley Renshaw, M. (1997), *The Travel Agent, 2nd Edition*, Sunderland: Business Education Publishers.

Cowell, D. (1991), *The Marketing of Services*, Oxford : Butterworth-Heinemann.

Fair CS Telemarketing (1996), *What role will it play?* LIMRA'S MARKETFACTS May/June: p7-9

First Choice History. URL: http://ww6.investorrelations.co.uk/firstchoice/EditHistory.shtml [5 October 2001]

Holloway, J.C. and Robinson, C. (1995), *Marketing for Tourism, 4th Edition*, Harlow: Longman.

Inkpen, G. (1994), *Information Technology for Travel and Tourism*, London: Pitman Publishing.

Kotler, P., Bowen, J. and Makens, J. (1996), *Marketing for Hospitality and Tourism*, London: Prentice Hall.

McIntosh, R., Goeldner C., and Ritchie, J. (1995), *Tourism: Principles, Practices, Philosophies, 7th Edition*: Harlow: John Wiley & Sons.

Lindsay, P. (1992), CRS Supply and demand, *Tourism Management* 13(1): 11-14.

Lumsdon, L. (1997), *Tourism Marketing*, London: International Thomson Business Press.

Middleton, V. (2001), *Marketing in Travel and Tourism, 3rd Edition*, Oxford: Butterworth Heinemann.

Mill, R. and Morrison, A. (1992), *The Tourism System: An Introductory Text 2nd Edition*, London: Prentice Hall.

Mintel (1998), *Directly Booked Holiday*, Mintel International Group Limited.

Mintel (2000), *Travel Agents*, Mintel International Group Limited.

Pender, L. (1999), *Marketing Management for Travel and Tourism*, Cheltenham: Stanley Thornes (publishers) Ltd.

Poon, A. (1988), Tourism and information technologies, *Annals of Tourism Research* 15 (4): 531-549.

Poon, A. (1993), *Tourism, Technology and Competitive Strategies*, Wallingford: CAB International.

Poon, A. (2001), Travel distribution: the future of travel agents, *Travel and Tourism Analyst* No.3: 57-80.

Richardson, D. (2000), First Choice tactics slammed by agents, *Travel Trade Gazette UK & Ireland*, July 24th: p.20.

Schulz, A. (1997), Electronic market co-ordination in the travel industry: the role of global computer reservation systems, in A. Min Toja (ed.) *Information and Communication Technologies in Tourism*, Proceedings of the international conference in Edinburgh Scotland, New York: Springer Wien: 67-73.

Sheldon, P. (1997), *Tourism Information Technology*, Wallingford: CAB International.

Sussman, S. (1994), The impact of new technological developments on destination management systems, in C. Cooper and A. Lockwood (eds.) *Progress in Tourism Recreation and Hospitality Management, Volume V*, Chichester: John Wiley & Sons: 289-296.

Tracey, P. (1989), Information technology - central reservation systems, *ETB Insights, Volume 2*, London: English Tourist Board: A2:1-8.

Travel Trade Gazette (2001), Expedia targets digital TV bookings, *Travel Trade Gazette UK & Ireland* July 23rd: p.6.

van der Heijden, J. (1996), The changing value of travel agents in tourism networks: towards a network design perspective, in *Information and communication technologies,* Proceedings of the international conference in Innsbruck, Austria, New York: Springer Wien: 151-159.

Vlitos-Rowe, I. (1992), Occasional Studies: Destination databases and management systems, *Travel and Tourism Analyst* No.5: 84-108.

Witt, S. and Moutinho, L. (1995), *Tourism Marketing and Management Handbook Student Edition*, London: Prentice Hall.

7

Transport for Travel and Tourism

David Holding

Learning objectives

This chapter examines the role of various forms of transport within the tourism industry. It enables the reader to:

- *understand the broad contribution of transport to tourism*

- *appreciate the business disciplines within which transport providers work*

- *appreciate how industry economics influence its marketing*

- *identify the relevance of environmental issues to tourism transport*

Introduction

Transport and tourism are synonymous. That is, transport is indispensable to the operation of the travel and tourism industry and, therefore, a knowledge of how it works is essential. This chapter begins by summarising the principal features of a transport system that are common to all the major forms or modes. The particular characteristics of each of the modes and current issues relating to tourism are then described. Finally, the contribution of transport to environmental impacts is discussed.

The importance of transport

Transport is important to the travel and tourism industry for four reasons:

i. Tourism implies movement

Virtually all tourism is based on experiencing different locations, for which transport facilities are essential. Not so widely recognised, however, is the scale and extent of the transport businesses that underpin that travel. For international tourism, airlines are the principal mode of travel (although globally, ground travel – by car or train – remain the most commonly used forms of transport) and, for example, British Airways – the largest airline in the UK – in 2000 had a turnover of £8,940m, employing 65,640 people. Even so, BA is small by comparison with the giants of the US industry.

At the same time, transport investment and infrastructure are vital to the commercial development of tourism in an area. Indeed, the historical role of the railways in the development of the British seaside resorts in the 19th Century (see Chapter 2) was mirrored by the contribution of air travel to the emergence of many international tourist destinations, such as The Gambia, the Maldives and the Caribbean islands, during the 20th Century. For example, traditionally the few visitors to the smaller Greek islands arrived by ferry from Athens (Piraeus) and the more adventurous still do, but the time taken (and inherent complexity) would be unacceptable to the mass market. It was only when an enterprising tour operator persuaded the authorities to allow military airfields to be used for charter flights that large-scale commercial development could begin.

This illustrates the important concept that, after cost, the main constraint on people's ability to travel is not distance but time; certainly, the growth of long-haul holidays shows that distance is not necessarily a deterrent as long as the journey can be made easily and rapidly. Conversely, some destinations, such as the St Moritz area of Switzerland and Positano/Amalfi on the Neapolitan Riviera, have remained exclusive partly because they are difficult to reach quickly and are, thus, only available to those with time to spare or fast personal means of transport.

ii. Transport is a product of the travel industry

Despite the growing importance of Internet sales, travel agents generate a large proportion of their income from selling transport services, as distinct from holiday packages – in particular tickets for air and rail travel, together with car hire, coach and ferry services. World-wide, typically 75 percent of all air tickets are sold by travel agents. Commission is paid on these sales, and it is necessary for the travel agent to have knowledge of services and facilities available.

iii. There is overlap between components of the travel industry

Some travel agents and tour operators are offshoots of transport companies, and vice-versa; the same organisation which puts the package together or sells it may be involved in providing the transport. Ferry companies, airlines, railways and coach operators offer extensive tour programmes of various kinds, while most charter airlines are connected financially with tour operators (the outstanding UK example being Britannia Airways, a subsidiary of Thomson Travel Group). The Virgin Group controls hotels, long- and short-haul aviation and two UK rail franchises, in addition to other activities outside transport.

iv. The quality of transport is important in the travel business

A tour operator contracting hotel accommodation seeks assurances about the standard of rooms, meals and other facilities. Less attention tends to be given to the choice of transport, but poor transport arrangements can spoil a holiday just as easily. However, people are increasingly conscious of quality and expect service of a high standard. Where that quality is lacking and an operator refuses compensation, successful legal action is possible – as occurred after a coach driver smoked throughout a holiday.

Elements of transport systems

Although various modes of transport perform different functions and have individual strengths and weaknesses, they all feature five essential elements in common:

- a *Way* or route on which travel occurs;

- *Vehicles* that perform that movement;

- *Terminals* between which they travel;

- *Control and communication systems* through which safety is ensured and those involved are kept informed; and

- *Skilled management and staff* who bring the elements together.

All these make up a transport system, and it is important to recognise the contribution of each.

The way

In the case of sea and air travel, the way is natural and 'free'. In principle, therefore, it can be used without restriction or cost, although safety demands that most air movements are subject to an air traffic control system, while ports and inland waterways usually involve artificial works which are charged for. Roads require construction and maintenance to reach a standard suitable for modern traffic; this is normally done by a public authority and the cost recovered by taxation on fuel and the use of vehicles. Occasionally, as with French autoroutes, a private company builds and maintains the route and then charges users a direct toll to use it.

Rail systems similarly require construction and, by their nature, can only be used by very specialised vehicles. Historically, most railways were built by the companies which owned and operated vehicles on them, but nowadays it is increasingly common for the track to be in different hands from the operator. Since the way is exclusive, the congestion found on roads can be avoided, but the specialised nature of rail construction incurs high costs which can only be justified by high levels of traffic.

The vehicle

This is the carrying unit on which people travel – the train, ship, coach or aircraft. Sometimes separate 'motive power' is used to haul carrying units, the obvious example being railway engines, but usually the power to achieve movement is produced within the carrying unit itself. Over the years, the trend has been for the average size of vehicle to increase in order to accommodate increased demand and obtain economies (for example, the introduction of the 'jumbo' jet in the 1970s). However, this can result in the inability to service some destinations (as with cruise ships) or demand heavy investment to accommodate them, such as in longer airport runways.

The terminal

The terminal could be defined as the place where people begin and end their journeys but, in practice, this is rarely true; few people live next to transport terminals and even fewer would like their holiday hotel to be next to the airport (although airport hotels do of course exist for other purposes). In fact, the terminal performs two functions. Firstly, it facilitates transfer or interchange between modes. For example, passengers boarding an international flight at a major airport might arrive by one of a variety of means, including:

- railway

- their own or a friend's car

- taxi

- another aircraft (interlining)

- hire car

- scheduled bus or coach

- touring or transfer coach.

Thus, a major function of an airport is to allow the smooth interchange from and to these other modes of transport.

The second function of a terminal is to consolidate traffic. Passengers normally 'interline', or change aircraft, because no convenient direct service exists. Therefore, the airport acts as a hub, a process which exists in most forms of transport and is becoming increasingly common. In this case, aircraft from regional centres feed into a major interchange, maximising the range of through-journey opportunities for passengers and creating higher passenger numbers for carriers.

Control and communication systems

For safety reasons, aircraft are subject to air traffic control systems which monitor not only take-off and landing but their movement while airborne. Similarly, railways are subject to control systems, traditionally referred to as 'signalling' but usually far more technically advanced than this suggests. It is these systems which make air and rail relatively safe in terms of accidents per passenger-kilometre.

In contrast, we enjoy a right to take a car or other vehicle onto the road system, however busy and congested it is. The purpose of control here is to improve safety and restrict movements once we are there, through traffic lights, roundabouts, speed limits, and so on. Similarly, once out of port ships can generally sail where their owners wish, although rules of navigation dictate how they should move when close to each other, and masters use navigational aids to avoid shallows and other dangers.

At airport or rail terminals, there are usually information screens which not only list arrivals and departures, but also give "real-time" information stating when the next or delayed services are expected to arrive. This is possible because those operating the control systems are permanently in contact – through radio and electronically – with the aircraft or trains they monitor and thus know exactly where they are. This is not usually the case with road vehicles, unless they are linked to a tracking system which reports their movements back to a control centre and so on to waiting passengers.

Management and staff

It is easy to underestimate not just the numbers of personnel involved in a major transport business but also the complexity of management. For example, a company such as GNER, the franchise which operates trains between London, North-East England and Scotland, employs 3,000 to operate its 112 departures per day and carries 14m passengers each year, requires all the usual management functions, such as HR, finance, IT and marketing, in addition to those carrying out specialist operating duties.

The following sections now consider different modes or forms of transport.

Road transport

The private car

In most developed countries, the private car is the most popular form of transport for leisure travel. Not only can it reach most destinations easily and luggage can be easily handled, but also car owners can make extra 'marginal' journeys at a low cost which becomes lower still as more people are carried. This popularity and convenience of the car is demonstrated by a survey of visitors to Stratford-on-Avon which found that 66 percent arrived by private car; 17 percent by touring coach; 6 percent by hire car; 5 percent by train, and 6 percent by other means (ETB 1995). More generally, over 80 percent of visitors to the English countryside travel by car, a proportion which rises to ninety percent in some national parks (Sharpley 1996).

The car's widespread availability has brought about two major developments within tourism:

i. the use of a family car for holidays abroad

There has been a rapid growth in independent overseas travel by private car, although crossing water adds disproportionately to total holiday costs, thus discouraging both island residents from holidaying abroad and those on 'the other side' from coming in. For this reason, together with the attraction of warmer weather, residents of France, Germany and Holland are much more likely to use their car for a holiday on the European mainland than to travel to the United Kingdom.

ii. car rental

Because people value the use of a car for mobility at home, but a destination is beyond the possible range for taking one's own, the car hire business has developed rapidly in resort areas. Hire cars are also available at airports and rail terminals for business or leisure use. Some holidays include 'fly-drive' as an integral part of the package, while others offer optional car hire at discounted rates within the resort.

Given the rapid growth in car ownership and usage, attention is inevitably focused on the environmental impacts of the car, particularly in more fragile areas. Many national parks, for example, are developing policies to encourage the use of alternative forms of transport. At the same time, one approach to 'managing' independent car-borne leisure travel by tourism bodies is to designate recommended routes. These can be lengthy stretches of major roads passing through scenically attractive areas, such as the Romantischestrasse and Weinstrasse in Germany, where the object is to persuade travellers to stop and spend in historic towns along the route. On a more local basis, 'scenic drives' may be promoted along a common theme such as fruit trees in blossom. These are geared more to the 'Sunday afternoon' motorist looking for somewhere to go, and may have the ulterior motive of attracting drivers away from popular destinations and roads which become congested.

Taxis and private hire cars

The role of taxis is, in effect, halfway between private and public transport. Visitors may well use taxis on a casual basis to reach locations where they lack the confidence to use public transport, whilst they may also find it the easiest way of reaching a city centre from an airport. Equally, a taxi may be an alternative to a hired car to reach an attraction which is not accessible by public transport. Sometimes it is accepted practice, for example when cruise ships call into a port, for visitors to hire a taxi with a driver for the time available; the driver knows the main attractions and takes his passengers for a personalised tour. Taxis are also used by tour operators and their resort representatives for transferring small numbers of visitors between airports and hotels.

Cycling

For the first half of the twentieth century, cycling was one of the commonest forms of transport, used for travel to work, school and leisure alike. While that has continued in some places (notably in some University cities and in Holland), the growth in car ownership has both led to cars replacing cycles for these journeys and made conditions more dangerous and unpleasant for the cyclists remaining.

Nevertheless, cycling has more recently re-emerged as a leisure activity, particularly in the form of 'mountain' bikes. Families often travel by car on holiday or for a day out with cycles fixed to the back or roof of their car to an area where quiet roads or tracks are available, whilst some bus and rail operators adapt vehicles to carry cycles and so offer a public transport alternative. Opportunities for leisure cycling have also increased. In the UK, for example, the charity Sustrans (Sustainable Transport) is using funds raised from local authorities and others to develop a national network of cycle routes. (See Figure. 7.1).

The National Cycle Network is a visionary project to provide a 10,000-mile network of cycle routes.

Originally launched with a £43.5 million grant from the Millennium Commission, the Network involves the active participation of more than 400 local authorities, the Department of the Environment, Transport and the Regions, and other public and private bodies.

The Network is a linked series of traffic-free paths and traffic-calmed and minor roads connecting urban centres and the countryside, and reaching all parts of the UK. These will provide a safe, attractive, and high quality network for cyclists and a major new amenity for walkers and wheelchair users.

More than 5,000 miles of signed and mapped routes opened in June 2000. Ten thousand miles will be completed by 2005. The Network will connect with hundreds of further extensions.

Among the 10,000 km already open, a 'Sea to Sea' route from the Irish to the North Sea has been created and the target is to achieve 17,000 km of track. The routes are not all in open countryside; it is estimated that over 20 million people will live within 3 km of a point on the network, so it will be possible to use it for local leisure and travel to work or education.

Inevitably, some of the network will be in the form of cycle lanes along roads carrying other traffic, but the maximum use is being made of disused routes, such as old rail tracks and canal towpaths.

Figure 7.1: *Sustrans cycle routes*

Scheduled bus and coach

Scheduled services are those that run to a fixed timetable and are not subject to cancellation if demand is insufficient. These are the forms of transport normally used least by tourists, but are important for particular locations and purposes:

Long-distance leisure journeys

In the UK, this market is dominated by two organisations, National Express and Scottish Citylink. Both run networks of inter-urban coach services and are, primarily, planning and marketing bodies which charter in coaches to meet their needs from large and small operators across the country. However, the image of one large organisation is created by a requirement that coaches on long-term contract are of a specified design and painted in a standard colour scheme. Virtually all demand is leisure-oriented in some form and its scale is such that National Express schedules around 700 coaches on an average day, with more on a short-term basis to meet peak demands. Most European countries do not have long-distance coach networks of the same kind because their Governments have preferred to encourage use of their railways, but they are expanding slowly.

Local services

These are used by tourists principally for short-distance travel within towns and cities; London Transport Marketing (1996) found that about 45 percent of overseas visitors used its buses during their stay, while just under 40 percent used taxis. Buses are also used to an extent to reach rural attractions from the bigger accommodation centres. For example, in North Wales a 'Snowdon Sherpa' system of connecting minibuses was originally intended to help solve parking problems at the foot of Snowdon, but has been developed to provide longer distance access from towns such as Llandudno and Portmadoc. In some countries, particularly Switzerland, extensive and high quality rural services are promoted strongly to tourists and are used as an environmentally-friendly alternative to local car hire.

The bus has a fairly captive market among visitors to some islands, the systems in Tenerife, Malta and Majorca all being well used. That in Tenerife (TITSA) is modern and professional, while the Maltese system traditionally uses ancient buses which are almost a working museum and tourist attraction in themselves; however, modernisation is now taking place.

Also included in this category are local sightseeing tours, which are common in larger cities but have also been expanding in smaller historic centres. The London survey mentioned above found these to be used by over 20 percent of overseas visitors. In the UK they commonly use old double-deck buses with the roof removed, which have a low purchase price and are a novelty for most visitors.

'Touring' coaches

These refer to non-scheduled services offered for leisure purposes. At one extreme is the day trip, designed either for the resident population or to take visitors to attractions in the wider area; the latter, of course, are often organised in conjunction with tour operators and sold by resort representatives. Within the resident market, demand has moved away from the traditional seaside resort towards theme parks and locations associated with television series. Major shopping centres and developments can attract large numbers. The Metro Centre near Newcastle can accommodate 370 coaches and receives close to this number in the weeks before Christmas, while the hypermarkets of Calais are popular further south. Other growth sectors have been open-air museums such as Beamish and Ironbridge, where the school trip market is important. The total value of the market for UK residents taking coach tours (i.e. at least one night away) is estimated at £643m per annum, with a further £396m coming into the UK from overseas groups (Confederation of Passenger Transport 1999).

Beyond the day trip come weekend and mid-week breaks and extended tours of between seven and fourteen days. These include both more traditional tours and also 'shuttle' operations, where parties are ferried to their accommodation with a minimum of stops, and then return home one or two weeks later.

Structure of the industry

The road transport industry includes all sizes of operator, with fleets varying from one coach to a thousand or more. However, the bigger fleets, which outside the UK are still often publicly owned, tend to concentrate on local bus work, and in the coach sector small firms predominate, many of whom sell direct by word of mouth, newspapers or through a small number of local agents. The elderly form a large part of the coach tour market, but growth can be achieved provided new customers are attracted; it is an expanding and increasingly prosperous sector of the population.

As coach operators do not normally have the bargaining strength to negotiate attractive rates with hotels and ferry companies, specialist tour wholesalers offer to coach firms a package of accommodation, if necessary with overnight stops, and ferry bookings at reasonable prices expressed as a figure per head (subject to a minimum break-even number). Operators have then only to add coach operating costs and a profit margin to arrive at a selling price for the tour.

Rail transport

The railways no longer hold the dominant position in leisure passenger transport they enjoyed in the nineteenth and early twentieth centuries. Although demand still exists for rail transport to traditional coastal resorts for day trips and holidays, commuters and business travellers are now more numerous on these routes than holidaymakers.

However, rail is important in certain niche markets and, where investment in new vehicles and infrastructure takes place, it can increase ridership and market share. Most European systems have developed more commercial approaches which identify distinct styles of operation, and set appropriate targets for them. We shall consider each of these principal sectors in turn and then look at the involvement of the private sector in preserved and narrow-gauge railways.

Inter-City services

The main characteristic of Inter-City services is that they provide fast, high-quality regular services – often running every hour – between principal centres. Business travellers are an important market and for them first-class coaches are provided with restaurant cars and possibly other services such as computer plug-in points. Fares are relatively high, through a higher charge for First Class, discriminatory pricing on the busiest trains (see below) and possibly a premium for travel on Inter-City trains as opposed to others. Not surprisingly, perhaps, Inter-City services are normally the most profitable in a rail system.

Most West European countries have invested heavily in new high-speed rail systems, some running internationally (e.g. the Thalys service from Paris to Brussels, Cologne and Amsterdam). Maximum speeds of up to 300 kph enable these trains to compete effectively not just with the car but with airlines, and they have taken much of the airlines' previous market share for centre-to-centre traffic. On Inter-City routes as a whole, however, few trains can be filled with business customers alone and other types of customer are encouraged through pricing mechanisms such as Senior and Young Person's Railcards and APEX tickets. Sales to visitors from overseas can also be important, for which most European railways maintain international offices. Unlimited travel tickets (in Britain the Britrail Pass) are also available, but are normally sold only through these offices to avoid their use by domestic customers. For example, many young Americans use the British system to attend the Edinburgh Festival each summer.

Regional services

These are passenger routes outside the main conurbations that are slower, make more stops and sometimes offer lower standards of comfort. Although it is hard to distinguish precisely, there are two broad categories, which we might call 'Express' and 'the rest'. Express routes are those which come closest to Inter-City in terms of fast services between regional centres, using trains of a high standard with limited catering services; examples are Newcastle-Leeds-Liverpool in the UK and Dusseldorf-Kassel in Germany. These Express routes also come closest to Inter-City in their financial performance, being expected to cover at least their direct operating costs.

The rest are a financial liability to any rail organisation and exist mainly for political and social reasons. They may fit the description 'branch lines' although, in the UK, most such lines were closed in the 1960s; an exception is in Cornwall, where a number of branch lines remain open because of a continuing role in bringing visitors to the area. More commonly, these routes are 50km or more in length, connecting outlying towns and remote areas to the core system. It is accepted that these lines cannot be profitable and are, therefore, subsidised by central or regional Governments.

However, opportunities exist to improve their financial performance because, as rural tourism and interest in outdoor activities has grown, so too has the potential for their use by visitors. Many such lines pass through National Parks and other scenically attractive areas where environmental pressures make it sensible to encourage access by rail rather than by road. The cost structure of railways means that it costs little or nothing to carry additional leisure traffic, and the income can be used almost entirely to reduce losses. Well-planned marketing programmes to increase such patronage are therefore likely to be highly cost-effective.

Urban services

Urban railways are often operated by local as opposed to nationally-controlled organisations. In much of Europe, new systems are being built and existing ones adapted. For example, in Stuttgart and other German cities the traditional street trams run by city authorities have been modernised and diverted underground in city centres, while the suburban trains of the state railway (DB) also run in tunnels under the centre. Visitors to cities, who often do not have private transport with them, will use local rail services if they are made attractive enough and promoted as an integrated system.

In London, 9 percent of all journeys on the Underground system are made by tourists and a survey found that 76 percent of visitors had used the Underground system the previous day. Additionally, nearly 30 percent of all overseas visitors to London used the national rail system at some time during their stay (London Transport Marketing 1996).

Ownership and control of railways

Historically, most large railways, like major airlines, have been owned by the state, not only because they are seen as having political or strategic importance, but also because they tend not to be commercially viable. Most railways are still Government-owned, although they may be set more specific commercial targets and be run in a more businesslike way than hitherto.

The international trend to privatisation has not yet affected most rail systems. However, the EU has encouraged member states to separate the provision of *infrastructure* (track, control and stations) from the *operation* of the trains themselves. Some countries are, therefore, setting up track-owning companies or authorities from which train operators 'rent' paths or slots. The UK Government's decision was firstly to separate the various elements of service provision and then privatise them in turn. An infrastructure company (Railtrack) - recently nationalised by the Government - owns all public track (other than that locally run in the major cities), the control systems and some stations. 25 Train Operating Companies (TOCs) pay access charges for use of the system, own the remaining stations, and lease the trains they run from leasing companies. Their income is obtained from fares and Government subsidy.

However, the ownership of trains is of little interest to passengers, who seek reliability, reasonable fares and comprehensive and unbiased information. These factors are particularly important to tourists who are unfamiliar with a system, and integrated charging can be important in marketing rail-based travel. For example, tour operators sell packages based on accommodation together with rail travel, which is priced on a zonal system according to distance from the destination. It would seriously undermine the marketing of these packages if some TOCs excluded their services or charged on a different basis.

Tourist and private railways

Although the large, public rail organisations make an important contribution to the movement of tourists, there are also railways which exist purely as tourist attractions or holidays in their own right.

Firstly, it is possible to run privately-owned locomotives (usually steam) over parts of the public rail system; the number of preserved locomotives makes this commonest in the UK. Secondly, the national rail systems can be used for luxurious trains, of which the Venice-Simplon Orient Express (VSOE) is the best known example. Here, privately-owned coaches are hauled by electric locomotives provided by the various national railways.

Alternatively, a private organisation may run a self-contained railway. These normally involve steam locomotives and, usually, these are lines which have been closed to conventional traffic, although some were never intended for passenger travel at all. For example, most of the narrow-gauge railways in North Wales, collectively promoted as the Great Little Trains of Wales, were built to carry slate from quarries to the sea. The popularity of such lines can be increased by attractive scenery and nearby major tourist attractions. The Keighley and Worth Valley Railway in West Yorkshire, for instance, has its headquarters at Haworth where visitors to the Bronte literary associations are numbered in hundreds of thousands.

The appeal of these preserved railways which are open throughout a season must be to a mass market where they compete with totally different attractions. However, although they must meet the same safety standards as a 'public' line, which involves considerable expense, they are helped by only having to run when they judge the market demands it and by the use of volunteers to carry out driving, manual and clerical work.

The Channel Tunnel and Eurostar

The Channel Tunnel between Folkestone in Kent (UK) and Coquelles near Calais (France) opened in May 1994. It is a rail tunnel through which two distinct types of passenger service operate – the Shuttle and Eurostar.

The Shuttle service is designed to carry cars, coaches and goods vehicles with their drivers and passengers, and operates only between terminals at either end of the tunnel. It competes directly with cross-Channel ferries (see next section), particularly those between Dover and Calais, but its effect has also been felt on the longer crossings north and west of the Straits of Dover. In 2000, the Shuttle carried 2.8m cars and 79,000 coaches (www.eurotunnel.com).

Conversely, Eurostar is a high-speed Inter-City service which operates principally from London to Brussels and Paris. Jointly owned by the National Express Group and British Airways in the UK, and by the Belgian and French state railways, its scheduled time of 3 hours from London to Paris and 2 hours 40 minutes to Brussels makes it particularly attractive to business travellers between city centres. By 2000, Air France had lost 60 percent of its Paris-London market to Eurostar, which carried a total of 7.1m passengers in that year (www.eurotunnel.com). However, competition between Eurostar and the airlines has succeeded in expanding the total market.

Between Folkestone and London, Eurostar trains currently run over the slow and congested tracks also used by local commuter trains. A fast Rail Link to continental standards is under construction, the first section of which should be completed in 2003, with the more difficult London section to follow in 2007. This will further improve journey time and reliability, so increasing the threat to the airlines.

Shipping

Much of Britain's growth as an industrial nation and as the centre of an empire was connected with its shipping industry. In the Victorian era, large companies such as Cunard and P&O emerged, involved in the transport of goods to and from overseas centres and the movement of emigrants and business people. However, while cargo shipping still exists in a modern, mainly containerised, form, the greater speed of aircraft made it impossible from the 1950s onwards for ships to compete for passengers, and this business has largely disappeared. Shipping is now important to tourism in three forms:

i. Local ferries

These operate principally inland on lakes but also over short distances along coastlines and in long inlets, such as the Norwegian fjords. These features often occur in mountainous areas which are attractive for tourism, and the lakes are part of the scenery that is marketed. Such terrain often makes overland travel difficult and it can be much quicker to travel from one side of a lake to the other by water than round the edge (for example from the French southern side of Lake Geneva to Lausanne in Switzerland on the northern bank). Similarly, it is an easier journey by water from one resort to another along the Italian Riviera than on land by road. Thus, ferries may form part of a local transport network for residents, but use by tourists is likely to predominate.

Such ferries have been a feature of the English Lake District since late Victorian times. The Furness Railway, wishing to reach the heart of the Lakes at Bowness and Ambleside, built a branch from its main line to the southern tip of Windermere at Lakeside, where a terminal and an imposing hotel were built, and its passengers could then travel by steamer along the lake. Today, the Lakeside and Haverthwaite Railway runs steam trains along the northern part of the line, connecting with the ships of Windermere Lake Cruises. The fact that original craft are still in use is one of the attractions, and in this way visitors are offered a package of travel by vintage train and ship.

ii. Sea-going ferries

These are distinguished by typically longer crossing times and, particularly with islands, their history is much more of necessity as opposed to leisure.

Traditionally, people wishing to travel from Britain to Europe or from Ireland to the UK mainland reached the port by train, crossed by ferry and continued by rail on the other side. Nowadays, however, the majority of passengers travel with vehicles which are also carried on the ferry, these being known as 'Roll-on/Roll-off or 'RoRo' ferries. Domestic routes, such as those to Ireland and the Scottish islands, continue to be important. Just under a million cars and many foot passengers travel by sea to or from Ireland every year, while the Scottish services, operated by Caledonian Macbrayne (West Coast) and P&O (Orkney and Shetland), in addition to being 'lifelines', have also become involved in tourism travel. Between them they carry about 250,000 cars annually.

Holidays involving taking the family car, and sometimes a caravan, to or from the European mainland enjoyed steady growth for many years and packages were developed, including ferry crossings and either fixed bookings or a series of "go-as-you-please" hotel vouchers. In recent years, however, the ferry companies have experienced increasing difficulties. From Table 7.1 it is evident that, over a ten year period, traffic on the Straits of Dover and English Channel routes began to fall in 1995, while on the North Sea the decline began earlier in 1993 (although a recovery can be seen from 1998 onwards).

Table 7.1: *Accompanied cars travelling by ship between the UK and European mainland, 1990-1999*

	Accompanied cars by ship (thousands)									
	1990	1991	1992	1993	1994	1995	1996	1997	1998	1999
North Sea	650	730	734	697	632	609	547	518	532	586
Straits of Dover	2,346	2,624	2,715	3,173	3,627	3,309	3,383	3,739	3,193	2,856
English Channel	1,140	1,257	1,295	1,369	1,436	1,422	1,292	1,357	1,370	1,349
ALL ROUTES	4,137	4,611	4,744	5,238	5,695	5,340	5,222	5,614	5,095	4,790

Source: Transport Statistics Great Britain 2000, DETR

The principal cause of this was the opening of the Channel Tunnel, where the shuttle service between Folkestone and Calais takes 35 minutes compared with at least 75 minutes by ferry. By mid-1996, the Shuttle was estimated to have around 45 percent of traffic across the Straits of Dover, equivalent to the combined business of the two largest ferry companies, and the over-capacity led to fierce price competition, particularly at off-peak times. Thus, although the total market continued to increase, ferry turnover fell, a problem aggravated in 1999 by the ending of duty-free sales within the EU.

Cruises

Like ferries, cruising has a long history. Developed from the luxurious liners that sailed across the Atlantic and to far-flung colonies, cruise ships traditionally had an image of being expensive and oriented towards rich, elderly passengers.

The strength of cruising is that it combines the opportunity to 'sample' a variety of destinations with an elegant lifestyle, with the added benefit that the accommodation travels to the destination. The main disadvantage is that, due to the labour costs of providing high standards of service, cruising is expensive. For example, the average price of cruise holidays bought in the UK in 1995 was an estimated £1,049 (MINTEL 1995).

Sometimes, cruises may depart from and return to tourists' home country but, since most cruise destinations are a substantial distance from customers' homes, it is often impractical to sail from the country of origin. As a result, the 'fly-cruise' has become increasingly popular, accounting for around 70 percent of the UK cruise market. Not only do customers can fly to join the ship at a suitable point, but also the cruise is able to consolidate passengers of different nationalities and so maximise carryings. For example, the world's largest cruise market is the USA and its principal cruising area the Caribbean; most cruises start at or near Miami, which both American and European customers can reach quickly by air.

In recent years, the traditional image of cruising as an expensive form of travel for more elderly customers has been addressed by cruise operators. The Caribbean, for example, has become an attractive destination for the young, partly due to the water-sports opportunities offered and partly by changing the style of shipboard activity towards the gym and swimming pool, and by moving towards healthier food. At the same time, the problem of high costs have also tackled by introducing short 'mini-cruises' at a low cost and hoping customers will then trade up and by reducing levels of service, including food (although in surveys, high standards of food and drink are highly rated). Moreover, tour operators have increasingly featured cruises in their brochure range, normally by selling the products of an existing operator. Airtours took this a stage further in 1995 by introducing cruises under their own name, targeted at the market in which the company already traded. As a result of these changes, UK sales of cruises increased from 301,900 in 1994 to 740,000 in 2000; as new destinations were brought on stream, the Caribbean lost some of its dominant position but still accounted for 41 percent of UK sales in 1999 (Coulson 2001).

For destinations, cruise ships do not always represent a suitable form of tourism. Cruise passengers tend to buy relatively little on shore, whilst the arrival of a cruise ship with 1,500 passengers can put enormous strains on local facilities. Thus, some Caribbean islands having developed an exclusive image for a small but wealthy market, fear that cruise business may lead to environmental damage and loss of this clientele. At least one island has withdrawn facilities for berthing cruise ships and, as shipping companies introduce new ships able to carry up to 6,000 passengers in their pursuit of economies of scale, this is likely to increase – if indeed ports are able to accommodate vessels of this size.

Air transport

Air travel is the means of transport most associated with the tourism industry, since it is a fundamental element of the mass package tour. This perception is confirmed by figures showing the number of UK residents leaving the UK by the three alternatives of air, sea and the Channel Tunnel (see Table 7.2). The figures also demonstrate that, while business travel and visiting friends and relatives (VFR) are important, holidays are the predominant reason for travel by all the modes.

Table 7.2: *Overseas visits by UK residents, 1999 ('000s)*

	Holiday	(of which inclusive tour)	Business	VFR	Other	Total
Air	25,282	14,998	6,400	4,974	854	37,510
Sea	6,483	2,923	875	1,069	1,640	10,427
Tunnel	2,898	1,135	886	554	1,605	5,994
Total	35,023	19,077	8,161	6,598	4,100	53,881

Source: Travel Trends 1999, HMSO

However, the UK aviation market is small by comparison with that of the USA, as can be seen by comparing passenger numbers passing through major airports and carried by the largest airlines (Table 7.3 and 7.4).

Table 7.3: *Passengers at major airports, 1998*

	Airport	Total Passengers (million)	International Passengers (million)
USA	Atlanta Hartsfield	73	4
USA	Chicago O'Hare	72	9
UK	London Heathrow	60	53
USA	Dallas Fort Worth	60	4
USA	Los Angeles	59	15
Germany	Frankfurt/Main	42	34
USA	San Fransisco	39	7
France	Paris Charles de Gaulle	38	34
Netherlands	Amsterdam Schipol	34	34

Source: ICAO, reproduced in Transport Statistics 2000 (DETR)

It can be seen from Tables 7.3 and 7.4 that, although the USA dominates the world's aviation industry, only a small proportion of its passengers fly internationally. British Airways, though eleventh in terms of total passengers carried, has the highest figures for *international* passengers and passenger kilometres. Similarly Heathrow, with 54.8 million international and 7.1 million domestic passengers in 1999, has the world's highest number of international users.

Table 7.4: *Passengers carried and kilometres travelled on scheduled flights by major international airlines, 1997*

	Airline	Total Passengers (millions)	Int. Passengers (millions)	Total Pass. km (billions)	Int. Pass. km (billions)
USA	Delta	103.1	7.2	160.3	36.9
USA	United	84.2	12.3	195.3	76.2
USA	American	81.1	17.1	172.1	55.9
USA	US Air/Piedmont	58.7	2.3	66.9	6.9
USA	Northwest	54.6	9.5	115.8	52.4
USA	Continental	38.8	4.9	70.9	17.4
Japan	All Nippon	36.8	3.0	51.2	18.3
Germany	Lufthansa	35.7	22.6	71.5	66.4
France	Air France	32.7	15.5	70.0	52.4
Japan	JAL	31.8	11.3	79.1	62.0
UK	British Airways	29.5	24.3	101.5	99.1

Source: ICAO, reproduced in Transport Statistics 2000 (DETR)

Note: It is likely that airlines based in Russia and China carry numbers which qualify them to appear in this table, but reliable figures are not available.

The USA's dominance can be explained by its advanced economy and its large geographical area, which not only contains a large population but creates a greater market for domestic travel within the country.

The relatively high cost of air travel and the need to site airports at some distance from city centres mean that the greater speed of aircraft only becomes an asset above a certain distance, usually about 500km. Below this rail, and sometimes car, can achieve comparable centre-to-centre time, the exception being where water forms a barrier. This is why, until the Channel Tunnel was opened, air had a near-monopoly of business travel over the fairly short distances between London and Brussels or Paris.

Of the 151 million passengers who passed through British airports in 1999, 133.5 million were making international journeys and only 17.5 million domestic. The latter market comprises principally:

- journeys linking cities over the 'magic distance where air becomes advantageous (e.g. London-Glasgow);

- services to offshore islands as in Scotland, Northern Ireland and the Channel Islands;

- 'interlining, where passengers transfer to or from an international flight.

Scheduled and charter aviation

The air passenger market can be divided in principle between scheduled traffic, where seats are purchased individually, and charter, where blocks of seats or the entire capacity of an aircraft, perhaps for a season, is sold to an intermediary. Most charter operations are in the form of Inclusive Tour Charters (ITCs), and it is the growth of these which made the European package holiday available to a mass market. More recently, long-haul destinations have been included in charter operations.

Charter operators achieve a much lower seat cost than the conventional scheduled flight, for a number of reasons:

- They usually fit more seats into a given type of aircraft than would a scheduled airline; a Boeing 757 would typically seat 180 for British Airways but 228 in charter use. The extra space is an important selling point to scheduled passengers, so it is difficult for the same aircraft to be used for a mix of scheduled and charter flights.

- The charter operator achieves a greater number of flying hours per day from its aeroplanes. The Managing Director of Monarch Airlines, claiming 11.7 flying hours per day compared with 6.8 hours at British Airways, commented:

  By a combination of differential pricing and clever marketing by the tour operators, charter airlines are able to sell capacity at times of day that are unthinkable for scheduled carriers and thus achieve very high levels of utilisation.

For example, Figure 7.2 shows a flight plan for a Boeing 757 of Britannia Airways as it was scheduled to operate on Fridays during summer 1997:

Figure 7.2: A charter flight plan

Depart	Palma	0120		*Arrive*	Birmingham	0340
"	Birmingham	0620		"	Naples	0905
"	Naples	1005		"	Birmingham	1250
"	Birmingham	1425		"	Corfu	1735
"	Corfu	1835		"	Birmingham	2155
"	Birmingham	2320		"	Palma	0140

- Whereas the scheduled airline may assume a relatively low load factor (i.e. percentage of seats filled), the charter operator assumes that 95 percent or more of seats will be filled. Furthermore, if this seems unlikely to be achieved, the operator will 'consolidate' groups of customers from different flights in a single departure. This results in the last-minute changes to flight arrangements that are unpopular with customers but keep costs down to the price they are willing to pay. The scheduled airline's lower load results from the fact that it must fly at scheduled times, irrespective of demand. Conversely, the charter operator flies only when the break-even load factor (typically 95 percent) has been achieved.

- Charter airlines are usually much smaller than scheduled airlines, which are often national 'flag-carriers' and in many cases state-owned, and therefore have relatively lower administrative costs. In particular, because the charter airline sells its seats in blocks to a few customers, its marketing costs are much lower. For example, Monarch Airlines claimed an advertising budget of £10,000 in relation to a turnover of £111million, and that its only other marketing costs were the salaries of a sales director, three salesmen and a typist – altogether no more than 0.2 percent of turnover. Conversely, British Airways' 2000 turnover of £8,940m was much greater, but its 'selling costs' were 13 percent of this figure, mainly as a result of agent commissions and its reservation system.

- They normally offer a lower standard of in-flight catering and, unlike many scheduled operators, charge for all drinks and other services, such as the use of headphones.

- They generally use smaller and regional airports, where handling and landing charges are lower than at the major international airports.

Despite the low prices achieved by charter operators, under certain circumstances scheduled operators also serve the ITC market. For example, blocks of seats on scheduled flights are commonly sold at discounted prices to tour operators willing to pay above the charter rate (for example, fly-cruise customers), whilst some tour operators offer destinations where demand cannot justify charter flights and, therefore, there is no option but to buy scheduled capacity. Some scheduled airlines also mount their own holiday programmes using existing flights, and switch aircraft which fly business routes during the week to serve holiday destinations at weekends.

Conversely, some charter airlines, knowing they will have spare capacity on particular flights, now sell 'seat-only' tickets, but their development has been limited. Despite the demand for cheap individual bookings to holiday destinations, charter operators sometimes feel it is not worth the cost of setting up the necessary distribution system, whilst countries wishing to protect their scheduled airlines discourage 'seat-only' sales through their regulatory system (see next section).

'No-frills' airlines

Perhaps the most significant recent development within Europe has been the growth of 'no-frills', or low-cost scheduled airlines such as Buzz, EasyJet, Go and Ryanair. This has been made possible by the relaxation of regulatory controls within the EU, but what distinguishes these airlines is the adoption of the same cost-cutting practices as charter airlines. There are variations in their systems, but generally:

- they use Internet or telesales bookings, thereby avoiding commissions to agents;

- they aim for high utilisation of aircraft through a long operational day and short turnrounds (20 minutes in the case of Ryanair). This is facilitated by carrying no cargo and limited catering;

- if catering is provided at all, it is basic and charged for, leading to a smaller cabin crew requirement;

- regional airports are used, where low handling charges are negotiated;

- aircraft have a high seating density similar to charter airlines;

- tickets are only sold for single sectors, eliminating complex financial reconciliation, handling of baggage and transfers at connecting airports.

Although the 'no-frills' airlines carry out extensive promotion of very low lead-in fares, they also charge at levels closer to their established rivals – but still good value – at peak times and when demand enables them to. Thus, while in April 2001 it was possible to fly with Ryanair from Stansted to Frankfurt/Hahn for £7 each way (plus airport departure tax), a flight to Ancona on a summer weekend in July 2001 was priced at £77 each way.

Currently, these airlines hold no more than a 6 percent share of the total scheduled market within Europe (Donne 2000), and not all are trading profitably. However, the leading operators are introducing new routes and expanding capacity at rates exceeding 20 percent per annum and it is clear that a large market is awaiting the opportunity of low-cost European travel.

Regulation in transport

Regulation is important because it has a major effect on the price, availability and quality of transport services for tourism.

Forms of regulation

Traditionally two types have been recognised:

i. safety or quality controls

External safety control, such as the high standards of maintenance and operating procedures required with aircraft, is generally accepted as socially beneficial and, therefore, this form of regulation generally attracts controversy only when it is shown to be absent. For example, the sinking of SS Titanic in 1912 led to regulation ensuring that every ship carries sufficient lifeboats for all its passengers. Quality controls include the professional qualifications of ships' masters, airline pilots and coach drivers, their working hours and the mechanical condition of the equipment they use.

ii. quantity controls

These may restrict entry to a route, the timetable offered or fares charged and are, therefore, far more controversial. Where deregulation has occurred in recent years, as in the US domestic air market and the British bus and coach industries, it is primarily the removal of quantity controls that has taken place.

In recent years, regulation has been imposed for further reasons – consumer protection and environmental reasons. Operators of air-based holidays are required to hold an Air Travel Organiser's Licence (ATOL), which is issued by the Civil Aviation Authority (CAA) in return for a financial bond. The purpose is to protect customers against the risk of either losing holidays they have paid for or of being stranded at the destination. All such organisers must display an ATOL number and logo in their publicity. Scheduled airlines carrying inclusive tour passengers and coach tour operators are now also subject to bonding.

The prime example of environmental controls is where limits are placed on night movements of aircraft at airports in the interest of local residents. Coach operators can also experience restrictions on the routes they use in areas congested by high levels of tourist traffic.

Who are the regulators?

The task of regulation is carried out partly by public bodies and partly by private or industry-based organisations, although often to meet a Government's wishes. In the UK, Government bodies include the CAA, which exercises both 'quantity' and 'quality control over British air carriers, is responsible for the Air Traffic Control system and operates a number of airports. Traffic Commissioners issue Operators' Licences (now issued according to safety criteria only) to bus and coach operators, and monitor their behaviour. Local councils control the issue of licences to taxi operators and, through powers to subsidise, can secure the availability of tourist-oriented bus and rail services.

Governments also support international bodies, among which is the International Civil Aviation Organisation (ICAO), a United Nations body which is mainly concerned with the technical side of air operations. In particular, it is concerned with the improvement of technical standards and with helping developing countries to bring their facilities to international standards. Similarly, following marine disasters such as the loss of the 'Herald of Free Enterprise' at Zeebrugge in 1987, the International Marine Organisation (IMO) has been studying the design of RoRo ferries, and new requirements of bulkheads to divide up vehicle decks are being brought into effect.

ICAO works closely with the International Air Transport Association (IATA), a trade organisation representing most international airlines. IATA is concerned with technical matters (hence its liaison with ICAO), and also provides financial and legal services for its members. However, it is best known as the body which still decides many of the fares charged by international airlines, a task which is delegated to it by individual Governments.

Regulation in international air transport

While control of domestic air routes is determined by the individual state, the international industry requires regulation at various levels. Indeed, whether a route between two states should exist at all is, firstly, a political decision made by the Governments concerned rather than the airlines. This is known as a *bilateral agreement* and specifies the number of airlines that are to operate the service. It is normally either 'dual designation', in which case only two airlines may operate (usually one from each country), or 'multiple designation', which allows a number of airlines to fly the route.

The agreement sometimes specifies that the fixing of detailed times and fares should be delegated to IATA, subject to Government confirmation. It also specifies which of a number of possible 'freedoms' apply. These 'freedoms' grant the airlines of one country the following rights:

1st   the freedom to fly over another country's territory without landing.

2nd   the freedom to land for technical, non-traffic reasons, such as refuelling.

3rd   the freedom to set down passengers, mail and freight taken on in the airline's the home country.

4th   the freedom to pick up passengers, mail and freight destined for the home country of the airline.

5th   the freedom to start flights in the home country (A), pick up passengers, mail and freight in country (B) and convey to country (C). An example of this 5th Freedom would be an American airline operating New York-London-Frankfurt which was permitted to carry London-Frankfurt traffic.

6th   the freedom to start in country (A), and operate via the home country (B) to country (C). Here an example would be a route operated by the Chinese airline Cathay Pacific from Bangkok through its base at Hong Kong and on to Tokyo in Japan.

The granting of the first and second freedoms is normally automatic. The third and fourth are negotiable, although possession of these freedoms forms the basis of most international services. The 5th and 6th freedoms are less commonly agreed although the deregulation of air services within Europe should in principle mean that all European airlines now enjoy all of these freedoms.

An airline wishing to take advantage of a bilateral agreement must next satisfy the licensing requirements of each state involved. This is normally a formality but gives the 'host' country an opportunity to ensure that visiting airlines meet its own quality standards. Similarly, the aspiring airline must meet its own state's requirements, partly on a quality basis but also to be recognised as a party to the bilateral agreement relevant to its intended destination.

The above applies to scheduled routes, but it cannot be assumed that a free market exists in the charter business, about which each state makes its own policy decision. Quality controls still exist to the same standards and in the USA, for example, where quantity controls are absent following deregulation of the domestic industry in the 1970s, there appears little need for a charter industry. On the other hand, most European countries favour charter flights as encouraging the growth of tourism whilst, until recently, Australia discouraged them, thereby delaying the growth of long-haul holidays.

Regulation within Europe

Despite the existence since 1993 of a Single European Market within the EU, the aviation industry is still strongly oriented to individual states. In 1992 the EU agreed its 'Third Aviation Package', which was a complex series of liberalisation measures (see TTA 1988; 1992). However, the most important points may be summarised as follows:

- In general, Governments can no longer control the fares charged by airlines.

- The bilateral agreements between EU member states are replaced by the freedom for airlines based in one state to fly between any of them. Not only can an airline fly any route from its home state to another EU state, but it can fly between two others; for example, the Irish-registered Ryanair flies between the UK and Germany. This is sometimes referred to as the 7th Freedom.

- An EU-based airline can now also fly internally within another member state. For example, Lufthansa could operate on the Paris-Nice route. This is known as 'cabotage' or the 8th Freedom.

However, it must be remembered that at least one of most city-pairs served by airline routes lies outside both the USA and the EU, where most deregulation/liberalisation has occurred. In these cases, bilateral agreements normally still have dual designation and the route can be served only by the two partners' national airlines.

Strategic alliances

The nationality or place of ownership of an airline is important in determining where it is permitted to fly. In the past this was not a problem, because most international routes were 'dual designation' with access limited to the national (and usually state-owned) airlines of the destination countries. Now that other airlines are permitted to compete on these routes, and that they are increasingly owned by the private sector, the issue of nationality becomes important. That is, if an airline, through changes in shareholdings, loses its national status it also loses the right to operate on routes based in its 'home' country.

Aviation, like most industries, is becoming global and economies of scale are identified from having world-wide coverage. However, the obvious approach of mergers between airlines may be closed to them because of their effect on national status. Airlines have, therefore, taken the alternative approach of forming strategic or marketing alliances designed to achieve the benefits of scale without losing national identity. There is no rigid formula but the following are common features:

- Cross-shareholdings at a level below 50 percent;

- Collaboration in maintenance of aircraft and stocking of spare parts;

- Mutual provision of handling services at "home" airports;

- Code-sharing, that is, the attachment of the flight code of one partner to the operation of another. For example, a KLM flight from Amsterdam to Berlin may also be listed with a flight number for its American partner NorthWest Airlines. This is to encourage a concept of through or connecting flights and to give a stronger presence on computer reservation screens;

- Jointly-planned scheduling to optimise connections at hub airports and maximise utilisation of aircraft;

- Inter-availability of tickets, standardised pricing and common reservation systems;

- Shared Frequent Flyer programmes, encouraging brand loyalty among customers.

Cost structures, capacity and utilisation

Fixed and variable costs

Like any business, transport experiences a mixture of fixed, variable and semi-variable costs. Similarly, what the economist calls 'joint costs' are experienced, the most important of which is that at some time a vehicle will probably have to return to the place where it began its journey. Therefore, the cost to a carrier of operating a journey must include the cost of coming back, and purely one-way traffic must pay exceptionally well if it is to be profitable. This does not necessarily mean returning directly; airlines, for example, often perform what are known as 'W formations' where routes are linked together, either to give good utilisation or to serve destinations where the airline lacks back-up resources (see Figure 7.3).

Figure 7.3: *The W formation*

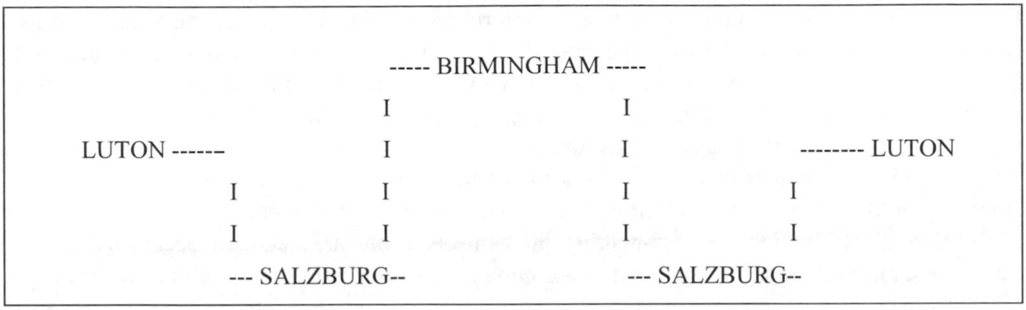

```
                    ----- BIRMINGHAM -----
                    I                    I
   LUTON ------     I                    I            -------- LUTON
           I        I                    I        I
           I        I                    I        I
           --- SALZBURG--           --- SALZBURG--
```

The incidence of fixed and variable costs determines what marginal costs will be, that is, the cost of providing an additional unit of capacity or the saving from removing a unit. Transport's units of production come in 'lumps' of fixed sizes; if a coach tour operator runs only 50-seat coaches, the minimum that can be added to or removed from an operation is this number.

Marginal costs can be very low or very high. The cost to the operator of an additional passenger on a train or plane which has empty seats is minimal; in the case of the train it is literally the cardboard in the ticket, while an airline must pay airport handling charges for each passenger and provide meals, but other cost changes are negligible. However, the point is eventually reached where no capacity remains and the marginal cost of the next passenger is then extremely high.

The significance of marginal costs varies between the modes of transport. Variable costs have traditionally formed a much greater proportion of total costs in road transport than rail, because rail provides its own track which must be paid for regardless of the level of use. Road users, on the other hand, pay for their track through taxation, which (especially fuel tax) varies directly with use. Variable costs are also high for airlines because of the high fuel consumption of aircraft. These differences are important because they affect the benefit to the operator from increasing or reducing the level of service.

Utilisation and load factors

We have already noted that one of the ways in which charter and 'no-frills' airlines are able to keep costs down is by maximising utilisation of their aircraft. This is because the high fixed costs remain the same regardless of distance or sectors covered; the fixed cost per flight or per passenger falls as it is spread over a greater number. Similarly, we have seen that total cost varies little with the number of passengers being carried and that costs are at their lowest per head when the load factor is maximised. It is therefore in operators' interest:

- to maximise the distance operated in service; and

- given fixed vehicle capacities, to maximise *use* of that capacity profitably in terms of the number of passengers being carried. Thus, it is usually not in operators' interest to create more capacity if it will remain partly unused.

Contributory revenue

When assessing the financial performance of a route, it should not necessarily be considered in isolation. Frequently, one part of a transport system feeds another, passengers transferring from a local to a long-distance service at an interchange point. If the local service, such as a rail branch line, is deemed to be uneconomic and closed, passengers using it for access to Inter-City routes will not necessarily make their own way to the railhead and many are likely to use cars for the whole journey. Thus, if the capacity of the Inter-City service remains the same, the seat stays empty and the fare income (much more than that for the local service) is lost. For this reason, it is worth looking at the contributory element in a loss-making service, since it could well be worth retaining as a 'loss leader' for the commercial route. Many airlines' domestic routes are loss-making in themselves but are retained because they feed traffic, which might otherwise be lost to a competitor, to profitable international routes.

Industry performance and marketing

The glamour associated with air travel and the enormous investment in aircraft and airports may suggest that aviation is highly profitable but, in general, this is not so. Scheduled airlines rarely achieve significant profits, and no large rail system is commercially viable. The challenge for these businesses, therefore, is to improve their load factors to nearer the levels of charter airlines. However, whilst this could easily be done by filling seats at low fares, it does not necessarily maximise revenues; for example, business travellers on airlines making last-minute journeys and willing to pay a high fare may find their chosen flight is full. The answer lies in yield management.

Reference has already been made to transport capacity being in 'lumps' of fixed sizes. The problem for operators in filling that capacity is that, with a few exceptions, demand for their product is 'derived' – it is not wanted as an end in itself but as a means to something else. People fly to Spain to acquire a suntan and, therefore, want a flight in August and not February. The carrier thus experiences peaks in demand which hinder attempts to secure full utilisation of capacity and which may mean that some equipment is not in use for part of the day or year.

Operators must first ensure that the costs of any under-used equipment are correctly allocated and fully recovered, probably in the form of peak premium charges. However, action can also be taken to minimise the effect of the peak. Some of this action may be operational, for example, by leasing extra vehicles for peak requirements, but the price mechanism can help towards this objective too, both by persuading some peak customers to switch and by generating new business outside the peak. Provided again that costing is accurate and fixed costs are allocated to the peak operations, lower but still profitable prices can be offered for this new business because only the marginal variable and semi-variable costs, plus ideally some contribution to fixed costs, need be recovered.

Elasticity of demand

Use of the price mechanism to influence patronage levels presumes that the public will in fact respond – what economists call 'price-elastic' demand. However, a number of hurdles must be overcome by the transport operator. Firstly, elasticity of demand can relate to factors other than price, in particular quality of service issues. Therefore there are limits to the extent to which price alone will affect patronage.

Secondly, it is important not to be too successful. Low prices which result in demand exceeding supply will bring a call for extra resources with a high marginal cost that would not be recovered. Finally, every operator has its existing customers who are paying the full price. It is vital not to allow these to 'trade down' to lower prices, a process known as revenue dilution, and so some kind of barrier or distinction must be created between the high- and low-price products in order to retain high-price traffic. This is the explanation of many of the restrictive conditions attached to reduced fares, which will now be examined.

Product differentiation and price discrimination

Transport operators have long practiced branding in the form of separate First and Second Class or Economy provision, Pullman cars and so on. These maximised revenue by ensuring that customers willing to pay a higher price did so, and the revenue is secured by a providing higher quality in some way – more comfortable and guaranteed seats, availability of meals, a quiet atmosphere for working, and so on. Much more widespread than in the past, however, is the carriage of passengers in the same facilities at widely differing prices, where barriers of an invisible kind are erected.

The best illustration of this are the rules conventionally attached to airlines' APEX fares, which are sometimes as low as 30 percent of Economy. These are subject to a limited number of seats on particular flights, often around midday when demand is low; a minimum advance booking period of 14 days, which is unsuitable for urgent business trips; a 'no refund or cancellation' condition; and, a rule that a Saturday night must fall between the outward and return journeys, which conflicts with the business traveller's normal desire to be home for the weekend but is acceptable to leisure travellers. These all minimise the 'dilution' of revenue from the valued business market but, as the number of reduced price offers has increased, can lead to a situation where passengers seated alongside pay fares varying by up to 300 percent. Airlines have therefore developed a 'business' or 'Club' class for those paying the full Economy fare, creating a separate cabin with better meals and other privileges. In turn, this has undermined the need for First Class and most airlines have now abolished it within Europe.

However, the operator's objective is to maximise not just seats filled but revenue, and both can be achieved by skilful use of market intelligence and sales data. Just as a tour operator observes sales carefully before deciding when and how far to discount, an airline can decide when, where and how many APEX seats to release. Thus, the ratio can vary not just between flights but day by day, the process aided by equipping aircraft with moveable screens and curtains to adjust the balance between Business and discounted passengers. Information from Computer Reservation Systems assists airlines in making these decisions, and load factors can be further improved by the use of Standby tickets, which are only validated close to the time of departure and when seats have not been filled by other means.

Seat reservations and overbooking

Air passengers assume that when a booking is confirmed a seat is assured, but this is not necessarily the case. Full-price scheduled tickets have a refund facility which airlines are anxious to retain for fear of upsetting high-fare regular business travellers. These, uncertain when they will be able to travel, sometimes buy several tickets in the knowledge that they can obtain a refund on those not used. The loss resulting from 'no-shows' can be considerable, so a practice has developed of systematic overbooking, whereby levels of 'no-shows' are established from records and a flight for which 5 percent of passengers typically fail to report might be overbooked by 3 percent. Sometimes the gamble fails and passengers with valid tickets find there is no room. On long-haul flights, it may be possible to upgrade some to First, while others are encouraged or obliged, with a variety of inducements, to transfer to other flights. The European Union has introduced a Regulation fixing levels of compensation for overbooked passengers and setting priorities in selection.

Environmental impacts of transport

All tourism activities have their damaging effects on the local and wider community (see Chapters 11 and 20), but transport has some of the most visible and severe of these. Few would consider airports and their surroundings physically attractive, air pollution levels are normally high, and the route to resorts is often littered with the ugly but necessary support businesses on which mass tourism depends. Even in the resort itself, we may notice large areas taken up by car parking both on and off the street, the smell of vehicle exhausts and nose-to-tail traffic at busy times. There are also the less obvious consequences, such as climate change.

Ample evidence exists of people's concern at these problems. For example, a survey of residents' attitudes to tourism in Stratford-on-Avon (ETB 1995) confirmed that traffic congestion, parking problems and general environmental damage were seen as disadvantages of the town's tourism business. 88 percent of residents believed that traffic congestion needed to be relieved, but there was not the same consensus on how to achieve it! As car ownership grows, both visitors and residents find it more difficult to imagine a lifestyle without it, while businesses in host areas consider car-borne trade vital to their prosperity. As a result, people's desire for action in general is contradicted by a wish that it should not affect them personally.

Nevertheless, attitudes may be changing slowly. A view has emerged in Europe that, rather than restrictions on car use deterring visitors, *too much* traffic can be a deterrent. Switzerland has a group of car-free villages which promote themselves jointly on that strength, and they have experienced growth in their share of the tourism market. An economic as well as an environmental case therefore exists for promoting sustainable forms of transport. Also, it is easy to forget that not everybody owns a car. Ownership rates vary widely between countries and regions but, even in prosperous areas, 10-15 percent of households may have no car, a figure which rises to over 50 percent in cities. Therefore, a resort or business which limits itself to car access ignores a substantial part of the market whilst, at some attractions, scarce land has to be devoted to car parking which, if visitors arrived by other means, could be put to more productive use.

A number of approaches to environmentally-friendlier transport are possible. Greater use of walking, horse-riding and cycling can be encouraged by the development of specialised routes. Local traffic management and restriction schemes can be implemented, but these tend to have no effect on the total number of cars coming into an area. The signing necessary to advise motorists of a restriction can itself be visually intrusive, but perhaps the biggest problem is the likely objections from businesses and residents.

An alternative approach is to encourage use of public transport, either for the 'trunk' journey to the holiday area or for local journeys within it. However, car-owners take their motorised lifestyle for granted and find the alternative inconvenient, probably expensive and unsuited to their image, and many projects have failed to achieve their objectives. As a minimum, in order to attract car users public transport must offer high quality in its operation and promotion, have reasonable and simple integrated pricing, appear 'seamless' and create an impression of user-friendliness. It helps if it can be sold as an attraction in itself, for example through the use of vintage equipment. Even this may not be enough and, therefore, to achieve any significant transfer from cars, it may be necessary to introduce traffic restrictions alongside. Here, here the pill can be sweetened with assurances that funding is committed to a high-quality alternative.

Two kinds of location lend themselves particularly to intervention of the kind described, namely, historic towns and protected rural areas, such as National Parks. In both cases, visitors are attracted by the traditional and 'heritage' aspects. Thus, conventional approaches to traffic planning, involving the widening of roads, demolition of buildings and construction of car parks, would remove the essential attraction of the visit and so threaten visitor numbers. As a result, many historic town centres are now pedestrianised, and the removal of traffic to achieve this is often assisted by a Park and Ride scheme which allows car users to park on the outskirts and use a dedicated bus (occasionally a train) to the centre.

National Park areas have found it more difficult to achieve progress, but the Lake District, for example, is currently developing a 'Strategic Gateway' west of Kendal. This will seek to intercept car traffic approaching the congested centre of the National Park by providing a Park and Ride facility on its outskirts.

Discussion questions

1.   *Where does transport serve tourism and other markets at the same time?*

2.   *Why do airlines and railways charge widely varying fares for the same journey?*

3.   *Can people's desire to use cars where they are environmentally unfriendly be put down entirely to selfishness?*

Further reading

Doganis, R. (2000), *The Airline Business in the Twenty-First Century*, London: Routledge.

Hanlon, P. (1999), *Global Airlines: Competition in a Transnational Industry (2nd Edition),* Oxford: Butterworth Heinemann.

Page, S. (1999), *Transport and Tourism*. Harlow: Longman.

Pender, L. (2001), *Travel Trade and Transport – An Introduction*, London: Continuum.

Shaw, S. (1999), *Airline Marketing and Management,* Aldershot: Ashgate.

Travel and Tourism Analyst. In every issue (published 5 times yearly), the first article is on a transport topic. See for example:

Peisley, T. (2000), Cruising in Crisis? *Travel and Tourism Analyst* No 5: 3-23.

References

Confederation of Passenger Transport (2000), *Coaches mean business – the role of the coach in the economy*, London: David Simmonds Consultancy and Cambridge Policy Consultants.

Coulson, B. (2001), *The Cruise Market*. Paper to conference of the Tourism Society: 'Transport and Tourism: Making the Right Connections'. Peterborough.

DETR (2000), *Transport Statistics 2000,* London: Department of Environment, Transport and the Regions.

Donne, M. (2000), The growth and long-term potential of the low-cost airlines, *Travel and Tourism Analyst* No.5: 1-15.

English Tourist Board (1995), Visitor Management in Action: Stratford-on-Avon's National Pilot, 1992-95. *ETB Insights*, *Volum. 7*: C25-37.

London Transport Marketing (1996), *Market Report,* London Regional Transport.

MINTEL (1995), *Cruises*, Leisure Intelligence Volume 1, 1995. London.

Quarmby, D. (1996), Travel for Pleasure and Profit, *Global Transport*, Winter 1996, London: Chartered Institute of Transport.

Sharpley, R. (1996), *Tourism and Leisure in the Countryside, 2nd Edition*, Huntingdon: Elm Publications.

TTA (1988), European Air Transport Liberalisation, *Travel and Tourism Analyst* No.6: 5-18.

TTA (1992), The European Commission's 3rd Air Transport Liberalisation Package, *Travel and Tourism Analyst* No.5: 5-22.

8

The Accommodation Sector

Bridget Major

Learning objectives

This chapter looks at the accommodation sector of the travel and tourism industry. It presents an overview of the types of accommodation available on the market and some of the current important strategies employed in the management and operation of this sector focusing, in particular, on the hotel industry. By the end of the chapter the reader will be able to:

- *appreciate the historical significance of accommodation and how the industry has developed to meet the needs of the modern day tourist.*

- *identify growth and marketing strategies within the accommodation sector and discuss the implications of these upon the structure of the industry in the future.*

- *understand the diversity of the industry and appreciate the scope of future provision in accordance with new market trends.*

Introduction

Accommodation is a fundamental part of the domestic and international tourism product. Moreover, the selection of accommodation and associated product expenditure is a major part of the tourist decision process. Medlik and Ingram (2000: 4) state that 'the primary function of an hotel is to accommodate those away from home and to supply them with their basic needs'. Recent years have witnessed increasing diversity in the provision of accommodation for the tourism industry which, in terms of scope, certainly makes this an interesting sector to study. At the same time, however, it is also challenging to keep pace with developments within the sector as the industry structure is in a constant state of flux.

The study of accommodation is inextricably linked to the concept of hospitality. Jones (1996: 1) states that 'hospitality is made up of two distinct services – the provision of overnight accommodation for people staying away from home, and the provision of sustenance for people eating away from home'. Here, we are concerned only with the former service, the latter being well beyond the purpose of this chapter. The importance of the accommodation sector to the tourism industry in terms of share of total expenditure is shown in Table 8.1.

Table 8.1: *Tourism expenditure as a percentage of the total, 1999*

	Overseas Visitors in UK	Domestic visitors	All visitors
Accommodation	33.3	34.0	34.0
Eating Out	20.6	26.0	23.5
Shopping	26.0	13.0	18.9
Travel in UK	9.2	19.0	14.7
Services	7.1	1.0	3.4
Entertainment	2.9	6.0	4.4
Other	0.9	1.0	1.0

Source: BTA in British Hospitality Association (BHA) Trends and Statistics (2001)

History of the accommodation industry

Overnight stays and the provision of accommodation are, of course, nothing new. Not only can we can look back as far as Roman times and even further to the renowned 'Inn' in the Bible for evidence of the provision of accommodation for travellers, but also the development accommodation has long been linked with the growth in travel. Journeys in the very early centuries were made on foot or horseback and often took many months to complete, necessitating overnight stays to rest. Many accommodation outlets at that time also supplied alcohol and were associated with unruly behaviour (threats to public order and temptations to indulge in adultery – perhaps not so different to today!). It was this that gave rise to the first regulation of the trade in the twelfth century, even prior to the introduction of taxation and licensing (Walton 2000: 57).

Throughout the Middle Ages, the first inns and guesthouses were developed primarily for travelling merchants and pilgrims. These would usually be established alongside the primitive road system and in private residences, offering hospitality for a small charge. However, as time progressed, the provision of accommodation developed in accordance with its markets as comparatively well off merchants began to seek more comfortable accommodation. Thus, the seventeenth and eighteenth centuries witnessed the emergence of the coaching inn and the spread of these throughout Europe. Travellers motives varied, of course. Merchants travelling for trade and business purposes obviously needed accommodation but, as discussed in Chapter 2, leisure travel and the European Grand Tour were increasingly popular at this time. Travellers were also undertaking religious pilgrimages or, for health reasons, visiting spas and resorts in Europe and so accommodation facilities were developed to meet the needs of all these different groups.

The development of the railways in the nineteenth century impacted hugely on the provision of accommodation. From the 1860s onwards, railway companies and related steamship companies began to build hotels at terminal stations in order to capitalise upon the regularity of rail services and the public's increasing desire and ability to travel for pleasure – indeed, reminders of this era remain evident today in some of the fabulous hotel buildings in cities throughout the world. Interestingly, international airlines were to have a similar influence on hotel development over a century later. The Le Meridien chain, for example, was originally established by Air France.

Following the patterns of innovation in transport, the structure and distribution of accommodation provision has been heavily influenced by the massive growth in the use of the private motor car. Roadside accommodation is, of course, very much in evidence today, but ever-increasing car ownership has meant that tourists can go wherever they want, thus spreading the demand for accommodation to some very out-of-the-way places. Where no accommodation is available, tourists often take their own, in the form of caravans, tents or boats.

As society has become more affluent and more leisure time has become available over the last century, the accommodation industry has developed to meet changing needs. In the UK, for example, the Holidays with Pay Act of 1938 stimulated the demand for 'mass tourism' and meant that, from the late 1940s, holidays could become a reality for many. As a result, holiday camps such as Butlins flourished and, indeed, many ideas from this period form the basis of holiday provision today. Sharpley (1999: 55) states that Butlin's first holiday camp, which opened in Skegness in 1936, was relatively luxurious. 'It comprised 600 chalets, dining and recreation facilities, a swimming pool, a theatre, tennis court, services such as child-minding and organised entertainment and, perhaps most important of all, modern sanitary arrangements'. (See also Ward and Hardy 1986). In short, then, the accommodation sector has developed and diversified to meet the evolving and changing needs of tourists and it is now a vast and complex industry which lies at the very heart of travel and tourism.

Categorisation of accommodation demand

The accommodation sector meets the needs of a number of different markets:

Business or leisure market

When examining the motives behind the selection of accommodation, a simplistic division can be made between accommodation for business or for recreation and tourism purposes. In reality, of course, such a clear cut division does not exist and many people travelling for the purpose of business or attending conferences will add on leisure time and become 'a tourist'.

Domestic or international market

Visitors from both markets are clearly important to the accommodation sector. Visitors from overseas, however, generate crucial foreign exchange earnings. Britain receives approximately 25 million overseas visitors each year, who spend nearly £13 billion (British Hospitality Association Election Manifesto 2001). The British Tourist Authority (BTA) has predicted that international tourists to the UK will spend in excess of £18bn a year by 2003, although there is concern that, in recent years, the number of incoming visitors has remained broadly static. Moreover, given the developments in the early half of 2001 related to the outbreak of foot and mouth disease, as well as the events of September 11th in the USA, the BTA's forecast would seem to be optimistic.

Commercial and non-commercial accommodation

Non-commercial accommodation can be defined as accommodation that is only concerned with the recovery of costs as opposed to making a commercial profit, such as privately owned holiday homes and yachts, tents, caravans and motor homes. Youth hostels and centres for young people's activity holidays can also be included in this category. Conversely, the commercial sector covers all forms of accommodation run as a business.

Serviced and non-serviced accommodation

A further distinction must be made between serviced and non-serviced (i.e. self-catering) accommodation. This is fairly obvious in the case of a four star hotel which relies heavily on its provision of service in attracting customers, whilst a rural bed and breakfast would also fit into this category. However, the distinction is less clear in the case of, for example, a French self-catering farmhouse holiday where the owner offers the provision of an evening meal and, more generally, there has recently been an increase in the demand for what is essentially non-serviced accommodation but with the option and flexibility of service provision if required. 'Apart-Hotels' fall into this category – the accommodation component is basically of a self catering nature, but the location of the apartment within an hotel means that the occupants may use hotel leisure facilities, restaurants and bars if they wish. Figure 8.1 summarises this categorisation of accommodation.

Figure 8.1: *Categorisations of accommodation*

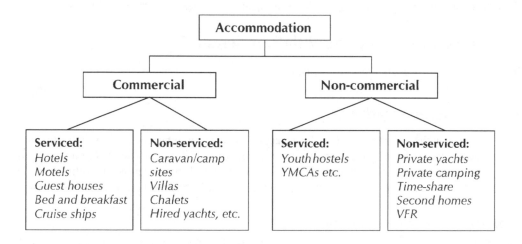

The variety and diversity of the accommodation sector

Accommodation has developed enormously since the first roadside inn and the present-day heterogeneity of the sector makes it difficult to produce managers with the relevant skills to run it. For example, the operation of managing and cooking for a chalet in a ski resort based on personal service for eight guests requires very different skills from that of the General Manager of a large multi-national hotel chain (although the underlying principals will essentially be the same). Similarly, the physical nature of one of the properties owned and let by the Landmark Trust (Figure 8.3) is very different from a city centre Marriott Hotel. It is, therefore, difficult to categorise such a range of accommodation types, examples of which are given below.

- Hotel - budget, mid-market, luxury
- Club Hotels
- Bed and Breakfast/Guest house

- Pubs
- Holiday Houses, Cottages and Apartments
- Camping and Caravan

- Home Exchanges
- Second Homes
- Timeshare Homes and Apartments
- Cruise Liners
- Yachts/Boats

- Train Accommodation

Within these accommodation types there are naturally a huge number of variables, such as location, markets, ownership (small family run business to multi-national chain), and levels of service provision. Table 8.2 compares the different types of accommodation used for domestic holidays in the UK.

Table 8.2: *Accommodation used for domestic holidays*

	Trips m	%	Nights m	%	Expenditure £m	%
Home of friend or relative	22.0	33	85	29	1,650	15
Hotel, motel, guest house	15.5	24	55	19	3,750	34
Own/timeshare property/static caravan	6.5	10	25	9	450	4
Camping/touring caravan	6.5	10	35	12	900	8
B & B, farm, hostel, university	3.5	5	10	4	550	5
Holiday centre (serviced or s/c)	3.5	5	12	4	650	6
Boat	0.5	1	3	1	200	2
Other self catering*	8.0	12	65	22	2,850	26
Total	**66.0**	**100**	**290**	**100**	**11,000**	**100**

*flats, houses, cottages, chalets; rented static caravans/mobile homes
Source: Mintel (2000) estimates based on United Kingdom Tourism Survey.

The economics of accommodation

The profitability of commercial accommodation is greatly influenced by occupancy rates. These represent the level of usage of hotel rooms or bed spaces and are usually expressed as a percentage figure. Care must be taken to differentiate between the four main types of occupancy rate, all of which will produce very different figures (see Bull 1991).

- The basic occupancy rate measures the percentage of rooms used by guests on a given night.

- The average occupancy rate measures the percentage of rooms used over a period (i.e. over a month or a year).

- The bed occupancy rate establishes how many guests are physically accommodated as a percentage of the maximum capacity; that is, is there one person or two in a double/twin room?

- The revenue occupancy rate, which compares the room revenue on one night with the theoretical maximum that could be charged. Therefore, it takes into account any discounted prices that may be offered.

Hotels generally have a variety of different charges for any one room. The published tariff of the hotel is known as the 'rack rate' which represents the price the hotel would ideally like to charge. In practice, however, the rack rate is often not used and prices vary according to whether they are for a tour operator, who often reserves rooms on 'allocation' for their guests, a corporate client for a conference or incentive stay, a large group booking, or simply because the demand for the hotel beds on that night is low and the market dictates a discounted price. Thus, the two key components of rooms revenue are the level of occupancy and the average achieved room rate. The latter only represents the price achieved on rooms sold, however, and bears little resemblance to the full or rack rate' (Knowles 1994: 86).

In addition to rooms revenue, hotels also earn income from direct and ancillary services, such as food and beverages, telephones, dry cleaning, currency exchange and in-house retailing. Frequently, such services are more profitable than the basic business of selling rooms.

Factors affecting profitability and pricing in the accommodation sector

Perishability

The accommodation product is highly perishable – if a room is not sold on a particular day, the opportunity to generate any revenue from that room will be lost for ever. Therefore, it is important for managers to be able to forecast demand as accurately as possible, to be aware of the external environment and to adjust prices accordingly. One common 'solution' is overbooking in the expectation that cancellations, for one reason or another, will offset this although yield management systems, which will be looked at later in this chapter, are increasingly being used to address the problem of perishability.

Seasonality

Tourist accommodation is subject to seasonality, which must be taken into account when pricing. For example, business and conference clients can often be an important source of business during the low season in resort hotels whilst, in city centre hotels which depend upon the business sector during the week, prices may be adjusted to attract short-break leisure customers over weekends and holiday periods. The importance of target marketing and tactical pricing is, therefore, crucial ensure a balanced flow of customers throughout the year. In fact, this is one of the most challenging areas for those involved in the management of tourism accommodation.

High fixed costs

The accommodation sector has very high fixed costs and these are proportionally far greater than the variable costs. Fixed costs are costs that are fixed irrespective of levels of occupancy achieved, such as capital costs for bank loans, finance arrangements, building maintenance and equipment. Variable costs, on the other hand, increase as occupancy levels increase, and include items such as food, drink and the cost of additional staff. The high level of fixed costs means that the break-even point is also relatively high, whilst revenue from sales will, in the longer term, need to be sufficient to cover both fixed and variable costs.

It is only once the accommodation unit has reached this break-even point (see Figure 8.2) that it can begin to make a profit. The break-even point represents the point at which total revenue is equal to both fixed and variable costs. A hotel will have a certain level of occupancy (calculated from revenue generated, not necessarily physical occupancy) that represents its break-even point. As the occupancy level is increased beyond the break-even level, profits accumulate as revenues exceed costs.

Figure 8.2: *The economics of accommodation: the break-even point*

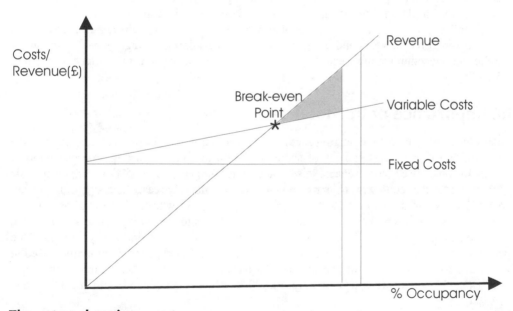

The external environment

One of the major problems facing the accommodation sector is the uncertainty and unpredictability of the external environment. This includes not only the business environment with its fluctuations in the economic cycle, where both leisure and business demand will drop sharply during periods of economic down-turn, but also events and factors which may dictate market circumstances. For example, a study of 193 UK hotels by consultants Pannel Kerr Forster Associates found that, during a recessionary year in the early 1990s, profits fell by almost a quarter, occupancies fell by an average 8 percent nationally, whilst average achieved room rates fell by an average 2.5 percent. This situation was reflected in the European hotel market generally. The Gulf War, also at that time, exacerbated the problem and many accommodation businesses suffered as a result of cancellations, in particular within the American market. More recently in the UK, the strong pound and a global economic slowdown has not helped in attracting tourists to the UK whilst, in early 2001, the foot and mouth outbreak had a disastrous impact on accommodation bookings. According to one survey in April 2001, 78 percent of hotels in England, 91 percent percent in Scotland and 95 percent in Wales were affected, with a third of UK hotels as a whole suffering a drop of more than 25 percent in business because of the outbreak. Moreover, about a seventh recorded drops of 50 percent or more (TravelMole 12/4/01). A similar, if not even more severe, problem also faced the self-catering holiday cottage and campsite accommodation sectors.

More generally, however, recent years have in fact been very good for the industry with the positive growth in occupancy levels and significant structural change in the industry. 'Hospitality is in an industry whose time has come. It is an industry, no longer a collection of seaside hotels and travellers' rests. Tourism is a major foreign exchange earner for the UK – and one now recognised by the government, if its reaction to the present foot and mouth outbreak is anything to go by' (BHA 2001).

Taxation

British accommodation providers face one of the highest rates of VAT on accommodation and restaurant meals in Europe and this is affecting the industry's ability to compete internationally. Issues such as this, coupled with the impact of substantial increases in property taxes in recent years and the introduction of the minimum wage, have compounded to make the accommodation sector a challenging area in which to achieve consistent profitability.

The importance of the hotel sector

As already noted, the accommodation sector is diverse but hotels, in particular, comprise the largest and most important category of accommodation providers. Through the provision of facilities for businesses, conferences, leisure and entertainment, hotels play an important role in society and the economy in most countries. 'In many areas, hotels are important attractions for visitors who bring to them spending power and who tend to spend at a higher rate than they do when they are at home. Through visitor spending, hotels thus often contribute significantly to local economies both directly, and indirectly through the subsequent diffusion of the visitor expenditure to other recipients in the community' (Medlik and Ingram 2000: 4). The definition of a hotel varies according to which source used, yet it is estimated that there are approximately 60,000 hotels and guest houses in the UK alone (BHA 2001.)

The pattern and structure of hotel ownership has been changing in many countries in recent years and, to an extent, now more closely mirrors other industries. Strategies have been imported from the United States and we have witnessed several companies enlarging their market share on a sizeable scale. Thus, although independently owned hotels may still be dominant in terms of number in the UK, with corporately owned hotels representing a small percentage of the total number of hotels, growth is, however, generally associated with the large hotel chains (listed on the stock exchange and with access to financial resources) utilising strategies such as mergers, acquisitions and alliances. Indeed, 'the hotel industry in the UK has changed beyond all recognition. Companies which were household names 25 years ago no longer feature in the list of top hotel groups' (Parker 1996: 39).

One of the current 'buzz words' in the hotel industry (as in many others) is globalisation; 'globalisation is popularly understood as a process which establishes a hotel company's presence on a worldwide basis. Globalisation is commonly perceived to have a standardising impact, as products and institutions originally offered only in the domestic market appear worldwide (Pine and Go 1996: 96). This is manifested in American incursions into the UK hotel industry – Blackstone/Colony has taken over the Savoy group, Starwood has acquired Sheraton, and Marriott expanded its base with acquiring Renaissance. However, the British hotel industry has been similarly active. For example, Bass bought Inter-Continental to enhance its Holiday Inn holding and thus became the second largest hotel group in the world, whilst Whitbread has acquired the master franchise for Marriott and also founded Travel Inn. At the same time, the recent merger of Granada with Compass has led to the sale of all the Forte Hotels except Travelodge and has opened up new opportunities for other companies (BHA 2001). In short, what we are seeing is transnational hotel corporations based in Europe, Asia and North America investing abroad, thereby creating a global market place (see Table 8.3).

Table 8.3: *Top 10 hotel groups worldwide*

	Hotel Group	Rooms	Hotels
1	Cendant Corp. (USA)	542,630	6,315
2	Bass Hotels & Resorts (UK)	471,680	2,886
3	Marriott International (USA)	355,900	1,880
4	Accor (France)	354,652	3,234
5	Choice Hotels International (USA)	338,254	4,248
6	Best Western International (USA)	313,247	4,037
7	Hilton Hotels Corp. (USA)	290.000	1,700
8	Starwood Hotels & Resorts Worldwide (USA)	217,651	716
9	Carlson Hospitality Worldwide (USA)	114,161	616
10	Hyatt Hotels/Hyatt International (USA)	85,734	195

Source: BHA (2000)

The UK hotel industry

As already noted, a lack of consensus exists with respect to the definition of an hotel. Additionally, hotels in the UK are not currently required to be centrally registered whereas, in many other countries, hotels can only be termed an 'hotel' after a compulsory inspection. Industry pressure now exists to introduce legislation making it compulsory for all hotels to be registered. This would, of course, be of considerable advantage to the Tourist Boards whose responsibility it is, by a process of independent inspection, to provide a classification and grading system. Thus, in the UK, hotels are generally defined as accommodation establishments which also have a licence to sell alcoholic drinks. This definition would also include pubs and inns with accommodation but excludes bed and breakfasts and guesthouses as they are normally unlicensed. A number of issues with respect to the UK accommodation sector deserve consideration:

Classification and Grading

A distinction needs to be drawn between registration, categorisation, classification and grading. These terms are often confused but can be explained as follows:

- *Registration* – relates to the basic listing of accommodation establishments and is not presently compulsory in the UK, with fewer than 23,000 of the estimated 60,000 'hotels' in the UK registered with a tourist board (Travel and Tourism Analyst 2000).

- *Categorisation* – refers to different accommodation types: hotels, bed and breakfast, self-catering cottages, etc.

- *Classification* – is concerned with the range of facilities and services provided by the accommodation unit.

- *Grading* – assesses the quality standards of the facilities and services provided.

In 1999, the English Tourism Council in conjunction with the AA and RAC launched new quality standards for serviced accommodation. The new harmonised scheme replaced the three separate schemes previously in existence, which were subject to much criticism on account of being complicated and confusing for consumers to understand. Thus, the new scheme is based on a scale of 1 -5 and features the symbols 'Stars for Hotels,' (replacing 'Crowns') and 'Diamonds' for Guest Accommodation (replacing 'Highly Commended/Commended').

Beioley (1999) states that 'accommodation rating schemes are seen by the tourist boards as a key tool for improving the experience of visiting Britain'. The main purposes are two fold:

- To aid consumer selection of accommodation by providing meaningful criteria which will assist judgement and comparison and provide assurances concerning the quality of facilities; and

- To encourage accommodation providers to upgrade their facilities, thus improving the stock of accommodation throughout the UK. Used appropriately, the scheme can be an excellent marketing tool for service providers.

The scheme, however, remains voluntary and although open to accommodation throughout the UK, Scotland and Wales have opted for their own rating systems. This, coupled with the lack of compulsory registration, has meant that despite the launch of the new scheme, this country still does not have a universally accepted system for grading hotels throughout the UK. Critics of the existing system argue that there are a growing number of complaints from domestic and overseas visitors concerning the quality of some hotels and that compulsory hotel registration would help counteract this. Furthermore, it would enable consumers to make more effective comparisons with hotels overseas. There is also a move for a common grading scheme to be introduced for all EU member countries. However, given the problems in implementing a grading and classification schemes in the UK alone, the successful introduction of a European Scheme would seem to be unlikely in the near future.

Independent schemes

Independent grading and classification schemes, such as those of Relais & Chateau, Wolsey Lodges and Michelin, continue to proliferate, often accompanied by their own guide books. Other independent guide books, such as the 'Which? Good Hotel Guide' and 'Good Pub Guide', Alistair Sawday's 'Special Places' and 'The Great British Bed and Breakfast', are also extremely popular, reflecting the growing niche of discerning consumers wishing to make their own arrangements. These guides provide all sorts of idiosyncratic information, including the owners peculiarities, pet facilities, decor schemes and local knowledge, and are often to be found in the 'Best Sellers' book listings.

Awards

Competition for special awards can help enhance accommodation quality and are popular with providers as a marketing tool. Awards have huge diversity, varying from 'Hotel (or Pub) of the Year' and 'Caravan Park of the Year' to 'Loo of the Year'!

Location

The hotel sector is highly fragmented; the 60,000 UK properties termed as hotels range from the small family owned and run hotel through to the large multi-national chain hotel. Location is one of the most important factors dictating an hotel's markets and, it could also be argued, success in terms of profitability. London hotels can almost be regarded collectively as a separate category, being the main destination for over 80 percent of overseas visitors (Mintel 2000) and the major centre for business meetings and conferences. London hotels have occupancy rates of over 80 percent for the last seven years, a figure unparalleled in any other European city (BHA 2001). At least 10,000 new hotel rooms were built in the capital between 1995 and 2000 and a target exists for a further 10,000 rooms before 2006 (BHA 2001.) The capital is not, therefore, as affected by the factors affecting price and profitability discussed earlier. Nevertheless, even London hotel bookings were affected by the foot and mouth outbreak in 2001, mainly as a result of negative press reporting overseas.

A large proportion of British hotels are located beside the sea, and many of these are still family owned and have been hard hit in recent times with the trend for overseas holidays. Therefore, they have attempted, where possible, to diversify their markets, in particular offering short breaks or selling themselves as conference hotels during low season.

Budget hotels

Budget hotels have boomed in the last decade in the UK, reflecting the demand for cheap, basic accommodation that has been a particular feature of accommodation provision for many years in both the USA and France. Forte were the first to capitalise on the demand in the budget sector with Travelodge chain. This brand went on to be developed by its subsequent owners, the Granada Group, and is the only chain currently not being sold off by the newly formed Granada Compass group.

Table 8.4: *Ten largest UK hotel groups, 2000 (by total number of bedrooms)*

Group Name	Hotels	Rooms
Forte Hotel Division (Granada Compass)	337	30,754
Whitbread Hotel Group	323	24,022
Hilton Group	81	15,869
Bass Hotels & Resorts	97	14,074
Thistle Hotels	56	10,718
Choice Hotels Europe (Friendly)	91	7,428
Corus (Regal Hotels)	97	6,764
Jarvis Hotels	65	6,635
Scottish & Newcastle	123	6,427
Queens Moat Houses UK	43	6,208

Source: Adapted from BHA Trends and Statistics (2001) and HCIMA Year Book (2001)

Note: At the time of writing (2001) the Granada Compass group currently consists of 47 Heritage Hotel, 7 Le Meridien, 4 London Signature Hotels and 200 Travelodge. The Compass group is however disposing of all its Forte hotel brands, with the exception of Travelodge.

Hotel branding

Market segmentation is a marketing strategy increasingly used in the accommodation sector. In particular, larger hotel chains have adopted this strategy, finding that the various segments require different product offerings that incorporate a tailored 'marketing mix'. They have, therefore, designed clearly identifiable branded products. 'Branding or, more specifically, a company's success or failure at building a brand, is perhaps one of the hottest topics for the industry at present. Operators are increasingly accepting the value of brands in delivering profits. The brand is becoming the key element of defining the market. Rather than who owns or who operates a hotel, it is the name of the brand under which it trades that is the key' (Travel and Tourism Analyst 2000: 66).

Table 8.5: *Leading hotel brands in the UK, January 2000*

Brandname	Owner	No. of hotels	No. of rooms
Best Western	Best Western	368	17,037
Hilton	Hilton Group	82	16,194
Posthouse	Granada	84	13,244
Travel Inn	Whitbread	230	12,461
Thistle	Thistle Hotels	51	9,789
Travelodge	Granada	178	9,350
Marriott	Marriott International	50	9,073
Jarvis	Jarvis Hotels	71	6,846
Moat House	Queens Moat Houses	40	5,779
Premier Lodge	Scottish & Newcastle	116	5,738

Source: Travel & Tourism Analyst (2000)

In terms of traditional consumer segmentation based on, for instance, socio-demographic information, such as age or occupation, we can relate some of the brands above to the market segments to which they most appeal. For example, the budget hotel brands Travel Inn, Express by Holiday Inn and Travelodge will appeal to families on the move, or those travelling on business on a limited budget. Heritage Hotels, conversely, may appeal to 'Empty Nesters' with more disposable income as their children have left home or 'Dinkies' (dual income no kids) who want an active leisure break, for which Heritage have become well known.

Similar applications of branding as a method of market segmentation occur throughout Europe and the evidence suggests that the brand grows up first with the domestic market, as in the case of the French owned Accor group, and then spreads overseas in accordance with the globalisation trend discussed earlier. Accor brands, such as Ibis, Hotel Mercure, Formule 1, Novotel and Sofitel, are to be found worldwide in the same way as British brands; research has shown that over 60 percent of adults recognise the top five brand names (Hilton, Holiday Inn, Forte, Posthouse and Travelodge) Mintel (2000).

Hotel ownership and growth strategies

It will by now be apparent that hotel ownership and is becoming increasingly complex, particularly with the current emphasis on globalisation strategies. Indeed, it is almost impossible to keep abreast of this very dynamic and fast moving industry, with changes in structure and ownership occurring on a seemingly daily basis. The methods and principles of expansion and diversification remain, however, the same and it is these upon which we shall now focus.

Ownership and management contracts

It is important to point out here that there is a clear distinction between the 'ownership' of hotel properties and their 'management.' An hotel may be owned by a company with no operational involvement with the hotel industry; various organisations, such as insurance companies, investment trusts and banks, are often owners of hotels, essentially viewing the financing of an hotel as a safe investment with a good return. Real estate investment trusts also often have ownership of hotels, whilst property developers, construction companies and landowners also have a logical interest in hotel ownership. However, travel and tourism organisations, including travel agencies, tour operators, airlines and theme park owners are increasingly turning to hotel ownership as vertical integration strategies within organisations are becoming more and more prevalent. For example, Airtours plc's acquisition of various hotels in recent years reflects this trend. In some developing countries, the government may invest in the purchase of a hotel and then try and engage a well known international hotel organisation to run it. The recognised brand will immediately give it a head start in terms of quality and reputation and experienced management means that it will have a greater chance of success.

Ownership is therefore both complex and various. In comparison, management contracts are, essentially, a straightforward means of running a hotel in which a hotel owner employs an agent to manage the hotel. In other words, the agent – sometimes an internationally recognised hotel chain, sometimes an independent management company – operates the hotel on behalf of the owners in return for a management fee. There are, naturally, advantages and disadvantages to both parties. However, it is an increasingly used strategy as it assists hotel chains to expand globally and rapidly whilst utilising capital provided by external investors, thereby avoiding the risks associated with ownership. Having said that, it is not unusual to find that the hotel may be partly owned by a management contract company who manages that contract, yet is also a franchisee of the hotel brand! This will be explained more fully in a moment.

Strategic alliances

Strategic alliances have become increasingly common in recent years, not only in the hotel industry but also in the airline sector (see Chapter 7). By linking up with another hotel chain, expansion can more easily and readily be achieved – very often in desired overseas markets. This strategy may take many forms, from joint marketing to a common reservation system but, generally, 'by using a common name, or one of the partners' existing names, it is possible to double a hospitality firm's portfolio overnight' (Knowles 1996: 249). Not surprisingly, partners are carefully selected, often with fairly similar properties and service standards, in order to fit in with existing or determined future markets.

The main advantage of strategic alliances is a sharing between alliance partners of their market, in particular the substantial sector of the frequent business traveller who will be able to utilise the increased number of hotels within the chain in a larger diversity of locations. Marketing advantages and economies of scale also occur and one of the major benefits is that the ownership of the property will not alter and the chain can still retain its independence. Strategic alliances are, therefore, a key route to achieve global expansion.

Case Study

Extract from the TravelMole Insider Electronic Newswire

www.travelmole.com 21 May 2001

Millennium and Maritim Hotels strike global alliance

Millennium & Copthorne Hotels PLC (M&C) and Maritim Hotels have announced a combined global marketing alliance to tap into each other's main geographical markets, in order to accelerate their worldwide expansion strategies.

The move grants each chain immediate penetration into those regions where its partner is particularly strong, and at relatively little expense. M&C has a strong presence in Europe, the USA and Asia, whilst Maritim's main hold is over Germany - one of the world's largest hotel markets. M&C last year bolstered its presence in Europe with the appointment of a Germany-based Sales Director for Central Europe.

Together, the two chains have a portfolio of 128 hotels with almost 35,000 rooms in Europe, the USA and Asia. The plan is for these hotels to be cross-sold by staff at both Maritim and M&C, enabling the two chains to help maximise incremental revenues in the medium to long term.

Kwek Leng Beng, Chairman of M&C, commented: "This is a 'win-win' situation for Maritim and M&C, as well as for our respective customers... Instead of buying hotel chains, this alliance allows us to compete and grow quickly. Germans are avid leisure and business travellers, and the country is ranked the top outbound country in the world. Now they will have an opportunity to stay at our hotels in Singapore and elsewhere".

Joint ventures

A joint venture is an agreement between the hotel operating company (often an international hospitality organisation) and another (non-hotel) organisation. Generally, the hotel operator is in full partnership by means of joint ownership of the hotel with another company and there will therefore be joint participation in any financial result. Real estate developers are often involved in such arrangements and joint ventures have been popular methods of expansion in areas where there is a comparatively low volume of modern hotel stock, such as in eastern Germany post-unification and in Eastern Europe more generally. The advantages are similar to those discussed under management contracts and, in this instance, the investors would be looking towards a longer-term capital appreciation.

Acquisition

Acquisition continues to remain a popular route to expansion, with the splitting up of the Granada Compass portfolio in 2001 (formerly Forte) being a good example of recent major acquisitions. Macdonald Hotels have purchased the Heritage Brand, Bass the Posthouse brand and the Japanese Bank Nomuera, the Meridien Brand. How these companies integrate their new acquisitions into their existing portfolios remains to be seen.

Franchising

Franchising is becoming almost a houschold word. MacDonalds, Burger King and Pizza Hut have been operated successfully for many years using this format, whilst many other internationally organisations operate on a franchise basis. In the context of accommodation in particular, the growing pressures of globalisation and greater emphasis on hotel brand awareness by customers has resulted in franchising becoming enormously popular as a method of spreading the market. It is, however, a frequently misunderstood concept and there are many definitions of it.

The relationship between the two parties, franchisor and franchisee, may be summarised as follows. 'Franchising can best be described as a system of distribution whereby one party (the franchisor) grants to a second party (the franchisee) the right to distribute products, or perform services, and to operate a business in accordance with an established marketing system' (Knowles 1996: 262). For this there is a fee, the arrangement of which varies considerably. The franchisee can then utilise the company's brand, logo, identity and operational systems including marketing and distribution practices. There are many advantages and disadvantages on both sides:

For the franchisor

- Income from fees;

- International growth and recognition of the brand product – without the huge financial outlay involved with acquisition;

- An opportunity to sell and market their product both nationally and internationally without prohibitive expense;

- The opportunity to maximise the usage and spread the costs of an international computerised reservation system;

but also

- A lack of quality control over franchisees and the danger that standards may fall therefore endangering the reputation of the chain;

- The costs of setting up will have to be met by the franchisor.

For the franchisee

- The opportunity to operate under the umbrella of a successful and well known brand which already has an international identity and fully functional operating systems;

- To be able to utilise a national or international organisation's computer reservation system (CRS) or Global Distribution System (GDS) thereby maximising market opportunities;

- To be able to participate in all marketing functions provided by the organisation;

- To benefit from the provision of management experience in all operational areas;

- To gain from economies of scale, guest loyalty schemes and referrals from other members of the chain;

but also

- The financial costs are considerable, not only fees, but also initial investment in ensuring that the property is converted to the franchisor's standards and staff trained accordingly;

- There is a loss of identity, sense of ownership and uniqueness in conforming to the new brand.

Critics of globalisation trends argue that hotel brands are making Europe's hotels bland. For example, an article in the Wall Street Journal (e-tid 20.04.01) entitled 'Endangered Species: Hotels with Character' suggests that, through franchising,' anonymous chains are gobbling up Europe's quaint inns'. However, there is no doubt that, as a method of expansion, franchising is a very successful format and one which will continue to grow in popularity.

Case Study

Extract from Electronic Travel Industry Digest (June 2001)

www.e-tid.com

Ramada returns to UK with Jarvis franchise deal 13/06/01. Jarvis Hotels has signed a 20 year franchise agreement with Marriott International. 55 properties will be rebranded as Ramada Plaza, Ramada-Jarvis or Ramada Resorts. John Jarvis, chairman and founder, said that the deal gives Jarvis access to Marriott's global reservation systems and Ramada's sales network. Marriott's mid-market Ramada brand has been absent from the UK for two years since four hotels were rebranded as Renaissance.

Consortia

Although the large international hotel chains may dominate the accommodation industry, the independently owned hotel sector, in terms of numbers, is still greater. In an attempt to compete in a global market place dictated by large organisations, these independently owned hotels frequently band together and consolidate their strength in the market place by forming consortia.

The key advantages of being a member of a consortium lie in the access to central marketing and distribution systems which will introduce the possibility of new domestic or overseas markets. They are, therefore, often termed 'Marketing Consortia'.

Main advantages of consortium membership

- Access to a CRS or GDS;

- Featuring in the consortium's guidebook (nationally or internationally distributed);

- Press exposure as a result of public relations activities featuring the consortium's brand name;

- Economies of scale in terms of purchasing power for hotel equipment, food, wine, etc.;

- Referrals from other consortium members;

- Access to professional advice on all operational issues; and

- The hotel still retains its independence, not only in name, but also in operational character.

The main disadvantage is the cost of membership, which is generally high in order to ensure that the provision of quality in terms of service and standards remains high throughout the chain and the brand name. In order for consortia membership to be effective, members seek like-minded hoteliers featuring similar products and levels of service. One of the most well known consortia is Best Western, often referred to as 'the world's largest hotel chain.' It is a membership association of independently owned and operated hotels and provides marketing, reservations and operational support to 4000 members in 80 countries. A recent advertising campaign features international landmarks, such as the Eiffel Tower and the Grand Canyon, thus demonstrating the idea that no matter where travellers go, they won't be far from a Best Western (source: e-tid.com). Other well-known consortia include Les Routiers, Monotel, The Leading Hotels of the World, Small Luxury Hotels of the World and Relais & Chateaux.

Other accommodation types

Despite the evident importance of hotels in terms of visitor numbers and expenditure on accommodation, many of the trends experienced by the hotel industry, such as branding, franchising and consortia membership, are replicated in other accommodation sectors.

Bed and Breakfast

Often referred to as 'the great British phenomenon', the bed and breakfast (B&B) concept has been copied all over the world and is now found in such far flung places as New York City. Generally, B&Bs are family owned and run, and popular on account of their value for money, heterogeneity (each different B&B provides a unique experience) and distribution – certainly, there are few places in the UK where some form of B&B cannot be found. This appeals to the increasing number of independent travellers packaging up their own holidays and staying somewhere economical for a short break or one or two nights before moving onto the next location. In 1998, the British spent nearly 11 million nights in B&Bs in the UK and overseas visitors over 9 million nights, together amounts to about 1 in 6 of all tourist nights. Total spend of visitors using B&B accommodation was £1billion (Beioley 2000).

The classification and grading scheme administered by the tourist boards incorporates B&Bs and, of those registered with the ETC, 37 percent are diamond rated and about half of these have en-suite facilities (Beioley 2000). Again, defining a B&B, as opposed to a hotel or guesthouse, is problematic and so statistics need to be treated with some caution. B&Bs generally consist of only a handful of rooms, so the distinction is made in terms of size and, often, cost as they tend to offer excellent value for money. B&Bs can, however, have a licence and many of them will now provide an evening meal.

The initial capital required to establish a B&B is often small and they are an important extra source of income to communities, particularly those in rural areas and farms in particular. The plight of many B&B accommodation providers was highlighted during the foot and mouth crisis in 2001, which seriously adversely affected many in the business.

B&B providers are becoming more knowledgeable and experienced and are increasingly segmenting and targeting their markets in order to overcome problems of seasonality. Marketing consortia also exist for B&B providers, such as Distinctly Different who offer B&B accommodation in buildings which have been converted from their original use, such as water and windmills, barns and even brothels! There is no doubt that the B&B is here to stay and that quality, specialisation and uniqueness will be the order of the day.

Camping and caravaning

This sector incorporates a wide variety of holiday types and has grown increasingly in terms of demand in recent years, both in the UK and abroad. The chief attractions are the freedom and flexibility it offers and the cost effectiveness of owning your own accommodation, although many tourists now opt for the expanding range of static mobile homes and tents provided by tour operators. General holiday trends with an emphasis on activity holidays, health and fitness have also provided a boost to this sector. Once again, membership organisations, such as the Camping and Caravan Club, and branding are becoming all-important distribution and marketing strategies. Classification and grading quality schemes also exist, accompanied by inclusion in guidebooks, and endorsed either by the tourist offices or independently run schemes, such as Alan Rogers' Good Camps Guide.

Timeshare

The timeshare industry in the UK is growing rapidly. There was a 13.6 percent increase in timeshare ownership between 1998 and 1999 and 1.5 percent of all UK households are involved in timeshare ownership (Mintel 2000). Timeshare appeals to a particular type of holidaymaker who likes to return to the same place each year and prefers self-catering. The emergence of club resorts in holiday complexes means, however, that many facilities are now on hand.

The ownership of a second home has different motivations attached to it compared with purchasing holiday accommodation and a full analysis is beyond the scope of this chapter. Nevertheless, despite the continuing negative publicity associated with time share ownership, the industry has become much more sophisticated and the emphasis has switched from hard sell approaches to marketing and meeting consumer needs. The industry is also a significant source of employment and income for local communities and, it is claimed, generates a higher level of tourist spending than hotel-based tourism (WTO 1996).

Holiday cottages

The self-catering market has developed considerably over recent years and holiday cottages represent only a part of the provision of this diverse sector. Cottages and houses are available for rental throughout most parts of the UK, (the French equivalent is the very popular *gite*), from either a tour operator, membership consortia, or directly with the owners themselves by way of an advertisement or web site. Like the bed and breakfast, they are generally privately owned and many are second homes and let out when the owners are not using them. They can provide a valuable contribution to the local economy as long as holidaymakers utilise local facilities and shops.

Case Study

The Landmark Trust

www.landmarktrust.co.uk

The Landmark Trust provides holiday accommodation with a difference. They are an independent UK building preservation charity who rescue worthwhile historic buildings from neglect and let them for holidays. The income from letting contributes to their upkeep. Holidaymakers can stay in accommodation ranging from manor houses to mills and follies to forts, thus having a unique and independent holiday experience. Demand for this type of accommodation is growing in accordance with increasingly discerning customer choice and also the knowledge that visitors are participating in a sustainable and worthwhile tourism venture.

Figure 8.3: *The Pineapple*

Cruise

The cruise market in the UK has more than doubled in the last 5 years, making it one of the fastest growing sectors of the outbound travel market (Mintel 2000). Cruises were previously associated with the elderly or wealthy but the traditional image is now disappearing and consumers are aware of the very broad range of holiday types which incorporate cruising. Short cruise breaks on the Mediterranean are now extremely popular and several large tour operators, such as Airtours and Thomson Holidays, have invested in cruise liners. A wide variety of other water based holidays providing accommodation is also available, such as yachting holidays (either participating in a flotilla holiday or chartering a 'bare' boat and making up your own independent itinerary) and canal boat holidays.

Technology

As in all sectors of the travel and tourism industry, technological developments have had a huge impact on the accommodation sector and there are almost daily developments. The most important areas are briefly examined here.

- Yield Management Systems are becoming increasingly utilised within the accommodation sector, especially as their performance continues to improve with technological developments. They are essentially computer software systems which aim to maximise profit and revenue by interpreting demand in accordance with room types available. There is no doubt that they are becoming a key tool for accommodation providers in order to overcome the problems of perishability and seasonality, but in order for them to be effective they have to be provided with essential and accurate historical booking patterns and information.

- Computer reservation systems (CRS) and global distribution systems (GDS) continue to play an important role, particularly for hotels which are members of a consortium or an international chain. The Hotel Electronic Distribution Network Association has reported that hotel bookings made through Amadeus, Galilieo, Sabre, Sahara and Worldspan grew 11.4 percent in 2000, with 48,787,000 bookings (Travelmole, 23/03/01).

- Utell (a subsidiary of Pegasus) is the hotel industry's largest third party marketing and reservations provider. It manages and produces very large hotel databases which provide a wealth of information on hotels around the world, as well as providing yield and other management systems for member hoteliers. The organisation has no affiliations with the hotels on their systems and acts effectively as a 'one stop shop' for travel agents. It is also linked to GDSs.

- On-line hotel reservations are expected to grow from the current rate of 4.9 percent to 15.4 percent within the next three years (TravelMole, 06/06/01). Hospitality companies are keen to reduce the currently very high costs of distribution, such as travel agency commission fees, GDS fees and the costs of multi-faceted distribution and the Internet is seen as providing limitless opportunities for implementing successful on-line marketing and distribution strategies (see also Chapter 18). However, simply having a web site will not be sufficient and the development of a formal e-strategy may be necessary to take full advantage of this new distribution channel. At the same time, evidence suggests an unwillingness on the part of consumers to book over the Internet, although consortia members have significantly benefited from Internet business through a central web site and reservations system.

- Recent research by Hilton (e-tid 21.06.01) has shown that WAP users are not so much using their appliances to make reservations with hoteliers but rather to cancel them, or to check in. This can have a beneficial impact on re-sale of rooms and therefore perishability and it is suggested that this trend may also benefit airlines who suffer from similar problems from 'no shows'.

The accommodation sector and sustainability

Accommodation providers play a very important role in providing a sustainable tourism product, not only in terms of the quality of the provision of the built environment (physical appearance and degree of harmony with surroundings) but also with respect to the volume and type of market segment that they attract and in their operational procedures. It is imperative that accommodation construction and the provision of leisure facilities, such as swimming pools and gardens, now take into account environmental factors, such as energy and water consumption, pollution, global warming and degradation of the natural environment. Accommodation providers can make significant cost savings through the adoption of environmentally friendly practices, such as a reduction in energy costs by utilising solar power where possible. Re-cycling and changes in operational practices, such as using real as opposed to paper napkins, can also lead to an improvement in quality standards. It is also becoming evident that accommodation providers are being progressively more consumer led in the demand for environmentally friendly tourism accommodation, although the success of environmental policies in the accommodation sector, as in all areas of tourism, is dependent upon the acceptance and positive support of tourists.

Case Study

Extract from the TravelMole Insider (19.10.00)

www.travelmole.com

Sydney's Green Games inspire hotel clean up

Sydney Olympic Park's Novotel and Hotel Ibis Homebush Bay have recently completed a comprehensive survey in order to the ascertain the impact of environmental initiatives on hotel guests and how, if at all, they affect the guest experience.

The survey, which was conducted in August, of 105 guests and 345 rooms highlights the public's increasing preference for 'environmentally friendly' business.

90 percent of guests polled said they preferred to stay in a hotel that cared for the environment (compared to 8 percent who were indifferent).

At home or at work, 91 percent of respondents indicated that they recycle, 82 percent said they reuse plastic bags, 50 percent said they opt for less packaging and 46 percent make compost.

Whilst 57 percent of guests opted to reuse their towels more than once to save water and washing detergents, a growing 35 percent of guests opted to reuse their sheets more than once for the same reasons - a new trend in hotels.

During their stay, 78 percent of guests used the recycling bins in the hotel rooms correctly (as compared with 95 percent of respondents who said they used the facility), 83 percent chose to use the soap dispensers rather than ask for individual soap cakes and whilst 58 percent used their operable windows rather than air conditioning, a staggering 98 percent identified the windows as one of the top three environmental initiatives.

Conclusion

The accommodation sector is a vitally important part of the travel industry. On account of its heterogeneity and diversity, however, it is impossible to analyse the industry as one body. In general terms, we are seeing a move from an hotel industry that was basically a collection of family owned and run accommodation providers to one where international chains are increasingly dominating the industry. Growth strategies, such as acquisitions, alliances and joint ventures, are proliferating as the demand for a global presence becomes ever necessary and the brand is becoming all-important in terms of standardisation and quality. New products, such as designer, boutique and townhouse hotels are emerging, as are new locations such as hotels next to sports stadia.

Independent hoteliers are, however, fighting back by joining marketing consortia, segmenting and targeting their market more effectively and providing products, which meet new consumers' needs in terms of taste and current trends. Holidaymakers, seeking more independent and specialised travel, can take advantage of new technology, such as the Internet, and are able to find a large array of segmented accommodation suitable to their particular needs. Providers of accommodation as an alternative to hotels continue to grow in popularity and the line between serviced and non-serviced is becoming more indistinct. Thus, there is no doubt that the accommodation sector will continue to diversify and, despite periodic setbacks in the external environment, it will continue to expand in accordance with the general trend in demand for travel and tourism products.

Discussion questions

- *Discuss the reasons for the adoption of growth strategies by hoteliers and the advantages and disadvantages of the main types.*

- *Examine ways in which the independent hotelier or accommodation provider can compete in today's competitive environment.*

- *What are some of the alternatives to hotel accommodation and why might these become increasingly attractive to consumers?*

Further reading

British Hospitality Association (2001), British Hospitality: Trends and Statistics.

Jones, P. (1996), *Introduction to Hospitality Operations*, London: Cassell - Part A.

Knowles, P. (1998), *Hospitality Management An Introduction, 2nd Edition,* Harlow: Longman.

Knowles, P. (1996), *Corporate Strategy for Hospitality*, Harlow: Longman.

Medlik, S. and Ingram, H. (2000), *The Business of Hotels, 4th Edition,* Oxford: Butterworth-Heinemann.

References

Beioley, S. (1999), Accommodation standards - what the customer wants, *Insights, Volume 10*, B47-B51, London: English Tourist Board.

Beioley, S. (2000), Diamonds are trumps - the bed and breakfast sector, *Insights. Volume 11*, B65-B80, London: English Tourist Board.

British Hospitality Association (2001), *British Hospitality: Trends and Statistics*, London: British Hospitality Association.

Bull, A. (1995), *The Economics of Travel and Tourism, 2nd Edition*, Harlow: Longman.

Electronic Travel Industry Digest. URL:http://www.e-tid.com [11th,18th & 20th April, 11th May, 14th & 21st June.

Jones, P. (1996), *Introduction to Hospitality Operations*, London: Cassell.

Knowles, P. (1998), *Hospitality Management An Introduction, 2nd Edition*, Harlow: Longman.

Knowles, P. (1996), *Corporate Strategy for Hospitality*, Harlow: Longman.

Landmark Trust, (2001), *Landmark Trust Handbook*.

Leisure Intelligence (2000), *Hotel Report*, London: Mintel International Group.

Leisure Intelligence (2000), *Holiday Property Abroad Report*, London: Mintel International Group.

Leisure Intelligence (2000), *Camping and Caravaning Report*, London: Mintel International Group.

Medlik, S. and Ingram, H. (2000), *The Business of Hotels, 4th Edition*, Oxford: Butterworth-Heinemann.

Parker, A. (1996), The changing face of the hotel industry, in R. Kotas, R. Teare, J. Logie, C. Jayawardena and J. Bowen. (eds.) *The International Hospitality Business*, London: Cassell: 39-41.

Pine, R. and Go, F. (1996), Globalization in the hotel industry, in R. Kotas, R. Teare, J. Logie, C. Jayawardena and J. Bowen . (eds.) *The International Hospitality Business*, London: Cassell: 96-103

Sangster, A. (2000), The impact of branding on the UK hotel industry, *Travel & Tourism Analyst*, (2) 65-82.

Sharpley, R. (1999), *Tourism, Tourists and Society, 2nd Edition*, Huntingdon: ELM Publications.

TravelMole Insider. URL:http://www.travelmole.com [19th October 2000, 19th June 2001].

Ward, C. and Hardy, D. (1986), *Goodnight Campers! The History of the British Holiday Camp*, London: Mansell Publishing.

Walton, J. (2000), The hospitality trades: a social history, in C. Lashley and A. Morrison (eds.) *In Search of Hospitality*, Oxford: Butterworth-Heinemann:

WTO (1996), *Timeshare: a new force in tourism*, Madrid; World Tourism Organisation.

9

Visitor Attractions in Tourism

Hans-Christian Andersen

Learning objectives

This chapter introduces the tourist visitor attraction as one of the main constituents in the tourism system. It enables the reader to:

- *appreciate the nature and specific features of the visitor attraction*

- *define the visitor attraction, in the light of the variety that exists in the sector*

- *explain salient aspects of the design and management of visitor attractions*

Introduction

The attraction – whether called the 'tourist' attraction or the 'visitor' attraction – has a central place in the tourism system. It includes a large number of very diverse phenomena, including architecture, nature, museums, public sculpture, theme parks, retail parks and events. In fact, the sector is so diverse that it is hard to find a definition that covers them all. Nevertheless, the importance of the visitor attraction (as it will be called here) is obvious: it helps 'make' a destination, sometimes it *is* the destination. It *attracts* tourists in some way, it gives the tourist a *motivation* for travelling and, therefore, it becomes a reason for paying a visit to a place. Everybody who is involved in tourism at any level will appreciate how crucial this makes the attraction in tourism generally. By definition, that which attracts a tourist also makes tourism possible, opening up opportunities in transport, catering, accommodation, guiding, publishing, souvenir production, and so on.

The purpose of this chapter is to look at the attraction in its own right, in order to understand what it is and how it works. It will also look at the particular issues which the tourism industry and tourism managers (and others working in the sector) have to deal with in relation to attractions at both the micro and macro levels.

The historical background

Have there always been attractions, and have they always motivated tourism? If, for the moment, we forget about any distinction between 'tourism' and 'travel', there were probably always visitor attractions of one sort or another. That is, it is likely that people have always travelled in order to see or experience something 'for its own sake', in addition to the other reasons they might have for going somewhere. Of course, we cannot know for certain why people travelled to Stonehenge, for example. Undoubtedly they went for religious reasons, to perform rituals or some other social or religious duty. However, it is also very likely that they went to a place like Stonehenge because it was – and is – such an exceptional monument, such a unique piece of religious architecture, so exciting in its own right. Thus, we cannot know, though we can guess or even assume, that visits to Stonehenge also led to some kind of activity in the travel, catering and accommodation sectors. The people who lived at the time when Stonehenge was in use were not radically different from us and it is, therefore, reasonable to imagine that what amazes and preoccupies us today could also have some kind of parallel then.

Moving forward in history to Ancient Egypt, Greece and Rome, there were certainly religious and civil monuments and institutions which people travelled to see for touristic reasons. During the time of the Roman Empires, Greece had already come to be seen as an artistic and cultural ideal which the Romans travelled to see and whose artistic works they reproduced for their own homes. By the Middle Ages, religious tourism became widespread, leading to the creation of pilgrimage 'trails' across Europe which Christian pilgrims would follow, collecting souvenir tokens at the great religious attractions so that they could eventually prove back home that they had been there. The great cathedrals and monasteries and sites of religious miracles and revelations became religious attractions, as they have remained to this day.

As already discussed in Chapter 2, modern tourism has its roots in developments going back several centuries. In Europe, its roots lie in the Grand Tour of the 17th and 18th centuries, when young noblemen toured Europe as part of their general education, to visit the sites that had come to represent the origins of their contemporary civilisation. Co-incidentally, these were also many of the sites which the ancient Romans had visited – for example, Athens – plus newer attractions dating from Roman times, such as Rome and Pompeii, and great cities which represented a more modern cultural tradition, such as Paris and Venice.

Of course, the Grand Tour was only for the few and, to a great extent, the wealthy. The 19th century, however, saw the development of a more widespread kind of tourism, resembling more closely what we see today. With industrialisation came the creation of a working class with – eventually – leisure time and a certain amount of surplus spending power: this was the foundation of a new mass market. The steam engine was the technological advance that made mass tourism possible: trains and ships could now transport people from place to place, quickly and reliably, according to fixed timetables. The way was open for Thomas Cook to bring that market and that technology together in the UK, to create a modern tourism which was less exclusive and which enabled the many to take shorter, cheaper holidays, following a predetermined route to destinations with a series of attractions appropriate to the kind of tourist that went there. Soon this new concept was spread across Europe, inviting new tourists to visit known attractions across the Continent and benefit from new transport and accommodation.

The destination and the attraction

The 'destination' is, effectively the 'unit' which the tourism industry puts together and which it then presents and markets to the tourist/visitor as a complex product. The destination needs to have a range of facilities for the tourist, such as accommodation and catering, for a range of customer types. It must also have the appropriate infrastructure to allow tourist to travel there (by road, rail, air) and move around within it (public transport, roads) and communicate (telephone, postal services, etc.).

More than anything else, however, it must offer a reason or a motive for tourists to go there – it must be able to attract tourists. It can do so in a number of ways. Ski resorts, for example, offer a well-defined range of winter sports-related leisure activities, based on the landscape. Some towns and cities are well-established and, over the centuries, have built up a longstanding reputation as tourist destinations, offering a particular kind of attraction, such as the cultural destinations of Florence, Paris or Dresden. In the UK, York in this category, though perhaps at a slightly more modest level. Some landscapes can have a similarly longstanding reputation, as is the case with England's Lake District, famous for its scenic qualities and its association with the Romantic poets. Importantly, age is not in itself a qualification for success. For example, Blackpool and Agia Napa are seaside resorts, differentiated not by age but by appealing to different kinds of tourists with different expectations.

Each of these types of destinations has something which will motivate tourists to go there. However, there also has to be enough of that 'something' for the tourist to do so – the destination needs 'critical mass' before tourists can be expected not only to visit but also to stay. In the UK, a tourist might decide to stay for a length of time in London and, perhaps for shorter periods, in a range of other cities. Official statistics can show which cities are most attractive in these terms (Table 9.1).

Table 9.1: *Top towns visited by overseas residents, 2000*

Rank	City/town	Visits
1	London	13,150,000
2	Edinburgh	910,000
3	Manchester	560,000
4	Birmingham	520,000
5	Glasgow	430,000
6	Oxford	410,000
7	Cambridge	370,000
8	Bristol	360,000
9	Bath	300,000
10	Cardiff	240,000
11	Nottingham	190,000
12	Newcastle-on-Tyne	180,000
13	Stratford-on-Avon	170,000
	Coventry	170,000
	Reading	170,000
14	Bournemouth	150,000
15	Leeds	140,000

Source: StarUK (2001)

Clearly, there is a connection between size and attractiveness, although size is not a sufficient reason for visiting in itself: all of the cities on the list have a variety of attractions to tempt the tourist. Of the cities listed in Table 9.1, London clearly has critical mass. Edinburgh is not only architecturally and historically attractive, but also has an annual Festival to attract visitors. Oxford, Cambridge and Bath are all traditional centres for visitors with their historical and cultural connections, whilst Glasgow, conversely, has only recently been established as a tourist centre.

Interestingly, although Stratford-on-Avon, because of its Shakespeare connections, is a standard stop on the tourist itinerary, it did not receive as many visitors in 2000 as did Newcastle-on-Tyne, which is now building up an image, along with Gateshead, as a tourist centre. This is principally because the latter two cities have decided to collaborate instead of competing – by sharing resources, they have a greater chance of achieving sufficient 'weight' as a destination. The two cities have also embarked on a programme of creating new facilities and attractions which, it is hoped, will help transform the reputation of the North East from being an area of heavy industry and coal-mining into being a cultural destination, potentially the European Cultural Capital in 2008. Included in this programme are the Millennium Bridge (opened in 2001), the Baltic Centre for Contemporary Art (to be opened in 2002) and the Gateshead Music Centre (under construction in 2001), as well as a sculpture trail along the River Tyne.

Defining the visitor attraction

Visitor attractions can be many things. They may be things which tourists travel purposely to see, such as a trip to India specifically to see the Taj Mahal, or which they visit when they are on their travels anyway ('when in the US, don't miss the Grand Canyon!'). They can be man-made (Sydney Opera House) or natural (the Lake District), it can be there anyway (St. Peter's Church in Rome) or it may have been constructed specifically as an attraction (Disneyland). It may be part of a destination (the Manneken Pis in Brussels) or it may the destination itself (inland resorts, such as Center Parcs).

From a tourism management perspective, the definition should embrace the concepts of both 'tourism' and 'management', thus permitting the inclusion of some things which are not *intended* to be visitor attractions, but which tourists visit anyway and in such numbers that the tourist flow has to be managed (as is the case with many religious buildings, such as Westminster Cathedral or the Blue Mosque). Conversely, it also makes us think carefully before we include the Sidney Opera House or Nelson's Column in London: they may help attract tourists to the destination, but they may not be managed specifically for that purpose, nor are they necessarily major reasons for visiting. However, a magnificent view of the Scottish Highlands can be included, as it can be deliberately managed by offering tourists a simple lay-by with a interpretation board explaining the landscape.

Several definitions of the visitor attraction exist. The Scottish Tourist Board (STB), for example, defines it as:

> *A permanently established excursion destination, a primary purpose of which is to allow public access for entertainment, interest or education, rather than being principally a retail outlet or a venue for sporting, theatrical, or film performances. It must be open to the public without prior booking, for published periods each year, and should be capable of attracting tourists and day visitors as well as local residents.* (STB 1991)

More simply, Middleton (1988), defines the visitor attraction as:

> *A designated permanent resource which is controlled and managed for the enjoyment, amusement, entertainment and education of the visiting public.*

Swarbrooke (1995) defines the attraction in the context of the destination:

> *Attractions are generally single units, individual sites or very small, easily delimited geographical areas based on a single key feature. Destinations are larger areas that include a number of individual attractions together with the support services required by tourists.*

Hanna (1997) formulates it in this way:

> *The attraction must be a permanently established excursion destination, a primary purpose of which is to allow public access for entertainment, interest or education; rather than being primarily a retail outlet of a venue for sporting, theatrical, or film performance.*

From these four definitions, it is evident that the visitor attraction must, in particular:

- be *permanent*, in the sense of being permanently established or regularly repeated, as in the case of a festival or sports event;

- not simply *frame* the actual attraction, as a theatre would;

- be *enjoyable* and function as part of the (tourist) visitor's *leisure time* but also possibly be *educational*;

- *attract visitors* (not only tourists but as members of the public), and be designed and managed to provide a *service* to *satisfy their needs*; and

- it may *charge*.

Therefore, this chapter will concentrate on the kind of facility that has been specifically designed and created to function as an attraction. In other words, many things attract visitors, but only some are primarily or entirely designed and managed for that specific purpose. These include:

- Museums (or special exhibitions in museums).

- Arts centres and arts museums/galleries.

- Nature centres, national parks and other managed landscapes.

- Historical buildings, open-air museums and managed townscapes.

- Theme parks and amusement parks.

- Visitor centres.

- Zoos and aquaria.

- Historical and archaeological reconstructions and research centres.

Amenities

All of these would normally have a number of standard features which would be part of the service to be provided (and therefore part of the experience to be managed). These features – or amenities – include (see Yale 1998):

- On-site amenities
  - Parking
  - Visitor Centres
  - Signs and labels, audio-visual presentations and guides and guidebooks
  - Shops, catering and lavatories
  - Litterbins, seating, lifts and on-site transport

- Off-site amenities
  - Signposts
  - Hotels

Classifying the visitor attraction

Having defined the visitor attraction, it is also important to find a means of classifying it in order to help isolate aspects that distinguish one type of attraction from another. Therefore, this section considers the criteria that can be used to distinguish different types of attraction and to provide an overview of this richly varied sector.

Attraction types

The degree of variety is clear from classifying which attractions by type. Such types include (Prentice 1999):

- Natural history attractions
- Science based attractions
- Attractions concerned with primary production
- Craft centres and craft workshops
- Attractions concerned with manufacturing industry
- Transport attractions
- Socio-cultural attractions
- Attractions associated with historic persons
- Performing arts attractions
- Pleasure gardens

- Theme parks
- Galleries
- Festivals and pageants
- Field sports
- Stately and ancestral homes
- Religious attractions
- Military attractions
- Genocide monuments
- Towns and townscape
- Villages and hamlets
- Countrysides and treasured landscapes
- Seaside resorts
- Regions

With the exception of 'Genocide Monuments', most, if not all, of these types may be represented in most areas. The drawback, however, is the very variety: there may be so many types that the classification becomes confusing. Equally, it could be argued that there are many more types. For example, is a 'theme' park the same as an 'amusement park? Is a 'region' not too large to qualify as a single attraction? In any case, classifications of this kind require constant updating to ensure that they include new types of attractions, such as the increasingly important themed retail parks.

Private - public

Other kinds of classification use broader criteria in order to help distinguish between the different types. One distinction is between privately-owned and publicly-owned attractions.

Privately-owned attractions

Normally, the primary concern of these attractions is to earn a profit for their owners/shareholders. This means that they have to focus carefully on what their customers want, so that they can attract them, not only once but for repeat visits. To do so, they need to focus on developments in their own sector in order to maintain or improve their competitive position. They also need to monitor their customers' levels of satisfaction through regular surveys.

For example theme parks, such as Alton Towers or Disneyland, are designed to attract and entertain large numbers of paying customers and are, therefore, closely focused on the needs and wants of their core visitors, as well as on their own need to survive and prosper. Attention is also paid to the activities of any competitors in their own industry or to other activities that compete for their customers' attention and money. They will also consider the (relative) importance of customers drawn locally, day-trippers and tourists coming from further afield and will work out to what extent they have to serve, say, overseas tourists as well as domestic ones. Marketing, as well as good business management generally, becomes a crucial factor in their success.

Publicly-owned attractions

These can be owned by local or national government and, therefore, can usually rely on an element of financial support from their owners. This sector includes attractions run by charitable trusts, such as the National Trusts for England and Scotland. Public-sector attractions include such facilities as museums and other public buildings, whose primary purpose is not usually to service tourists but which may nevertheless do so. Thus, they are usually service institutions, created to meet the needs of the local population, although this is not always the case. For example, the Burrell Collection in Glasgow was created by a rich collector, who donated it to Glasgow without attempting to discover whether there was a real local *need* for such a collection.

Publicly-owned attractions are usually created to meet non-tourist needs. Thus, museums normally exist to educate the local population in an aspect of their own heritage, to collect, preserve and exhibit artefacts and to make them accessible to the public. In the case of the national museums in the UK, the purpose is the same at the national, and possibly even international, level. Charitable trusts, such as those owning and managing the National Trusts' properties or other attractions, such as the Centre for Life in Newcastle, do not have to make a profit. However, they do have to earn their own revenue – the National Trust, for example, depends entirely upon members subscriptions, entry fees at its sites, donations, retail activities and special appeals for its income.

Similarly, publicly-owned museums (most are either publicly-owned or are run as charities) are nowadays expected to raise their own revenue through retailing other commercial activities, such as corporate hospitality. In the case of charitable trusts, all revenue is earned (or donated), meaning that they are increasingly 'commercial' in their attitude to management and to the visitor: their management is inevitably coloured by the need to attract and please visitors. This is also increasingly the case for attractions owned by local and national government, which is why it is possible to deal with them all under the same heading of 'attractions management'. But, significantly, such attractions may also be subsidised, allowing them to focus on the local audience rather than tourists.

The distinction between privately and publicly owned attractions may only seem one of degree: they may all seem to be run along commercial lines, using modern management methods. However, the actual difference should not be underestimated. In practical management terms, it is often the case that an attraction within the publicly-owned sector will not only *distinguish* itself from the privately owned sector, but will also *distance* itself from it on qualitative grounds, arguing that the two types of organisations are fundamentally different. One exists to make profit (by serving the customer explicitly), whereas the other aims to add to the quality of life of members of the community (by helping the visitors discover their identity and heritage or discover their position as citizens). Thus, in their day-to-day work, these privately and publicly-owned institutions will prioritise differently when balancing the needs of their specialist staff (perhaps researchers and scientists employed in a museum) against the needs of operations managers (looking after the running of the building as a visitor attraction) and the visitors (who may be students, schoolchildren, tourists, families etc.).

Natural, man-made or special events

It is possible to distinguish between attractions that are:

- natural
- man-made
- man-made and purpose-built to attract tourists
- special events

Natural attractions

These include landscape features, which, for one reason or another, attract the attention of visitors. The Foot and Mouth crisis in the UK in 2001 confirmed the fact that the farming industry helps to maintain the landscape for tourism purposes as well as for agriculture. Without the constant attention from farmers, the cultural landscape would lose qualities that currently attract tourists. However, landscape may be more explicitly designed and managed as a tourist attraction through, for example, the provision of managed paths for walkers, huts for climbers and visitor centres which can both act as information offices and interpretation centres. The National Parks are prime examples of this kind of landscape management.

Man-made attractions

Man-made attractions are features in landscapes or townscapes (or entire townscapes) that have been created by human beings for purposes other than tourism. These include religious buildings, castles, examples of special architecture (which may be special because it is typical of an historical period or of a particular architect's work), or areas in towns and cities of particular aesthetic or historical value. Also included in this category are ruined buildings, which are often preserved for historical or other reasons and presented as tourist attractions.

The National Trust is a good example of an organisation devoted to the preservation and interpretation of buildings (and landscape features) that are significant parts of England's national heritage, from ancient times to (almost) the present day. The Trust presents buildings in a manner that makes them accessible in intellectual terms to the visitor (that is, which allows the visitor to understand what their significance is). At the same time, it is increasingly adopting modern teaching and learning methods to make the visit not only educational but also entertaining.

Man-made, purpose-built attractions

Attractions built with the specific purpose of attracting tourists include theme parks and amusement parks, holiday centres, such as the Center Parcs or Disneyland, and recent attractions, such as Newcastle's Centre for Life and Edinburgh's Dynamic Earth. These latter attractions combine the theme park with the educational facility, but they are not there specifically to serve the local community: they appeal to a national (and possibly an international) audience. Thus, they fulfil a dual attraction and the public service role, exemplifying the trend towards mixing both entertainment and education in new contemporary attractions. Theme parks, conversely, aim specifically to earn a profit by providing an experience and facilities that will attract visitors.

Special events

Festivals and sports events, such as the Olympics, are examples of special events that play a large part in contemporary tourism. Festivals – in particular arts festivals – are numerous in the UK. Major examples are the Festivals in Edinburgh, Chichester and Glyndebourne, which attract audiences and performers from all over the world. Because they are recurrent, they can become part of a region's or a city's tourism strategy. Some festivals, such as the Munich Beer Festival, are not only visited but also copied in other countries and others occur in a similar form, such as the Newcastle Hoppings, a great, annual meeting of travelling show-people.

Managing the special event as an attraction largely involves the same skills as other kinds of attraction management but also involves specific aspects, such as programming, arranging venues, co-ordinating sales and merchandising. Customer research is a difficult aspect of the special event, in particular where the free event is concerned. If, for example, a festival takes place in the streets of a town, it is difficult to estimate the number of people attending and why they have come. However, as is the case with other attractions, the special event will also provide opportunities for a range of local and other entrepreneurs and suppliers in the tourist business, including catering and accommodation.

The nature of the visitor attraction product

All attractions serve visitors directly by providing the kind of experience that is appropriate to the tourist (and to others), which includes a *core experience* (heritage, architecture, mountain-climbing, fun and excitement, learning, art) set among a variety of other facilities which service the visitors and provide employment and other opportunities for local people.

As with the tourism product as a whole, the attraction is a service and, therefore, displays the characteristics of intangibility, inseparability, heterogeneity and perishability (see Chapter 6). This means, amongst other things, that people are central to the attractions industry: employees must be appropriately trained to deal with visitors. It also means that the attractions industry – like tourism generally – belongs to a sector, the service industries, which is becoming increasingly important in contemporary industrialised societies. Citizens are increasingly used to acting as customers for services and the demand for quality service and professional management grows ever stronger. This affects all parts of the industry, including the not-for-profit element (see also Chapter 5).

The market for attractions

Given the sensitivity of tourism in general to a variety of external factors (see Chapter 3), it is difficult to measure and accurately predict the market for attractions. Nevertheless, in recent years, the 'travel facilities and attractions'[1] market has enjoyed some growth, though spread unevenly across the market. Figure 9.1 summarises recent developments:

Figure 9.1: *The market for travel facilities and attractions*

- The market for travel facilities and attractions in the United Kingdom grew by 12.4 percent over the 1995-1998 review period, reaching an overall value of £2,608.3 million in 1998.

- All sectors benefited from the increasing popularity of the United Kingdom as a tourist destination, attracting foreign tourists with large disposable incomes, resulting in escalating consumer expenditure throughout the United Kingdom travel and tourism industry.

- The travel facilities and attractions market also benefited substantially from the rising number of United Kingdom residents holidaying in the United Kingdom rather than travelling abroad. Similarly, the market benefited from the increasing incidence of United Kingdom residents enjoying weekend breaks and visiting tourist attractions.

- The strength of the United Kingdom travel facilities and attractions market is expected to continue into the near future. Over the 1998-2003 forecast period, growth of 30.9 percent is expected, underpinned by the focus on millennium celebrations and increased commercialisation of all attractions, with the overall market reaching value sales of £3,413.6 million in 2003.

Source: Euromonitor (1999)

This would suggest that:

- the facilities and attractions market is a market in growth and therefore worth investing in;

- the UK attracts increasing numbers of relatively wealthy tourists;

- more British tourists holiday at home and more British tourists go on weekend breaks; and

- more growth is expected.

The events of 2001, in particular the Foot and Mouth crisis and the terrorist attacks in the USA, cast some doubt on these projections. Nevertheless, it is reasonable to expect that the market will return to where it recently – that is, the estimated market growth may not happen by 2003 but it will happen eventually.

Supply-side aspects

In 1999, the English Tourism Council (ETC) published a report which reveals a great deal about the 'shape' of the visitor attractions market from the supply side. It is summarised in Figure 9.2:

Figure 9.2: *The supply of attractions in the UK*

•	There are at least 6,215 attractions in the UK; 74 percent of these are in England.	
•	The attractions sector is split as follows (**top 10 categories**):	

Museums and Galleries	1,756	28%
Historic Properties	1,521	24%
Visitor Centres	489	08%
Gardens	378	06%
Workplaces	382	06%
Wildlife Sites	315	05%
Country Parks	290	05%
Farms	247	04%
Steam Railways	106	02%
Leisure Parks	85	01%
Other	646	10%

• Although only 4 percent of attractions are in London, they account for 13 percent (52,860,000) of visits.

Source: ETC (2000a)

Heritage in the UK visitors attractions market

The dominant position of 'Museums and Galleries' and 'Historic Properties' in the UK market should be noted. Many of these attractions are non-profit-making, being funded by national or local government, and often they do not charge admission or do not charge much (as in the case of many museums) or they are run by trusts (as in the case of the National Trust). There is a tendency, at the moment, for these sectors to become increasingly dependent on earned revenue (as opposed to funding from the public purse), although the present government has made national museums free of charge. This benefits all visitors, from local, socially excluded schoolchildren to wealthy foreign tourists. In all, some 41 percent of all attractions in the UK did not charge for admission in 1999, suggesting that they could be an important service to the visitor, adding to the leisure experience without costing the visitor anything.

In 1999, visitor attractions earned an estimated £1.4 billion gross revenue, of which 49 percent from came from entrance fees or donations (donations are preferred by some attractions such as some cathedrals and museums), whilst 41 percent was earned through sales of merchandise in shops and 10 percent came from catering (ETC 2000a). These revenue figures do not, of course, include income from public-sector bodies in the shape of grants. As long as public funds go into the attractions sector, competition will always seem unfair. Local museums do not usually have to fend for themselves financially, unlike, say, a local theme park. On the other hand, the local museum usually serves quite different purposes from the theme park: where the former aims to educate, the latter seeks to entertain. The two are not, however, mutually exclusive.

The London/South-East factor

Of the 404 million visits in 1999, by domestic and international visitors, the vast majority (81 percent) was to attractions in England and a large proportion of those were in London and the Southeast. There is nothing surprising in this. Some of the most famous heritage attractions and museums are in or near the capital, and the largest theme parks are constructed where they will have the largest catchment area – that is in the South and the Southeast of England, which also has the largest population density. The large attractions are visited both by international, national and local visitors and will locate where they can reach those audiences.

It is clear that the domestic and foreign markets present different challenges to the tourism marketer (Table 9.2). Domestic tourists are more focused on the 'other England' than are foreign tourists, whose interest is clearly in the London and the South East. To the latter, the United Kingdom appears, at first sight, to be divided into the London area and the not-London area.

Table 9.2: *Leading UK destinations for domestic and foreign tourists (all purposes), 1999*

Region	Domestic tourists (% trips)	Overseas tourists (% trips)
Heart of England	13	7
London	12	45
West Country	12	6
East of England	11	6
Southern	9	8
South East	8	9
Other England	20	9
Scotland	7	7
Wales	7	3
Northern Ireland	1	-
Total	100	100

Source: Mintel (1999)

The ability to attract visitors: size matters

The market is not only concentrated in terms of where the attractions are, but also in terms of their ability to attract an audience: attractions with over 200,000 visits make up 7 percent of all attractions, but account for 58 percent of visits. Thus, the market is heavily concentrated on a relatively small number of attractions with a very large number of visitors. This does not mean, however, that smaller attractions cannot exist or survive in the market. As ETC (2000a) report points out, '57% of attractions receive fewer than 20,000 visits per year; three quarters (76%) receive less than 50,000 visits'.

Evidently, because they are all 'attractions', all the sites included in the ETC (2000a) report clearly belong to the same sector. However, that is not to say that they are also in the same *market* seen from the customers' view. Not only geography but size determines that, for example, Metroland in Gateshead does not at any level compete with Alton Towers. That is important for both: they are not competing for the same customers, one does not threaten the existence of the other.[2]

Attractions over-supply

Attractions of different sizes are designed and operated at very different levels; it is also a sector with a great turnover. For example, it is known that at least 859 attractions closed throughout England between 1978 and 1999 whilst, between 1990 and 1999, over 1,200 new attractions opened to the public (South West Tourist Board 2001). These figures could be taken to mean that the market for visitor attractions is buoyant. However, the reality seems to be different: there is an *oversupply* of tourist attractions in the UK. It appears that '[d]emand for attractions is slowing' and that the 'average number of visits per attraction is declining, yet supply is increasing.' (ETC 2000a).

The National Lottery

One possible reason for this oversupply in the UK is the role played by the National Lottery, in particular in the construction of the Millennium projects, such as the Millennium Dome in London. In many ways, these projects are exciting opportunities for the areas where they are built. They potentially enhance the lives of local people as well of visitors generally. They are also, generally speaking, exciting as buildings: they add to the quality of the built environment and contribute to a general upgrading not only of the UK as a tourist destination but as a place to live. However, the Millennium projects – like some other Lottery-funded projects, not least new arts venues – have been criticised on several grounds.

- Being publicly-funded and owned, they are seen as competition for the commercial, for-profit sector. There is nothing new in the public sector owning attractions in the UK, and they are not in a majority, with 69 percent (4,139) of attractions being privately owned (including charitable trusts); of the remainder, 1,406 are owned by local authorities and 453 by the Government. However, the arrival of new publicly-funded attractions in an already crowded market is seen by some commercial operators as excessive and unfair competition.

- There is a suspicion that some of the Lottery-funded projects are based on over-optimistic business plans with exaggerated expectations of visitor numbers (indeed, some projects, such as the National Centre for Popular Music in Sheffield, have since closed). Although potentially drawing increased numbers of visitors to a region, new attractions also threaten existing ones, particularly if the overall market remains static in terms of revenue and/or visitor numbers.

Table 9.3: **S**ummarises the status of major lottery-funded projects in the UK

Table 9.3: Lottery-funded attractions[3]

Name	Place	Status	Problem?
Centre for Life	Newcastle	Highly popular	Well-visited
Dynamic Earth	Edinburgh	Highly popular	Well-visited
Earth Centre	Doncaster	Staff numbers reduced	Low visitor numbers
Eden Project	Cornwall	Highly popular	Well-visited
Nat. Centre for Popular Music	Sheffield	Temporarily closed	Low visitor numbers
National Glass Centre	Sunderland	Staff laid off	Low visitor numbers
National Space Centre	Leicester	(recently opened)	Difficult location
Tate Modern	London	Highly popular	Well-visited

The attractions sector, therefore, seems to be skewed in ways that seem important:

- museums, galleries and historic houses make up the largest number of attractions;

- London and the South East attract the largest number of tourists, with London being the be preferred destination for international tourists;

- there is oversupply in the sector;

- competition is coming from new directions; and

- currently, in the year 2001, the tourism sector generally is facing major crises, nationally and internationally, which can limit the number of overseas tourists but which may also strengthen domestic tourism.

These factors might influence the attractions owner (and various organisations with an interest in the success of attractions) to consider:

- whether this means that attractions outside the museums/heritage sector will be less successful;

- whether the dominance of London in the tourist market is inevitable;

- whether it will be necessary to respond to oversupply by reducing the number of attractions or by attracting more visitors;

- whether the sector will be able to meet the new competition and the changing market conditions; and

- how the sector can best respond to national and international crises.

The answers to these issues relate partly to changes which individual attractions have to make, partly to changes at governmental level or at the level of lobbying groups and professional organisations. Ultimately, they all have to do with the strategy of visitor attraction management and with the business environment within which that strategy is worked out.

Feasibility studies and attractions design

Management is about controlling resources and delegating work and, in the case of the attraction, those tasks start before the attraction opens its doors for the first time. The modern attraction is a sophisticated 'machine', designed, equipped and manned to give visitors an enjoyable and memorable experience. This section looks at some of the processes that this involves. By outlining the process of creating a new attraction, it throws light on aspects of attractions planning that are applicable in a range of situations, from the development of a small theme park to a major heritage site or, indeed, the continuing development of an existing attraction.

Planning and preparation

The planning and preparation of a new attraction must be carried out with great care so as to ensure that the original concept is not only practicable and marketable, but also that:

- it will be able to attract investors;

- once opened, that it will be manageable;

- over the years, that it will have potential for further development; so that

- it can continue to attract visitors.

The process can be illustrated as in Figure 9.3

Figure 9.3: *The attraction, from idea to realisation*

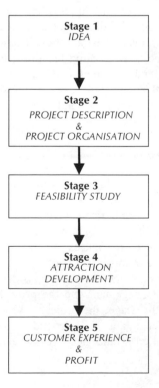

Stage one

At the initial, idea generation stage, the new idea for an attraction is measured against whether, at this stage, there is likely to be sufficient back-up, resources and perceived need for it. Subsequently, the concept development can start, addressing questions such as:

- what is it you want to achieve and why?

- does the idea seem simple, unique, innovative?

- does it, at this early point, appear viable, given the competitive environment and the resources that would be needed?

Stage two

The project development stage is a more 'real' phase. A team of people must be identified to create a real project out of the idea and the concept, who can provide expertise at all levels of the development of the project, who can timetable and organise the actual venture, and the legal and financial expertise. At this point, detailed costings of building and running the project will also be undertaken to help with financial projections. In short, the project organisation will involve the establishment of a team to turn the project from plan to reality, with changing membership so that it can deal with different tasks as the project develops.

Stage three

The first task in the feasibility study is to establish whether a market exists for the new attraction, firstly through secondary research (using existing, published sources), then through the commissioning of primary research that aims to establish who the visitors would be, where they would come from geographically, what their socio-demographic profile is, and so on. A second phase would establish where the best location is (assuming that this is not a natural or heritage attraction tied to an existing location), in particular with respect to proximity to major cities, how much land is needed, and whether the right infrastructure and labour force exist. An environmental audit would also be considered, given not only the interest in sustainable tourism but also national and international rules and regulations concerning environmental protection.

Stage four

The feasibility study allows the project developer to complete the project description and project organisation, moving forward to the actual attraction development stage, planning the construction of the attraction in detail, with financial costings. At this stage, the project developer is aiming to create a workable plan for how the original idea of the project can materialise as a real attraction with real experiences and facilities for the visitors, created within given financial and physical constraints. Here, not only is the nature of the individual 'ride' or stage on the visitor's tour through the attraction considered: attention is also paid to the actual building materials, queue management and the provision of catering for visitors with different purchasing power. At this stage, the project developer also takes into account budgeting and the raising of finance. The latter will depend on the quality of other planning work done so far, given that investors would need reassurance that the project would, indeed, be feasible.

Stage five

This stage involves the realisation of the project and, therefore, requires concentration on:

(a) the customer experience, which is all-important for the continued success of the project; and

(b) making a surplus on the activities of the attraction, if in the private/charitable sector, or at least balancing the books, if in the public sector.

The first issue requires constant research into customer satisfaction levels through, for example, questionnaire completion or focus groups. The second requires an equal level of vigilance in keeping an eye on whether all parts of the attraction are achieving the anticipated results, and on plans for future investment requirements. Both can be seen as an attempt to maintain the momentum that has been built up during the entire planning process, as described above.

In reality, the development of an attraction is a much more is a lengthy process than described here, involving repeats of many of the stages as new ideas are brought forward and as new constraints are encountered. Similarly, large numbers of specialists of different kinds may be involved in the project planning and development, as new issues of the practical implementation and funding arise. The attraction that finally opens may well be the result of a series of compromises, yet it may still be a success as long as the process is managed and guided firmly throughout the process and any changes are made with due regard for the original vision of the project. Once the attraction is open to the public, it will be subject to evaluation not only by technical and other specialists but also by its customers who will be the ultimate arbiters of what works and what does not. Their views will be important, as the attraction develops and perhaps expands throughout its lifetime, to take account of changing fashions in the leisure market.

Management issues

The visitor attraction, as defined in this chapter, requires management. This implies that it is usually staffed with several people with different duties relating to the maintenance of the building and serving the visiting members of the public.

Managing a visitor attraction is like managing any other organisation. There is a core product or a core product range. It has to be marketed to customers and it is important, therefore, to try and find out what those customers need and want. At the same time, income and expenditure have to be planned, monitored, controlled and reported, whilst there will be staff to manage, sometimes with very different kinds of expertise and duties. Finally, the attraction has to be operated on a day-to-day basis, as well as developed on a longer-term basis. In this respect, the visitor attraction is like any other organisation and it is necessary to pay attention to the kinds of management issues that normally arise, particularly:

- Operations management

- Marketing

- Finance

- Human Resource Management

Operations Management

Operations management is concerned with the day-to-day running of the attraction. Given that visitor attractions are services, people are central to the process, both as visitors and as attraction staff and management. Even where the attraction is in itself important – as in the case of major heritage attractions such as Stonehenge – the attraction does not fully come into its own until it has an audience, a visitor, who has decided to devote resources, such as time and money, to experiencing the attraction.

Operations management is there to ensure that the attraction functions properly; that any machinery is functional and safe; that catering outlets and shops are stocked and open; that staff are present and correct; that all facilities are presentable; and, that the site in general is tidy. In other words, although others have planned, designed and built the attraction, operations management is there to ensure that it operates as it should. Operations management is on the frontline between attraction and visitor. Issues such as queue management, problem solving and safety concern are in its remit. This is, therefore, the area within attractions management that will be particularly interested in quality management, possibly in accordance with accepted quality standards, such as those represented by ISO 9000.

Marketing

Marketing (see also Chapter 18) is the management discipline that brings visitor attractions' unique strengths together with the 'target visitor', by creating a story around the attraction that will appeal to that visitor. Successful marketing depends on a thorough understanding of the 'core experience'. In general terms, that is what the visitor is primarily looking for – 'a good day out, exploring our heritage', perhaps, or 'a day with my friends on the scariest rides available in theme parks' – and which the visitor attraction than seeks to turn into a 'real' experience. That real experience is a composite product. It comprises many sub-components, including the moment the visitor becomes aware of the visitor attraction through, for example, advertising; the process of buying the entrance ticket; going on the rides; and, using the ancillary services which the visitor attraction has to offer, such as catering, that ideally makes the visit even more enjoyable and merchandise from the shop provides opportunities for shopping both for gifts and souvenirs.

Visitor research is the fundamental route to marketing success in the visitor attraction. Regular questionnaire exercises monitor the satisfaction level of existing visitors, whilst specially commissioned research investigates the expectations and motivations of non-visitors, both those who are currently visitors at other attractions and those who are not yet visitors but might be converted. Armed with knowledge about visitors, the attraction can attempt to aim its promotion as directly as possible at potential visitors, by selecting to advertise or otherwise publish in appropriate media, promoting through other appropriate channels (e.g. flyers at tourist information offices and hotels) an perhaps even promoting through directly mail to the target audience.

Finance

Finance is usually concerned with two aspects:

- day-to-day finance, in the sense of looking after the cash flow that results from revenue earning at the entrance and at other outlets and franchises within the attraction.

- the raising of finance for new projects: capital expenditure.

The finance department will monitor income and expenditure in order to ensure that the attraction is solvent and that it achieves the appropriate financial result. The main income for the attraction may come from admissions, which means that the attraction must pay careful attention to pricing and the relationship between the price and value which the visitor feels that the attractions visit represents. The modern services customer looks for value for money and it becomes one of the central tasks of attractions management to find out how that can be provided at each individual attraction.

Instead of the admissions price, the attraction may rely on the 'average spend' of the visitor during the visit. This can enable the attraction to lower its admission price (thereby removing a financial barrier to visiting) in the expectation that the visitor will spend additionally at outlets within the attraction. Shopping is a staple part of the attraction visit in the UK and visitors expect to find appropriate merchandise, at a range of prices, as part of the service. The budget is the main instrument for financial control, enabling the financial officer to check forecasts against actual performance and suggest ways of dealing with temporary problems.

Human resource management

Human resource management is concerned with how staff are best recruited, trained and employed at the attraction (see Chapter 14). Staff salaries is likely to be the largest item on the attractions overall costs and the temptation – indeed, the need – may well be for managers to seek to reduce staff costs by making staff more efficient and productive. This may happen through the employment of temporary staff or through multi-skilling of existing staff, to ensure that they are able to function at more than one point in the attraction experience. Given that the attractions market is seasonal with the majority of visitors arriving during peak holiday times, a flexible workforce is a must for many attractions which need to close down, wholly or in part, during the low season. This makes staff motivation a constant issue in the visitor attraction; it is not easy to maintain morale in a workforce which is not prepared to offer permanent employment to its staff. Since staff are crucial in delivering a high-quality visitor attractions experience, that becomes a major issue for the attractions manager who must maintain staff morale and staff numbers at a sufficient level to keep the visitor satisfied.

Quality management

Nowadays, the concept of quality prevails in the business in general, and in the tourism sector in particular. As previously seen in Chapter 5, quality management is an essential task in tour operations, and the same is true for attractions management.

Quality in attractions related to at least two different areas. Firstly, since the attractions product is an 'experience, the staff delivering that service need to be skilled both in the particular jobs they carry out, such as manning rides, guiding tourists, or guarding sensitive areas, and in human relations, so that they know how to interact with visitors in an appropriate manner. Secondly, the attraction normally uses a range of 'hardware'. This may include machinery that is part of the experience which needs to be safe for the public to use and at an appropriate level of quality. The attraction also relies on a variety of produce bought in for sale to the public, such as food, drink, guidebooks, and merchandise. All of this has to be of the right quality and therefore the attractions manager is responsible for ensuring that suppliers meet the attraction's quality demands.

Getting quality levels right

Quality levels have to be appropriate for the attraction, but determining quality is difficult. Quality is relative; there is no scientifically-based scale to indicate when the right level has been achieved. However, there are other ways of measuring it. For one thing, quality levels must reflect the image of the attraction: the attractions manager must know what the attraction ought to be able to deliver to the customer. That particular decision must be made with reference to what kind of person the attraction wishes to attract and what that customer is entitled to expect; meeting customer expectations is an important part of deciding quality levels. Customer expectations will be coloured both by what the attraction itself offers and by what other attractions and other service organisations have to offer: the competition is always a factor in creating customer quality perception.

The attraction can turn this to its advantage by benchmarking itself against other, similar organisations in the industry, so that it can decide at what point it reaches appropriate quality levels. It may also adopt quality assurance standards through schemes such as the International Standards for Quality Management Systems: ISO 9000. It may also adopt the Total Quality Management (TQM) approach which aims for the implementation of a culture of quality throughout the organisation.

Although these ideas have long been current in general management, the attractions industry remains slow in their adoption. However, the demand from the public for good quality – or even excellence – will not go away and the industry will have to consider how to approach it. The Scottish attractions industry has introduced a quality scheme to help visitors know what service levels to expect at the visitor attraction. The English attractions industry has, however, refused to introduce a similar scheme, and now finds itself the subject of an 'attack' from the Consumer Association (Wniter 2000), which has published its own Guide to Tourist Attractions, judging each on:

- **Quality of attraction** (welcome, what there is to see and do, interpretation, guides, range of appeal).

- **Standard of facilities** (restaurant, shops, toilets, parking, maintenance).

- **Value for money.**

World Heritage

The World Heritage Committee (WHC), a part of UNESCO, is an attempt to create not only a network of globally important heritage sites but also a global set of standards for heritage attractions. In order to qualify for inclusion in the network, sites must conform to criteria specified by the WHC. Currently, the WHC includes 690 cultural and natural sites across the world, preserved so that future generations can inherit the treasures of the past. Among the UK sites are Stonehenge, Hadrian's Wall and the Old and New Towns of Edinburgh.

The WHC is not only concerned with heritage in an abstract sense; it also has views on how that heritage can be preserved and made available to visitors in a more specific sense. Thus, the WHC stipulates that any site included on the official list must have 'agreed plans, (e.g.

regional, conservation plan, tourism development plan)' (WHC 2001) and that it must address issues of, among other things, management, finance and visitor facilities.

Hadrian's Wall

Hadrian's Wall was placed on the list of World Heritage sites in 1987. It is a requirement from the UK government (in line with the WHC requirements listed above) that this long site, stretching across 12 local authorities, should have a management plan. This plan aims 'to balance and accommodate the different and sometimes potentially conflicting) interests of those whose purpose of to management and conserve the Site and those who use it' (Underwood 2001). Part of the purpose of the management plan is to balance the economic need to attract tourists with the need to ensure that the site is not eroded by too many visitors. This, the plan states, will happen through '[t]argeted tourism marketing campaigns … that bring added value from tourism to the area'. Similar plans exist for other sites in other countries, helping not only to identify internationally significant heritage sites but also to ensure that they are preserved and managed, so that they can serve the several purposes they have to serve as part of local and global history and culture, as national status symbols and as tourist visitor attractions.

Visitor attraction organisations

By creating a trade association, businesses can achieve several important things. They are able to speak with one voice, putting their industry's case to government, when they negotiate national regulations and legislation. They are also able to establish and maintain agreed quality levels within the industry. It is sometimes argued that, as a tourist destination, the UK lags behind other countries where customer care is concerned. A national organisation could help improve this situation.

Trade associations

Since the visitors attractions sector is so varied, setting up a truly representative network in the UK has proved to be difficult. However, several associations have been formed:

- The Association of Leading Visitor Attractions (ALVA) has some thirty members (out of the approximately 6,000 that make up the sector) who between them attract over 85 million visits annually, including Tyne and Wear Museums, Blackpool Leisure Beach, Stonehenge and Longleat. ALVA is involved in a benchmarking project for the sector (Locum Destination, 2000).

- The Historic Houses Association (HHA) is a trade association for stately homes, lobbying about taxation issues and co-ordinating its members' tourism and commercial activities, such as weddings and film location work. Among its members are Alnwick Castle and Burghley Castle.

- The British Association of Leisure Parks, Piers and Attractions (BALPPA) represents the interests of 250 of the UK's commercial leisure parks, piers, zoos and static attractions.

- The International Association of Amusement Parks and Attractions (IAAPA), with more than 5,000 members in 91 countries, aims to promote professionalism in the amusement industry and to represent the industry before government.

- The Association of Scottish Visitor Attractions (ASVA) is concerned with providing the Scottish visitor attractions sector with services that help the development of its members by supplying information about trends in the industry and arranges staff development courses and workshops in topics of interest to members. It also supports product development by providing consultancy and 'mystery visits' to allow managers to understand where there might be room for improvement.

National (state) organisations

There are also national organisations concerned with the standard of visitors attractions. The Scottish Tourist Board (STB) runs several quality assurance schemes, one of which grades visitor attractions according to the standard of services they provide, classifying them as *Highly Commended* (a very good overall standard), *Commended* (a good overall standard) and *Approved* (an acceptable good overall standard (Perthshire Tourist Board 2001). The English Tourism Council (ETC), responding to a general decline in the English visitor attractions sector, has developed an attractions strategy, which aims to 'improve the sustainability of attractions, encourage them to embrace change and be more customer orientated and to inform relevant organisations of the operational context, characteristics and needs of attractions' (ETC 2001). This not only indicates where some of the industry's structural problems lie, it also implies that a centralised strategy for the entire industry may help solve its problems.

In this context, the Regional Tourist Boards must not be forgotten They are responsible for creating the regional matrix of destinations and attractions will provide not only a regional strategy to guide members of the industry but also a forum for local attractions.

Conclusion

The centrality of the visitor attraction, as part of the tourism system, is clear – along with the other elements in the system, it helps make the destination what it is. The exciting thing about visitor attractions, from the manager's point if view, is the great variety that exists in the sector; the challenge of managing them and making them successful is endless. In addition, the visitor attraction has the potential to make a difference, not only to the economy of the destination (and, sometimes, the wealth of its owner). It can also make a difference to the visitors who may not only be entertained by it but who may also learn from it and take new knowledge back into their lives from it. Its attraction can, to coin a phrase, be endless to all those who come into contact with it.

Discussion questions

1.   *Where, in your opinion, do the most pressing issues lie for the visitor attraction today: on the supply side or the demand side?*

2.   *Is it ever possible for a visitor attraction to say that the visitor is **not** the most important factor in the attraction's success?*

3.   *Read the two cases at the end of this chapter. What are the most important differences and similarities between the two visitors attractions and what would you do to make the Innsbruck museum more accessible to the ordinary visitor?*

Footnotes

1. The "attractions and travel facilities" involved here are: Theme parks, Casinos, National parks, Museums, Zoos.

2. Both are "big" in their own sectors, Metroland being the largest indoor amusement park in the UK.

3. Nick Mathiason (1999). "Cultural revolution's cul-de-sac". *The Observer*, October 31st.

   Maev Kennedy et al. (2000). "Millennium projects pass the numbers test." *The Guardian*, May 27th.

   Hugh Pearman (2000): "Mr. Big's kingdom." *The Sunday Times*, May 21st.

Further reading

Drummon, S, and Yeoman, I. (eds.) (2001), *Quality Issues in Heritage Visitor Attractions*, Oxford: Butterworth-Heinemann.

ETC (2000), *Sightseeing in the UK 1999*, London: English Tourism Council.

Getz, D. (1997), *Event Management and Event Tourism*, New York: Cognizant Communications.

Hall, C. M. and McArthur, S. (1998), *Integrated Heritage Management: Principles and Practice*, London: The Stationery Office.

ICOMOS. (1993), *Tourism at World Heritage Cultural Sites* (rev. ed.). Washington: ICOMOS/WTO.

Prentice, R. (1993), *Tourism and Heritage Attractions*, London: Routledge.

Richards, G. (ed.) (2001), *Cultural Attractions and European Tourism*, Wallingford: CABI Publishing.

The following are useful websites:

Association of Leading Visitor Attractions, The (ALVA): www.alva.org.uk

Association of Scottish Visitor Attractions, The (ASVA): www.asva.co.uk

British Association of Leisure Parks, Piers and Attractions, The (BALPPA): www.balppa.org/

Department for Culture, Media and Sport, The (DCMS): www.culture.gov.uk

English Heritage: www.english-heritage.org.uk

English Tourism Council, The (ETC): www.englishtourism.org.uk

Historic Houses Association, The (HHA): www.hha.org.uk

International Association of Amusement Parks and Attractions, The (IAAPA): http://www.iaapa.org/

International Festivals and Events Federation, The (IFEA): http://www.ifea.com/

National Piers Society, The: www.piers.co.uk

National Trust, The: www.nationaltrust.org.uk

Scotexchange tourism industry page: www.scotexchange.net

Scottish Tourist Board, The (STB): www.visitscotland.com

Star UK, Statistics on Tourism and Research: www.staruk.org.uk

References

British Renaissance Starts Here, Special Issue: How the Lottery is Changing the Shape of the Country. *Sunday Times Magazine,* 30th April 2000.

Confederation of British Industry (1998), *Attracting Attention: Visitor Attractions in the New Millennium* London: CBI Publications.

Deloitte and Touche (1997), *A Survey of Continental Visitor Attractions*, Deloitte and Touche.

Dcloitte and Touche (1998), *UK Visitor Attractions*, Deloitte and Touche.

Drummon, S. and Yeoman, I. (eds.) (2001), *Quality Issues in Heritage Visitor Attractions*, Oxford: Butterworth-Heinemann.

ETC (2000), *Sightseeing in the UK 1999*, London: English Tourism Council.

ETC (2001), *Action for Attractions Strategy*, www.englishtourism. org.uk.

Euromonitor (1999), *The UK Market For Travel Facilities & Attractions: Main Findings,* London: Euromonitor.

Hanna, M. (1997), *Sightseeing in the UK 1996*, London: BTA/ETB Research Services.

Kennedy, M. *et al.* (2000), Millennium projects pass the numbers test, *The Guardian,* May 27th.

Leask, A. and Yeoman, I. (eds.) (1999), *Heritage Visitor Attractions*, London: Cassell.

Locum Destination (2000), Benchmarking Attractions, in *Locum Destination*, No. 1.

Mathiason, N. (1999), Cultural revolution's cul-de-sac, *The Observer*, October 31st·

Middleton, V. (1988), *Marketing in Travel and Tourism*, Oxford: Butterworth-Heinemann.

Mintel (1999), *The British on Holiday at Home*, http://sinatra2.mintel.com/sinatra/ mintel/d/f/home.

National Statistics/Star UK (1998), *Survey of Sightseeing in the UK 1998*, www.englishtourism.org.uk/.

Pearman, H. (2000), Mr. Big's kingdom, *The Sunday Times,* May 21st.

Perthshire Tourist Board (2001), www.Perthshire.co.uk.

Prentice, R. (1993), *Tourism and Heritage Attractions*, London: Routledge.

Scotexchange (2001), New Horizons: International Benchmarking and Best Practice for Visitor Attractions, www.scotexchange.com.

South West Tourist Board (2001), *Stronger Attractions*, http://www.swtourism.co.uk/rnd/ consultationpapers/ETCATTRACTIONSSTRATEGY.pdf.

StarUK/National Office of Statistics (2001), *Tourism Facts and Figures,* http://www.staruk.org.uk/.

STB (1991), *Visitor Attractions: A Development Guide*, Edinburgh: Scottish Tourist Board.

Swarbrooke, J. (1995), *The Development and Management of Visitor Attractions*, Oxford: Butterworth-Heinemann.

Thybo, Eva (ed.) (2000), *Udvikling af attraktioner*. ("Developing attractions"). Copenhagen: Danmarks Turistråd, Arbejdsmarkedets Feriefond, Turismens UdviklingsCenter.

Underwood, Sue (2001), *Hadrians's Wall World Heritage Site Management Plan 2001-2007: Summary of Consultation Draft*. Hadrian's Wall WHS Management Plan Committee (www.hadrians-wall.org/).

Winter, K. (2000), *The Which? Guide to Tourist Attractions*, London: The Consumer Association.

Yale, P. (1998), *From Tourist Attractions to Heritage Tourism, 2nd Edition*. Huntingdon: Elm Publications.

Appendix

Visitor Attraction Cases

The two cases below offer insights into to quite different visitor attractions. Read both separately and together, they throw light on some of the current issues in this type of attraction, in particular in the areas of interpretation and customer service.

Case One

The Space Centre at Leicester

© H. C. Andersen

'When I visited the National Space Centre at Leicester in June 2001, I arrived by train. I had expected to find signs at the station telling me how to get there but none were present. I took a taxi and expected that the taxi driver would be able to find the National Space Centre but discovered that at first he was not sure where it was. It was a very new attraction, but as a tourist-student I was a little disappointed. However, as the taxi driver got nearer to the attraction, road signs – both general road signs and the characteristic brown attraction signs – began to announce where we had to go to find it.

Once we were at the National Space Centre, the unusual architecture of the new building was in itself enough to tell me that we were there. I had, in fact, spotted the unusual building from the train and guessed that it had to be one of the new Millennium buildings. Progressive architecture has become a distinctive part of the contemporary attraction in the UK, often made possible by funding from the National Lottery. A large car and coach park was the first facility I encountered, although the taxi could drive close to the main entrance and did not have to enter the car park as such.

There were signs telling me where to find the main entrance although the modern architecture made it difficult for me to recognise the front door as such. As a visitor, I expect to be guided all the way to the attraction nowadays, without having to ask directions, just as I expect to be able to find products in the supermarket without having to ask staff.

There were parking spaces for the disabled near to the entrance and disabled access was available everywhere. That, of course, is becoming a legal requirement but it is also satisfying in itself to see that provision is made for disabled visitors so that they do not feel disadvantaged when they enter and use the building. Of course, I am talking about physical access for the physically disabled: there are many other kinds of disability which do not require special access but which may require other facilities such as signs in braille or large letters for visually impaired visitors, or induction loops for the hard of hearing.

Once you enter, a large Soyuz spacecraft, hanging from the ceiling, clearly signals to the visitor what kind of attraction we are in: one dealing with science and technology. Of course, that is what you expect when you visit a National Space Centre, but it is also the responsibility of attraction designers to make it obvious from the start what we are dealing with. In this case, although this is not a museum as such, the Space Centre does in fact own and exhibit important artefacts, including the Soyuz spacecraft. We are not just visiting a virtual reality experience, we will see authentic objects, we are facing reality, although as the exhibition then shows us, we are also in the world of conjecture, speculation and, most importantly, calculation. After all, this is about space, and much of it is still unknown.

That means that the Centre has to be well organised: otherwise, how can it take us through material that seems quite abstract at times? The exhibition itself has been thematically organised: we can explore a series of themes, each interesting in its own right, and together they form an overall picture of contemporary space exploration, carried out in space and from Earth. There are many interactives, including computer interactives and various 'toys' allowing us to learn about things like gravity. It soon becomes clear that you come to this attraction to learn things and I suspect that one of the major target audiences is schools.

A special information area tells us about space exploration here and now, with a large screen for the projection of images from, for example the Internet. There is a completely up-to-date cinema with the capacity for film screening with audience feedback. There is a hall for special exhibitions, a lecture room, a restaurant and a cafeteria, toilets (of course) and a gift shop with space-related gifts for any purse. The catering is not very space orientated – I wondered if they would be selling space food in tubes and that kind of thing. The merchandise plays, very obviously, to people's interest in science fiction, but it also includes some fairly sophisticated items like rockets. In addition, you can buy a guidebook and, if you want to and have the computer access, a homepage on the net.

The Space Centre has a large tower, the spectacular and very obvious architectural feature, covered in inflated plastic material and heated by heaters designed to look like solar panels. Inside the tower are two full-size rockets as well as more exhibitions on each of the floors off the tower space, including full-scale models of satellites. Of course, there is a lift for those who do not want (or are not able) to walk upstairs. You expect that kind of facility, but this lift is special: it is rattly and shaky. The reason is that it is exactly the same kind of rattly lift that takes NASA astronauts up to the cockpit of the space shuttle. Now, that is mixing customer facility with exhibition design in the most elegant and pleasing way.

This is how a really well-designed attraction works: it is a single experience, it offers a quality exhibition and a quality environment with good quality facilities. This should help ensure that the visitor has an enjoyable time, stays as long as possible (but not for too long: you also need to move people through the attraction) and has opportunities to spend, so that the attraction can earn the revenue it needs to.

The National Space Centre has been developed to attract a number of different audiences. It targets the educational market very clearly with excellent educational facilities including the schools space resource building at the entrance to the centre. This is not surprising: Leicester University, which has been instrumental in developing the Space Centre, is in itself a national centre for space research, as it has been for decades. That is also why it seems aimed at schoolchildren. But it is also aimed at tourists, who may not want to spend their entire holiday at Leicester itself but who may day-trip from London. It certainly has the facilities to satisfy that market, although only time will tell whether it can actually attract them.

They may be able to get to the Space Centre on the new City Tour coach, which takes the visitor to main sights and attractions in Leicester. The centre is meant to be part of a wider launch of Leicester as a tourist destination and there are clear hopes that tourism will form part of the economic regeneration of the City. Many cities are trying this approach at the moment and it is one of the exciting aspects of visitor attractions that they are in such a central position in the tourist economy now and that so much money is being invested in them. Again, only time will show whether there is an audience, of schoolchildren, families, tourists and others to fill this attraction, and the many others which have appeared in Britain in the last ten years.'

Case Two

The Anatomical Museum, Innsbruck, Austria.

© H. C. Andersen

'I had a scary experience on my holiday one year ago. My parents took me to something called the 'Anatomical Museum' in a city in Austria called Innsbruck. The whole family had 'passe' which we could use for two days, and the 'Anatomical Museum' was one of the things we could see. So we went.

The Anatomical Museum is in a building called the 'Anatomical Institute'. It is part of the University. At first we could not find it. It was not at the address on the map that we got with the passes. We had to walk past the University Hospital through several streets before we got to a big house in a quiet street. There were no signs in the street but there was one on the house: That was the Anatomical Institute. First we went into the basement. There was nothing there. We went upstairs to a corridor with cases with glass fronts. It was spooky: the cases were full of skulls with maltese crosses painted on them in black, and green oak leaves. The ceiling was high and the corridor was very dark and quiet. On one door was a large sign saying 'Strictly no unauthorised admittance.' We could not find the museum anywhere, so my dad knocked on some doors and eventually a man came out. He looked surprised, but then he said he would open up for us. They were closed, we said, but dad had a brochure which he got with the pass and it said that they were open on Tuesdays and today was Tuesday. The man had a key and opened the door. He walked into a dark room and switched the ceiling strip lights on, one by one. Then he waved us in and left us.

We were in a brightly lit room surrounded by display cases. But the first thing you really noticed was the smell: a kind of musty, chemical smell. To the left and right were display cases full of specimens. I have always been interested in the skeleton and muscles and there was skeleton and muscles everywhere, in bottles and in boxes, in rows on shelves and so on. Even an entire person, in a glass case. At the back of the room was this huge skeleton which belonged to a man who had been very tall when he died five hundred years ago. Behind him was a collection of skeletons of animals: dogs, seals, horses, everything.

We were all very quiet in there. My sister went out first. Mum did not seem to know where to look. Daddy was taking pictures. I was thinking about tomorrow when we were going riding at a riding school.

We did not stay long. Afterwards we went to a place called a 'Konditorei', where you get coffee and cakes. We talked about the museum. My sister thought it was scary. She hated the lights. My mum was not sure it was a good place for children. The smell was a bit much, too. I thought it was OK but not that interesting. Some of the books they have in the library showed the human anatomy better. The skulls were cool, though. My dad said he was not sure what all the exhibits were. There was so much in that one room and some of the labels were hand-written. All in all, we thought it was quite interesting, though, and we had never seen anything like that before. Anywhere.'

Section 3

Planning and Managing Tourism

Tourism, both as a social activity involving millions of people travelling nationally and internationally and as a complex, global industry that enables people to participate in tourism, does not exist in a vacuum. That is, tourism is not developed and promoted for its own sake but for its potential contribution to economic growth and socio-cultural development in destination areas. However, like all economic activities, costs are also incurred which, in the case of tourism, are manifested in the various impacts of tourism on the environment and local communities. There is, therefore, an evident need to plan and manage tourism effectively so that, on the one hand, its contribution to development is optimised whilst, on the other hand, its less desirable consequences are minimised.

At the same time, all sectors of the tourism industry operate with a national and international political and economic context. For individual businesses, this means facing up to the challenge of operating in a highly competitive international market, whilst the operations of all businesses within the industry are constrained or subject to political and legislative structures, as well as transformations within the social, economic and technological environment, to which they must respond in order to survive.

This third section introduces these business-specific and broader planning and management challenges facing the tourism industry. It commences with an overview of the need for planning before looking at the need for and means of resource management and the role of government in tourism planning and management. Subsequent chapters then consider specific operational issues, such as human resource management, financial management and marketing, as well the influence of legislation and technological advance on the manner in which tourism is supplied. The final chapter serves to remind the reader that tourism is, essentially, a social activity – without people wishing to be tourists, there would be no need for a tourism industry (although the industry itself plays a significant role in creating the demand for tourism) – and the relationship between tourism and destination societies in particular must also be planned and managed.

10

Planning for Tourism

Richard Sharpley

Learning objectives

The purpose of this chapter is to examine the role and objectives of, and approaches to, planning in tourism. Having completed this chapter, the reader should be able to:

- *understand the need for and role of planning in tourism*

- *identify the objectives of planning tourism*

- *explain the different approaches to planning in relation to different tourism contexts*

- *appreciate the contribution of the public sector to the planning of tourism*

Introduction

Tourism development is not an end in itself, but a means to an end. In other words, destinations do not develop attractions, facilities and amenities for the simple purpose of attracting and satisfying the needs of tourists. Rather, they seek to attract tourists or, more precisely, tourist spending, for the contribution that it can make to the wider economic and social development of destination areas. Indeed, as previously outlined in Chapter 3, it has long been recognised that international tourism can be an important means of achieving development and, as a result, many countries have embraced tourism as an integral element of their development strategies (Jenkins 1991).

Similarly, domestic tourism development makes an important contribution to local economic and social regeneration. In the UK, for example, many inner city regeneration projects have been based upon tourism, the most widely cited example, perhaps, being Bradford, which established itself as an unlikely but successful destination during the 1980s. Many dockland areas, such as Bristol and Liverpool, have also developed a range of tourist facilities and attractions whilst, throughout Europe, tourism is widely considered an effective means of addressing the economic and social decline of peripheral rural areas (Cavaco 1995; Hoggart *et al.* 1995; Sharpley and Sharpley 1997).

In short, the fundamental role of tourism is, essentially, to 'ensure the steady acceleration of economic and social development and progress, in particular in developing countries' (WTO 1980: 1), as well as contributing to local and regional regeneration in developed countries. In turn, this suggests that there is a need to plan tourism so that it fulfils this role effectively. That is, tourism development must be planned so that, beyond providing satisfying experiences for tourists, destinations themselves benefit economically and socially from tourism whilst the costs to the destination – the economic, environmental and socio-cultural impacts – are minimised.

However, whilst it is easy to justify the need for effective planning in tourism, the actual planning process is, for a number of reasons, rather more complex:

- Planning occurs at different levels, or 'scales' (see Gunn 1994: 25) in the tourism system, from the development of specific attractions or facilities, through destination/resort planning, to regional or national plans for tourism. The objectives of planning may vary at each level. At the site level, for example, planning may focus on design issues whilst national tourism planning may be concerned with employment opportunities.

- Different types of organisations may be involved in the planning process, including businesses in the various sectors of the tourism industry, government bodies and non-profit or 'voluntary' organisations, each of which may have different objectives dependent on their role in the tourism system.

- The overall approach to planning is likely to vary according to the specific characteristics or needs of the destination or type of tourism. Rural tourism planning, for example, embraces a different set of challenges and objectives compared with, say, urban tourism development. Nevertheless, regional or national development needs should, ideally, provide the focus for tourism planning to ensure that broader developmental needs are met. This, in turn, points to the need for integration across the tourism planning spectrum.

Evidently, then, tourism planning is a complex, multi-layered process, a full consideration of which is well beyond the scope of this chapter (see, for example, Gunn 1994; Hall 2000; Inskeep 1991; WTO 1994). The purpose here, therefore, is to explore the basis of planning, its role and objectives within the tourism development process, different approaches to planning and the need for planning to be located within broader national development objectives. The first question to be addressed, however, is what *is* planning?

What is planning?

Planning, according to Murphy (1985: 156), is 'concerned with anticipating and regulating change in a system, to promote orderly development so as to increase the social, economic, and environmental benefits of the developmental process'. In other words, planning is a process whereby a variety of future decisions or actions are mapped out in order to achieve desired outcomes in appropriate ways. In the context of this chapter, this means that planning is directed towards developing tourism in a manner that is appropriate to the needs of the destination community, to the capacity of the environment to absorb tourism and tourists, and to the needs of tourists themselves, optimising the desired outcomes whilst minimising the costs or negative impacts.

Implicitly, therefore, the ability to plan effectively is dependent upon the existence of goals or objectives; it is not possible to plan without having a reason for planning, a goal to aim for. Such goals might be set as part of the planning process or they may already exist as an element of broader local, regional or national policy. In either case, though, planning is guided by policy. Thus, if a destination's *policy* is to develop smaller-scale, up-market tourism, it will *plan* its accommodation and other developments, as well as its marketing and promotion activities, accordingly.

It is apparent, then, that planning is a much broader or more complex task than simply producing a plan. As Hall (2000: 7) observes, 'planning as a process must... be distinguished from a plan', the latter representing a set of decisions or actions that are, in effect, the outcome of planning which, itself, is guided by policy. Moreover, planning does not stop once a plan has been produced. A plan must also be implemented or put into action and, once this has occurred, the results must be evaluated, reviewed and, if necessary, fed back into the policy/planning process (see Figure 10.1).

The model shown in Figure 10.1 demonstrates a typical planning process. Though simplifying what, in practice, may be a lengthy and complex task (see WTO 1994: part 1), it nevertheless shows that planning in tourism is neither a 'one-off' event, nor simply the formulation or production of a plan. Indeed, the most important element of the planning process is, perhaps, the monitoring and evaluation of the outcomes, for tourism development not only results in a variety of environmental, economic and social consequences for the destination (both positive and negative), but also must be measured against the broader goals or objectives of developing tourism in the first place.

Figure 10.1: *The planning process*

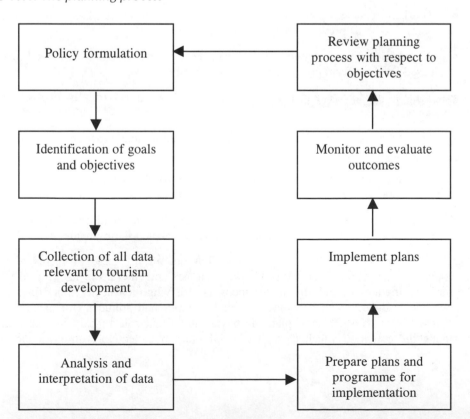

Thus, in short, tourism planning is a constant, cyclical process embracing policy formulation, the preparation and implementation of plans for tourism development, and the monitoring and reviewing of outcomes.

The role of planning in tourism development

Planning is an essential element of successful tourism development. In other words, experience has shown that, where tourism has been allowed to develop unconstrained by planning and control, not only do destinations suffer a variety of environmental and social problems but also, in the longer term, they may experience difficulty in continuing to attract tourists. In short, if unplanned, tourism can destroy itself, with consequential economic consequences for the destination. Conversely, many other destinations have shown that 'the planned approach to tourism can bring benefits without significant problems, and maintain satisfied tourist markets' (WTO 1994: 3).

To a great extent, the nature of tourism as both an economic and social activity demands that it be planned effectively. That is, tourism is characterised by a number of 'fundamental truths' (see McKercher 1993) which point to the need for tourism to be planned to avoid causing social problems, environmental degradation and limited long-term benefits. McKercher's 'truths' may be summarised as follows:

- Tourism development consumes resources, creates waste and pollution and has specific infrastructure needs which may impact negatively on fragile environments.

- Tourism potentially over-consumes resources; that is, it may be developed beyond the environmental and social capacity of destinations, resulting in negative impacts on the environment and local communities.

- Tourism depends upon and competes for scarce resources. Thus, tourism may conflict with or prevent other uses of a resource.

- As a private-sector dominated industry, development decisions are likely to be based on short-term profit maximisation objectives.

- Tourism is diverse and multi-sectoral. Therefore, it is virtually impossible to control.

- Tourists are consumers who principally seek pleasurable experiences. Generally, they do not wish to 'work' at tourism (see Chapter 4).

- Tourism is entertainment, so cultural resources (festivals, shows, museums) must be adapted or 'commodified' to meet the needs of tourists.

- Tourism is consumed on-site, pointing to the inevitability of tourist-host encounters and stresses on physical infrastructure and environment.

It is evident that planning can 'solve' some, but not all, of these problems of tourism development. For example, the tourist is the customer and, therefore, as with all products and services, the tourism industry should focus on satisfying their needs rather than, as some would naively suggest, trying to modify their behaviour and attitudes (for example, Wood and House 1991). Nevertheless, planning has an important role to play in constraining or restricting the extent to which these 'truths' of tourism collectively diminish the benefits accruing from tourism development. Indeed, planning fulfils a number of significant functions:

- It provides the framework for establishing and assessing the objectives of tourism development – it is all too easy to justify tourism simply on its contribution to 'development' (see below).

- It encourages the integration of tourism development into broader development policies in the destination area.

- It ensures that, as far as possible, the resources upon which tourism depends are maintained and enhanced for both present and future use.

- It provides the framework for co-operative actions and decision-making amongst all stakeholders (i.e. private and public sector organisations and all elements of the tourism sector) involved in the development process.

- It focuses on developing and promoting tourism of an appropriate type and scale in order to optimise the economic, social and environmental benefits of tourism within the context of local needs.

- It establishes an overall 'design' for the development of a destination.

- It sets the yardsticks by which the outcomes of tourism development can be measured and evaluated against the overall objectives of such development.

There is no doubt that 'the planned approach to developing tourism at the national and regional level is now widely adopted as a principle' (WTO 1994: 4). Less certain, however, is the extent to which plans are implemented. In other words, although most, if not all destinations have tourism development plans, in many cases there is little evidence that those plans have been carried through to fruition. As suggested later in this chapter, this frequently results from an ineffective balance between the role of the industry (the private sector) and government (the public sector). Nevertheless, planning provides the means for controlling and directing tourism development to the benefit of the destination and, in principle, ensuring that it contributes to broader objectives. What, then, are these objectives?

The objectives of tourism planning

In a general sense, the objective of tourism planning is to ensure that the desired benefits of tourism development to all stakeholders – destination communities, tourism businesses and tourists themselves – are optimised. Typically, such benefits are referred to collectively as 'development', a term which is usually taken to mean progress or improvement in people's social and economic status although, as considered below, the meaning of the term is rather more ambiguous that might be expected.

At the same time, however, the purpose of planning tourism is also to minimise the negative consequences of developing tourism. That is, it has long been recognised that the development of tourism can result in variety of impacts on destinations. These include, of course, environmental impacts, such as pollution (including so-called 'architectural pollution', epitomised, perhaps, by the concrete jungles of over-developed coastal resorts), social impacts, such as the disruption to local people's daily lives, and economic impacts, such as the costs of refuse collection, policing and so on (see Mathieson and Wall 1982; Croall 1995; Chapters 11 and 20).

Thus, tourism planning has two broad sets of objectives:

- *'developmental' objectives*: those that are concerned with achieving some benefit for the destination environment and community, and

- *'management' objectives*: those that are concerned with guiding the nature, rate and scale of tourism development to minimise its negative consequences.

The specific objectives within each category will, of course, vary according to the characteristics of the destination in terms of its stage of economic and social development, its environmental diversity and robustness/fragility, the extent to which tourism has already been developed, its geographic location in relation to potential tourist markets and so on, and its broader developmental objectives. It is, therefore, difficult to highlight specific objectives of tourism planning as they are likely to vary from one destination to another.

Nevertheless, Gunn (1994: 11-18) suggests that, generally, for the 'betterment of tourism there are at least the following four planning goals', three of which fall under the 'developmental objective' umbrella, and one under the 'management objective' umbrella.

i. Enhanced visitor satisfaction

Though not, arguably, the principal objective of tourism planning, tourism 'begins with the desires of travellers to travel and ends with their satisfactions derived from such travel' (Gunn 1994: 11). In other words, if people did not wish to be tourists, there would be no tourism industry. Thus, it is vital for a destination not only to attract tourists in the first place, but also to ensure that their needs / expectations are, as far as is possible, satisfied. Moreover, in an increasingly competitive international tourism market, it also necessary to focus continually on improving or enhancing the tourist experience as part of the planning process (hence, the need for the evaluation and review stage in planning). If this is not done, tourists may simply go elsewhere.

This objective also points to the need for integrated planning in tourism. The extent to which tourists are satisfied with their holiday experience is not simply related, for example, to having good food, sunny weather and a comfortable hotel. Rather, tourists evaluate their experience of the 'total tourism product', which represents a combination of both tangible and intangible factors (see Figure 10.2). Therefore, planning must, ideally, embrace all sectors of the tourism industry at all stages of the demand process (see Chapter 4) to ensure satisfying tourist experiences.

Figure 10.2: *Elements of the total tourism experience*

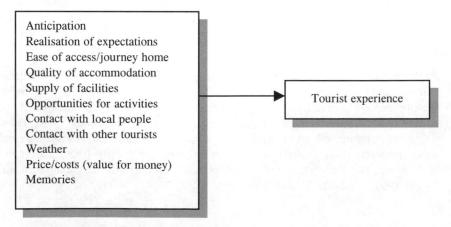

ii. Improved economy and business success

The main purpose of developing tourism has long been, and largely remains, to achieve economic growth and development in destination areas. That is, tourism is usually developed for its potential economic benefits, including foreign exchange earnings (international tourism is an export), income to local businesses, employment and the 'multiplier effect' (see Chapter 17). The economic benefits of tourism are summarised in Figure 10.3.

One objective of tourism planning, therefore, is to maximise these benefits by ensuring, for example, that sufficient support and incentives are provided at the national level to encourage entrepreneurs to invest in tourism, that appropriate tourist markets are attracted, that education and training are provided for employees, that other sectors of the local economy (e.g. food production, transport providers and so on) are able to benefit from tourism, and that policies are in place to encourage local ownership of tourism development.

iii. Protected resource assets

It has long been recognised that tourism development has adverse impacts on the resources upon which it depends (Croall 1995). This reflects the broader conflict between, on the one hand, the exploitation of natural resources to achieve development and growth and, on the other hand, the need to protect and conserve resources. Certainly, since the late 1960s, concern for the environment has become a dominant political and economic factor and there is no doubt that environmentalism, manifested in, for example, increasing membership of conservation organisations, the emergence of green political parties, and the activities of organisations such as Greenpeace and Friends of the Earth, has done much to raise global environmental awareness.

Figure 10.3: *The economic benefits of tourism*

Direct benefits	Indirect benefits
• Foreign exchange earnings	• Linkages throughout the economy
• Business income	- construction sector
- owners earnings	- food production sector
- employee earnings	- transport sector, etc
• Employment	• Multiplier effect: spending from primary income, which generates
- private sector	- income
- public sector	- employment
• Government earnings	- government earnings
- Income tax from employment /corporation	
- VAT/import duties, etc	
- Local business taxes	

The growth of environmentalism in general has been mirrored by increasing concern for the impacts of tourism in particular (see Dowling 1992). Indeed, the rapid growth in international tourism from the 1960s onwards has been matched by a no less rapid growth in calls to manage the development of tourism so that its environmental consequences are minimised. Not only does this make sound economic sense – any business has an interest in maintaining its resource base to ensure its longer-term survival – but, as a resource dependent industry (Chapter 11), tourism depends upon a healthy, attractive environment in order to continue to attract tourists. Therefore, a fundamental 'management' objective of planning is resource protection, focusing upon the design, location and scale of facilities and infrastructure, the appropriate type of tourism (for example, small scale versus mass tourism), and targeted marketing and promotion.

iv. Community and area integration

In addition to its environmental consequences, tourism also has an impact on local communities in destination areas. Ideally, such consequences should be positive as the primary purpose of tourism development, as observed at the beginning of the chapter, is the social and economic development of local communities in destination areas. In other words, tourism is developed in order to improve the lives of local people and, although this is often the case, there are also many ways, of course, in which tourism has an adverse effect on locals.

Thus, a final objective of tourism planning, according to Gunn (1994), is community and area integration. That is, tourism planning should be directed towards integrating tourism into the social and economic life of local communities and areas not only so that the negative impacts are minimised but also, and perhaps more importantly, so that the needs of local people and local development plans figure prominently in tourism planning.

These objectives of tourism planning are not necessarily mutually exclusive. Indeed, as discussed shortly, although different approaches to planning can be related to different objectives, the last decade or so has witnessed the virtually global acceptance and endorsement of an approach that attempts to combine and achieve all of these objectives – sustainable tourism development.

However, before going on to look at the different perspectives on planning, it is important to consider briefly what is meant by the term 'development' as the overall objective of tourism planning. That is, although tourism is usually justified on the basis of its potential contribution to the development of destination areas, until recently little attempt has been made to define what development is and, consequently, to consider whether tourism is in fact an appropriate means of achieving it (see Sharpley and Telfer 2002).

What is development?

It is likely that, although most people refer to 'development', few would be able to define what they mean by it. This is due, in part, to the fact that it is an ambiguous term to describe both the process which a society moves through from one condition to another, and also the goal of that process. That is, the development process in any country or society may result in it achieving the state or condition of development, although even that it is not a static, final condition – Britain, for example, though a 'developed' country, is still undergoing development.

At the same time, however, the difficulty in defining development also stems from a lack of consensus over the aims or gaols of development. Traditionally, it was equated with economic growth. As the national economy grows the national productive capacity (usually measured as Gross Domestic Product, or GDP) increases and, as long as national output expands at a faster rate than the population growth rate (i.e. per capita GDP is increasing), then development is said to be occurring. Certainly, throughout the 1950s and 1960s, international policies for promoting development were based on economic growth strategies and, to a great extent, tourism's contribution to development remains based on economic indicators – employment, income, foreign exchange earnings, and so on.

However, by the late 1960s it had become clear that, in many countries, economic growth was not only failing to solve wider social and political problems but was actually causing or exacerbating them. As a result, the objectives or meaning of development gradually moved beyond the goal of economic growth to embrace the broader social needs of reducing poverty, improving employment opportunities and so on. Indeed, many policy makers rejected economic growth as the objective of development; people, rather than things, became the focus of attention. In particular, the notion of economic growth was challenged by Seers (1969), who asserted:

> *The questions to ask about a country's development are therefore: What has been happening to poverty? What has been happening to unemployment? What has been happening to inequality? If all three of these have declined from high levels, the beyond doubt this has been a period of development for the country concerned.*

He later added self-reliance, or reducing dependence on other countries, as a further objective of development. In other words, for a country to be achieving development, it must be in control of its own development process and guiding it according to its own needs.

Thus, development, whilst still requiring economic growth, is a more complex and multi-dimensional process requiring the transformation of social and political, as well as economic, structures; it is the process whereby a whole society advances from a condition that is unsatisfactory to one that, according to that society's needs and values, better provides for the overall well-being of its members. Typically, therefore, development, as both a process and a gaol, embraces a number of dimensions:

- *economic*: the creation of wealth and the equitable access to resources and material goods;

- *social*: health, education, employment and housing opportunities;

- *political*: human rights, political freedom and the ability of societies to select and operate political systems that best suit their needs or structure;

- *cultural*: protection/strengthening cultural identity and self-esteem; and

- *environmental*: all development should occur within the ability of the environment to sustain such change and development.

As an example of these elements of development, the OECD has identified a number of goals as part of a new international development strategy (Figure 10.4).

The question then, of course, is: to what extent can tourism, as a specific economic sector and development option, contribute to these broad goals? Undoubtedly, tourism makes a contribution to economic growth and diversification, but less certain is its contribution to socio-cultural, political and environmental development. Nevertheless, some advance can potentially be made, particularly is the appropriate approach to tourism planning is adopted.

Figure 10.4: *International development goals*

Development goals for 2015
Shaping the 21st Century

Economic well-being

- Reduce extreme poverty by half

Social development

- Universal primary education

- Eliminate gender disparity in education by 2005

- Reduce infant and child mortality by two-thirds

- Reduce maternal mortality by three-fourths

- Universal access to reproductive health services

Environmental sustainability and regeneration

- Implementation of a national strategy for sustainable development in every country by 2005, so as to:

- Reverse trends in the loss of environmental resources by 2015.

Source: OECD (1999)

Approaches to planning

Just as the objectives of tourism planning will vary according to the particular needs and characteristics of different destinations, so too will the approach to tourism planning vary. To an extent, this will be determined by the scale of planning.

Tourism planning scales

Generally, there are three levels, or scales, at which tourism is planned:

i. The site scale

Probably the most common form of tourism planning is at the site scale; that is, at the level of individual projects, developments or properties. At this level, planning is most likely to be concerned with factors relevant to the physical scale and design of the development with respect to both the environment (e.g. using appropriate materials, a design that is appropriate to the character of the area and that is on a scale that does not place excessive pressure on local resources) and to potential or desired tourist markets. Frequently, the physical design of the project will be constrained by local planning restrictions – in the English national parks, for example, all proposals are rigorously scrutinised by the relevant National Park Authority – whilst the size and type of business proposed will be subject to a variety of factors, such as location, transport services, other local attractions and services, information and marketing services, and so on. Thus, even at the site level, tourism planning cannot be divorced from a variety of wider external influences and relationships.

ii. The destination scale

In order to achieve local developmental goals, it is important to plan tourism at the destinational scale. In a sense, this represents the collective planning of all site-level developments within a broader plan for the destination as a whole, the objective usually being to provide a critical mass of facilities and attractions sufficient to satisfy the needs of tourists. Typically, such planning will address issues such as:

- The number and variety of facilities and attractions (accommodation, restaurants, shops, etc) to meet the needs of a number of different tourist markets;

- Limits on the scale and character of development to retain the desired 'feel' of a destination;

- Public facilities for the use of both residents and tourists (parks, museums, sports centres, etc); and

- Efficient and attractive transport services within the destination.

Generally, destinational planning is concerned with providing the optimal tourist experience, thereby underpinning tourism's contribution to local economic and social development, whilst being sensitive to the potential social, environmental and economic impacts of tourism development on the destination.

iii. The regional scale

At the regional (or national) scale, tourism planning is undertaken to ensure that tourism is planned and managed within the parameters of regional (or national) development policy. Thus, different destinations in the region are, in principle, planned and developed as part of a cohesive overall tourism development plan so that, for example, the problem of seasonality may can be addressed – one resort may cater principally to a summer-sun market whilst, elsewhere, business/conference tourism may be developed. At the same time, regional planning can focus on the development of transport systems that benefit all tourism development in the region whilst it is also necessary to plan at the regional or, in the case of smaller countries, such as island micro-states, to ensure that the development of the tourism sector is integrated with the planning and development of other sectors, such as industry, forestry, agriculture, housing, and so on.

Planning approaches

Hall (2000) describes four different approaches to the planning of tourism which, to an extent, reflect increasing knowledge and awareness of the impacts of tourism and the of the need for an integrated approach to planning and managing tourism development.

i. 'Boosterism'

Boosterism is a simplistic or naïve approach to planning based on the assumption that tourism development is inherently a 'good thing', that it will inevitably bring benefits to the destination. Thus, environmental considerations are submerged by the belief that local resources should be exploited for tourism, whilst local communities are rarely involved in the planning and decision-making process. The objective of boosterism is to maximise the potential growth and, hence, economic return (in the short term) from tourism with scant regard to longer term consequences for the destination's environment and communities and, as Hall (2000: 21) comments, 'may be more aptly described as a form of non-planning'. The hosting of mega-events, such as the Olympic Games, is a continuing example of boosterism.

ii. The economic approach

The economic approach to planning regards tourism as an industry which can be used to achieve certain economic objectives (the economic benefits of tourism referred to earlier). In other words, it is based on the assumption that tourism is an effective means of achieving economic growth, regeneration or diversification and, therefore, the focus of tourism planning is on economic returns and the ways in which these can be optimised. As a result, greater attention is paid to economic objectives than to social and environmental issues, and planning centres on marketing and promotional activities designed to attract the type or number of tourists who will provide greatest economic return. In Cyprus, for example, the Cyprus Tourist Organisation (CTO) has long had the policy of increasing overall tourist numbers, but now focuses on attracting 'up-market' tourists in order to maximise per-head tourist spending (Sharpley 2001). Arguably, the economic approach remains dominant in tourism planning, despite the popularity of sustainable tourism development (see below).

iii. The land use approach

In comparison to the economic approach, land use-based tourism planning recognises the interdependency between tourism and the physical environment and, as a result, primacy is given within the planning process to minimising the impact of tourism and tourists on the environment. In a general sense, land designations, such as the establishment of national parks and other forms of protected areas, are a major planning tool designed to integrate the exploitation of the environment for tourism with the overarching objective of conservation. However, more specific planning controls and visitor management techniques, such as zoning (both land-base and marine), interpretation, directional signing and marketing, are also common elements of tourism planning in environmentally sensitive areas. At the same time, environmental impact assessments (EIA) are increasingly being undertaken as an integral part of tourism planning to ensure that proposed developments will not have excessive impacts on the environment.

iv. Community tourism planning

In response to the growing recognition of the socio-cultural impacts of tourism and the need to better direct tourism planning towards satisfying the specific needs of local communities (as well as optimising the visitor experience), the concept of community-based tourism planning emerged in the 1980s as a potential means of balancing the needs of tourists with those of local people in destination areas (see, in particular, Murphy 1985). The community approach to planning is essentially a 'bottom-up' form of planning where the views and attitudes of local residents are incorporated into tourism plans and, ideally, where local residents also play an active role in planning and managing tourism. The purpose of this approach is to 'empower' local communities so that:

- they do not feel exploited by tourism or that their society and culture is being 'commodified';

- they enjoy some degree of control over the rate and nature of tourism development;

- their economic and social needs form the basic objectives of tourism planning;

- they have some control over local resource use; and

- they benefit directly from tourism development.

The extent to which community tourism planning is feasible in practice remains open to debate. Not only is it difficult to encourage widespread public participation, but local political structures may discourage the handing over of power to the community at large. At the same time, community/public involvement may lengthen the planning process, whilst certain stakeholders, such as the owners of local businesses or local landowners, may seek to dominate or impose their will on the decision-making process. As a result, as Hall (2000: 32) observes, community involvement in tourism planning is, more usually, a form of tokenism.

Undoubtedly, there are examples in practice of all four approaches to tourism planning and, frequently, situations where a combination is adopted. The most common approach to tourism planning, however, is probably the one which attempts to combine the economic benefits of tourism (the economic approach) with environmental compatibility (the land-use approach) and community empowerment (the community approach) whilst minimising environmental degradation and social impacts. In other words, tourism planning, whether at the site, destination or regional scale, is most usually undertaken according to the principles of sustainable tourism development.

Sustainable tourism development

Since the mid-1980s, the concept of sustainable tourism development has become almost universally accepted as a desirable and politically appropriate approach to, and goal of, tourism development. It has achieved 'virtual global endorsement as the new [tourism] industry paradigm' (Godfrey 1996: 60) and, from the local to international level, innumerable sectoral and destinational organisations within the tourism industry have produced sustainable tourism development plans and policies. At the same time, sustainable tourism development has been a dominant theme in tourism research; not only are 1990s particularly memorable for the volume of literature related to the topic but also 'defining sustainable development in the context of tourism has become something of a cottage industry' (Garrod and Fyall 1998).

However, despite the widespread acceptance of and adherence to the principles of sustainable tourism development (see Figure 10.5), the extent to which it represents a universally viable or applicable approach to tourism planning and development remains the subject of intense debate (see Butler 1998; Sharpley 2000). This lack of consensus has arisen primarily from the two distinct ways in which the concept of sustainable tourism development is interpreted. According to Hunter (1995), 'those who insert the word 'tourism' between 'sustainable' and 'development' [should] ensure that, under all circumstances, the resultant principles of sustainable tourism development are the principles of sustainable development'.

Figure 10.5: *Principles of sustainable tourism development*

- Tourism should be planned and managed within environmental limits and with due regard for the long term appropriate use of natural and human resources.

- Tourism planning, development and operation should be integrated into national and local sustainable development strategies.

- Tourism should support a wide range of local economic activities, taking environmental costs and benefits into account, but it should not be permitted to become an activity which dominates the economic base of an area.

- Local communities should be encouraged and expected to participate in the planning, development and control of tourism, with support from central government, to ensure the equitable distribution of the benefits of tourism.

- All organisations and individuals should respect the culture, the economy, the way of life, the environment and political structures in the destination area.

- All stakeholders within tourism (businesses, local communities and tourists themselves) should be educated about the need to develop and participate in more sustainable forms of tourism.

- Research should be undertaken throughout all stages of tourism development and operation to monitor impacts, to solve problems and to allow local people and others to respond to changes and to take advantage of opportunities.

- All agencies, organisations, businesses and individuals should work together to avoid potential conflict and to optimise the benefits to all involved in the development and management of tourism.

This, certainly, was the original approach to sustainable tourism development, an approach which envisaged tourism as a means of achieving or contributing to the broader sustainable development of destination areas. Inevitably, of course, this then begs the question: what is sustainable development? The fact that there exists some 70 definitions of sustainable development suggests that there is no simple answer to that question! Nevertheless, it can be seen as an approach to development that is:

> *holistic* – it must be viewed as an approach that addresses global problems of poverty, health, education, pollution, resource exploitation and degradation and other challenges of underdevelopment with global solutions.

> *equitable* – it seeks to provide equal opportunities and access to resources for present and future generations.

> *future oriented* – the focus is on future generations, and their ability to satisfy their needs.

> *environmental* – the defining element of sustainable development is that it should be within the global ecosystem's capacity to sustain development.

As such, sustainable development is an approach which seeks to achieve the broad objective of development described earlier in this chapter (i.e. social, political, cultural development) combined with environmental sustainability.

Not surprisingly, perhaps, given the nature and characteristics of tourism, sustainable tourism development has come to be seen in a much more specific, tourism-centric way, as 'tourism which is in a form which can maintain its viability in an area for an indefinite period of time' (Butler 1993: 29). In other words, rather than being seen as a contributor to the wider (sustainable) development of destination areas, which is, of course, the primary justification for planning and developing tourism in the first place, sustainable tourism development is, more commonly, associated with sustaining tourism itself. In other words, although the term sustainable tourism development is politically attractive, it is, in practice, little more than an adaptation of the land-use approach to planning referred to above.

This is not to say that, under specific circumstances, 'true' sustainable tourism development cannot be achieved on a local, small-scale basis. However, on a global scale a variety of factors militate against the achievement of sustainable tourism development, not least the way in which tourists themselves consume tourism (Sharpley 2000). Therefore, in the context of tourism planning, it is, perhaps, more realistic to plan for environmentally benign forms of tourism which, nevertheless, optimise the economic benefits to local communities.

Who plans for tourism?

The final issue to be addressed in this chapter is where the responsibility lies for the planning of tourism. More specifically, we have seen that tourism planning is a complex and continuous process that links policy objectives in general with the planning and implementation of tourism development in particular. This implies that, although tourism is primarily a private sector dominated industry and much planning at the site/destinational level will be undertaken by tourism businesses themselves (albeit normally within the parameters of local or national planning regulations and development objectives), there is, nevertheless, an important role that is fulfilled by government in tourism planning. Indeed, as tourism is increasingly viewed as a means of achieving regional economic regeneration or national development, it is inevitable or, indeed, essential, that governments play a role in the tourism planning process. The purpose of this section, therefore, is to consider why and how government should be involved in tourism planning.

The role of government in tourism planning

The role of government in tourism in general is covered in greater detail in Chapter 12. In the specific context of planning, however, government policy has an inevitable impact on tourism, whether intentional or not. For example, economic policies which influence exchange rates or interest rates will impact upon tourism, as does transport policy, taxation policy, employment policy, licensing laws, and so on. Thus, in the UK, the high level of duty on fuel has undoubtedly has undoubtedly had a negative impact on international tourism to the country, whilst the introduction of the minimum wage has also had an impact in what is traditionally a lower-paid industry. At the same time, it could be argued that government should be involved in tourism planning for the simple reason that, financially, the public purse benefits significantly from tourism. Again in the UK, the tourism industry as a whole contributes some £1.5 billion in taxation each year.

There are, however, a number of specific reasons why government should play a leading role in the planning of tourism. In particular, it is government that:

- establishes or defines the policy objectives of tourism development (for example, employment generation, economic growth, social development, inner city regeneration, etc.);

- sets out the types of tourism to be developed – domestic and /or international, mass or niche market, etc.;

- defines broader development objectives and approach – sustainable development versus 'traditional' economic growth;

- determines the extent of tourism development (i.e. a smaller contribution in a mixed economy or the principal sector of the national economy);

- controls the rate of tourism growth and development to:

  - ensure social adjustment to tourism

  - respond to and provide for related infrastructural needs

  - introduce policies for human resource training and development

  - avoid distortion in the national economy

- introduces planning laws and regulations, establishes environmental protection measures (e.g. national park designation), and so on; and

- can influence tourism through its international policies with respect to, for example, bi-lateral air agreements (see Chapter 7) or visa requirements.

Of course, not all governments will be concerned with all of these issues, whilst the extent to which governments involve themselves directly in tourism planning also varies. Much depends upon the prevailing political ideology, the stage of development of the economy as a whole and the tourism sector in particular, the importance of tourism to the economy, and a variety of other factors. However, it has been suggested that, generally, there are two forms of government involvement in tourism (see Jenkins 1991 and Hall 2000 for more detail).

i. Passive involvement

In many countries, in particular in the industrialised, developed nations, the involvement of government in tourism planning can generally be described as passive. That is, beyond setting broad policy objectives for tourism development and, in most cases, establishing a national tourism organisation to market and promote the country as a destination, the government is not directly involved in the planning and management of tourism at the national level. Indeed, according to Jenkins (1991), passive involvement is limited to:

(a) *mandatory activities* – the introduction of legislation relating to all sectors, but which may impact on tourism, such as regulations with respect to investment incentives, the employment of foreign nationals or the minimum wage.

(b) *supportive actions* – these are activities, such as general training programmes, that are *not* aimed at the tourism sector in particular but may nevertheless have some supportive influence.

ii. Active involvement

In less developed countries, government involvement in tourism planning tends to be more active, usually because the private sector lacks the necessary expertise or capital to take the lead in developing tourism. In other words, the government recognises that its active participation is necessary in the planning and development process. This takes the form of:

(a) *managerial activities* – the government not only sets out policies and objectives for tourism, but also establishes the necessary legislative and organisational framework to led the development of tourism. For example, it may set up a tourism development fund to provide incentives or designate tourism development areas.

(b) *developmental activities* – the government adopts an operational role, not only planning but investing in and running services and facilities such as hotels and travel agencies.

In the UK, the government has long adopted a 'hands-off' or passive role in tourism planning. Indeed, successive policies have been designed to further reduce public involvement in and support for tourism, with even the national and regional tourist boards being expected to finance themselves increasingly through commercial activities. However, some intervention in tourism planning at the national level will always be necessary and, given the contribution of tourism to the British economy, it is not surprising that there have long been calls for a more active role in tourism on the part of the government.

Conclusion

Tourism planning is a vital element of the overall tourism development process, yet it is also highly complex. It is vital because it helps to ensure that the development of tourism is directed towards the achievement of regional or national objectives, and that such objectives are not met to the cost of the destination's physical, social and cultural environment. It is complex because it involves all stakeholders at every level or scale in the tourism system. The primary challenge, then, is to ensure that appropriate policies exist, supported by legislative and economic frameworks, to ensure that all those involved in the planning process work towards common aims and objectives.

Discussion questions

1. *Why is it necessary to plan for tourism?*

2. *To what extent do you consider that the economic approach remains the most widespread approach to tourism planning?*

3. *Should all governments take an active role in tourism planning and management?*

Further reading

Gunn, C. (1994), *Tourism Planning: Basics, Concepts, Cases*, London: Taylor and Francis.

Hall, C. M. (2000), *Tourism Planning: Policies, Processes and Relationships*, Harlow: Pearson Education Ltd.

Inskeep, E. (1991), *Tourism Planning: An Integrated and Sustainable Development Approach*, New York: Van Nostrand Reinhold.

Sharpley, R. and Telfer, D. (eds.)(2002), *Tourism and Development: Concepts and Issues*, Clevedon: Channel View Publications.

References

Butler, R. (1993), Tourism: an evolutionary perspective, in J. Nelson, R. Butler and G. Wall (eds.) *Tourism and Sustainable Development: Monitoring, Planning, Managing*, University of Waterloo, Dept. of Geography: 27-43.

Butler, R. (1998), Sustainable tourism – looking backwards in order to progress?, in C. M. Hall and A. Lew (eds.) *Sustainable Tourism: A Geographical Perspective*, Harlow: Longman: 25-34.

Cavaco, C. (1995), Rural tourism: the creation of new tourist spaces, in A. Montanari and A. Williams (eds.) *European Tourism: Regions, Spaces and Restructuring*, Chichester: John Wiley & Sons: 129-149.

Croall, J. (1995) *Preserve or Destroy: Tourism and the Environment*, London: Calouste Gulbenkian Foundation.

Dowling, R. (1992), Tourism and environmental integration: the journey from idealism to realism, in C. Cooper and A. Lockwood (eds.) *Progress in Tourism, Recreation and Hospitality Management, Volume IV*, London: Bellhaven Press: 33-46.

Garrod B. and Fyall, A. (1998), Beyond the rhetoric of sustainable tourism?, *Tourism Management* 19(3): 199-212.

Godfrey, K. (1996), Towards sustainability? Tourism in the Republic of Cyprus, in L. Harrison and W. Husbands (eds.) *Practising Responsible Tourism: International Case Studies in Tourism Planning, Policy and Development*, Chichester: John Wiley & Sons: 58-79.

Gunn, C. (1994), *Tourism Planning: Basics, Concepts, Cases*, London: Taylor and Francis.

Hall, C. M. (2000), *Tourism Planning: Policies, Processes and Relationships*, Harlow: Pearson Education Ltd.

Hoggart, K., Buller, H. and Black, R. (1995), *Rural Europe: Identity and Change*, London: Arnold.

Inskeep, E. (1991), *Tourism Planning: An Integrated and Sustainable Development Approach*, New York: Van Nostrand Reinhold.

Jenkins, C. (1991), Tourism development strategies, in L. Lickorish (ed.) *Developing Tourism Destinations*, Harlow: Longman: 61-77.

Mathieson, A. and Wall, G. (1982), *Tourism: Economic, Physical and Social Impacts*, Harlow: Longman.

Murphy, P. (1985), *Tourism: A Community Approach*, London: Routledge.

OECD (1999), *Development Indicators*, www.oecd.org/dac/Indicators/htm.goals.htm.

Seers, D. (1969), The meaning of development, *International Development Review* 11(4): 2-6.

Sharpley, R. (1999), *Tourism, Tourists and Society, 2nd Edition*, Huntingdon: Elm Publications.

Sharpley, R. (2000), Tourism and sustainable development: exploring the theoretical divide, *Journal of Sustainable Tourism* 8(1): 1-19.

Sharpley, R. (2001), Tourism in Cyprus: challenges and opportunities, *Tourism Geographies* 3(1): 64-86.

Sharpley, R. and Sharpley, J. (1997), *Rural Tourism: An Introduction*, London: International Thomson Business Press.

Sharpley, R. and Telfer, D. (eds.) (2002), *Tourism and Development: Concepts and Issues*, Clevedon: Channel View Publications.

Wood, K. and House, S. (1991), *The Good Tourist: A Worldwide Guide for the Green Traveller*, London: Mandarin.

WTO (1980), Manila Declaration on World Tourism, Madrid: World Tourism Organisation. WTO (1994), National and Regional Tourism Planning: Methodologies and Case Studies London: Routledge.

11

Tourism and the Environment

Graham Mowl

Learning objectives

This chapter introduces the environmental consequences of tourism development and possible strategies for reducing its negative environmental impacts. Having read this chapter you should be able to:

- *appreciate the importance of the physical environment as a resource for tourism development*

- *describe the different positive and negative environmental impacts of tourism*

- *identify the various factors that determine the scale and extent of environmental impacts*

- *describe the different strategies that tourism planners and managers can use to alleviate some of the negative consequences of tourism*

Introduction

> '*The environment is the foundation of the tourist industry.*' (Mathieson and Wall 1982: 97).

From the intrepid trailblazer back-packing through Laos and Cambodia to the sun-loving package tourist basking on the beaches of the Costa del Sol, tourists decisions to visit particular destinations are strongly influenced by their perception of their differing environments. Moreover, how they get there, where they stay, and whatever they do whilst staying there will all have a discernible impact on the physical environment. In short, tourism is what we refer to as an **environmentally dependent industry**. The physical environment is a fundamental part of the tourism product and, as tourists, we seek out different and distinctive environments. However, in doing so, we may threaten the very nature and physical well being of these environments; our actions may even end up destroying the very thing that attracted us in the first place.

As already shown (see Chapters 2 and 3), international tourism has increased rapidly since the 1950s to become one of the world's largest industries. There are over 600 million international arrivals per year and a choice of over 200 foreign destinations. As a result, very few countries in the world do not attract any foreign tourists at all. However, since the heyday of mass international tourism in the 1960s, concern about the environmental consequences of tourism development has grown. During this period, people have become more aware of environmental issues generally as the environmental impacts of rapid economic growth have become increasingly experienced both locally and globally.

Importantly, however, although the deleterious impact of human activity on the physical environment is by no means a new phenomenon, what is new is the scale and severity of this impact. Indeed, there are now very few places on earth which have not been subject to some form of human interference and economic exploitation. At the same time, global news media networks have heightened our awareness of environmental issues and it is perhaps not surprising, therefore, that people are becoming more aware of the impacts that tourism in particular can have upon the physical environment.

Tourism is a form of exploration and, throughout history, explorers have always gone in search of new lands, partly out of curiosity but also out of a desire or necessity to discover new resources for exploitation. The success of the capitalist enterprises which make up the tourism industry is, therefore, partly dependent upon their ability to 'discover' and market new destinations for our consumption. However, although tourism is sometimes described as a 'smokeless industry', as an activity it has several important and unique characteristics (see Figure 11.1 below) which mean that, in many cases, it is far from being environmentally benign. From deforestation in the Nepalese Himalayas to the threatened extinction of loggerhead turtles on the Greek island of Zakynthos, there are now many well documented examples from all over the world of where tourism is a contributor to some form of environmental damage.

Figure 11.1: *Some potentially environmentally threatening characteristics of tourism*

- Unlike the consumption of most manufactured goods, in the case of tourism the customer (tourist) must go to the point of production to consume the product. A defining characteristic of tourism is, therefore, travel and, in the modern age, most travel necessitates the consumption of fossil fuels. Moreover, there is a social cache associated with distant travel whereas the constraints of modern life dictate that such journeys should be completed as quickly as possible. These dual demands for travel over greater distances and speeds further increase the consumption of fossil fuels. Tourism essentially encourages millions of people to travel much greater distances, consuming more fossil fuels, than they would otherwise normally do in their daily lives.

- Tourism tends to be a relatively short-term, transitory experience characterised by a rather escapist philosophy. For most people, tourist activity is restricted to, at most, a 2-week holiday each year. Tourism encourages consumerist behaviour, as there is a tendency for most people to consume proportionately more of certain products and services whilst on holiday than they would normally do at home (e.g. food and drink, clothing, souvenirs, fuel, water, suntan lotion, tobacco). Consequently, tourism is a wasteful industry and encourages the consumption of both renewable and non-renewable resources.

> - Our cultural fascination for and attraction to relatively pristine natural environments (e.g. lakes, mountains, forests, coasts, and islands) necessitates that tourism development often takes place in relatively fragile and previously undisturbed ecosystems.
>
> - Tourism is a complex and multi-faceted industry and so are its associated impacts. Several different industries (e.g. transport, construction, hospitality, services, and entertainment) contribute to the making of the tourism product and each has distinctly different environmental impacts in terms of their nature, location, scale and severity. The environmental impacts of every tourist trip are not, therefore, just limited to one particular location (e.g. the destination area) but can be geographically widespread.

Before discussing the environmental impacts of tourism in some detail, it is worth noting that the study of them is by no means a straightforward task, for a number of reasons:

- It is often difficult to differentiate between the environmental changes attributable directly to tourism and those caused by other human activities.

- The environmental impacts of tourism may not always be immediately obvious as it may be sometime before perceptible changes to land, air, water, flora or fauna become apparent.

- It is necessary to consider the indirect as well as direct effects of tourism development on the environment. Direct effects may be relatively obvious and are usually experienced in and around the tourist destination areas themselves. However, environmental impacts can also occur elsewhere in areas that are either on transit routes to the destination or are linked to them in some way through the supply of goods, labour or services to the tourist industry. For example, tourism development has been a catalyst for rural to urban migration in some developing areas, leading to the abandonment of low-paid agricultural employment in favour of more lucrative work in the tourism industry. The consequent reduced labour input in agricultural areas is likely to precipitate some form of environmental change as agricultural infrastructure is no longer fully maintained.

- Frequently, there is a lack of sufficiently detailed information about what environmental conditions were like in the destination area before tourism development took place (e.g. an inventory of local flora and fauna or measures of seawater quality) and so it is difficult to derive a precise baseline from which comparisons can be made.

It is sometimes easy to place the blame for environmental damage, such as coastal pollution, on the tourism industry, in particular when other factors may have already been contributing to the problem long before any significant tourism development took place. It is also worth considering, as emphasised in the next section, that not all of the environmental changes induced by tourism development are necessarily negative.

Different types of relationship between tourism and the environment

According to Mathieson and Wall (1982), there are three possible relationships between tourism and the physical environment (see also Budowski 1976).

i. Neutrality

This is, perhaps, the rarest and almost certainly the most short-lived condition. Neutrality exists when there is little or no interaction between tourists and the physical environment. Thus, this relationship is only experienced, if at all, in the very early stages of tourism development when there are only small numbers of tourists and no additional facilities provided. However, it is difficult to envisage how even a small number of visitors would not create extra demands for local resources and, thus, disturb the human-environment equilibrium in some way. After only a short time, as the destination becomes more popular, this relationship is likely to be destroyed by the additional environmental pressures created by tourism development. It would be naïve to assume, though, that, prior to the arrival of tourism, all societies coexist in a state of neutrality with the physical environment and that only tourism disturbs this equilibrium.

ii. Opposition or conflict

The most widely commented upon relationship between tourism and the environment (see below), this is where the interests of tourism and the environment are in opposition to each other so that, as tourism develops, natural resources are degraded and eventually destroyed. Many argue that this condition is particularly caused when rapid growth in visitor numbers (e.g. Butler's (1980) development stage) coincides with unplanned, uncontrolled, profit-led forms of tourism development (e.g. Spain's Costas during the 1960s).

iii. Harmony or symbiosis

Symbiosis occurs where there are positive benefits provided by tourism development to the physical environment and vice versa. In this context, tourism is seen as a lesser evil than other forms of development as the revenues from tourism may be ploughed back in to the preservation or protection of fragile ecosystems that may otherwise have been developed or destroyed. As an environmentally dependent industry, it is obviously in tourism's long term interests to protect the environment for the enjoyment of future generations. However, as discussed later in this chapter, this goal may be practically very difficult to achieve in a climate of increasing tourism demand.

Factors influencing the nature and scale of environmental impacts

Before looking at some examples of the negative environmental impacts of tourism, it is first necessary to consider some of the factors that are likely to determine the nature and scale of the environmental impacts. Some of these factors relate to the environment itself, whereas others relate more to the socio-political context in which tourism takes place and the type of tourists attracted to the destination.

According to Burns and Holding (1995), the factors affecting the environmental impacts of tourism include:

- **The scale of tourism development and rate of growth**. Sometimes, tourism development occurs so rapidly that there is not time to develop sufficient infrastructure and sanitation services to cope with the increased demand;

- **The fragility and sensitivity of the environment**. Some ecosystems are more sensitive to environmental changes than others (e.g. coral reefs and wetlands) or take longer to recover from any environmental damage (e.g. mountain environments);

- **The sensitivity of the development in terms of its integration with the local environment and cultur**e. For example, the design of tourist related buildings are not always in keeping with local architectural styles, leading to a form of aesthetic pollution. Also, the building materials used may have been imported from elsewhere, creating further environmental costs in transportation;

- **The political context of development**. In some destination areas there is neither the political infrastructure nor the will necessary to ensure proper development planning and control and, as a result, resorts may be developed in a very piece-meal, 'laissez-faire' fashion;

- **The range of development incentives and the importance attached to tourism by national and regional government**. Development incentives offered by local, national or inter-national government bodies (e.g. EC) might influence both where tourism development occurs and the type of development initiated. Some national governments in the developing world, for example, have offered incentives to encourage inward investment (e.g. by foreign transnational tour operators) in their tourism infrastructure. Their need for foreign exchange earning and capital investment in tourist infrastructure, such as airports and resort complexes, has sometimes taken precedence over a concern for the impacts of such development on the local environment.

- **The cultural attitudes of local people to the environment**. Cultural attitudes to the environment vary from place to place. Some cultures regard certain environments as sacred – for example Ayers Rock (Uluru) is a sacred site for Australian Aborigines – and so are likely to strongly resist certain forms of tourism development in such areas (e.g. airstrips, hotel complexes). In Western Christian societies, the Romantic Movement of the eighteenth century fundamentally changed cultural attitudes towards wild landscapes, such as forests, mountains and moorlands, inspiring the creation of protected areas such as the US National Parks.

- **The type of tourists attracted to the destination and the characteristics of their behaviour**. Some tourists create more environmental damage than others simply because of both their actions and their attitudes towards the environment. The type of accommodation stayed in, the extent and mode of travel to and around the destination, the places visited, the activities engaged in, and what is actually consumed whilst on holiday will all have an influence on the degree of environmental stress created by each individual tourist. Clearly, a cycling holiday around your own country, staying in locally owned bed and breakfast accommodation and eating local organic produce will cause less environmental damage than, for example, flying to Nepal for a trekking holiday involving overnight stays in tourist lodges which consume large quantities of local fuel wood to provide hot water and cooked meals.

- **The availability of information to educate the tourist**. The more information tourists have about the potential environmental consequences of different forms of behaviour, the less likely they are to engage in behaviour that they know to be harmful to the environment. Many tourists are simply not aware of the environmental implications of their actions (e.g. the damage done to coral reefs by trampling on them and breaking off pieces as souvenirs) and, therefore, by improving most tourists' basic environmental awareness, many problems could, in principle, be alleviated.

- **The volume of tourists using the destination**. In some areas, even a few tourists can create a perceptible environmental impact if there are insufficient local resources (e.g. food, water, shelter) and inadequate infrastructure to meet these additional demands. Nevertheless, we tend to assume that more tourists mean more damage. This is only really the case when the carrying capacity of an environment is exceeded, when additional numbers do create additional damage.

- **The physical robustness or fragility of the environment to different types of tourist activity**. Some ecosystems are more sensitive than others to the kind of environmental pressures initiated by the increased presence of tourists. The trampling of plant species in mountain environments, for example, is a particular problem because their relatively cold temperatures, short growing seasons and poor quality soils mean that regeneration of damaged vegetation is a lengthy process.

Tourism and environment in conflict

Academics have tended to approach the study of the environmental impacts of tourism in a number of different ways. For example, Mathieson and Wall (1982) simply divide the physical environment up into its constituent parts (e.g. vegetation, wildlife, air, water, and land) and report on the impacts of tourism on each of these separate elements. Although perhaps the most straightforward, this approach can, however, be a little misleading as it is possible that any one tourism development or activity could impact on all of these elements either simultaneously or sequentially. For instance, the clearance of vegetation for the construction of a ski piste may not only lead to the loss of wildlife habitat but can also expose the soil to increased rates of erosion and, consequentially, alter sediment loads in local rivers and streams because of increased run-off. Ultimately, it may also contribute to increased levels of carbon dioxide in the atmosphere because of deforestation as well as perhaps reducing the overall aesthetic appeal of the area. Therefore, just one form of tourism development impacts upon flora, fauna, land, air and water.

An alternative approach, then, is to study the environment as an integrated, holistic system and, therefore, structure the analysis around different aspects of tourism development. At the same time, it is also necessary to consider the environmental impacts of tourism at different stages in the tourism system. For example, there are impacts created in the generating areas, during transit, at the destination area itself and in other areas linked into the tourism system by the supply of tourist goods and services.

Perhaps the most comprehensive and integrated framework for studying the environmental impacts of tourism was developed by the OECD in the mid 1970s (see Figure 11.2) as part of their tourism and environment programme (Pearce 1989). The framework focuses upon a number of tourism-generated stressor activities (e.g. resort construction, generation of wastes and tourist activities), the nature of the stresses themselves and the primary (environmental) and secondary (human) responses to this environmental stress.

Figure 11.2 *OECD framework for the study of tourism and environmental stress*

Stressor activities	Stress	Primary response (environmental)	Secondary response - reaction (human)
1. *Permanent environmental restructuring* (a) Major construction activity • Urban expansion • Transport network • Tourist facilities • Marinas, ski lifts • Sea walls (b) Change in land use • Expansion of recreational lands	Restructuring of local environments • Expansion of built environments • Land taken out of primary production	Change in habitat Change in population of biological species Change in health and welfare of man Change in **visual** quality	*Individual* - impact on aesthetic values *Collective measures* • Expenditure on environmental improvements • Expenditure on management and conservation • Designation of wildlife conservation and national parks • Controls on access to recreational lands
2. *Generation of waste residuals* • urbanisation • transportation	Pollution loadings • Emissions • Effluent discharges • Solid waste disposal • Noise (traffic, aircraft)	Change in quality of environmental media • Air • Water • Soil Health of biological organisms Health of humans	*Individual defensive measures* Locals • Air conditioning • Recycling of waste materials • Protests and attitude change Tourists • Change in attitude towards the environment • Decline in tourist revenues *Collective defensive measures* • Expenditure on pollution abatement by tourist-related industries • Clean up of rivers, beaches
3. *Tourist activities* • skiing • walking • hunting • trial bike riding • collecting	Trampling of vegetation and soils Destruction of species	Change in habitat Change in population of biological species	*Collective defensive measures* • Expenditure on management and conservation • Designation of wildlife conservation and national parks • Controls on access to recreational lands
4. *Effect on population dynamics.* • Population growth	Population density (seasonal)?	Congestion Demand for natural resources • Land and water • Energy	*Individual* - attitudes to overcrowding and the environment Collective - growth in support services, e.g. water supply, electricity

Source: Pearce (1989) after the OECD

The OECD identify four environmental stresses related to tourism, which are considered below.

Permanent environmental restructuring

The first major source of environmental stress identified by the OECD is described as permanent environmental restructuring. This is caused by major construction activity, such as the building of new resorts and associated infrastructure (e.g. roads, airport terminals and runways, railways). Such development leads to a change in the physical fabric of an area.

The ribbon-style beach resort developments along the most of the Spanish Costas provide a striking example of this transformation. The famous British novelist Laurie Lee, looking back on his visit to the area in the 1930s, described it as 'a beautiful but exhausted shore, seemingly forgotten by the world. I remember the names San Pedro, Estepona, Marbella, and Fucngirola. They were salt-fish villages, thin-ribbed, sea-hating, cursing their place in the sun. At that time one could have bought the whole coast for a shilling. Not Emperors could buy it now.' (Lee 1992: 353-4). Indeed, over a period of just 40 years, the Costa del Sol has been transformed from a relatively barren coastline dotted with poverty-stricken fishing villages into a virtually unbroken strip of high rise hotels, apartments, motorways, marinas and urbanisations stretching nearly 60 kilometres from Malaga in the east to Estapona in the west (Barke *et al.* 1996).

The planned coastal resorts of the Languedoc-Roussillon development on France's western Mediterranean coastline are another extreme example of this form of permanent environmental restructuring. Resorts in this area were planned on a grand scale, with ribbon-style coastal developments like those found in Spain and on the neighbouring French Riviera deliberately avoided. Despite this, the development did involve the wholesale drainage and 'reclamation' of large areas of wetland, including coastal marshes and saltwater lagoons leading to a loss of habitat for many wetland species of flora and fauna (Pearce 1987).

As well as wetlands, coral reefs are another coastal ecosystem that has come under threat because of the construction of coastal tourism resorts. Coral reefs are thought to be home to 25 percent of all known marine species and constitute the second most biologically diverse ecosystem on earth. They are, however, very sensitive to environmental change and require specific water quality conditions to survive, hence their limited geographical distribution. For healthy growth, the coral requires fairly constant sea temperatures of between 25 and 29 degrees Celsius, a shallow platform less than 100 metres below sea level and clear, highly oxygenated water that is free from sediment and pollution. Although coral reefs have become a tourist attraction in their own right, such as the Great Barrier Reef, tourism development and the activities of some tourists threaten them.

The construction phase of tourism development – digging of hotel foundations, clearance of vegetation, road construction, and so on – often leads to increased sediment loads in the coastal waters surrounding the development. The consequent clouding-up of coastal waters can starve coral of essential sunlight and, effectively, choke the reef to death. The dumping of inadequately treated sewage into coastal waters from resorts can also effect the vitality of coral reefs by increasing salinity and reducing dissolved oxygen levels. Additionally, of course, tourists themselves contribute directly to coral damage by both walking on reefs and plundering them for souvenirs. The extensive reef systems off Egypt's Red Sea coast attract thousands of divers to resorts such as Sharm el Sheik and Naama Bay but, according to

Goudie and Viles (1997), 73 percent of coral reefs off the coast of Egypt have been adversely affected by tourism.

Another obvious consequence of the permanent environmental restructuring that accompanies most tourism development is a change in land use patterns, usually with predominantly urban land use replacing predominantly rural. This transition is often quite rapid and not only leads to a change in wildlife habitats but also a change in the livelihoods of the local human population, with employment opportunities in the construction and hospitality sectors replacing those in traditional primary industries such are agriculture and fishing. In southern Andalucia (i.e. the Costa del Sol), where agriculture tended to be dominated by a relatively small number of large landowners (*latifundia*) and the majority of the generally poor local population either relied on migrant work elsewhere on seasonal employment as landless day-labourers (*braceros*), such a transition has been mostly welcomed and the environmental changes accepted (Barke *et al.*1996).

Elsewhere, though, where tourism development has been externally imposed on an indigenous population without their support and has involved the enforced confiscation of their land and the diversion of water resources to the tourism industry (e.g. Goa, India), such changes have not been universally welcomed and local farmers and environmentalists have formed protest groups to resist these forms of development (Lea 1993).

The construction of coastal resorts is not the only form of tourism development to cause permanent environmental restructuring. Mountain areas are the second most popular location for tourism yet these areas are particularly sensitive to environmental change because their cold temperatures, short growing seasons and poor quality soils mean that regeneration of damaged vegetation is a lengthy process (Holden 2000). According to the World Tourism Organisation figures, winter sports are estimated to account for about 4 percent of all international tourist arrivals and the construction of ski resorts to satisfy this demand can lead to considerable and irrevocable environmental change. In addition to the visual impacts associated with the construction of an urban environment within an often remote mountain setting, the creation of ski runs, depending on altitude, usually necessitates deforestation resulting in a loss of wildlife habitat. The removal of vegetation is also likely to increase surface run-off and may precipitate hydrological changes together with gullying and even landslides. There is also evidence of an increased incidence of avalanches and mudslides due to the removal of trees and other vegetation for ski resort development (Simmons 1988).

The generation of wastes and pollution

The second major source of environmental stress created by tourism development is the generation of new or increased waste materials and, consequently, the pollution of air, land and water resources. The pollution of air and water resources resulting from wastes generated by tourism is a problem on a global as well as a local scale.

The transportation of tourists is, not surprisingly, a major source of air and noise pollution. Air and car transport contributes significantly to both local and global atmospheric pollution. According to the United Nations Environment Programme (UNEP), it is estimated that approximately 2 million tons of aviation fuels are burned each year, producing 550 million tons of greenhouse gases and 3.5 million tons of chemicals responsible for acid rain (WTO 1997). It is also estimated that, in the US, aircraft contribute 10 percent to CO^2 emissions and that globally airlines account for 2-3 percent of CO^2 and NO^2 emissions (Burns 2000; Pearce 1989).

Cars are, however, the main mode of tourist transportation and by far the biggest contributor to atmospheric pollution. According to Cooper *et al* (1998), within Europe alone – by far the biggest tourist generating area (see Chapter 3) – the car accounts for 83 percent of tourist passenger miles. Air pollution is no respecter of national boundaries and the knock-on effects of atmospheric pollution, such as acid rain, may well in turn contribute to the degradation of tourism resources, such as ancient monuments and coniferous forests. In addition, the increased local air pollution levels experienced in both major transit and destination areas at peak times can have an adverse effect on the health of the local population. There are clearly considerable secondary human costs of increased air pollution in terms of paying for the amelioration of the local effects (e.g. repairing damaged stonework, treating asthma sufferers, installing air conditioning). Globally of course, the consumption of fossil fuels by tourist related transport is also a major contributor to the creation of greenhouse gases and possible future global warming.

However, these negative aspects of tourism must be put within some sort of perspective. It is worth pointing out that sustaining other aspects of our everyday western lifestyles, such as travelling to work, school, and the shops, the production of consumer goods and the supply of domestic gas and electricity, contributes far more to the consumption of fossil fuels and air pollution loads.

As well as contributing to air pollution, tourism development is also a major polluter of the world's water resources. Throughout its history, tourism development has been drawn to water resources of one kind or another. As described in Chapter 2, from the seventeenth century onwards, the European aristocracy's belief in the curative properties of sea bathing and spa waters greatly influenced the pattern of tourism development (Towner 1998). The Romantic poets, painters and writers of the late eighteenth and early nineteenth centuries also helped fashion a taste for lonely lake shores, meandering rivers and dramatic coastal scenery amongst the social élite (Andrews 1989). Even in the contemporary period, tourism's umbilical link with water has continued with the western fashion for sun, sea and sand holidays and the popularity of water sports.

Often, however, resorts have developed without the prior construction of adequate sewage facilities and so our seas, lakes and rivers have acted as cheap and convenient depositories for untreated effluent. While tourism is by no means the only contributor to marine and fresh water pollution, its role has been significant in many parts of the world. Coastal pollution through the inadequate disposal of human sewage not only threatens marine life (see the section on coral reefs above), but can also have a negative effect on human health, possibly causing anything from a mild stomach upset to typhoid through either bathing in infected waters or eating contaminated seafood. In addition, the effects of water pollution can be off-putting for visitors because it is both unsightly and smells unpleasant. In recent years, many European resorts have been encouraged to clean up their coastal waters under the European Blue Flag initiative and, as a result the quality of bathing water and the cleanliness of beaches in many resorts has improved significantly. Thus, at the launch of the campaign in 1987, only 244 beaches in Europe satisfied the Blue Flag's water quality standards; by 2001, however, they had granted the award to 2041 beaches in 21 different countries (see Table 11:1). Nevertheless, despite these measures, in the Mediterranean basin only 30 percent of over 700 towns and cities on the coastline treat their sewage before discharging it into the sea (Holden 2000). Moreover, such voluntary regulations are only applicable inside Europe and the costs of improving coastal sewage infrastructures may be prohibitive for many resorts in developing nations.

Table 11.1: *Numbers of awarded Blue Flag beaches and marinas in 2001 in the different European countries*

Country	Beaches	Marinas
Belgium	7	4
Bulgaria	9	0
Croatia	16	14
Cyprus	34	0
Denmark	188	79
Estonia	2	3
Finland	6	30
France	403	85
Germany	33	204
Greece	351	8
Ireland	75	4
Italy	154	40
Latvia	3	0
Netherlands	18	30
Norway	1	6
Portugal	133	7
Slovenia	4	3
Spain	390	85
Sweden	60	74
Turkey	99	11
United Kingdom	55	26
Total	2041	713

Source: Foundation for Environmental Education, Blue Flag Campaign, 2001

As well as contributing to the disposal of untreated sewage, tourism is also partly responsible for the water pollution caused by the fertilisers and herbicides that are used extensively in the maintenance of golf courses and hotel gardens.

Tourism is generally a rather profligate activity; we consume more and we waste more when on holiday. Consequently, the industry produces large quantities of solid wastes. Improper disposal of solid wastes generates litter and resort areas can start to look and smell unpleasant with rubbish attracting vermin and possibly affecting human health. Disposal techniques include landfill and incineration, but these are not without their own environmental impacts potentially leading to the contamination of land, water and air. Not all of the solid waste produced by the tourism industry is biodegradable either and, in some locations, disposal opportunities are more limited than others. There have even been reports from the Masai Mara game park in Kenya of elephants being poisoned by eating zinc batteries that had been left on a tip outside one of the tourist lodges (Holden 2000).

One only has to think of the hundreds of different holiday brochures lining the walls of your local travel agent, and how these are replaced and discarded at least once every year, to realise that the tourism industry is an inherently wasteful one. Nevertheless, it is clearly not in the industry's best interests to foul-up resorts with untreated effluent pumped into the seas and piles of uncollected garbage left around the hotels. Somewhat ironically, although most tourists are very wasteful, they also like to visit clean, pristine environments and other people's dirt puts them off, as does the potential threat of communicable illnesses spoiling their holiday. The impact on human populations of the generation of wastes by the tourism industry is not just about the impact on human health, but also the escalating financial costs involved in pollution abatement measures and in cleaning-up already polluted environments in order to maintain their attractiveness.

Whose responsibility it should be for meeting the costs of cleaning up after the tourists is, however, a matter for speculation. In many resort areas, the local population bears the greatest burden of these costs through the local taxes they pay for public services, yet we might ask ourselves why the polluter (the tourist) doesn't pay more towards the costs of 'cleaning-up'.

Tourist activities

The third source of environmental stress and, perhaps, the one that is most widely documented is that which results directly from the recreational activities of tourists themselves. Mention has already been made about how the souvenir collecting antics of some tourists can threaten the vitality of coral reef ecosystems, but there are many other ways in which the activities of tourists can disturb, damage and even destroy sensitive flora and fauna.

Some forms of tourism, such as safari tourism, are explicitly designed to bring tourists into close contact with wild nature. In some of the more popular game parks, such as the Masai Mara in Kenya, the breeding and eating habits of some wild animals, including the rare black rhino, cheetahs and lions, have been disrupted by the intrusive activities of tourist buses. There are reported instances of up to 40 minibuses at a time around a single animal (Mathieson and Wall 1982; Shackley 1996). Through close contact with some animal populations, particularly fellow primates such as gorillas, tourists can also inadvertently spread human ailments, such as colds, flu, pneumonia and measles. For other species with no source of protection, these illnesses can often be fatal (Ryan 1989).

Other forms of tourism also impact directly upon wildlife. Ryan (1991) describes how, on the Greek island of Zakynthos, the breeding habits of loggerhead turtles were severely disrupted by tourism development until the Greek authorities took action to protect this endangered species. The turtles lay their eggs on what have now become popular tourist beaches. If the eggs manage to survive the beach activities of the tourists then it is when they hatch that the young turtles are in most danger. The lights and noise from the tourist resorts can disorientate the turtles and, instead of heading for the sea by the light of the moon, they can head straight for the headlights of motor vehicles or the bright lights and noise of the local taverna or disco! Failing to reach the sea, many young turtles were dying on the roads or of dehydration. However, the introduction of building restrictions and strict controls on the use of the beaches at certain times have helped protect the turtle population (Williams 1998).

Other seemingly innocuous activities, such as walking and trekking, also pose a considerable environmental threat in some areas. The trampling of vegetation and compaction of soils along popular recreational paths and trails has attracted a considerable amount of research (e.g. Liddle 1975). In mountain environments, where the vegetation recovery process tends to be very slow, trampling by walkers can reduce vegetation cover and species diversity with more resilient species becoming dominant around heavily used areas (see Figure 11.3). The widening and erosion of heavily used footpaths in several of the National Park areas in England and Wales has resulted in costly repairs and maintenance for the park authorities, with duckboards and gravel having to be used along parts of the Pennine Way to prevent further environmental damage.

Figure 11.3: *Effects of trampling at tourism sites*

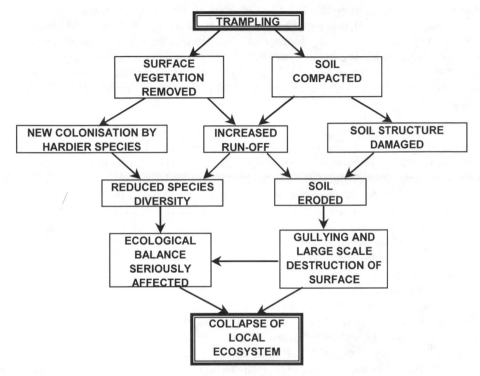

Source: Williams (1998)

The impacts of trekking in the Nepalese Himalayas have also attracted a considerable amount of academic attention (Holden 2000; Nepal 2000). The Nepalese Himalayas now attract well over 100,000 trekkers a year (Nepal 2000) and, in the Sagarmatha National Park and Annapurna Conservation Area in particular, the relatively high numbers of visitors have created a number of environmental problems. The littering of tracks in remote mountain locations with garbage has become a particular problem – Nepal (2000) estimates that an average trekking group of 15 generates 15kg of non-biodegradable, non-burnable garbage in just ten days. The other major issue, though, has been the accelerated deforestation of some hillsides in order to supply fuel wood to the numerous trekking lodges that offer tourists hot showers, cooked meals and a welcoming real fire. Deforestation has exposed some hillsides to soil erosion and gullying.

In other parts of the world, forest fires sometimes caused by the careless activities of tourists, such as not properly extinguishing campfires, barbecues or cigarette butts, have also damaged areas. Thus, some tourist activities are not only clearly a threat to the physical environment in some areas, but there is also a considerable financial cost involved in repairing damaged environments and in setting up appropriate controls on access and on certain activities. Resource management techniques that are commonly employed to protect the environment are introduce later in this chapter. However, the final area of tourist related environmental stress identified by the OECD is that associated with population dynamics, in particular population growth as a result of tourism development.

Effect on population dynamics

The seasonal increases in population densities experienced by most resort areas create a number of environmental impacts. The most obvious of these is the physical congestion and over-crowding experienced at key tourist sites, such as beaches, ski-slopes, and historic town centres, during peak periods of demand (Pearce 1989). In some popular resorts, the population density during the peak season may be as much as twenty times higher than that experienced during the low season. In Torremolinos on the Costa del Sol, for example, the official population of 33,055 swells to over 200,000 in the summer months (SUR in English, September 6th-12th, 1996).

Congestion is not only unpleasant for the tourists. It can also inconvenience members of the local population not directly involved in tourism who are delayed by traffic jams and have to compete with tourists for access to local services such as shops, banks, and restaurants. Tourists and locals also compete for relatively scarce natural resources, such as land and water, with the behaviour of many tourists sometimes exacerbating the situation. Whilst on holiday, most western tourists on average consume a much greater quantity of water than they would normally do at home. For many package tourists, it has also become an essential part of the holiday experience to stay in relatively luxurious hotels. Operational standards in these establishments help perpetuate an expectation on the part of the tourist that sheets and towels will be laundered daily. Also, the daily activities of the average sun, sea and sand seeker encourage the excessive use of water in the form of regular showers and baths to remove the bodily accumulations of sand, salt water and sun tan lotion acquired from an average day on the beach. The hospitality industry, therefore, consumes copious amounts of water when compared to both other industries, such as agriculture, and to local residents. It has been calculated, for example, that 100 luxury hotel guests would consume as much water in 55 days as 100 urban families consume in two years and 100 rural farmers in three years (Salem 1994). In areas where water resources are scarce anyway due to climatic conditions, excessive water usage by tourists can be a particular problem. Not surprisingly, many Mediterranean sun, sea, and sand destinations fall into this category (see Figure 11.4).

Another consequence of increased population densities as a result of tourism is the stress placed on inadequate local transport infrastructures, together with increased levels of local pollution levels due to the number of idling engines in slow moving traffic.

Figure 11.4: *Tourism and water resources on the Costa del Sol*

Cost of water protest in Marbella *Sur in English,* September 23rd-29th 1994	**Further drop in Costa reservoir water level** *Sur in English,* October 28th-Nov. 3rd,1994
Andalucian government seeks urgent measures to alleviate prolonged drought. *Sur in English,* September 23rd-29th 1994	**Water cuts inevitable until it rains: Marbella has no water between midnight and six in the morning** *Sur in English,* Dec 9th-15th 1994.

The Costa del Sol is located on the southern coast of Spain and, as the local newspaper headlines above suggest, it is an area that regularly experiences long periods of drought. (e.g. 1994-5). Many of the rivers in this area are dry from one year to the next and are seasonally used as convenient transport routes by the local population. In the height of summer, one is more likely to see cars and motorbikes running up and down the river beds than water!

Irrigated agriculture (e.g. citrus fruit, vegetables and salad crops), supplying food to the local tourist industry as well as for export to the rest of Europe, competes with the tourism hospitality sector for water resources. In addition, the Costa del Sol also has one of the highest spatial concentrations of golf courses in Southern Europe with over 30 courses located along a 125km stretch of coast (Priestley 1995). The use of extensive sprinkler systems to keep the hundreds of greens and fairways in lush, verdant condition for the thousands of golf tourists requires the use of considerable water resources. According to the US National Golf Foundation, maintaining the turf grass on one golf course requires between 500,000 and 800,000 gallons of water per day.

In recent drought years, the situation has reached crisis point with water having to be rationed for a few hours a day for the local population in resorts like Torremolinos and Marbella whilst supplies to the hotels were unaffected. Considerable amounts of local taxpayers money has had to be invested in the construction of expensive sea water desalinisation plants in order to cope with the fresh water shortfall.

Tourism and the environment in harmony

So far, we have only examined the negative environmental impacts created by some forms of tourism development. However, tourism is by no means the main cause of environmental damage around the world. Other industries, such as mining, logging, petrol-chemicals and even agriculture, pose a much more significant threat to the physical environment. Moreover, in some circumstances, tourism development can actually be the driving force behind schemes to protect environmentally sensitive areas and prevent other potentially more damaging forms of development taking place. Without tourism, for example, it is unlikely that protected areas such as the national parks in both the US and the UK would have ever been established. In many areas, tourism provides an economic rationale for the maintenance of a healthy and attractive physical environment. In general, when tourism impacts upon the health of the physical environment then it threatens to impact upon its own health and future well being as tourists are not normally attracted to degraded, congested, dirty and polluted environments. Therefore, it is in the long-term interests of the tourism industry, unlike some other industries, to sustain the quality of the environment for future generations of tourists.

Mathieson and Wall (1982) identified four different ways in which tourism makes a positive contribution to the conservation of the physical environment:

i. Rehabilitation and restoration

Tourism provides the economic rationale for the rehabilitation and restoration of historic sites, buildings and monuments. The funds generated by tourist admission fees are now often used to refurbish and restore historic houses, castles, and other heritage attractions.

ii. Transformation

Tourism has been responsible for the transformation of old redundant sites into completely new tourist facilities and attractions. This has been particularly the case with industrial heritage attractions in the UK, where run-down dockside and canal areas have been transformed by urban development corporations into vibrant riverside areas with smart shops, restaurants, cafes and bars (e.g. the Quayside area in Newcastle upon Tyne, the Albert Dock in Liverpool, and Salford Quays near Manchester). Mothballed coal mines have also been transformed into heritage attractions with cafes, shops and interactive sight and sound museums, such as the Woodhorn colliery near Ashington, Northumberland. These new attractions also have the effect of relieving congestion at other popular attractions.

iii. Conservation

Tourism provides the incentive for the conservation of natural resources. As noted above, tourism and recreation have usually provided the main rationale for the establishment of protected areas such as national parks and nature reserves. Indeed, many would argue that there is little point in preserving unique and spectacular environments unless people are able to see them and that it is the demand created by tourists that gives the environment value and creates the need for protection. It is also recognised that, if it was not for the establishment of national parks in East Africa to protect one of the world's largest wildlife populations, then some of the greatest wild species on earth such as lions, leopards, giraffes, zebras and elephants could have been threatened with extinction through poaching and over-hunting. It is tourism, though, in the form of safari tours, that has provided the main justification for wildlife preservation by creating a valuable source of foreign exchange, income and employment in developing countries such as Tanzania and Kenya.

iv. Planning and administration

Finally, tourism has often been the impetus for the introduction of planning and administration controls in some areas in order to restore and maintain environmental quality and to ensure the provision of satisfying experiences for visitors. Such planning initiatives, although more often than not introduced in response to resource damage, have also produced other benefits for the local community in terms of the wider adoption of environmental planning and development control. In addition, some authors have argued that tourism itself has been instrumental in promoting environmental awareness and the broader appreciation of conservation issues.

Figure 11.5 below provides a summary of the positive and negative environmental consequences of tourism development. Having discussed these negative and positive impacts in some detail, we can conclude that the environmental costs associated with tourism development are by no means inevitable. In fact, in many areas tourism offers a much more environmentally friendly alternative to other forms of economic development and it is in the best long-term interests of tourism to preserve environmental quality. However, in order for the positive environmental benefits of tourism to be realised, development needs to be carefully planned and controlled, with the local population both involved in development decisions and sharing fully in the sustained financial rewards that can accrue from sustainable tourism development (but, see Chapter 10).

Figure 11.5: *Balance sheet of the environmental impacts of tourism*

Area of effect	Negative Impacts	Positive Impacts
Biodiversity	• Disruption of breeding/feeding patterns • Killing of animals for leisure (hunting) or for souvenirs • Loss of habitats and change in species composition • Damage/destruction of vegetation	• Encouragement to preserve flora and fauna as attractions • Establishment of protected or conserved areas primarily to meet tourist demands
Erosion and Physical damage	• Soil erosion • Damage to sites through trampling • Overloading of key infrastructure (e.g. water, sewage, transport)	• Tourism revenue used to finance ground repair and site restoration • Improvement to infrastructure prompted by tourist demand
Pollution	• Water pollution through sewage disposal, fuel spillage, construction activity and rubbish discarded by tourists • Air pollution (e.g. vehicle emissions) • Noise pollution (e.g. construction work, traffic, bars and discos etc) • Disposal of solid waste materials (e.g. landfill) • Littering	• Cleaning programmes to protect the attractiveness of environment to tourists (e.g. European Blue Flag initiative)
Resource Base	• Depletion of ground and surface water • Diversion of water supply to meet tourist needs (e.g. golf courses, pools, hot showers etc) • Depletion of local fuel sources (e.g. firewood • Depletion of local building-material sources	• Development of new/improved sources of supply
Visual/structural change	• Land transfers to tourism (e.g. from agriculture) • Detrimental visual impact on natural and non-natural landscapes through tourism development • Introduction of new architectural styles • Changes in (urban) functions • Physical expansion of built-up areas	• New uses for marginal or unproductive lands (e.g. beaches, moors and mountains) • Landscape improvement (e.g. to clear urban dereliction) • Regeneration and/or modernisation of built environment • Reuse of disused buildings (e.g. conversion of derelict coal mines into heritage attractions)

Source: Adapted from Hunter and Green (1995); Williams (1998)

The next section considers some of the management and planning techniques that are employed to control the environmental impacts of tourism. However, if tourism development occurs without detailed planning and is dominated by the interests of external agents, such as foreign tour operators, whose primary motivation is providing short-term profit for their share-holders and hedonistic pleasure for their customers, then this harmonious relationship between tourism and the environment is likely to be threatened as the human and physical resources of the destination area are rapidly exploited and degraded.

Resource management techniques for controlling the environmental impacts of tourism

The now well-documented environmental costs associated with some forms of tourism development have led to the increased application of planning and resource management strategies in many destinations in an attempt to avoid the same problems and to, instead, generate potential environmental benefits from tourism development.

These different planning and resource management strategies can be divided into five distinctive but complimentary approaches:

- Spatial planning strategies

- Alternative development strategies

- Education and marketing techniques

- Access control measures

- Site management techniques.

Spatial planning strategies

Essentially, these are measures designed to encourage tourism development in alternative locations and relieve pressure on sensitive or already degraded sites. A number of different spatial planning techniques have been used, including the strategy of concentrating tourist numbers at specially designed 'hardened' sites, sometimes referred to as 'honey-pot' sites. In several national park areas this is achieved by providing free car parking facilities in certain areas, perhaps accompanied by information and interpretation boards as well as other facilities such as picnic tables, public toilets and even cafes. Visitors may also be encouraged to stay near to the site by promoting well-marked trails. Access to other areas may be physically restricted or simply not encouraged through lack of parking, limited access roads or absence of marked trails.

In contrast, an alternative spatial planning strategy is to disperse rather than to concentrate visitors. The aim of this policy is to spread any potential benefits to a wider area and to dilute visitor numbers at the most popular sites to ensure that carrying capacities are not exceeded. Dispersal may be achieved by creating new attractions or alternative resorts elsewhere, or by directing visitor traffic to alternative areas by the use of sign posting and marketing. The consequences of such an approach, however, may be to attract a greater number of visitors to the area rather than to help disperse the existing numbers more evenly around the area. Thus, the unintended net outcome may be increased environmental pressures over a larger area. It is, therefore, believed that dispersal techniques are only effective in low-use places, such as in some of the larger, less accessible US wilderness areas, whereas concentrating visitors and their impacts is most effective in popular locations (Cole 2000).

Zoning is one of the most popular town and country planning strategies and involves identifying certain areas of land where some land uses are considered desirable (e.g. residential, industrial, commercial, recreational, agricultural) and are, therefore, encouraged whilst other less suitable land uses will be restricted through planning legislation and control. This approach is designed to minimise the potential for land use conflicts. For example, busy tourist developments do not always make the most suitable neighbours for quiet residential areas and a coal-fuelled power station is unlikely to be chosen as the ideal view from the window of a luxury hotel complex. In countries with strong planning legislation and procedures, zoning can be used effectively to improve the visitor experience and to minimise conflicts between host and guests. However, there is a danger that the over-zealous use of land use zoning can produce physically isolated modern resorts devoid of local character and interest.

Zoning may also be used on a micro scale in order to avoid user conflicts between different types of recreational activities. For example, zoning strategies are commonly used in the management of water resources – all over the world, popular beach and lakeside resorts tend to allocate separate areas of the water for jet skis, powerboats, windsurfs, sailing dinghies and bathers in order to avoid accidents and user conflicts.

Alternative development strategies

There are a number of alternative development strategies that can be implemented in order to manage the environmental impacts of tourism. Firstly, alternative types of tourism development such as 'soft' and 'green' tourism can be encouraged. Soft tourism attempts to restrict development to more environmentally tolerable levels and tourist activity is, therefore, restricted to existing developments. The only growth that is encouraged is that which complements other major economic activities, such as agriculture, rather than supplanting or threatening them. Activities such as farm tourism are, therefore, encouraged and small-scale accommodation provision, such as family-run bed and breakfasts or campsites, may be favoured rather than large scale hotel developments.

Green tourism has, unfortunately, become a rather meaningless term as it is often wrongly used to describe many different types of tourism activity, not all of which are necessarily designed to minimise environmental impacts and to foster environmentally friendly behaviour. Some tour operators, for example, have tended to jump on the green bandwagon, promoting an array of eco-tourism products as 'green' simply because they bring the participant into close (and therefore potentially very damaging) contact with wild nature. However, there is an attempt to encourage forms of tourism development that do potentially make a more positive contribution towards the environment. For example, holidays are available that combine more environmentally friendly forms of transportation, such as railways and cycling, with accommodation provision on organic farms. Less extreme, perhaps, were the efforts made by the UK Government's then Rural Development Commission (now part of the Countryside Agency) to encourage the English hospitality industry to adopt more environmentally friendly forms of consumption. The Commission produced a 'do-it-yourself guide to greening the tourism business' in which they encourage enterprises to look carefully at their purchasing policies, energy consumption and waste generation, suggesting action that they can take, such as recycling, reusing or reducing, in order to be more environmentally responsible (Rural Development Commission 1996).

A third type of alternative development strategy is to create new resources and attractions nearer to existing centres of population in order to increase capacity, reduce motor vehicle travel and reduce overcrowding at more environmentally sensitive sites. The creation of urban forests, city farms, and water parks, together with improved recreational provision along regenerated riversides and canal areas in and around many British cities, are a good example of this approach.

Education and marketing techniques

There are a number of measures, collectively described as education and marketing, that are designed to influence the attitudes and behaviour of both visitors and/or staff employed in the tourism industry.

One strategy that can be employed to reduce the environmental impacts of tourism is to educate industry staff more thoroughly in environmental conservation issues. This may involve appraising staff of the ways in which they can reduce energy consumption and produce less waste during their day-to-day working activities. In the US, a number of environmental educational schemes (e.g. 'Soft Paths' and 'Leave-No-Trace') have been developed by the National Park Service and other organisations in order to educate key workers, such as park rangers, and visitors in low-impact behaviour within wilderness areas (Cole 2000). In a similar way, some package tour operators are trying to improve the local environmental awareness of their resort representatives so that they can positively influence their customers' behaviour by, for example, warning visitors of the environmental threat posed by collecting souvenirs from coral reefs.

Visitor behaviour can also be influenced by the provision of multi-lingual information and interpretation boards located strategically around environmentally sensitive sites explaining the environmental threats posed by certain forms of behaviour. This approach has been adopted in an effort to protect the fragile dune systems along France's popular Vendéen coastline.

It is well known that marketing has a powerful influence on tourist behaviour patterns and this is particularly the case when tourists have limited access to other information about a destination area. Therefore, some local authorities may heavily promote less sensitive environments and less environmentally damaging activities whilst restricting the availability of information about those sites which they consider are under threat. In many cases, strategic marketing techniques are used as a complimentary measure to other educational techniques.

Access control measures

The fourth method of minimising the degradation of popular but sensitive tourist environments is to introduce any one of a number of access control measures. These tend to be the most controversial of the resource management techniques as they tend to be exclusionary, restricting resource access perhaps to only a limited number of individuals and sometimes coupled with both temporal and spatial restrictions.

Some destination areas protect their environmental assets by maintaining exclusivity by effectively pricing themselves out of the mass market. Only the very rich can afford to visit these areas and so visitor numbers are restricted and carrying capacities are never exceeded. The small Himalayan kingdom of Bhutan, for example, has one of the most exclusive tourism development policies in the world. Since the 1980s, it has restricted its visitor numbers to fewer than 3,000 a year by only granting access visas to those who have purchased their exclusive package tours.

Alternatively, some heavily used areas may restrict visitor numbers by introducing quotas and permits. Spain's number one tourist attraction, the Alhambra Palace in Granada, sells time-allocated tickets to visitors each day on a first-come, first-served basis. Only a certain number of visitors are given access to certain parts of the palace complex at any one time and once the capacity has been reached, no more tickets are sold. In a similar way, in order to visit the Upper Mustang region in northern Nepal, tourists are obliged to obtain a permit and, although these only cost a fairly modest sum, only 1000 permits are issued each year to tourists belonging to an agency-handled tour group. In an attempt to reduce the pressures on local supplies of fuel wood and to prevent further deforestation, the Nepalese government also insists that trekking groups take with them their own supplies of kerosene (Nepal 2000).

Access to protected areas may also be controlled by only permitting entry at a limited number of entry points, whilst physically controlling vehicular access to the park area can also be used to restrict visitor numbers. Gating all access points to the park area and only permitting vehicular access to residents is one example of this form of access control. Alternatively, placing physical limitations on car parking availability within and around the park area can also be an effective measure for controlling numbers. Some of these schemes have been implemented in Britain's national park areas. In the Peak District, for example, the capacity of the main Dove Dale car park was reduced in an attempt to reduce the flow of walkers through the popular but sensitive limestone gorge (Ryan 1991).

Some more remote areas can control access by choosing to remain physically inaccessible to all but the most intrepid visitors. Not developing transport infrastructure, such as road, rail, air and sea links, can be perhaps the most effective means of controlling visitor numbers.

Site management techniques

Finally, there is a range of local site management techniques that can be implemented to protect sensitive areas and to allow the regeneration of already damaged sites.

The creation of sign-posted walks, together with the provision of information points along the route, can be used to encourage visitors to use paths which have been designed to sustain high pedestrian flows and discourage them from using more fragile areas. In addition, a number of 'site-hardening' measures can be implemented to protect vegetation and reduce soil compaction and erosion around heavily used sites. Several different techniques have been used to prevent path erosion and widening due to excessive trampling. In the Peak District, paths have been re-laid using synthetic materials, such as nylon netting, as a permeable base but then overlain by natural local materials such as gravel produced from gritstone and basalt (Ryan 1991). These paths produce a much more hard-wearing surface than the underlying peat, which was subject to severe erosion in heavily used areas. In a similar way, footpaths through the sand dunes along the French Vendéen coast have been replaced with boardwalks to protect the grasses and maintain dune stability.

Where possible, site-hardening techniques try to make use of local materials and maintain the natural appearance and aesthetic appeal of the area under threat.

Table 11.2 below, compiled by the WTO, provides a summary of some the resource management strategies discussed in this chapter.

Table 11.2: *Planning and management strategies for alleviating tourism impacts*

Policy/planning	• Development plans which include tourism and which set out zones or sites for tourist use, determine rights of access to areas, and consider what sort of activities are suitable for the area.
	• Develop and enforce regulations to control aspects of development and tourist activity.
	• Require environmental impact assessments and monitoring for tourist developments.
	• Use economic mechanisms such as subsidies to encourage more sustainable practices and 'user pays' to control use and provide income for conservation and rehabilitation of the environment.
Development/ Construction of Facilities	• Consider choice of sites and site design carefully to ensure minimal impact.
	• Use minimal impact construction techniques.
	• Use native species for landscaping and appropriate architectural styles.
Management of Resources	• Conduct environmental audits.
	• Develop and use recycling, waste minimisation and energy efficiency programs.
	• Use environmentally friendly products and technologies.
Management of Visitors	• Design systems which control visitor flows.
	• Use interpretation/education to encourage sustainable behaviour.
Adapting the Environment	• Harden sites for protection
	• Provide facilities which influence visitor activities.
Marketing and Promotion	• Consider tourism concepts and products better suited to the environment.
	• Provide accurate information in advertising to ensure that visitors have appropriate expectations.
Education	• Use effective interpretation services to encourage visitors to engage in more sustainable behaviours.
	• Provide environmental education for tourism personnel.
	• Develop codes of conduct for tourist, staff, operators and other tourism sectors.
Research and Monitoring	• Support research which seeks to improve understanding of the tourism-environment relationship.
	• Evaluate the effectiveness of any programs and activities conducted.
	• Monitor environmental quality.

Source: World Tourism Organisation (1997)

Conclusions

Although virtually any form of tourism activity will have some impact on the physical environment, these impacts are not necessarily always negative. In fact, we have argued here that it is in the tourism industries long term interests to try and engender a symbiotic relationship with the physical environment as this is a key, but potentially fragile, resource for the future sustainability of the industry. Achieving this kind of relationship is not, however, always possible and development of any kind always leads to some form of environmental change. It is necessary, therefore, to think in terms of the limits of acceptable change and to introduce planning and management measures, such as those discussed above, that are designed to reduce the environmental impacts of tourism to acceptable levels. For this to be possible, however, there needs to be the necessary political will and planning infrastructure which enables local populations, as well as representatives from the tourism industry, to be involved in the tourism planning and development process as stake holders.

Discussion questions

1. *What types of tourism activity do you think are the most damaging to the physical environment, and why?*

2. *Make a list of all the products you usually consume whilst on holiday (e.g. sun tan lotion, water, ice cream, alcohol etc.). Think about where each of these products is produced and discuss what environmental impacts may result from their manufacture, transportation, and consumption.*

3. *Why does the nature and extent of the environmental impacts of tourism vary from one destination area to another?*

4. *What measures can be implemented by local governments to alleviate some of the negative impacts of tourism development?*

Further reading

Holden, A. (2000), *Environment and Tourism*, London: Routledge.

Williams, S. (1998), *Tourism Geography*, London: Routledge. *Chapter 5.*

Hall, C. M. and Lew, A. A. (1998), *Sustainable Tourism: a Geographical Perspective*, New York: Longman.

References

Andrews, M. (1989), *The Search for the Picturesque: Landscape, Aesthetics and Tourism in Britain 1760-1800*, Aldershot: Scolar Press.

Barke, M., Towner, J and Newton, M. T. (1996), *Tourism in Spain: Critical Issues*, Oxford: CAB International.

Budowski, G. (1976), Tourism and environmental conservation: conflict, coexistence or symbiosis?, *Environmental Conservation* 3(1): 27-31.

Burns, P. M. and Holden, A. (1995), *Tourism: a new perspective*, Hemel Hempstead: Prentice Hall International.

Butler, R. (1980), The concept of a tourism area cycle of evolution, *Canadian Geographer* 24: 5-12.

Cole, D. N. (2000), Biophysical impacts of wildland recreation use, in W. C. Gartner and D. W. Lime (2000), *Trends in Outdoor Recreation, Leisure and Tourism*, Wallingford: CAB International: 257-264.

Cooper, C., Fletcher, J., Gilbert, D., Wanhill, S. and Shepherd, R. (1998), *Tourism: Principles and Practices, 2nd Edition*, Harlow: Longman.

Goudie, A. and Viles, H. (1997), *The Earth Transformed: an Introduction to Human Impacts on the Environment*, Oxford: Blackwell.

Holden, A. (2000), *Environment and Tourism*, London: Routledge.

Lea, J. P. (1993), Tourism development ethics in the Third World. *Annals of Tourism Research*, 20(4): 701-715.

Lee, L. (1992), *Red Sky at Sunrise*, London: Viking.

Liddle, M. J. (1975), A selective review of the ecological effects of human trampling on natural ecosystems, *Biological Conservation*, 7:17-34.

Mathieson, A. and Wall, G. (1982), *Tourism: Economic, Physical and Social Impacts*, New York: Longman.

Nepal, S. K. (2000), Tourism in protected areas: the Nepalese Himalaya, *Annals of Tourism Research*, 27(3): 661-681.

Pearce, D. (1989), *Tourist Development, 2nd Edition*, Harlow: Longmans.

Priestley, G. K. (1995), Sports tourism: the case of golf, in G. Ashworth and A. Dietvorst (eds.) *Tourism and Spatial Transformations: Implications for Policy and Planning*, Wallingford: CAB International: 205-224.

Rural Development Commission (1996), *Green Audit Kit: the DIY guide to greening your tourism business*, Bristol, Rural Development Commission.

Ryan, C. (1991), *Recreational Tourism,* London: Routledge.

Salem, N. (1995), 'Water Rights', *Tourism in Focus*, 17, 4-5.

Shackley, M. (1996), *Wildlife Tourism*, London: International Thomson Business Press.

Simmons, P. (1988), 'Après ski le deluge', *New Scientist*, 1, 46-9.

Towner, J. (1997), *An Historical Geography of Recreation and Tourism in the Western World 1540-1940*, Chichester: John Wiley & Sons.

Williams, S. (1998), *Tourism Geography*, London: Routledge.

World Tourism Organisation (1997), *International Tourism: A Global Perspective*, Madrid: WTO.

12

Government, Governance and Tourism

Ken Harrop and Janice McMillan

Learning objectives

Most undergraduate students of tourism pursue their courses within business studies or hospitality and leisure management frameworks. Travel and tourism, however, raise intensely political issues for the institutions and processes of government. Accordingly, this chapter is intended to enable the reader to:

- *understand the essential nature of politics*

- *appreciate the dimensions of governmental involvement in the business of tourism*

- *demonstrate an understanding of some of the relevant administrative architecture*

- *discuss the effectiveness of these arrangements, and their capacity for solving, or perhaps creating, problems*

- *be familiar with the emergence of a more issue-based, outcome-oriented, joined-up model of governance.*

Introduction: the essence of politics and government

Politics can sometimes be a bit of a dirty word. Most 'ordinary' people seem to love to hate it. 'They should keep politics out of sport'; 'they bring politics into everything these days' or 'politics and business don't mix' are typical, sincere laments. Such refrains, however, reveal a profound misunderstanding of the nature of politics and its all-pervasive, everyday significance. Times of war remind us that there's only one thing worse than too much politics, and that's too little.

A frequently heard grumble is that politics is too adversarial, with politicians squabbling and arguing with each other 'like children', instead of pooling the best minds for the good of the country. Politics, however, *is* a 'disputatious' (Crick 1995) or 'quarrelsome' (Gilliatt 1987) activity. It is an adversarial business. The configuration and organisation of the House of Commons – its opposing front benches separated by two swords' length and one foot – symbolically reminds us so. The cut and thrust of debate is intended to be a more acceptable currency of political discourse than more violent ways of expressing purposive choice. The party-system has tended to produce a more 'temperate politics' than some of its early observers feared (Humphreys 1992). However, that is not to ignore the reality that the institutionalised politics of 'London SW1', in the case of England, are perceived by apparently large numbers of the population to be of decreasing interest and relevance in their own lives; their belief in the capacity of the institutions of representative democracy to deliver has diminished.

In the political science literature, politics, being about choices, competing preferences and alternative priorities, informs many typical definitions. However, it should be noted that politics is not only about arranging for these more-or-less legitimate differences to be articulated, expressed, heard and debated, but also involves making collective decisions and together agreeing ways forward. Without this second dimension, politics would indeed be a dark and destructive pursuit.

Definitions of politics

- politics 'considers conflicts of interests and values and how they are or can be conciliated' (Crick 1995: 3).

- 'political activity is a … universal phenomenon. It involves disagreements and the reconciliation of those disagreements (Ball and Peters 2000: 27).

- 'people or groups of people who want different things – be it power, money, liberty, etc. – face the potential or reality of conflict when such things are in short supply. Politics begins where their interests clash' (Jones *et al.* 2001: 8).

- 'politics may be defined briefly as a process whereby a group of people, whose opinions or interests are initially divergent, reach collective decisions which are generally regarded as binding on the group, and enforced as common policy' (Miller 1987: 391).

- 'politics is the activity by which groups reach binding collective decisions through attempting to reconcile differences among their members' (Hague and Harrop 2001: 3).

- 'Choice, preference, priorities, they are the currency of politics, and those who translate them into practical policies are politicians' (Wilson and Game 1998: 219).

The business of tourism and leisure throws up practical examples on an almost daily basis. In the wake of terrorist atrocities in New York, Washington and Pennsylvania on September 11, 2001, was it right to postpone golf's Ryder Cup competition? Should motor-racing's Formula 1 circus have raced in Indianapolis or not? At the same time, was it right to switch Glasgow Rangers' European football tie from Dagestan to 'neutral' Poland on account of the former's proximity to war-torn Chechnya? Should the former undisputed world heavyweight boxing champion and convicted rapist Mike Tyson have been allowed into the UK in 2000 to fight in Manchester? And what about the Miss World contest in India in 1996, when protestors from the Indian Forum for Awakening Women announced their intention to set fire to themselves at the pageant as an expression of opposition? What should have been the response of the Indian Authorities to such a clash of culture and values? Should Miss World have been banned? Should the protestors have been permitted to go ahead with deliberate and public self-immolation? Should protestors have been taken into protective custody for 'their own good'? Should the authorities have done nothing and allowed events to take their course? Are there any right or wrong answers at all? Such questions take us to the heart of classical political theory.

In the advanced liberal democracies of the so-called 'free' world, politics tend to be a secular business (Crick 1995). The currency of politics is different from that of religion; there is no holy writ, neither eternal truth nor tablets of stone – only complex problems capable of relatively temporary resolution in terms of shifting political values. Conditions and attitudes change. In this sense, there are no right or wrong answers for at the heart of secular politics lies the 'principle of uncertainty'.

Politics and tourism

The travel and tourism industries, arguably the largest of global businesses, raise many virtually intractable political issues, such as the balance between development and conservation, the relative distribution of positive and negative external effects, the relationship between host, indigenous cultures and incoming visitors, and long-term sustainability – all at the global, national and local levels. Therefore, given (i) the nature of politics both as an activity and as a field of study and (ii) the nature of the global business of tourism and its consequences, a prominent place for tourism on the political agenda would seem assured. However, this has tended not to be the case (Hall 1994).

'Tourism is widely regarded as the world's largest industry. However, despite the significant role of tourism in national and regional economies, and its social and environmental effects, the political aspects of tourism are rarely discussed in the tourism literature. Given the vast seasonal intra and international movements of people which modern travel represents and the impacts of tourism on many destinations, it must therefore strike the student of tourism that the rarity of academic research on the political dimensions of tourism is somewhat surprising' (Hall 1994: 3).

There are several reasons for this state of affairs. For one thing, governments and politicians tend to play down the intensely political nature of tourism. This is reflected in, for example, their historic reluctance to develop systematically clear policies for tourism (clearly connected with other policy fields such as energy, environment or transport), as well as their disinclination to commission fundamental research (as opposed to collecting visitor numbers or developing marketing strategies). Academics and scholars are also to blame, for they are not inclined to view tourism as a serious subject of enquiry - more to do with holidays than proper, serious work. There are also significant methodological challenges (Hall 1994).

Nevertheless, the hand of the state is ever discernible in the scale, distribution, character and organisation of tourism. Each aircraft flight, or package holiday or overnight hotel stay bears witness to the extent of governmental influence. Take a typical tour operator's brochure from any 'high-street' travel agency, for example. The hand of government is likely to be evident in the choice of available holiday destinations, points of departure, prices, resort information, the use of photographs, textual content, codes of practice, consumer protection provisions, currency regulations, travel advice and so on. Indeed, as discussed in Chapters 5 and 15, tour operations are highly regulated at both the national and European levels. The purpose of this chapter, therefore, is look at the relationship between tourism and government, focusing in particular on the influence of changing 'styles' of government on tourism. The first task, however, is to review the public administration of tourism in the UK (for a detailed account, see Holloway 1998).

Government and tourism: aspects of the administrative architecture in the UK

In everyday parlance, the term 'government' may be used to convey several different meanings. These include a vague sense of authority, power and order, control by a political party such as the 'Labour Government' or a particular administration, maybe as in 'the Blair government', or a collective of official institutions such as 'government departments' and 'local government'. It may even be used when referring to particular organisations, such as the Ministry of Defence or the Treasury. All of these uses are legitimate. Underlying them all, however, is a deeper meaning, for 'government' conveys a sense of the settled (but not permanent) and agreed formalisation of power and authority which provides a framework within which political discourse can be managed, disagreements can be debated, collective choices made and policy directions set out. In a sense, but not entirely, it's the problem-solving end of politics. Not entirely though, for government policies can themselves cause their own problems. Some would argue, for example, that Mrs Thatcher's economic policies in the 1980s created major problems of social distress and civil unrest whilst, more generally, Dunleavy (1995) has written of the catastrophic unintended consequences of 'policy disasters'.

The United Kingdom is a relatively small, centralised (albeit of late increasingly devolved) unitary state. Even so, governmental arrangements for the tourism, leisure and cultural industries are characterised by a high degree of organisational pluralism and institutional fragmentation. Indeed, many governmental bodies are involved in the tourism business, although many of these are not primarily or exclusively concerned with the business of tourism. Therefore, many of the effects of their policies or influence are indirect. Let us take central government as one example.

Central government and tourism

Central government has, for the past couple of centuries at least, exercised significant indirect effects on the development of the tourism industry. For example, nineteenth century legislation providing for Bank Holidays and paid leave for industrial workers (together with the development of the railways of course) contributed to the development of the Victorian seaside resort (see also Chapter 2). The official promotion of education, literacy and other 'self-improving' pursuits, coupled with the suppression of 'undesirable' leisure activities, such as gambling, drinking or cock-fighting (Henry and Bramham 1989), also shaped the infant leisure and cultural industries. Moreover, nineteenth century foreign, penal and agricultural policies still exert discernible effects in present day patterns of international tourism, especially in the Visiting Friends and Relatives (VFR) sector. For example, condoning, in the name of agricultural improvement, the clearance of crofting communities in Caithness, Sutherland and elsewhere in favour of the Cheviot sheep (Prebble 1969) was no more an instrument of tourism policy than was British penal policy in the nineteenth century. However, in 'forcibly' relocating British nationals in Australia, Canada, New Zealand, the United States and elsewhere, a significant contribution would be made to the future VFR market. More recently, in the 1980s and 1990s, employment policy, the deregulation and privatisation of the transport sector, as well as the policies of the European Union on consumer protection or monetary integration and the single market, have all had very major consequences for the travel and tourism industries.

Government's first formal support for tourism came about in 1929 when the Department of Overseas Trade made a grant of £5000 to the Travel Association of Great Britain and Northern Ireland (TAGBNI), successor to the Come to Britain movement (Cooper *et al.* 1998). TAGBNI would, in the inter-war years, become the British Travel Association, though still a voluntary as opposed to a statutory body. Apart from continuing grant-aid to this voluntary body, providing extra funds for local authorities which were seaside resorts and a piece of legislation in 1948 relating only to Northern Ireland, nothing too much changed in terms of central government's interest in tourism until 1969 (Harrop and Long 1994). It was in that year that the Development of Tourism Act 1969, was passed.

Hailed as the first piece of comprehensive legislation systematically to address the needs of the tourism industry, the Act provided for the creation of several new statutory boards – the British Tourist Authority (BTA), the English Tourist Board (ETB), the Scottish Tourist Board (STB) and the Wales Tourist Board (WTB) – as well as development grants and an accommodation grading scheme. It was a turning point, heralding as it did the creation for the first time of national arrangements for developing tourism and allocating public funds. However, the Act was articulated against a background of economic crisis and the need to generate earnings and income from wherever; tourism was seen as a major source of 'invisible' earnings and the 1969 Act may have owed as much to this imperative as to a clear commitment to tourism.

This would help to explain one of the apparent paradoxes of the past thirty years. On the one hand, there has been no shortage of central government involvement in tourism, at least not if measured by the number of departments either directly or indirectly involved. On the other hand, policy has tended to remain general and vague – long on 'motherhood and apple pie', but short on specifics.

Government institutions and tourism

With reference to the first point above (the number of departments involved in tourism), Central Government in the UK has a number of institutional forms, especially:

- the large, well-known Departments of State, such as the Home Office, the Foreign and Commonwealth Office, the Treasury, the Department for Education in its various names and, similarly, Environment and Transport, to name but several. Many of these are relevant to an understanding of the Travel and Tourism business. Some examples might include:

Foreign Office:	conduct of foreign and international relations, travel advice
Home Office:	immigration and security matters
Environment:	the countryside, local government and planning
Agriculture:	countryside matters
Trade and Industry:	hotels, travel agents, business

Indeed, it would be more difficult to think of Central Government Departments without consequences for tourism than to draw up an inventory of those which do have.

- Secondly, there are the Executive Agencies. These were created after publication of the Ibbs or 'Next Steps' Report in 1988 on management and efficiency in the Civil Service. These Executive, or 'Departmental', Agencies are semi-autonomous organisations which carry out many of the routine, administrative functions of central government – 'freeing-up' the centre to concentrate on policy-making. Well-known examples include the Social Security Benefits Agency and its former sister, the Contributions Agency, now merged with the Inland Revenue. They are by no means all based in London, let alone in Whitehall. Many Agencies are relevant to the business of tourism. These include the UK Passport Agency (set up in 1991); the Meteorological Office (1990); Historic Royal Palaces (1989); the Ordnance Survey (1990); CADW Welsh Historic Monuments (1991); and Historic Scotland (1991).

- In addition, the territorial Departments – the Northern Ireland, Scottish and Welsh Offices – traditionally exercised responsibility for tourism in their respective geographical areas until devolution took effect.

In the absence of a dedicated Tourism Ministry, until 1992 responsibility for tourism lay with a designated 'lead' Department. Until 1985, this was the Department of Trade and Industry (tourism means business being the message), when responsibility then passed to the Department of Employment (tourism means jobs). There it remained until the creation of the Department of National Heritage in 1992 and now, the Department for Culture, Media and Sport (DCMS) following its creation after Labour's General Election victory in 1997.

The debate leading up to the creation of the Department of National Heritage in 1992 was an interesting one. It brings us to the second element of our paradox; that is, despite extensive government involvement, overall policy direction remained vague and uncertain. The Commons' own Trade and Industry Committee in 1985 commented:

> *The truth is that the Government cannot quite decide what its own role is... The Government minimises the appearance of involvement by reducing policy aims to statements of the obvious but maintains the fact of involvement in the tourist boards and the grants provided through them. The trouble is that this actual financial commitment is then left without there being any clear specific strategy to guide its use* (House of Commons Trade Committee, quoted in Cooper *et al.* 1993: 148).

In the same vein, a retiring Chair of a Regional Tourist Board felt compelled to write in the Board's 1993-94 Report that central government had 'failed to provide the leadership necessary to encourage the development of the tourism industry... there is still no coherent national policy on tourism'.

Reflective of such concerns and criticism, the case for a single, integrated 'Department of Leisure' had gained momentum during the 1980s (Adams 2000; Harrop and Long 1994). It culminated in the creation, after John Major's General Election victory in 1992, of the Department of National Heritage. In rather rapid succession its Secretaries of State were David Mellor, Peter Brooke, Stephen Dorrell and Virginia Bottomley. Tony Blair, on the back of 'New Labour's' May 1997 General Election triumph, recast it as the Department for Culture, Media and Sport – partly because the word 'heritage' is backward-looking ('heri' in Latin, like 'hier' in French, means yesterday) and sent out inappropriate messages for the modernising Mr Blair. The Secretary of State for Culture, Media and Sport throughout the Blair government's first term (1997-2001) was Chris Smith. After Labour's return to office in June 2001, he was replaced by Tessa Jowell.

The Department for Culture, Media and Sport is responsible for:

- the arts
- broadcasting
- cultural objects
- film
- the government's art collection
- heritage
- libraries
- the millennium
- museums and galleries
- the national lottery
- new media and information services
- the press
- the royal estate
- sport and recreation
- tourism

The Department for Culture, Media and Sport's overall aim was to improve the quality of life for all through cultural and sporting activities, and to strengthen the creative industries. In doing so, it was expected to:

- bring excitement into the life of the nation and the work of government;
- make things of quality available to the many, not just the few; and
- create the jobs of the future.

On the tourism front, the setting-up of the Tourism Forum in November 1997 was interpreted as signalling a re-positioning of tourism at the centre of the Government's cultural initiatives and an honouring of its promise in *Breaking New Ground*, published whilst still in opposition, to 'implement a committed strategy to assist the development of tourism and hospitality'. In February 1999 appeared *Tomorrow's Tourism*, the Government's strategy for tourism. Recognising tourism as 'one of our most important industries... (because)... it generates wealth, it creates jobs, it promotes entrepreneurship, it provides social and environmental benefits, and supports local diversity and cultural traditions' (DCMS 1999: 8), the need for a government strategy for tourism was explicitly acknowledged. Characterised by, firstly, diversity and fragmentation, secondly, seasonal and sometimes fickle demand, thirdly, an inadequate understanding of its market and, fourthly, a reliance on infrastructure determined by central and local government in other policy fields, such as transport or planning, the tourism business needs a clearly articulated and joined up strategy (DCMS 1999: 9). Committing itself to work in partnership with the industry towards shared objectives and common targets, the publication of *Tomorrow's Tourism* probably marked the most comprehensive governmental arrangements for tourism since the Development of Tourism Act thirty years earlier. It is a significant attempt to address the policy vacuum for tourism and to deliver on the very least that the industry might reasonably expect of government, namely the enunciation of a clear overall policy:

> *At the national level, tourism is in the first instance a government responsibility to formulate a tourism policy, which may be translated into a plan... when the role of tourism is defined, the policy provides a statement of the means by which the objectives are to be attained... such ... as the administrative arrangements, the respective rules of the private and public sectors and the fiscal arrangements.* (Burkart and Medlik 1992).

Tourism: other institutional arrangements

Despite the complexity of the arrangements described above, there are other relevant items of the administrative 'furniture' to be cited. These may be briefly summarised as:

- sub-national government

- public bodies

- supra-national government

i. Sub-national government

In the absence of constitutional guarantees to the regions of the UK, sub-national government has tended to focus on local government. During the past decade, however, the picture has become more complicated. The Conservative government, for example, created Government Offices for the Regions (such as the Government Office for the North East (GONE)). Bringing together the work of some, but by no means all, central government departments on a regional basis, these Offices are involved in local economic development strategies, often with a strong cultural dimension, and the administration of European funds. Additionally, the Blair government's agenda of democratic modernisation has seen the introduction of devolved structures. The Scottish Executive, for example, exercises responsibility for tourism as part of the work of its Department for Enterprise and Lifelong Learning. The organisation of the Scottish Executive does not, however, reflect the configuration of responsibilities of the Department for Culture, Media and Sport for in Scotland, sport, the arts and culture lie within the Education portfolio. Wales now has its own National Assembly and Northern Ireland its Executive. In London, there is an Elected Mayor (Ken Livingstone, who has not always been at one with his own party in national government, as evidenced by disagreement over the future of the London Underground for instance) and a 25 member Greater London Assembly. All English regions have appointed (not elected) Regional Development Agencies and non-statutory Regional Chambers. Fully elected Regional Assemblies for the English Regions remain a possibility. For the student of tourism, the reformed administrative architecture of government beyond Whitehall perhaps serves to compound an already complex picture.

As for local government, there is a comprehensive cover of directly elected, multi-purpose primary local authorities. Again, the arrangements are complex and a review of local government structures in the mid-1990s made the pattern even more complicated than before. In England, Wilson and Game (1998) drew up a list of 387 principal authorities as follows:

- 34 Non-metropolitan County Councils, e.g. Northumberland or Hampshire.

- 238 Non-metropolitan District Councils, e.g. Carlisle, Tynedale or The Wrekin.

- 36 Metropolitan District Councils, e.g. Newcastle upon Tyne, Birmingham or Liverpool.

- 46 Unitary Councils, e.g. Stockton, Stoke-on-Trent or Bristol.

- 32 London Borough Councils, e.g. Tower Hamlets, Kensington and Chelsea or Islington.

- 1 City of London Corporation.

In Scotland, 1996 saw a two-tier system of regional and district councils replaced by 32 unitary authorities. Examples include Perth and Kinross, Argyll and Bute or City of Aberdeen. In the same year, Wales similarly adopted a system of 22 unitary authorities, such as Blaenau Gwent, Wrexham or Ceredigion. Northern Ireland has an arrangement of district councils, such as Belfast and Armagh.

In very general terms, local authorities have been the principal public service providers of leisure services in the arts, sport and physical recreation, and tourism (Harrop and Long 1994). They provide an extensive range of facilities, venues and activities, from orchestras to football pitches, ice-rinks to caravan sites and lifeguards. However, their activities relating to tourism fall under two main headings. First are their statutory responsibilities, such as physical planning, development control, inspection and regulation, environmental health or licensing, for example. Additionally, however, they provide many discretionary services, including promotion and publicity, information centres, conference facilities, heritage attractions and social tourism schemes. For the past twenty years, local authorities have engaged in tourism development as a means of economic regeneration in, for example, Bradford, Glasgow, Sheffield, Sunderland and Wigan. They provide financial support to the Regional Tourist Boards and, in partnership with other agencies, increasingly participate in the development and implementation of tourism development strategies. Recent trends have seen development strategies increasingly integrated into broader economic development or local and regional cultural strategies.

Public bodies

There are many other public bodies which are relevant to an understanding of government and tourism. Sometimes misleadingly referred to as 'quangos', these are part of the 'non-elected' state, including NHS Health Trusts or Learning and Skills Councils. Their members are appointed, not elected.

There are two main types relevant to an understanding of tourism. First, those organisations specifically concerned with the tourism business. Several of these were created by the 1969 Development of Tourism Act, including the British Tourist Authority, the English Tourist Board, the Scottish Tourist Board and the Wales Tourist Board (Adams 2000; Harrop and Long 1994). Focusing on the development of tourism within their particular territorial jurisdiction, these Boards are heavily involved in promotion, marketing and publicising the tourist product. After an increasingly controversial political history, the English Tourist Board was recast in 1999 as the English Tourism Council as part of the new support structure for tourism in England referred to in *Tomorrow's Tourism*. The national Boards and Council work in close partnership with the network of Regional Tourist Boards (Adams 2000).

In addition, there are many other public bodies which are not specifically or primarily concerned with tourism (their principal roles lie elsewhere) but which nevertheless have engaged in tourism development for a number of reasons, or which exert indirect effects. These fall into three main areas:

- arts, culture and heritage;

- environment and the countryside; and

- economic development.

They include the Arts Council, Regional Arts Boards, English Heritage, the Countryside Agency and (in Scotland and Wales) the Countryside Councils, English Nature and Scottish Natural Heritage, the Forestry Commission and various economic development bodies. The legacy of the Urban Development Corporations, wound up in 1998, is also clearly evident. All are significant elements in the overall picture.

Supra-national government

Last, but by no means least, mention must be made of the work and influence of the European Union (EU), an example of supra-national government in the form of an economic and political union. Its overall purposes – to restore economic prosperity to a war-ravaged Western Europe after 1945 and to win lasting peace in a world region which had twice within a generation embroiled the rest of the world in almost total warfare – went far beyond tourism. Indeed, no powers relating to tourism were conferred upon the European Commission (and its predecessors) either by the founding Treaty of Rome in 1957 or subsequent Treaties, such as Maastricht. This was not the case with agriculture, fisheries, transport, regional, energy or competition policies, where specific powers were conferred. Nevertheless, the European Union has had major effects in travel and tourism in member states. These can be classified under three headings:

- measures following from the pursuit of the internal market;

- indirect measures from other policy concerns; and

- specific tourism initiatives.

i. The internal market

In this first category, one might note:

- the role of the Single European Act 1987, in providing for the free movement of goods, persons, services and capital and moving by 1993 towards a frontier-free Europe. This has progressively led to the relaxation and abolition of frontier controls and a relatively passport-free 'Schengenland'.

- deregulation of air transport.

- abolition of duty free sales for travellers between EU member states.

- mutual recognition of training and educational qualifications.

- deregulation of coach transport.

- a Union-wide framework of company law.

- the single currency, or 'Euro'.

ii. Indirect measures

From other policy commitments include:

- consumer protection initiatives including the package travel directive in 1993.

- denied-boarding compensation (aircraft).

- competition and its effects on civil aviation including transatlantic mergers.

- environmental standards such as bathing water quality.

- cultural tourism, including the European City and Capital of Culture initiatives.

iii. Specific tourism initiatives

Which include:

- Initial Guidelines on Tourism, 1982.

- European Year of Tourism, 1990.

- Community Action Plan to Assist Tourism, 1991.

- Philoxenia – the proposed First Multiannual Programme to assist European Tourism, 1997-2000.

Competitiveness, quality and sustainability have increasingly become the watchwords of EU thinking.

Towards governance?

Governmental involvement with the businesses of travel and tourism is, therefore, complex and multi-layered, extending from the local to the supra-national. This multi-level governance is the outcome of several pressures, including globalisation and Europeanisation. For the UK, there have also been internal pressures which have impacted on governmental arrangements.

Government in the UK has undergone considerable change over the part twenty-five years or so. These changes have not only led to a new operating code in the public services but also to the partial break-up of the unitary state, with powers being devolved from Westminster to the Scottish Parliament and to the Welsh and Northern Irish Assemblies. These constitution-changing moves have resulted in a further loss of central government control and renewed calls for regional government in England. Some of these have clearly been noted in our review of the administrative furniture. Here, we assess these changes in greater detail and consider some possible consequences of, and for, a 'Disunited Kingdom'.

The Westminster Model

For many years, the Westminster Model provided an organising perspective for understanding British Government, a way of characterising its main features (Rhodes 1997a). Through its longevity, it became the traditional way of thinking about and describing British government. Most lay people would use it unwittingly in any discussion of how the British state functions. Its survival has been perpetuated by the lack of a viable alternative organising perspective.

In the political science literature, the Westminster Model is defined in various ways. Its essence, however, has been concisely captured by Rhodes, who identifies the defining characteristics as focusing on: parliamentary sovereignty; strong Cabinet government; accountability through elections; majority party control of the executive (that is, Prime Minister, Cabinet and the civil service); elaborate conventions for the conduct of parliamentary business; institutionalised opposition, and the rule of debate (Rhodes 1997a: 3).

The Westminster Model's mainstream status has been strengthened by its applicability to other countries which have developed systems of government similar to Britain's. In other words, the Westminster Model has applicability beyond the parliament which gave it its name. The perspective is transferable and portable.

However, the dominance of the Westminster Model is now being challenged. It is argued that it no longer fully or accurately describes the organisation and operation of the state and power in Britain. It is unlikely that the model will ever completely disappear from political science as an organising perspective. It may not accurately capture the move to governance, but will continue to have relevance to understanding the institutions of UK government.

From government to governance

The role and power of the British State has changed. We talk today not of *government* but of *governance*. Governance is about a new way of governing, a changed order. This changed order means a new way of thinking about British government is required, a new way of thinking about and defining the various power relationships. One such way of thinking which has been suggested as overcoming the weaknesses of the Westminster Model is the concept of a 'Differentiated Polity'.

Rhodes (1997a) characterises the Differentiated Polity as 'functional and institutional specialisation and the fragmentation of policies and politics'. He argues that the Differentiated Polity perspective has several advantages over the Westminster Model for conceptualising and understanding the governance of Britain:

- the Differentiated Polity allows fuller appreciation of the limits of the Westminster Model;

- it raises important and distinct questions about government in Britain;

- it identifies and explains the major issues and problem facing policy makers today.

The Differentiated Polity framework, therefore, has a value beyond academic debate concerning the organisation and management of British government. It is about how the state, in its manifest and manifold complexity, affects everyday lives.

For many years, the Westminster Model may have been the dominant perspective. During the past quarter of a century, however, much has changed. The very conception of a public sector, its purpose and role, structures, institutions, resourcing and management practices have all been radically transformed in a process which continues under Mr Blair's premiership (Harrop 1999). Although the signs were there to see long before 1979, it was Mrs Thatcher who set about public service reform with energy and enthusiasm. Partly because of the Westminster Model itself perhaps, the overly bureaucratic state could be lampooned as self-serving, conceited, wasteful, inefficient, disabling, hidebound and insufficiently attentive to the public who, snared and entangled, struggled in a deadly web of 'red tape'. Riding the ideological chariot of the 'New Right' into battle, for Mrs Thatcher the moment was opportune. And after the so-called 'winter of discontent' in 1978-79, there was little popular support for much of the public sector. They may not have liked Mrs Thatcher very much, but they had no affection either for local government, for example.

Contemptuous of the performance of the public sector, Mrs Thatcher embarked upon her wide-ranging reform agenda. Nothing less than wholesale change would do. Particular emphasis was laid on 'rolling back the frontiers of the state' and lifting the yoke of public bureaucracies from the people, on reducing the burden of pubic expenditure and making efficiency savings. Clear themes became discernible and a guiding ideological rationale (Rhodes 1997a):

- the large-scale privatisation of public assets (including for example British Airways in 1986 and the British Airports Authority in 1987);

- the marketisation and compulsory commercialisation of what remained in the public sector (including the purchaser – provider split in the National Heath Service and compulsory competitive tendering and contracting out in local government);

- the break-up (and in some cases abolition) of public sector bureaucracies and the introduction of alternative delivery systems;

- the introduction and adoption of private sector methods and styles of management;

- de-concentration and devolution of the administrative work of central government (by creating the Executive Agencies, for example);

- a growth in regulation though output control; and

- tighter central resource control.

In the whirl of furious activity, however, not everything was well or carefully thought through. Some of the reforms may have been less than successful because insufficient attention was given to the underlying values and purpose of public services, and the complex challenge of their management. The result was an interesting mix of unplanned, as well as planned, outcomes. The concept of a Differentiated Polity captures something of the unintended, as well as intentional, results of the reforms as the authority of the unitary state diminishes and the ability of central government to control the system is reduced. This may not have been Mrs Thatcher's intention.

Under Tony Blair the genie of devolution has been uncorked. The result has been the emergence of real policy differences geographically. In Scotland, for example, there are no tuition fees for students in higher education and financial arrangements for care of the elderly are less punitive. Nor do arrangements for the public administration of cultural services reflect those in England. It may be impossible to recork the bottle. 'Balkanisation' of the polity could be an unintended consequence of the honourable devolution of power and authority. The balance between freedom and order, always difficult to strike, has shifted.

The consequences of reform

There are several unintended consequences of public sector reform which have important implications for democracy and how the British public is governed, and which also impact on government's management of travel and tourism. The impact of these consequences is augmented by the fact that they will not be easy to undo, meaning that today central government is governing with imperfect control, a situation which looks likely to continue well into the new millennium. The most serious unintended consequences concern accountability, steering and fragmentation (Rhodes 1997b).

Accountability, steering and fragmentation

One of the main objectives of the Thatcher reforms was the break up of public sector bureaucracies, a fragmentation which would free mangers from the constraints of rule-bound administration. However, fragmentation has led to a situation which is harder for the centre to control. Within a framework of networks and 'collaborative governance', many organisations provide public services. The challenge of devising an overall strategy and securing its implementation becomes more difficult for central government. Another stated reason for pursuing a policy of public sector fragmentation was to improve accountability. With smaller organisations, the role of individuals and organisations in policy outcomes would be more easily identifiable and, consequently, they could be more easily held to account. However, an opposite outcome may be identified; that is, fragmentation has blurred accountability. The myriad of organisations now involved in the provision of public services means that it is harder to distinguish the precise influence on policy outcomes. The buck stops where? Accountability is as slippery as a bar of wet soap.

Furthermore, the fragmentation of the public sector means that control and steering are major problems facing government. The numbers of interested parties involved in service provision means that the centre cannot clearly control their actions. Moreover, implementing parties will interpret policy to suit best their own purpose. Policy outcomes are, therefore, diluted. This dilution of policy may also result in more policy being generated to plug the gaps in policy outcomes. A vicious circle thus develops. The centre cannot steer the system through traditional means. It is arguable that, under Mrs Thatcher, these unintended consequences led to a situation of decentralisation to centralise – in other words, in order to control the system, central government had to increase control over resources, thus defeating a main aim of the reform programme. There are no easy solutions to the problems of governance.

As far as the territorial settlement is concerned, the creation of the Scottish Parliament and Welsh and Northern Ireland Assemblies has already moved the UK from the traditional understandings of a unitary state towards disunity. The consequences of these moves are, to a certain extent, dependent on the resultant degree of disunity. It has been argued above that the creation of these devolved structures may add to the problems already apparent in the move from the Westminster Model to a Differentiated Polity. Any further realisation of regionalisation or regionalism through the establishment of regional government in England would necessarily compound the problem.

Regionalisation may ultimately result in the break up of the UK, but what of the standing of the separate emerging administrative units? Scotland may have difficulties in asserting itself in negotiations with the EU and other governments. What chance have the English regions? A more likely outcome is, perhaps, the creation of a regional tier of government in the UK, but then where would this leave Scotland and Wales? Would there be calls for Scottish and Welsh regionalisation? After all, the Highlands and Islands of Scotland may consider its claims for a degree of self-government as valid as that of, say, the South West of England. The ultimate irony, however, would be a situation where the regions of the UK achieved devolved government and found themselves more constrained as a result. The greater the differentiation the greater the integration needs to be to maintain the whole. Again, checks and balances, freedom and order.

Government and governance, travel and tourism

What, then, are the implications of this shift towards governance for travel and tourism?

The UK is no longer the unitary state it once was (perhaps it never was all that united?). Government has undergone, and is likely to continue to undergo, great change. The way we think about and explain British government has shifted away from the Westminster Model towards the organising perspective of a Differentiated Polity. Regionalisation is alive, if not always well. The haste to reform has, however, raised new challenges of governance. Publish in haste, repent at leisure was the warning of the wise; reform in a rush and rue the wreckage might be the advice to the legislator. The privatisation of the railways is not the only example – remember dangerous dogs? For tourism policies, what are the implications?

Ironically, in some ways, the history of policies for tourism and travel in the UK displayed many of the features and problems which are now being identified as problematic in the differentiated polity – namely fragmentation, lack of accountability and steering. Undoubtedly, many elements of government and the public sector were relevant to understanding the overall picture. However, the development and implementation of clear policies, systematically connected to other considerations and integrated into other policy fields such as energy, environment or transport, remained weak. The effects of public policy were largely unknown and business lamented the lack of a guiding framework for action. Indeed, various organisations, such as the Tourism Society, have long called for a more cohesive policy framework for tourism.

New Labour's chosen solution, within its general modernisation programme for government, was to think in terms of joined-up solutions for joined-up problems – joined-up governance, in fact.

The publication in February 1999 of *Tomorrow's Tourism*, its new strategy for 'a growth industry for the new millennium', has already been mentioned in this context. Its raft of recommendations, proposals and action points revolved around a number of key themes:

- to provide a new support structure for tourism in England, including the creation of the English Tourism Council to replace the English Tourist Board;
- to develop and promote quality tourism experiences;

- to provide better information about tourism;

- to promote improved career opportunities including a careers festival;

- to promote the wise growth of tourism through sustainable development; and

- to widen access to tourism, especially for those on low incomes, families, the elderly and the disabled.

One of its provisions was for convening, each March, an annual Tourism Summit of Ministers, officials and senior representatives from the industry. Its papers and proceedings, publicly available, provide a picture of joined-up governance in action (http://www.culture.gov.uk). The second Tourism Summit (March 6, 2001) reviewed progress on the initiatives and action points agreed by Ministers at the first Summit. Chaired by then Secretary of State for Culture, Media and Sport, Chris Smith, the Summit participants (16) included another seven Ministers, representatives of the National Assembly for Wales, the Northern Ireland Executive and HM Treasury, as well as the Chairmen of the English Tourism Council, the British Tourist Executive and senior officers of the British Hospitality Association and the Better Regulation Task Force. The following progress updates were presented:

- *Ministry of Agriculture, Fisheries and Food*

    - Foot and Mouth disease outbreaks and the effects of restrictions

    - Rural Enterprise Scheme

    - Local food promotion

- *Department of the Environment, Transport and the Regions*

    - Signage of tourist attractions

    - Spending Review

    - Rural Bus Challenge

    - 'Traveline', the new information system

    - Alternatives to the car for leisure travel

    - 'Waterways For Tomorrow'

    - Bathing Water Directive Standards

    - Rural White Paper

    - Urban White Paper

- *Department for Education and Employment*

    - Standards in further education

    - Learning Skills Council

- *Foreign and Commonwealth Office*

    - Leave and multi-entry visas

    - UK portable website

    - Sustainable tourism

- *Home Office*

  - Modernisation of licensing laws

  - Sunday dancing

  - Gambling review

  - Easing UK entry procedures

- *Department of Trade and Industry*

  - Small Business Service

  - Knowledge Economy White Paper

  - Best practice forum to strengthen competitiveness through management skills and business procedures.

- Other progress reports were made by HM Treasury, the National Assembly for Wales, the Northern Ireland Executive, the English Tourism Council and the British Tourist Authority.

New agenda items focussed discussion on resort regeneration, better regulation of hotels and restaurants and the BTA's *First Impressions* survey. The Tourism Summit, in the words of its Chairman, 'had demonstrated its worth in concentrating minds on the needs of tourism', and would reconvene one year hence, although officials would meet more frequently in order to maintain the momentum. 'Joining-up' is not, however, a simple task. One preferred way of going about it is to create co-ordinating organisations and mechanisms (the Tourism Summit may be an example of the latter). However, such arrangements may add to the complexity by increasing the number of interests to be joined-up.

There are some possible strategies, however, for overcoming the challenges of governance. These strategies are as applicable to travel and tourism policies as to any other policy area. Stoker (2001) suggests three ways of improving co-ordination in an effective system of multi-level governance:

- the use of contracts or concordats can express joint commitments to spend money and achieve improvements;

- joint budget holding can guarantee co-ordination of policy working; and

- summits or regular meetings of key actors can dissipate conflicts between different levels of government.

He contends that the agenda is not about choosing between these options, but about finding space and scope for them all. The future lies not in establishing exclusive areas of jurisdiction, but in finding ways to co-operate.

Such new ways of governing will not appear, however, without change in the behaviour of key actors. Crucial to New Labour's modernisation programme and prospects for good multi-level governance are the key skills of diplomacy and negotiation. These lie at the root of the new governance and are skills which need to be developed and effectively deployed. Mindsets have to move on. The distance to be travelled may be significant. The travel and tourism business, however, demands effective policy co-ordination. A complex and fragmented business in a labyrinth of multiple interdependencies, the portfolio cannot be detached from other concerns. Itself a sensitive barometer of economic and political factors, such as economic well-being or safety and security, tourism in turn exerts its own external effects (on the planning process, for example, on transport networks, pollution and congestion, land use, environment or the physical infrastructure such as water supply and sewage disposal to name only a few) and, in addition to its obvious purpose such as offering good holidays, pleasure, relaxation and enjoyment, it can contribute to so many other concerns of public policy, including economic development or regeneration and social inclusion initiatives. It deserves and demands joined-up governance. The historical baronies of policy making and implementation have not tended to serve it well.

The modernisation of government is generally to be welcomed, but how effective will the emerging arrangements be? The past couple of years have been interesting and challenging ones for tourism. The year 2000 saw a fuel supply crisis, major disruption to rail travel and widespread flooding in the UK. The following year, 2001, was marked by major outbreaks of foot and mouth disease at home and the terrorist events of September 11 in New York, Washington and Pennsylvania. How well was government able to cope? Were its responses qualitatively improved? That is the acid test of it all for government and the tourism business must make their way together in a real world not always of their own choosing, and one in which there are no easy answers.

Discussion questions

1. Critically evaluate the effectiveness of the connections and relationships between government and tourism in the UK or elsewhere. How well do the arrangements work?

2. To what extent did the publication of Tomorrow's Tourism mark a genuine turning point in tourism policy in the UK?

3. Joined-up problems demand joined-up solutions which require joined-up governance is the thinking of Mr Blair's government. How well are the new arrangements able to deal with the unforeseen challenges which affect the tourism industry?

4. Discuss the view that government is nothing more than a nuisance without which the tourism business could operate more efficiently and effectively.

Further reading

Elliott, J. (1997), *Tourism: politics and public sector management*, London: Routledge.

Hall, C. M. (1994), *Tourism and Politics: Policy, Power and Place*, Chichester: John Wiley & Sons.

Holloway, J. C. (1998), *The Business of Tourism, 5th Edition*, Harlow: Longman. Chapter 15.

Pearce, D. (1992), *Tourist Organisations*, Harlow: Longman.

References

Adams, I. (2000), *Leisure and Government*, *3rd Edition*, Sunderland, Business Education Publishers.

Ball A. R. and Peters, B. G. (2000), *Modern Politics and Government, 6th Edition*, Basingstoke: Macmillan.

Burkart, A. J. and Medlik, S. (1992), *Tourism: Past, Present and Future*, *2nd Edition*, London: Butterworth Heinemann.

Cooper, C., Fletcher, J., Gilbert, D. and Wanhill, S. (1993), *Tourism: Principles and Practice*, London: Pitmans.

Cooper, C., Fletcher, J., Gilbert, D., Shepherd, R. and Wanhill, S. (1998), *Tourism: Principles and Practice*, *2nd Edition*, Harlow, Longman.

Crick, B. (1995), What is politics?, *New Statesman and Society, Political Studies Guide*: 3-5.

DCMS (1999), *Tomorrow's Tourism: A growth industry for the new Millennium*, London, Department of Culture, Media and Sport.

Dunleavy, P. (1995), Policy disasters: explaining the UK's record, *Public Policy and Administration* 10(2): 52-69.

Gilliatt, S. (1987), Being political: a quarrelsome view, *International Political Science Review*, 8(4): 367-384.

Hague, R. and Harrop, M. (2001), *Comparative Politics and Government, 5th Edition*, Hampshire, Palgrave.

Hall, C. M. (1994), *Tourism and Politics: Policy, Power and Place*, Chichester: John Wiley & Sons.

Harrop, K. (1999), The political context of public services management, in A. Rose and A Lawton (eds.) *Public Services Management*, Harlow: Pearson Education: 3-25.

Harrop, K. and Long, P. (1994), Government and tourism, in P. Callaghan, P. Long and M. Robinson (eds.) *Travel and Tourism, 2nd Edition*, Sunderland: Business Education Publishers: 161-193.

Henry, I. and Bramham, P. (1993), Leisure policy in Britain, in P. Bramham, I. Henry, H. Mommaas and H. Van der Poel (eds.) *Leisure Policies in Europe*, Wallingford: CAB International: 101-128.

Holloway, J. C. (1998), *The Business of Tourism, 5th Edition*, Harlow: Longman.

Humphreys, A. (1992), The arts in eighteenth century Britain, in B. Ford (ed.) *Eighteenth Century Britain: The Cambridge Cultural History*, Cambridge: Cambridge University Press: 3-46.

Jones, B. *et al.* (eds.) (2001), *Politics UK, 4th Edition*, Harlow, Longman.

Miller, D. (ed) (1987), *The Blackwell Encyclopaedia of Political Thought*, Oxford, Blackwell.

Prebble, J. (1969), *The Highland Clearances*, Harmondsworth, Penguin.

Rhodes, R. A. W. (1997a), *Understanding Governance*, Milton Keynes: Open University Press.

Rhodes, R. A. W. (1997b), From marketisation to diplomacy: It's the mix that matters, *Australian Journal of Public Administration* 56: 40-53.

Stoker, G. (2001), Top heavies, *The Guardian*, June 13.

Wilson, D. and Game, C. (1998), *Local Government in the United Kingdom, 2nd* Edition, Basingstoke, Macmillan.

13

Organisational Behaviour in Tourism

Gill Forster

Learning objectives

By the end of this chapter students should:

- *have sufficient knowledge and understanding of organisational behaviour so that they can comprehend the ways in which people are managed in organisations*

- *identify individual and group differences*

- *understand the implications for managers of individual and group differences*

- *express knowledge of the work of a number of writers and researchers who have made a contribution to the field.*

Introduction

Organisational behaviour is part of the multi-disciplinary field of studying organisations. It explores issues in organisations at the micro level, that is, at the individual and group levels. In other text books, you will also see the terms organisation theory and organisation analysis, both of which, conversely, usually focus on the macro level, or the organisation as a whole. Some commentators argue that these two (the micro and the macro) cannot be separated – understanding behaviour at one level automatically requires understanding of factors at other levels (Rollinson *et al.* 1998). However, for the purposes of this chapter, we shall take the first approach; that is, that organisational behaviour looks at behaviour in organisations at individual and group levels.

Why study behaviour in organisations?

There are two main reasons why students of travel and tourism should study behaviour in organisations. First, organisations, in their many forms, are a dominant institution in the modern world. Most people will find that their lives are, to some extent, affected by the existence and behaviour of organisations and so it is important that we try to understand them better. Second, those who manage or aspire to manage in organisations need to understand the factors that influence behaviour in order to help them manage people more effectively. In practice, individuals interact as people who bring their personalities, problems and interests with them into the work situation, and this influences how well they fit into the roles that the organisation gives them.

The rest of this chapter explores four main areas:

* personality
* attitudes and perception
* motivation
* groups and teams.

Personality

Why study personality?

From a managerial perspective, personality is an important issue because it is believed by many that personality is related to job performance and career success (Huczynski and Buchanan 2001). Organisations want certain personality types working for them – for example, people who are committed, conscientious and career-orientated. Knowing about personality helps managers in two ways. Firstly, it helps them to select the appropriate person for the job and the organisation through the use of psychometric testing and, secondly, it helps them to understand the individuals under their management, so that they can manage them and their work environment more effectively.

Definition of personality

Personality refers to the psychological qualities that influence an individual's characteristic behaviour patterns, in a distinctive and consistent manner, across different situations over time (Huczynski and Buchanan 2001). However, whilst personality theory looks at patterns of behaviour that are consistent, this does not mean that personality cannot be flexible. We know that the conscientious, quiet young man in sales can become a rampaging lager lout when on holiday! Behaviour we exhibit depends in part, therefore, on the social context.

There are two main approaches to personality. The first is based on the belief that personality is inherited – it is determined by genes and the biochemistry of our brains. Indeed, some psychologists would even go so far as to say there is a 'criminal' gene. All of this implies that your personality is fixed at birth, if not before, and that life's experiences do little or nothing to alter it. Other psychologists, however, argue that personality is shaped by environmental, cultural and social factors, and that our feelings and behaviour patterns are learned through observing and imitating others. Thus, our personality is flexible and changes with experience.

This ongoing argument between psychologists is referred to as the 'nature versus nurture' debate. Those approaches which favour 'nature' as dictating behaviour are called *nomothetic* approaches; those which believe that it is situational factors which influence our personality are called *ideographic* approaches. The following sections consider these approaches in more detail.

(a) Nomothetic approaches to personality

The nomothetic approach to the study of personality emphasises the identification of universal personality traits and looks for systematic relationships between different aspects of personality. This approach can be divided into *trait* theorists and *type* theorists.

Traits

A trait is a relatively stable quality or attribute of an individual's personality which influences behaviour in a particular direction. Traits include, for example, shyness, sociability and conscientiousness and trait theorists describe people in terms of a number of personality dimensions.

Catell's 16 personality factor questionnaire

Catell (1965) identifies two types of traits

- surface traits that are directly observable in behaviour

- source traits that cannot be observed directly and the existence of which can only be inferred

He claims that these traits are the fundamental factors or building blocks that make up personality (Rollinson *et al.*1998) and his research led him to identify 16 traits that were said to be the fundamental dimensions of personality (see Figure 13.1). Through data, such as ratings by other people of an individual's behaviour, self ratings and objective performance measures, an individual's personality traits can be identified through his questionnaire.

Two points need to be made regarding this questionnaire:

1. The sixteen factors are bipolar dimensions of personality. Therefore, whilst an individual can be located somewhere between practical and imaginative, these are two opposing characteristics and not a scale which measures how reserved or outgoing the person is.

2. Each factor is independent of the other factors.

Despite criticisms of being over-simple, Catell's questionnaire is used a lot by organisations for recruitment and selection.

Figure 13.1: *Catell's 16 personality factors*

Low score description	Factor	High score description
Reserved, detached, critical, aloof: *sizothymia*	A	**Outgoing**, Warm hearted, easygoing, participating: *affectothymia*
Less intelligent, concrete thinking *lower scholastic mental capacity*	B	**More intelligent**, abstract thinking *higher scholastic mental capacity*
Affected by feelings, emotionally less stable, easily upset: *lower ego strength*	C	**Emotionally stable**, faces reality, calm, mature: *higher ego strength*
Humble, mild, accommodating, conforming: *submissiveness*	E	**Assertive**, aggressive, stubborn, competitive: *Dominance*
Sober, prudent, serious, taciturn *desurgency*	F	**Happy-go-lucky**, impulsively lively, enthusiastic: *Surgency*
Expedient, disregards rules, feels few obligations: *weaker superego strength*	G	**Conscientious**, persevering, staid, moralistic; *stronger superego strength*
Shy, restrained, timid, threat sensitive *threctia*	H	**Venturesome**, socially bold, uninhibited, spontaneous: *parmia*
Tough minded, self-reliant, realistic, no-nonsense: *harria*	I	**Tender-minded**, clinging, over-protected, sensitive: *premsia*
Trusting, adaptable, free of jealousy, easy to get along with: *alaxia*	L	**Suspicious**, self-opinionated, hard to fool *protension*
Practical, careful, conventional, regulated by external realities, proper: *praxernia*	M	**Imaginative**, wrapped up in inner urgencies, careless of practical matters, bohemian: *autia*
Forthright, natural, artless, unpretentious: *artlessness*	N	**Shrewd**, calculating, worldly, penetrating: *shrewdness*
Self-assured, confident, serene *untroubled adequacy*	O	**Apprehensive**, self-reproaching, worrying, troubled: *guilt proneness*
Conservative, respecting established ideas, tolerant of traditional difficulties: *conservatism*	Q₁	**Experimenting**, liberal, analytical, free thinking: *radicalism*
Group dependent, a 'joiner' and sound follower: *group adherence*	Q₂	**Self-sufficient**, prefers own decisions, resourceful: *self-sufficiency*
Undisciplined self-conflict, follows own urges, careless of protocol: *low integration*	Q₃	**Controlled**, socially precise, following self-image: *high self-concept control*
Relaxed, tranquil, unfrustrated *low ergic tension*	Q₄	**Tense**, frustrated, driven, overwrought *high ergic tension*

Source: (Rollinson *et al.* 1998:83)

Eysenck's type theory

Type theories place people into predetermined categories on the basis of characteristics that are said to give rise to certain types of behaviour. Eysenck (1947) based his 'type theory' on extensive empirical work, which led him to believe that there are two fundamental dimensions of personality:

- Extroversion – Introversion.

- Neuroticism – Stability

These dimensions give four personality types – stable extroverts, unstable extroverts, unstable introverts and stable introverts. These types are sometimes known by the same names used by Hippocrates, when, centuries ago, he identified four personality types (see below). As Figure 13.2 demonstrates, each type is associated with a number of specific personality traits.

Figure 13.2: *Eysenck's personality types*

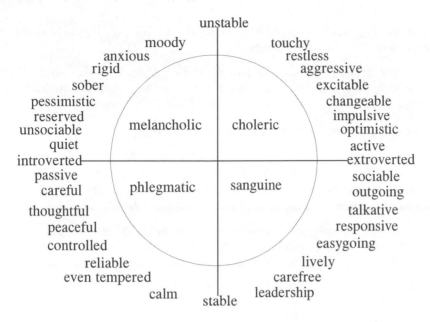

Source: Rollinson *et al.* (1998:84)

Extroverts are generally found to be sociable, outgoing and carefree, but can be aggressive, quick-tempered and sometimes unreliable. Introverts are the opposite. Neurotics can be unstable, anxious and finicky and suffer from lack of self-esteem, whereas stable people show the opposite tendencies.

Eysenck regarded personality as largely inherited; whilst people become diverse and individualistic as they gain a wider experience of the world, their reactions to the experience depend very much upon their personality type. Therefore, hereditary factors are assumed to have a strong enduring influence.

(b) Idiographic approaches to personality

Unlike nomothetic approaches, the idiographic approach to the study of personality emphasises the uniqueness of the individual, challenging the assumption that we can all be measured and compared on the same dimensions. They deal with the individual as an integral whole and focus on the development of the personality.

The psychodynamic perspective

There are common assumptions that underpin all psychodynamic theories:

- the psychological determination of behaviour. That is, mental activity precedes physical activity;

- the unconscious has a prominent role in determining behaviour and, at times, unconscious thoughts can force their way into the consciousness;

- all behaviour is goal directed, although humans are not always aware of what those goals might be;

- adult personality usually results from childhood experiences, so there is a strong emphasis on personality development.

Rather than simply seeking to describe and measure personality, the psychodynamic approach is the only one that seeks to explain in a detailed way how an individual's personality comes to be what it is (Rollinson *et al*. 1998: 70-71).

Freudian conception of personality structure and dynamics

One of the most famous personality theorists is, of course, Freud. He believed that a person's psyche has three components. They are not 'physical' parts of the brain but, rather, abstract concepts that describe driving forces behind behaviour. These components are also at different levels of depth in the mind:

1. *The Id.* This is the biologically driven component of personality that consists of inherited drives which demand immediate gratification of all that is pleasurable. It is with us from birth and makes no distinction between right and wrong.

2. *The Ego.* This develops out of the Id. It attempts to balance the Id's demands against the reality of the external world, and therefore is the force that keeps the individual together as a whole.

3. *The Superego.* This component reflects the learned rules of society which are absorbed during upbringing. It exerts moral restraint by forbidding certain actions.

Freud (1901) perceived adult personality dynamics as a conflict between the id, the ego, and the superego. In a well-adjusted person, the ego manages to balance the needs/desires/expectations of the id and the superego with the external reality of any given situation. This is a difficult thing to achieve when the id is always driving the person to gratify needs with no thought to the consequences and the superego is constantly driving to resist gratification! If the id or the superego is stronger than the ego, permanent anxieties can be present. These include, for example, 'denial', when the individual refuses to recognise a change which can be harmful and so ignores it, and 'regression', which refers to the ego taking the person back to a form of behaviour that was successful in coping with a similar situation, for instance, bursting into tears when being reprimanded at work.

Carl Rogers' person-centred theory

Rogers (1951) believes that, in order to understand people, it is necessary to understand how they view themselves and the world around them. Central to his ideas is the individual's concept of self. There is the 'actual' self which the individual believes himself/herself to be and the 'ideal' self – the self as the person would like to be. Rogers argues that most people behave in a way that tries to maintain congruence between what they do and their concept of self and, therefore, if you believe you are sociable and outgoing then you are likely to behave in this way. Thus, the behaviour of individuals can be predicted to some extent by finding out what they think of themselves. However, Rogers also believes that people are always striving for the ideal self, towards 'self-actualisation'. This has important implications for organisations in terms of motivation, as considered later in the chapter.

Implications for organisations of personality

Knowledge of personality is of benefit to the organisation in a number of ways:

1. For recruitment and selection purposes. Nomothetic approaches, which use data from questionnaires to identify different personality traits or types, help organisations to make decisions about who is the best person to join their organisation. Most organisations have their own cultures and accepted patterns of behaviour. Thus, personality differences means some people are likely to fit into an organisation better than others. In addition, jobs differ in terms of the personal characteristics that they require and so an individual's personality could have an impact on his or her suitability for certain roles.

2. To predict job performance. Again, some personality theories postulate that certain personality types may perform more effectively than other personality types.

3. For counselling/employee welfare purposes. Many organisations today have set up Employee Welfare or Employee Assistance Programmes in order to help employees who may be suffering from work related stress, personal problems, and so on.

Perception

Why study perception?

We all perceive the world around us in different ways; we attach different meanings, interpretations, values and aims to our actions. What we do in the world depends on how we perceive ourselves and our social and physical environment, and on how we perceive our circumstances. Our personal perception of reality shapes and directs our behaviour. Therefore, if we are to understand why someone behaves in a certain way then, first of all, we need to discover how they perceived the context and their place in it. We need to be able to understand why they perceived things differently in the first place.

Definition of perception

Perception is the dynamic psychological process responsible for attending to, organising and interpreting sensory data. We each have a similar nervous system and share more or less common sensory equipment so, to this extent, we process and interpret incoming data in a similar way. However, we have different social and physical backgrounds which give us different values, beliefs, knowledge, interests, expectations and, therefore, different perceptions. We do not behave in, and respond to, a 'real world' – we behave in, and in response to, the world as we perceive it. In short, we each live in our own perceptual world.

Perceptual sets

A perceptual set is an individual's predisposition to respond in a particular manner. As already stated, perception is an information processing activity – it involves ordering and attaching meaning to 'raw' sensory data. Sensory apparatus is bombarded with vast amounts of information, both internal to us, such as hunger or pain, and external to us from people, objects and events. We are constantly sifting and sorting out this information, making sense of it and interpreting it. The process we go through is influenced by learning, motivation and personality, factors which give rise to expectations which, in turn make us more or less ready to respond to certain stimuli in certain ways and less ready to respond to others.

Perceptual sets and assumptions

Much of perception can be described as classification or categorisation. We categorise people as male or female, lazy or energetic, and so on. These categories are learned – we are not born with neat classification schemes. What also has to be remembered is that what we learn is often culture bound or culture specific. Cultural factors play a significant role in determining how we interpret available information and experience. We tend to select information that fits our expectations and pay less attention to information that does not. When we have complete or ambiguous information we 'fill in the gaps' from our own knowledge and past experience, or what we have 'learned'. This can lead to two phenomena which can give rise to problems in organisations and elsewhere:

i. Stereotyping

Defined as attributing a person with qualities assumed to be typical of members of a particular category because the person falls into that category, stereotyping is a bias in person perception. Stereotypes are overgeneralisations. For example, 'Germans are loud and fight over sunbeds on holiday', or 'British holidaymakers just want Blackpool with sun' are both wildly inaccurate generalisations.

ii. Halo/horns effect

This is a form of stereotyping, when our judgement is based on something that we have noticed about a person, for example, how they dress or how they have behaved in a situation at work. From this we make huge assumptions about the person and their behaviour.

The halo effect is when our assumptions are positive, such as when we assume that a person who dresses smartly must be efficient and well organised. Conversely, the horns effect is a negative one. For example, a person who was five minutes late for the meeting must be lazy, disorganised and not competent in his job. Despite efforts to train interviewers and appraisers in objectivity and impartiality, these phenomena are apparent in a number of organisation activities, such as recruitment and selection and performance appraisal (Jacobs and Kozlowski 1985, cited in Rollinson *et al.* 1998)

> *Errors in perception can be overcome by taking more time and collecting more information. Marketing/Customer Service Departments spend vast resources finding out customers' perceptions of their product or service. Direct Holidays, for example, are currently looking to expand into the Irish marketplace. Their research involves identifying Irish perceptions of what constitutes a 'good holiday' in order that they can provide a product which appeals. They do not intend to fall into the trap of British Airways who, in their attempt to incorporate cultural diversity on their flights to Egypt, did not make themselves aware of all the facts. To improve customer service they introduced Arab music, coffee and dates served by multi-national cabin staff on all their flights between London and*

Egypt. However, it was not Egyptian music, and Egyptians prefer to drink mint tea. British Airways had, unfortunately, 'stereotyped', categorising all Arabs together rather than perceiving each Arab state as separate.

Definition of attitudes

An attitude can be defined as a persistent tendency to feel and behave in a particular way towards some object (Luthans 1995: 121). Attitudes have the following characteristics:

1. they are held towards something specific that is part of the world of the attitude holder;

2. they reflect the attitude holder's experience of that aspect of his or her world;

3. to a large extent, they are learned from experience and are relatively enduring;

4. since the definition implies feeling and evaluation, attitudes have a bearing on how the individual reacts to the object;

5. because attitudes involve mental processes, they are not tangible objects that can be observed directly and their existence can only be inferred.

Attitudes have three basic components (Breckler 1984 in Luthans 1995) and the more consistent they are with one another, the more stable the attitude.

*   The cognitive component, that is, the perceptions and beliefs about the object. For example, a positive attitude towards a country – Switzerland is clean and well-organised.

*   The affective component, or the emotional feelings. Switzerland is inspirational because of its breathtaking mountain scenery.

*   The behavioural component, that is, the tendency to act towards the object, in this case Switzerland, in a consistent and characteristic way. For example, going on holiday there every year, encouraging your friends to visit, etc.

Functions of attitudes

Attitudes serve a useful purpose to the individual – they are part of an individual's psychological makeup and develop and change in a response to the person's current needs (Rollinson *et al.* 1998). In a work related context, attitudes help predict worker behaviour. For example, if an attitude survey shows that workers are upset by the change in working hours, and the next week absenteeism begins to increase, management may be able to conclude that a negative attitude towards working hours led to an increase in worker absenteeism.

Job satisfaction

Job satisfaction is one of the work related attitudes that receives the most attention both in the literature and in organisations. There are three important dimensions to job satisfaction:

1. It is an emotional response to a job situation, so it is not tangible.

2. It is often determined by how well outcomes meet or exceed expectations. Therefore, if people feel they are working harder than other people in the

department but are receiving fewer rewards, then they will probably have a negative attitude towards work, their superior and colleagues. However, if they feel that they are being treated well then they will have a positive attitude.

3. It represents several related attitudes. Smith, Kendall and Hulin (1969) suggest that there are five dimensions to the attitude all of which reflect responses to the job (Luthans 1995, Rollinson *et al.* 1998). These are:

    - *The work itself* – to what extent does the job provide the individual with tasks, opportunities for learning and taking responsibility?

    - *Pay* – is the financial reward received adequate and is it equitable compared to what other people receive?

    - *Promotion Opportunities*

    - *Supervision* – the extent to which the person concerned derives satisfaction from his relationship with his immediate superior. Is the supervisor supportive, both technically and interpersonally?

    - *Co-workers* – the degree to which co-workers are technically competent and socially supportive.

Implications of job satisfaction to organisations

Whether or not this is the case, organisations take a great deal of interest in the extent to which people are satisfied in their work because of its potential effects. For example:

1. *Employee Turnover*. Research would indicate that where job satisfaction is high, labour turnover is reduced (Rollinson *et al.* 1998).

2. *Employee Absenteeism*. When people are not satisfied in their work, they tend to absent themselves on a more frequent basis. This could be as a result of stress, illness, lack of motivation or because they are looking for jobs elsewhere.

3. *Employee Productivity*. The interest in job satisfaction stems from the fact that, for many years, there has been the assumption that a 'satisfied' worker is a 'productive' worker. However, this debate is ongoing, with some writers believing that rewards play a much greater part in job satisfaction than was first believed (Podsakoff and Williams 1986 in Rollinson *et al.* 1998). Another issue is about whether satisfaction leads to performance, or whether good performance leads to satisfaction.

Attitudes of Employees in the Cypriot Hotel Industry: A Pilot Study

Since the 1960s, Cyprus has successfully developed into a major, mass tourism destination but now, after many years of growth, the island's tourism industry faces a less certain future. In order to survive and prosper within an increasingly competitive marketplace, there is a need for Cyprus to reassert its reputation for high levels of service and hospitality. This, of course, is dependent upon the co-operation of the workforce, particularly within the hotel industry.

In 1999, a pilot study was undertaken to find out employees' attitudes towards their work within the hotel industry and towards tourism/tourists. Whilst attitudes towards the tourism industry and working within it were, in general, positive, the findings highlighted a number of implications for management. These were:

- A need for training in order to improve levels of service. It was recommended that this training should not only focus on specific skills such as handling customer complaints, but a total quality approach should be adopted through the development of communication and teamwork to improve customer service.

- A review of remuneration packages. Whilst wage levels within the Cypriot hotel industry remain linked to a national bargaining process, hotel managers were asked to consider introducing a performance-related element into future wage negotiations.

- Job security. Hotel work is often seasonal, which means a lack of job security to many employees. Although this problem is related to the overall characteristics of tourism in Cyprus, the authors of the study believed that attempts could be made by management to work with the tourism authorities and tour operators to develop new products/markets which might reduce some of the impacts of seasonality on employment.

See Sharpley and Forster (2000)

Implications of perception and attitudes for organisations

Managers need to be aware of:

- how perception may influence an individual's behavioural pattern in relation to other people in the organisation, for example, stereotyping, and seek to overcome this through appropriate selection of staff, training, etc.;

- how values and attitudes develop in the individual and how these relate to the organisation. In any change situation in the organisation, whether it be changing the organisation's culture, structure or HR systems, all will require a change in attitudes;

- the extent to which the individual's job provides him/her with what s/he values in a work situation. If not, absenteeism, sickness and eventually leaving the organisation will occur.

Motivation

Why study motivation?

To managers, motivation has great practical significance. Everything that is achieved by an organisation is achieved because of the human activity within it and an organisation's success is dependent upon the extent to which its employees are willing, and able, to channel their energies into performing their tasks. Because of this, managers must know what motivates people and be able to create the conditions which will enable people to perform effectively.

Definition of motivation

Rollinson *et al.* (1998: 148) define motivation as:

> *a state arising in processes that are internal and external to the individual, in which the person perceives that it is appropriate to pursue a certain course of action (or actions) directed at achieving a specified outcome (or outcomes) and in which the person chooses to pursue those outcomes with a degree of vigour and persistence.*

This definition refers to three components of behaviour that has an impact on performance:

- the *direction* of behaviour – what does the person want to do?

- the *intensity* of behaviour – how hard is the person going to try to go in that direction?

- the *persistence* of behaviour – how willing is the person to keep going in this direction even if there are obstacles in the way?

Theories of motivation

Motivation theories attempt to provide a framework which can predict behaviour, especially behaviour at work. Some focus on how people can be motivated to work harder for the benefit of the organisation whilst others seek to improve an individual's sense of satisfaction and fulfilment at work. At the same time, however, many theories also address the fact that each individual is unique and, therefore, not everyone will be motivated in the same way.

A number of text books divide motivation theories up into content and process theories. Content theories are concerned with why do people work and provide a universalistic approach to what motivates. Process theories identify factors that affect people's willingness or persistence to work.

Three waves of motivation

Watson (1986), however, identifies three categories of motivation theories which he calls 'waves'. The first wave represents the oldest way of thinking, the second more recent, and the third, the most up to date set of ideas. It must be noted that one wave does not replace another. Indeed, Watson (1986: 89) claims that 'the three groupings have little validity beyond the function which they are intended to serve: that of helping the reader find a way through a potentially frightening mass of different ideas and theories'.

Wave 1: people as machines

This wave represents the earliest thinking put forward, which includes the prescriptive approach of Taylorism, or Scientific Management. F. W. Taylor was the first to propose work study, bonus schemes, and time and motion studies, and underpinning his ideas was the belief that employees are economic animals, motivated purely by money, who generally prefer management to do all their task related thinking for them. All management had to do, therefore, was to work out the most efficient way of organising work and then introduce a payment by results system of remuneration so that workers would be motivated to apply themselves to maximum effect to the task in hand and achieve high outputs. This, of course, would produce results which would benefit both the employee and the employer. In this wave, therefore, workers are viewed as machines – both in the manner they are required to work and in the way they are 'fed' with cash in proportion to their output (Watson 1986).

Motivation and retention in call centres

Call centres are in danger of becoming the dark satanic mills of the 21st century as the industry gains a reputation for sweatshop practices and assembly-line methods (Management Today 1999, in Maude 2000: 3).

Maude (2000) researched into what motivates people to work in a call centre for a travel company, and what it is about the job that makes them stay. She believes that, despite the long unsociable hours, the high targets, low pay and weekend work associated with the travel industry, people still find this environment dynamic and attractive to work in. In her report, she puts forward the view that the reputation of call centres, as cited above, stems from organisations operating in industries such as telecommunications where consultants have a specific 'script' to keep to and the job is far more repetitive and unchallenging than the job of a sales consultant in the travel industry.

Her findings, however, do not support this view to any great extent. Whilst 'bonuses' and 'incentives' in travel companies appeared to be wider ranging than in other industries, including, for example, education trips, 'travel bank' bonuses for achievement of personal targets each month, free travel insurance and reduced rate travel, employees' opinions were much the same as elsewhere. They felt that the basic salary is too low, targets are unrealistically high, there is inconsistency in incentives and, more importantly, they did not feel valued or recognised by the senior management for good work done.

Maude's (2000) overall conclusion was that:

- The senior management did not meet simple psychological expectations such as praise, recognition and appreciation. Instead, they provided negative feedback and there were repercussions for failure of achievement.

- Reward systems barely met the individual's extrinsic or intrinsic needs.

See Maude (2000)

Wave 2: People with needs

Under this heading are the approaches of human relations and democratic humanism, schools of thought that attempt to influence managerial practice in terms of improving the human lot, arguing that a human does not become a machine at work whilst existing only as a person outside its doors.

Theorists in this wave emphasise the social needs of people at work and their desire for 'belonging' in some way. They argue that employees' productivity is more affected by their need to be secure, involved and recognised (intrinsic needs) than by physical conditions or level of monetary reward (extrinsic needs).

Figure 13.3: *Need-hierarchy based approaches to motivation*

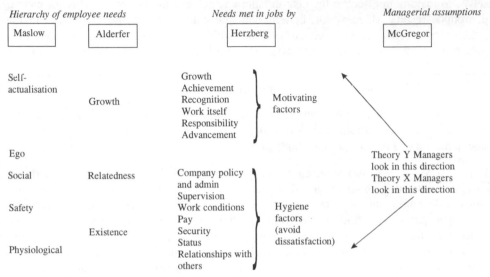

Source: Watson (1986:109)

Maslow: Hierarchy of needs (1943)

Maslow's basic proposition is that people are wanting beings – they always want more, and what they want depends on what they have. He places their needs in a hierarchy of importance, like a pyramid:

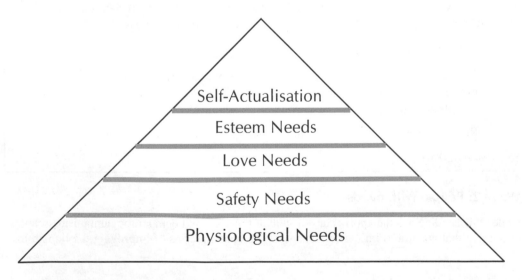

- *Physiological Needs* – food, drink, sex and sensory satisfactions

- *Safety Needs* – security, freedom from pain or harm

- *Love Needs* – Need to belong and affiliate with others

- *Esteem Needs* –prestige, status, and appreciation, sense of achievement

- *Self-actualisation* – the need to reach one's full potential

The pyramid is generally regarded as a fixed order, with individuals progressing up it from the physiological needs to self-actualisation. Once a lower level has been satisfied, it no longer acts as a strong motivator and the next higher level of hierarchy demands satisfaction and thus becomes the motivating influence.

There are, however, a number of problems relating this to a work situation:

1. People do not necessarily satisfy their needs, especially higher level needs, just through the work situation.

2. Individual differences means that individuals place different values on the same need. For example, some people prefer what they see as job security in a public organisation – a tourism department in a local authority – to a more highly paid but less secure job in a commercial tourism organisation.

3. It is unclear which needs lead to which behaviours or which behaviours are determined by which need (Foster in Chmiel 2000).

Alderfer's ERG Theory (1972)

Alderfer uses similar ideas to Maslow's, but proposes only three levels: Existence (E), Relatedness (R) and Growth (G). As Figure 13.3 shows, these approximate to Maslow's levels, although there is an important difference. That is, Alderfer sees needs as lying along a continuum, so that a number of needs are activated or being satisfied at the same time, rather than consequentially as in Maslow's model. Furthermore, he argues that if one set of needs are not being satisfied, the ensuing frustration of satisfaction will force the individual to refocus their efforts on another set of needs. For example, if you are finding that your work does not give you the opportunities and feeling of self-worth that you need, then you may focus more on your personal relationships outside work.

Herzberg's two-factor theory (1959, 1966, 1976)

Herzberg's research revealed that there are two different sets of factors affecting motivation:

(a) *Hygiene factors*, such as working conditions, salary, status, security and relationships with superiors, which lead to dissatisfaction if they did not meet the expectations of the individual, and

(b) *Motivating factors*, which include receiving recognition, being given responsibility, personal growth and achievement.

Evidently, hygiene factors relate to Maslow's lower level needs, whilst motivators relate to his higher level needs. Herzberg argues that addressing hygiene factors will prevent dissatisfaction but will not create motivation to work. Therefore, to motivate employees, attention must be given to the motivators. This means designing jobs so that workers themselves take responsibility for planning their work, choosing appropriate methods and so on; in other words, the direct opposite of Taylorism.

McGregor: X and Y theory

McGregor (1957, 1960) identifies two basic styles of management. Theory X assumes that people dislike work and will avoid it if they can, meaning that the manager has to control and coerce people towards meeting organisation objectives. McGregor argues that the theory operates as a self-fulfilling prophecy. That is, it actually brings about the kind of behaviour it assumes to be inevitable, either through an employee's passive acceptance of the situation leading to a lack of initiative and creativity, or becoming resentful and uncooperative (Watson 1986). Theory Y, however, operates under the assumption that people want to take responsibility and that most people are creative and want to take the initiative – they are just waiting for management to give them the opportunity! This means that managers should use a participative style rather than an authoritarian one.

McGregor's theory sets up two extremes of how managers tend to think about employee motivation, and is useful in showing how self-fulfilling prophecies occurring in the motivational area can restrict, or improve, performance.

The theorists in this wave have contributed to the debate about motivation by raising many basic questions about the assumptions managers may have about employee behaviour, or indeed, nature. However, there are drawbacks to this approach:

1. Their psychological universalism infers, to some extent, that cultural and social processes do not have much impact upon an individual's behaviour.

2. More attention is required about how people might want different things from work, or might want different things at different times.

Wave 3: People and processes

This wave of theory produces a more sophisticated view of human beings and their mental processes. People are not just led by their needs, but are creative and assertive, and they calculate what is worth putting into work for what they will get out of it. These theories are more successful in highlighting the differences between individuals and their differing motivational states. They emphasise the process by which individuals think, calculate and pursue purposes.

Adams: Equity theory

Adams (1963, 1965) suggests that people balance what they put into their work with what they get out of it in the light of what they see other people putting in and taking out of similar situations (Watson 1986:118). This means that if a reward is perceived as unfair, an individual will balance this out by putting less effort into the situation. However, the reverse has not been proven: that a perceived over generous reward will not motivate the individual to put more effort in, they will merely perceive it as their 'good fortune'.

Vroom: Expectancy theory

Vroom (1965) suggests that people are influenced by the expected results of their actions. There are five conditions needed before motivation exists. Individuals:

1. have to believe that the effort make will achieve effective performance;

2. have to see that appropriate performance will lead to their receiving rewards to perceive the available rewards as attractive;

3. must have the appropriate skills and knowledge to achieve effective performance;

4. must have an appropriate perception of the role they are filling. That is, they must be aware of all internal and external factors, such as performance targets or maintaining good relationships with superiors and peers, which influence the extent to which their objectives will be fulfilled.

Figure 13.4: *The expectancy view of work motivation*

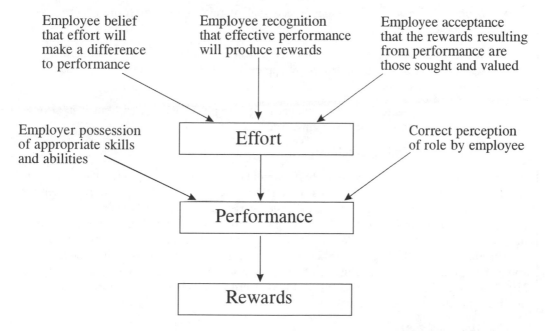

Source: Watson (1986:119)

The advantage of expectancy theory is that it provides a practical framework to managers for analysing work motivation – it provides a checklist of factors and provides the relevant links between them.

Incentive Travel as a Motivation to Employees – does it work?

Incentive travel is used by a number of companies to motivate employees. They are generally companies, or departments of companies, that depend heavily on sales and so need to find incentives to motivate staff. That individual who meets or exceeds performance targets is rewarded with an 'extraordinary travel experience' (Society of Incentive Travel 1996) for being such a high achiever.

After money, incentive travel appears to be the most popular reward (Fisher 2000). Reasons given are:

- It offers intrinsic psychological aspects such as relaxation away from the stresses of everyday live.

- It illustrates management's acknowledgement of the achiever's efforts showing that no expense is spared to show appreciation, thus boosting the individual's sense of self worth.

- It has 'trophy value' – the individual is not simply winning a trip but it is also the manner and level of luxury involved.

- Peer recognition boosts self esteem.

According to Ricci and Holland (1992), winning an incentive trip sets the individual amongst the elite group of employees as it is considered an exclusive reward. Incentive travel participation is a combination of basic work motivation ideas, competition, peer recognition, status, self-esteem and fantasy goal fulfilment. Although an attractive theory, however, more recent research suggests the ultimate travel prize is not always a 'satisfactory carrot' (Burleigh 2001:42). That is, it does appear to increase the motivation of some, but not all, employees. Burleigh's work supports the argument of Holmes and Smith (1987) that travel will only be successful if the reward is perceived to be reasonable to attain and it is attractive to the individual.

Source: (Burleigh 2001)

Implications for organisations

- Motivation approaches and theories have been considered to give variable insights into the nature of employee behaviour and offer some practical guidance for those involved in the management of employees for enhancing employee performance.

- There is no simple link between motivation and job satisfaction.

- Theories acknowledge to a greater or lesser extent the differences between individuals as to what motivates them, but *culture* has received less attention. Many writers assume that what has been found in developed western countries is likely to be true for any other culture, but organisations also need to think about subcultural differences in motivation, such as gender differences.

- Contemporary theories emphasise the need for the employer or manager to be more than a source of financial rewards and to understand the needs of the workforce, to consider the issue of job design and to enhance the well being of those below him or her.

- No set of theories can be regarded as the whole story; taken together they all have something useful to offer. They provide four general lessons:

  (a) When an employee becomes motivated, this is the outcome of a psychological process. Managers cannot observe this process at work, nor can they apply or supply motivation directly to employees. However, an employee's level of motivation can be influenced to some extent by the manager creating conditions that the individual finds stimulating and encouraging.

  (b) Managers need to be sensitive to variations in individual needs, goals, preferences and abilities – not everyone is motivated in the same way in the same set of organisation circumstances.

  (c) The needs of the individuals can change over time so organisations must be prepared to adapt to those changing needs. Provision of an encouraging work environment has to be kept under constant review.

  (d) Whilst it is not only work that motivates individuals, organisations still need to provide a motivating work experience that gives sufficient diversity, opportunity and challenge to satisfy needs. It is half the battle won.

Groups and teams

Why study groups and teams?

Most people working in any organisation will spend a lot of their time working in groups, and effective group working is fundamental to the achievement of any organisation's goals and objectives. Therefore, a knowledge of groups and teams, and how they function, is vital for any manager, potential manager, or individual working in an organisation.

Definition of a group

Schein (1980) defined, in psychological terms, a group as any number of people who

- interact with one another;

- are psychologically aware of one another;

- perceive themselves to be a group; and

- purposefully interact towards the achievement of particular goals or aims.

Formal and informal groups

Groups have tremendous influence over an individual's behaviour whilst an individual's behaviour also has great influence over the group.

Formal groups are those groups that are brought into existence by the structure of an organisation, for example, departments, task groups, command groups.

Command groups are permanent groups of people all under a single manager who perform similar activities, such as in a call-centre. At TravelBag, for example, command groups will all be situated in the same room, but one command group will sell holidays to Australia, one to the United States and so forth.

Task groups are temporary formal groups formed for a specific short-term purpose or special project, and they are dispersed as soon as the task is completed; for example, a group of people are brought together to write and print a brochure for a particular destination. The group of people will be from different departments in the organisation, as graphic designers, copy writers, account managers, marketing managers and sales representatives are all required to input their own specific expertise into the project.

Schein (1980) lists six formal functions of groups:

1. They work on complex tasks not easily undertaken by the individual.

2. They are a means of stimulating creativity and generating new ideas.

3. They act as a liaison/co-ordination mechanism which integrates different parts of an organisation.

4. They are there for problem solving purposes where multiple viewpoints are important.

5. They implement decisions so that a common objective or goal can be set for a number of people.

6. They are useful as a socialising device so that a common message, especially with respect to an organisation's culture, can be communicated and reinforced.

Informal groups are not set up by the organisation, but tend to run parallel to formal groups. They exist for a different purpose, however, which is principally to satisfy the social needs of their members. Membership of an informal group is voluntary and joining also involves the consent of existing group members. This means that an informal group can often exert a more powerful influence over an individual's behaviour than a formal one.

The benefits of informal groups are that they:

1. fulfil the members' social needs, that is, friendship and social interaction;

2. develop, test and confirm a person's sense of identity and self-worth;

3. establish and test beliefs, reality, experience and meanings;

4. reduce feelings of insecurity, anxiety and powerlessness; and

5. achieve mutually agreed informal aims and objectives.

(Schein 1980, quoted in Rollinson *et al*. 1998: 296)

As Rollinson *et al.(*1998) argue, it is likely that managers will focus more on the formal groups than the informal groups but, generally, the two complement one another. Even if an individual has not much say in which formal group he must belong to, the group can fulfil some of the informal group functions – working on a task, sharing the experiences, implementing decisions can give people a sense of self-worth and accomplishment.

Group formation and development

All groups go through various stages of development from inception to maturity, when they can start to perform effectively. Tuckman (1965) identifies the various stages of group development in his Integrative Model.

Stage 1 – Forming

The group is a collection of individuals brought together. As a result, they devote a lot of attention to getting to know one another rather than to the task in hand.

Stage 2 - Storming

This stage is characterised by interpersonal conflict; personal agendas and goals surface as people get to know one another and begin to express their views more openly. It is an uncomfortable stage for everybody involved, and concessions need to be made so that the group can move onto the next stage.

Stage 3 - Norming

The rules for a group's way of functioning start to emerge, and group norms are formulated to predict future behaviour, such as keeping to deadlines. Distinct roles start to emerge and signs of co-operation and sensitivity are much in evidence.

Stage 4 – Performing

At this final stage of development, the group becomes capable of effective functioning; task aspects and social aspects complement one another. Members are supportive, and trusting, of one another. They are much better equipped to perform their role effectively.

Tuckman added one further stage which is particularly relevant to today's working conditions – that of *adjourning,* when the group is disbanded because people leave or its task has been completed. Adjournment is often accompanied with sadness and a sense of loss.

This particular model is useful for two reasons. Firstly, it provides guidelines to anyone who is starting up a new group and, secondly, it explains why some groups are never effective. Belbin (1981, 1993), however, provides another explanation as to why groups do not always perform as effectively as hoped, or predicted.

Group effectiveness

An effective group is one in which both task and socio-emotive needs are met, and this occurs when individual members occupy compatible roles. Belbin, (1981, 1993) identifies what he believes to be nine key roles in an effective group. The central thrust to his argument is that effective groups and teams seldom consist of people who are of the same type, but of people who have different and complementary skills and expertise. Effective and creative teams require a balanced mix of individual characteristics. If the tasks change then individual roles will change, and if a team is small then people will occupy more than one role.

Figure 13.5: *Belbin's 9 team roles*

- **The Plant.** This role requires someone who is creative, imaginative and unorthodox. Plants solve difficult problems, but they ignore details and are too preoccupied to communicate effectively.

- **The Resource Investigator.** Resource Investigators are extrovert, enthusiastic and communicative. They explore opportunities and develop contacts. Sometimes though they are over optimistic and they lose interest once the initial enthusiasm has passed.

- **The Co-ordinator.** This role requires someone who is mature, confident and a good chairperson. They are able to clarify goals and promote decision making as well as being good delegators. However, they can be seen as manipulative.

- **The Shaper.** Shapers are challenging, dynamic and they thrive on pressure. They have to drive and courage to overcome obstacles, but they can provoke others and hurt people's feelings.

- **The Monitor-Evaluator.** Monitor-Evaluators are strategic and discerning. They see all options and **judge** accurately. However, they lack drive and the ability to inspire others. They are also overly critical.

- **The Team-Worker.** A role that requires someone who is co-operative, mild, perceptive and dynamic. Team-workers listen, build, avert friction and calm the waters. They can also be very indecisive in crunch situations and can be easily influenced.

- **The Implementer.** The Implementer is disciplined, reliable and efficient. They turn ideas into practical actions. However they can be inflexible and they are slow to respond to new possibilities.

- **The Completer-Finisher.** The Completer-Finisher is painstaking, conscientious but also anxious as they search out errors and omissions. They always deliver on time and are **reluctant** to delegate.

- **The Specialist.** This role requires someone who is single-minded, self-starting and **dedicating**. They provide knowledge and skills that are in rare supply. However, they tend to dwell on technicalities and overlook the big picture.

Source: Adapted from Belbin (1993)

Definition of a team

Whilst to some people the terms 'group' and 'team' are interchangeable, most theorists make a distinction between the two. Unsworth and West (in Chmiel 2000) believe that a number of conditions must be satisfied before a group of people can be called a team. These are that they:

- have shared goals in relation to their work;

- interact with one another in order to achieve those shared objectives;

- have well defined and interdependent roles; and

- have an organisational identity as a team with a defined organisational function.

Thus, teams go beyond traditional formal work groups by having a collective, synergistic (the whole is greater than the sum of its parts) character. Teams can be formed for any purpose. For example:

1. *Advice teams* – a team created primarily to provide a flow of information to management to be used in its own decision making, like a committee. It is sometimes responsible for implementing those decisions.

2. *Quality circles* – these teams consist of employees from the same department who meet for a few hours each week to discuss ways of improving their work environment. Quality circles began in manufacturing companies in Japan, but now they are applied extensively in the service industries, government agencies and the voluntary sector.

3. *Cross-functional team* – this is a team composed of employees from about the same hierarchical level but from different work areas or functions within the organisation. They are brought together to complete a particular task, such as quality and customer service improvements, and operate in a similar way to task groups in that they are 'temporary' and individuals remain members of their specific department or function. They are very often used by organisations to implement quality and customer service improvements.

The disadvantages of groups and teams

Whilst there are a number of apparent advantages to group and team-working, as demonstrated above, there are also a number of disadvantages:

Intergroup conflict

Because an effective and cohesive group has its own norms and values, there is always an in-built potential for conflict and, therefore, co-operation between groups cannot be taken for granted. Furthermore, winning can become all important as groups compete with one another for sales targets, customers and so on, so that other groups become the 'enemy'.

Group polarisation (risky shift)

This refers to the tendency of some groups to opt for much riskier decision alternatives than individuals would make. This comes about, perhaps, because of the diffusion of responsibility that comes with working in a group, the fact that taking risks have some degree of social prestige with the group, and because as the group becomes more accustomed or familiarised with the risky decision as they talk about it, it appears less risky. Furthermore, those most likely to speak out in group decision meetings are often those who have most influence in the group and their suggestions are sometimes adopted without full consideration (Stoner 1961, in Rollinson *et al.* 1998).

Groupthink

This can be explained as impaired decision making by a group because their desire for being unanimous overrides examining the consequences of a decision. The concept was developed by Janus (1972) after researching into the invasion of Cuba 1961. Historical evidence revealed that John Kennedy and his group of expert advisors were driven by seeking group consensus when making an important decision rather than basing it upon information and reality. As a result, the invasion failed (Unsworth and West, in Chmiel 2000).

Implications for organisations of groups and teams

- Organisations should not feel threatened if informal groups emerge. They are created to meet the socio-emotive needs of the individuals, which formal groups cannot always do.

- Organisations need to be aware that it takes time for a collection of individuals to develop into an effective group. If the organisation tries to hurry the process in a way that leaves some of the issues at one stage unresolved, the eventual effectiveness of the group can be seriously impaired.

- Organisations need to be aware that group effectiveness can crucially depend on an appropriate mix of different but complementary roles.

- Whilst there are a number of advantages to groups, organisations should also recognised that there are potential problems in highly cohesive groups. This includes intergroup conflict and impaired decision making.

Conclusions

This chapter has attempted to give an overview of some of the main theories which help us to understand aspects of individual and group behaviour. Individuals come together within an organisation to achieve some common purpose, but the way that these individuals are 'organised' and how the organisation 'treats' them will affect their perceptions of that organisation and the work that they do and, subsequently, their behaviour within that organisation. Therefore, managers have to be aware of a number of issues. Firstly, they have to realise that the environments in which people live and work influence their behaviour. If the external environment changes, then the needs of the people will change with it, and so must the organisation's capability to meet those needs by creating a stimulating and rewarding working environment.

Secondly, managers must understand that all people cannot be 'managed' in a similar way. Whilst some individuals may respond to the 'carrot and stick' approach of scientific management, others place far greater importance on feeling valued for the work that they do. Managers, therefore, need to be sensitive to the variations in individual needs, goals, preferences and abilities in order to get the best out of their people.

Discussion questions

1. *Compare and contrast nomothetic and idiographic approaches to personality. Which do you think is of the greatest use to organisations and why?*

2. *Man is only truly motivated by money. To what extent do you agree with this statement?*

3. *Identify when you were part of a group, either at work or university. Using Tuckman's model of Group Development:*

   • *Trace the stages that you went through, providing examples of behaviour for each stage.*

   • *Identify the problems your group encountered at each stage.*

   • *How could any of the problems have been overcome?*

Case study

Sophie is aged 23, and left school when she was 18 after successfully passing three A' levels, one being in business studies and two in languages. She works in the sales department of a leading tour operator, Viva L'Espagna, and sells villa/apartment holidays in Spain. Her job is essentially tele-sales, although she is at times allowed to do promotional work at exhibitions. In her department there are ten other people on the same grading as Sophie, three people on the grade above and the office manager, Daniel.

Each year all the members of the department have staff appraisals, where they discuss their performance over the previous year and set performance targets for the coming year. At her last appraisal meeting, Daniel had told her that he was concerned about her level of motivation as at times her performance had been below the level expected of her and she didn't seem to be committed to, or as interested in her job as they would have liked.

Sophie said that she had been doing the job for three years and that she frequently found it 'boring'. She also said that she had been disappointed not to have been promoted to the higher grade in the round of promotions that had taken place last year. This disappointment was exacerbated by the fact that each year the organisation took on a travel and tourism work placement student who, because of their theoretical knowledge and future potential in the industry, automatically took on a supervisory role. Therefore, despite lack of work experience, they were placed above her by the organisation. She didn't have anything against the students personally, but the whole situation made her feel demotivated and devalued. She was an experienced member of staff and her prospects at the organisation were zero as far as she was concerned. Sophie concluded her appraisal interview by saying that as things stood, she really had no alternative but to find work elsewhere.

Task

Analyse this case study and using some of the theories and ideas that you have learned from the chapter, provide recommendations to Daniel as to how he should manage this situation.

Further reading

Foster, J. (2000), Motivation in the Workplace, in N. Chmiel (ed.) *Introduction to Work and Organizational Psychology. A European Perspective* Oxford: Blackwell: 302-326.

Pugh, D. and Hickson, D. (1989), *Writers on Organizations, 4th Edition*, London: Penguin: *Pages 167-170.*

Sharpley, R. and Forster, G. (2000), Attitudes of Employees in the Cypriot Hotel Industry: A Pilot Study, *Cyprus International Journal of Management* Vol 5, Nos 1 & 2: 30-38.

Unsworth, K. and West, M. (2000), Teams: the Challenges of Co-operative Work, in N. Chmiel (ed.) *Introduction to Work and Psychology: A European Perspective*, Oxford: Blackwell: 327-346.

Watson, T. (1986), *Management, Organisation and Employment Strategy: New Directions in Theory and Practice,* London: Routledge. *Chapter 4.*

References

Belbin, R. M. (1981), *Managerial Teams,* London: Heinemann.

Belbin, R. M. (1993), *Team Roles at Work,* Oxford: Butterworth-Heinemann.

Brooks, I. (1999), *Organisational Behaviour: Individuals, Groups and the Organisation*, London: Pearson Education Limited.

Burleigh, S. (2001), *An Analysis of the Effectiveness of Incentive Travel as a Tool for Motivating Employees,* unpublished dissertation, University of Northumbria.

Foster, J. (2000), Motivation in the Workplace, in N. Chmiel (ed.) *Introduction to Work and Organizational Psychology: A European Perspective* Oxford: Blackwell: 302-326.

Freud, S. (1901), in D. Rollinson, A. Broadfield and D. Edwards (1998) *Organisational Behaviour and Analysis. An Integrated Approach*, Harlow: Addison, Wesley Longman: 70-75.

Huczynski, A. and Buchanan, D. (2001), *Organizational Behaviour: An Introductory Text, 4th Edition,* Harlow: Pearson Education Limited.

Janis, I. L. (1972), *Victims of Groupthink* Boston: Houghton Mifflin.

Luthans, F. (1995), *Organizational Behaviour, 7th Edition*, New York: McGraw Hill.

Maude, S. (2000), *Motivation and Retention of Call Centre Sales Consultants*, unpublished dissertation, University of Northumbria.

Pugh, D. and Hickson, D. (1989), *Writers on Organizations, 4th Edition*, London: Penguin.

Rollinson, D., Broadfield, A. and Edwards, D. J. (1998), *Organisational Behaviour and Analysis. An Integrated Approach*, Harlow: Addison Wesley Longman.

Rogers, C. R. (1951), in D. Rollinson, A. Broadfield and D. Edwards (1998) *Organisational Behaviour and Analysis,* Harlow: Addison, Wesley Longman: 80.

Schein, (1980), in D. Rollinson, A. Broadfield and D. Edwards (1998) *Organisational Behaviour and Analysis. An Integrated Approach* Harlow: Addison Wesley Longman: 296.

Sharpley, R. and Forster, G. (2000), Attitudes of Employees in the Cypriot Hotel Industry: A Pilot Study, *Cyprus International Journal of Management* Vol 5, (1 & 2): 30-38.

Smith P. C., Kendall, L. M. and Hulin, C. L. (1969), in D. Rollinson, A. Broadfield and D. Edwards (1998) *Organisational Behaviour and Analysis* Harlow: Addison Wesley Longman: 137-138.

Stoner, J. (1972), in D. Rollinson, A. Broadfield and D. Edwards (1998) Harlow: Addison Wesley Longman: 318.

Tuckman, B. W. (1965), Development Sequence in Small Groups *Psychological Bulletin* 63(3):384-399.

Unsworth, K. and West, M. (2000), Teams: the Challenges of Co-operative Work, in N. Chmiel (ed.) *Work and Organizational Psychology: A European Perspective*, Oxford: Blackwell.

Walton, J. (1999), *Strategic Human Resource Development* Harlow: Pearson Education Limited.

Watson, T. (1986), *Management, Organisation and Employment Strategy: New Directions in Theory and Practice*, London: Routledge and Kegan Paul.

Watson, T. (1995), *Sociology, Work and Industry, 3rd Edition*, London: Routledge.

14

Human Resource Management

Helen M Douglas

Learning objectives

This chapter introduces the main issues managers need to consider in handling their staff. It enables the reader to:

- *assess the contribution HRM can make to the overall success of the business if it is linked with the business strategy.*

- *explain the techniques which can be used to assess the supply and demand for employees and the actions to be taken to ensure that these are balanced in line with the overall business needs.*

- *identify the stages involved in deciding upon the need for staff, advertising the vacancy and encouraging applicants to respond, and then deciding upon which, if any, individual to select.*

- *define and explain the constituent elements of the training cycle*

- *outline the different ways staff can be given feedback on their performance and consider how to conduct an appraisal interview.*

- *assess the range of benefits which can be given to employees and how these can be managed to help the organisation achieve its objectives.*

The role of human resource management

Definitions

There are a number of definitions of human resource management. Most simply, it may be described as *getting the right number of the right people into the right place at the right time.*

Although a succinct statement, this nevertheless sums up a lot of the activities of human resource management in any business or organisation, including those in the travel and tourism sector. The emphasis on the 'right number' refers to human resource planning and its attempts to relate the number of people employed to the amount of work to be done. The need to have the 'right people' shows the need to have well-designed recruitment and selection procedures to choose people who will fit into the organisation. However, that is not the end of the story, as these people must then receive appropriate training and coaching to help them develop their skills.

Mention of the 'right place' and the 'right time' again refers to human resource planning, but it goes further. Recruitment and training, together with performance management, must be used to develop individuals so that they have the ability to make a worthwhile contribution when the time comes for promotion or there is a need for reorganisation. This requires forward planning in an attempt to foresee the directions in which the organisation will have to move.

Another definition suggests that the key purpose of human resource management is to 'enable management to enhance the individual and collective contributions to the short and long-term success of the enterprise' (Personnel Standards Lead Body 1993).

The human resource management cycle

There has been considerable discussion of the concept of 'strategic human resource management' (Fombrun *et al.* 1984). One of the main features of the concept of human resource management is that it is a coherent approach, as demonstrated in Figure 14.1:

Figure 14.1: *The human resource management cycle*

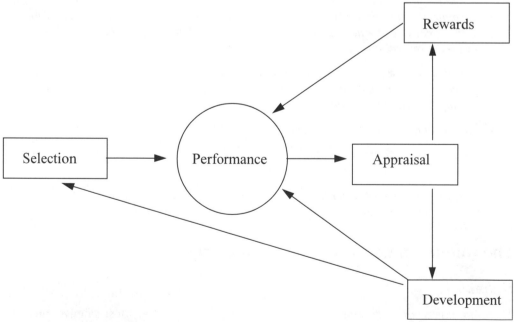

Source: Fombrun *et al.* (1984)

This model provides the outline structure of this chapter: an organisation, whether in travel or tourism or any other industry, must plan how many people it requires of what types and then select the best people. Having selected them, they must use a variety of techniques to ensure they obtain the necessary development. This will include providing training to ensure they perform effectively, appraising them to establish their development needs, and rewarding them appropriately to ensure they are motivated to achieve the necessary level of performance.

Human resource planning

Definitions

Human resource planning is an essential feature of human resource management. Indeed, the above the definition of human resource management, *getting the right number of the right people into the right place at the right time*, could also be used as a definition of human resource planning as it includes the key concept of matching the number of people to the amount of work to be done. Thus, human resource planning can be treated in its widest sense of making the best of the human resources available to the organisation.

There are number of other definitions of human resource planning, perhaps one of the most helpful being *a strategy for the acquisition, utilisation, improvement and retention of an enterprise's human resources* (Department of Employment 1974). Let us examine this definition in more detail:

- A **strategy** implies a relatively long term plan which has been devised bearing in mind other aspects of the organisation's operations.

- **Acquisition** refers to recruitment and selection, and then subsequent promotions and transfers.

- **Utilisation** means that having employed a group of people, they must be used in an efficient manner to attain high productivity.

- **Improvement** refers to training and development, and also to performance appraisal as a means of identifying training needs.

- **Retention** means that the organisation must provide work organised in a way to motivate the staff, with adequate financial compensation and opportunities for promotion.

It is evident from the above that human resource planning incorporates much of what is considered to be the subject matter of human resource management. Thus, it is a product of the techniques of human resource management designed to match the demand for staffing with the supply available.

The need for human resource planning

In the current financial climate, most organisations are having to become increasingly cost-conscious. At the same time, in an increasingly competitive industry such as travel and tourism, organisations are faced with the need to improve efficiency, which in turn means maximising the return on all available resources, whether these be financial or human.

Organisations will usually set themselves a number of goals in relation to their staffing. There is a tradition in the travel industry of high levels of seasonal, part time, casual and female labour and these groups tend to be associated with high labour turnover. This can cause particular problems for the human resource planner who needs to ensure the right number of people are employed, as too many means an unnecessarily high wage bill, whilst too few may mean that sales targets cannot be met. They need the right balance of people, with neither too many managers compared to the number of workers, nor an inexperienced workforce without adequate supervision and leadership. The skills of the staff must be in balance so that the range of jobs can be covered.

These goals can be placed in two categories. The first is to ensure that there is the right number of the right people to do the job efficiently now. The second looks to the future to ensure that there will be the right number of the right people in a few years time, even though it is not known what the exact requirements may be five years hence.

Atkinson (1984) introduced the concept of the 'flexible firm', and suggested there were three kinds of flexibility:

- **Functional flexibility,** so that employees have multiple skills and can be moved between a range of jobs;

- **Numerical flexibility** by the use of part time and temporary contracts so that the numbers of employees can be easily increased or decreased in line with the demand for labour;

- **Financial flexibility,** which provides for pay levels to reflect the state of supply and demand in the external labour market.

The concept of the flexible firm involves employing a core of permanent, full time, relatively well paid and well trained staff, supported by peripheral workers who move in and out of the labour force in line with demand. The peripheral workers can have a range of different types of contract; for example, Lunn Poly employ part timers who can be asked to work anywhere between 4 and 37 hours a week, although the average is around 18.

There is, then, an evident need for organisations to carry out human resource planning. However, it has been observed that there are so many problems to overcome, and so many uncertainties in the local, national and international environment, that it is pointless spending a lot of time and effort on an activity which so frequently produces the wrong answers. In particular, the travel and tourism industry has a number of features which can make predicting staffing needs very difficult. For example, the demand for holidays can be affected by a range of factors, from weather conditions to the strength of sterling, while industrial action by air traffic controllers and political unrest generally have an impact somewhere in the world each year. This may make the task more problematic, but does not mean it should not be attempted at all!

Stages of human resource planning

It is possible to identify a number of stages in human resource planning:

- Assessing demand – this involves looking at the objectives the organisation is trying to achieve overall, and then assessing the number of people it will require.

- Assessing supply – this involves taking an inventory of the number and type of people employed today, and then making a projection of how the position is likely to change in future years.

- Balancing supply and demand – there is likely to be a disparity between the number of people available and the number of people needed.

- Human resource planning – this involves determining the necessary actions so that the supply of labour matches the demand for labour.

An organisation must satisfy three conditions if the above stages are to be carried out effectively:

i. Human resource planning must be fully integrated with corporate planning

It is impossible to make decisions about staffing requirements unless decisions have also been made about the products and services the organisation will offer in the future. Decisions must also be made about the human resource policies of the organisation, for example, in terms of the levels of training to be offered and the salary levels to be paid.

ii. Comprehensive human resource records and statistics must be available

It is impossible to forecast the level of staffing available unless there are accurate and up-to-date records and statistics available. Human resource planning requires both information on individual employees, and also statistical information on trends in the labour force, such as the number of people leaving over a year.

iii. The organisation must define its objectives

The organisation must decide the period over which the forecast should be attempted, and also the degree of accuracy and detail which it requires. There will be certain areas which are critical to the success of the organisation, and on which the human resource planner should concentrate attention.

For example, a travel agency chain may set itself the target of increasing the number of travel shops by 5 percent in the next 12 months, or a tour operator may decide to enter the cruise market, or a theme park may decide to build a number of new rides and a hotel. All of these decisions require resources to make them happen, whether capital, material or human, and planning to ensure that things happen at the right time.

However, staffing requirements are expressed not only in terms of quantity, but also in terms of type and quality. Thus, it is insufficient to say we need 10 people to fill 10 posts; they must have the knowledge and experience to be able to do the 10 jobs. This implies a need to conduct a 'skills audit' to discover the skills and abilities of the existing staff and an analysis of the job descriptions of the vacant posts to ensure that the right people are recruited.

Human resource forecasting

An organisation has to predict the number of people it will need in the future. These people are only available from two sources: those people who are currently working within the organisation, and those people currently outside the organisation. Whilst seemingly obvious, this indicates clearly the two sources which the human resource planner must investigate.

i. within the organisation

This requires an analysis of the skills and experience of current employees, their length of service, training potential, and also their personal preferences. Some assessment of the likelihood of them leaving the organisation must also be made.

ii. outside the organisation

This requires an analysis of the availability of people with specific skills outside the organisation. Even in times of high unemployment, certain occupational groups will still be in great demand. Some assessment must also be made of the likelihood of the organisation being able to attract the people it will require.

Assessing staffing supply

The purpose of human resource planning is to estimate the size of any future shortages or surpluses in particular skill groups so that action can be taken if necessary. In order to succeed at human resource planning, it is essential to have an accurate picture of the organisation's existing labour resources and then to assess the extent by which this stock will have been reduced by labour turnover by the end of the forecast period. At the same time, an assessment must be made of the extent to which the future requirements for labour will be available.

Internal supply

Human resource records should record the number of staff in different categories, their age, sex and length of service. Records must be kept of the absence levels of staff in specific occupations and also on the turnover of staff. It may be helpful to conduct exit interviews to establish the reasons why staff are leaving the organisation. The information gained will allow predictions to be made about the numbers of days likely to be lost through absence, and also how many staff are likely to leave the organisation. The age and length of service of employees may also affect future wastage rates. Younger employees are more likely to leave the organisation than older employees, and people who have a longer length of service are less likely to leave than those who have only been with the organisation for a shorter period of time.

External supply

An estimate must be made of the supply of labour outside the organisation. This is based on the total population figures, but also on the numbers in particular age groups, for example school leavers or university graduates. The educational system will also determine the numbers available with particular qualifications at a range of levels; for example, over the last ten years there has been a tremendous increase in the number of travel and tourism graduates in the labour market. There are also social factors which influence the number of people available, such as the availability of child care provision.

Effect of new technology

It has been said that Britain is undergoing a second Industrial Revolution, brought about by the increased availability and sophistication of computers. New technology has an impact both on the demand for different products and the methods used to provide different goods and services. For example, within the travel industry there has been a move towards 'ticketless' travel which has reduced the commission available to travel agents. The availability of new machinery can either be used to increase the output from the same number of staff or to maintain the output level with a smaller number of staff. However, increased automation may also call for different skills from employees and may also change the way in which work is organised. This is already happening in travel agencies, where some employees are mainly booking clerks, entering details in a computer, while others are able to make full use of the available technology to provide high quality advice on a range of destinations.

The human resource plan

The next step is to draw up a plan to ensure that the future demand for labour will be met by the appropriate level of supply. More specifically, it will specify future recruitment requirements, training and development to be undertaken, and any necessary redundancies. The process of forecasting future labour requirements may also indicate areas in which improvements in productivity could be made.

Perhaps the most important point to remember about human resource planning is that even detailed human resource plans are useless in themselves. Their only value lies in providing the manager with information to make decisions. If the figures show that absence or labour turnover is rising in a particular department, then **action** must be taken to find out the reasons why so that further action can be taken to reduce it. Monitoring is vital so that any change in the actual position compared to the forecast position will be noticed and then action can be taken either to change the trend or to change the forecast. The result of this may be to modify long term plans, policies or objectives.

Recruitment and selection

The previous sections on the role of human resource management and on human resource planning have stressed the need to select the 'right people', and this is achieved by using recruitment and selection techniques. The CIPD publish a Code of Practice (1995) on Recruitment which 'aims to promote and maintain high standards of professional practice by encouraging recruiters to adhere to best practice'. The Code contains advice and guidance on a range of aspects, including ensuring equality of opportunity.

It is helpful to divide the process into four distinct stages and examine each one in turn:

Recruitment:

1.   Assessing the job

2.   Attracting a field of candidates

Selection:

3.   Assessing the candidates

4.   Placement and follow up

Assessing the job

The first question to be asked is 'Do we need to fill this vacancy?' In the current climate, where many organisations are attempting to reduce their numbers by natural wastage, the answer to this question may well be 'no'. However, if the question is not asked at all then there is no opportunity to examine the work done by the post-holder in an attempt to see whether it could be reorganised in a more efficient manner. One technique which may be helpful in examining the work done is job analysis which is an analytical study of a job to determine the essential component factors.

The job analyst will ask four basic questions to determine what a job involves:

- what the job holder does

- how the job holder does it

- why the job holder does it

- what does the job involve

Job description

The information about a job will normally be presented in the form of a Job Description. This will detail the organisational position of the job in terms of department, location, who the post-holder reports to, and which posts they are responsible for. The job description will also outline the resources available to the post-holder and any specific constraints. The main part of the job description comprises a list of the duties and responsibilities involved in the job, together perhaps with some indication of the amount of time spent on individual activities. There has been a move away from detailed job descriptions in some organisations as it is felt they can inhibit flexibility. However, there is still a need for some indication of the personal competencies which are necessary to perform a particular job. Armstrong (1999: 280) draws a distinction between work-based or occupational competencies, which refer to what people should be capable of doing and the standards that people are expected to attain, and behavioural or personal competencies, which are the personal characteristics of individuals which they bring to their work roles.

Person specification

When all the above information has been collected, it will be possible to determine the knowledge and skills required to perform the job successfully. A popular classification of human attributes which can be useful in compiling a person specification is Rodger's Seven Point Plan. The purpose of the Plan is to set a standard under a range of headings against which individual candidates may be measured. The Seven Point Plan covers:

- Physical make up (e.g. clear speaking voice)

- Attainment (e.g. academic and other achievements)

- General intelligence (e.g. other evidence of mental ability)

- Special aptitudes (e.g. foreign languages)

- Interests (e.g. physical, mental or social)

- Disposition (e.g. preference for working in a team)

- Circumstances (e.g. where they live and how far they have to travel to work).

When preparing the person specification, requirements should be stated under each heading. The temptation will often be to draw up an over-idealised specification, perhaps requiring

GCSE Maths when really an understanding of how to calculate percentages would be sufficient. It may be helpful to consider those attributes which are essential, those which are desirable and those which are undesirable and would automatically disqualify any individual who possessed it. An example of the latter may be an applicant for a position of regional sales manager who has a conviction for driving while under the influence of alcohol.

Attracting a field of candidates

There are three main sources of recruitment : internal sources; external agencies; and advertisements.

Internal sources

There may well be somebody already employed in the organisation who could perform the job competently. Indeed, some organisations have an agreement with their staff that all vacancies should be advertised internally to give existing staff a chance of promotion. However, there should be a balance between bringing in people with new ideas from outside the organisation and offering promotion prospects to existing employees. An advantage of promoting existing staff is that their abilities are well known whilst their knowledge of the organisation should allow them to make a more immediate contribution in their new job than an outsider.

External agencies

There are a range of different agencies, some of which are Government funded and others which are operated privately. Job Centres are located in most suburban shopping centres and provide a basically free service to both employers and job seekers. They tend to concentrate mostly on manual and clerical jobs, although they provide specialised services for particular groups, such as disabled workers and the long term unemployed. Careers Services are particularly useful for school and college leavers as they have close links with educational institutions. Private agencies frequently specialise in certain fields, such as travel and tourism, or in particular areas of the market, such as secretarial staff, IT staff, drivers or temporary workers. These agencies charge the employer for their services.

Advertisements

Most organisations will use advertisements at one time or another, and they can form a substantial part of recruitment costs. They must be written very carefully and be placed in the appropriate place at the right time if they are to prove cost-effective. The aim of recruitment advertising is to produce a compact and well-qualified field of candidates who are motivated to accept the job. This implies that sufficient candidates must apply to offer a reasonable selection, but not so many that they present an administrative burden. The candidates should meet the requirements of the person specification, and they should have obtained a favourable impression of the organisation.

It may be helpful to state in the advertisement that a copy of the job description will be sent with the application form. This will give potential candidates a much better idea of what the job entails and enable them to decide at an early stage if they feel that the job is not what they are looking for. This will save the employer administrative time and expense in dealing with applications which will not lead to an appointment. It also recognises that recruitment is a two-way process and that the candidate needs to have the information to select a suitable employer in the same way the employer selects a suitable candidate.

Application forms

A well designed application form will request the information which is required in a systematic manner. A specific item of information will be in the same position for each candidate which should allow speedier comparisons. There should be sufficient space in which to write the required information. Many application forms for more senior positions require the candidate to state at some length why they feel their experience and qualifications make them a suitable contender for the job.

Assessing the candidate

The first two stages should have produced a shortlist of qualified candidates. The subsequent selection stage, using a range of selection methods, then involves deciding on the most suitable. The most common selection method is the interview which may be supplemented by selection tests, group selection methods, and references.

Selection tests

A range of tests are available which are designed to assess various attributes. These include tests of practical skills, such as filing or typing, and verbal and numerical abilities. There are also psychometric tests designed to provide information on personality characteristics. Many of these must be administered by a trained psychologist to facilitate interpretation of the results.

Group selection methods

These involve bringing a group of candidates together and giving them tasks to do. This is often used to recruit tour operators' overseas representatives, where their ability to get on well with other people and be able to present material clearly and concisely can be assessed. They may be given a topic to discuss, be asked to deliver a 'welcome talk', or sell excursions. Trained observers watch each individual's contribution and make an assessment of their personal skills and their ability to work with a group of people. These exercises may be time-consuming, but properly used can obtain information which would be very difficult to obtain using other methods.

References

The purpose of a reference is two-fold. Firstly, it is designed to obtain, in confidence, factual information about a prospective employee and, secondly, it may ask for opinions about their character and their likely suitability for the post in question. Some people argue that references rarely supply any useful information, while others argue that they provide a valuable safety net. They are probably most useful when they ask for specific information on starting and leaving dates, salary history, and sickness record.

Selection interview

The interview is trying to find an answer to two simple questions: can they do the job, and will they do the job? At the same time, however, as well as trying to select the best candidate for the job, the interview is also trying to persuade the candidate to accept the job. The majority of candidates will be unsuccessful but it is, nevertheless, important that they too receive a favourable impression of the organisation. That is, there may be a temptation in times of high unemployment to feel that it is less important to try to sell the job because it is a buyer's market. However, if the organisation is trying to recruit the best people for the job, those people are likely to receive offers from other organisations as well. Thus, it is equally important to convince the candidate that the job is right for them as to assess whether they are right for the job.

Research has shown that interviews can produce very poor selection decisions – most people only have to look around their own organisations to see evidence of this. Better results can be obtained if the interviewer has been trained, and if they carry out adequate preparation prior to the interview. The interview room itself should be free from interruptions and arranged for either a formal or an informal interview as appropriate. A one-to-one interview may be conducted fairly informally around a coffee table but a panel interview involving three or more interviewers may dictate a more formal seating plan.

One-to-one interviews

A single trained and experienced interviewer may well produce the best results. The candidate is likely to be more relaxed in this situation and the conversation will, therefore, flow more easily. The main problem, however, is that the organisation then relies on the judgement of one individual who may be biased in certain directions. This type of interview is more common in the private sector.

Panel interviews

These can vary in the number of interviewers, although they have been known to enter double figures. The smaller the numbers, the more likely they are to be effective as large numbers are very difficult to control. The panel members should agree beforehand on their respective roles and they should be carefully controlled by a chairperson. The advantages of a panel interview are that the people involved can share the responsibility for making the decision and that experts in particular areas can ask questions on their own specialism.

During the interview

At the start of the interview, the interviewer should try to create a rapport so that the candidate begins to relax and settle down. Typically, the interviewer may ask about the candidate's travelling arrangements, how well they know the area or some other non-threatening topic of conversation. Inexperienced interviewers tend to ask "Did you find us easily?" and then launch straight into the interview. It is well worth taking more time to relax the candidate, particularly if they are young or obviously nervous. The interviewer will often tell the candidate a little about the organisation and the specific job applied for. Care must be taken not to talk for too long as the candidate will probably be nervous and unable to easily absorb the information.

The actual questions should then be put to the candidate and the interviewer should carefully listen to the answers. This can be quite difficult in practice, as the inexperienced interviewer will tend to be thinking about how to ask the next question rather than listening to the answer from the last one. Thus, a useful technique is to follow up each question with at least one supplementary question designed to probe what the candidate has just said.

Different techniques are useful in different situations. Leading questions will usually provide little information as to the candidate's true feelings, whilst multiple questions can lead to confusion. Generally speaking, open questions are more useful than closed questions as they encourage the candidate to talk. One technique which can produce reasonably consistent and reliable results is the 'behaviourally situated' interview. This technique is based on the belief that past performance is the best predictor of future performance. The candidates are asked pre-prepared questions such as:

- describe a situation where you used your influencing skills to achieve a successful result, or

- describe a situation where you had to overcome difficulties to complete a task.

The questions are chosen to reflect the type of situations which are likely to be crucial to effective job performance. It is important that the interviewer should really probe to discover exactly what the candidate **did** to achieve the outcome.

It has been suggested that the interviewer should talk for no more than 30 percent of the time because while they are talking they are not learning anything. It may be helpful to take notes as a reminder of the answers, particularly if a number of candidates are to be seen at the same time. The candidate should also be given the opportunity to ask any questions they might have and then the interview should be brought to a close. The interviewee should be told when they can expect to receive any information and also how to claim their expenses if appropriate. Each candidate should feel that they have had a fair hearing and have been given sufficient information so that they can make their own decision as to whether they would like to do the job if it were offered. It is much better that a candidate refuses a job offer because they feel the job is unsuitable rather than accepting, only to leave the organisation after a short period of time.

After the interview

Any notes which have been made during the interview should be written up immediately afterwards, before the next candidate is seen. The selection decision is then made by comparing all the available information on a candidate with the requirements of the job. It may be helpful to use some form of rating scale based either on the Seven Point Plan or on the specified criteria for the job as a systematic means of recording information on each candidate. If a number of interviewers have seen the same candidate there may be some fairly lengthy discussions before a measure of agreement can be reached. Candidates who are unsuccessful should be informed promptly and courteously.

No matter how carefully the recruitment and selection procedures have been carried out, the new employee will still need assistance if they are to become fully effective as quickly as possible. The administrative details must be handled competently and the new employee must receive appropriate induction training. Even an experienced operative will require training in the particular procedures to be adopted in their new organisation, as well as needing information on the organisation itself and such practical matters as stationery supplies and when they will be paid.

Training and development

Training is of vital importance if the organisation is to ensure that it has the right people available at the right time. It should be considered as an investment in the organisation's most valuable resource, the people it employs. However, in times of financial difficulty it is often one of the first activities to be curtailed. In the past, a lot of training has undoubtedly been carried out for its own sake rather than helping the organisation to meet specific objectives. The aim then should be to ensure that training is designed to meet specific needs.

Potential benefits of training

Training is provided to:

- provide specific skills – it can be easier to train your own staff in essential skills rather than relying upon the labour market to provide them;

- improve performance and productivity – teaching the best methods of working can increase the quantity and quality of the output;

- reduce wastage – employees who make mistakes are wasting both time and perhaps materials;

- reduce accidents – the correct method will also be a safe method;

- reduce labour turnover – employees who are unsure about what they are supposed to be doing and who receive complaints because they make mistakes are more likely to be absent or to leave the organisation; and

- individual advancement – employees will improve their personal position by acquiring new skills.

Many employees have a probation period during which their performance is closely monitored and they receive training and feedback on how well they are adapting.

It is sometimes said that training is designed to effect a change in three main areas, namely, knowledge, skills and attitudes. Knowledge-based training is sometimes called education as it involves the assimilation of a number of facts, for example, the codes used for different airports. Skills-based training will enable the trainee to **do** something at the end of the training, for example, type at 40 words per minute. Training designed to change attitudes can be the most difficult, such as encouraging a calm and patient response when faced with an irate and demanding customer.

Although all training will be directed towards bringing a change in knowledge, skill or attitudes, or a combination of them, it is possible to identify particular types of training:

Induction training

This can fall into two categories. Firstly comes the introduction to the organisation which every new employee will need. The second part involves initial training related to the specific job they will be required to do.

Skills training

This is an extension of the induction training and is designed to enable employees to perform all parts of their job competently.

Management training

This may be carried out within the organisation, or by attendance on external courses, and is designed to encourage the skills required to manage other people.

There will be a wide range of training needs in any organisation and only a limited amount of money available in the budget. In these circumstances, decisions must be made as to which activities take priority so that the training provided will be both relevant and cost-effective. The best way of achieving this is by drawing up a training policy which has the support of the highest level of decision makers within the organisation. Decisions have to be made about the staff and resources which are to be devoted to training, as these in turn determine the actual training carried out.

Training cannot be carried out in isolation; it must be integrated with the other activities of the organisation. Thus, if the policy is to recruit school leavers and then train them, the resources must be available to do this. If the organisation is installing new machinery or expanding into new markets then the staff must be trained in the necessary skills. Training is simply one more method of helping the organisation to achieve its overall objectives.

The training cycle

If training is to be carried out in the most efficient manner, it is important that it is approached in a systematic fashion. There is a Four Step Approach, the Training Cycle, which can be applied to all types of training at all levels.

Figure 14.2: *The systematic training cycle*

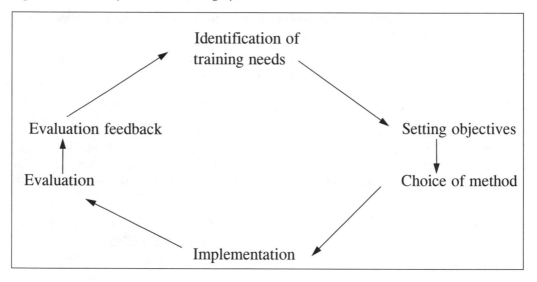

Source: adapted from Kenney and Reid (1988)

i. Identify training needs

It seems obvious to say that it is necessary to find out what training people need before giving them any training yet, in many organisations, this does not happen. People are sent on training courses because their colleagues have been sent on the same training course, rather than because the course is actually right for them.

In order to determine an individual's training needs, it is necessary to carry out a training needs analysis. Examine their job description to see what they are required to do and then interview the individual and their supervisor to see what they can do already. The difference between the two is called the Training Gap and it is here that training should be directed. There are also other ways of deciding what training needs to be done and these are more suitable for deciding what training requires to be done on an occupational or departmental level and on the organisational level. Training may be related to:

ii. Set the objectives for training

Training may be related to:

- changes in legislation: this can involve changes in policies, practices or procedures

- changes in equipment: people must be trained to operate and maintain the new equipment

- changes in product: there may well be new techniques involved

- productivity figures: these may indicate where improvements can be made.

- accident figures: high numbers of accidents may indicate training should be given in safe working practices.

- wastage figures: large amounts of spoiled materials may indicate a need for training

- customer complaints: those may indicate where things are going wrong

- labour turnover: people who are finding it difficult to do their jobs are more likely to leave the organisation.

A word of caution is necessary, as there may be an assumption that training can solve all problems. It is true that training may be able to help in all of the above examples, but it will be only of limited assistance if the problems basically stem from obsolete equipment and poorly-designed procedures.

iii. Plan the training

Once decisions have been made about who needs what training, then further decisions must be made about how this is to be achieved. In particular the following questions must be answered:

- WHO: who will carry out the training?

- WHERE: where will the training take place?

- WHAT: what specific knowledge, skills and attitudes will be included?

- WHEN: when will be the date, time and duration of the sessions?

Having answered these questions, then arrangements must be made for the people, equipment and rooms to be made available as required.

On-the-job and off-the-job training

There is sometimes an assumption that training only takes place in a classroom away from the job. In reality, people learn most about their job by actually doing it. Effective learning takes place when people are given an opportunity to practice particular skills and are then given feedback on their performance. It may well be that a short period of off-the-job training can best be followed by guided practice on-the-job, by somebody who has been trained in instructional techniques.

iv. Evaluate training

Most organisations will have carried out the previous three steps, to a greater or lesser extent, when arranging a training programme. However, in many cases little or no attempt is made to systematically evaluate the training with the intention of feeding back these results to future training programmes. It is no wonder that training is one of the first areas to be cut back if there is no data available on the extent to which it is helping the organisation to achieve its overall objectives.

Evaluation can be carried out at different levels and thus provide answers to different questions:

- Did the training achieve what it set out to do?

- Were the original objectives appropriate?

The success of a training programme can also be measured at different points in time:

- *Reaction evaluation*: this involves asking the trainees to assess how much they learned and whether they 'enjoyed' the training. This is the most common form of evaluation, but is of limited usefulness.

- *Learning evaluation*: this involves testing the employees at the end of the course to see if they have achieved the objectives. To be fully effective, a test should also be given prior to the course to ensure that the learning is a result of the course.

- *Performance evaluation*: this involves making an assessment of the performance of the trainee when they have returned to their job to see if they are implementing their training in practice.

- *Organisational evaluation*: this is the ultimate test which is designed to show whether the organisation as a whole is performing better as a result of the training.

It will be clear that the most valuable information relating to the impact on the organisation is the most difficult to obtain and is most affected by external variables. Thus, although British Rail invested a great deal of money in their 'Charm Schools' which were designed to improve the social skills of their staff, it is impossible to say whether this alone contributed to increased passenger revenue. However, it undoubtedly led to a reduced number of complaints about the attitudes of certain members of staff, which could in itself be considered to be sufficient justification for the training.

The costs involved in training must be carefully controlled to ensure both that the most cost-effective methods are being used and that benefits to the organisation outweigh the money spent on training. It is only by monitoring the situation closely that the organisation will be able to maximise the benefits of an investment in training. At the end of the day, training must be seen to be producing the desired results in terms of contributing to the overall organisational objectives.

Performance appraisal

In every organisation, there is a need regularly and systematically to take stock of current manpower. The aim is to assess people's performance in existing jobs and their potential for future jobs. The technique used to achieve this is performance or staff appraisal. Properly conducted, performance appraisal can achieve the following:

- It gives line managers the opportunity to assess employees' strengths and weaknesses;

- It gives employees the opportunity to assess their current position within the organisation, and to review their personal future;

- It provides the opportunity for action to be taken to provide training and development which will enable the individual to more closely match the requirements of the job.

The importance of the word 'action' must be noted. Undoubtedly the most frequent criticism of appraisal schemes is that much talking is done and many forms are filled in, but nothing actually **happens** as a result.

In essence, appraisal entails one individual sitting in judgement on another. Many managers dislike the idea of 'playing God' and employees may be reluctant to receive criticism, particularly if they feel the organisation itself is making it difficult for them to achieve their goals. Some organisations try to shift the focus of appraisal so that the manager helps the employee to identify their own strengths and weaknesses and from there pinpoint their own training and development needs. The success of this sort of approach will depend on the relationship which exists between the manager and the employee.

Staff appraisal ranges from intermittent, informal and often ill-informed discussion between managers and individual members of staff, to highly formal appraisal procedures, based on extensive sets of forms and laid down times, rules, and frequency of assessments. Generally, an important point is that any decisions made as a result of the appraisal process should be based on sufficient, relevant and objective information.

Value of performance appraisal

Appraisals are not an end in themselves, but a means to an end. Research has shown that appraisal schemes aim to achieve one or more of the following purposes:

- to improve current performance;

- to identify future potential; and

- to link pay realistically with performance.

It is, of course, very difficult for any one scheme to successfully achieve all of the above. For example, if one is attempting to improve current performance, this assumes a fairly frank discussion about strengths and weaknesses. However, if the employee is aware that a future pay increase rests upon their performance during an appraisal interview, they are likely to be less forthcoming about their weaknesses and concentrate on their strengths.

A similar distinction can be drawn between schemes which aim to improve current performance, and those which aim to identify future potential. The former will require detailed discussions with the employee in order to review past performance, set performance targets, and motivate the employee to achieve these. However, the latter objective requires less discussion with the employee as the information required to identify 'high flyers' can perhaps be more readily obtained from other sources.

Designing a scheme

When designing the scheme, early consideration must be given to the categories of staff which it is appropriate to include and whether it will be necessary to incorporate different aims and procedures as a result. Some organisations only include white-collar staff in their scheme, or white-collar staff between certain levels.

Acceptability of scheme

The scheme must be designed to suit the needs of the organisation and must have the full support of senior management. It must also be acceptable to line managers, employees and the trade unions, if appropriate. Trade unions have a traditional mistrust of appraisal schemes as they feel it allows scope for management to show favouritism. To achieve acceptability the scheme must be fully explained to all parties, training must be given to the managers involved, and the system should be designed to involve a minimum of bureaucracy.

Performance and Reward

If a decision has been taken that pay increases will in some way be linked with an assessment of performance rather than using an incremental payment scheme, then this process should be separate from the process used to help the individual improve their current performance. The reasons for this are set out below:

- a full and frank exchange of views becomes less likely;

- it may be better to link pay with some objective measures rather than a manager's subjective judgement;

- managers may avoid differentiating between their staff and give everyone the same increase; and

- Those disadvantages may at least be minimised by separating the two processes in time and also preferably in paperwork and procedures.

The appraisal interview

This forms the basis of the scheme and is conducted at regular, usually annual, intervals. It is not intended as a substitute for day-to-day management, so feedback, both positive and negative, should be given as appropriate as near as possible to the specific events. Its purpose is to take an overview of the last year's performance and from there plan an appropriate course of action for the future. This is done by taking into account both the needs of the organisation and the personal preferences of the individual.

The interview can be seen as rather threatening by the employee, so care must be taken to ensure a genuine two-way flow of information. If handled well, the employee can leave the interview feeling that there has been an opportunity to discuss in detail their hopes and problems, and feeling that action will be taken to sort out specific issues. On the other hand, if handled badly, the employee may feel resentful because the manager did not listen to the comments and opinions expressed and used the interview as an opportunity to criticise.

Objective setting

The most effective interviews usually involve the evaluation of performance against pre-set targets which had been **jointly** set by the manager and employee. There may be the disadvantage that the interview concentrates on only a limited part of the job as a result. The main advantage is that results-oriented appraisal is likely to be more impartial and therefore may be more acceptable to the parties involved.

Paperwork

It has already been said that appraisal is a means to an end but, if an organisation produces elaborate documentation, then the completion of the forms themselves is seen as being increasingly significant. If managers are unconvinced about the usefulness of the exercise, or feel uncomfortable about the process, they may conduct the interview at a superficial level in order to complete the form.

Certain basic information will be required, such as the job description for the post, any statements of objectives agreed previously, plus basic human resource information on the employee. In addition, the following types of forms may prove helpful:

- self-appraisal form: used by the employee prior to the interview to assist them in thinking about their own performance

- free written report: either a blank sheet of paper, or including a number of headings, which encourage the managers to comment as they see fit without being over-constrained

- comparative rating form: the manager is asked to rate the employee on a number of scales covering different aspects of job performance

- combination report: this combines rating scales with an opportunity for more descriptive comment.

Whichever forms are used, simplicity in design and ease of use are vital factors to be considered.

Employee rewards

The notion of 'reward' includes both financial and non financial benefits which are given to the employee. The financial rewards include basic pay, commission, overtime, and bonuses. However, some organisations also provide other benefits, sometimes known as indirect pay, in the form of pensions, life assurance, health assurance, and subsidised loans. Annual holidays are not strictly remuneration but are also regarded as a benefit. Non-financial benefits may include recognition as an 'employee of the month', or the opportunity to attend training courses.

An employee reward system 'consists of an organisation's integrated policies , processes and practices for rewarding its employees in accordance with their contribution, skill and competence and their market worth' (Armstrong 1999: 569). The purpose of a reward system is to attract, retain and motivate staff, and its success can be measured by how well it achieves these things. Both the employer and the employee have different requirements from a reward system and sometimes these may be in conflict with each other. The employer will, in general, want to minimise the expenditure on wages, whilst the employee will want to maximise their earnings. The employer will want as much work as possible, at the appropriate quality, while the employee will want stable earnings. The employee will want to feel they receive a 'fair' reward for their efforts compared with other people in the organisation and with similar jobs outside.

The level of pay in any organisation is determined by a combination of a number of factors. These include the external value of the job as determined by market forces, the comparative value of jobs within the organisation, sometimes determined by job evaluation, the value of the person as measured by performance appraisal or other measures and, in some cases, the influence which can be exerted by trade unions. There is generally believed to be a certain balance between supply and demand so that people who have skills which are in short supply will be able to command more than those who have skills which are easily obtained elsewhere. This is one of the reasons why pay is low in the travel and tourism industry, as many of the jobs require relatively low skills levels and therefore replacement staff can be found easily.

A number of people in the industry receive a form of bonus or commission dependent upon the sales which they receive. This can take a number of forms, such as £X per booking or passenger, or the opportunity for top sales people to 'win' a holiday. It can also take the form of a bonus paid to everybody depending on the sales or profit made by the whole organisation. The idea is to relate the efforts of the worker or the team of workers to a reward. The major variable is the ratio of effort to earnings: in some schemes this is set so very little effort can produce proportionately high earnings whereas in others a lot of effort can produce a small increase in pay.

The human resource management approach would look at the extent to which the payment system matches other parts of the overall human resource strategy and the extent to which it contributes to the overall corporate strategy. For example, an organisation which was trying to provide a high **quality** service should not have a payment system which only rewarded the **quantity** of output. Alternatively, an organisation should not only reward individual achievement if the employees need to work together as a team in order to perform the job effectively.

The reward system is a very powerful expression of what the organisation values and is prepared to pay for and it plays a significant part in the communication of the organisation's values, performance, standards and expectations.

Discussion questions

Think about any organisation with which you are familiar and ask yourself the following questions:

1. *Are employees aware of the overall business strategy?*

2. *How are people managed to help the organisation achieve this strategy?*

3. *Do staff receive sufficient training to enable them to do their jobs?*

4. *Have the managers received training to enable them to manage their staff?*

5. *How do staff receive feedback on their performance?*

6. *Is there a link between an individual's performance and the amount of pay they receive?*

For all of these questions think about why this is the case and how it happens.

Further reading

Beardwell, I. and Holden, L. (1997), *Human Resource Management: A Contemporary Perspective*, London: Pitman.

Bratton, J and Gold, J. (1999), *Human Resource Management: Theory and Practice,* London: Macmillan.

Torrington, D. and Hall, L. (1998), *Human Resource Management*, London: Prentice Hall.

References

Armstrong M, (1999), *A Handbook of Human Resource Management Practice*, London: Kogan Page.

Atkinson, J. (1984), *Manpower strategies for flexible organisations*, Personnel Management, August: 28-31.

Beardwell, I. and Holden, L. (1997), *Human Resource Management; A Contemporary Perspective*, London: Pitman.

Department for Education and Employment (1997), *Employment News*, June.

Department of Employment (1974), *Company Manpower Planning*, HMSO.

Fombrun, C. J., Tichy, N. M. and Devanna, M. A. (1984), *Strategic Human Resource Management*, New York: John Wiley & Sons.

Harrison, R. (1999), *Employee Development*, London: CIPD.

Institute of Personnel and Development (1995), *Codes of Practice*, IPD.

Kenny, J. and Reid, M. (1988), *Training Interventions*, London. IPM.

Mullins, L. (1992), *Hospitality Management - A Human Resource Approach*, London: Pitman.

Personnel Standards Lead Body (1993), *A Perspective on Personnel*, London.

Torrington, D. and Hall, L. (1998), *Human Resource Management*, London: Prentice Hall.

Tourism and the Law

David Grant and Stephen Mason

Learning objectives

This chapter introduces the reader to the English legal system as a foundation for a more thorough consideration of the most important areas of law relevant to the travel and tourism industry. Having read this chapter, the reader will be able to:

- *understand the sources of English law and to differentiate between criminal and civil law*

- *appreciate the scope and importance of the Package Travel Regulations*

- *explain contract law as it relates to the travel industry*

- *identify and explain the pieces of legislation relevant to criminal offences that may be committed by tour operators.*

Introduction

This chapter is divided into two sections. The first describes briefly the English legal system and is intended to provide a basic understanding of the legal framework within which the travel industry must operate. The second gives a broad outline of some of the most important areas of law that are of particular relevance to the package travel industry.

The English legal system

The purpose of this first section is to explain the sources of English law and, in particular; to differentiate between civil and criminal law. In other words, it explains where laws come from and the different kinds of law that exist.

ources of law

Broadly speaking, there are two sources of law in England - legislation and case law. Legislation is law made by Parliament and is the collective name for what are also known as Acts of Parliament or statutes. Case law is law made by the courts and is also known as the common law or judicial precedent.

(a) Legislation

An Act of Parliament, or a statute, is a law which has been passed by Parliament after being subjected to a rigorous scrutiny by both the House of Commons and the House of Lords (often after an equally rigorous consultation process outside Parliament). This process includes a formal introduction into one House by means of a *first reading* of what is then known as a *bill*. Then there is a full scale debate on the merits of the bill during the *second reading*. After the second reading the bill goes through the *committee stage* where it is looked at in some detail – often clause by clause. Finally, it is returned to the floor of the House where, after a *report stage*, it receives its *third reading*. Then the bill is sent to the other House where it undergoes a similar process. If it survives all this it then receives the *royal assent* and becomes law.

Parliament only has time to deal with about 70 or 80 new statutes a year. Examples of statutes passed in recent years that have had a direct bearing on the regulation of the travel industry include the Trade Descriptions Act 1968, which concerns false trade descriptions, and the Consumer Protection Act 1987, which is about misleading price indications. Further examples are the Unfair Contract Terms Act 1977 and the Misrepresentation Act 1967.

(b) Delegated legislation

Apart from Acts of Parliament, another very important form of legislation is *delegated legislation*. For a variety of reasons, including lack of time, lack of technical expertise or the need for speed, Parliament often delegates the making of legislation to an inferior body – usually a minister but sometimes a local authority. Much law is therefore made without proper Parliamentary consideration and is usually done by way of an enabling Act – an Act of Parliament which contains a power enabling a minister, or whoever, to make delegated legislation.

One example of delegated legislation of direct relevance to the travel industry is the Civil Aviation (Air Travel Organisers' Licensing) Regulations 1995 (SI No 1054 1995), otherwise known as the ATOL Regulations. These Regulations provide that tour operators who offer air-inclusive package holidays must be licensed and bonded by the CAA. Although they were first passed in 1972 they have been amended on a number of occasions. However, the most important example of delegated legislation relevant to the travel industry is the Package Travel, Package Holidays and Package Tours Regulations 1992 (SI No 3288 1992). In this instance, the enabling Act is the European Communities Act 1972 which was passed when the UK joined the EEC and provides that European legislation can be enacted in the UK by means of delegated legislation. This was how the EC Directive on Package Travel, Package Holidays and Package Tours 1990 became part of English law.

(c) European legislation

Increasingly, much English law comes from Brussels rather than Westminster and it is necessary, therefore, to give a brief explanation of the types of legislation that we are subject to as members of the European Union.

i.   **Treaties:** the European Community Treaty (the Treaty of Rome), as amended by Treaty on European Union (the Maastricht Treaty) and the Treaty of Amsterdam, are all *primary* sources of European law and are *directly applicable* in the UK by virtue of the European Communities Act 1972 s.2(2). This means that they create rights in English law without the necessity for legislation by Parliament.

ii.   **Secondary sources:** these include *Directives* which in general are not directly applicable in the UK unless Parliament gives effect to them by statute or delegated legislation. As explained above this is how the Package Travel Regulations came into being. *Regulations* are a form of European legislation which, in general, are directly applicable.

Occasionally, European secondary sources of law are regarded as being directly applicable without Parliament having implemented them by means of domestic legislation. For instance, if the UK had not complied with its European obligations by bringing the Package Travel Directive into force by 31 December 1992, the Directive would nevertheless have been directly applicable in the UK. What this means is that a UK citizen who was adversely affected by the failure of the UK government to bring the EC Directive into force could *sue the government* for the losses caused by the failure. Thus, if a tour operator had become insolvent before the Government had implemented the requirements about security, the consumers harmed by this failure could claim compensation from the Government. This situation actually arose in Germany in 1993, as illustrated by the following case.

> *Dillenkofer and Others v Germany* (Case C-178,179,188-190/94). A German tour operator became bankrupt before the German government had implemented the Directive. German consumers who lost out as a result sued the German government to recover their money. The European Court of Justice held they were entitled to be compensated by the government which had failed to implement those provisions of the Directive which would have protected consumers in the event of a tour operator's insolvency.

Note that the Directive is directly applicable against the state – known as *vertical* applicability – but it does not create rights as between individuals (*horizontal* applicability).

(d) Case Law

A large part of English law is to be found not in statutes but in case law – decisions made by the judges in individual cases which create *precedents* which are then *followed* by other judges. A system of *binding precedent* (otherwise known as *stare decisis*) has evolved, whereby once a court has decided a case then the rule or principle that it establishes is binding in later cases. The rule that the case establishes is also known as *ratio decidendi* – the reasons for the decision. The judge in a subsequent case has no choice in the matter, he *must* follow the previous *ratio* no matter how much he disagrees with it. The reason for this is to establish consistency in the law. If a judge could decide a case according to whatever principles he chose then it would be difficult for anyone to know where they stood in any particular situation.

It could be argued that a disadvantage of such as system is that lacks flexibility and, consequently, the law is unable to grow or adapt to changing circumstances and unjust decisions are perpetuated. However, the system in general does possess sufficient flexibility to overcome the problems of excessive rigidity. Firstly, it is possible for a court higher up in the hierarchy of courts to *overrule* a previous decision of a lower court. For instance, the Court of Appeal can overrule decisions of the High Court, and the House of Lords can overrule decisions of the Court of Appeal. (A case is *overruled* when a court in a *later* case decides that the *ratio* of the first case is wrong. A case is *reversed* when a court to which that case is appealed decides that the decision of the lower court was wrong.) Note that it is higher courts that bind lower courts, not vice versa.

Secondly, a subsequent court can *distinguish* the decision of a previous court and refuse to follow it. To distinguish a previous case is not to disagree with the principle or rule that it lays down but simply to say that the facts are sufficiently different to justify coming to a decision which is not based on that principle. For example, the case of *Jarvis v Swans Tours* [1973] 1 All ER 71 establishes that in holiday cases a plaintiff is entitled to damages for distress and disappointment. But how far does this principle extend? *Hayes v Dodd* [1990] 2 All ER 815 decided that, where a contract is not for the purpose of providing peace of mind or freedom from distress, damages for distress and disappointment are not recoverable. So what about a 'flight-only' contract to a holiday destination? Is this to be decided according to *Jarvis* or *Hayes*? It would be possible for a judge, if he so wished, to distinguish the facts of such a case from either *Jarvis* or *Hayes* - giving him the freedom to decide the case as he saw fit. This would not require him to ignore or overrule these decisions – merely to say that the factual situation he is dealing with does not fit comfortably within the principles established by those cases and therefore need not be followed. One County Court case does address just this issue.

> *Lucas v Avro* [1994] CLY 1444. The plaintiff had bought 'flight-only' tickets from the defendants. The return flight returned almost 24 hours later than the plaintiff expected because of a mistake on the ticket. Avro admitted breach of contract and paid damages of £165 for hotel, taxi and telephone expenses and loss of earnings. However, the plaintiff also claimed damages for distress and disappointment. It was held that, as the contract was not one to provide either freedom from distress or to provide peace of mind, such damages were not recoverable.

It remains to be seen whether the reasoning in this case will be adopted by the higher courts.

Finally, it is possible, if all else fails, for legislation to be passed to overrule inconvenient or unjust precedents. This is effectively what the Package Travel Regulations have done to large parts of the common law relating to package holidays. For instance the decision in *Wall v Silver Wing Surface Arrangements* (1981, unreported), a High Court decision which was followed in a number of County Court cases, laid down that a tour operator was not liable to clients who were injured on holiday by the negligence of the hotel they were booked into. Now, Regulation 15 of the Package Travel Regulations provides that a tour operator is responsible for the negligence of suppliers.

Civil and criminal law

Broadly speaking, the criminal law is concerned with offences that are regarded as being sufficiently serious or anti-social that, when they occur, the state should intervene to maintain order or to protect citizens who may be unable or unwilling to protect themselves. This intervention will usually take the form of an individual being *prosecuted* by the state in a criminal court and, if the *defendant* is found *guilty*, then *punishment* such as a fine or imprisonment will be imposed. This clearly applies to 'traditional' crimes, such as murder, manslaughter, arson, rape or theft, but the criminal courts also deal with large numbers of 'regulatory' offences, such as parking on double yellow lines or failing to label the contents of processed food properly. These are not criminal offences in the traditional sense but, in order to regulate a complex modern society, it has become necessary to categorise such activities as criminal and to impose criminal penalties simply in order to ensure that the traffic on our roads can flow freely or we can eat food confident in the knowledge that it is properly labelled.

A number of statutes that impact heavily on the travel industry fall into this latter category, including the Trade Descriptions Act 1968, the Consumer Protection Act 1987 and many of the provisions in the Package Travel Regulations 1992 relating to the provision of information. Lord Scarman has said of the Trade Descriptions Act:

> "…. it is not a truly criminal statute. Its purpose is not the enforcement of the criminal law but the maintenance of trading standards. Trading standards, not criminal behaviour are its concern." (*Wings v Ellis* [1984] 3 All ER 577.

The civil law, on the other hand, is largely concerned with disputes between individuals. Two of the most important areas of civil law are contract law and the law of torts, in which the dispute will often resolve itself into a situation where a *claimant*, formerly called a *plaintiff* (the person with the grievance) is *suing* a *defendant* in a civil court. If the defendant is found *liable*, then the court will endeavour to find a *remedy* – usually financial compensation called *damages* but, occasionally, an *injunction* or an award of *specific performance*.

Frequently, the same set of facts can give rise to both criminal and civil liability. For example, if a tour operator describes a hotel in a misleading fashion, such as stating that the hotel has a children's swimming pool when it doesn't, this may give rise to a criminal prosecution under s.14 of the Trade Descriptions Act 1968 or Regulation 5 of the Package Travel Regulations. It may also give rise to a civil action for breach of contract or misrepresentation. If the misrepresentation was deliberate, then this amounts to the tort of deceit. The tour operator may end up paying both a hefty fine for the criminal offence and substantial damages for the civil liability.

Package travel law

Building upon the overview of the English legal system, this second section looks at those aspects of the law, both civil and criminal, that have most bearing on the package travel industry. More specifically, it considers those parts of the law that govern the relationship between tour operators and their clients. Some of this law, such as the law of contract, is of general application in that it applies to all businesses but some, such as the Package Travel Regulations 1992, is specifically aimed at the travel industry.

This section covers four main areas:

- the civil liability of tour operators as defined by the Package Travel Regulations (PTR)

- the law of contract and its relation to the Package Travel Regulations 1992

- tour operators' criminal liability under the Package Travel Regulations, the Trade Descriptions Act 1968 and the Consumer Protection Act 1987

- the protection the law gives to consumers when their tour operator becomes insolvent.

The liability of hotels, airlines, railways, ferry operators, coach operators and other travel industry businesses who do not come within the ambit of the Package Travel Regulations are not covered here as they fall outside the scope of this chapter.

Civil liability: the Package Travel Regulations 1992

Scope of the Regulations

The purpose of the Regulations is to regulate conventional package holidays, such as two weeks of sun, sea and sand in the Mediterranean and other similar arrangements. On this everyone is agreed but, unfortunately, the scope of the definition of a 'package' in Regulation 2 is so wide that it goes far beyond conventional package holidays. There is an amazing variety of travel and holiday arrangements over which fierce arguments rage about their inclusion in the definition of package, such as overnight ferry trips to the Continent; business travel; holiday camps and caravan sites; 'tailor-made' packages put together by travel agents; sleeper accommodation on the newly privatised railways; holidays provided by local authority social services departments for their pensioners; and activity holidays provided by schools or local education authorities. Interestingly, the Association of British Travel Agents (ABTA), the main trade association, has issued guidelines on the scope of the Regulations which disagree fundamentally on the extent of the definition.

We are concerned here with examining the scope of the definitions in the Regulations with a view to determining what falls within the Regulations and is subject to its regime and what falls outside and remains regulated solely by the common law.

i. The definition of 'package'

The Regulations define 'package' in the following manner:

> *2(1) 'Package' means the pre-arranged combination of at least two of the following components when sold or offered for sale at an inclusive price and when the service covers a period of more than twenty-four hours or includes overnight accommodation:*
>
> *(a)   transport;*
>
> *(b)   accommodation;*
>
> *(c)   other tourist services not ancillary to transport or accommodation and accounting for a significant proportion of the package,*
>
> *and*
>
> *(ii)   the submission of separate accounts for different components shall not cause the arrangements to be other than a package;*

> (iii)   the fact that a combination is arranged at the request of the consumer and in accordance with his specific instructions (whether modified or not) shall not of itself cause it to be treated as other than pre-arranged.

Thus, for there to be a package there has to be

- a pre-arranged combination

- sold at an inclusive price

- consisting of two of the following:

  - transport

  - accommodation

  - other tourist services

At the margins. all these terms cause difficulties. For instance, is a 'fly drive' package caught by the Regulations because it is only two forms of transport? Or what about package put together by travel agents? Are they 'pre-arranged' combinations? Does the term 'other tourist services' include services for businessmen? Despite the fact that the Regulations are now several years old, many fundamental questions like this remain unanswered. However, the vast majority of holidays sold by major tour operators, like Thomson, Airtours, JMC and First Choice, undoubtedly fall within the Regulations.

ii. Upon whom is liability imposed?

The regulations impose liability on 'the organiser' and 'the retailer'.

1.   The Organiser

2(1) 'Organiser' means a person who, otherwise than occasionally, organises packages and sells or offers them for sale, whether directly or through a retailer.

The test here is how frequently the organiser arranges packages, not, as in other consumer protection legislation, whether the organiser acts in the course of a business. The definition will clearly catch conventional tour operators but, importantly, it will also catch most travel agents in its net. If 'tailor-made packages' are regarded as 'pre-arranged', then it will be very rare indeed that a travel agent can say that he does not 'otherwise than occasionally' put a package together. In this context it is important to note that the term organiser cuts across the more conventional terms of principal and agent. That is, to be an organiser it is not necessary to be a principal and, by the same token, an agent is not precluded from being an organiser simply because he is an agent; the criterion is whether a person 'organises' a package, not whether they act as principal.

The chief significance of being labelled an organiser is that the liabilities are much greater that those of a retailer. The organiser is responsible for the performance of the whole package but the retailer's liabilities are much more narrowly defined. There are also additional criminal offences for organisers to fall foul of.

2.   The retailer

2(1) 'Retailer' means the person who sells or offers for sale the package put together by the organiser.

The definition clearly covers the activities of travel agents. Under the Directive, member states had the option of imposing liability on either organisers or retailers or both for failures in the package itself. It is generally believed that the Regulations do not impose such extensive liabilities on retailers but they do make them subject to the provision of information regime (Reg. 5 and possibly also Regs 7 and 8) and they incur civil liability under Reg. 4 for providing misleading descriptive matter. However a recent case has imposed liability on a travel agent.

> *Hone v Going Places* (2001, Court of Appeal). The claimant, who was on a package holiday, was injured during an emergency evacuation of an aeroplane following a bomb scare. Both the tour operator which organised the holiday and the airline which provided the flights were bankrupt and not worth suing so the claimant sued the travel agent through whom the holiday had been purchased. During the purchase of the holiday the travel agent had not made it clear that they were only acting as an agent for the tour operator; they had given the impression that they were the principals selling the holiday. The Court of Appeal held that they would be treated as 'organisers' because they had held themselves out as such. (Note that although the travel agents could be sued as organisers they were ultimately not liable because the court said that there was no failure to take reasonable care of the claimant.)

As previously stated, a travel agent who puts a package together and sells it in his own name falls within the definition of organiser rather than retailer and is, therefore, subject to the more stringent liabilities in the Regulations. Similarly, the agent who packages extra elements with a conventional package is likely to be classified as an organiser rather than a retailer.

iii. In whose favour is the liability imposed?

The Regulations impose civil liability on the organiser and, in some cases, the retailer, in favour of 'consumers'.

> *2(2) ... 'consumer' means the person who takes or agrees to take the package ('the principal contractor) and elsewhere in these Regulations 'consumer' means, as the context requires, the principal contractor, any person on whose behalf the principal contractor agrees to purchase the package ('the other beneficiaries') or any person to whom the principal contractor or any of the other beneficiaries transfers the package ('the transferee')*

Traditionally in English Law, only a party to a contract is entitled to take the benefit of it. In other words, there have been doubts as to the extent to which members of a client's family who are named on the booking form but who may not be party to the contract would be entitled to the benefits of the contract - see *Jackson v Horizon* [1975] 3 All ER 92 and *Woodar v Wimpey* [1980] 1 All ER 571. The problem also extends to members of a party where one person has made the booking on behalf of others.

However, the definition of 'consumer' in the Regulations, making what amounts to a revolutionary change to a long established rule of English law (which still applies to all but package holiday contracts) goes some way to eliminating these problems. Furthermore, if a consumer transfers his booking to another person, as he is sometimes entitled to do now under Regulation 10, the transferee stands in the same position as the original consumer.

Contract

(a) Making the contract

A contract can be defined as a *legally binding agreement*. Legally binding simply means that it is an agreement recognised by the law which can be enforced if necessary by the courts. Briefly, the elements of an enforceable contract are that:

- the parties have come to an *agreement;*

- the agreement is *intended to be legally binding;*

- each party has provided the other with *consideration;*

- the contract is in the right *form*; and

- the parties each have the *legal capacity* to make the contract.

Apart from the first of these requirements, we can dispose of the other elements briefly because they do not cause much problem in holiday contracts. However, it is important to look at how agreement is arrived at in more detail.

Intention: as far as intention to create legal relations is concerned, in general most commercial transactions are intended to be legally binding and certainly a contract between an individual and a tour operator for the provision of a holiday would be enforceable.

Consideration: consideration means that each party has given something or done something of value for the other. Consideration is the price one party pays to enforce the promise that the other party has made. So, in a holiday contract, the consideration provided by the consumer is the price he pays, or promises to pay, for the holiday. The tour operator's consideration is his promise to provide the holiday in exchange for the price.

Capacity: if a party does not have the legal capacity to make a contract, it is not binding on him. Persons falling into this category would be drunks, the insane and minors. The former two categories are of marginal legal importance and as for minors they do not in practice create problems for tour operators.

Form: some contracts must be in the right form. As far as package holiday contracts are concerned, the Package Travel Regulations 1992 provide in Regulation 9 that all the terms of a contract must be reduced to writing and a copy given to the consumer before the contract is made, unless this is impracticable. Even where it is impracticable to do it before the contract is made, a copy must be provided to the consumer in every case. If this is not done, the consumer has the right to cancel the contract.

Offer and acceptance

Turning now to *agreement*, before there can be a legally binding contract the parties must have reached an agreement. Lawyers break down the process of agreement into two parts. One of the parties must have made an *offer* to the other party which the other party has *accepted*. An offer can be defined as a statement by one party that he is prepared to be bound by the terms of his offer if the other party accepts his offer. An acceptance is an unequivocal agreement to the terms of the offer. An offer must be distinguished from an *invitation to treat*. An invitation to treat is where a party sets the ball rolling by indicating that he is prepared to consider offers from the other party. In other words, he is not yet prepared to commit himself to making a firm offer but he wishes to enter into negotiations. In a package holiday context, the tour operator usually makes an invitation to treat when he publishes his brochure. In effect, he is saying that he has holidays available for sale and if members of the public come forward and make an offer to buy a holiday then the tour operator may then accept the offer.

In this process of offer and acceptance, there are a number of other rules:

- an offer can be withdrawn at any time before it is accepted but the withdrawal of the offer must be communicated to the other party before it is effective.

- an offer will lapse after a stated time, or after a reasonable timer or after it has been rejected.

- a counter offer amounts to a refusal to the offer, which then lapses.

- silence does not amount to consent; for example, the statement 'I will assume we have a contract unless I hear to the contrary' will not bind the other party, even if they do not reply.

(b) The contents of the contract

As part of the bargaining process, before a contract is concluded the two parties will make a variety of statements to each other, either orally or in writing. Some of these statements may end up as part of the contract and some may not, and those which end up as part of the contract may vary in importance. This section is concerned with how to classify these statements. It is important to be able to do this because the rights of the parties clearly depend upon whether a statement is part of the contract or not, and if it is, the relative importance to be attached to it.

i. Terms, representations and mere puffs

The task of classification is complicated by the fact that English law distinguishes between three different types of statement. Firstly, there are those statements which end up as *terms of the contract* which, if broken, give the victim a straightforward action for *breach of contract*. These are the things which the other party has *promised* you will get. In a package holiday context, it will be a term of the contract, for instance, that it is a four star hotel, that the clients will get a balcony and private facilities, that there are three pools and two bars, that it has a children's club, and so on. Generally, these are all statements which are printed in the brochure and are what the operator has *contracted* to provide.

Secondly, there are statements which *induce* the other party to enter into the contract but do not become terms of the contract. These are known as *representations* and, if they are *false*, they give rise to an action for *misrepresentation*. An action for misrepresentation is not as straightforward as an action for breach of contract and the remedies available may be inadequate in some circumstances. Often it is difficult to distinguish between a term and a representation but, for example, it would *probably* only be a representation if an operator, having described the hotel, then went on to describe the resort as having a 'wide range of shops'. The operator is contracting to provide an hotel with particular facilities but then, in order to encourage the client to enter into the contract, he makes other statements which will influence the client's decision but which do not form part of the contract. If the resort turns out not to have a wide range of shops, the client can sue for misrepresentation but not for breach of contract.

Thirdly, there are statements which have no legal force at all. These are known as 'puffs' or 'mere puffs' and a victim of such a statement has no redress at all. In one case, *Hoffman v Intasun* (1990, High Court, Unreported), the plaintiff tried to make out that because of the extravagantly worded statements made at the beginning of a 'Club 18-30' brochure, the defendants, Intasun, had *contracted* that they owed her an especially high standard of care. The judge rejected this approach. He decided that the statements had no contractual effect at all. This is what he said:

> "I am asked to say that because of the advertising – what lawyers call "puff" – in the early part of the brochure, the Defendants were undertaking to give an especially high standard of care. That is an argument that I reject. Puff is puff, and if that is what lawyers call it, lay people have their own expressions for it which are perhaps less flattering. Everybody knows that travel agents [sic] set out to create an atmosphere on paper of a wonderful holiday and marvellous value for money. It cannot possibly be said that a visitor to the Tyrol can sue the travel company for breach of contract if he fails to have any respiratory defect in regarding the breathtaking views of the mountains there – and so on. I look for example at how the Club reps are described on page 8 of the brochure. Mr Eccles [counsel for Intasun] in his opening drew my attention to it specifically saying that the reps were the life and soul of the party, hard working, good timing, trouble shooting, guitar playing, beach partying, smooth operators. I do not know if Miss Gail Tarburn [the Intasun rep] can even play the guitar and I am certain that it could not form any part of a breach of contract if she cannot."

Much of the advertising hype that goes into the front of brochures falls into this category, with statements that make the holiday sound good but do not amount to specific contractual promises. Examples are to be found in most brochures – 'picturesque villages set amidst glorious scenery' – 'quality hotels' – 'the number one choice for families' – 'the holiday of a lifetime' – 'the most beautiful locations around the Mediterranean' – 'hand picked accommodation' – 'a luxury cruise around the glittering Caribbean', and so on.

Thus, not only do terms have to be distinguished from representations, they both have to be distinguished from mere puffs.

ii. Conditions, warranties and innominate terms

Terms can be classified into either *conditions* or *warranties*. A condition is a major term of the contract which, if broken, provides the victim of the breach with not only a right to damages but also the right, if they wish, to terminate the contract altogether. A warranty, on the other hand, only gives rise to an action for damages. There is no right to terminate the contract for what is regarded as a breach of a minor term of the contract. There is also an intermediate form of term – called an *innominate* term – which cannot immediately be classified as either a condition or a warranty. Its classification depends upon the nature and severity of the breach.

iii. Express and implied terms

Terms can be further classified into *express* terms and *implied* terms. An express term, as its name suggests, is one which is expressed in some way, either in writing or orally. An implied term is one where the term is not expressed but can nevertheless be implied into the contract. Terms can be implied either *in fact* or *in law*. The following travel law case, decided before the Package Travel Regulations were passed, revolved around the issue of implied terms and illustrates the problem vividly.

> *Wall v Silver Wing Surface Arrangements* (1981, Unreported), A party of holidaymakers were injured in a hotel fire in Tenerife. They had been unable to escape down the fire escape because the hotel owners had padlocked the gate at the bottom. In the contract between the clients and the tour operators nothing was expressly stated about safety at the hotel but the clients alleged that there was an implied term in the contract that they would be reasonably safe in using the hotel for the purposes for which they had been invited to be there. Ultimately the court held that there was no such term but it had to make a difficult choice between protecting the interests of the clients by implying a term relating to their safety and the interests of the tour operator by not extending its liability to all the components of the package.

iv. The Package Travel Regulations and the classification of terms

The classification of terms in a package holiday contract is no longer simply a matter for the common law, but is heavily affected by the Package Travel Regulations. For instance, Reg. 6 states that all the *particulars* in the brochure (whatever that means) are implied warranties. On the face of it this has two major effects. Firstly, it potentially upgrades just about every statement in the brochure to at least a term of the contract – representations and puffs alike. Secondly, it appears to classify all statements as minor terms of the contract.

As far as this second effect is concerned, closer examination of the Regulations shows that this is not entirely so. For instance, Regulation 9 explicitly states that it is an implied *condition* that certain information must be supplied to the consumer before the contract is made. In addition, there are other regulations which have the same effect. Reg. 12 permits a consumer to withdraw from the contract if significant alterations have been made to the contract before departure and Reg. 14 effectively gives the consumer the right to terminate a contract if, after departure, a significant proportion of the services cannot be provided.

v. Exclusion clauses

One very important type of term, which will be looked at in more detail in a subsequent section, is the exclusion clause – also known as an exemption clause or an exception clause. These are clauses where one party to the contract endeavours to escape liability for breach of contract by inserting a clause into the contract excluding his liability.

vi. Liability under Regulation 15

Until 1992, the position at common law was that tour operators were not liable for the defaults or negligence of their subcontractors (or suppliers as they are often called). This was the issue which was at the heart of the *Wall* case referred to above. Although it had been the fault of the hotelkeeper that the fire escape gate had been padlocked, no blame could be attributed to the tour operator in the case. On the contrary, the judge said that the tour operator was a reputable company that had acted properly throughout. It had selected a modern hotel and monitored it for safety and there was nothing more that could reasonably be expected of them.

In practice, this approach meant that because most of a package is made up of elements subcontracted to others – airlines and hotels – much of what went wrong with a package could not be made the legal responsibility of the tour operator. This often left clients either without a remedy or the difficult task of suing a foreign hotel or airline. However, regulation 15 of the PTR changes all that. It provides:

> *15(1) The other party to the contract is liable to the consumer for the proper performance of the obligations under the contract, irrespective of whether such obligations are to be performed by that other party or by other suppliers of services but this shall not affect any remedy or right of action which that other party may have against those other suppliers of services.*

> *15(2) The other party to the contract is liable to the consumer for any damage caused to him by the failure to perform the contract or the improper performance of the contract unless the failure or the improper performance is due neither to any fault of that other party nor to that of another supplier of services, because –*

> (a) *the failures which occur in the performance of the contract are attributable to the consumer*

> (b) *such failures are attributable to a third party unconnected with the provision of the services contracted for, and are unforeseeable or unavoidable, or*

> (c) *such failures are due to –*

> > (i) *unusual and unforeseeable circumstances beyond the control of the party by whom this exception is pleaded, the consequences of which could not have been avoided even if all due care had been exercised; or*

> > (ii) *an event which the other party to the contract or the supplier of services, even with all due care, could not foresee or forestall.*

The effect of this is that if part of what the tour operator has promised to the client is to be performed by subcontractors, the tour operator is nevertheless held responsible if things go wrong unless he can prove one of four things:

- it was the consumer's own fault

- it was the fault of a third party unconnected with the contract

- it was caused by *force majeure*

- it was caused by some other event which the tour operator couldn't predict or avoid.

(c) Misrepresentation

In the previous section, we saw that some pre-contractual statements did not become terms of the contract but were only *representations*. If these representations turn out to be false, then the victim may have an action for misrepresentation. To succeed in an action for misrepresentation it must be established that:

- one party to the contract

- made a false statement of fact

- to the other party to the contract

- which induced the other party to the contract to enter into it

Statement of fact

Statements of opinion, or intention, or statements as to the future are not statements of fact and are therefore not actionable. Thus, if a tour operator prints in his brochure a statement that all clients will be accommodated in twin rooms with ensuite bathrooms and he fully intends to fulfil this promise (and has contracts with hotels to substantiate his statement), then he cannot be sued for misrepresentation if, for instance, the hotelier lets him down and his clients are all accommodated in single rooms with no bathrooms. At the time the statement was made it was neither true nor false, merely a statement of intention. It would be different, however, if the tour operator had never intended to fulfil his promise. In those circumstances, he would be making a false statement (albeit implied) about his intention to fulfil the contract. In the words of one judge "The state of a man's mind is as much a fact as the state of his digestion."(*Edgington v Fitzmaurice* (1885) Ch D 459.)

Inducing the contract

The victim of the misrepresentation only has a remedy if he can show that the statement induced the contract. If the statement had no effect upon his decision to make the contract, it is not actionable. Thus, if an 85 year old booked a holiday at an hotel where the tour operator's brochure indicated that water sports were available, when in fact they were not, he would not be able to claim for misrepresentation unless he could show that the statement influenced him to book the holiday – which seems most unlikely.

i. Types of misrepresentation

Once it has been established that a misrepresentation has been made, it is necessary to determine what type of misrepresentation it is. This is because the remedies for misrepresentation are determined according to the type of misrepresentation. There are three types of misrepresentation.

- *Fraudulent misrepresentation* – where the representor made the statement knowing it was false or was reckless as to its truth.

- *Negligent misrepresentation* – where the representor made the statement honestly believing it to be true but having no reasonable grounds for that belief

- *Innocent misrepresentation* – where the representor made the statement honestly believing it to be true and having reasonable grounds for that belief.

Putting it more broadly, the difference between the three types depends on whether the person making the statement acted dishonestly, carelessly or innocently.

ii. Remedies for misrepresentation

There are two remedies for misrepresentation, damages and rescission. Rescission is a drastic remedy which involves calling the contract off altogether and restoring the parties to the position they were in before the contract was concluded. It is available for all three types of misrepresentation automatically but can be lost in certain circumstances, such as by lapse of time, by affirmation or if the parties cannot be restored to their original position because for instance the subject matter of the contract has been consumed. This would apply in a holiday case if the clients only discovered the misrepresentation when they arrived in resort.

For fraudulent misrepresentation, damages are awarded at common law because a fraudulent misrepresentation amounts to the tort of deceit. For negligent misrepresentation damages are awarded under s.2(1) of the Misrepresentation Act 1967. There is no right to damages for innocent misrepresentation except in one case. Under s.2(2) of the Misrepresentation Act the court has a discretion to award damages in lieu of rescission if it thinks it just to do so. Thus, if a representee has a right to rescind the contract for innocent misrepresentation, he may be awarded damages instead – but only if he has not lost his right to rescind for other reason, such as lapse of time.

(d) Regulation 4

Regulation 4 creates a statutory right to compensation for the consumer that cuts across the traditional boundaries of the common law. It imposes civil liability on both organisers and retailers if they supply misleading information. It states:

> *4(1) No organiser or retailer shall supply to a consumer any descriptive matter concerning a package, the price of a package or any other conditions applying to the contract which contains any misleading information.*
>
> *4(2) If an organiser or retailer is in breach of paragraph (1) he shall be liable to compensate the consumer for any loss which the consumer suffers in consequence.*

There is liability if the plaintiff can show that

- a tour operator or travel agent
- supplied
- to a consumer
- a brochure
- that contained misleading descriptive matter
- concerning a package or its price
- and the consumer suffers as a consequence

The liability is imposed for supplying misleading descriptive matter. The implication here is that it will cover written matter but not oral statements. The word *matter* suggests something tangible. It will obviously cover brochures and other brochure-like leaflets and it would most probably extend to videos of holiday destinations. It probably does not extend to window displays or window cards because the requirement is that the matter be *supplied to* the consumer and it cannot be said that such matter is supplied to the consumer. Press advertisements are a different matter. It is a moot point whether it can be said that the operator or the retailer have supplied the matter. It comes in a paper or journal supplied by a publisher or newsagent.

The other qualification is that liability is only imposed where the consumer, as a result of the misleading information, suffers in consequence. For the consumer to show that as a consequence of the descriptive material he suffered loss, there will have to be some evidence of cause and effect. He will have to show that he relied upon the information, otherwise how can it be said that he suffered loss as a consequence? In this respect, it is similar to an action for misrepresentation.

A significant point is that the travel agent, as well as the tour operator, could incur liability, thus making them strictly liable for brochure errors they might know nothing about – and with no defence. The only way to combat this liability is to ensure that the agency agreements they have with operators contain indemnity clauses. Whether they do may very well be a matter of bargaining power.

(e) Exclusion clauses

In this section, we will look at the extent to which it is possible for a party to exclude his liability for breach of contract. In other words, can a party who is in breach of contract escape liability by relying upon a term in the contract stating that in the event of a breach he will be under no liability?

As far as tour operators are concerned, the legal obstacles that have been created mean that, for all practical purposes, they are unable to exclude their liability to consumers and can only limit their liability in very restricted circumstances. Both the common law and statute have combined to produce this situation.

i. Common law

Although the judges baulked at striking out exclusion clauses simply on the grounds that they were unreasonable, they nevertheless created a number of hurdles before an exclusion clause could be relied upon.

Notice: for an exclusion clause to be effective it has to be incorporated in the contract. Failure to do so means that it cannot be relied upon.

> *Olley v Marlborough Court Hotel Company* [1949] 1 KB 532. A guest had valuables stolen from her room because of the negligence of the hotel. The hotel relied upon an exclusion clause on the bedroom wall to avoid liability. It was held that the contract for the room had been made downstairs at the reception desk at which time the guest had no notice of the exclusion clause. It was held that the clause was ineffective as it had not been incorporated into the contract.

Construction: if the words used by the party trying to escape liability do not cover the kind of breach that occurred the clause will not help them.

> *Spencer v Cosmos, The Times*, December 6th, 1989; LEXIS, CA. The plaintiffs had been expelled from their hotel for alleged rowdy behaviour. They sued their tour operator for breach of contract. The tour operator could not prove that the plaintiffs had been rowdy. In their defence they argued that an exclusion clause in their contract protected them even against wrongful expulsions. It was held by the Court of Appeal that " ... the clause does not even set out to exclude claims in contract for failure to provide the services comprised in the holiday" and they permitted the plaintiffs' claim.

ii. The Unfair Contract Terms Act 1977

The Unfair Contract Terms Act 1977 (UCTA) regulates exclusion clauses in most types of contract, not simply holiday contracts. It has the effect of making some exclusion clauses void altogether and many others valid only if they can satisfy a reasonableness test. The main provisions are found in sections 2 and 3.

Section 2 provides:

2(1) A person cannot by reference to any contract term or to a notice given to persons generally or to particular persons exclude or restrict his liability for death or personal injury resulting from negligence.

2(2) In the case of other loss or damage, a person cannot so exclude or restrict his liability for negligence except in so far as the term or notice satisfies the requirement of reasonableness.

Thus, if a tour operator negligently causes death or personal injury to a client, this cannot be excluded at all. Even if the damage is not death or personal injury, for example, loss or damage to baggage, this liability can only be excluded if the tour operator can establish that it would be reasonable to exclude this liability – which might prove difficult.

Thompson v LMS [1930] 1 KB 41. The plaintiff was injured when she stepped down from a train which had pulled up short of the platform. The defendants escaped liability because their exclusion clause had been incorporated into the contract by means of a notice on the back of her ticket. The case was decided in 1930. Today, the railway would be found liable because s.2(1) of UCTA would prevent them from relying on an exclusion clause which protected them against negligence causing death or personal injury.

Section 3 provides:

3(1) This section applies as between contracting parties where one of them deals as consumer or on the other's written standard terms of business.

3(2) As against that party, the other cannot by reference to any contract term –

(a)   when himself in breach of contract, exclude or restrict any liability of his in respect of the breach, or

(b)   claim to be entitled –

(i)   to render a contractual performance substantially different from that which was reasonably expected of him, or

(ii)   in respect of the whole or any part of his contractual obligation, to render no performance at all,

except in so far as (in any of the cases mentioned above in this subsection) the contract term satisfies the requirement of reasonableness.

A holidaymaker will benefit from the protection of this section if they can demonstrate that

* either they dealt as consumer, or

- they dealt on the other party's written standard terms of business, and

- they suffered from one of three types of exclusion clause:

  - one which excludes or restricts the liability of the other party, or

  - one which the other party claims entitles him to offer a substantially different kind of performance, or

  - one which permits the other party not to perform at all, and

- the tour operator cannot prove the term is reasonable.

The first and third types of exclusion clause are relatively straightforward to understand. The second is illustrated by this case:

> *Anglo-Continental Holidays Ltd v Typaldos Lines (London) Ltd* [1967] 2 Lloyd's Rep. 61. The plaintiffs were travel agents who had booked a party onto the defendant's ship, Atlantica, for a cruise to Israel. With less than two weeks to go, the defendants substituted a much inferior ship, the Angelika, and an equally inferior itinerary. The plaintiffs cancelled the cruise, refunded their clients' money and sued the defendants for breach of contract. The defendants relied on an exclusion clause which stated: "Steamers, Sailing Dates, Rates and Itineraries are subject to change without prior notice". The case was decided at common law in favour of the plaintiffs but today it would be decided under UCTA and the decision would probably be the same. The defendant's would not be permitted to substitute an inferior ship and itinerary because this would be 'substantially different from that which was reasonably expected'.

Deals as consumer: this is further defined in section 12. It covers persons who do not make the contract in the course of a business contracting with someone who does make it in the course of a business. Thus, it would cover holidaymakers contracting with tour operators but not businesses who purchase packages. Note that the definition of consumer in this legislation differs from the definition in the PTR and in other consumer protection legislation, such as the Consumer Protection Act 1987, which will be examined later.

Dealing on written standard terms of business: this simply means that the business relying on the exclusion clause uses a standard set of terms and conditions on which to contract. Given that most tour operators have a set of such terms, then most people who contract with them will get the benefit of s.3.

The rationale for both s.2 and s.3 is to offer protection to those classes of contractor who find themselves at a disadvantage or where the ability to negotiate is virtually non-existent – private individuals and those who have to contract on someone else's pre-printed terms and conditions.

iii. The Package Travel Regulations

The provisions in the PTR relating to exclusion clauses are to be found in Reg. 15. Reg. 15(5) contains a blanket prohibition on exclusion clauses.

> *15(5) Without prejudice to paragraph (3) and paragraph (4) above, liability under paragraphs (1) and (2) above cannot be excluded by any contractual term.*

However, there are two major exceptions found in Reg. 15(3) and (4).

Reg. 15(3) provides

> *15(3) In the case of damage arising from the non-performance or improper performance of the services involved in the package, the contract may provide for compensation to be limited in accordance with the international conventions which govern such services.*

There are international conventions covering carriage by air (The Warsaw Convention), carriage by sea (The Athens and London Conventions) and carriage by rail (The Berne Convention). Under these conventions, the carriers are entitled to limit their liability for death and injury and loss or damage to baggage to relatively modest sums. However, under Reg. 15(1) and (2), the tour operator is responsible not only for the actions of themselves but also their suppliers, such as air and sea carriers. The immediate practical effect of this would be that if, say, an airline carrying a tour operator's clients crashed, the airline could limit its liability but the tour operator could not. Thus, the main burden of compensation would fall on the tour operator rather than the airline, even though it would be the airline that actually caused the crash. To redress the balance, the PTR permits the tour operator to limit his liability in the same way that the airline (or cruise line, or railway) could. Of course, this will only happen if the tour operator incorporates an appropriate term in his contracts. It does not happen automatically.

Reg. 15(4) provides

> *15(4) In the case of damage other than personal injury resulting from the non-performance or improper performance of the services involved in the package, the contract may include a term limiting the amount of compensation which will be paid to the consumer, provided that the limitation is not unreasonable.*

Fortunately, most complaints about package holidays are 'quality' complaints that do not concern death or personal injury. In those circumstances, the PTR permits tour operators to limit their liability to sums which are 'not unreasonable'. Tour operators take advantage of this provision in two different circumstances. Firstly, they often print tables of compensation to cover situations where they make major changes before departure. The compensation offered rises as the date of departure approaches. The amounts vary from operator to operator but often the sums are quite derisory and would quite clearly fail the test, leaving the tour operator exposed to a larger claim. Secondly, there is often a 'catch-all' clause stating that the tour operator limits its liability to a maximum of, say, twice the price of the holiday. Such a sum would, in fact, compensate consumers for all but the most disastrous of holidays and, given that the legislation permits the operator to *limit* his liability (i.e. it envisages that the tour operator will be able to escape paying full compensation in some circumstances), this would probably be regarded as a reasonable sum.

iv. The Unfair Terms in Consumer Contracts Regulations 1994

Unlike UCTA and the PTR, the Unfair Terms in Consumer Contracts Regulations (UTCCR) cover not only exclusion clauses, but also terms which are simply unfair. In this respect, the UTCCR is much wider than the other two. For instance, if I promise that you will be accommodated at a four star hotel but insert a clause into the contract saying that I will not be liable to you if you are accommodated in a lower rated hotel then I am *excluding* my liability. On the other hand, if I say that in the event of you wishing to cancel your holiday you must pay 100% cancellation charges no matter how long before departure it is you cancel, then I am not excluding my liability but imposing a term on you which is unfair. The UTCCR covers both type of term but UCTA and the PTR only cover the former.

To gain the protection of the UTCCR it has to be established that

- a consumer

- made a contract with a supplier

- which contained unfair terms

- which were not individually negotiated

Consumer: this term is defined to cover any natural person who makes a contract for purposes that are outside his business (Reg. 2(1)). Thus, businesses and companies are outside the protection offered by the Regulations.

Supplier: this means anyone supplying serviccs in thc coursc of a business (Reg. 2(1)). Tour operators would fall within the ambit of this definition.

Unfair terms: these are terms which contrary to the requirement of good faith cause a significant imbalance in the parties' rights and obligations to the detriment of the consumer (Reg.4(1)).

Individually negotiated: terms which have not been individually negotiated are subject to the Regulations. This corresponds to the requirements in UCTA relating to written standard terms of business.

Illustrative terms: Schedule 3 to the Regulations contains an 'indicative and illustrative' list of terms which may be regarded as unfair. Contained in this list are examples of standard exclusion clauses which would also be caught in most cases by UCTA, but one type of term that is potentially unfair which is listed in the Schedule is a clause 'requiring any consumer who fails to fulfil his obligation to pay a disproportionately high sum in compensation'. Tour operators are in the habit of requiring consumers who cancel their holidays to pay cancellation charges, usually on a sliding scale that rises to 100 percent as the date of departure nears. Some of these scales might be open to attack under the UTCCR on the grounds that they are disproportionately high.

Consequences of finding a term unfair: if a term is unfair then it is void and the tour operator cannot rely upon it.

The role of the Office of Fair Trading (OFT): the OFT is given powers under the legislation to investigate unfair terms in contracts drawn up for general use and in appropriate cases he may bring an action for an injunction against the person using the term to have it restrained. Currently the OFT is in the process of investigating cancellation clauses in tour operators contracts.

Terms which reflect other legislation: one drawback for consumers wishing to employ the UTCCR against tour operators' contracts is that, under Reg. 3(1) and Schedule 1, the Regulations do not apply where the contract incorporates a term which is there to 'comply with or which reflects' other legislation. However where contract terms go beyond what is permitted in this other legislation the UTCCR can be invoked. The OFT has already used its powers to require airlines to amend their standard conditions of carriage where they have not complied with the Warsaw Convention and they have made numerous requests for tour operators to change their terms and conditions.

(f) Remedies

If one party to the contract breaks it, then the other party is entitled to a remedy. The usual remedy in contract is damages, that is, financial compensation designed to put the victim of the breach in the same position as if the contract had been performed (*Robinson v Harman* (1848) 1 Ex 850). However, package holidaymakers also benefit from a range of other remedies created by the PTR which are in addition to damages and are not available in other areas of contract. These include the right to be offered an alternative holiday if, before departure, the tour operator makes a substantial change to the holiday booked, and the right to be repatriated if the tour operator cannot provide what he promised.

i. Damages

In order to compensate the consumer for breach of contract, three heads of damage are recognised

- Damages for difference in value

- Consequential loss

- Damages for distress and disappointment

Damages for difference in value: where the tour operator has provided a holiday which is worth less than the holiday he contracted to provide, the holidaymaker is entitled to the difference in value. A straightforward example of this principle is the following case.

> *Mcleod v Hunter* [1987] CLY 1162. The tour operator promised a luxurious villa but what they provided was a cramped apartment. The court assessed the difference in value as £439. This was in addition to damages for distress and disappointment.

Consequential loss. When the breach of contract results in the holidaymaker having to expend further sums in order to rectify the breach, damages for consequential loss can be claimed. Sometimes these damages are referred to as out of pocket expenses.

> *Harris v Torchgrove* [1985] CLY 944. The court awarded £40 damages for parking expenses because the promised parking at the apartment was not available and a further £300 for the cost of extra meals taken in restaurants because the apartment had no oven and the fridge was 'eccentric'.

Note that difference in value claims and consequential loss claims cannot be combined to give double compensation. For instance, if a tour operator promises full board but no evening meals are provided, the consumer cannot claim both the difference in value between half board and full board and also the out of pocket expenses for purchasing restaurant meals in the evening.

Damages for distress and disappointment: Holiday contracts are almost unique because in appropriate cases the courts will award damages for distress and disappointment caused by a breach of contract. Such damages are not available generally in the law of contract. The rule was established in the following case.

Jarvis v Swans Tours [1973] 1 All ER 71. The plaintiff booked a holiday in the Tyrol at Christmas. He was promised a 'house-party' atmosphere; 'gemutlichkeit'; fondue parties; yodler evenings; afternoon tea and cakes; etc. The hotel was virtually deserted, the skiing was very restricted, almost none of the services were provided and the hotel proprietor spoke no English. The Court of Appeal awarded the plaintiff £125 damages on a holiday that cost £64. Lord Denning said, "In a proper case damages for mental distress can be recovered in contract ... One such case is a contract for a holiday, or any other contract to provide entertainment and enjoyment. If the contracting party breaks his contract, damages can be given for the disappointment, the distress, the upset and frustration caused by the breach.

The rationale behind the decision is that where the purpose of the contract is to provide peace of mind and enjoyment then such damages can be claimed, but not for everyday commercial transactions where the provision of pleasure is not the essence of the contract.

Mitigation of loss: A victim of a breach of contract cannot simply sit back and collect damages. They must take reasonable steps to mitigate their loss and failure to do so can mean that they will lose their damages. In holiday cases, one of the simplest ways to mitigate your loss is to complain to the tour operator or its representative who may then be able to put things right. Reg. 15(9), in fact, requires tour operators to put a term into their contracts obliging consumers to complain at the earliest opportunity if they have a problem.

Czyzewski v Intasun (1990) County Ct. Unreported. The plaintiff complained of an 'offensive' toilet. After several unsuccessful attempts to repair it the hotel offered him an alternative room but for some reason he declined to take it and remained in his room for the rest of his holiday. The court awarded him only £50 damages based on the limited amount of time he would have had to spend in the room if he had accepted the alternative.

ii. Remedies for pre-departure changes

Under Regulations 12 and 13, a consumer is entitled to remedies other than damages. These Regulations provide

12 In every contract there are implied terms to the effect that –

(a)   *where the organiser is constrained before the departure to alter significantly an essential term of the contract, such as the price (so far as regulation 11 permits him to do so), he will notify the consumer as quickly as possible in order to enable him to take appropriate decisions and in particular to withdraw from the contract without penalty or to accept a rider to the contract specifying the alterations made and their impact on the price; and*

(b)   *the consumer will inform the organiser or the retailer of his decision as soon as possible.*

13(1) The terms set out in paragraphs (2) and (3) below are implied in every contract and apply where the consumer withdraws from the contract pursuant to the term in it implied by virtue of regulation 12(a), or where the organiser, for any reason other than the fault of the consumer, cancels the package before the agreed date of departure.

13(2) The consumer is entitled –

(a)   *to take a substitute package of equivalent or superior quality if the other party to the contract is able to offer him such a substitute; or*

(b)   *to take a substitute package of lower quality if the other party to the contract is able to offer him one and to recover from the organiser the difference in price between the price of the package purchased and that of the substitute package; or*

(c)   *to have repaid to him as soon as possible all the monies paid by him under the contract.*

13(3) The consumer is entitled, if appropriate, to be compensated by the organiser for non-performance of the contract except where –

(a)   *the package is cancelled because the number of persons who agree to take it is less than the minimum number required and the consumer is informed of the cancellation, in writing, within the period indicated in the description of the package; or*

(b)   *the package is cancelled by reason of unusual and unforeseeable circumstances beyond the control of the party by whom this exception is pleaded, the consequences of which could not have been avoided even if all due care had been exercised.*

Thus, under Regulation 12, if a consumer can establish that a tour operator has

- altered significantly
- an essential term

he has the choice of either

- withdrawing from the contract, or
- accepting the change with a rider to the price.

Presumably, if there is such a major change, then the consumer will withdraw unless the tour operator offers enough by way of compensation. If the consumer does withdraw, or if the operator cancels the holiday for any reason other than the consumer's fault, then the consumer is entitled to the following choices:

- a substitute holiday of equivalent or superior quality, or
- a substitute holiday of inferior quality plus the difference in value, or
- a full refund, and
- compensation, except where the contract was cancelled for *force majeure* or because of lack of minimum numbers.

iii. Remedies for post-departure changes

Where problems arise with the holiday after departure this is dealt with by Reg. 14 which provides

> *14(1) The terms set out in paragraphs (2) and (3) below are implied in every contract and apply where, after departure, a significant proportion of the services contracted for is not provided or the organiser becomes aware that he will be unable to procure a significant proportion of the services to be provided.*

> *14(2) The organiser will make suitable alternative arrangements, at no extra cost to the consumer, for the continuation of the package and will, where appropriate, compensate the consumer for the difference between the services to be supplied under the contract and those supplied.*

> *14(3) If it is impossible to make arrangements as described in paragraph (2), or these are not accepted by the consumer for good reasons, the organiser will, where appropriate, provide the consumer with equivalent transport back to the place of departure or to another place to which the consumer has agreed and will, where appropriate, compensate the consumer.*

Thus, if the consumer can show that

- a significant proportion of the services are not to be provided, or

- the tour operator becomes aware that they cannot be provided

the tour operator must

- make suitable alternative arrangements for the continuation of the holiday, or

- if it is impossible to make alternative arrangements transport the consumer home again

- and, in both cases, compensate the consumer where appropriate.

Criminal liability

This section of the chapter is concerned with the criminal offences that a tour operator might commit. There are three pieces of legislation that are relevant, the Trade Descriptions Act 1968 which regulates false trade descriptions, the Consumer Protection Act 1987 which regulates misleading prices, and the Package Travel Regulations which regulate both descriptions and prices. The offences are usually tried in a magistrates' court where the maximum penalty is £5,000 per offence but, in extreme cases, an offence under these provisions could be tried in the Crown Court before a jury and the maximum penalty would be an unlimited fine. The offences fall into a category of criminal offence labelled as regulatory offences; that is, they are not concerned with traditional types of criminal behaviour but are intended to improve trading standards.

(a) The Trade Descriptions Act 1968

Section 14 of the TDA sets out two offences:

14(1) It shall be an offence for any person in the course of any trade or business–

(a) *to make a statement which he knows to be false; or*

(b) *recklessly to make a statement which is false;*

as to any of the following matters, that is to say –

(i) *the provision in the course of any trade or business of any services, accommodation or facilities;*

(ii) *the nature of any services, accommodation or facilities provided in the course of any trade or business;*

(iii) *the time at which, manner in which or persons by whom any services, accommodation or facilities are so provided;*

(iv) *the examination, approval or evaluation by any person of any services, accommodation or facilities so provided; or*

(v) *the location or amenities of any accommodation so provided.*

To put it another way, for the prosecution to succeed it must prove that the tour operator

- made a statement
- in the course of a business
- relating to one of the categories in section 14 (for example, the facilities or the accommodation)
- that was false
- and the statement was made knowingly or recklessly.

Statements: a wide interpretation has been given to this word. It has been held to cover not only written statements but also photographs (*Yugotours v Wadsley* [1988] Crim LR 623); artist's impressions (*R v Clarksons Holidays Ltd* (197257 Cr App R 38); and oral statements (*Herron v Lunn Poly (Scotland) Ltd* [1972] SLT 2).

In the course of a trade or business: most tour operators, when they sell holidays, are doing so in the course of a trade or business. As with most businesses, there will be those who only participate at the margins and there are those who organise holidays for groups of friends and, therefore, questions may be raised as to whether they are acting in the course of a business. However, for most tour operators, this is not an issue.

The statement must fall within the categories listed in section 14: only if a tour operator makes a false statement falling into one of the categories listed in Section 14 can a prosecution succeed. The list, however, is quite comprehensive and most of the statements that a tour operator makes in a brochure would be covered by the list. For instance, *Herron v Lunn Poly* [1972] SLT 2 was a prosecution under s.14(1)(b)(i) for a false statement relating to the provision of any services, accommodation or facilities. That case concerned an hotel and its facilities which were incomplete when the clients arrived. *R v Clarksons* (1972) 57 Cr App R 38 was a prosecution under both s.14(1)(b)(i) and (ii) that is, not only for the provision of the services, but also the nature of any services, accommodation or facilities. *British Airways Board v Taylor* [1976] 1 All ER 65, which concerned a passenger who was 'bumped' from a scheduled flight after he had been given a confirmed booking, was a prosecution under s.14(1)(b)(iii) for a false statement as to the time at which any services are provided. (See also *R v Avro plc* (Court of Appeal, 14th January 1993)). *R v Sunair* [1973] 1 WLR 1105, included a count for contravening s.14(1)(b)(v) relating to the location and amenities of any accommodation provided. The prosecution concerned the non-availability of promised facilities.

The statement must be false: clearly, a statement that the hotel is only 100 metres from the beach when, in fact, it is 500 metres is a false statement and a tour operator would be rightly convicted, but some statements are much more difficult to label as true or false.

> *Thomson Travel Ltd v Roberts* (1984) 148 JP 666. A tour operator published a brochure which described an hotel as having a 'beach'. The so-called beach was a man-made construction consisting of an area of sand approximately 51 yards long and 17 yards wide retained behind a concrete wall bordering the sea. Access to the sea was by ladders down to water level at which point the depth of the sea was equivalent to the shallow end of a swimming pool. Before it could be decided whether the tour operator had made a false statement about the beach the court had to decide what was meant by the word 'beach'. Only after deciding that what existed at the hotel could not be described as a beach could the court then go on to say that a false statement had been made about a beach.

It has also been held that statements as to future intention are not capable of being either true or false. At the time they are made they are merely promises which may or may not be fulfilled. Given that much of a tour operator's brochure consists of promises as to the future, this has caused some difficulties.

> *Sunair v Dodd* [1970] 2 All ER 410. A tour operator published a brochure describing the facilities at an hotel as "all twin-bedded rooms with private bath, shower, WC and terrace". Clients who read the brochure in January 1969 and made a booking on the basis of the brochure description discovered, when they arrived at the hotel in the summer, that their rooms did not have balconies. At the time the brochure had been published the tour operator had a contract with the hotel for rooms with twin beds and balconies. It was held by the Divisional Court that what the brochure statement meant was that the tour operator was offering to supply rooms with twin beds and balconies and as this was a statement as to future intention it could not be classified as a false statement when it was published. The tour operator was therefore not guilty.

Note, however, that the situation would have been very different if the tour operator had had no contract with the hotel for the rooms described and no intention of providing such rooms. In that case there would have been a false statement – as to the state of mind of the tour operator.

The statement must have been made knowingly or recklessly: to secure a conviction, the prosecution must establish that the statement was made knowingly or recklessly; that is, they must prove a state of mind. In legal terms, they must prove *mens rea* – a guilty mind. Case law, however, has developed to a stage where it can be said that the offence approaches strict liability, that is, liability without fault.

> *Wings v Ellis* [1985] AC 272 A tour operator published a brochure which described an hotel as having air-conditioning. This was false but, at the time the brochure was published, the tour operator did not know this. As soon as they discovered the false description, they issued errata to all existing clients and told all sales staff to bring the false description to the attention of new clients when they booked. Despite these precautions, a client managed to book a holiday without being informed that the hotel had no air-conditioning. Thus, the position was that the tour operator knew that the statement was false but it did not know that the statement was being made. If they had done so, they would have seen to it that the statement was corrected. On appeal to the House of Lords, it was held that *Wings* were rightly convicted. The offence in section 14(1)(a) is to make a statement which he knows to be false, and this is what *Wings* had done. Thus *Wings* were convicted even though it might be said that they were not at fault – they were doing their best at the time to avoid committing the offence.

Wings was a case under s.14(1)(a) involving knowledge. The following case, which is not a travel case but where the principles are the same, involves a s.14(1)(b) offence which requires recklessness. Again, it shows that the case law imposes a liability much stricter than one would suspect when first reading the statute.

> *MFI Warehouses Ltd v Nattrass* [1973] 1 All ER 762. The defendants published an advertisement which contained a false statement. The advertisement had been drafted by a director and approved by the chairman. The latter had considered the advertisement for about 5-10 minutes but had not specifically considered whether it contained any false statements. On appeal to the Divisional Court, it was held that the defendants had recklessly made a false statement. Recklessness is actually defined in the Act in the following terms "a statement made regardless of whether it is true or false shall be deemed to be made recklessly ..." Literally this meant not having regard to the truth of the statement, which is what had happened. The chairman had not thought about the falsity of the statement.

Who must make the statement? An offence under the TDA requires the prosecution to prove a state of mind – knowledge or recklessness. However, most defendants will be companies who have neither minds nor bodies. The law solves this problem by requiring the prosecution to establish that one of the 'directing minds' of the company, for example, a director or managing director or company secretary, had the requisite state of mind.

> *Airtours v Shipley* (1994) Divisional Ct. Unreported. The defendants had published a brochure which stated that a hotel had a pool when it didn't. They were found not guilty on appeal because they demonstrated that the 'directing minds' of the company had not acted recklessly. They had established a 'due diligence' system which established that they had had regard to the truth or falsity of the statements in the brochure.

(b) The Consumer Protection Act 1987

The Consumer Protection Act is concerned with misleading prices. Section 20 creates two offences: giving a misleading price indication (s.20(1)); and giving a price indication which subsequently becomes misleading (s.20(2)).

Section 20(1) provides

> *20(1) Subject to the following provisions of this Part, a person shall be guilty of an offence if, in the course of any business of his, he gives (by any means whatever) to any consumers an indication which is misleading as to the price at which any goods, services, accommodation or facilities are available (whether generally or from particular persons).*

Section 20(2) provides

> *20(2) Subject as aforesaid, a person shall be guilty of an offence if –*
>
> (a)   *in the course of any business of his, he has given an indication to any consumers which, after it was given, has become misleading as mentioned in subsection (1) above; and*
>
> (b)   *some or all of those consumers might reasonably be expected to rely on the indication at a time after it has become misleading; and*
>
> (c)   *he fails to take all such steps as are reasonable to prevent those consumers from relying on the indication.*

Thus, for the prosecution to succeed under s.20(1), they must show that

- a person in a course of a business of his
- has given a misleading indication
- about the price, or
- the method of calculating the price
- of goods, services, accommodation or facilities
- to a consumer.

And, under s.20(2), the prosecution must show that

- a person in the course of a business of his
- has given an indication of the price or its method of calculation
- which has subsequently become misleading, and
- some consumers might still be relying upon the original indication, and
- he has not taken reasonable steps to correct the indication.

A person in the course of a business of his: as with the TDA, the CPA is only aimed at offences committed in the course of a business. The difference between the two is that, under the CPA, the offence can only be committed by someone acting in the course of a business *of his*. The importance of this is that employees cannot be prosecuted under the CPA whereas they can be under the TDA.

Misleading indication: this is defined very widely in s.21(1) and s.21(2). It would include, for instance, not making it clear that supplements and tax had to be added to the price in the pricing panel; not explaining that prices were based upon two sharing a room; not making clear that under-occupancy supplements were payable; and, not making it clear that insurance was a compulsory extra.

Consumer: this term is defined in s.20(6) as being any person who might wish to be provided with the services otherwise than for the purposes of a business of his. Thus, purchasers of business travel would not be protected but ordinary members of the public would. Note that no purchase has to be made – it covers any private individual *who might wish* to purchase the services.

(c) The Package Travel Regulations 1992

The PTR contain a number of criminal offences but the most important is to be found in Reg. 5. It covers both misleading descriptions and misleading prices. It provides:

> *5(1) Subject to paragraph (4) below, no organiser shall make available a brochure to a possible consumer unless it indicates in a legible, comprehensible and accurate manner the price and adequate information about the matters specified in Schedule 1 to these Regulations in respect of the packages offered for sale in the brochure to the extent that those matters are relevant to the packages so offered.*

> *5(2) Subject to paragraph (4) below, no retailer shall make available to a possible consumer a brochure which he knows or has reasonable cause to believe does not comply with the requirements of paragraph (1).*

The prosecution must, therefore, establish in relation to tour operators that

- an organiser
- has made available a brochure
- to a possible consumer
- which does not indicate adequately, accurately, legibly or comprehensibly
- information listed in Schedule 1.

In relation to travel agents, the prosecution must establish, in addition, that the travel agent knew or had reasonable cause to believe that the brochure did not comply.

Schedule 1 to the Regulations lists the following information:

1. *The destination and the means, characteristics and categories of transport used.*

2. *The type of accommodation, its location, category or degree of comfort and its main features and, where the accommodation is to be provided in a member State, its approval or tourist classification under the rules of that member State.*

3. *The meals which are included in the package.*

4. *The itinerary.*

5. *General information about passport and visa requirements which apply for British citizens and health formalities required for the journey and the stay.*

6. *Either the monetary amount or the percentage of the price which is to be paid on account and the timetable for payment of the balance.*

7.   Whether a minimum number of persons is required for the package to take place and, if so, the deadline for informing the consumer in the event of cancellation.

8.   The arrangements (if any) which apply if consumers are delayed at the outward or homeward points of departure.

9.   The arrangements for security for money paid over and for the repatriation of the consumer in the event of insolvency.

The effect of Reg. 5, taken in conjunction with Schedule 1, is to ensure that *if* a tour operator publishes a brochure, then it must contain certain information that relates to the most important elements of a package holiday. Note that there is no requirement that a tour operator must publish a brochure.

A possible consumer: as with the CPA, there is no need for the prosecution to show that a purchase had been made by a consumer, simply that a brochure had been made available. Thus, simply displaying an inaccurate brochure would be sufficient. Note that the definition of consumer in the PTR is different from that in the CPA. 'Consumer' in the PTR covers anyone who agrees to take the package and, thus, it extends to packages bought in the course of a business.

Adequately, accurately, legibly, comprehensibly: legibly presumably means that if the print cannot be read by someone with good eyesight, then it does not comply with the Regulation. Comprehensible means that it can be understood, thus obscure and overly legalistic language will be penalised. Accurate is a word that is currently causing problems to tour operators who have adopted a practice called 'fluid pricing' (i.e. where they print a price in a brochure which is a maximum price but then indicate that discounts are available for early bookers). It is argued that the price is not accurate because a consumer cannot ascertain in advance from the brochure what price he will pay. Adequate means that there must be enough information on which the consumer can make an informed choice.

Knowledge or reasonable cause: a travel agent is in a different position to a tour operator. For a tour operator, the offence is one of strict liability; that is, the prosecution do not have to prove fault to prove their case, However, with travel agents the offence, as with the TDA offences, requires *mens rea*, a 'guilty mind'.

(d) Defences

All the offences we have looked at, under the TDA, the CPA and the PTR, have defences. Some are specialised and only apply to the particular legislation, but there is one which is of general application. This is known as the 'due diligence' defence. It appears in slightly different terms in each piece of legislation but essentially it has the same effect whatever the legislation. Reg. 24 of the PTR provides:

> *24(1) Subject to the following provisions of this regulation, in proceedings against any person for an offence under regulation 5,7,8,16, or 22 of these Regulations, it shall be a defence for that person to show that he took all reasonable steps and exercised all due diligence to avoid committing the offence.*

The corresponding provision in the TDA is found in s.24 and in the CPA at s.39. The essence of the defence is that tour operators will escape conviction if they can establish that they were not at fault, because they took all reasonable precautions and exercised all due diligence to avoid committing the offence. Note that the burden of proof is on the tour operator rather than the prosecution and that the burden is difficult to discharge, as illustrated by the following case.

> *Buckinghamshire CC v Crystal Holidays Ltd* (1993) Div. Ct. Unreported. The defendants published a brochure in which they stated that there was a golf course at a particular resort. In fact when the brochure was originally published the golf course was only in the course of construction but everyone confidently believed that the course would be open by the time the season started. Unfortunately because of bad weather the golf course did not open on time. The defendants were prosecuted under the TDA for making a false trade description. Their defence failed because the prosecution pointed out that they could have prevented the commission of the offence simply by changing the wording of the brochure to say that they expected the golf course to be open at the beginning of the season. The judge said, "... it seems to me that once one is able to identify a precaution which one can properly be described as a reasonable precaution which was not taken, such as the different wording ... being put in the brochure in this case, then that really is the end of the case so far as [the defence] is concerned."

Nowadays, most tour operators have adopted 'due diligence' systems to ensure that the information in their brochures is thoroughly checked before it is published. In the *Airtours v Shipley* case referred to above, this is what saved them from conviction. Note, however, that the due diligence system was used in that case to prove that Airtours had not acted recklessly under s.14(1)(b) rather than as a due diligence defence under s.24 of the TDA. Technically there is a difference but the effect was the same.

Protection against insolvency

Expenditure on the average family holiday usually ranks as one of the two or three largest items of expenditure in the family's annual budget. In the vast majority of cases, the money has to be paid in advance to the tour operator. The obvious danger with this is that, if the tour operator becomes insolvent, consumers will lose their money. The problem is exacerbated if the clients happen to be abroad at the time. Prior to 1992, there were various voluntary and statutory schemes in place to protect consumers if this happened. Thus, if a consumer booked an air package holiday they were protected by the Air Travel Organisers' Licensing (ATOL) scheme which required air package tour operators to take out a bond to be paid out to clients in the event of the tour operator's insolvency. ABTA also operated a scheme whereby their members, whether air package operators or not, were also required to have bonds to protect their clients. However, the protection was not universal and it was possible for a client to book a holiday with a non-bonded operator and lose their money. Many bus tour operators fell into this category.

Now, the PTR requires all tour operators to be able to provide evidence of security for the return of pre-payments and for repatriation (Reg. 16). The Regulations provide that this can be done in a number of ways:

- by bonding
- by insurance
- by establishing a trust fund

If a tour operator chooses to protect his clients by bonding, then the level of the bond is determined by whether or not the tour operator is a member of an 'approved body' which has a reserve fund or not. The bonding level is higher for approved bodies with no reserve fund to make up the shortfall if the bond is insufficient. Approved bodies are organisations such as ABTA and AITO. Arrangements falling within the ATOL scheme are automatically covered by the new requirements.

Because bonds and insurance are relatively expensive to acquire many smaller, particularly domestic tour operators, are attracted by the possibility of trust funds. These work by having the pre-payments paid into a trust fund and only paid out again once the holiday has been completed. The arrangements for policing these schemes are weak and there is a real possibility of fraud associated with them.

Discussion questions

1. *Do you think the Package Travel Regulations should be extended further e.g. to cover all overseas travel products bought through a travel agent?*

2. *Is it right that a tour operator can be made liable for the negligence of his suppliers or do you think it should only be liable for its own negligence?*

3. *When you read the terms and conditions in the back of a tour operator's brochure do you understand them? Do you think anybody reads them? Does it matter?*

4. *How much does consumer protection cost?*

5. *Do you think it is a good idea to make criminals out of tour operators?*

Further reading

Grant, D. and Mason, S. (1998), *Holiday Law, 2nd Edition*, London: Sweet & Maxwell.

Saggerson, A. (2000), *Travel Law and Litigation, 2nd Edition*, CLT Professional Publishing.

16

Financial Management for Travel and Tourism

Nigel Evans

Learning objectives

This chapter introduces the ways in which the effective management of a travel and tourism company's finances can be achieved. On completion of this chapter, the reader should:

- *understand the scope and relevance of treasury management to travel and tourism companies*

- *understand the types of foreign exchange risk encountered by international travel and tourism companies*

- *understand ways in which foreign exchange risks can be managed by travel and tourism companies*

- *understand how international travel and tourism companies undertake cash management activities.*

Introduction

Although the travel and tourism industry covers a diversity of different organisations, including tour operators, airlines, hotels and travel agencies, financial management is important to all of them. Financial management is that part of the total management function concerned with the effective and efficient raising and use of funds.

Finance, like physical resources, has a large number of competing uses, is scarce but can be obtained at a price, and is bought and sold in markets. Financial management is concerned with managing this scarce resource so as to ensure that:

- sufficient *finance* is available at the right time;

- *finance* is obtained at the least possible cost; and

- *finance* is used in the most profitable ways.

The scope of financial management

Financial management can be seen as a function of management concerned with managing the financial aspects of a company's activities, just as the marketing function and personnel functions, for instance, are concerned with the managing of products and the managing of people, respectively. Financial management encompasses a broad range of activities including:

- financial planning, control and reporting;

- budgeting;

- treasury management.

Of these, this chapter will focus specifically on *treasury management*, as this area of financial management has a considerable significance for most companies operating in the international travel and tourism industry.

Treasury management

Over the last two decades, increasing attention has been paid to the Treasury aspect of financial management. It has become a specialist aspect of financial management with a professional body, The Association of Corporate Treasurers, founded in 1979.

The increasing internationalisation of business and the extreme volatility of exchange rates (following the breakdown of the previous fixed rate regime in the early 1970s), together with volatility of interest rates, has forced many businesses to concentrate resources and attention on this aspect of their business. Since travel and tourism is the most international of businesses, treasury management is of particular importance.

Treasury management is concerned with the management of a company's cash so as to ensure:

- the *right* amount of cash is available;

- in the *right* place;

- in the *right* currency;

- at the *right* time.

In managing the company's cash in such a way, Treasury management is about minimising risks, (such as minimising exposure to movements in foreign exchange and interest rates and minimising the financing costs of the business), and maximising returns, specifically, maximising the returns on surplus funds. Since maximising returns entails taking risks, decisions have to be made which require compromising some degree of profitability in return for a reduction in risks.

The role of the treasurer

The role of the 'treasurer' or 'treasury manager' is still developing but, in broad terms, it can include any corporate activities or services directly associated with banking and the financial and currency markets. Indeed, many companies (and most in travel and tourism) may not have a treasurer or a treasury department as such. The responsibilities may be split across several departments or operations, or carried out by outside financial institutions or consultants.

In most cases, however, whether treasury management is centralised or decentralised, is carried out internally or is delegated to outsiders, some degree of management of cash activities takes place and overall responsibility is vested in one person, if not the treasurer, the financial director.

Arguably, this area of management is poorly understood and managed by many travel and tourism companies, particularly small and medium sized enterprises.

The relevance of treasury management to travel and tourism

The importance of treasury management can be attributed to two particular factors that affect the industry:

Managing foreign exchange

The industry operates internationally producing international flows of funds in various currencies. Tour operators and airlines typically have a very large *exposure* to movements in foreign exchange rates, almost certainly far larger than for most companies of a similar size engaged in other areas of the economy, for instance, manufacturing companies. The very purpose of these companies implies that they are international in their activities, thereby leaving them exposed to international risks associated with foreign exchange transactions.

So for instance,

(a)   a French airline may:

- sell tickets in many currencies

- buy its fuel and aircraft in US dollars

- pay most of its staff and report its profits in French francs (or euros).

(b)   similarly, a British outbound tour operator may:

- receive most of its income in sterling

- buy aircraft fuel and pay leasing costs in US dollars

- pay its staff in sterling

- pay its hoteliers and other suppliers in various currencies, including euros and US dollars.

Cash management

The industry is highly seasonal, which usually leads to a highly seasonal pattern of cash flow. At certain times of the year, companies may have large cash balances and, at other times of the year, many companies need to borrow money in order to maintain payments to suppliers (creditors). The industry is also cyclical in nature, in that cash flows are very responsive to changes in the general level of economic activity.

In terms of cash management, tour operators and travel agents are typically low margin businesses, deriving important parts of their income not from operating profits (through the selling of holidays), but from interest income derived from investing cash surpluses they may be holding at certain times of the year.

So, for instance, a British tour operator may:

- receive revenue from customers before the company has to pay its suppliers

- invest this revenue to produce interest income

- view the interest income derived as a major source of the company's profitability.

We will now look in greater detail at these two important aspects of treasury management.

Foreign exchange management

The profitability of any company that trades internationally is affected by changes in foreign exchange rates. As Lockwood (1989) states:

> *as a large part of the travel and tourist industry is concerned with persuading and assisting people to cross national boundaries and thus to buy goods and services priced in a foreign currency, the identification and management of exchange rate exposures is vital to the profitable operation of a travel and tourist business.*

Thus, foreign exchange management is very significant for many travel and tourism businesses. The lack of stability caused by the continual changes in exchange rates between currencies creates uncertainty. Specifically, uncertainty is created as to:

- what foreign income will be worth when it is received

- what payments will cost when they have to be made, and also

- what the value of foreign assets and liabilities might be in the future.

The overall foreign exchange position of a company may be complicated as illustrated by the position of British Airways. The British Airways Annual Report and Accounts for 1998-99 states that:

> *The group does business in approximately 140 foreign currencies, which account for approximately 60 % of Group Revenue and approximately 40% of operating expenses. The Group generates a surplus in most of these currencies [i.e. revenues are greater than costs]. The principal exceptions are the US dollar and the pound Sterling in which the Group has a deficit arising from capital expenditure and the payment of some leasing costs, together with expenditure on fuel, which is payable in US dollars and the majority of staff costs, central overheads and other leasing costs, which are payable in pounds Sterling.*

British Airways, consequently, has a highly complex foreign exchange position, but it is imperative to the profitability of such a company that this exposure to foreign exchange rate movements is recognised and managed appropriately.

In all cases, risk attributed to foreign exchange rate movements arises out of uncertainty about the future exchange rate between two currencies. This risk would be minimised if it were possible to predict future rate movements. Unfortunately, however, it is not possible to do so with any degree of accuracy and for a company to try to do so can be financially dangerous. Therefore, given that foreign exchange rates cannot be predicted, another option might be to pass on to the customer the effects of any adverse movements in exchange rates and, hence, the company would incur no impact. In most cases, however, the highly competitive nature of the travel and tourism business prevents higher costs being passed on to the customer in this way. For instance, if Spain as a destination increased in price as a result of an appreciation of the Spanish peseta or euro, (making Spanish hotel costs more expensive to foreign customers), over time customers might switch to say Turkey as a cheaper alternative.

Furthermore, because many tour operators now have 'no surcharge guarantees', it effectively means that increased costs resulting from adverse foreign exchange rate movements cannot be passed on to the customer. At the same time, even if 'no surcharge guarantees' are not given, passing on increased costs can be difficult, as the Association of British Travel Agents (ABTA) Code of Conduct requires members to absorb unforeseen costs up to 2 percent of the original holiday cost. Similarly, although the European Community Package Travel Directive (see Chapter 15) allows tour operators to impose surcharges to pass on the increased costs arising from adverse movements in currency (or fuel) rates, the directive stipulates that a maximum surcharge of 10 percent can be levied, with any increase over and above this level having to be absorbed by the operator.

Clearly, then, it is prudent to manage these risks, although it is common in the industry for the risks to be ignored, especially by smaller companies. We can identify three different types of foreign exchange risk or exposure a company may be faced with.

Transaction exposure

Transaction exposure arises 'because the cost or proceeds (in home currency) of settlement of a future payment or receipt denominated in another currency may vary due to changes in exchange rates'(Buckley 1992).

Transaction exposure relates to the foreign exchange exposure where contracts have already been entered into. When a company has contracted to receive or pay an amount of money in a foreign currency at some time in the future, a risk is incurred. The specific risk is that adverse exchange rate movements between now and the time of the eventual cash receipt/payment which will increase the amount to be paid out or decrease the amount to be received.

For example, a UK tour operator selling holidays to America would receive its income in pounds sterling, but has to make payments to hoteliers and other suppliers in US dollars. In order to make the payments, the company would at some stage have to convert sterling into US dollars. This would entail a risk that the US dollar might rise in value (appreciate) against sterling, thereby making the payments more expensive in sterling terms. Assume, for instance, the company had costed its hotel beds in its American programme at a rate of $1.70

to the pound (i.e. 1 pound buys 1.70 US dollars), and that the total cost to purchase the required bed spaces was $1,700,000. The cost in sterling to the company would be $1,700,000/1.70 = £1,000,000. Now, if the rate subsequently fell to $1.60, the cost would increase to $1,700,000/1.60 = £1,062,500.

Translation exposure

Buckley (1992) states that 'translation exposure arises on the consolidation of assets, liabilities and profits denominated in foreign currency in the process of preparing consolidated accounts'. The concept is also known as *accounting exposure.*

For example, if a UK hotel company purchases a hotel in Australia, it acquires an asset priced in Australian dollars. Each year, when the balance sheet of the business is prepared, the value of the hotel would be translated into sterling at the prevailing rate on the balance sheet date. The hotel might therefore be worth less in sterling terms as shown in the balance sheet of the company.

In general, the management of translation exposure receives less active management attention than the management of transaction exposure. It might be argued that such an exposure is not a real exposure, since the asset itself remains unchanged; that is, the company still owns the same hotel. However, if at any time the company wishes to sell the hotel and wants to realise its value through the repatriation of the proceeds to the host country, then the revenue received will be affected by the prevailing exchange rate. Therefore, to give a true and fair picture of the current value of foreign assets and liabilities, it is necessary for them to be re-valued in the balance sheet of a company.

Consequently, under UK accounting convention (Statement of Standard Accounting Procedure 20), translation exposure is seen as a potential risk that might be incurred and is reported through a movement in reserves on the balance sheet. All foreign assets and liabilities are translated into domestic currency at the rate of exchange ruling on the balance sheet date (the *Closing Rate Method*) or the average rate throughout the year (the *Average Rate Method*).

Economic exposure

Economic exposure (sometimes referred to as political exposure) arises from the effect of adverse exchange rate movements on future cash flows, where no contractual arrangement to receive or pay money has yet been made. This kind of exposure is longer term in nature and often difficult to quantify exactly and forecast accurately.

For instance, suppose a specialist tour operator operates most of their programme to one country, such as The Gambia, then the company will have an economic exposure to that country and its currency. In some cases, the political and economic circumstances are very uncertain and if, for example, the government should be replaced in a violent way, (as occurred in The Gambia in 1994), customers will be reluctant to book holidays to that country, thereby severely limiting the revenues of the specialist tour operator.

Another example of such a risk might relate to the effect that relative exchange rate changes have on demand. For instance, if the value of the euro appreciates versus sterling whereas the value of the Turkish lira falls, it may well lead over time to a reduction of demand for

Greek holidays among British customers and an increase in demand for competing Turkish holidays. Consequently, a company selling Greek holidays would suffer a fall in revenues.

Thus, movements in foreign exchange rates lead to a number of different problems or exposures for travel and tourism companies. These exposures can be dealt with in a number of ways, the most obvious way being to avoid the exposures altogether, either by trading in domestic markets only or by passing the exposure over to suppliers or customers. However, these alternatives are seldom possible in international travel and tourism and so other management methods have to be employed in order to reduce the risks

The management of transaction exposure

The first step in managing transaction exposure is to identify the magnitude and the timing of the risks involved. An exposure occurs as soon as the commitment to buy or sell in a foreign currency is taken and a company needs to build up an overall picture of these commitments in order to work out total transaction exposure. This information can then be presented on an exposure summary.

To demonstrate how we can show the risk and how that risk can then be managed, we will consider a simple example using a fictitious UK tour operator, Stateside Travel. The major part of the business of Stateside Travel is selling package holidays to the USA to British customers. The operator also has a smaller operation selling British holidays in America. This produces both payments and receipts in US dollars. Table 16.1 shows a summary of Stateside's total transaction exposure for US dollars. A similar table would be produced for each currency for which an exposure exists.

Table 16.1: *Stateside Travel – US $ transaction exposure ($000's)*

	Mar	Apr	May	Jun	Jul	Aug	Sept	Total
Payments	(600)	(900)	(1100)	(1250)	(1350)	(1500)	(900)	(7600)
Receipts	50	100	100	150	200	250	50	900
Net cash flow	(550)	(800)	(1000)	(1100)	(1150)	(1250)	(850)	(6700)
Cover	300	600	800	900	950	1000	700	5250
% Cover	55	75	80	82	83	80	82	78
Net exposure	(250)	(200)	(200)	(200)	(200)	(250)	(150)	(1450)

In this example, Stateside has a larger amount of US dollar payments (because it has to pay its American suppliers) than receipts. These payments, therefore, have to be met using funds from elsewhere. In other words, the company has at some time to purchase US dollars with sterling and thus has a US dollar exposure.

There are a number of methods that could be used to manage such an exposure. These include:

(a) Matching (sometimes termed 'netting')

The company could develop an American source of income to offset against the payment. That is, it could use US receipts to directly make US payments. The company could do this by developing its American sales of UK holidays, the effect of which would be to equalise receipts and payments, payments being made from the money derived from receipts. Since in such a case no foreign exchange purchases would be necessary, the company can be said to have *covered* its exposure. However, such a position is difficult for a company to achieve, at least in the short term, because different products grow at different rates.

(b) Forward foreign exchange contracts

A forward foreign exchange contract allows a company to:

- arrange to enter into a binding contract with a bank;

- to buy or sell at a specific future date, an agreed amount of a foreign currency;

- at a rate of exchange that is determined 'now', that is, when the forward contract is made; and

- the rate agreed will be linked to the current or *spot* exchange rate, with an adjustment made (the *premium* or *discount*) for forward value.

Forward contracts allow a company that knows it will have to buy or sell a foreign currency at a date in the future to make the purchase or sale at a predetermined rate of exchange. The company will, therefore, know in advance either how much local currency it is likely to receive (if it is selling foreign currency to the bank), or how much local currency it must pay (if it is buying foreign currency from the bank). The contract is entered into now for an agreed date in the future (the *maturity* date) at which time the currencies are actually exchanged. Note the premium or discount is added or deducted from the spot rate and represents an adjustment for the interest rate differential between the two currencies.

Taking out forward cover by means of forward foreign exchange contracts is by far the most common method of covering known transaction exposures. There are, however, costs involved with forward contracts. In some cases, banks demand collateral of up to 20 percent of turnover in order to agree to transact forward contracts with smaller companies. Also, if the foreign currency is trading at a premium to the home currency, it makes it more expensive to buy in the future than the current prevailing spot rate. However, the fact that foreign costs and receipts are known exactly in advance is an important benefit in that uncertainty is removed. Furthermore, knowing in advance the costs of foreign currency purchases or the revenues to be received as a result of foreign currency sales can allow a company to put these details into its calculations when formulating brochure prices. The company, therefore, protects itself against the risk of adverse currency movements between the time it makes the forward contract and the time the foreign currency actually needs to be delivered or received at some future date.

This can be illustrated by referring again to the Stateside example. At the start of the season, Stateside has estimated that in June, for instance, payments exceed receipts by $1.1 million. That is, there is a net exposure of this amount in June. There are three ways in which this shortfall can be met:

(i)   The company could purchase the necessary US dollars now and retain them on deposit earning interest until required. This necessitates the immediate availability of sterling to pay for the US dollars and ties the money up in a foreign currency until it is needed.

(ii) The company could leave the transaction until the US dollars are required in June. This would, however, leave the company open to the risk of an adverse movement in exchange rates. If, for instance, the US\$/£ rate is now \$1.75 (in late February when the forecast cash flow was drawn up) and this rate it is assumed is maintained until June, the US dollars would cost the company 1,100,000/1.75 = £628,571. If, however, the rate between US dollars and sterling fluctuates, so the rate had moved to say \$1.55 (quite possible in the timescale), the US dollars would cost 1,100,000/1.55 = £709,677, that is, an additional cost of £81,106. In an industry such as travel and tourism, where 10 percent profit margins are commonplace, an adverse rate movement such as that outlined above of some 13 percent could completely eradicate all profits.

(iii) The company could arrange a forward foreign exchange contract with a bank. The bank would, for instance, arrange to sell US dollars to the company at US\$/£ 1.74 on 1st June. This transaction would cost US \$ 1,100,000/1.74 = £632,184, that is, £3,613 more than if the current or spot exchange rate had been applied. However, in this case the company would have paid for the certainty that, whatever the prevailing rate might be on 1st June, it could nevertheless purchase its requirements at the agreed rate and that no funds need to be transferred until that date.

Forward cover is, however, an acceptable means of covering exposure only where there is a reasonable degree of certainty as to the size and timing of foreign currency receipts and payments. Nevertheless, it is usually taken out on the basis of forecasts which will almost certainly turn out to be wrong (especially given the volatility of travel and tourism demand). Therefore, in order to deal with this problem and to introduce a degree of flexibility, other ways have been developed to cover foreign exchange exposure, most notably foreign currency options.

(c) Foreign currency options

A foreign currency option can be described as a method by which the buyer has the right, but is not obliged, to buy or sell a certain quantity of a currency at a specified rate of exchange (*the exercise price*) within a certain limited time or at the end of that period. Thus, the primary difference between a currency option and a forward contract is the absence of the obligation to buy or sell the currency once the option contract is entered into. This facility gives the contract a greater degree of flexibility, since if cash flows fail to materialise, then the contract can be allowed to lapse without being exercised; that is, no currency is exchanged. Additionally, if rates move in a favourable direction, then the contract can also be allowed to lapse. The company can take advantage of the favourable rate through the purchase of the currency needed at the time it is required.

The increased flexibility of foreign currency options also makes them more expensive than forward contracts but, in industries such as travel and tourism that often have highly volatile and unpredictable cash flows, the increased flexibility may be highly desirable for at least a part of the cover taken out.

In the Stateside example, the cover taken out (whether in the form of forward contracts or options), is shown. The difference between the net cash flow and the cover represents the proportion of the cash flow remaining at risk from exchange rate movements. For instance, in the example, Stateside needs to pay \$1,100,000 in June of which \$900,000, or 82 percent, has been purchased (forward contracts and options), leaving $200,000 at risk from adverse currency movements.

The managing of the risks arising from transaction exposure, often referred to as *hedging* the risk, can be illustrated by looking at the approach of two companies, British Airways and Thomson, as shown in Figure 16.1.

Figure 16.1: *Managing foreign currency transaction exposure at British Airways and Thomson*

British Airways

The broad spectrum of currencies in the business, many of which are linked in their movements to the US dollar and the pound sterling, gives the Group a measure of protection against exchange rate movements and reduces the overall sensitivity of the Group's results to exchange rate fluctuations. Nonetheless, the Group can experience adverse or beneficial effects. For example, if the pound sterling weakened against the US dollar and strengthened against other major currencies, the overall effect would be likely to be adverse, while the reverse would be likely to produce a beneficial effect.

The Group seeks to reduce its foreign currency exposure arising from transactions in various currencies through a policy of matching, as far as possible, receipts and payments in each individual currency. Surpluses of convertible currencies are sold either immediately (*spot*) or forward for US dollars and pounds sterling.

Source: British Airways Report and Accounts (1998-99)

Thomson Travel Group

A substantial proportion of the Group's revenues are denominated in sterling. However, the Group's UK air inclusive holiday activities, a majority of the Group's costs are denominated in currencies other than sterling, notably US dollars, Spanish pesetas, Greek drachmas and, in the future, euros (following the introduction of the European Monetary Union). A strengthening of these currencies impacts upon profitability. Each season Thomson Travel Group enters into forward contracts to 'hedge' its estimated costs in foreign currencies and at April 1998 had hedged its estimated costs up to the end of the summer 1999 season.

Source: Thomson Travel Group plc Mini Prospectus for share offer April 1998

The management of translation exposure

Translation exposures are different to transaction exposures in that they represent potential changes in the profitability of a company. Only when assets are sold or when liabilities are settled do these risks directly affect profitability. However, translation exposure can lead to very large changes in the size of a company's reserves and so most companies attempt to manage the total size of their translation exposure in some way.

The most common method of managing translation risks is by *matching* foreign currency assets and liabilities, so that a company has equal amounts of assets and liabilities denominated in a particular foreign currency. As a result, the assets and liabilities are translated at the same rate and, consequently, the effects of a revaluation of assets and liabilities offset each other. If, for example, Hilton decided to build a hotel in Germany (an asset), the company might may finance it by borrowing in local currency, namely euros. The euros borrowing, which would be a liability on the balance sheet, would be translated into pounds sterling for the accounts at the same rate as the hotel. Consequently, an increase or decrease in the value of the hotel is offset by a corresponding increase or decrease in the value of borrowings. Also, the stream of earnings from the hotel can be used to repay the interest on the loan.

Figure 16.2: *Managing foreign currency translation exposure at Airtours*

Airtours

The groups net assets in currencies other than sterling are hedged to reduce the effect of currency movements on the Group's sterling balance sheet. The group's policy is to minimise this effect primarily through matching the currency assets with centrally held currency liabilities by using currency foreign exchange contracts and debt.

Source: Airtours Annual Report and Accounts 2000

Another method of managing translation exposure could be through the use of forward contracts. This method of management is often viewed as being inappropriate, since contracts have to be taken out for a specified period of time, (the maturity of the contract), whereas the asset or liability that is to be covered by the contract may have no known maturity date. That is, it is not known when the asset will be sold or the liability will be settled, and the risk realised.

The management of economic/political exposure

Since economic or political exposure is difficult to measure and forecast, it is also difficult to manage effectively. Such risk can, of course, be avoided entirely if a company declines to trade internationally, but this is rarely an option in travel and tourism.

The main method of managing the risk that can be employed is through diversifying the product and, thus, spreading the potential risks. A company will normally seek to have a balanced portfolio of products that cover different countries and currencies diversifying products in such a way lessens exposure to any one country or currency. If, for instance, in the case of a company that sold holidays to Croatia, the company also sold holidays to other parts of the Mediterranean, only part of the business would be affected if hostilities were to break out in Croatia.

In managing the economic risks, British Airways Annual Report and Accounts states that 'exchange rates can affect demand for services, especially from leisure travellers whose decision whether and where to travel may alter as a result of exchange rate movements. While it is not possible to quantify this effect, British Airways does monitor exchange rate movements in an attempt to anticipate likely changes in the pattern of demand' (British Airways 1998-99).

Foreign exchange risk management strategies

Different companies implement very different strategies for dealing with the various risks described. The reasons for these differences on how to manage the risks stem, fundamentally, from management attitudes to taking risk. Some company managers are *risk averse* in their attitudes to taking risks, in that they will attempt to cover all foreign exchange exposure. Conversely, other managers may accept risks, due to either a lack of understanding or to a readiness to speculate in the hope of gaining increased profitability from favourable foreign exchange rate movements.

Three strategic options can be considered by management in relation to taking out cover against foreign exchange exposures:

(i) Doing nothing

A firm may be unaware of the risks or the opportunities for reducing the risks. This may well be the case, for instance, with small tour operators who may worry about the operational aspects of the business to the exclusion of the financial risks. Alternatively, the firm may take the view that exchange rates will remain unchanged or move in its favour. Effectively, such a firm would be said to be speculating.

(ii) Covering everything

This is the only way to avoid all risk, but the total costs involved in terms of commissions to banks, premiums and collateral may be substantial. However, once the cover has been taken out, and the costs are known, they can then be included as part of the calculation for working out holiday costs.

(iii) Selectively cover

By hedging only a proportion of the total risk, total costs can be reduced, for example, 70 percent of transaction exposure. This strategy covers the majority of the risk whilst leaving some room to benefit from favourable exchange rate movements should they occur. It also allows for errors in forecasting.

Cash management

Travel and tourism companies make profits from their operations, such as selling accommodation, holidays, airline tickets and so on. However, they also derive substantial revenue from investing the cash that they receive from their customers. Indeed, in some cases, it represents the major source of income to companies in the industry.

Cash management is concerned with the investing of cash surpluses and financing of cash shortages. During the course of trading, companies often generate *surplus* cash for which there is no current requirement. This cash surplus can be invested in order to obtain income in the form of interest receivable. At other times, however, even the most successful of companies may encounter periods of cash shortages during which cash has to be borrowed and interest paid. The task of a *cash management* is to manage the cash in such a way so as to maximise the amount of interest receivable and minimise the amount of interest payable.

All companies have a need to hold cash or have the ability to borrow cash. Cash is used to pay creditors (suppliers) which for a tour operator, for instance, might include airlines, hotels, ground handling agents, and travel agents. This cash expenditure is used to provide a service, such as a holiday, to customers. The service is sold to debtors (customers) who pay cash to the company. This cash flow cycle is illustrated in Figure 16.3.

Figure 16.3: *The cash flow cycle*

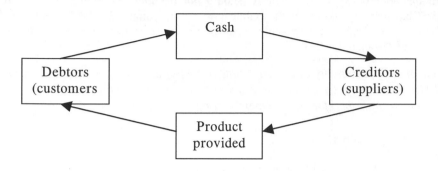

The importance of cash management in travel and tourism

An important feature of travel and tourism products is that, usually, a full cash payment is received for the product before it is provided. For instance, the holiday business generates substantial positive cash flows as passengers traditionally pay in advance, while the holiday companies themselves pay their suppliers in arrears. This is in sharp contrast to other sectors of industry, such as manufacturing, where the product normally has to be produced before it is sold to the customer and cash is received by the company.

This feature of travel and tourism has a highly significant effect on company cash flows. Cash management is, consequently, one of the most important aspects of financial management in many travel and tourism businesses, with many companies within the sector holding large amounts of surplus cash for periods of the year. The income earned on these surplus cash balances is important. Indeed, in a business where trading margins are often low (or even negative), interest income is often a vital source of income. Taking the Airtours Group (which includes Airtours Tour Operations, Going Places travel agencies and the airline Airtours International) as an example, profit figures reveal substantial interest income even over a period of relatively low interest rates (see Table 16.2).

Table 16.2: *Airtours profits (£mn), 1999 and 2000*

	2000	**1999**
Profit from operations	38.0	125.9
Bank Interest receivable	38.2	40.7
Operating profit and interest receivable	76.2	166.6

Source: Airtours plc Annual Report and Accounts (2000)

Table 16.2 illustrates the significance of interest income and, hence, of cash management to a company such as Airtours. In both years, interest income was highly important to overall group profitability (although interest expenses were also incurred on loans and lease agreements). In 1999 and 2000, the group had significant amounts of cash and bank deposits amounting to £554.2m and £793.3m respectively.

The pattern of earnings demonstrated by Airtours is repeated throughout the travel and tourism industry. Hence, the importance of, in effect, 'making money out of money', as well as from the operations of the business, should not be under-estimated. David Crossland, Airtours Chairman, speaking on the publication of his company's 1992 results in January 1993, gave an indication of the significance of this area of management to his company. There is, says Crossland (1993):

> *a degree of seasonality to this cash flow, but even at its lowest point in February 1992, Airtours' net cash balances did not fall below 65 million. Effective cash management is therefore a very important part of managing the business.*

Seasonality of cash flow

Travel and tourism has one of the most highly seasonal patterns of demand for any product or service, with less variation than the demand for Christmas cards or air conditioners, but more than nearly all high value individual purchases (Bull 1995). This seasonality is largely due to climate, but is also related to factors such as school holidays, festivals, and historic travel patterns.

Seasonality of demand for the product leads to a highly seasonal pattern of cash in-flows and out-flows. Consequently, at some times of the year, companies often have large surplus cash balances to invest whilst, at other times, only small amounts of cash may be available to invest or it may even be necessary to borrow in order to meet cash requirements. If we take, as an example, a typical UK tour operator selling mass-market package holidays largely to Europe, the company is greatly affected by the seasonality of the product which directly affects its cash management. Such an operator may have a number of operating characteristics:

- the bulk of holidays sold would be summer sun with the season lasting from April to September, but with the peak months being July and August during school holidays.

- summer sun holidays are typically booked in three distinct periods:

  the early booking period starting in August or September, when a significant number of people book. This applies especially to families, and those who are tied to taking holidays between certain dates, or are trying to take advantage of particular offers such as 'free child places', or low deposits.

  the post Christmas period from January to March which is usually the largest *booking* period, and during which customers may be targeted with a second edition of the brochure.

  the late booking period, from April onwards, which has become increasingly *significant* in recent years, and maybe a time of intense competition as operators try to sell remaining capacity and vary prices in order to do so.

- many tour operators have attempted to widen their range of activities, and reduce the effects of seasonality, by, for instance, introducing winter sun and skiing programmes. The winter sun season normally lasts from October to April, whilst the skiing season normally lasts from December to April with peaks in February and at Easter. In most cases, the combined size of these programmes is far smaller than the summer programme, representing perhaps 25 percent of the summer programme in terms of receipts. Bookings for the winter sun and skiing programmes are taken throughout the summer and autumn, but the winter ski programme in particular is subject to a great deal of late booking in late autumn and early winter as customers wait to see what snow conditions are likely for the season.

- the tour operator will have a number of seasonal costs such as airline fuel, staff working at resorts, and accommodation charges. However, the tour operator will also have a high level of costs that have to be met throughout the year, such as the costs of head office staff, aircraft maintenance, and computer facilities.

The characteristics of the tour operating business outlined above have certain implications for cash management. Cash builds up and declines in a seasonal way and, therefore, the cash position of a typical tour operator will vary greatly over the course of a normal year, as shown in Figure 16.4.

Figure 16.4: *The cash flow profile of a tour operator*

The cash flow profile shown in Figure 16.4 is, perhaps, typical of a mass tour operator in a

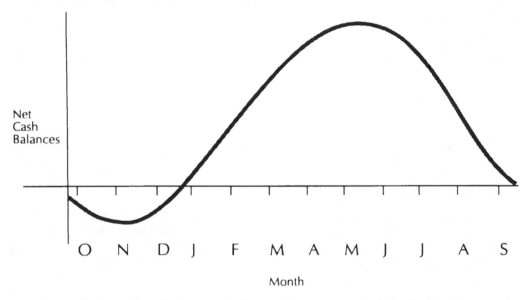

normal year. It shows that during certain times of the year, particularly the first five months of the calendar year, large surplus cash balances are free to be invested until the cash is needed to pay bills during the summer season and for the remainder of the year. The size and timing of the cash balances and the interest to be earned from the invested balances will vary from year to year, since the profile of bookings and level of interest rates also vary from year to year.

The period of greatest risk for many travel and tourism companies, however, usually comes in the autumn and winter. Cash balances have been run down as seasonal payments have been made during the preceding summer season and the bulk of bookings for the subsequent season have yet to be made. The position is often exacerbated by companies offering favourable payment terms to customers whereby a low initial deposit is required and, as a result, companies often have to rely on bank support to help them through this period. The problem may be compounded, however, if the early summer booking period for the forthcoming season and winter ski and sun bookings are poor, and post Christmas bookings are delayed.

In a case where a bank (or other party) fails to lend the necessary support, insolvency is the inevitable result. Insolvency, (the inability to pay bills as they become due), has often befallen companies in this sector when revenue from expected bookings has failed to materialise. When a company reaches an insolvent position, it normally leads to the company's failure and liquidation. A company can sometimes survive for many years without making profits or making very low levels of profit but, if they run out of cash, it is difficult for them to survive because employees and creditors must be paid. Many travel and tourism companies routinely rely on banks to provide short term finance for a part of the year, but it is when these negative cash balances are larger or more prolonged than usual and banks feel unable to provide finance that problems occur.

Cash forecasting

An essential starting point for efficient cash management is to produce cash flow forecasts. Cash flow needs to be carefully planned and monitored so that the necessary action can be taken when cash surpluses or deficits are indicated. The main purposes of cash flow forecasts are:

- to plan/forecast the organisation's cash shortages or cash surpluses over the forecast period, and

- to monitor how actual cash in-flows and out-flows vary from forecast cash flow.

Detailed cash flow forecasts should, ideally, be produced for all travel and tourism businesses, and these forecasts should be continually updated as and when new information becomes available. The cash flow forecast involves the calculation of future cash in-flows (receipts) and cash out-flows (costs), but it is usually easier for a business to forecast its costs than its revenues.

Costs are made up of major items such as salary costs, administrative costs, accommodation costs, and transportation costs. Many of these costs can be estimated in advance with some degree of accuracy since they are subject to contracts agreed before the costs are incurred. Furthermore, uncertainties with regard to costs can be minimised by management actions. For instance, the costs of foreign currency and jet fuel purchases can be established in advance through purchasing forward contracts. In the case of receipts, however, the forecasting process is much more difficult and usually less accurate since, ultimately, the forecast depends upon the attitudes of customers. Customers can be fickle and their attitudes are influenced by a range of factors and events, such as wars, political instability, recession, unemployment and mortgage rates. Nevertheless, despite the inherent difficulties and inaccuracies involved in forecasting, it is an important management activity and an essential pre-requisite for successful cash management.

An example of a cash flow forecast for a tour operator is shown below in Figure 16.5. This cash flow forecast follows a similar pattern to the cash flow profile of a tour operator shown in Figure 16.4

Figure 16.5: *The cash flow forecast for a tour operator (£000s)*

	Oct 1999	Nov 1999	Dec 1999	Jan 2000	Feb 2000	Mar 2000	Apr 2000	May 2000	June 2000	July 2000	Aug 2000	Sep 2000	Total
Inflows:													
Receipts from debtors	300	610	2,300	3,300	2,615	2,600	3,550	6,530	6,600	7,701	7,733	2,050	45,889
Interest income					13	23	33	44	47	29	17	4	210
	300	610	2,300	3,300	2,628	2,623	3,583	6,574	6,647	7,730	7,750	2,045	46,099
Outflows:													
Payments to creditors	900	905	1,000	1,000	1,083	1,078	1,648	5,539	8,062	8,545	8,565	1,869	40,194
Salaries	160	160	250	250	250	250	640	640	640	640	640	640	5,160
Admin	35	35	35	45	45	45	45	45	45	45	45	45	510
Interest payments	5	10	15	5									
	1,100	1,110	1,300	1,300	1,378	1,373	2,333	6,224	8,747	9,230	9,250	2,554	45,889
In-flows less out-flows	800	500	1,000	2,000	1,250	1,250	1,250	350	-2,100	-1,500	-1,500	-500	200
Opening balance b/f	-200	-1,000	-1,500	-500	1,500	2,750	4,000	5,250	5,600	3,500	2,000	500	
Closing balance b/f	-1,000	-1,500	-500	1,500	2,750	4,000	5,250	5,600	3,500	2,000	500	0	

The forecast shown indicates that, for nine months of the year, the company involved has a positive net cash balance. That is, it has a surplus of cash over and above the amount that is necessary in order to pay its bills. For the remaining three months, the company has a negative net cash balance. That is, it has a deficit of cash and must find other sources of cash in order to pay its bills as they become due. The questions posed by such a cash flow are:

- how are the cash surpluses to be invested?

- how are the cash deficits to be financed?

Principles of investing surpluses and financing deficits

If surplus cash is available, an investment decision is required. This decision will be based on a consideration of the pertinent facts:

- the size of the amounts available;

- the period for which the cash is available;

- whether there is a possibility that the cash will be required sooner than forecast in order to make unexpected payments; and

- a knowledge of the competing institutions with which funds can be placed and the terms and rates that they are prepared to pay in *bidding* for the cash.

The aim of the investment should be to secure the maximum interest possible consistent with a satisfactory level of risk and the required level of liquidity (Samuels, Wilkes and Brayshaw 1990). Liquidity is the ability to access the funds invested as and when required.

Similarly, a cash deficit requires a decision as to how the deficit is to be financed. The decision will also depend on the length of time financing is required, the size and certainty of the financing requirement and knowledge of the terms and rates upon which cash will be *offered*.

Investment of cash surpluses

Cash can be invested and deficits financed in a number of ways. As with most forms of investment, returns on the investment of surplus cash will be higher if the level of risk accepted is higher, if the funds are invested for long periods, and if a longer period of notice to uplift the funds is accepted. That is, the consideration of investments in detail is concerned with risk, maturity dates, and liquidity.

There are many ways in which short term funds can be invested that vary in relation to risk, maturity dates and liquidity. Four of these methods of investing short-term cash surpluses at relatively low levels of risk are now outlined.

(i) Call accounts

Call accounts are similar to personal deposit accounts and are provided by all banks. They provide flexible accounts whereby cash can be called upon, should it be needed, at short notice, such as on the same day, with one or two days' notice or sometimes with one weeks' notice. In return for the flexibility, a fairly low interest rate is applied to such accounts and the rate of interest varies in accordance with money market rate movements.

(ii) Term deposits

All major banks take cash on term (or time) deposits in amounts from about £50,000 upwards. A term deposit is an investment of a fixed amount of cash for a fixed period of time (i.e. there is a set maturity date for the investment) and at a fixed rate of interest. Consequently, the cash is tied up for a set period of time so that this form of investment offers a low level of liquidity and requires a good knowledge of expected future cash flows. If the cash was to be required at an earlier date, the deposit could in some circumstances be *broken* (received back earlier than the maturity date), but a penalty would be applied. The rate of interest earned on term deposits is fixed at the time the deposit is made, but is likely to be substantially higher than on call accounts due to the lack of flexibility with such a deposit. Term deposits can be made for periods ranging from overnight to several years.

In addition to the large British commercial banks, there are over 400 foreign banks in the City of London that quote competitively for term deposits. Therefore, the market for such cash deposits is large and extremely active (especially in the major currencies), and it pays a company to shop around for the best rates available at the time.

The term deposit represents the primary investment method used by most Travel and Tourism businesses. Airtours, for instance, 'invests surplus funds on term deposits with mainstream banks but, as the rates decline, it has indicated that it is examining other areas of investment for these funds' (Accountancy Age 28/1/93).

(iii) Certificates of deposit

A certificate of deposit (CD) is a certificate acknowledging a deposit issued by a bank. These are issued for periods ranging from three months to five years on amounts usually over £50,000, and carry a fixed rate of interest which is likely to be at a rate similar to a term deposit of the same maturity. The main advantage of the CD over a term deposit is that it is a *negotiable* form of investment and is, consequently, more liquid. That is, if the investment needs to be realised, the CD can be sold to another party at a price agreed through negotiation. In London and other financial centres, there are large *secondary* markets for CDs so that buyers can usually be found if CDs need to be sold.

(iv) Commercial paper

Large companies with good credit ratings can raise short-term finance by issuing commercial paper. Only larger companies can normally raise finance in this way, but all companies can use the market to invest during the short term. Commercial paper represents a promise to pay back the investment by the company that issues the commercial paper at a fixed maturity date (typically between 7 days and three months), in return for cash deposited.

One company can invest in another's commercial paper. For instance, Thomson might purchase Shell Oil Company commercial paper. The *instrument* is like a certificate of deposit, negotiable, so that the investment can be sold if it is no longer required, thereby providing flexibility.

The market for commercial paper has grown considerably in recent years and interest rates (agreed at the time of purchase) tend to be slightly higher than those available on term deposits or CDs, reflecting a slightly higher level of risk.

Financing of cash deficits

At certain times of the year, many travel and tourism organisations have cash deficits which have to be financed in some way. Cash deficits can be variously financed but, before resorting to external sources for the necessary finance, there are a number of broad methods of easing temporary cash shortages that a company will probably wish to consider. Some of these measures might include the following:

(i) Postponing capital expenditure

Some capital expenditure items are more important and urgent than others. It might be imprudent to postpone expenditure on fixed assets (such as new aircraft) which are needed for the growth and development of the business. It may, however, be possible to postpone some capital expenditure without serious consequences, such as the routine replacement of company cars.

(ii) Accelerating cash in-flows which would otherwise be expected in a later period

The most obvious way of bringing forward cash in-flows would be to press debtors (customers) for earlier payment. This might be achieved, for instance, through early payment discounts or through providing commission incentives to agents to collect and pass on cash from customers at an earlier date. Such actions must, however, be seriously considered before they are taken, since they might result in some loss of goodwill with customers.

(iii) Decelerating cash out-flows

Longer credit might be taken from suppliers, by taking longer to pay hotels, airlines, and so on. The longer credit might be the result of a negotiated agreement or a decision may be taken unilaterally to take longer to pay bills. Such a policy might run a serious risk of incurring bad feeling among suppliers and make renewing contracts difficult or expensive.

(iv) Reversing past investment decisions

Some assets are less crucial to a business than others, so that if severe cash flow problems occur, the option of selling off investments or property might have to be considered.

Although internal methods of avoiding cash deficits may be implemented, most companies will need to obtain short-term finance from external sources at some time. This need for short-term external finance is either because they do not want to use the internal methods, or because there is still a cash shortfall after the internal methods have been exhausted. There are many methods of obtaining short-term finance for a business including short term loans, factoring, commercial paper, sale and lease-back of assets. By far the most popular form of short-term finance in the UK is provided by banks in the form of overdrafts. The overdraft has a number of characteristics:

- it is a very flexible form of finance with limits on borrowing set by negotiation;

- it gives enterprises the scope to move freely within these limits and only be charged on the outstanding debit balance (although small commitment fees on undrawn balances are often charged);

- overdrafts can generally be arranged quickly;

- the rate of interest charged normally fluctuates with market rates; and

- technically, the overdraft is 'repayable (to the bank) on demand', but usually some notice is given of repayment.

The overdraft is a very flexible and commonly used method of short term financing. However, the fact that the finance can be recalled on demand, or at least at short notice by banks, has often given cause for concern and sometimes has led to the insolvency of travel and tourism companies. For instance, the failure of Barclays Bank to agree to an annual overdraft facility to provide finance for the slack winter period for Exchange Travel (then the country's seventh largest travel agency group), was the event that pushed the company 'over the edge' into failure in September 1990.

Good cash management practice involves the building of a relationship between the bank and the company so that the bank fully understands the company's financing requirements. Requests for overdrafts do not then come as a surprise to the bank but are seen as a normal part of the company's operations. Consequently, overdrafts are often renewed from one period to the next or agreed on an annual basis without problems.

Conclusion

This chapter has considered two aspects of financial management that are of vital importance to an international business such as travel and tourism, namely foreign exchange management and cash management. It has argued that these two areas (that are normally seen as being part of the treasury area of financial management) are vital to the well being of most travel and tourism companies. These two areas of management concern are important primarily because:

- in the case of foreign exchange management, the risks stemming from movements in foreign exchange currency rates are so large that if they are not managed in an appropriate fashion, profits derived from the operations of the business can be completely eliminated and the business as a whole placed at risk; and,

- in the case of cash management, the short term investing of cash balances is often a major source of income for travel and tourism companies, so that it is imperative that these balances are managed in an active way and invested at competitive market rates, thereby maximising profitability, whilst cash deficits need to be planned for and financed appropriately.

These two areas of travel and tourism management have received little attention in the travel and tourism literature, but their importance to the profitability and well being of many companies in the sector should not be under-estimated.

Discussion questions

1. *What are the three categories of foreign exchange risk? Provide an illustration of each of these risks from the Travel and Tourism industry.*

2. *What steps can a manager of a Travel and Tourism company take to manage the risks arising from the volatility of foreign exchange rates?*

3. *What is meant by the term 'cash management'? Explain the significance of cash management to Travel and Tourism companies.*

Further reading

Buckley, A. (2000), *Multinational Finance, 6th Edition*, London: Financial Times Prentice Hall.

Lockwood, R. D. (1989), Foreign exchange management, in S. Witt and L. Mountinho (eds.) *Tourism Marketing and Management Handbook*, Hemel Hempstead UK: Prentice Hall: 175-178

Ross, D. (1996), *International Treasury Management, 3rd Edition*, London: Euromoney Publications.

Samuels, J., Wilkes, F. and Brayshaw, E. (1995), *Management of Company Finance, 5th Edition*, London: Chapman and Hall.

Vogel, H. L. (2001), *Travel Industry Economics – A Guide for Financial Analysis*, Cambridge: Cambridge University Press.

References

Accountancy Age (1993), Interview with David Crossland, 28th January.

Airtours plc (2000), *Annual Report and Accounts 2000*.

Association of British Travel Agents (ABTA) Code of Conduct for Members, in *ABTA Members' Handbook 2000*, London: ABTA.

British Airways (1999), *Annual Report and Accounts (1998-99)*.

Buckley, A. (2000), *Multinational Finance, 6th Edition*, Harlow UK: Financial Times Prentice Hall.

Lockwood, R. D. (1989), Foreign exchange management, in S. Witt and L. Moutinho (eds.) *Tourism Marketing and Management Handbook*, Hemel Hempstead, UK: Prentice Hall: 175-178.

Samuels, J., Wilkes, F. and Brayshaw, E. (1995), *Management of Company Finance, 5th Edition*, London: Chapman and Hall.

Thomson Travel Group plc (1998), Mini Prospectus for share offer April 1998.

Travel and Tourism Economics

Nigel Evans

Learning objectives

After completing this chapter, the reader should:

- *understand the nature of economics as it affects travel and tourism*

- *understand the concepts of demand and supply for travel and tourism products*

- *understand how prices are determined by the interaction of demand and supply*

- *understand how price elasticity affects the demand and supply of travel and tourism products*

- *be aware of the macro economic effects of tourism and, in particular, the use of tourism multipliers*

Introduction

The study of economics is usually defined in terms of scarcity. How can the imbalance between scarce resources on the one hand, and people's needs and 'wants' on the other, be reconciled? The basic economic problem is that resources are finite whereas people's needs and wants appear to be unlimited and, consequently, exceed the resources available in order to satisfy these needs and wants.

Economists usually divide resources (sometimes referred to as 'factors of production') into those which can be considered 'free' and those which are scarce. Free resources are those resources available in such abundance naturally (such as air and the sea) that there is no need for an allocative mechanism to allocate them to users or consumers. Scarce resources, conversely, are those which are limited in their supply relative to the demand of consumers.

These resources are often categorised as:

- Land – including not only the land resources themselves but the earth's mineral resources;

- Labour – the human skills used in the creation of wealth; and

- Capital – the man made resources that have been created using the other two resources. Machinery and financial resources are included in this category.

Everyone needs air, food and water in order to support life and have basic wants, such as clothing and shelter, but once these basic needs and wants have been satisfied more advanced wants present themselves, such as wanting to travel or wanting to take a holiday. Business is involved with combining the factors of production in order to produce goods and services which are wanted by consumers.

The existence of this imbalance between resources on the one hand, and consumers' needs and wants on the other, means that choices have to be made in the allocation and distribution of resources to consumers. Economics, then, is largely concerned with analysing the problems of choice arising from this scarcity and, in so doing, gaining an understanding of the behaviour of households and firms in the economy.

Tourism economics

In a tourism context, the economics of tourism has been defined by one writer as being

> concerned with the use of scarce resources, labour, capital, land, and environmental resources, to produce the product, tourism, and with the distribution of this product between different consumers (Sinclair 1991).

It should be noted that in this definition, environmental resources are differentiated as a separate resource (rather than included as part of the 'land' resource). In so doing, the underlying critical importance to the tourism product of the environment in terms of air and water quality and the aesthetic beauty of nature and the landscape is recognised.

Indeed, Bull (1995) argues that the basis for tourism lies in building upon these 'free' resources (or 'renewable resources' as they are sometimes termed), with a mixture of public sector and private sector resources. These free resources, together with the other scarce resources, are combined to form what most tourists perceive as the tourist 'product' they consume and which suppliers produce. As Bull (1995) points out, in today's world there are few truly free resources since any human activity makes demands on the world's resources and, as a consequence, ultimately someone will have to pay a price.

Figure 17.1 shows Bull's interpretation of the way in which resources are combined in travel and tourism to produce the tourism product.

Figure 17.1: *Resources used in travel and tourism*

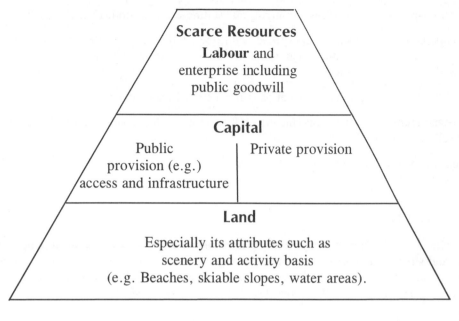

Source: Bull (1995)

All of the resources have competing demands made upon them so that, if they are used for one form of development, they cannot be used in other ways. For example, a large flat land coastal area might be suitable for the development of a resort area for tourism or as a site for heavy industry. If tourism is chosen ahead of heavy industry, an opportunity to develop heavy industry on this site has been lost and the cost of this choice is known as the 'opportunity cost', which represents the potential economic returns that are being given up in favour of developing tourism.

Economics, then, can be viewed at two levels. The *micro* level considers individual businesses and consumers and the *macro* level considers the economy as a whole in a particular area or in relation to the national or international economy.

Microeconomics in tourism is, therefore, concerned with how economic decisions are reached at the level of the individual tourism business or the individual tourism consumer. Key questions to consider include:

- What makes consumers decide which tourism products they are going to buy, and in what quantities?

- How do specific tourism businesses, decide what tourism products are going to be sold and distributed to consumers and in what quantities?

- How are the market prices for buying and selling tourism products arrived at?

Macroeconomics in tourism is concerned with the study of the total (usually termed aggregate) effects of economic phenomena affecting the local, national or international economy. Key questions include:

- What factors determine the level of aggregate tourist spending?

- What is the aggregate economic effect of tourism on the economy through the so-called 'multiplier' effect?

In this chapter we will consider some of these questions first at the micro level and thereafter at the macro level.

Economic choices

The cornerstone of economic analysis at the micro level is the consideration of supply and demand and the interaction between them. Every individual demands goods and services (products) and, when all these demands are put together, the resulting aggregate demand is what the industry must supply if all consumers are to achieve satisfaction.

The interaction of the forces of supply and demand determine the price of a product. Products have a price because they are useful (or have *utility* to use the economists' jargon), and because they are scarce. Their usefulness is shown by the fact that consumers demand them and scarcity is revealed by the unwillingness of firms to provide unlimited amounts of a product. Neither demand nor supply are static but vary with changing conditions. Furthermore, the nature of demand and supply will vary according to the nature of the product in question.

Before going on to consider the nature of demand and supply in tourism, it is necessary to consider briefly where the interaction of these forces takes place in a market.

> *Markets are situations where potential buyers and sellers of products come together in order to exchange.*

To an economist, the term 'market' does not represent the geographical place where buyers and sellers meet but, instead, refers to all those buyers and sellers who exert an influence on the price of a product. Some markets are world-wide, such as the markets for oil, gold or foreign exchange, whereas others are more localised, such as the markets for holidays or transportation.

In analysing markets, economists distinguish between *perfect* and *imperfect* competition in markets. All markets have some imperfections, but economists often study perfect markets as they provide useful insights to the theoretical behaviour of markets and demonstrate what would happen if all the imperfections were to be removed.

> *A perfect market exists where there are a large number of buyers and sellers and no individual buyer or seller has enough market power to influence the market price.*

In a perfect market:

- individual firms must sell at the prevailing market price;

- all buyers and sellers have the same information about prices;

- the consumer will act rationally by purchasing at the lowest available price;

- the product is uniform across the market (i.e. it is homogeneous);

- there is freedom of entry into the market for new sellers; and

- it is easy and cheap to transfer purchases from one seller to another.

These conditions, outlined above, ensure that price differences in the market are rapidly eliminated and that one market price is established for each product.

In the real world, of course, perfect markets do not exist, although some markets, such as the market for foreign exchange, come close. All markets exhibit some degree of imperfection. Reasons for this include:

- suppliers creating the impression that their products are different or better than those of their competitors;

- the loyalty of consumers to particular products preventing rational buying decisions being made;

- buyers and sellers not having complete access to information on prices; and

- an individual buyer or seller (or a group of buyers and sellers) being powerful enough to influence the price of the products on offer.

At the opposite end of the spectrum of market types from perfect markets are monopolistic markets where there is only one seller in the market, and the seller thereby has a very large influence on the price (unless the market is regulated by outside bodies). For example, the aviation market is heavily regulated by government agencies.

Having briefly considered the nature of markets, we can now move on to consider demand and supply and how they interact in markets through the *price mechanism*.

Demand

The concept of demand

> *Demand represents the quantity of a product buyers are willing and able to buy at a particular price over a specified period of time.*

Demand to an economist is not quite the same as wants. Everyone might want to go on a round-the-world cruise, but not everyone has the ability to pay for it. Thus, wants are unlimited, but demand is limited by the ability to pay.

Several factors influence the total market demand for a product such as:

- the price of the product;

- the price of competing products;

- the size and distribution of household incomes;
- fashion and tastes;
- opportunities for consumption (e.g. leisure time).

Central to a consideration of demand is the theory of demand which states that:

> *Other things being equal, the quantity of a good or service demanded is inversely related to its price.*

In other words, as the price goes down the quantity demanded goes up and, conversely, as the price goes up the quantity demanded goes down.

The demand curve

This relationship between demand and price is usually shown graphically as a demand curve. A demand curve can be drawn:

- for an individual consumer: or
- (more usually) a *market* demand curve which represents the aggregate quantity of a product demanded by all consumers together, at a given price.

A demand curve is constructed from a *demand schedule*, which shows the quantities of a product that are demanded at different prices. Figure 17.2 shows a typical demand curve DD which plots the relationship between price and the quantity demanded.

Figure 17.2: *The demand curve*

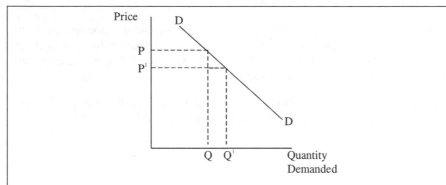

Changes in demand caused by changes in price are represented by movements along the demand curve, from one point to another. In Figure 17.2, for instance, if price is reduced from P to P¹ the Quantity Demanded increases from Q to Q¹.

Note that the demand curve is drawn as a straight line. Straight line demand curves are often drawn in economics for illustrative purposes because it is more convenient to draw them in this way. In reality a demand curve's shape is more likely to be concave indicating that there are progressively larger increases in the quantity demanded as the price falls.

The market demand curve generally slopes downwards to the right because:

- as prices fall the product becomes cheaper relative to other products and, therefore, expenditure will shift to the product whose price has fallen. That is, a fall in the relative price of a product increases the demand for it – *the substitution effect*. (An increase in the relative price of a product decreases the demand for it).

- A fall in the product's price means that people with lower incomes will be able to afford it and the overall demand therefore increases. That is, a fall in the absolute price of a product increases in the demand for it – *the price effect*. (The converse is also true if the product's price rises).

Analysis of a given demand curve gives a great deal of information about the nature of demand for a particular product. In particular two factors are of interest:

1. the shape or slope of the demand curve; and

2. the position of the demand curve.

The shape or slope of the curve is a reflection of its steepness, and tells us how sensitive demand is to changes in price; that is, the *elasticity of demand*. This is discussed in more detail in a later section. The position of the curve refers to its position in relation to each axis. As already established, changes in price result in movements along the curve.

Changing conditions of demand in tourism

However, factors other than price will also affect demand. These factors will alter the position of the demand curve, causing the curve to shift its position to the left or to the right. These factors can be referred to collectively as the conditions of demand.

In Figure 17.3, demand increases for some reason, such as an increase in overall levels of income, and this is reflected in a shift to the right; from curve DD to curve D^1D^1. Every point on curve D^1D^1 is further from the Y axis, indicating that at every price level demand is stronger and a greater quantity is being demanded.

Figure 17.3: *Changing conditions of demand*

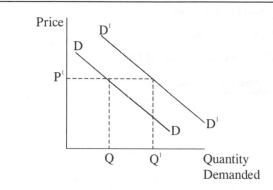

Changes in demand caused by changes in the conditions of demand are represented by a shift in the demand curve to the left or the right. In Figure 17.3, for instance, at price P^1 the quantity demanded increases from Q to Q^1.

Many factors other than price are likely to influence demand for any product and, in the case of tourism, these factors are numerous and the interaction between them complex. Some of the factors are economic, whilst further factors are related to the competitive environment and others are more social or cultural in their nature. Here we will consider firstly the economic factors before going on to consider the non-economic factors affecting demand.

Tourism is, in many ways, an unusual product in that consumers must physically go to the place of production (the tourist destination) to acquire the product, and the travel element is part of the product itself. The distinguishing features of tourism as a subject for economic analysis are enlarged upon by Sinclair and Stabler (1997) in the extract in Figure 17.4.

Figure 17.4: *The application of economic concepts to tourism*

'The application of economic concepts, theories and methods raises fundamental issues concerning both the characteristics of tourism which distinguish it from other commodities and the core elements of economics as a discipline. Tourism is distinct, even as a service activity, in that it is usually purchased without inspection, consisting of a range of goods and services which are consumed in sequence, including transportation, accommodation and natural resources. Because both natural and human-made resources are a substantial proportion of total inputs, it comprises a set of industries and markets involving significant no-priced features, such as the positive benefits which are associated with attractive and freely available environments and the negative effects of pollution (positive and negative externalities). It is, thus the unusual composite nature of tourism, frequently taking place in different countries, which requires specific analysis'.

Source: Sinclair and Stabler (1997)

Since economic conditions prevailing in the destination area can be quite different from those prevailing in the tourist generating area, variables in both areas and the comparison between them need to be assessed when considering their effect upon aggregate demand. Table 17.1 outlines some of the major economic factors influencing tourism demand.

Table 17.1: *Economic factors influencing tourism demand*

Tourism Generating Area	• Levels of personal disposable income
	• Distribution of incomes
	• Holiday entitlements
	• Value of currency
	• Tax policy and controls of tourist spending
	• Company competitive environment
Tourism Destination Area	• General price level
	• Quality of tourism products
	• Economic regulation of tourists
'Link' Factors	• Comparative prices in generator and destination areas
	• Promotional effort by destination in generating area
	• Exchange rates
	• Time/cost of travel

Source: Adapted from Bull (1995)

In assessing the nature of demand, it is important to realise that products are sold in competition with each other in order to gain consumers' scarce resource – their income. For example, different tour operating companies vie with each other to fly customers to the same destination, destinations compete with each other to achieve the maximum number of tourist visits and customers can choose which airline to fly on between two points.

Consequently, a change in the demand for one product can result in a change in the demand for another product and result in a shift in the demand curve facing the companies or destinations concerned. For example, an increase in market share for Thomson tour operating products (a shift in its demand curve to the right) may result in a fall in the market share for Airtours' tour operating products (a shift in its demand curve to the left). In other cases, products that appear to be unrelated are found to have a considerable influence on each others' demand. For example, since consumers only have a finite amount of *disposable income* (their income available to spend in a discretionary manner after essentials have been paid for), an increase in the demand for cars may result in a fall in the demand for holiday products.

Products where the market demand is in some way related are referred to as either *substitutes* or *complements*.

Substitutes: are products that are alternatives to each other, so that an increase in the demand for one product is likely to cause a decrease in the demand for another product. Examples of substitutes include:

- differing brands of the same product, such as Thomas Cook travel agencies versus Lunn Poly travel agencies;
- differing modes of transport, such as bus versus air and car journeys;
- differing decisions on high value purchases, such as the decision to purchase household equipment rather than travel and tourism products.

Complements: are products that tend to be bought and used together, so that an increase in the demand for one is likely to lead to an increase in the demand for another. Examples of complements are:

- hotel rooms and bars, restaurants and night clubs. If demand for bed-spaces at a destination increases it is likely that demand will also increase for restaurants, bars, night-clubs and so on in the vicinity;
- flights and airport facilities. If demand increases for flights from a particular airport the demand for airport facilities such as car parking, surface transportation, shopping and catering will also increase.

Other non economic factors can also have an effect upon tourism demand resulting in a shift in the demand curve. These factors include fashions and tastes, and seasonality.

Fashion and tastes change over time. In Europe, for example, mass tourism mainly from northern Europe to southern Europe has shown enormous growth in the post war period spurred largely by the advent of jet aircraft and the development of a sophisticated travel industry. But within this overall picture of growth, changes have occurred from one season to the next, with Spain, for instance, being out of favour one year and resurgent the next. Recent years have also seen the rapid growth of long haul travel, encouraged by the introduction of larger more fuel efficient long range aircraft and the growth of the tourism infrastructure in many of the tourist receiving countries concerned. Consumers tastes also change as, for instance, more activity oriented holidays are demanded and consumers demand independent arrangements rather than mass packaging.

Tourism is highly seasonal in its pattern of demand. As such the product is not unique since cars, heating products and ski equipment also face seasonal fluctuations in demand, but it is certainly an important characteristic of tourism that requires consideration when assessing demand. BarOn (1975) identified several factors contributing to the seasonality of demand in tourism. The principal factors he identified in his study in terms of recreational travel were climate, festivals and special events and academic holidays. Typically, a UK seaside resort, for instance, will have a high season, an off peak season and a low season. The high season is perhaps the school holiday period of July and August with off peak periods either side of these months and a low season for the rest of the year. Resorts attempt to extend their high season demand as much as possible into the off peak periods. In Blackpool, for instance, conferences and its famed illuminations extend the period of high demand into the autumn.

Changes in any one of the factors outlined in Table 17.1 above (or, indeed, a combination of these factors) will affect demand in some way. In reality, the analysis of such changes is complicated, not least by the non availability of reliable data.

Table 17.2 summarises some of the likely effects of changes to the conditions of demand.

Table 17.2: *The likely effects of changes in the conditions of demand*

Demand curve shifts to the left	Demand curve shifts to the right
• Fall in income (normal products)	• Rise in income (normal products)
• Rise in income (inferior products)	• Fall in income (inferior products)
• Rise in price of complementary products	• Fall in price of complementary products
• Fall in price of substitutes	• Rise in price of substitutes
• Fall in quality	• Rise in quality
• Unfashionable	• Fashionable
• Less advertising	• More advertising
• Less leisure time	• More leisure time
• Fall in population	• Rise in population

Source: Adapted from Tribe (1995)

Note that in Table 17.2, reference is made to *normal* and *inferior* products. Most products are normal products where demand increases as income goes up. Some products, however, are bought as cheap substitutes for other products and are termed inferior. As income increases, consumers switch to the normal products and, therefore, demand goes down as income increases.

An example is provided by the demand for airline seats by businesses in times of recession. In an economic recession (where business income decreases), businesses switch their employees from business class to economy class in order to save money. As the economy improves (and business incomes increase), businesses switch back to make fuller use of business class products. In terms of demand from business travellers, therefore, economy class can viewed as an inferior product.

Supply

The concept of supply

Supply represents the quantity of a product that existing suppliers or suppliers coming into the market would be willing to make available at a particular price over a specified period of time.

Several factors influence the total market supply for a product. These factors include:

- the price obtainable for the product;

- the price of competing products;

- the cost of providing the product;

- changes in technology;

- the ease with which providers of products can enter or leave the market - *barriers to entry* or *barriers to exit*; and

- the extent to which the market is regulated by governments or other bodies.

Central to a consideration of supply is the theory of supply which states that:

> *Other things being equal, the quantity of a product supplied is directly related to its price.*

In other words, as the price goes up the quantity of a product that suppliers will wish to supply goes up and, conversely, as the price goes down the quantity of a product that suppliers will wish to supply also goes down.

The supply curve

This relationship between supply and price is usually shown graphically as a *supply curve*. A supply curve can be drawn for:

- an individual supplier; or

- (more usually) for all firms which provide the product. This aggregate supply curve for all suppliers is the *market* supply curve.

A supply curve is constructed in a similar manner to a demand curve (from a schedule of supply quantities at different prices), but shows the quantities that suppliers are willing to provide at different price levels.

Figure 17.5 shows a typical supply curve SS which plots the relationship between price and the quantity supplied.

Figure 17.5: *The supply curve*

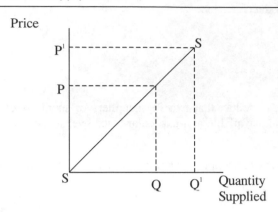

It should be noted that a supply curve shows how the quantity supplied will change in response to a change in price. Changes in supply caused by changes in price are represented by movements along the supply curve, from one point to another. In Figure 17.5, for instance, if price is increased from P to P¹ the quantity supplied increases from Q to Q¹.

The market supply curve generally slopes upwards to the right because at higher prices supplying additional quantities of a product is financially more attractive to companies.

A great deal of information about the nature of supply for a particular product can be discovered by analysis of the supply curve. In particular, (as with demand) two factors are of interest:

1.   The shape or slope of the supply curve; and

2.   The position of the supply curve.

The shape or slope of the curve is a reflection of its steepness and tells us how sensitive demand is to changes in price i.e. the *elasticity of supply*. This is discussed in more detail in a later section. The position of the curve refers to its position in relation to each axis. Changes in price result in movements along the curve.

Changing conditions of supply in tourism

As with shifts to the demand curve, factors other than price, referred to collectively as the conditions of supply, will alter the position of the supply curve, causing the curve to shift its position to the left or to the right. In Figure 17.6, supply increases for some reason. This could result from lower operational costs, improved technology or a reduction in taxation for instance.

Figure 17.6: *Changing conditions of supply*

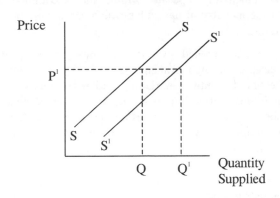

In Figure 17.6, changes in the conditions of supply are reflected in the supply curve's shift to the right; from curve SS to curve S¹S¹. Every point on curve S¹S¹ is further from the Y axis, indicating that at every price level quantities supplied are increased. At price P¹ the quantity supplied increases from Q to Q¹.

Many factors other than price are likely to influence supply for any product, as outlined above. In the case of tourism in particular perhaps two aspects can be highlighted: firstly, so called barriers to entry and secondly the relative inflexibility of supply.

Barriers to entry describe the barriers preventing potential suppliers coming into the market to compete for sales. Economists talk in terms of the relative size of these barriers. In some cases, the barriers are virtually impossible to overcome, as, for example, where the government grants one company a monopoly to provide flights or rail services on certain routes. In most cases in travel and tourism, the entry barriers are not insurmountable, but large variations occur in the various sectors. In the tour operating and travel agency sectors, barriers are generally thought to be quite low. This was indicated by the conclusions drawn from the UK Monopolies and Mergers Commission Report, published in 1998, which made a detailed investigation of the UK travel industry. In the transportation and accommodation sectors, however, entry barriers are often quite high, with significant capital requirements and brand loyalties in both sectors and additionally important regulatory barriers in the transportation sector. Significant barriers to entry include:

- Government requirements for companies to hold bonds or licenses in order to operate. These requirements often apply to travel agencies, tour operators and airline routes. For example, UK air inclusive tour operators require a licence in the form of an Air Travel Organisers' Licence (ATOL) issued by the Civil Aviation Authority, the UK regulatory body for air travel. The licence specifies the number of passengers that a particular tour operator can carry and thereby restricts the ability of new entrants to the market to trade at whatever level they choose;

- Some tourism enterprises have requirements for significant quantities of capital in order to start up. For example, aircraft, accommodation and cruise ships require considerable initial capital investment. However, the separation of ownership of the assets from their management can lead to the costs being borne by another company and thereby a reduction in start up costs. Various forms of management contracts, leasing and franchising operate within the accommodation and transportation sectors of the industry in particular which can lower start up costs for firms entering the industry.

The Holiday Inns hotel chain, owned by the UK brewing group Bass, for instance, has grown largely through franchising with Holiday Inns as the franchiser providing the brand identity, marketing and reservations support but with the capital for hotel construction being provided by other companies – the franchisees. It is common for property companies and pension trustees to own the physical fabric of hotel buildings but to place the management of the hotels in the hands of a well known international hotel operator such as Hilton or Marriott through management contracts (see also Chapter 8). Airlines have been able to start up with comparatively low initial outlays through leasing their aircraft requirements rather than outright purchases. In doing so, start up airlines, such as Easyjet, have been able to gain access to a modern fleet while deferring payments until cash-flow from ticket sales builds up.

- Planning restrictions or competing land uses may limit the degree to which new resorts and attractions can be developed. For example, large new hotel developments are usually restricted in national parks and other protected areas.

- Established companies in a sector may act in a way that restricts competitors coming in to the market to compete by the use of price wars and other tactics. For example, the low cost airlines operating in Europe, such as Ryanair and Easyjet, have frequently accused the large full service carriers, such as British Airways and Aer Lingus, of using unfair pricing methods to limit competition on certain routes. The accusations have focused on the use of *predatory pricing* (using profits generated by other routes in order to offer fares on one route at unprofitable levels), in response to their own low-cost operations.

In most areas of travel and tourism, supply is relatively inflexible, at least in the short term. Supply in the industry is usually referred to in terms of capacity. Most travel and tourism enterprises have the aim of operating at full capacity and, in the short term at least, this capacity cannot easily be varied. Thus, hoteliers measure their occupancy levels, transport providers measure load factors, tour operators measure the percentage of total capacity sold, and many tourist attractions measure their usage rate.

A distinction must be made between the short run and long run responses of supply and demand. In the case of supply, many tourism products, such as hotel rooms, airline seats and cruise ships, require heavy investment and additional capacity cannot be brought on stream quickly. Similarly, tour operators can often find it difficult to alter capacity quickly. Contracting of accommodation and transport arrangements, and the printing and distribution of brochures may take place many months prior to travel and, therefore, flexibility can be limited. However, it is true to say that many companies are expecting ever greater flexibility from their suppliers in order to effectively match their supply with demand.

As a result of the inflexibility experienced in the supply of travel and tourism products, suppliers will do what they can in the short run to adjust demand (instead of supply) so as to equal capacity supply through altering prices or through promotional efforts (Bull 1995). Indeed, oversupply caused by the relatively low entry barriers and continual striving among operators for increased market share led UK tour operators to repeatedly try to stimulate demand through lowering prices (Evans and Stabler 1995). These 'price wars' have been a characteristic feature of the UK outbound tour industry at various times (particularly in the early 1970s and mid 1980s) and led to an erratic record of profitability. Since the early 1990s, however, the picture has changed as the maturing industry has targeted profitability rather than market share as the key objective and has generally been able to avoid damaging price wars by more closely matching supply to demand.

The price mechanism

Having considered supply and demand separately, we can now bring them together through a consideration of the *price mechanism*.

> *The price mechanism is a system where the economic decisions in the economy are reached through the workings of the market: changes in the relative scarcity of goods and services are reflected in changes in prices and these price changes produce incentives for producers to reallocate available resources towards reducing market shortages and surpluses.* (Beardshaw *et al.* 2001)

The price mechanism does not require co-ordination or intervention, the necessary adjustments occurring automatically as a result of the separate decisions taken by a large number of individuals, all seeking to pursue their own best interests. Supply and demand are brought together by the price mechanism to create a situation of stability (*equilibrium*) where an equilibrium *price* for a product prevails.

> *The equilibrium price for a product is the price at which the volume demanded by consumers and the volume that firms be willing to supply the product are the same.*

In a competitive market, price acts as a mechanism which signals demand and supply conditions to producers and to consumers.

In order to understand how the equilibrium situation comes about and an equilibrium price is established we can consider the action of consumers' demand on the one hand and firms in the way in which they supply on the other. If demand for a product exceeds its supply, consumers must either stop demanding what is unobtainable or must be prepared to pay more in order to achieve satisfaction. At a higher price, producers will be prepared to supply more of the product thereby satisfying the demands of consumers. On the other hand, if the price of a product is at such a level that producers want to supply more of the product than consumers are willing to buy, then supply must be reduced or the price must be reduced so as to stimulate demand.

Figure 17.7 shows the interaction of demand and supply through the price mechanism and the establishing of an equilibrium price.

Figure 17.7: *The interaction of demand and supply through the price mechanism*

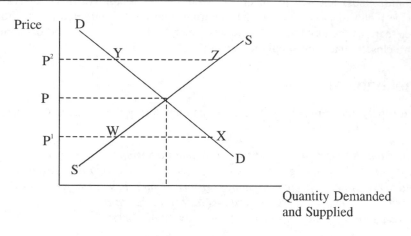

At price P^1 there is an excess in the demand of consumers over the quantity supplied at that price shown by the distance WX. The reaction of suppliers in such a case would be:

- To increase output; and/or

- To increase prices.

The opposite will be the case at P^2 where there is an excess in the quantity that suppliers want to supply over the quantity demanded shown by the distance YZ. Output and/or prices would fall in this case.

Price P shows the equilibrium price at which the amount that sellers are willing to supply exactly matches the amount that consumers are willing to buy.

The forces of supply and demand will always push a market towards its equilibrium price, as suppliers and consumers react to the signals given by the market.

Elasticity

The concept of elasticity

In previous sections, mention was made of the importance attached to the study of the steepness of the demand and supply curves. The steepness, or elasticity, indicates how responsive supply or demand is to a change in one of the variables influencing demand or supply.

> *Elasticity is a measure of the responsiveness of demand or supply to a change in one of the variables influencing demand or supply.*

There are a number of variables influencing demand and supply such as income levels, availability of competitors' products and price, and consequently there are a number of different types of elasticity. Here we will consider price elasticity.

From an economic perspective price elasticities are important for the suppliers of tourism products, since they have an impact on their total revenues. Since total revenues = price ×

quantity sold, any change a supplier makes to the price of the product directly affects the total revenue, but by how much? Will an increase in price lead to higher or lower total revenues? The answer lies in the study of elasticity.

Price elasticity of demand

Price elasticity of demand measures the responsiveness of demand to a change in price and can be expressed by the formula:

$$\frac{\text{Percentage change in quantity demanded}}{\text{Percentage change in price}}$$

Where demand is elastic it means that demand is highly responsive to changes in price whereas where demand is inelastic demand is relatively unresponsive to price changes. Figure 17.8 shows graphically a range of possibilities for price elasticity of demand.

Figure 17.8: *Price elasticity of demand*

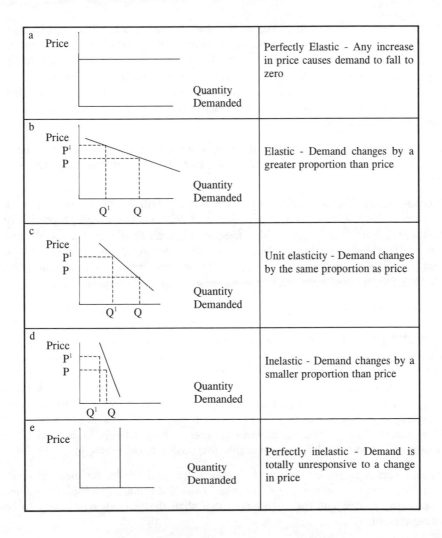

The main factors affecting price elasticity of demand in tourism are:

- The availability of substitutes – the greater the degree of competition and hence the availability of substitutes the more elastic demand is likely to be.

  In the UK, for instance, out-bound recreational tourism is highly competitive, with many companies and destinations competing. Over 1,500 companies have Air Travel Organisers Licenses, giving them the authority to operate air inclusive tours. Hence, this sector is usually considered to be highly elastic, with consumers very sensitive to price changes and willing to switch suppliers readily in order to save money.

  Some air routes, on the other hand, are highly regulated through inter-governmental bilateral agreements. Hence, in some cases routes are operated by a very limited number of airlines (often the national 'flag carriers'). Consequently, airlines operating such routes are faced with relatively inelastic demand curves as consumers wishing to fly between the two points have a limited choice.

- The time period – over time, consumers' demand patterns are likely to change. An increase in the value of the pound relative to the Turkish lira, but not the Greek drachma (or euro) is unlikely to make an initial impact on demand. In the longer term, however, as consumers become aware of the better value on offer in Turkey relative to Greece, their preferences will switch to Turkey rather than Greece. In other words, the elasticity of demand for Greece is likely to become more elastic over time.

- Proportion of income – the higher the proportion of a consumer's income that a particular product takes up, the greater the price elasticity of demand is likely to be.

  Thus, generally, the price elasticity for a holiday will be relatively high as it represents a high value item of expenditure and accounts for a high proportion of consumers' disposable income. Consumers will search for the best available deal as it is a significant purchasing decision. On the other hand, the market for ball-point pens is likely to be relatively inelastic, since they represent low value items accounting for a small proportion of consumers' disposable income.

- Luxury versus necessity – generally, the price elasticity of demand for luxury products is lower than that of necessities. Those that seek luxury are usually prepared to pay a premium in order to obtain it and demand is therefore relatively inelastic, whereas those who regard travel and tourism as a necessary part of their lives are likely to be relatively elastic in their demand. For instance, rooms in luxury hotels are sold to clients on the basis of the standard of facilities and service available rather than on the basis of price so that customers are relatively unresponsive to price changes. On the other hand, a mass market tour operator selling mainly family holidays sells to customers who are likely to demand value for money and who are likely to be highly responsive to price changes.

- Business versus pleasure – business travellers are likely to be far more inelastic in their demand than leisure travellers, since time and reliability are highly valued as opposed to price and the employer rather than the individual is likely to be footing the bill.

Price discrimination

An understanding of price elasticities of demand for a product can allow a company to sell basically the same product to different groups of customers (market segments) at different prices so as to increase revenues. This so-called *price discrimination* is common in travel and tourism with many airlines, transport operators and hotels, for example, operating such a pricing strategy. This serves to underline the importance of elasticity as an economic concept.

Three conditions for price discrimination to take are necessary:

- There must be market imperfections. In particular, there is likely to be a situation of monopoly power that allows companies to charge higher prices. Otherwise, companies would always compete to ensure that the lowest price was achieved.

- The product cannot be re-sold. If a product could be bought at the lower price in one segment of the market and then re-sold at the higher price in another segment, it would undermine direct sales to the higher price segment and ultimately prices in the two segments would equalise.

- Crucially, the seller must be able to identify different market segments exhibiting different price elasticities of demand. The market may be segmented for example by age, different times of use, and business versus leisure.

An airline, for instance may distinguish between two basic segments of the market on a particular route: business travellers and leisure travellers. As already noted, business travellers are likely to have a more inelastic demand curve than leisure travellers, because business travellers usually have to make the trip at a particular time whereas leisure travellers are usually more flexible in their requirements. The lack of flexibility in the business travel segment (the more inelastic demand curve) allows the supplier to charge higher prices to this segment and thereby increase total revenues.

Figure 17.9 shows the effects of price discrimination on a travel business

Price discrimination resulting from differences in elasticities of demand explains why:

- hotels offer lower rates at weekends;

- airlines are able to charge more for full economy tickets which can be altered than they charge for advance purchase tickets the terms of which cannot be altered; and,

- rail operators are able to charge more for early morning services.

Figure 17.9: *Prices set by a price discriminating travel business*

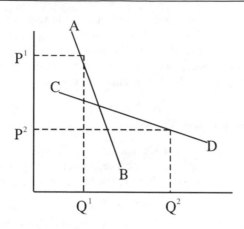

Here, the line AB represents the relatively inelastic demand of business customers whereas line CD is the relatively elastic demand curve for leisure customers. The graph shows that quantity Q^1 can be sold to business customers at the higher Price P^1 while an additional quantity shown by the distance Q^1 to Q^2 can be sold to leisure customers at the lower price of P^2. The total revenue for the travel business through being able to segment the market into business and leisure customers is $(P^1 \times Q^1)$ + $P2(Q^1-Q^2)$. If the business were to have sold all its capacity at P1 the revenue achieved would only have been $P^1 \times Q^1$ whereas if all sales had been at P^2, then total revenue achieved would have only been $P^2 \times Q^2$. Therefore price discrimination allows for total revenues to be increased.

Yield management represents a sophisticated form of price discrimination. Computer technology allows travel companies to identify patterns of demand for a particular product and then set prices in such a way that allows revenue to be maximised. An individual or company's historic buying behaviour can be analysed and prices set accordingly. A supplier can also build up sophisticated data bases of buyer behaviour patterns that allows it to make strategic pricing decisions in order to gain a competitive advantage over rivals. American Airlines, for example, using a sophisticated yield management system, gained an advantage over competitors in early 1992. Full fares were reduced and all but two basic discount fares were eliminated. Other airlines had no option but to reduce fares in a similar manner (or react in some other way), despite being unable to accurately assess the impact of such moves (Collison 1995).

Another form of yield management is the so-called fluid pricing adopted by major UK tour operators in recent years. Fluid pricing allows the tour operator to adjust prices in the important 'late booking' period (eight weeks or so before departure) in order to react to changing demand conditions and the actions of competitors. In so doing, tour operators are able to increase flight load factors and maximise occupancy in resorts and thereby optimise revenues.

In the past, UK customers had grown accustomed to 'late offers' advertised in travel agents' shop windows or on Teletext. Tremendous savings over brochure prices were sometimes available due to the excess supply over demand and intense competition. In recent years, however, as tour operators have become more sophisticated in managing their capacity and in pricing their products, late offers are often likely to mean an increase over the brochure price (although they are still heavily promoted in the traditional ways).

Fluid Pricing - An Illustration

The staff of the late bookings section of Airtours, bear more than a passing resemblance to a group of City dealers. What they do, however, is not to trade currencies or sell shares. On the basis of up-to-the minute information about their competitors in the UK's they seek to adjust their own prices to maximise profitability. Travel agents, whether multiple chains or independent shops, look up destinations on screen. The prices they see are set and communicated to them by the tour operators, which arrange flights and accommodation. Airtours changes its prices several times a day.

Along with the rest of the holiday industry, Airtours makes much of its cost-cutting campaigns. But like all companies, it strives to charge whatever the market can bear, pushing prices up when demand is strongest. Late bookings indeed play a central role in determining a holiday company's profitability. The companies begin selling summer holidays in the August of the summer before, when they publish the first edition of their brochures. In January, they publish a second edition, with either higher or lower prices, depending on how sales are going and what competing companies are doing. It is in the last eight weeks before departure that price competition becomes most intense. A third of holidays are sold during this period.

Apart from trying to get the highest price possible, the late booking team tries to ensure that all the company's airline seats are filled. Tour operators pay for most of their accommodation in holiday resorts only if they use it, although they do guarantee to fill a certain proportion of beds. If bookings are disappointing they do not end up owing hoteliers large sums of money.

Airline seats are another matter. The seats have to be paid for whether they are filled or not. Flights that depart with empty seats represent a loss for the tour operator. The Airtours late booking team's first task of the morning is to look at the prices competitors have set overnight. They do this by using the computer information available to travel agents. Airtours owns the Going Places travel agents' chain, which sells holidays organised by other operators as well. This gives Airtours access to other operators' prices.

If a competitor drops the prices on holidays to a particular destination, Airtours will not necessarily do the same. The competitor's price reduction could be temporary: the company might be attempting to fill a particular aircraft or ensure it can sell its guaranteed beds. On other occasions, the price drop might signal an attempt to take market share from rivals like Airtours. The team says it gets to know the psychology of rival price setters, as well as customers. A further aspect of the process carried out by the team is to closely monitor how soon each individual week's capacity will sell out given current sales trends. If for instance capacity for Majorca four weeks hence given current sales trends is likely to be completely sold out by week two, prices will be raised so as to achieve additional margin on sales and take e advantage of the strong effective demand.

(Adapted from *Financial Times* 27th January 1994)

Price elasticity of supply

Price elasticity of supply measures the responsiveness of supply to a change in price and can be expressed in the formula:

$$\frac{\text{Percentage change in quantity supplied}}{\text{Percentage change in price}}$$

Where supply is elastic, it means that supply is responsive to changes in price whereas, where supply is inelastic, supply is relatively unresponsive to price changes. Figure 17.10 shows graphically a range of possibilities for price elasticity of supply.

Figure 17.10: *Price elasticity of supply*

a 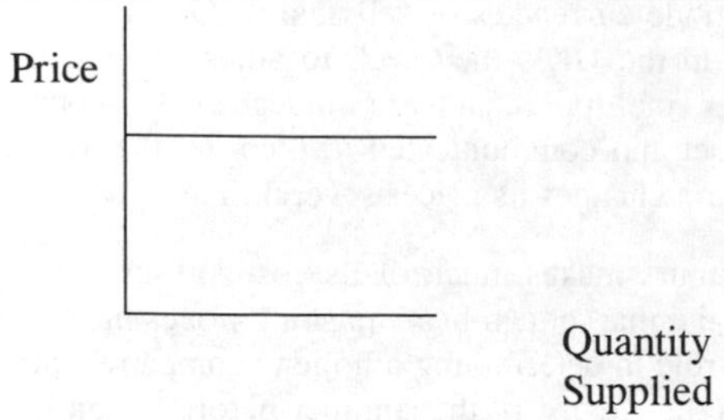 Price Quantity Supplied	Perfectly Elastic - Any decrease in price causes supply to fall to zero
b 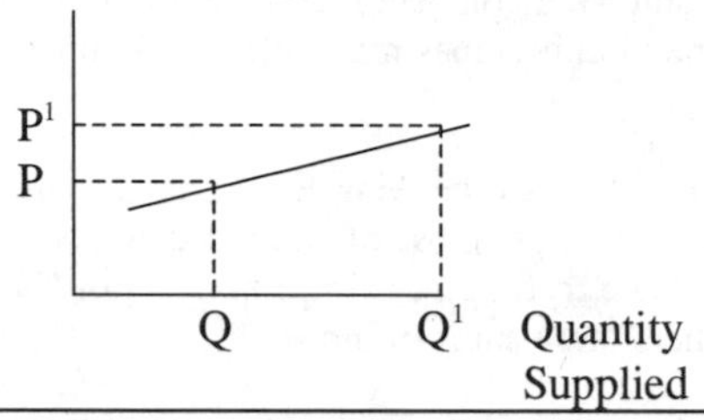 P¹ P Q Q¹ Quantity Supplied	Elastic - Supply changes by a greater proportion than price
c 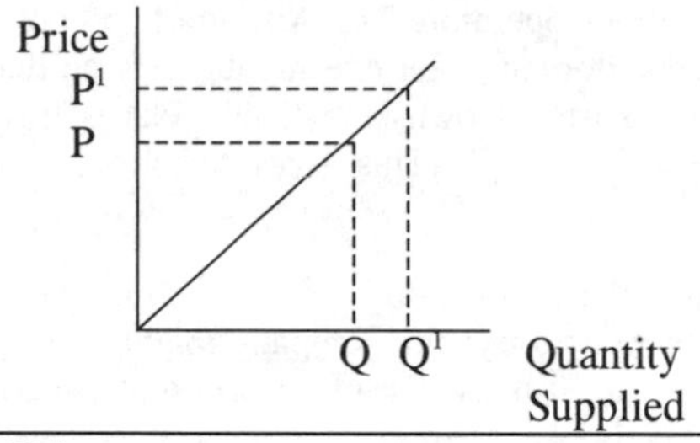 Price P¹ P Q Q¹ Quantity Supplied	Unit elasticity - Supply changes by the same proportion as price
d 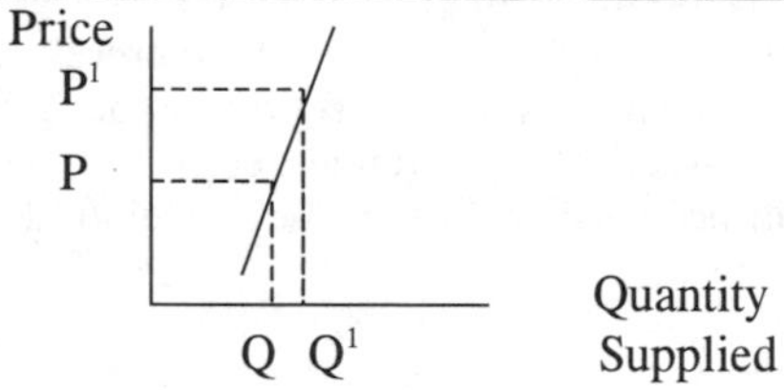 Price P¹ P Q Q¹ Quantity Supplied	Inelastic - Supply changes by a smaller proportion than price
e 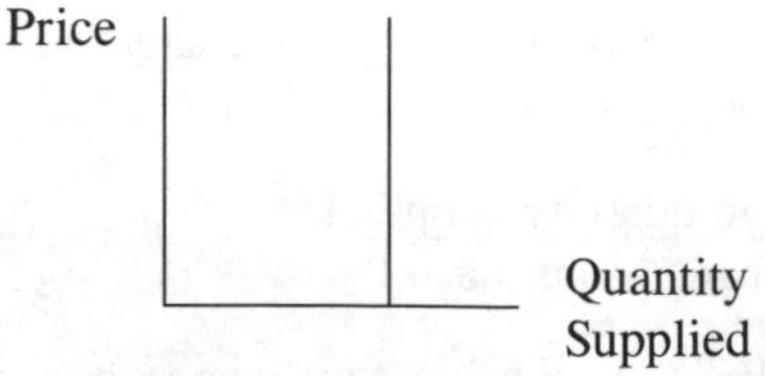 Price Quantity Supplied	Perfectly Inelastic - Supply is totally unresponsive to a change in price

The main factors affecting price elasticity of supply in tourism are:

- The Time Period – generally, the longer the time period allowed the easier it is for supply to be changed in response to price changes. In other words supply becomes more elastic over time.

  For example, suppose that there is an increase in the demand for hotel rooms in a city (shown by a rightwards shift in the demand curve for hotel rooms). The capacity of hotels in that city is limited by the number of rooms available in the hotels. Efficiencies might be possible allowing available rooms to be used more intensively and so supply is not perfectly inelastic, but there is a limit to this process so that supply is relatively inelastic. As a result of the supply shortage, in the short-term there is likely to be a large increase in price. In the longer term, the increased price levels attainable will encourage entrepreneurs to open new hotels. In the long term, therefore, supply is more elastic as capacity is expanded to meet demand.

  In some recent years, tour operators operating from the UK have cut their summer capacity (supply) in the period leading up to Christmas in order to match supply more closely with expected demand prior to the main booking period. As the actual season approaches, it becomes progressively more difficult to trim capacity as contractual arrangements with consumers and suppliers would entail financial penalties.

- Capacity utilisation – in the case of manufactured goods, stocks are held at retailers, wholesalers or factories. Modern 'just-in time' production methods are designed to reduce stock levels and make production more responsive to demand. A manufactured product's elasticity of supply is thus elastic to the extent that stocks can be released or production schedules altered to the level of demand.

  In the case of tourism, a service product, the position is different. No stocks are held and the product is 'perishable', in that the product is available at a certain date and price and if not consumed at that date disappears forever. Stocks in tourism terms are measured in terms of the amount of spare capacity that is available for certain dates. If spare capacity is easily obtainable, then supply will be relatively elastic but, if on the other hand, capacity is fully utilised, supply will be relatively inelastic.

  For example, a hotel with 100 percent occupancy will experience perfectly inelastic supply (in the short term). Since no beds are available, supply cannot be increased, regardless of the price. However, if the hotel is say, only 30 percent full on a particular night since there is spare capacity available the position with regard to elasticity is somewhat different. The product, a hotel room on a particular night, is perishable and, importantly, there are many fixed costs (rent, rates utility costs, salaries and so on) the hotel must pay for regardless of occupancy levels. Thus, there is a strong incentive for the hotelier to substantially reduce the price of the product in order to derive some revenue for that night to contribute towards the costs; in this case, the supply is relatively elastic.

- Flexibility of capacity – in some cases, capacity can easily be shifted from one market to another whereas, in other cases, it is much more difficult to change the focus of capacity.

- For example, a cross-channel ferry operator can adapt to changing demand patterns by moving a ship from the Dover - Calais route to the longer western channel routes. A small family run city centre hotel cannot easily become an exclusive 'town-house' hotel as this depends upon reputation, decor and cuisine which cannot be changed quickly. Supply is relatively elastic in the case of the ferry but relatively inelastic in the hotel case.

Supply, demand and elasticity – conclusion

This chapter has briefly examined the cornerstones of micro-economic analysis, namely, demand and supply, and has considered the elasticity of both concepts. It is of considerable economic importance for a tourism enterprise or a tourism destination to be able to measure and forecast the demand and supply for their products. In so doing, businesses can successfully match up supply with demand, plan effective use of resources for the future, and maximise their revenues.

Knowledge of price elasticity is crucial when making pricing decisions since, if the price elasticity of a product is known, a tourism product supplier can increase total revenues by making an appropriate adjustment to the price of the product. Conversely, an understanding of elasticity of demand and supply allows companies to forecast the impact changes in demand or supply will have on prices.

In practice of course, as Lundberg *et al.* (1995) point out, it is not so simple because price clasticities vary considerably between products and change over time. Furthermore, price elasticities are impacted by a multitude of factors that are difficult to model and, in some cases, reliable data is extremely difficult to obtain and interpret.

Having looked at some of the important micro-economic aspects of travel and tourism, this chapter now turns to briefly examine the macro-economic consequences of tourism – the economic impacts of tourism.

Economic impacts of tourism

The development of tourism may lead to positive impacts on a country's economy though improvements in its balance of payments, earnings in foreign exchange and through the *multiplier* effects (detailed below), as well as an increase in employment opportunities. These are widely discussed in the tourism literature (for example, Bull 1995).

The economic impacts of tourism will also apply on a regional or local scale and can be increased through tourism related events such as local festivals and events and larger 'hallmark' events, such as the Olympic Games and football's World Cup. Indeed, there is increasing recognition of the economic impact of events and festivals in particular. Even small-scale sports events and cultural festivals are now viewed as contributing to a local community's tourism and economic prospects, as well as to its recreational and cultural well-being.

The magnitude of the economic impact of tourism is determined a number of factors. Fletcher (1995) identifies the most critical factors as being:

- the level of economic development of the host economy;
- the degree of diversification of economic activity; and

- the extent to which the economy is dependent upon imports of goods, services and capital.

Economic impact assessments

In assessing the economic impact of tourism, it is not sufficient to simply look at the value of tourism receipts. The direct expenditure by tourists triggers expenditure on other goods and services by tourism businesses, which must also be measured in order to estimate accurately the total value of tourism. Economic impact assessments usually include a multiplier calculation to demonstrate that expenditure has both direct and secondary benefits to the economy.

This 'multiplier effect' measures the impact of extra expenditure introduced into the economy and which filters through it thus stimulating other sectors of the economy. The multiplier principles of assessing the economic impact of tourism is derived from several major studies that have been carried out in the UK and around the world that seek to assess the economic benefit derived from tourism.

> *A Tourist Income Multiplier is a coefficient which expresses the amount of income generated in an area by an additional unit of tourist spending (Archer 1982).*

In other words, if the total known tourist spending in an area is, say £1 million and this generates, say £800,000 of additional income for other (non tourism businesses) in that area, the value of the multiplier is 0.8.

The multiplier effect is based on the premise that firms in the local economy are dependent upon other firms for their supplies and that, consequently, any changes in the level of expenditure, as with tourists entering the area, will bring about a change in the local economy's overall level of income. These changes may be greater than, equal to, or less than the value of the change in expenditure that brought them about. That is, the multiplier may be greater than, less than or equal to 1.

Money will flow initially to 'front-line' establishments linked with tourism, such as hotels, attractions, restaurants and gift shops, which provide services directly for the tourist. This expenditure will be used by the recipients in various ways:

- a proportion will leak directly out of the local economy in that goods and services are bought from outside the area;

- a proportion will be used to purchase local goods and services;

- a proportion will be used to pay wages and salaries and become part of household income; and,

- a proportion will be used to pay taxes, licences and fees.

These are all direct effects.

The leakages will be lost to the local economy and in the same way that imports at the national level represent income for foreign nationals. However, the businesses, individual households and government which receive money in payment for their goods and services will also make purchases which will be spent in the same way as the direct effects shown above.

These are all secondary effects.

This multiplier effect, whereby the initial direct expenditure filters down through the economy and thereby generates additional secondary effects in subsequent tertiary rounds of expenditure, is shown in Figure 17.11.

Figure 17.11 *The income multiplier process*

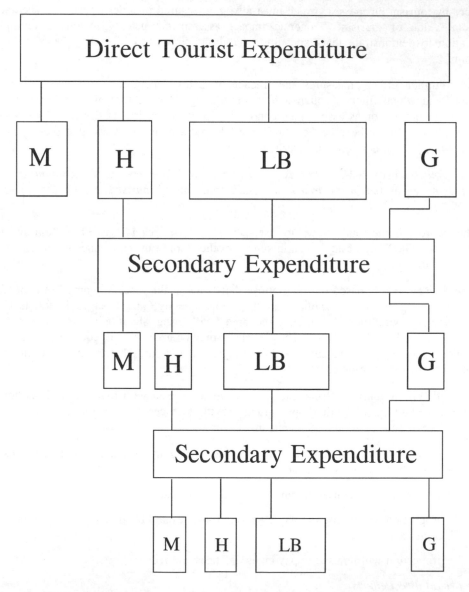

Key:

M	=	Imports or Leakages from the regional economy
H	=	Household income
LB	=	Local Businesses
G	=	Government

It is conceptually possible (but in practice difficult), to measure various types of multiplier. For example, additional expenditure of £1m may generate:

- output of £2.5 million within an economy (*output multiplier*);

- direct and secondary income of £0.5 million to nationals in the area (*income multiplier*);

- extra jobs totalling 380 of which 180 are created as a result of secondary effects (*employment multiplier*).

In the example above, the output multiplier therefore is 2.5, the income multiplier is 0.5 and the employment multiplier is 1.9 (380/200).

Most studies carried out in the UK, North America and elsewhere have concentrated on studying the income multiplier. A selection of tourism income multipliers from a multitude of individual studies are shown in Table 17.3.

Table 17.3: *Selected tourism income multipliers*

Counrty/Region/City	Tourism income multiplier
United Kingdom	1.73
Republic of Ireland	1.72
Dominican Republic	1.20
Bermuda	1.09
Fiji	1.07
Missouri, USA	0.88
Hong Kong	0.87
Walworth County, Wisconsin, USA	0.78
Iceland	0.64
British Virgin Islands	0.58
Victoria, Canada	0.50
Carlisle, UK	0.40
Edinburgh, UK	0.35
East Anglia, UK	0.34

Source: Cooper *et al.* (1998)

The results shown in Table 17.3 need to be interpreted with some care since they were determined using detailed variations in methodology. However, the results clearly show a distinction between the economic impact at the national level and the economic impact at the regional or city level, and the results also show higher coefficients for North America than are to be found in the UK.

The higher figures at the national level, and particularly for island economies, reflect the extent to which the sectors of the economy are linked together. For an island economy, for instance, it is likely that most of the goods and services would have to be serviced from within the island itself to be cost effective. Similarly, in the case of US states and counties, higher coefficients are to be observed than in the UK, reflecting the extent to which these regions and counties trade with the rest of the country. Given the relative distances between centres in the US compared with the UK, it is not surprising that regions and counties in the US are more self-sufficient, sourcing goods and services from within the region or county resulting in a higher income multiplier.

In the UK, the impact of tourism expenditure is diminished by the high level of leakages of business payments to firms located outside the region. For example, a hotel is likely to have employees who live outside the local area and some of their supplies will be provided by suppliers from outside the local area. Higher coefficients are likely to be observed in island economies or where a population centre is comparatively remote from other centres of population. In both these cases, the area has to be fairly self contained due to the access difficulties thereby leading to higher coefficients.

Tourism satellite accounts

As mentioned previously, measuring multipliers is conceptually possible but in practice very difficult due to the very nature of tourism. Difficulties include:

- the definition of tourism. There is no universally accepted definition of tourism, despite efforts by the World Tourism Organisation to encourage adoption of their definitions and statistical methods;

- tourism is not an industry in the traditional sense. However it is defined, tourists make purchases in many traditional industries, while non-tourists purchase tourism products or commodities; and

- measurement is laborious. To collect reliable data for multiplier analyses requires extensive, expensive and time-consuming fieldwork.

As a result of these difficulties, 'the tourism industry has defied easy analysis' (Smith 1995). However, in response to the complicated nature of tourism and the difficulty in obtaining reliable data, one approach that has been tried (in Canada, for instance), is the Tourism Satellite Account (TSA). The TSA represents a new accounting framework for tourism based upon Canada's system of national accounts.

A full description and analysis of TSAs is beyond the scope of this chapter, since they are highly complex. Briefly, however, the TSA is envisaged as 'an information system that collects, orders, and interrelates statistics describing all significant and measurable aspects of tourism within a framework that organises tourism data according to the 'real world' relationships from which they originate' (Canadian National Task Force 1987). As such, the TSA concept can be viewed as having the potential for providing data on national tourism industries that are, for the first time, credible, consistent, and coherent with statistics available for traditional industries (Smith 1995).

Conclusion

Tourism will generate a variety of economic problems, which can be studied at the micro or at the macro level. The nature of tourism is, however, complex as it is comprised of a range of inter-connected components. Consequently, the assessment of the interaction of supply and demand at the micro level and of the economic impact of tourism at the macro level is a complex task. Conceptually measuring and forecasting tourism demand and supply and its the economic impact may be relatively simple but, in practice, collecting and interpreting such information is extremely difficult.

Discussion questions

1. *What are the main characteristics of price discrimination? Provide an example from travel and tourism.*

2. *Identify four factors affecting price elasticity of demand in travel and tourism and briefly assess their potential impacts.*

3. *What is the meaning of the tourism multiplier effect?*

4. *When analysing the supply curve in tourism, identify three conditions of supply other than price, which affect the position of the curve.*

Further reading

Baum, T. and Mudambi, R. (1999), *Economic and Management Methods for Tourism and Hospitality Research*, Chichester: John Wiley & Sons.

Beardshaw, J., Brewster, D., Cormack, P. and Ross, A. (2001), *Economics: A student's Guide, 5th Edition,* Harlow UK: FT Prentice Hall.

Bull, A. (1995), *The Economics of Travel and Tourism, 2nd Edition*, Harlow: Longman.

Cooper, C., Fletcher J., Gilbert D. and Wanhill S. (1998), *Tourism: Principles and Practice, 2nd Edition*, Harlow: Longman.

Cullen, P. (1997), *Economics for Hospitality Management,* London: Thomson Business Press.

Fletcher, J. (1995), Economic impact, in S. Witt and L. Moutinho (eds.) *Tourism Marketing and Management Handbook*, 2nd *Edition*, London: Prentice Hall.

Lundberg, D., Stavenga, M. and Krishnamoorthy, M. (1995), *Tourism Economics*, New York: John Wiley & Sons.

Sinclair, M. T. and Stabler, M. (1997), *The Economics of Tourism*, London: Routledge.

Tribe, J. (2000), *The Economics of Leisure and Tourism, 2nd Edition*, London: Butterworth-Heinemann.

Vogel, H. L. (2001), *Travel Industry Economics – A guide for financial analysis*, Cambridge: Cambridge University Press.

References

Archer, B. (1982), The value of multipliers and their policy implications, *Tourism Management* 3(2): 236-241.

BarOn, R. (1975), *Seasonality in Tourism - a Guide to the Analysis of Seasonality and Trends for Policy Making*, Technical Series No.2, London: Economic Intelligence Unit.

Beardshaw, J., Brewster, D., Cormack, P. and Ross, A. (2001), *Economics: A student's Guide, 5th Edition*, Harlow: FT Prentice Hall.

Bull, A. (1995), *The Economics of Travel and Tourism, 2nd Edition*, Harlow: Longman.

Collison, F. M. (1995), Airline competition, in S. Witt and L. Moutinho (eds) *Tourism Marketing and Management Handbook, 2nd Edition*, Harlow: Prentice Hall: 18-28.

Cooper, C., Fletcher J., Gilbert D. and Wanhill S. (1998), *Tourism: Principles and Practice, 2nd Edition*, Harlow: Longman.

Evans, N. and Stabler, M. (1995), A future for the package tour operator in the 21st Century, *Tourism Economics - The Business and Finance of Tourism and Recreation*, 1(3): 245-263.

Fletcher, J. (1995), Economic impact, in S. Witt and L. Moutinho (eds.) *Tourism Marketing and Management Handbook, 2nd Edition*, Hemel Hempstead: Prentice Hall: 455-463.

Lundberg, D., Stavenga, M. and Krishnamoorthy, M. (1995), *Tourism Economics*, New York: John Wiley & Sons.

Sinclair, M. T. (1991), The economics of tourism, in C. Cooper and A. Lockwood (eds.) *Progress in Tourism Recreation and Hospitality Management, Volume 3*, London: Belhaven Press, 1-27.

Sinclair, M. T. and Stabler, M. (1997), *The Economics of Tourism*, London: Routledge.

Smith, S. (1995), The tourism satellite account: perspectives of Canadian tourism associations and organisations, *Tourism Economics* 1(3): September 1995: 225-242.

Tribe, J. (1995), *The Economics of Leisure and Tourism*, Oxford: Butterworth-Heinemann.

18

Marketing for Tourism

Caroline Barrass

Learning objectives

This chapter introduces the concept of marketing and its application to a range of tourism organisations and will enable the reader to:

- *describe the activities involved in the marketing process*

- *identify the primary elements of the marketing mix and extended mix used by tourism organisations and the way in which they can be used*

- *recognise the terminology used in marketing*

- *identify the characteristics of marketing in the travel and tourism industry*

Introduction to marketing

Previous chapters have outlined the complexity of the many different organisations and industries which provide services and products for visitors or travellers of all types. This mixed bag of service providers is often termed 'the travel and tourism industry' or 'the tourism industry', despite the fact that it encompasses many different classifications of industry and organisation, and serves many different consumer groups. This chapter will, therefore, refer to other industries, such as accommodation and tour operations, as 'sectors' within the more global definition 'tourism industry'.

Hotels, restaurants, tour guides, tour operators, tourist boards and other businesses or organisations involved in tourism often act cohesively in order to market their products and services more effectively. Indeed, many of the major tourism marketing events, as well as more general promotional activity, are undertaken jointly by tourism organisations, such events or activities including tourist board promotions; overseas trade missions (for example, those undertaken by the British Tourist Authority); trade shows, such as The World Travel Market, and joint advertising. As Seaton (1996) observes, those businesses defined under the 'tourism industry' banner are able to achieve greater visibility by acting cohesively together, although in subsuming them under one label, we ignore the fact that there are few common denominators aside from their provision of services for tourists or local visitors.

From the outset, therefore, it should be recognised that each industry involved in the activity of promoting tourism has slightly differing characteristics and approaches to marketing. Assistance in understanding these differences can be found in texts which examine the subject of marketing in more detail. However, it is beyond the scope of this chapter to examine these differences in depth and, therefore, further reading on distinct areas are suggested at the end of this chapter.

Definitions of marketing

Firstly, it is important to define what is meant by the term marketing, for to do so helps to clarify its overall purpose as well as presenting a more holistic picture of the marketing process. The Chartered Institute of Marketing, a professional and awarding body for practitioners in marketing, defines it as follows:

> *Marketing is the management process responsible for identifying, anticipating and satisfying customer requirements profitably.*

This statement has a number of important indicators as to the scope, purpose and process of marketing. Firstly, a business must identify for whom it is designing products and services, and it must anticipate the needs and wants of both existing and potential and consumers. Assuming that these needs and wants of consumers have been forecast correctly and that a product has been designed to suit them, the business should then focus on satisfying their needs successfully satisfy so that they will want to return and give the company more business. More simplistically, therefore, marketing can also be described as providing the right product, at the right place and the right time.

The central focus of marketing, then, is the consumer. In other words, the popular notion that marketing is to do with advertising and promotion, or that it is really selling in disguise, oversimplifies the total process. In reality, marketing is a broader, logical process consisting of many activities which are central to satisfying the consumer and ensuring the future prosperity of the organisation.

Marketing activities

Marketing involves not just the department or function responsible for marketing activity but the whole organisation, and marketing planning takes the form of both strategic and operational (or tactical) planning. Whilst the operational plan for any business or organisation usually covers a period of approximately one year, the strategic plan covers a longer time scale, generally three to five years. However, a particular feature of some sectors of the tourism industry where competition is most intense, for instance tour operating (see Chapter 5), is the emphasis on tactical planning – it could be argued that the dynamic nature of the business renders longer-term strategic planning an almost impossible task. Therefore, this chapter will concentrate on the marketing activities which are considered to be primarily operational or tactical. Nevertheless, this specific focus helps to highlight and explain the preliminary and formalised planning processes that most market oriented companies undertake.

McDonald explains the relationship between the two planning (operational and strategic) stages as follows:

A written strategic marketing plan is the backcloth against which operational decisions are taken on an ongoing basis (McDonald 1995).

The former part of the planning process, therefore, involves preparing for strategic planning – a simple explanation of this process is that it explains 'where we are now' as an organisation and 'where we want to be' at a point in the future. This chapter is more concerned with the processes which follow strategic planning and the techniques which marketing can employ to determine 'how' the organisation's objectives can be achieved, or how it can get to where it wants to be.

The activities associated with longer-term strategic planning and operational planning are fully outlined in McDonald (1995). However, the key activities in marketing are summarised in the following sections.

The planning cycle

Figure 18.1 presents a simplified adaptation of the planning cycle, describing the primary planning phases and the important activities undertaken within the marketing process.

Figure 18.1: *The planning cycle*

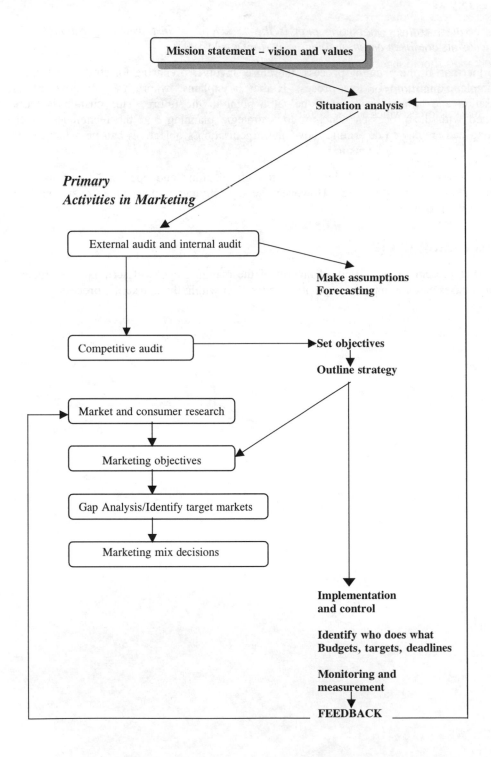

Situation analysis – external and internal audit

Situation analysis involves research into both the company's external operating environment and its own structures, processes, aims and objectives. The results of this research may affect what the company decides its course of action should be in the long-term, or what its strategic plans should incorporate. A situation analysis will cover, amongst other things:

- the organisation's position in the market;

- market forces which will affect the organisation's position and abilities;

- competitive activity and analysis; and

- internal analysis or audit of the organisation and its functional abilities and resources.

There can be a number of variables over which the organisation has little or no control, and the results of the audit tend to dictate the parameters within which an organisation can operate. It also gives an outline structure for future short-term plans and objectives (see McDonald (1995) and McDonald and Payne (1996)).

Market research

Before any marketing activity can be planned, an organisation needs basic information on which to base its future plans. Therefore, one of the primary roles of marketing is to conduct research. All of the primary activities involve research and there is a constant loop or feedback which enables organisations to make both strategic and tactical decisions.

Analysis and activity – market and consumer research

Before detailing its marketing plans, an organisation requires some of the following fundamental information.

i. Market research

- the size and nature of the market

- the nature of products and services on offer

- the nature of competing products and services

ii. Consumer research

- identifying consumer groups to whom the product will appeal

- identifying the validity (size, reachability, etc.) of target consumer groups

- identifying consumer tastes and preferences

- identifying consumer behaviour and changes – i.e. forecasting

The results of this research will largely determine what the organisation produces, for whom, when and in what quantities. In other words, it principally determines how and on what the activities of the organisation will be focused.

The marketing plan

Based upon the market and consumer information derived from the research and the subsequent strategic plan, the organisation must now decide on a more immediate course of action. These actions should enable it to achieve its more long-term objectives. This operational marketing plan tends to cover a shorter period (usually one year), and its purpose is to determine in more detail how the company will achieve its objectives.

The marketing plan incorporates activities generally referred to as:

The marketing mix

Marketing mix is the term normally used to refer to the combination of tools and methods adopted by an organisation to achieve the desired outcomes of the marketing plan. These tools, often referred to as the four 'Ps', are summarised as:

- *product* – the type of product the organisation produces, its characteristics, brand identity/image, and so on;

- *price* – the anticipated costs of production and distribution and the return that will achieve at the price which the market finds acceptable and which achieves the corporate objectives;

- *promotion* – the way in which the product is marketed the product to the consumer, deciding the nature of its appeal;

- *place* – the way in which the product is distributed to the consumer and its general accessibility.

In addition, there are other variables which organisations, particularly those in a service related industry such as tourism, can manipulate in order to change the nature of the offering and stimulate demand. These include areas such as people and processes, and are discussed later in the chapter in the context of the marketing mix and the extended marketing mix.

The nature of marketing planning is cyclical and should easily respond change. In other words, constant change in the external environment or in consumer preferences means that marketing must be a flexible process which incorporates ongoing feedback and research. Owing to the dynamic nature of tourism, it is particularly essential that organisations are able to be proactive and flexible.

Segmenting, targeting, positioning

A primary purpose of marketing is to identify those groups of people for whom the organisation will produce products or services. An important element of this process is to correctly identify those groups to be specifically targeted, knowing that they bring a greater chance of the product or service being successful (where the product is designed specifically to their requirements). Correct targeting of priority groups will also result in the organisation itself being more successful, as the purpose is to target those groups which will enable the organisation to meet its objectives. These priority or target groups may have more individual characteristics which help to define what the specific appeal of the product or the organisation might be. This, in turn, helps the organisation to:

- position the product in the consumers mind;

- position the product against competing products or services (product or competitive positioning);

- design campaigns which highlight the benefits to the consumer; and

- re-position the product (for example, to a new segment of consumers).

Segmentation

If the organisation is to utilise its marketing resources correctly or efficiently, it must have a clear picture of the groups of individuals who will use its product or services. The process of identifying and describing these groups of individual consumers is called segmentation. A segment is a group of people who have similar characteristics.

The marketing effort must be sufficiently different and appealing to these groups of consumers or segments so as to stimulate a recognition of a need or desire for the product or service. Thus, those organisations which do not correctly identify their market segments are likely to waste money by producing what has been termed 'a blanket approach' – that is, by treating everyone the same. The majority of organisations find that they need to adopt a differentiated approach to individual consumer groups or segments and to design products for their specific needs and, of course, to tailor their marketing campaigns to them.

What is a market segment? – criteria for identification

According to Engel *et al.* (1993), the objective of segmentation is to identify groups within the broader market that are sufficiently similar in characteristics and responses to warrant separate treatment. They suggest that there are four basic criteria which can be employed to identify a segment (Engel *et al.* 1993: 693-6):

- *Reachability*: can the group be identified and can it be isolated into a distinct group?

- *Identification of causal differences*: is it possible to identify the motivations and influences which define the group?

- *Economic potential*: is the segment large enough or valuable enough to warrant individual attention?

- *Possession of required marketing resources*: will the resources or effort required match the return?

Segmenting the market – methods and practices

There are many methods used by marketers to segment the market, some of which are more recognised or widely used than others. Government data collected through census or by similarly rigorous methods are often used as an initial basis for identifying groups by, for instance, age, socio-economic group, size of group or percentage of the population. These methods are not, however, sufficient on their own to describe the many different characteristics of consumer segments. Therefore, most organisations seek to use a number of methods to build up a clearer picture of their target audience. This is generally termed multivariate analysis; that is, the use of more than one method.

Marketing text books refer to and describe many different forms of segmentation, some of which are designed and researched by advertising agencies, which are useful for particular consumer or product markets. Some indication of size of segments is necessary and advertising agencies or professional research companies are sometimes in a better position to research and identify the size of specific product or consumer markets and the characteristics of groups contained within them.

Since there are many different types of organisation which make up the tourism industry, many different methods of segmenting consumer markets are used. However, only some of the more common methods are reviewed here (for more detail, see Engel *et al.* 1993).

i. Demographic segmentation

Demographic segmentation allows marketers to divide the market by known factors about the population, such as age, gender, occupation, education, nationality, family size, family life-cycle or life-stage. These tend to be reliable and measurable factors as they are primarily contained in regular government data or census details.

ii. Socio-economic groups

Socio-economic groupings are often referred to in marketing text books as the familiar categories of A, B, C1, C2, D and E. This classification has, however, become outdated, primarily because this segmentation method was used to link a household with an individual's (the head of the household) occupation and, therefore, income level. The household's socio-economic category was linked to class structures and, for marketers, was useful in identifying their likely purchasing habits or needs, level of education and so on.

However, a variety of social transformations, such as changes in types of occupation, the level of education required and relative salary levels, have changed household characteristics, with the result that these traditional segmentation methods are no longer applicable. Therefore, the government has revised the old classification system into the current National Statistics, Socio-Economic Categories or Classifications (NS-SEC) system. Details of the methods and reasoning behind this can be found on the government website (ONS – Office for National Statistics) and on the website for the Institute for Social and Economic Research at the University of Essex (see www.open.gov.uk; and www.iser.essex.ac.uk).

From 2001, the reference for the household is now the person with the highest income, whether male or female. The new national statistics for socio-economic classifications contains 17 categories in eight sub-groups; these can be aggregated to produce approximated socio-economic groupings. It is still, essentially, an occupationally-based classification but it has been adapted to cover other groups in the adult population who cannot be classified by occupation, such as full-time students and the unemployed. This method of classification provides a useful method of segmenting the market, but would generally be used in conjunction with other methods (see Figure 18.2).

Figure 18.2: *The national statistics socio-economic categories*

Socio-economic group: old classifications	Socio-economic group: new classifications
A: Professional classes	**1:** Higher Managerial and professional occupations
B: Managerial/technical	**1.1:** Large employers and higher managerial occupations
C1: Skilled blue-collar	**1.2:** Higher professional occupations
C2: Skilled and manual	**2:** Lower managerial and professional occupations
D: Semi-skilled	**3:** Intermediate occupations
E: Unskilled	**4:** Smaller employers and own account workers
Other	**5:** Lower supervisory and technical occupations
	6: Semi-routine occupations
	7: Routine occupations
	8: Never worked and long-term unemployed or sick

Note: Full details of the 17 sub-groups (fourteen functional and three residual operational categories) representing the variety of labour market positions and employment statuses can be obtained from the web site www. Statistics.gov.uk.

Source: Office for National Statistics

Age

Sometimes, large portions of a consumer market can be identified by age grouping. According to Yale (1998), tour operators providing for the holiday market in the UK can be seen to provide for three distinct groups identified by age and life-stage, or early middle and late adulthood. These are:

- The Youth Market   (18-30 years old)
- The Family Market   (25-50 years old)
- The Third Age Market   (50+ years old)

Within each of these broad notional age boundaries, there exists of course a myriad of similarities and differences which tour operators must provide for. Sub-groups may include, for example, the more active, the wealthy early retired, older parents, fixed-income singles, single parent families, and so on.

A glance at a range of tour operator brochures provides some clues as to what additional methods are used to further segment each age group. Take, for instance, a range of brochures catering for the 'third age' or over 50s group. This group could potentially cover an age range of 40 years and, not surprisingly perhaps, different brochures tend to illustrate the other variables which describe the target segments. At the same time, the actual names of the tour operators' programmes, such as 'Golden Years', 'Young-at-Heart' and Thomsons 'A la Carte' also give an indication of what these variables are (see also the Saga Holidays case study below). Nevertheless, segmenting according to one variable, such as age, remains an over-simplistic approach which may result in, for example, the provision of holidays which do not take into account the varying needs of consumers within particular age groups – it is feasible, for example, for a 50 year old to enjoy the same leisure lifestyle as a 30 year old.

Family life cycle

A method which overcomes some of the pitfalls of segmenting by age alone is the family life cycle or life stages. This method recognises that some people may be in the same life stage but at different ages. For example, many people are choosing to have children later in life and have more in common with other people in the same life stage (i.e. younger married couples with dependent children). It is also recognised that a high incidence of divorce has created a new category of the bachelor stage, namely, the 'second-time-around single'. However, these singles may not be in early adulthood. Many marketers in the holiday industry are, therefore, interested in identifying the life-stage rather than age of consumers. Many of their brochures reflect this by using older models with young families, or by portraying images of youthful and wealthy older age groups (see Figure 18.3 for the Family Life Cycle).

Figure 18.3: *The Family Life Cycle*

Bachelor stage:	Young and single
Newly married:	Married couples, no children
Full Nest 1:	Married couples with dependent children (sub categories toddlers and children over 6)
Full Nest 2:	Older married couples with dependent children
Empty Nest:	Older married couples with no children at home (sub categories of working and retired)
Solitary Survivors:	Older single people (sub categories working or retired)

Case study: Saga Holidays

Saga have been in the holiday business for more than 40 years and specialise in holidays for the 50+ market. Despite a stereotypical image of catering for the older market, the type of product that they produce is varied and geared to a very wide age range of people. They claim a customer base whose ages range from 50-90, and provide holidays from coach tours using student accommodation, to luxury cruises. (They do believe, however, that the majority of their client base consists of the more economically well off).

Saga identify target groups via a number of methods, including those which give an indication of their socio-economic status and lifestyle. Some of this information is available to Saga from other sections of their company which deal with products designed for retired people, such as investments and insurance. They also use geo-demographic indicators, such as Acorn and Mosaic, to pinpoint households. They also identify some of their most important target consumer groups by regular or occasional usage, whilst lifestyle descriptors, such as ' independent elders' and 'better off retireds', are also used to segment their market. The changes in life expectation and the general health and wealth of the 50+ market have meant that Saga's product and marketing policies have had to keep pace with this changing group of people, which no longer consists of one segment but many differing segments, all of which require different approaches.

Segmentation by geodemographics

Groups of consumers living in similar housing may well have similar incomes, similar lifestyles and similar wants and needs, as they often share common demographic characteristics. Geo-demographic segmentation, which combines a number of geographical and demographic details, is a commonly used method of pin-pointing specific geographical locations or types of housing which contain potential groups of consumers with similar characteristics. ACORN and MOSAIC are two commonly known systems (see Figure 18.4 below). Companies which specialise in collating this data offer a method of identifying the characteristics of households, consumer behaviour, and lifestyle types. Many tourism companies find it useful to identify postal areas where potential client types may exist, as this assists them in planning promotional activities such as advertising and direct mailing.

Figure 18.4: *Geodemographic segmentation methods*

ACORN

A	Agricultural areas
B	Modern family housing, higher incomes
C	Older housing of intermediate status
D	Poor quality older terraced housing
E	Better off council estates
F	Less well off council estates
G	Poorest Council estates
H	Mixed inner metropolitan areas
I	High status non-family areas
J	Affluent suburban housing
K	Better-off retirement areas

Categories and Components:

ACORN Category	ACORN Group	% of Population
A: Thriving	1: Wealthy Achievers, Suburban Areas	15.1
	2: Affluent Greys, Rural Communities	2.1
	3: Prosperous Pensioners, Retirement Areas	2.6
B: Expanding	4: Affluent Executives, Family Areas	4.0
	5: Well off Workers, Family Areas	7.8
C: Rising	6: Affluent Urbanites, Town and City Areas	2.5
	7: Prosperous Professionals, Metropolitan Areas	2.2
	8: Better off Executives, Inner City Areas	3.7
D: Settling	9: Comfortable Middle Agers, Mature Home Owning Areas	13.5
	10: Skilled Workers, Home Owning Areas	10.7
E: Aspiring	11: New Homeowners, Mature Communities	9.5
	12: White Collar Workers, Better Off Multi-ethnic areas	4.1
F: Striving	13: Older People, Less Prosperous Areas	3.7
	14: Council Estate Residents, Better Off Homes	10.9
	15: Council Estate Residents, High Unemployment	2.8
	16: Council estate Residents, Greatest Hardship	2.4
	17: People in Multi-ethnic, Low-Income Areas	2.0

Specialist tour companies, such as Cox and Kings may, for instance, wish to identify the 'high status non-family areas', and Saga the 'better off retirement areas' profiled by Acorn. Geo-demographics can also be useful for organisations in identifying where shops or services should be located.

Lifestyle and psychographic segmentation

These methods of segmentation aim to probe deeper into the characteristics of the consumer by identifying such things as their interests in life, their attitudes, values and aspirations. They attempt to identify the type behaviour consumers may demonstrate and to predict behaviour based on a knowledge of similarity of lifestyles, attitudes and motivations. Lifestyle segmentation assumes that we can relate certain products or services to certain types of lifestyle and consumer. Sometimes, these reflect aspirations or the type of 'lifestyle' some groups or individuals would like to lead, and many tourism organisations, such as hotels, can use this knowledge to target consumers – see also Chapter 4 for details of the Values and Lifestyle Scale (VALS).

Benefits and behavioural segmentation

These methods attempt to describe groups of consumers by the way in which they use products and the benefits they seek from them. Many organisations identify regular and occasional users, both of whom may require differing product characteristics. For example, regular users of an airline may be prepared to pay extra for a product, or anticipate added value, in the form of additional services such as a special business lounge.

Knowledge about the usage habits of consumers can assist with loyalty schemes or pricing structures. They are also useful for highlighting the way in which tourists use and choose products or services. For example, special occasions are often a time to dispense with usual buying routines, hence consumers may be more likely to use a different type of hotel for a honeymoon, or take additional treats such as champagne and flowers in the room on anniversaries. The benefits that groups of people seek from the product may also change the way in which products are designed – for example, all-inclusive holidays offer the benefits of a carefree holiday with little budgetary planning.

Analysis of market segments and selection of target markets

The detail of some market segmentation methods could lead marketers to over-rate the value of some of the more descriptive lifestyle classifications, or to believe that all information on the consumer is relevant. Engel *et al.* (1993) offer some advice regarding the trend towards greater multi-variate and descriptive analysis of market segments: 'Ask yourself of what practical value are the descriptors? Is the information interesting but irrelevant? And what will I do differently now that I have this information?' (Engel *et al.*1993:701).

Conversely, however, a business which chooses to describe its market segments in overly simplistic, out-of-date terms, or by product alone, may find itself 'out of step' with its customers and, hence, it may fail to communicate with them effectively.

The selection of the most appropriate target market segments for some travel and tourism organisations can be a difficult process. For example, in the case of tour operators the majority of larger companies will produce packages for a wide variety of differing segments and generally try to identify those which assist in profit objectives. That is, they seek the most lucrative segments or those which assist in the achievement of strategic advantages, such as market share (see also Chapter 5).

For tourist destinations, the choice of target segments may be limited to those which the tourism development strategy has identified as being the most beneficial guests (although not all destinations, off course, enjoy the luxury of being able to 'choose' their customers. Frequently, it is the tour operator that determines the characteristics of tourist flows to a destination). Their choices may focus on aspects other than finance, such as socio-cultural benefits, and may require some of the more immediately financially lucrative target markets to be ignored. Generally, however, whatever the options, the organisation must decide which segments have the greater priority, as the development of the marketing mix and complementary budgets will be tied to those priority groups.

Characteristics of the tourism industry and positioning strategies

The tourism industry, like many others, reacts to the particular nature of the environment and the structure of the market in which it operates. This brings about differing approaches to segmenting the market, and differing strategies for segments and product groups. Companies sometimes work on determining 'competitive market structures' – that is, grouping products or brands on the basis of competition boundaries. It can be recognised that, in the tourism market, there are specific areas where brands compete more strongly with one another than with other similar products.

For example, stronger brands and vertically integrated organisations, such as JMC or First Choice, may concentrate their marketing effort on dealing with the competition offered by others operating on a multi-market, multi-product basis (such as Thomsons or Airtours), rather than on smaller operators using the same destinations and offering similar packages. Similarly, major tourist destinations in the world, such as Greece and Spain, may compete more directly with one another for various tourist segments from the UK than do France and Spain as two of the largest destinations for UK tourists.

Differing market strategies and mixes in a fragmented market

A recent feature of the market for tourism is that many tour operators and destinations which catered for what was termed the 'mass market' are now attempting to respond to the growing trend towards a more fragmented market and tourists who require more individually tailored holidays (niche markets). This they have done by bringing out a wider variety of products to suit individual market segments and, as a result, in some product areas the larger operators might see their more direct competition to be a specialist or smaller operator. This highlights the need for distinctly different marketing strategies for particular market segments and products, with a different marketing mix.

As an example, the competition between JMC and Thomsons for their main multi-product summer programme might be such that they are forced to manipulate price rather more than other elements of the marketing mix. They might also have to concentrate a higher degree of their marketing budget on advertising and promotion. On the other hand, a smaller specialist operator, such as Abercrombie and Kent, competing with Thomsons in a tourist location may offer added value and expertise and a greater personal service element to the product. Thomsons may, in turn, may have to manipulate its product mix or perceived value in order to compete with the smaller operator. In this case, either operator may invoke the extended marketing mix (see below) and the emphasis may be on elements other than price, such as people and the service they give. Similarly, destinations such as Spain have the challenge of remaining appealing to the established market segments of the 'Costas' whilst promoting to smaller, and potentially more lucrative, segments who require differing product benefits. The marketing mix they invoke for these segments may therefore have to be very different.

The control of variables - the nature and characteristics of services and tourism marketing

In the marketing of tourism products, it is acknowledged that there are a number of variables over which the industry has little control and which characterise the tourism product These variables tend to focus on economic and political influences over which organisations in the tourism field have either little or no control. These variables, such as pdi (personal disposable income), are used by market intelligence agencies, such as Mintel, to forecast the nature of the market. Mintel maintain, for instance, that pdi has a direct correlational effect on the number of holidays the consumer is able to take in the year, and anticipated growth or decline in pdi will, therefore, have a direct influence on trends in holiday taking (Mintel 2001).

The levels of activity and spend in the tourism market are also affected by potential changes in the economic and political environment, including inflation levels, mortgage rates, interest rates and exchange rates, all of which may have a greater or lesser effect on consumer confidence and spending. Other variables of particular concern to those involved in tourism are wars and political instability. All organisations, therefore, seek to reduce risk by research; that is, they undertake economic forecasting and acquire other market intelligence which enables them to make realistic strategic and tactical plans.

Once organisations have defined those variables which will have most influence over the ability of the consumer to purchase, they must decide upon ways of overcoming some of the difficulties and then decide upon more direct activities. These direct activities focus on those variables which marketers are more able to control and are more widely known as the marketing mix, the extended marketing mix or services marketing mix. Marketers must seek to find the correct 'mix' which will achieve success for the organisation and satisfy consumers.

The marketing mix and extended marketing mix

As discussed above, the most widely accepted and used definition of the marketing mix is the four 'Ps', which incorporates product, price, place (distribution) and promotion. In service industries and in tourism in particular, it is considered that this mix can be extended to include other activities and that these can assume just as much importance. Indeed, the four 'Ps' approach has been widely criticised for its limitations and many commentators have offered advice on the application of an extended mix and the nature of services (Gronroos 1990; Cowell 1994, 1997; Kotler and Armstrong 1996; McDonald and Payne 1996; Zeithaml, Parasuraman and Berry(1985); Zeithaml and Bitner 2000).

Cowell emphasises that the marketing mix is a guide and a framework for action, not simply a theoretical idea (Cowell in Baker 1997: 671). Marketers should, therefore, be prepared to adapt and adopt the correct mix according to their particular industry and organisational conditions and, most particularly, according to the needs of the target market segments they have decided to cater for. One of the principal reasons for adopting an extended mix is the nature of the delivery of services, such as tourism, where in order to differentiate one product from another, factors such as the management of service quality through *people, processes and physical evidence* are important. These additional variables in the production process can affect the response of the consumer more readily. As far as possible, marketing must influence performance and delivery of the product.

The role of customer service and the control of quality are, therefore, heavily emphasised in tourism organisations (see Chapter 5). Companies such as British Airways spend sizeable portions of their marketing budget ensuring that the product is made more tangible and that customer experiences and perceptions are more consistent. The extended marketing mix of people, processes and physical evidence provide more ways in which marketers can control the delivery (see Zeithaml and Bitner (2000) for further reading).

Product

The nature and characteristics of the tourism product

i. Inseparability and heterogeneity

As has already been observed in the discussion of marketing mix, one of the features of tourism products is that production and consumption are not entirely exclusive. This inseparability is created because services which are part of the production process are only 'produced' at the time of consumption. For example, a night in an hotel or a flight on an aeroplane only occurs the service is 'consumed'. Because people are so much a part of this production process, another feature of tourism products is their lack of standardisation or 'heterogeneity'. As previously stated, marketers must try to make the product conform to the same standard so that it perceived the same by all users.

ii. Intangibility

Tourism products incorporate many elements, but a particular feature of tourism is that many of these elements are intangible – they are not physical goods, but experiences and feelings. In short, the nature of many holiday products is such that consumers could be said to buy on trust. As demonstrated in the above section, the producer seeks to control as many of these intangible variables as possible in order to make the product more tangible for the consumer (see section below on product analysis).

iii. Perishability and seasonality

Tourism products are highly perishable; unlike manufactured goods, they cannot be stored and sold at a later date. Therefore, the costs involved in their production can increase if, for example, tours are not filled to capacity, some departure dates remain unsold, or aircraft seats remain unsold. These are some of the factors which affect the pricing of tourism products, since producers must sometimes allow for a level of unsold capacity which can increase the individual costs of a holiday.

It is sometimes the seasonal nature of the tourism product which increases the risk and, therefore, tourist attractions and tour operators must ensure that they are able to make the most of peak seasons. Cash flow tends to be poor and sometimes non-existent in shoulder and off-peak seasons, whilst for those with high fixed costs or assets which remain dormant (aircraft, ships, coaches, hotels), the problem of seasonality is greater. Marketing efforts must, therefore, be focused on achieving prices which achieve the highest rate of return in peak season, and prices which stimulate demand in low seasons, thus increasing the likelihood of full use of assets.

Product analysis

Product analysis is an element of the marketing process that helps an organisation to identify the ways in which it can adapt and improve products in relation to customer needs and competitor products. It also assists the organisation in identifying features and benefits which can be highlighted in promotional campaigns.

Shoshtack (1977) has attempted to analyse products by identifying their relative importance to the core service, demonstrating how important some of the more peripheral services are in making the product more tangible for some consumers. The importance of components within the structure may change for different consumers – with airlines, for example, business class travellers may value reclining seats and more leg room, whilst a leisure passenger may value speed of service and ancillary services, such as duty free shopping. Both, however, experience the same core service – the flight.

The concept of a core which satisfies the most fundamental or basic needs arises from Kotler's (1994) Five Product Levels model, in which he suggests that marketers should attempt to enhance the set of attributes and conditions that customers normally expect with an augmented level, one which distinguishes their product from others. By augmenting the product, marketers will be satisfying more than the basic needs of customers and be supplying additional benefits which also differentiate the product from its competitors.

There are many other useful models which assist organisations in comparing and improving upon products. A SWOT analysis (strengths, weaknesses, opportunities and threats), for instance, may prove useful in comparing competing products. Alternatively, an analysis of the benefits which consumers derive from products helps the organisations to distinguish them from the integral features, thus providing marketers with material for promotional campaigns.

It is harder is to develop new products for the tourism market, as opposed to other markets, since it is generally much more difficult to pre-test service related products. Some tour operators will pre-test new products by pilot launches to specific geographical regions or release programmes with limited departure dates. Hotels and purpose built attractions may test concepts and reactions to interior decor. The retail trade and tourist boards can attempt to simulate the holiday experience through videos and computer generated graphics. In general, however, much of the industry relies on experience and the post-purchase evaluations of consumer satisfaction. When compared to some industries in manufacturing, the costs of the research, introduction and testing of new products for tourism are relatively low.

Product life-cycle

Since manipulating the features and design of the product is one of the primary ways in which marketers can ensure success, it is inevitable that they will also be interested in how much adaptation of the product can take place before consumers tire of the product and it becomes obsolete. The product life-cycle concept proposes that every product has four basic stages, namely, *introduction, growth, maturity and decline*. It is the job of marketing to assess the life of individual products in order to:

- assess and predict the length of the adoption stage of a new product;

- determine at what stage in the process each product in the organisation's portfolio is;

- adapt products to stem the decline or renew interest (extending the lifecycle);

- assess when products need to be deleted; and

- assess when new products need to be introduced.

There are a number of pitfalls in predicting the life-stages of products, and the intense competition in the tourism industry with its characteristic price wars could lead to a misinterpretation of the pattern of growth and decline. The popularity of products is clearly not just influenced by their path to obsolescence and caution is needed in interpreting the pattern of sales.

Figure 18.5: *The Product Life-cycle*

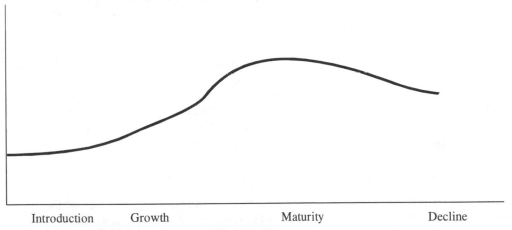

| Introduction | Growth | Maturity | Decline |

At the introduction stage, cost is the primary factor and it is not until the growth stage, when sales begin to rise, that marketing can be sure of some return on their investment. A mistake that some companies make is to underestimate the length of the adoption process and pull to the plug on new products too early. Equally, overestimation will increase costs with no return. Growth may also be affected by a number of other factors, such as the introduction of competitive products. At the maturity stage, it may be that a smaller number of producers battle it out for market share; during this stage it may be difficult to tell whether sales have reached saturation and a decline is likely.

Price

Influences on pricing

There are many influences on pricing, including:

- demand;

- supply (availability);

- costs;

- competition;

- government policies on pricing;

- consumer legislation; and

- competition.

In addition, there are many other constraints which influence the way in which organisations price their products. These include the health of the economy, personal disposable income levels, exchange rates, interest rates, mortgage rates, and so on. Corporate objectives and the margins required by shareholders and other investors will also be influential on pricing policy.

Whilst it is important that marketers decide upon the correct price for the product which suits the market segment at which it is aimed, it must be remembered that many constraints influence their ability to use price as a tool to manipulate consumer response.

Supply and demand and pricing policy

Some sectors of the tourism industry are said to be characterised by price wars. These are, sometimes, the inevitable result of over-capacity in airlines, shipping, and to a lesser extent, hotels, and reflect the extent to which supply or demand influences pricing. Principles or producers with spare capacity resulting from lower demand or increased supply will sell at cheaper rates in order to cover existing or high fixed costs, or cut prices in the belief that a reduction in price will lead to a subsequent increase in sales.

Market share and pricing policy

In recent years, price wars and discounting have been the major characteristic of the larger, vertically integrated companies who combine the functions of tour operator, travel agent and charter airline. These reflect the extent to which both perishability and the fight for market share influences pricing.

These larger companies have produced larger tour operating programmes, sometimes flooding the market with products, in order to preserve or win market share. When these efforts fail, products often have to be put back on the market in different forms or through different distribution channels and, generally, at lower or discounted rates.

Those companies without adequate resources cannot generally price products for market share. Nor should companies with either substantial borrowings and poor performance pursue pricing for market share, as banks may 'pull the plug' at the wrong time whilst shareholders may object to policies which reduce margins. Thus, market share is not a realistic option for many companies; indeed, some markets may remain stagnant with little growth in volume. Nevertheless, growth can be achieved not only by selling more of a product but also by selling the same volume, but at higher prices. For some, but relatively few, organisations in the tourism industry, this is the only option.

Pricing methods

i. Target rate of return

Prices are decided on the basis of achieving a particular return on the assets employed in an organisation. Investors in a business may simply set a target with which they will be happy.

ii. Cost based methods

Based on accounting disciplines of costing, this method is easy for many organisations to understand and use. Costs can be split into two types, fixed and variable. Fixed costs are those which do not vary with 'output', or the amount of the service provided. Variable costs, conversely, are those which do increase as more of a service is provided.

These two cost elements can be combined with revenue – which should increase as the service is sold – to give a picture of when an operation becomes profitable. Known as Break Even Analysis or Cost/Profit/Volume (CPV) Analysis, the interaction of these elements can be shown graphically.

In reality, in some businesses it may be difficult to allocate overheads or fixed costs to some products. Some businesses may want to be flexible and operate differing prices and pricing methods to achieve different objectives which stimulate demand. Therefore, contributions to cost (marginal cost pricing) is a more realistic proposition for some companies, as the range offered may support the sale of other products, or utilise spare capacity (e.g. transportation).

iii. Promotional and psychological pricing

Promotional pricing may be employed to destroy rival products or pricing policies. It may also be used as the lead-in price for a brochure where, for example, £399 is perceived as removing a barrier price of £400 or over. However, it would normally be viewed as a short term strategy as its objectives are achieved at the cost of profit.

iv. Competitive based pricing

Some industries are constrained in the way they price products and can only sell at what is termed the going rate, that is, the rate which the competition is charging. However, this method should be used with caution as it also means that costs should be relatively the same for both parties. Many organisations are forced into this situation when competition is intense and the public have got used to what they consider to be the 'going rate' for a product – as is very much the case with the mass, package holiday market.

v. Premium and destroyer pricing

These methods represent the opposite ends of a scale. More successful companies with well-known brands and highly regarded products are in a position to be price leaders in a market and achieve a premium price over others. Generally, there are good reasons for being able to achieve this, such as providing a higher quality service or providing a specialist or unique service.

At the opposite end of the scale, destroyer aims to undercut competitors in order to remove them from the market. This type of pricing can result in negative implications for the consumer as, once competition is removed, so too are the barriers for increasing prices and, therefore, such actions may be swiftly followed by price rises.

Place

Distribution and promotion often play inter-related roles in the marketing of travel and tourism products. The decisions facing most organisations are either to market direct to the consumer or to market their products via an intermediary, such as a travel agent. This still leaves the problem of how to distribute information and inventory (available capacity) to the travel agent. The nature of distribution services has changed considerably in the past twenty years as more and more ways of delivering the product direct to the consumer or more speedily business to business have been developed (see Chapter 6 for more detail). For example, on a business to business basis CRS's – global reservations networks – allowed travel agents and producers to access inter-related products, such as airlines, hotels and other services and for organisations to communicate. These systems are now becoming redundant as agents are able to access inventory and information on the Internet via separately controlled networks (which the public are not allowed access to).

Importantly, time is often saved and fewer brochures are needed if the public is able to access information direct from producers' web-sites and make some decisions before contacting travel agents. In these instances, the consumer is going direct to the producer for information but is still using the agent for booking purposes. Many organisations have developed call centres for the same purpose.

There has been much discussion on the value of the Internet as a distribution tool. Before making any decisions on more direct methods of distribution and promotion, it is necessary for marketers to decide what use the majority of people will make of these services. For example, it must be ascertained whether consumers will use services, such as the Internet, as a tool for collating information (accepting promotional material) or whether they would wish to undertake transactions using the Internet (a distribution tool).

Air travel is one product which has been successfully distributed on the Internet. Ryanair, for example, have achieved 70 percent of their bookings through their web site, another 23 percent are made by phone and only 7 percent through agents (Mintel 2001b: 11).

One of the major advantages of the Internet is that it may lower the cost of distribution for many organisations. For products such as ferry crossings, it offers another method of distributing information on fares and sailing times which are quicker than brochure distribution and more flexible. The Internet has also provided an opportunity for new types of distribution service which differ from retail agents. These distribution services may concentrate on one type of service or one consumer segment. They aggregate services to capture whole product or consumer markets, whilst providing an opportunity for a more efficient service for consumers wanting to compare services, prices and times (Barrass 1998). Thus, sites such as Ferrybooker.com are able to offer information on all ferry services on one site (Mintel 2001: 23).

Keynote maintain that four times as many tourists considered the Internet and travel books a better source of information than travel agents and tour operators (Keynote 2001: 51). Nevertheless, many organisations still believe that there are limitations to distributing products through the Internet. These limitations are: a reluctance to use technology; security concerns (with credit card transactions, bank details); ease of access to inventory; ease of access to correct information; and the lack security associated with dealing face-to-face or verbal communication.

Travel agents are still the primary method by which people in the UK access information on holiday products and make reservations. Agents can provide a professional service with additional information and advice, which should be impartial. There has been much discussion as to how impartial this advice can be when many agents are part of vertically integrated companies who have an interest in promoting their own products. Therefore, the European Competition Commission have taken an active interest in the growing integration of the European travel industry and have issued guidelines for agents which enable the public to identify where an agents is offering products which are owned by the group. The nature of travel agents is changing and many companies are developing new types of agency which no longer perform traditional roles but, which offer the benefits of new technology, such as the Internet alongside personal contact.

Whilst it is the marketer of tourism products who must decide on the best method of distribution for their product, it is still the consumer who makes the decision which method they prefer to use. Most organisations now seek to determine how particular market segments will react to and use different distribution systems and the preferences of important target market segments are taken into account. The type of holiday product and the typical consumer give some indication – for example, the Internet is apparently the ideal method for adventure travel operators as the profile of their consumers closely matches that of consumers likely to participate in adventure travel. It also suits the many small companies involved in this area, as distribution through agents would be difficult if not impossible. Indeed, approximately 85 percent of sales for adventure travel companies is by direct booking (Millington 2001). Specialist tour operators in general are hoping to develop their brands via the Internet, whilst the Association of Independent Tour Operators (AITO) has used it to raise the profile of its members and their products and as a communications tool (Mintel 2001).

In addition to consumer preference, tour operators and others must consider the cost of distributing products. If distributing through travel agents, they must decide whether they will distribute on a blanket approach to each agent or whether they will selectively distribute to a small number of agents or selected chains. Many organisations do not have the choice as, with such a wide variety of products on offer, travel agents must be selective about how many they stock and some producers may have no option but to sell direct.

Promotion

It is the responsibility of marketing to communicate factors about an organisation and its products. The purpose of communications can vary; for instance, it may be used for establishing an identity for a product, creating a corporate image for an organisation or creating awareness of a destination. The promotional efforts of organisations should generally be focused on their selected target market segments. It is one of the responsibilities of marketing not only to identify the various audiences but their characteristics. They also need to analyse the characteristics of their products and the appeal they have for their audience. This knowledge will enable clear directions to be given to those preparing the promotional plan as to the purpose of the campaign.

The purposes of campaigns are very varied. Tour operators or destinations, for example, may find it necessary to place advertising which raises awareness of a destination whereas established consumer segments, who are already knowledgeable on products and destinations, may need more persuasion to choose the product in preference to others. The purpose of the campaign, therefore, may be to create more favourable attitudes or to stimulate consumers to purchase.

As discussed shortly, there are a number of ways in which we can communicate with chosen audiences. However, the choice of the promotional effort or mix of the communications package will depend upon many factors, including:

- the size of budget;

- the objectives of the promotional campaign;

- the size and nature of the target audience; and

- the geographical spread of the target audience.

The primary concern is to establish clear objectives or goals for the campaign and then to monitor and measure the responses to it. Without monitoring and measurement, no organisation can clearly determine whether its success is due to marketing effort and the cost effectiveness of that effort.

Elements of the promotional mix

i. Advertising

Marketing must carefully select media by identifying the typical readership, viewers or listeners and matching the medium to their target audience. There are many considerations which affect choice and it is suggested that marketing must look not only at the absolute cost of advertising (time or space purchased) but also at the relative costs of advertising, 'that is, the cost of contacting each member of the target audience' (Fill 1995: 310). A wide range of media may be used for advertising, including:

- TV

- Radio

- National and local press

- Trade and professional journals

- magazines

- Posters/bill boards

- Direct mailing

For each method, details of advertising rates, readership and reach are published and part of the research and planning process is also to determine the medium most likely to be cost effective and with which the audience is most likely to identify.

ii. Public and press relations

Press and public relations campaigns form a major part of the additional activities which can enhance communications strategies. The influence of media coverage, in particular on the holiday product, has proven to be enormous. It is not just consumer programmes which review holiday products that are influential – the image of destinations created by TV programmes have also been instrumental in developing tourism and have been shown to have a far more powerful effect than traditional advertising (for example, 'Heartbeat' on Goathland and 'Peak Practice' on Crich/Amber Valley area of Derbyshire). Marketers know that filming in a location is likely to enhance or build an image for a destination and arouse awareness and curiosity.

iii. Direct marketing

Direct mail, telemarketing and the Internet are all forms of communication which are increasingly used in the travel and tourism industry. Direct mail and telemarketing have the advantage of being more easily monitored and, therefore, the response more directly measurable. Direct response methods, such as promotional coupons, are also used successfully to promote holiday products. Unlike the Internet, the cost of these is more directly measurable.

iv. Brochures and printed materials

The brochure is still the primary selling tool for the majority of the travel and tourism industry, including destinations, although the Internet is bringing about change on this front. The nature of the holiday product means that it is information intensive and the brochure has been the primary tool through which all information is distributed. It is, however, a costly business and marketers must consider how many brochures they need to distribute. The real cost of brochure production and distribution can be measured by assessing the number of bookings received to the number of brochures distributed. The conversion rate for most organisations is, in fact, staggeringly low and the real costs of 'wastage' (brochures taken but not used as a booking medium) are high.

v. Direct selling

A large proportion of business to business activity is undertaken by direct sales. However, the role of selling in the travel industry is often a controversial one, especially when considering the role of the travel agent. Face-to-face selling, therefore, has less of a role than, say, telesales throughout most of the industry. In reality, the purchase of holiday products involves complex decision-making, often by groups of people, some of whom take differing roles (for example, buyers or influencers). The direct selling role can therefore be controversial. However, some organisations have attempted to use direct selling when people's responses are known to be less guarded, such as in the selling of time-share in holiday resorts.

Discussion questions

1.   *Explain the processes and methods by which consumers are identified and marketing efforts directed towards them.*

2.   *What are the major characteristics and difficulties associated with the marketing of travel and tourism products and services?*

3.   *What elements make up the marketing and extended marketing mix and how can these be manipulated in the marketing of travel and tourism products?*

4.   *Attempt the segmentation exercise below.*

Segmentation exercise

Take a range of brochures intended for the following groups and try to identify and describe in more detail the market segments they cater for and their position in the market:

- *Youth Market*

- *Family Market*

- *Third Age*

Identify from the brochures other ways in which these target market segments can be identified.

Devise a market map by creating two relevant axes (e.g. High Activity to Low Activity, Budget to Luxury), identifying each brands position within the axes.

Further reading

Brent, J. R. & Goeldner, C. R. (1994), *Travel, Tourism, and Hospitality Research: A Handbook for Managers and Researchers*, Chichester: John Wiley & Sons.

Brunt P. (1997), *Market Research in Travel and Tourism*, Oxford: Butterworth Heinemann.

Horner, S. and Swarbrooke J. (1996), *Marketing Tourism Hospitality and Leisure in Europe*, London: Thomson International Business Press.

McDonald, M. (1995), *Marketing Plans*, Oxford: Butterworth Heinemann.

McDonald, M. and Payne, A. (1996), *Marketing Planning for Services*, Oxford: Butterworth Heinemann.

Pender, L. (1999), *Marketing Management for Travel and Tourism*, Cheltenham: Stanley Thornes.

Seaton, A. and Bennett, M. (1996), *Marketing Tourism Products, Concepts, Issues, Cases*, London: Thomson International Business Press.

References

Barrass, C. (1998), *An Exploratory Study on Internet Marketing Strategy and its Impact on Passenger Shipping*, Unpublished MA thesis, University of Northumbria.

Cowell, D. (1994), *The Marketing of Services, 2nd Edition*, Oxford: Butterworth Heinemann.

Cowell, D. (1997), in Marketing, Michael J. Baker, Butterworth Heinemann 3rd ed: pg. 671

Engel, J. F., Blackwell, R. D., Miniard, P. W., (1993), *Consumer Behaviour, 7th Edition*, Fort Worth: The Drydeen Press.

Fill, C. (1995), *Marketing Communications*, Trowbridge: Prentice Hall.

Gronroos, C. (1990), *Services Marketing and Management*, Lexington, MA: Lexington Books.

Horner, S. and Swarbrooke, J. (1996), *Marketing Tourism Hospitality and Leisure in Europe*, London: Thomson International Business Press.

Keynote (2001), *Current Issues - Travel Agents and Overseas Tour Operators*.

Kotler, P. (1994), *Marketing Management: Analysis, Planning, Implementation and Control, 8th Edition*, London: Prentice Hall International.

McDonald, M. (1995), *Marketing Plans*, Oxford: Butterworth Heinemann.

McDonald, M. and Payne, A. (1996), *Marketing Planning for Services*, Oxford: Butterworth Heinemann.

Millington, K. (2001), Adventure Travel, *Travel and Tourism Analyst*, No. 4: 65-97

Mintel (2001), *Crossing the Channel*, Leisure Intelligence UK Report, London: Mintel International Group Limited.

Mintel (2001b), *Directly booked holidays*, Leisure Intelligence UK Report, London: Mintel International Group Limited.

Pender, L. (1999), *Marketing Management for Travel and Tourism*, Cheltenham: Stanley Thornes.

Seaton, A. and Bennett, M. (1996), *Marketing Tourism Products, Concepts, Issues, Cases*, London: Thomson International Business Press.

Shostack G. (1977), Breaking free from product marketing, *Journal of Marketing* 41(2): 76.

Yale, P. (1998), *The Business of Tour Operations*, Harlow: Longman.

Zeithaml, V. and Bitner, M. (2001), *Services Marketing: Integrating Customer Focus Across The Firm*, McGraw-Hill Higher Education.

Zeithaml, V., Parasuraman, A. and Berry, L. (1985), Problems and strategies in services marketing, *Journal of Marketing* 49(1): 33-46.

Web-Sites

www.open.gov.uk (ONS- Office for National Statistics)

www.iser.essex.ac.uk - Institute for Social and Economic Research at the University of Essex

www.aito.org.uk - Association of Independent Tour Operators

www.competition-commission.org

19

eBusiness and Travel and Tourism

Alain Young

Learning objectives

This chapter considers the impact of eBusiness and the Internet on the travel and tourism industry. It enables the reader to:

- *appreciate the specific characteristics of eBusiness and their implications for travel and tourism businesses*

- *understand the potential contribution of eBusiness to the marketing of travel and tourism*

- *appreciate the impact of the Internet on the structure and operations of tourism businesses*

- *identify and explain the benefits of eBusiness for public sector tourism organisations*

Introduction

Information technology has always played an important part in much of the travel and tourism industry (see Chapter 6). However, perhaps the most significant and exciting development in the sector in the last few years has been the emergence and development of the Internet. The Internet has grown from a small network of computers, set up in the USA the late 1960s for defence purposes, into today's global network linking millions of computer users around the world. Private users and small companies can connect to the Internet via the phone line using a modem and by opening an account with an Internet Service Provider (ISP), whilst larger companies or organisations will have dedicated connections provided by telecommunications companies.

Digitised business or managerial information can be disseminated throughout the network and specially designed computer applications can analyse this information and respond accordingly, thereby interacting with customers, other businesses and organisations. This activity is now known as eBusiness or eCommerce.

The purpose of this chapter is to provide an overview of the role of eBusiness in the tourism sector and, in particular, to consider how it is affecting both industry players and customers. It also goes on to look at some future developments in eBusiness technologies and the implications that these may have for those involved in tourism. It does not, however, delve into Internet engineering and communication technologies but, nevertheless, assumes that the reader understands basic Internet concepts, terminology and, indeed, jargon. Examples of interesting or useful web sites are given in parentheses throughout the chapter.

Definitions

eBusiness is business or management activity conducted by electronic means over computer networks. It is more commonly referred to as eCommerce; however, eCommerce tends to focus on the transactions between customers and suppliers, whereas the term eBusiness can encapsulate the total business process, both within and without the firm, including the relationship between customer and supplier. eBusiness, then, affects a variety of business activities, such as marketing, human resource management, procurement and distribution, as well as having implications for the state in terms of the law, taxation and government regulation. Most notably, however, it is changing consumer behaviour whilst, at the same time, providing the consumer with increased power and choice.

Therefore, the scope of eBusiness extends well beyond the popular view of web pages being used to advertise and sell things. The components of eBusiness will include email, interactive websites, mobile phones, television and, possibly, other household appliances!

Characteristics of eBusiness

Global reach

The Internet is a global network which means that eBusiness has, theoretically, a global reach. However, although this characteristic is true as far as communication is concerned, the picture is more complicated when the distribution of tourism products is considered. It is not practical, for example, for a British travel agent to sell a Spanish holiday to a customer in Australia because the customer would, of course, have to come to the UK to take the holiday.

Global reach is also constrained by consumer protection law and other kinds of regulation both of the tourism sector in particular and, increasingly, of eBusiness generally. This will affect the ability of tourism firms to market their products on a global basis and may mean that companies engaged in eBusiness will have to adapt their activities and procedures in order to comply with such regulations in different parts of the world. At the same time, consumers are wary of buying from sites overseas because consumer law has not yet caught up with the new legal situation being created by the Internet. For example, if a consumer in Brazil arranged to rent a country cottage from a web site in Sweden and a dispute over the transaction arose, to which country's consumer protection law could that customer appeal? In other words, in the age of the Internet, an important yet unresolved question is which country's laws protect the consumer when they are making purchases across national boundaries? (Waldmeir 2001).

This is one reason why some companies have localised domain names as well as the more common international dot.com (.com) suffix. An example of this is *eBookers*, the online travel agency that has a main site at www.ebookers.com as well as various international sites, including www.ebookers.com/fr for France, and www.ebookers.no/ for Norway. Indeed, some sites' computers advise surfers that they should go to their 'national' site. *Expedia*, (http://www.expedia.com/) does this, reminding customers that they cannot buy American air tickets if they are browsing from outside the USA.

Of course, different rules and regulations may not be the only reason for a firm to have a variety of localised domain names – there are good marketing reasons for them as well. Potential customers may feel more confident interacting with a web site presented in their own language and with one that appears to be based in their own country.

In some cases, government regulation may lead to companies leaving particular geographic locations precisely because they can set up and conduct business anywhere by using the Internet. For example, in 1999, the large bookmakers *Coral* and *William Hill* threatened to move their operations overseas to reduce the tax burden imposed on those who bet. A private bookmaker, *Victor Chandler International*, had set up an offshore operation on Gibraltar and was able to reduce the tax on betting. The big bookmaking companies were being squeezed by the rival operation's success.[1] In late 2001 the taxation rules on betting were changed and taxes that were imposed on the customer are now levied on the bookmakers' profits. This change was largely as a result of the increase in betting on the Internet (BBC 2001).

Disintermediation/reintermediation

It was believed that one of the consequences of the growth of the Internet and the development of eBusiness would be the elimination of intermediaries between supplier and customer, a process that has been termed 'disintermediation' (see also Chapter 6). This potentially occurs because the Internet allows customers to communicate directly with the supplier or producer of a product. Thus, a potential package holiday customer can buy plane tickets from an airline, accommodation from a hotel, car-hire from a hire company, and so on (in effect, creating their own package), and this can all be carried out if the suppliers have a 'web presence'. This means that, in theory, the need to have travel agents based in the high street is unnecessary. However, this process of disintermediation has not yet happened, for several reasons:

- it is very difficult for individuals to buy the components of their holiday by surfing the Internet – it is time consuming and, in the long run, usually more expensive because individual consumers cannot benefit from the economies of scale that are available to travel agencies and tour operators.

- new intermediaries have emerged that specialise in marketing travel products on the Internet. Companies such as *Travelocity*, (www.travelocity.com), *Expedia* (www.expedia.com) and *Lastminute* (www.lastminute.com) now allow customers to search, select and buy tourism products in one place.

- sometimes the new intermediaries get it wrong and do not provide the customer with the best deal.[2]

- the development of the new intermediaries, referred to as 'reintermediation', has meant that many of the traditional travel agencies now also have web sites to market their products. Originally, these sites were advertisements for their high street shops and had no interactive facilities at all. Many, indeed, directed surfers to their branches by providing phone numbers. However, they have now developed into sophisticated sites from which to market their products (www.lunnpoly.com and www.firstchoice.co.uk).

It does seem likely that there may be a slight fall in the number high street travel agencies over the coming years, in much the same way that the UK banking sector closed unprofitable branches during the late nineties. However, the traditional agencies that are now trading on the Internet appear to be seeing this as complimentary to their marketing strategy in respect of their 'bricks and mortar' presence, rather than as a replacement. This begs the question, though, of whether the Internet is allowing these particular companies to reduce costs. Indeed, the setting up Internet operations as well as having shops may, in fact, have the opposite effect and actually increase costs.

Virtualisation

The Internet allows companies to contract out business activities to other firms more easily. An airline, for example, could outsource its aircraft, catering, in-flight and ground services, and so on, to specialist firms. Whilst this has always been possible in the past, the Internet makes this much less difficult and it can be much more efficiently organised. This is because all the suppliers could be locked into the airline's computer network where communications and operations between all the parties can be managed electronically. In some cases, the contracted company could even be based in another country.

Automation

eBusiness is ideal for automating business processes. Costly manual processes involving paper, telephones and the staff to carry them out can be, to a large extent, eliminated or reduced. Storage efficiencies can also be achieved because most information can be held on electronic databases for easy retrieval, comparison and manipulation. This, in turn, allows companies to obtain information at a very detailed level both in terms of its internal processes and its customers. This all leads to cost reductions and to other benefits both for the supplier and the customer.

Cost reduction

As already mentioned above, eBusiness technologies allow companies to reduce costs, primarily because the physical requirements of information collection, manipulation, analysis and storage can be radically reduced. Furthermore, because customers interact with web sites in order to collect much of this information, human intermediaries, such as telephone sales staff, can also be reduced in number. Thus, 'cost reduction in service is largely achieved by moving towards customer self-service, with the help of technology. Part of the cost reduction can be passed on to the customer' (Timmers 1999: 22). Indeed, some corporate customers are already switching from using traditional travel agencies to book business travel arrangements, to booking online (Rice 2001).

Collaboration

The Internet allows companies and their suppliers to be electronically linked via 'sub – networks' called *intranets* or *extranets*. An intranet is a closed network within a particular company or organisation. An extranet is a network that may link a company with its suppliers or other stakeholders. In other words, suppliers have access to a particular company's network to exchange information – the general public would not, however, have access to this network. Three major areas where the Internet is making an impact in collaboration are in product development, procurement and joint marketing.

i. Product development

Companies can involve their suppliers in the development of new products through network technology. Boeing, the aircraft manufacturer, has, for example, engaged a specialist company, Aeronet, to build it a wide-ranging intranet that allows suppliers and subcontractors to obtain technical information about its planes. Boeing's suppliers and customers can now directly download information, such as maintenance manuals and engineering drawings, that used to be distributed in 'hard' form (Nairn 1998). Keeping and supplying information in this way means that, when updates are necessary, the company does not have to order another print run of documentation – it just updates the digital information on its server. Again, this information would be available only to authorised individuals or organisations like the maintenance staff of airlines that fly Boeing aircraft, and would not be accessible to the casual net 'surfer'.

ii. e-Procurement

e-Procurement is the procurement and tendering of goods and services using electronic means. Many airlines now do business with their suppliers electronically. For example, a company in the USA, *FreeMarkets*, has recently signed a contract with the *Oneworld* airline alliance of 31 airlines. The company, which has been working with airlines and other aviation related industries since 1998, believes that it has saved an estimated $2.7 billion for its customers (www.ebizchronicle.com).

iii. Joint marketing

The Internet allows tourism principals, such as airlines, to jointly market their products, thereby avoiding other travel intermediaries. The Orbitz site, which was established by five US airlines, (www.orbitz.com), promotes itself as offering 'access to the most low airfares on the Internet, plus great values on rental cars, hotel rooms, and more. In addition, Orbitz brings you the latest in fare-finding technology, so you can be sure that you're getting the most complete list of available airfares.' This is just one example of how airlines are moving into areas that were once the preserve of the travel agent. Furthermore, some of the new start-up companies are now collaborating with older, more traditional companies in their marketing strategy. For example, in 2001, *Lastminute* and *Thomas Cook* established an arrangement whereby Thomas Cook would be the preferred supplier of airline tickets (*Financial Times* 2001).

Marketing and eBusiness

The most immediate effect of the growth of the Internet in the tourism sector has been its use in marketing. Many early web sites acted as promotional tools for tourism enterprises, whether they were large tour operations companies or small rural hotels. To use the Internet for marketing is relatively simple, inexpensive and extremely cost effective. A bed and breakfast business can, for example, design its own web page, arrange with an Internet Service Provider to put it online and, after registering it with a few search engines, wait for the customers to make enquiries. Many of these sites still exist but, as Internet technologies and software applications have developed, larger tourism businesses have been looking for more than just a means to promote their products and interactivity, multimedia presentations and page customisation have become commonplace (www.thomascook.co.uk).

Interactivity – getting the customer close to you

Before the advent of the Internet, consumers were largely passive recipients of promotional information provided to them by the tourism industry. The Internet, in contrast, allows customers to interact with the medium, actively seeking out the information they desire. This also means that the companies providing this information can react to this activity by identifying what the consumers' interests and needs are. More tailored information can then be sent back to the surfer and the cycle of information exchange is repeated. A simple example of how a web server can interact with a surfer is at '*Ask Jeeves*', a search engine (www.ask.co.uk). If an enquiry is made about a specific country or destination, the results page will include advertisements for that country. It is likely that regular surfers will revisit the same sites, thereby allowing the companies to further refine their knowledge of the customer. This has several implications has far as interactivity is concerned:

- Sites must be available constantly as, nowadays, customers may want to buy products at any time of the day or, indeed, night. This has implications for staffing and servicing – especially if a site is complemented by the human touch through help lines and so on.

- Sites must be easily 'navigable' so that interactivity can be made as straightforward as possible. This means that web site design and site 'stickiness' becomes critical.

- Companies need to try to enter into closer relationships with customers once they can identify who they are. This entail, for example, encouraging customers to give more information about themselves through the completion of forms or the 'personalisation' of their own version of the company's web site.

- Customers can now search for tourism services much more quickly and efficiently on the Internet. This means that comparisons can easily be made between companies and the competition between them is intensified.

Market Research – getting closer to the customer

Interactivity is one way in which tourism companies can obtain information about their customers but other eBusiness technologies can also provide sophisticated tools for carrying out market research. When surfers browse web sites, information can be obtained regarding their interests and activities either overtly or surreptitiously. This information can then be stored, retrieved and analysed, although any eBusiness operation that does this is still subject to the Data Protection Act, 1998.

Some techniques that are commonly used to gather information on customers are given below:

- Electronic order forms
- Electronic registration

- 'Cookies'

i. Order forms

An obvious and open way of acquiring information is for companies to ask surfers to provide them with information. If a customer is looking to book a holiday they will have to provide information about himself or herself to the operator in question. This is normally done by completing a form online. The form itself can ask questions that are not directly related to the ordering of the holiday and the customer can, if he so wishes, provide this additional information. The details on the form can then be processed to complete any order that has been made by the customer. However, the information, because it is provided electronically, can be analysed and stored for further market research.

ii. Registration

Sometimes, web sites encourage surfers to register themselves with the web site and this, again, helps firms obtain useful information regarding their wants and needs. Once registered, users will be offered additional benefits over and above those offered to casual surfers. For example, page customisation might be available where customers can adjust the 'look'n'feel' of the page to suit their own tastes, or regular emails will be sent to those registered regarding special offers.

iii. Cookies

A less transparent way of obtaining information on surfers is to send a 'cookie' to the surfer's computer after they have loaded a web page. A cookie is a small file that is stored on the users computer by the company's web site. It will contain information regarding the consumer's activity on the web. This may be information about what the customer has ordered on the Internet in the past, or about which advertisements have attracted his attention. When the customer revisits the web site in question, the cookie is accessed so that the customer, and his web activity, can be identified. The web page can then be 'personalised' for that customer.

In some cases, the management of cookies can be highly sophisticated. For example, information can be contained in the cookie regarding the frequency or likelihood that a customer may place an order. This means that, when a regular customer returns he, or rather his surfing activity, is directed to much faster computer servers so his order can be processed more quickly. Casual browsers, identified by their cookies, are directed to slower servers.

Cookies and similar software are giving rise to some concern about privacy on the Internet and many surfers object to the idea of outsiders placing files, however small, on their computers. Some browsers now allow surfers to choose whether to accept cookies before they are downloaded (www.opera.com); however, if cookies are refused in this way, it may mean that the customer is unable to access the site.

The new capability to gather large quantities of information about customers using customer interaction, and the processing of it using electronic databases, means that companies can develop both the ability and the flexibility to be able to offer customised products to individual customers – one-to-one marketing.

Promotion – getting the message to the customer

Early web sites concentrated almost entirely on promotion. They were effectively little electronic posters or brochures – 'brochureware' (Chen 2001). One major advantage over physical promotional tools like brochures, is that tourism suppliers are able to rapidly update their information regarding prices, timetables and product attributes etc. online. Some consequences of how promotion has been affected and developed by the Internet are given below.

Web page design

As with all promotional devices, design is critical. Too many pages look cluttered and confusing and this detracts from the promotional effect. Clean design with a logical navigation system is critical if a page is to be effective as a promotional tool.

Corporate identity and branding can also be reinforced using the web page. As noted above, existing travel and tourism companies are already present in cyberspace. Their web sites will have been designed so that their corporate identities are highly visible and integrated into their overall real world brand image.

Advertising

Soon after the emergence of the Internet as a marketing tool, 'banner' advertising developed whereby tourism companies could buy space on more generic Internet portals (http://uk.dir.yahoo.com/Recreation/Travel/). Banner advertising consists of a small advertisement or *banner*, usually placed at the top of a web page, where a firm can promote its products. If a customer clicks on the banner, he gets taken to the site advertised. It is thought, however, that the 'click through rate' for banner advertisements is only about 0.5 percent. Another form of advertising is 'interstitial' advertising, where a small additional window opens when a web page is accessed. However, a reading of the popular computer press indicates that these forms of advertising are extremely irritating and software now exists to prevent them loading on to a web page, thereby defeating the purpose of the practice. Any company thinking of using this form of advertising needs to think carefully about whether more people may be put off the product than be attracted to it.

The Internet also encourages 'affiliate' advertising. This is where a firm with a complimentary product places small advertisements on another company's web sites. A car hire company might buy some space on a tour operator's site, for example, or an airline might use a hotel site to promote itself (http://berlin.hyatt.com/bergh/).

Finally, technology is now becoming so sophisticated that 'geo-location software' has been developed that enables companies to identify where a particular surfer lives. This means that advertisements and other promotions can be targeted at people's browsers based on their location, and of course, location can be an indicator of age, lifestyle and class. This targeting can be further refined depending on the time of day or day of the week. For example, an airline could promote discounted tickets for weekend travel to potential customers within a defined radius of a particular airport. The advertisement would only appear on those customers' screens – it would not appear on screens outside the designated zone even if those surfers were looking at the same web page (Hunt 2001).

Email

Email can also be used to promote goods and services on the Internet. Unsolicited emails, however, are viewed with suspicion by many surfers. Therefore, companies that want to use email as a promotional tool will ask site visitors to register their interest with a particular site, thereby inviting emails about special offers, late availability, or new products (www.klm.com and www.britishairways.com). Email can also be customised to reflect a particular company's corporate identity; however, this does not seem to have caught on and most emails still appear to surfers as plain text (Halpern 2000). This may be because some email programmes have difficulty handing such content.

Text messaging

Text Messaging (SMS) is now increasingly being used as a promotional technique. It is especially useful when used tactically. In the summer of 2000, a company called *Worldpop* (www.worldpop.com) began promoting clubs, and other products, in Ibiza using text messaging. Clubbers needed to register to receive the SMS service and about 800 did so. The SMS system was also used to control capacity at certain clubs, advising clubbers where the longest queues were. This kind of promotional strategy is likely to grow in the future as it offers firms the ability to target carefully selected audiences with specific information while at the same allowing them to measure the response. *'Mobiles offer marketers the ultimate direct, personalised, time- and location-sensitive method of advertising'* (Day 2001).

Market Development – getting more customers

As the Internet makes international markets more accessible, it allows organisations in the tourism sector to attract customers and visitors from far and wide. A country house hotel or a National Park can use the Internet in this way; for example, both the Langley Castle Hotel in Northumberland (www.langleycastle.com) and the Dartmoor National Park (www.dartmoor-npa.gov.uk) have web sites that can now be used to market both organisations around the world.

The Internet has enabled companies reach parts of the market that might once have been difficult and expensive to attract. For example, a specialist firm that offered walking holidays would, in the past, have probably concentrated on reaching its target market through specialist magazines and the weekend leisure supplements in newspapers. By going online, the company has the ability to reach a much wider market – especially if it makes sure it has registered with several search engines. (www.nzwalkingcompany.com). 'If you run a small travel agency or tour operation, it is very important to realise that it pays to specialise on the Web. Specialist operators and agents will not only be sought out by travellers for their specific expertise, but there is actually less competition' (Travel Trade Gazette 2001a).

The Internet has also allowed new business models to develop. One of these is the online auction. Instead of an auctioneer gathering together a lot of potential customers in one physical space, an online auctioneer gathers them together in cyberspace. Surfers can log on to dedicated web sites and make offers for the products that are for sale. The web based travel site *Priceline* (www.priceline.com) offers customers the chance to bid for air tickets online. Other generic sites like *eBay* (www.eBay.com) also offer this facility for all kinds of tourism products.

Product characteristics and distribution

The characteristics of a particular product are crucial when considering whether that product can be sold and distributed over the Internet. 'Digitised' products, like software, or 'digitisable' products, such as music, can easily be delivered through computer networks to customers' computers. Small products, such as books or CDs, can be transported via conventional delivery systems like the post or courier services. In both these cases, distance is not a particular issue. However, with some services it might be. For example, if a plumber used the Internet to advertise and promote his services he could still only operate within the geographical area in which he did before. A plumber in London, however stylish and sophisticated his web page, could not really offer to carry out repairs in Los Angeles. So how does this affect tourism products?

Tourism products are intangible yet they do have certain tangible aspects – an air ticket is tangible, the flight itself is intangible. This means that an air ticket can be ordered over the Internet and can be delivered to the customer by post, courier or at the departure airport itself. Interestingly, the function that the air ticket performs, that is, to show a check-in clerk that a customer has paid for a trip to a particular destination, can be now be digitised. If the customer is sent a code by a computer instead of a paper ticket, that code can perform the same function of an ordinary ticket. The budget airline EasyJet uses this system (http://easyjet.com/en/info/howToBook.html). This model extends to other to other tourism products like hotel accommodation or theatre bookings.

Digitising the tangible aspects of the tourism product, like a ticket or a hotel reservation, means that tourism companies will need build in added reassurance for customers who may not feel that they have bought anything because they do not have any physical evidence to prove that they have done so. Therefore, email, containing a unique reference number, is usually used to confirm that a purchase has been made.

Furthermore, the more complicated a product, the more difficult it might be to sell over the Internet. An air ticket, virtual or otherwise, is far simpler to sell through the Internet than a package holiday. A package holiday contains far more variables than a simple ticket – variables such as full-board or half-board, length of stay, type of hotel, transport from the airport, day trips, insurance, child prices, food, etc. Therefore, the customer may want the reassurance of a human salesperson with whom to discuss such things, as well as tangible objects like glossy brochures, complicated forms and baggage tags (Wall Street Journal 2001).

Market segmentation

The fact that the product can be digitised and distributed electronically may have implications for segmentation in tourism marketing. Tourism consumers, as in all markets, can be segmented along certain lines based on behaviour, culture and needs. Those who currently use the Internet tend to be from the more affluent and better-educated groups and they may have less fear about making eBusiness transactions. This means that companies that traditionally target this kind of customer are able to make more of the Internet than others. Youth market segments are also prime targets for tourism eBusiness whereas the grey market might be less so (www.gite.com).

eBusiness and Staffing

Tourism businesses wanting to become ebusinesses will need to think about having to recruit new people to handle this new way of doing things. Most of these staff are likely to come from the information technology sector but some may need to bring with them new skills in relation to marketing and operations. Firms can, of course opt to retrain existing staff but, given the technological nature of eBusiness, this may sometimes be difficult. An alternative, especially for a large operation, is to engage the services of specialist companies who can set up the appropriate web structures to do business online. In 1995, Japan Airlines contracted IBM to explore 'the opportunity to launch e-commerce services via the Web' (www-3.ibm.com).

eBusiness technologies also allow for more home working and distance working as working with the Internet means that workers do not have to occupy one building in a particular location. Furthermore, eBusiness is not constrained by the traditional working day and the workforce will need to be managed so that 24-hour cover is given. This also means that opportunities for part-timers may increase – maybe at the expense of full-time workers.

Restructuring and redundancy

The development of an eBusiness may have the effect of 'flattening' the management structure. For example, if a travel agency company wanted to move out of the high street and sell its products on the Internet, it would want to close its high street shops down. This would lead to redundancies, unless those staff could be easily relocated and retrained. It would also be likely that the network of shops would be replaced by a single operation in a large office with smaller number of workers. There would be less need for these workers to interact with customers as most of the business, formally carried out face to face in the travel agencies, would take place electronically. These workers too would be managed by fewer managers. All the hierarchies that previously existed in the agencies would have disappeared, being replaced by a flatter, broader structure located in one place. Finally, it might even be more cost effective to have this new operation based abroad. So, in this scenario, the dynamics of eBusiness have removed a travel agency's presence in the high street, reduced its workforce, flattened its management structure and moved its operations overseas.

Public sector tourism

So far this chapter has dealt with eBusiness as applied to the private sector. However, the public sector can also benefit from eBusiness. Public sector tourism is involved in the promotion of tourism in geographic areas usually to promote economic development. For example, in former industrial areas, many local authorities are keen to promote tourism to replace jobs and economic activity lost with the decline of older industries (www.durham.gov.uk), whilst others may be concerned with managing tourists within certain geographic boundaries (www.cumbria.gov.uk).

As with the private sector, public sector tourism can use the Internet to market tourism. Destinations and attractions can be marketed on the Internet and local authorities and tourist boards draw together many of the tourism operators and attractions in a particular area, and promote them on a single web site under one local or regional umbrella (www.zurichtourism.ch). This allows small operators, like bed and breakfast operators, and museums, organisations and firms that are never awash with money, to benefit from the power of eBusiness without having to invest in the technology themselves (www.wooler.org.uk).

The public sector, however, can do more with Internet technologies than just promoting a particular area. The large number of small businesses that make up tourism can be brought together by public sector bodies via the Internet. Local authorities can easily communicate with these businesses using the Internet. Tourism policy, marketing plans, and other issues involving tourism can also be disseminated through the Internet to all those involved in tourism in a particular locality.

Other public sector bodies can also use the Internet to enhance their services. National parks, for example, can use the Internet to communicate with potential visitors about weather conditions or special events. They can augment their education and interpretation services (www.nnpa.org.uk) and thcy can manage the park more effectively in terms of communications with remote field offices, inventory management, and so on by using the Internet.

Finally, public sector bodies can also use the Internet to disseminate information regarding tourism to those who have a professional interest like companies, researchers and academics (www.tourismtrade.org.uk).

Future developments

The eBusiness revolution started with access to the Internet via personal computers. While the personal computer will remain a key device for many tourists and tourism companies when engaging in eBusiness, new hardware is also being seen as crucial to the development of eTourism. Perhaps the most important of these will be the mobile phone but PDAs (Personal Digital Assistants) and other electronic devices, such as televisions, will also begin to play a role in eBusiness.

The personal computer allows surfers to browse at leisure looking for tourism products but the advantage with the mobile phone is that most of the time they are switched on. This means that those that can interact with the Internet are online all the time, and when they are on the move. This 'nomadicity' offers many opportunities for eBusiness, especially when it comes to engaging in short tactical communications with owners. 'Current uses of mobile devices take into account the limitations and focus on providing targeted information that frequently requires only short responses. Once the current limitations are overcome, increased sophistication of mobile applications is anticipated. Further application enhancements are expected in the areas of localisation, personalization, and instant connectivity.' (www.dmreview.com). Telephones also have a familiarity that computers do not, thereby avoiding the fear some people might have when using 'new technology'.

The two areas where mobile phones will prove critical are text messaging (SMS) and third generation mobile telephony services (3G).

i. SMS

SMS is proving to be a very attractive way for suppliers to maintain contact with customers. This comparatively simple technology has achieved the same level of market penetration in three years that took email twenty years. Already, many airlines offer a mobile call service regarding flight schedules and other information that connects directly to subscribers' phones (www.china-airlines.com/us/index.htm). Furthermore, there are now companies that provide a price comparison service on the Internet for consumer goods (www.pricerunner.com). These sites can be accessed via mobile phones to carry out instant price comparisons based on product search criteria. It seems inevitable that this kind of facility will soon exist for travel products. SMS is also now being developed to handle more sophisticated information like simple graphics and sound.

ii. 3G

In the late 1990s, I-mode and WAP (Wireless Application Protocol) phones were introduced. These were the first attempts at providing Internet access from a mobile phone. I-mode is however, confined to Japan and WAP to Europe. Although I-mode has proved popular, WAP has failed to take off in Europe, mainly because the technology is still an ineffective way of communicating with the Internet – it is slow and expensive and unable to handle much more than textual information. The real advance in Internet connectivity will come with 3G phones, which will be able to handle far more sophisticated information, including multi-media applications, at a much higher speed – expected to be 40 times faster than WAP.

In 2000, Swissair introduced a service for selected mobile phone users where the checking-in process could be done from a mobile phone using WAP technology. This kind of service is likely to increase with the advent of 3G services where, for example, travellers will be able to make and adjust booking arrangements for air trips and accommodation from their mobile phones. Payment for theses services will be charged on the basis of the service provided, or the quantity of bytes downloaded, rather than the time spent on the phone. Furthermore, with the development of 'agents' or 'bots' (http://botspot.com), tourists will one day be able to ask these software entities, via their computers or phones, to search for specific travel products online and report back with the results.

Related to these developments are biometric technologies, which might remove the need for passwords, boarding cards and even, one day, passports (http://webusers.anet-stl.com/~wrogers/biometrics/). The technology is based around certain unique physical attributes of the human body, such as the iris or the face. Some airlines have already begun to experiment with this when screening passengers boarding planes.

Conclusion

eBusiness in tourism has grown significantly in the past few years and looks to grow even faster in the years to come. This growth originated with simple web applications and has now developed to include mobile phone technologies. Research carried out by Energis indicates that travel and tourism is believed by industry experts to be the leading sector in eBusiness development in the future (Travel Trade Gazette 2001b). Moreover, Forrester Research (www.forrester.com), estimate that between '2001 and 2004 more than $212 billion of business and leisure travel services will be bought online in the US, Canada, and Europe.'

The Gartner Group (www.gartner.com) sees eBusiness as going through four phases (Leemakdej 2001). These are:

(i) The 'cyberspace placeholder' phase, where businesses used the Internet to advertise their products;

(ii) The Common Gateway Interface (CGI) phase, which saw the beginnings of interaction between surfer (customer) and server (supplier);

(iii) The transaction phase, by which time firms were creating 'virtual stores' and began to integrate their online presence with existing information systems; and

(iv) The transformation phase, whereby companies' web resources will connect with their suppliers information systems to improve supply chain management, while at the same time integrating the management of human resources, processes and production.

The nature and characteristics of each of the myriad of organisations that make up the tourism sector will determine how fast each one goes through these four 'phases' – some, like major airlines, are nearing phase four. It seems inevitable, however, that those companies that fail to understand the potential offered by eBusiness will struggle to survive – today eBusiness *is* business.

Discussion questions

1. Which particular characteristics of the Internet/eBusiness are likely to be of particular benefit to the tourism industry?

2. How serious is the threat of eBusiness to the travel agent?

3. What is the potential contribution of the Internet to the marketing of tourism products?

4. What are the implications of eBusiness for the future structure and operations of travel and tourism businesses and organisations?

Footnotes

1. "People that ... [bet this way] ... will pay either 3% tax - if they bet on the phone - or no tax at all, if they bet on the Internet. Those that walk into a high street shop to bet face a 9% tax." As a consequence the Treasury could lose an estimated £50 million a year through offshore betting. http://news.bbc.co.uk/hi/english/business/newsid_703000/703770.stm

2. The author tried to book a flight to Paris from Newcastle in 1999. There is a direct route from Newcastle to Paris. However, Expedia insisted that the only way to Paris was via Brussels.

Further reading

Alford, P. (2000), *E-Business in the Travel Industry*, London: Travel & Tourism Intelligence.

Chen, S. (2001), *The Strategic Management of e-Business*, Chichester: John Wiley & Sons.

Currie, W. (2000), *The Global Information Society*, Chichester: John Wiley & Sons.

Inkpen, G. (1998), *Information Technology in Travel and Tourism*, Harlow: Addison Wesley Longman.

Lawrence, E. et al. (2000), *Internet Commnerce*, Chichester: John Wiley & Sons.

Nokes, S. (2000), *startup.com*, Harlow: Pcarson.

Timmers, P. (1999), *Electronic Commerce*, Chichester: John Wiley & Sons.

References

BBC (2001), *Radio 4 News Report*, 6th October 2001.

Chen, S. (2001), *The Strategic Management of e-Business*, Chichester: John Wiley & Sons.

Day, J. (2001), Hard sell in your hand, *The Guardian*, March 19th 2001.

DMReview, *Mobile eBusiness* Magic White Paper, http://www.dmreview.com/portal.cfm?NavID=95&Topic=65&PortalID=196, 2001.

ebiz Chronicle (2001), http://www.ebizchronicle.com/news01/apr/apr12.htm, April 2001.

Financial Times (2001), *Lastminute signs deal with Thomas Cook as losses mount*, ft.com staff, February 12th 2001.

Halpern, L. (2000), You've got email: are you using it?, *The Guardian*, November 30th 2000.

Hunt, J. (2001), We know where you live, *The Guardian*, October 22nd 2001.

IBM (2001), *Japan Airlines: Building an e-business on IBM technology*, http://www-3.ibm.com/e-business/casestudy/44720.html, November 2001.

Leemakdej, A. (2001), The four e-phases: All elements of business being linked online, *Bangkok Post*, August 2001.

Nairn, G. (1998), Business benefits come first, *Financial Times*, March 4th 1998.

Rice, K. (2001), Companies force web travel, *Financial Times*, June 4th 2001.

Timmers, P. (1999), *Electronic Commerce*, Chichester: John Wiley & Sons.

Travel Trade Gazette (2001a), E-Commerce Articles: Will Online Travel Survive?, *Travel Trade Gazette*, September 24th 2001.

Travel Trade Gazette (2001b), E-Commerce Articles: Putting e-Travel in Context, *Travel Trade Gazette*, June 2001.

Waldmeir (2001), Treaty threatens e-commerce, *Financial Times*, May 30th 2001.

Wall Street Journal (2001), Cruise lines go online - to tout travel agencies, *US Abstracts*, August 23rd 2001.

20

Tourism and Society

Richard Sharpley

Learning objectives

This chapter explores the relationship between tourism and the societies that both generate and receive tourists. On completion of the chapter, the reader will:

- *appreciate the two-way nature of the tourism-society relationship*

- *understand the social influences on the demand for tourism*

- *recognise the influence of modern society on tourist behaviour*

- *understand the factors that influence the degree of social impact experienced in destinations*

- *appreciate the impacts of tourism on host societies.*

Introduction

Tourism is, essentially, a social phenomenon. It is about millions of individuals who, travelling nationally or internationally, temporarily leave their own society and visit and impact upon the societies in which other people live. It is about tourists who are motivated and influenced by their own social environment, who carry with them a set of socially patterned values and expectations, and who interact with people in other places and societies which, frequently, possess a completely different set of social structures and values. In other words, tourism is about people, tourists, visiting other societies and undergoing experiences that may influence their own or their hosts' attitudes, behaviour, expectations and, ultimately, lifestyles.

In short, a direct relationship exists between tourism and the societies that both generate and receive tourists. The purpose of this chapter is to explore the nature and characteristics of this relationship. It introduces a number of issues and concepts that are fundamental to the understanding of the ways in which societies influence, and are in turn influenced by, tourism, and it discusses the implications of the tourism-society relationship for the effective management and planning of tourism. First, however, it is necessary to determine the form of this relationship to provide a framework for the chapter.

Tourism and society: a two-way relationship

The relationship between tourism and society is manifested in two ways or, more specifically, in two directions (see Figure 20.1). Firstly and, perhaps, most visibly, the development of tourism inevitably results in both positive and negative consequences for destination societies. Indeed, the rapid growth of mass, international tourism since the 1960s has been mirrored by ever increasing concern about the impacts of that growth on local people in tourism destinations, concern that was reflected in early writing on the subject (see, for example, Young 1973; Turner and Ash 1975; de Kadt 1979). These issues are addressed in the latter part of this chapter.

Figure 20.1: *Tourism-society relationships*

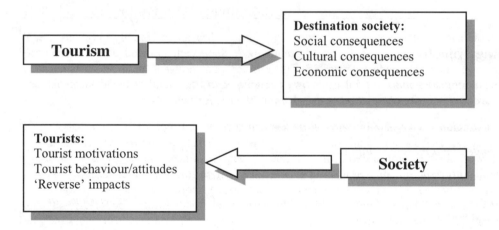

Secondly, tourism is itself influenced or impacted upon *by* society. As history shows (see Chapter 2), mass tourism has evolved as a result of transformations and developments in society; it is, in a sense, a social victory (Krippendorf 1986). More importantly, however, society has been, and continues to be, a powerful force in shaping the character of tourism. That is, as introduced in Chapter 4, a variety of social factors are instrumental in determining the motivation for and style of tourism, influencing how, when, where and why people participate in tourism. It is upon these factors that the first section of this chapter now focuses.

Social influences on tourism

Tourism is a social activity. That is, it is an activity which is undertaken by ever-increasing numbers of people, either individually or in groups and most typically for leisure or holiday purposes, and which normally involves inter-action with other people, whether fellow tourists or local people in tourist destinations. It is also, however, a form of consumption. In other words, people *buy* tourism; they buy, in effect, blocks of time which are filled with a variety of services and experiences provided, for the most part, by the tourism industry.

As with many other forms of consumption, there are a variety of reasons why people choose to buy tourism as opposed to other products or services in the first place and, having done so, why they choose particular styles of tourism. Thus, although tourism is seen by many as simply a means of escape or relaxation, (the term 'holiday' being synonymous, perhaps, with having a break or resting from work), there are, in fact, a variety of underlying social factors which influence why and in what form people participate in tourism. Indeed, it has been argued that 'explaining the consumption of tourist-services cannot be separated off from the social relations within which they are embedded' (Urry 1990a: 23). This suggests that, in order to understand the consumption of tourism and, for practical purposes, to be better able to explain and predict changes in the demand for tourism, it is important to consider those social factors which influence tourists' roles and behaviour. Here, we shall be primarily concerned with:

- extrinsic influences on tourist motivation

- tourism as a consequence of modern society

- tourism as an authentic experience

- post-modern tourism and travel in 'hyper-reality'

Extrinsic influences on tourist motivation

As shown in Chapter 4, the tourism demand process is triggered by motivation; it is person-specific motivation that translates people's needs and wants into goal-oriented behaviour and influences their tourism decision-making process. The motivational stage is, therefore, a key factor in understanding how and why people participate in tourism.

It was also noted that, just as there are many different forces and pressures that influence the motivation for tourism, there are many approaches to researching or explaining it. For the most part, however, there are two distinct perspectives on tourist motivation. Firstly, motivation is more traditionally considered in relation to the intrinsic personal or psychological needs of tourists themselves – that is, motivation is seen as a psychological concept. Secondly, there are undoubtedly a number of extrinsic, social determinants of tourist motivation. These are forces that emerge from tourists' social environment which influence or shape their needs and wants and, hence their consumption of tourism. It is these latter, extrinsic motivational factors which concern us here.

i. Tourist typologies and motivation

A number of authors have developed typologies, or categorisations, of tourist roles and behaviour as a basis for understanding the motivations of different types of tourists. Some concentrate on the intrinsic, psychographic characteristics of tourists, such as the psychocentric-allocentric continuum devised by Plog in the 1970s and referred to in many tourism texts. However, Erik Cohen developed two typologies which relate tourist behaviour to their home social environment and which are therefore of relevance here.

Both of Cohen's typologies are based on the notion of a familiarity-strangerhood continuum. He suggested that different tourists are more or less able to withstand the 'culture-shock' of travelling abroad and that, as a result, they are motivated to seek out forms of tourism that offer either novelty (i.e. the strange or new) or the familiarity of home. In other words, he proposed that tourists travel within an 'environmental bubble' which, depending where they are positioned on the line between familiarity and strangerhood, they are more or less able to break out of whilst on holiday. Thus, in his first typology (Cohen 1972), he described four types of tourist:

- **The organised mass tourist:** travels on an organised package tour, stays in hotels which recreate the home environment, remains largely within the hotel complex unless on organised trips and avoids all contact with local people or culture.

- **The individual mass tourist:** similar to the organised mass tourist in that the holiday is organised and packaged, but occasionally ventures out to seek novelty by, for example, hiring a car to visit local attractions or facilities. Thus, unlike the organised mass tourist, the individual occasionally escapes from the environmental bubble.

- **The explorer**: unlike the organised or individual mass tourist, the explorer is a 'traveller' rather than a 'tourist', makes his/her own travel arrangements, avoids the 'tourist trail' and seeks out local culture. However, escape from the bubble is not total; reminders of home (a newspaper, familiar food) are needed, as is contact with fellow travellers.

- **The drifter:** at the opposite end of the familiarity-strangerhood continuum to the organised mass tourist, the drifter has no fixed itinerary, attempts to merge into local communities and customs and avoids all contact with tourists or the tourism system. The desire for novelty is greatest and escape from the environmental bubble is almost complete.

Although this typology represents a useful basis for predicting tourists' behaviour based upon their relationship with their home society, it is largely descriptive rather than analytical. That is, although it suggests *how* different people will behave as tourists, it does not explain *why*. As a result, Cohen proposed a second typology (Cohen 1979), still using the notion of the familiarity-strangerhood continuum but also introducing the idea that tourists' desired experiences will be very much dependent their experience of their home environment. That is, he argued that some people feel entirely familiar and happy with their home society; they feel they belong where they live/work and that what Cohen describes as their 'spiritual centre' is firmly rooted at home. They therefore have no need to seek reality or meaning elsewhere and their desired tourism experiences will reflect this. At the other extreme, however, are those who have no sense of belonging or no sense of place in their home environment. They feel like a stranger, or alienated, at home; their spiritual centre lies elsewhere and, as a result, they are motivated to seek out places, cultures or experiences that provide them with that sense of place or belonging which is lacking at home.

Cohen developed this concept into a five-fold typology:

- **Recreational tourist:** has no desire or need for novel experiences and, therefore, seeks out recreational, play forms of tourism.

- **Diversionary tourist**: does not feel alienated yet nevertheless seeks some diversion or change from the home environment.

- **Experiential tourist**: neither identifies with nor rejects the home environment and, therefore, is motivated to seek novelty or strangerhood as a tourist but inevitably returns home.

- **Experimental tourist:** feels very much alienated and therefore seeks reality and meaning elsewhere. However, some link with the home environment remains.

- **Existential tourist:** the opposite to the recreational tourist, the existential tourist feels no sense of belonging at home and travels to find reality, meaning and a sense of place elsewhere.

Figure 20.2: *Cohen's 'phenomenology' of tourist experiences*

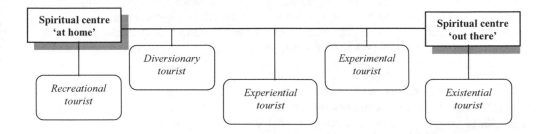

There are a number of weaknesses inherent in these and, indeed, in most typologies (see Lowyck *et al.* 1992; Sharpley 1999). In particular, they over-generalise tourist motivations; they are static, in as much as they do not allow for variable behaviour over time; they overlook many other factors that influence tourists' motivations; and, they tend to subordinate the ability of individuals to make their own decisions to the influence of their relationship with their home society. Nevertheless, they do provide a foundation for understanding that tourist motivation is influenced, in general, by the relationship of individuals with their home society and, in particular, by specific features or social factors that frame that relationship.

For many people, one of the most important or influential extrinsic factors that motivates them to participate in tourism is work. Indeed, tourism can be seen as the antithesis to work, the chance to escape, unwind and relax. However, as we shall now discuss, the relationship between work and tourism may be more complex than is at first apparent.

ii. Work and tourist motivation

Tourism and work are inter-related in as much as work provides both the means (income) and the motivation for tourism. At the same time, tourism, as a form of recreation, enables people to return to work refreshed and, literally, 're-created'. However, the relationship between work and tourism is not so straightforward as this. Different types of work are more or less stressful, challenging, stimulating or physically tiring, whilst work itself means different things to different people. To some, it may be simply a means to an end, a way of earning a living; to others it may be a way of life. In other words, different types of work, different work environments and people's differing approaches to work all combine to result in an enormous variety of personal needs and, hence, tourist motivations. As has been argued elsewhere, 'the experience of work in industrial societies...forms the context for the experience of leisure' (Clarke and Critcher 1985: 17).

Of course, work is not the only extrinsic motivating factor and nor does it apply to a number social groups. Nevertheless, there are three ways in which work and tourist motivation are related:

(a) Work and tourism in opposition

Alternatively described as the compensatory model, this proposes that the experiences of work and tourism are in opposition to each other. That is, the individual is motivated to seek out forms of tourism that that offer a distinct change of experience, or even lifestyle, from that found at work. Tourism thus compensates for what is lacking at work. In theory, this relationship should operate in both directions: those in monotonous, repetitive, unchallenging jobs might be expected to seek out holidays that offer excitement and that are stimulating whilst, alternatively, those who have stressful, challenging jobs might be motivated to have quieter, restful holidays where they can 'switch off'.

Interestingly, however, this model has been found to be most applicable to those in lower status jobs, where tourism compensates for deficiencies at work and, by implication, at home. Thus, people are motivated to save up for a holiday where they can indulge in a lifestyle that can normally only be dreamed of. By escaping to a fantasy life of staying in hotels and enjoying standards of service that are in direct contrast to normal, day-to-day life, tourists experience an inversion of reality; they become, as one commentator described, king or queen for a day (Gottlieb 1982).

The opposition/compensatory model can also be used to explain the motivation to escape the constraints imposed by work and, indeed, from social constraints in general. People at work are normally restricted by time commitments and codes of dress and behaviour, as well as by socially imposed values. Conversely, tourism offers the opportunity to indulge in 'ludic' behaviour, behaviour that represents play or freedom from the rules and regulations of work and home society. Such behaviour may be described as simply 'letting your hair down' and not only compensates for the rigid, social structure of normal life but also prepares tourists to re-enter that structured, everyday existence.

(b) Tourism as an extension of work

In comparison to the opposition/compensation model described above, the extension theory suggests that there is little or no distinction between work and tourism. In other words, tourism complements, rather than contrasts with, work. Thus, those who are employed in challenging, stimulating jobs and who enjoy a position of responsibility are more likely to choose independent and similarly stimulating types of holiday, whereas people in regulated, routine and passive jobs will be motivated to participate in equally passive, less stimulating forms of tourism. They will choose the mass produced package holiday which, in effect, mirrors the production-line environment of the workplace. The extreme case, of course, would be where there is no distinction at all between work and tourism, where work is carried over into tourism, such as a history teacher touring historical sites.

The implication of this approach is that, as general work practices change, so too will the demand for tourism. Thus, as societies transform into post-industrial, service based economies, changes in work practices may well have an impact on tourist motivation.

(c) Neutrality between tourism and work

Unlike the previous two models, where there exists a causal relationship between the nature of work and tourist motivation, the third model proposes that work has little or no effect on the patterns of tourism demand. In other words, there is no link between the two; work becomes, in the context of tourism, simply a means to an end, a source of income to pay for tourism. This suggests that other factors will be more influential than work in determining tourist motivation, although it is probably true to say that, for the majority of tourists, work remains the dominant extrinsic motivating factor.

iii. Social determinants of tourist motivation

Even where work and the work environment represent powerful influences on tourist motivation, a number of other extrinsic pressures may be significant determinants of tourist motivation and behaviour. Such pressures emanate from four main sources (see Moutinho 1987 for more detail):

- **Family influences:** For many people, one of the most significant influences on their attitudes and behaviour is their family. It is the family, particularly parents, that initially provide the values and behavioural codes that frame people's social existence and, frequently, continue to do so throughout their lives. In other words, many aspects of people's behaviour, including their consumption of tourism, may be subject to the influence of their family. The VFR (Visiting Friends and Relatives) market is, of course, motivated by the desire to visit relatives or, more specifically perhaps, the need for love and affection. However, other types of tourist behaviour, such as visiting particular destinations or going on camping holidays, might be influenced by childhood experiences or family tradition.

- **Reference groups:** Just as the family is the initial source of social values and attitudes, so too may reference groups determine people's behaviour. A reference group is any group that an individual turns to as a point of reference for beliefs and attitudes, a group against which the individual can judge his or her own beliefs and behaviour. Reference groups may take various forms, such as ethnic groups, work colleagues or other social associations, such as environmental pressure groups, and they are either normative (influencing general values) or comparative (influencing specific values). They may also be a powerful influence on tourist motivation, as in, for example, people being motivated to go on environmentally friendly, eco-tourism holidays as a result of reference to conservation organisations.

- **Social class:** Members of particular social classes tend to have similar lifestyles and values and it is likely that they will follow similar standards of behaviour. Therefore, although some would argue that traditional social class divisions are less evident or meaningful in today's post-industrial society, social class is, nevertheless, an important motivational factor. For example, different destinations may be categorised by the social class of the majority of visitors and it has been argued that, whilst the working classes traditionally prefer mass, collective forms of tourism, the middle classes seek out more solitary, individualistic or 'romantic' forms of tourism (Walter 1982).

- **Culture:** The culture of a society, its values, morals, behavioural codes as well as its more tangible identifying characteristics, such as language, dress and art forms, may be a strong influence on tourist motivation and consumption. In some cultures, tourism may be more deeply rooted or have greater significance than in others, whilst other factors, such as destination choice or types of tourism, may be culturally determined. For example, the importance of pilgrimage in Islamic culture is a powerful religious tourism motivator.

- **Social values:** As a specific category of cultural motivator, various social values may be an important determinant of tourist motivation. For example, the term 'mass tourism' has increasingly been used in a derogatory sense to describe particular forms of tourism and particular destinations. That is, mass tourism, the 'degenerate offspring' (Crick 1989) of early travel, has come to be viewed as a potentially destructive force and 'mass tourist' is, in effect, a socially defined label attached to particular types of tourist. This negative connotation of mass tourism/tourists has evolved into a social value and, although large numbers of people evidently still enjoy being mass tourists, many may be motivated to seek out forms of tourism that are more exclusive or 'better'; in a similar vein, the so-called 'good tourist' (Wood and House 1991) has evolved as a result of alleged widespread environmental concern, itself an emerging social value (but, see Chapter 4).

Tourism as a consequence of modern society

So far, we have been looking at specific extrinsic factors, or particular social forces and pressures, that influence tourist motivation. In other words, we have been concerned with specific factors *within* society that motivate tourists. It is also important, however, to appreciate how overall changes in the character of society as a whole have had an impact on tourist motivation and behaviour.

It is paradoxical that, whilst modern, industrial society has provided the means of mass tourism in the form of fast, safe and economical transport systems, higher living standards, socially sanctioned leisure time (i.e. holidays with pay, bank holidays, etc.) and the tourism industry, it has also created the need for tourism. That is, modern society not only provides the opportunity for mass participation in tourism, it also motivates people to do so. For many tourists, the annual holiday represents the chance to rest, to recover from the stresses and strains of modern life. It has become an essential ingredient in people's lifecycles; in order to survive in modern society, people must, periodically, escape from it. In a sense, therefore, society itself represents the ultimate motivation for tourism.

What, then, are the characteristics of modern society that have created this need amongst large sections of the population to escape? The answer lies in the factors that have led to a sense of alienation, a feeling of not belonging, of not having a sense of meaning or purpose in life. These factors are the work practices, activities, technological advances, expectations and social values that together constitute the modern way of life, and which create a sense of alienation in a number of ways:

- **alienation at work:** modern work practices, such as the division of labour, automation and the centralisation of various functions, have separated people from the product of their labour. They are simply cogs in the system.

- **alienation from community:** greater mobility and technical advances in communication, most recently mobile phones and computer-based communication systems, have reduced the sense of community. People are more independent, live further from work or family and friends, and no longer need to communicate face-to-face.

- **alienation from nature:** urban living separates people from nature and the natural world.

In a sense, people have also become alienated from themselves. Modern society provides products to make every task easier and faster, yet technological advance diminishes human contact and reduces the need for social interaction. In a society dominated by economic growth, people's expectations and values are guided by materialism and the need for acquisition. As life gets faster, people have less time and the realities of modern life are, for many, a source of stress, disenchantment and dissatisfaction. In short, people lack a sense of meaning in modern society, they have lost their self-identity.

Of course, not all people suffer from this sense of alienation and not to the same degree. Indeed, many people undoubtedly live happy and fulfilled lives in modern society. Nevertheless, the inherent alienating characteristics of society are considered by many to be a major extrinsic tourism motivating factor (see Dann 1977; Krippendorf 1986; MacCannell 1989) and, whether to simply unwind on a beach or to search for meaning and a sense of place elsewhere, millions of people each year are motivated by their society to escape, albeit temporarily, from it.

Tourism as an authentic experience

One implication of the alienating characteristics of modern society discussed in the previous section is that not only are people motivated to escape temporarily from society, but also to seek out meaning and reality, or what is frequently termed 'authenticity', elsewhere. In other words, tourists are motivated by the desire for authentic experiences that compensate for the deficiencies of modern life.

The extent to which tourists do in fact seek reality or authenticity has long been debated in the literature. On the one hand, it has been suggested that all tourists are satisfied with inauthentic, staged, 'pseudo-events' and experiences and, like Cohen's organised mass tourists discussed earlier, have no need or desire to experience the reality/authenticity of destination societies and cultures (see Boorstin 1964). On the other hand, it has been argued that all tourists do in fact seek authenticity, that tourists are, in effect, modern day pilgrims seeking a sense of meaning and purpose in life through their touristic experiences (MacCannell 1989).

In practice, most people fall between these two extremes. That is, there is no doubt that many people have no need or desire to immerse themselves in the authentic culture of destinations. For them, both modern society and the mass package tourism that reflects that modernity satisfy them completely. However, there is also no doubt that many more do seek out some form of authentic experience whilst on holiday, though not to the extent suggested by MacCannell. This then begs the question, what is an authentic tourism experience?

Strictly speaking, the term authentic means genuine or real. Therefore, an artefact in a museum, or a painting in a gallery, may be described as authentic (as opposed to fake) if it is known or recognised to as being the genuine article. In the context of tourism, however, the meaning of 'authenticity' is rather more ambiguous and it is used in two particular ways:

- **authentic destinations:** authenticity is often used to describe the works of art, cuisine, dress, language, festivals and other rituals or other cultural characteristics of a destination. As long as something is produced or enacted according to local custom or tradition, then it is deemed authentic.

- **authentic travel**: authenticity is also used to describe (and sell) specific types of travel. These are usually specialist, niche forms of tourism, often involving overland travel, and are described as authentic to distinguish them from mass market, packaged holidays or travel experiences.

In both cases, however, authenticity also connotes tradition and pre-modernity. In other words, authentic tourist destinations are perceived to be those which have not yet become, in comparison to western, industrialised societies, modern. Hence, authentic destinations are perceived to be those which are, primarily, in the less developed regions of the world. Similarly, authentic travel reflects the styles and forms of transport or travel that pre-date the modern, mass package tour, such as travelling on the Orient Express to Venice. Thus, the desire for authentic experiences is the desire to experience the pre-modern, or the past. Thus, tourism becomes, in a sense, a form of time travel.

The extent to which tourists desire, or are able, to have authentic experiences is open to debate. For example, MacCannell (1989) argues that all tourist experiences are, to a lesser or greater extent, staged and that the authentic can never be experienced. Others, conversely, suggest that the notion of authenticity is an individual experience. That is, individual tourists, based upon their personal motivations, perceptions and experience, make their own sense of each tourism setting or occurrence. The important point here, however, is that the tourism industry has recognised and is responding to widespread demands for authentic tourism experiences, as evidenced by:

- the use of authenticity as a marketing tool, where destinations or types of travel are promoted and advertised in a way that matches the perceptions of potential tourists (though not necessarily reflecting the reality of the destination), and

- the development of attractions, facilities, rituals or events that possess the aura of authenticity.

It is, therefore, paradoxical that, although tourism is primarily promoted as a means of social and economic modernisation and development, many tourist destinations will only remain attractive to tourists 'so long as they remain undeveloped and, hence, in some way primitive' (Silver 1993: 310). Implicitly, tourism will then increasingly become a system of illusions or what, as we shall now see, has been described as travels in 'hyper-reality' (Eco 1995).

Post-modern tourism and travel in 'hyper-reality'

So far in this chapter we have been looking at the ways in which modern society can influence or shape the demand for tourism. In particular, we have been considering both the overall characteristics of modern society and a variety of specific social factors which, in one way or another, contribute to the explanation of why and how people participate in tourism.

However, one other variable in the relationship between tourism and society has been overlooked, namely, changes in modern society itself. In other words, whilst there can be little doubt that many tourists are motivated by the desire to escape *from* modern society and that their behaviour may be conditioned to some extent by their relationship *with* society, it has been assumed that 'modern society' is a constant, fixed factor. Certainly, a number of characteristics that have been discussed here are typical to most modern societies. However, it is important to recognise that the nature of society results from a combination of economic, political, social and cultural processes which together create the framework for social life. These processes are constantly adapting and changing and so the nature, or 'condition', of modern society is also in a constant state of change. Indeed, it has been suggested by some that, as many modern societies become post-industrial, with their economies becoming increasingly dependent on the tertiary, service sector, they are transforming into culturally 'postmodern' societies (see Harvey 1990; Urry1990b).

It is difficult to grasp the notion that society or, more specifically, the social and cultural character of life in modern society, is undergoing an identifiable process of transformation from one condition (modern) to another (postmodern). Indeed, the entire concept of postmodernism is a controversial topic. Nevertheless, many social, cultural and economic forms in modern societies are undoubtedly undergoing change and, whether or not they are inter-related and represent an all-embracing cultural transformation into what may described as postmodernism, they potentially influence the demand for tourism.

An in-depth analysis of postmodernism is, of course, beyond the scope of this chapter. Briefly, however, it is seen as representing the end of the ordered, structured and defined state of (socially) modern society where strict distinctions were evident in most structures and institutions. In other words, the modernisation and industrialisation of societies resulted in most spheres of social life, including work, leisure, social class, gender roles, high and low, or popular culture, and even the past and the present, being strictly demarcated. More recently, however, there has been an evident breaking down, or de-differentiation, of many of these social structures. For example, boundaries between social class have become less distinct, societies are becoming multi-ethnic, the past, rejected by modernists in favour of scientific progress, has merged into the present as concern grows for conserving or recreating history, and there has been a fusion of popular, mass culture with high culture, such as the use of classical music to promote sporting events. In particular, it is claimed that there is a diminishing distinction between reality and representations of reality and, in the extreme, image may actually replace reality, such as in the case of computer games. Thus, postmodernism can be characterised by:

- a plurality of viewpoints and ideas;

- the fusion of distinct areas of social and cultural activity;

- lifestyles increasingly dominated by spectacle, image and visual media;

- the merging of the past into the present; and

- the breaking down of traditional social structures.

There are a number of ways in which this de-differentiation of postmodern society influences or shapes tourism. For example, the popularity of historical sites and events as tourists attractions, conveniently packaged by the so-called 'heritage industry', is evidence of the merging of the past into the present, whilst the growth of urban or industrial city tourism or the fusion of shopping and tourism activities within the context of shopping malls demonstrates how both the time and the place where people participate in tourism is less distinct.

However, the influence of postmodern culture on tourism is arguably most evident in the development and popularity of sites or attractions that are representations or images of reality and which present the tourist with 'hyper-reality'. For example, many historical attractions represent the past through a variety of interpretative techniques which artificially recreate the past as a modern spectacle, so that 'fantasy is potentially as real as history' (Walsh 1992: 113). Similarly, genuine historical artefacts are frequently placed in recreated settings, which may be a room set or an entire village, complete with the appropriate sounds and smells, in order to 'bring to life' what might be otherwise mundane or uninteresting articles. In both cases, the artificial creation is often devoid of any true analysis of the past.

The development of themed restaurants or dining areas, often within shopping malls, is a further example of postmodern tourist facilities which attempt to recreate the 'reality' of, say, dining out in Greece or Italy whilst. Similarly, inland resorts or holiday villages which are based around themed tropical swimming centres are quintessential postmodern tourist sites, being simulated environments superimposed on reality. More generally, many tourist sites and attractions have become famous as symbols or signs of a particular place or culture rather than in their own right. In other words, postmodern tourists are motivated to seek out images or representations of cultures or countries rather than to understand the true meaning of such sites. Thus, tourists visit the Taj Mahal as a sign of 'Indian-ness' or the Eiffel Tower as a sign of 'French-ness'.

In the extreme, images and recreations may be copies or simulations for which no original exists. One example of this is the successful promotion of Santa Claus as a tourist attraction in Lapland (Pretes 1995), whilst many tourists are drawn to the Peter Rabbit exhibition in the English Lake District, an attraction based entirely on the children's stories of Beatrix Potter, who lived in the region. Indeed, it was once proposed that the Lake District be promoted as 'Peter Rabbit Country', which would have been doubly ironic for a region which, for many, is a modern-day representation of an imagined rural past made famous by the poems of Wordsworth and the paintings of Turner. In short, postmodern travel in hyper-reality is tourism in constructed reality, the ultimate form of which is likely to be manifested in virtual reality or virtual travel.

The socio-cultural consequences of tourism

It is, perhaps, inevitable that the development of tourism impacts upon destination societies and cultures. In fact, in some respects it would be considered unfortunate for tourism *not* to result in certain consequences for destinations, for the simple reason that tourism is usually promoted with the aim of achieving economic and social development and diversification. Therefore, social consequences of tourism in the form of higher income, greater employment opportunities, improved education and healthcare facilities, infrastructural developments and an overall improvement in local communities' quality of life are largely welcomed.

At the same time, given the nature of tourism, other socio-cultural impacts are also inevitable. That is, all tourists travel to destinations, carrying with them their values, beliefs, perceptions and behavioural modes as a form of cultural baggage. Whilst on holiday they interact with members of the local, host community and this interaction brings about social consequences, whether simply as a result of the physical presence and behaviour of tourists or because of the cultural gap that exists between tourists and their hosts.

Some of these consequences may, again, be beneficial; indeed, tourism is seen by some as a vehicle to greater international harmony and understanding (WTO 1980). Unfortunately, however, more often than not it is the negative, emotive consequences of tourism that gain most publicity or notoriety, in particular the consequences of mass tourism: 'tourists seem to be the incarnation of the materialism, philistinism and cultural homogenisation that is sweeping all before it in a converging world' (Macnaught 1982). It is for this reason that the solution to the 'problem' of mass tourism is seen to lie in the development of responsible, alternative (to mass) forms of tourism.

Many of the social consequences of tourism are well known and some, such as the problems of tourism-related child prostitution or the displacement of communities to make way for tourist development, have been publicised globally. However, for our purposes here, it is first important to develop an understanding as to why and to what extent socio-cultural consequences occur. Therefore, this section of the chapter will consider:

- factors that determine the extent of socio-cultural change

- the nature of tourist-host encounters

- host attitudes towards tourists

- social impacts on tourists.

The chapter will then conclude with a brief outline of the socio-cultural impacts of tourism and an introduction to the concept of sustainable tourism as a potential solution.

Factors determining socio-cultural change

Although it is likely that all destinations experience social and cultural consequences of tourism development, the degree to which these consequences are felt or are manifested is dependent upon a number of factors. As a general rule, the greater the difference between the cultural and economic characteristics of the destination and those of the tourists' own society, the more significant are the social and cultural impacts likely to be (WTO 1981). More specifically, however, the extent of tourism-induced socio-cultural change may be influenced by:

- **the types or numbers of tourists**: normally, it is considered that higher numbers of mass tourists will impact more on host societies than relatively few explorer-type tourists. However, it can also be argued that an independent traveller visiting an isolated community may have more of an impact than, say, large numbers of tourists in a purpose-built, self-contained club resort.

- **the size and development of the tourism industry:** the larger the tourism industry relative to the size of the local community, the greater is its impact likely to be. However, the more established or mature the industry, the less likely are significant socio-cultural changes to occur.

- **the relative importance of the tourism industry**: the consequences of tourism will be felt more keenly in destinations that are highly dependent on tourism than in more mixed economies.

- **the pace of tourism development**: it has been found that socio-cultural impacts are more likely to be experienced when the development of tourism is rapid and uncontrolled.

It is also important to consider the extent to which tourism, as opposed to other pressures and influences, leads to social and cultural change in destination societies. That is, all societies are dynamic; they are in a constant state of change and no society is immune from outside influences. Tourism is undoubtedly one of these external influences but, frequently, tourism *contributes to*, but does not *cause*, social and cultural change. In other words, global information systems, the activities of multi-national corporations or the general processes of industrialisation and urbanisation potentially have a far greater impact on social structures and values yet, all too often, it is tourism that is blamed for what are seen as undesirable changes. Therefore, care must be taken to determine the precise components of social and cultural change.

The nature of tourist-host encounters

As pointed out earlier, it is virtually impossible to be a tourist in isolation. Tourists inevitably come into contact with local people in destination areas and, even if such encounters are brief, such as when buying a souvenir in a shop, a variety of social processes are at work which determine the nature of that encounter. This, in turn, goes a long way to determining or explaining the potential socio-cultural consequences of tourism because, generally speaking, the more unbalanced or unequal the encounter or relationship, the more likely it is that negative impacts will occur. Thus, understanding the nature of tourist-host encounters is of fundamental importance to explaining and minimising tourism's socio-cultural consequences.

Of course, there are potentially as many types of encounter as there are tourists and hosts but, nevertheless, it is possible to make a number of observations about the nature of tourist-host encounters. In general, the greater the economic, social and cultural gap between the tourist and host, the less balanced will their encounter or relationship be. For example, the relative wealth of tourists compared to that of their hosts, particularly in less developed countries, is a fundamental difference that may lead to feelings of resentment or inferiority on the part of local people. However, differences in values and attitudes may also be significant. More specifically, four other characteristics of tourist-host encounters have been identified (see Mathieson and Wall 1982: 136):

- most encounters are transitory or fleeting, the resultant relationships being shallow and superficial;

- most encounters are constrained by temporal restrictions (the two weeks of the holiday or the tourist season) and by the location or spread of tourist facilities and amenities;

- most encounters are pre-planned or lack spontaneity as hospitality becomes commercialised; and

- tourist-host encounters tend to be unbalanced, local people perhaps feeling inferior or subservient to tourists.

To this list a further characteristic may be added, namely, that many tourists travel with an apparent lack of knowledge, understanding or sensitivity to local culture or customs in destination areas. Whilst this raises broader issues about tourists' motivation and behaviour and questions of responsibility that are beyond the scope of this chapter, it represents a potential barrier to meaningful or balanced encounters and, hence, raises the potential for negative social consequences. Similarly, although it is dangerous to generalise the varied and complex social processes involved in encounters between tourists and local people, it is likely that some or all of the other characteristics will be identifiable in many such encounters. Thus, it would appear that some form of negative impact is the inevitable result of the typically unbalanced or unequal nature of inter-action between tourists and hosts.

This, however, need not always be the case. It is possible for tourists to develop meaningful relationships with local people, particularly when they frequently visit one destination, and, as we shall now consider, much also depends upon the attitudes of local people towards tourists.

Host attitudes towards tourists

It is widely accepted that tourists are people characterised by a range of expectations, attitudes, motivations and modes of behaviour and that these differences can result in a variety of tourism impacts and encounters with local people. It is important to recognise, however, that local communities are also made up of individuals who themselves possess an enormous variety of attitudes, values and perceptions. In other words, local people may have varying degrees of either positive or negative attitudes towards tourism and tourists, attitudes which are a vital consideration in tourism planning and management. It is essential that local communities are favourably disposed towards the development of tourism; if not, the possibility of a community backlash may arise, leading to an unwillingness to support or work in the tourism industry or, in the extreme, demonstrations of outright hostility towards tourists. Thus, the attitude of the host community is an important variable in the extent to which the socio-cultural consequences of tourism are both perceived and accepted.

Research into host attitudes towards tourists have found that, not surprisingly, positive attitudes amongst local communities are positively correlated to employment and place of residence. That is, those who are employed in the tourism industry and who live close to tourist areas are more favourable towards tourists. At the same time, research has also shown that local people often balance the benefits and costs of tourism development and that positive attitudes may be evident even where socio-cultural costs are incurred. For example, it was found that in Santa Marta, a coastal resort in Colombia, residents felt that, overall, tourism had been beneficial, particularly in terms of employment and infrastructural developments, despite higher seasonal food prices and a greater incidence of robberies and other illegal activities (Belisle and Hoy 1980).

Importantly, however, the attitudes of local people can also vary according to the stage of tourism development in destination areas. That is, the perceptions of host communities and the degree of socio-cultural impact change over time and may be directly related to the stage of tourism development that a destination has reached. In a widely quoted model, Butler (1980) suggests that resorts pass through a 'life-cycle' similar to the product life-cycle theory in marketing. In the early stages of development, when there are relatively few visitors and local people offer hospitality on an informal basis, tourist-host relations are likely to be good and negative impacts minimal. However, as the resort progressively develops, attracting increasing numbers of mass tourists, tourism becomes more commercialised and local people become ambivalent or apathetic towards tourists, feelings which may in the long run be transformed into annoyance or hostility if the resort stagnates or goes into decline. It is also at these latter stages in the life cycle of a destination that the socio-cultural consequences of tourism may be most keenly felt, when the potential benefits of tourism become outweighed by the negative and costs experienced by the local community.

In reality, few, if any, tourist destinations progress through to the decline stage, although the history of a number of traditional British seaside resorts appears to match closely Butler's model. Equally, open hostility or antagonism towards tourists is rare. That is, local communities more often than not tolerate tourists and accept the socio-cultural consequences brought about by tourism, although one exception to this is the case of the village of Agia Napa in Cyprus. Following the rapid development of the once small village into a mass tourism resort, the entire original village relocated a few kilometres away to avoid the problems and social impacts of tourism.

However, the important point is that, given the nature of tourism and the characteristics of tourist-host encounters, some degree of tourism-induced socio-cultural change or impact in destination communities is inevitable. Indeed, to expect otherwise is unrealistic because tourism, like any other business, incurs 'production' costs. Such costs are usually financial, such as investment in tourism facilities and infrastructure, but negative consequences for host communities should also represent, in effect, a debit on the tourism development balance sheet. The challenge for tourism planners and managers is then to ensure that these costs do not outweigh the benefits that tourism brings to destination areas.

Socio-cultural impacts on tourists

Before introducing finally the range of socio-cultural consequences of tourism that may be experienced by host communities, one issue that deserves consideration is the extent to which tourists, rather than hosts, similarly experience such consequences. That is, attention is generally focused upon the impacts of tourism on destination areas but, socially and culturally, tourism is a two-way process and, frequently, local cultures and people impact significantly on visitors.

At a basic level, such impacts occur when tourists become the victims of crime or health problems. Indeed, becoming the target of criminal activity has always been regarded as one of the risks of travel and tourism, as have health problems. More recently, however, the opening up of more distant or exotic locations to mass tourism has resulted in increasing incidence of tourists contracting serious diseases, such as malaria, whilst an increase in the number of cases of 'old' diseases, such as diphtheria, which have been virtually eradicated in Western societies, has been directly associated with the growth in tourism to previously inaccessible areas.

However, a variety of other 'reverse' socio-cultural impacts can be identified, including:

- the internationalisation of fashions and tastes in clothing, music, art forms, cuisine and so on;

- a reduction in national xenophobia resulting in a greater awareness and acceptance of different cultures;

- the verification or changing of tourists' perceptions of different places, peoples and cultures; studies have also shown that tourists often return home with a more positive attitude towards their own society and culture; and

- the adoption by tourists, on either a temporary or permanent basis, of new cultural practices.

Little attention has been paid to these socio-cultural impacts of tourism on tourists and tourism generating societies and it is likely to be a fruitful area of research. Nevertheless, the fact remains that the majority of the socio-cultural consequences of tourism are experienced by destination societies and it is no coincidence that the rapid growth in international tourism has been matched by increasing concern about the impacts of that growth. More often than not it is the negative consequences that attract most attention but, as we shall now see, tourism may also bring benefits to host societies.

Tourism's socio-cultural consequences: an overview

Given the extent of concern about and research into the impacts of tourism development, it is not surprising that there is a wealth of information and case studies in the tourism literature. Therefore, the discussion here is limited to an introductory overview of the topic (see Sharpley 1999 for more detail).

Although the effects of tourism on host societies are often collectively referred to as socio-cultural consequences or impacts, it is useful to distinguish, albeit somewhat artificially, between social and cultural consequences. Thus, social consequences can be thought of as the more immediate effects of tourism on local people and their quality of life, whereas cultural consequences are longer term changes that occur in the context of social values, attitudes and behaviour, as well as changes in the production of cultural art forms and practices.

i. Social consequences

The more immediate, social consequences of tourism result from both the overall development of tourism and also the more specific inter-action between tourists and local people.

Firstly, tourism is primarily developed as a means of wider social and economic development. The potential beneficial social consequences are, for example, infrastructural improvements, the protection or improvement of the physical environment, and the provision of services and facilities that benefit tourists and locals alike. More specifically, tourism provides income and employment opportunities and, in the longer term, the resources for investment in essential social services, such as education and health. In particular, the employment opportunities offered by the development of tourism have, in many societies, brought a new freedom and independence and an improved social condition for many women.

However, the extent to which these benefits accrue to destination societies is often limited. It is widely accepted, for example, that many tourism-related jobs are low grade and low paid, whilst more generally, tourism rarely fulfils its role as a vehicle to economic and social development. Furthermore, negative social impacts may occur, such as changes in community structures. It is often the case, for example, that younger people are drawn from inland rural areas to the coast or cities to work in the tourism industry. This rural-urban migration pattern often results in a population imbalance in rural areas and the polarisation of local societies between younger, more affluent groups and the older, perhaps more traditional generations.

Secondly, the physical presence of tourists, their behaviour and their inter-action with local people impacts upon local communities in a variety of ways. Some of these may be immediate, such as inappropriate behaviour, displays of conspicuous consumption or simply the inconvenience caused by large numbers of holiday makers, causing annoyance or resentment amongst the local population. Other consequences include:

- **the demonstration effect:** tourism introduces new or alien values or lifestyles in destination areas. Local people may attempt to emulate behaviour or styles of dress, or to strive to achieve levels of wealth, demonstrated by tourists.

- **crime:** although there is little evidence to directly link increases in crime with the development of tourism, there is little doubt that where there are significant numbers of tourists criminal activity is also evident. This may result in increased expenditure on law enforcement, the growth in activities such as gambling and black-market operations, increased crime against residents and, potentially, a reduction in tourism as experienced by Florida in the early 1990s.

- **religion:** in tourism destinations, religious buildings, shrines and practices have become commoditised. That is, they have become an attraction and a part of the tourism product, gazed upon and 'collected' by tourists. As a result, there is frequently conflict between local communities, devout visitors and tourists as religious rituals or places of worship are disrupted by tourists.

- *prostitution:* although care must be taken in apportioning the blame on tourism, there is no doubt that, in many destinations, tourism has led to an increase in prostitution. The social impact of this can be devastating, particularly in the case of child prostitution and the spread of sexually transmitted diseases.

ii. Cultural consequences

Over time, the culture of host societies may change and adapt either directly or indirectly as a result of tourism. Much of the literature is concerned in particular with the way in which cultural forms, such as arts and crafts or carnivals, festivals and religious events become adapted, trivialised, packaged and commoditised for consumption by tourists, and there is certainly no doubt that this occurs on a wide scale. For example, many art forms become mass produced as souvenirs (i.e. 'airport art') whilst, frequently, cultural rituals are transformed and staged for tourists, becoming devoid of all meaning to the participants. It is also true, however, that tourism also encourages the revitalisation or resurgence of interest in traditional cultural practices and there are many examples of how tourism supports the redevelopment of traditional art forms and production techniques.

Less visibly, tourism also contributes to broader, deeper cultural transformations in destination societies. These are changes that occur in a society's values, moral codes, behavioural modes and identifying characteristics, such as dress and language. As mentioned earlier, it is difficult to separate the influence of tourism from other factors which induce cultural change but, nevertheless, it is generally accepted that tourism can accelerate this process, largely through what is known as acculturation.

Acculturation is the process whereby, when two cultures come into contact (for example, through tourist-host encounters), over time they will become more like each other through a process of borrowing. By implication, if one culture is stronger or more dominant than the other, then it is more likely that this borrowing will be a one way process. The extent to which tourism contributes to the acculturation process will vary depending on a variety of factors, such as the cultural gulf between the tourist and the host and the influence of other forces yet in many instances cultural change can be directly attributable to tourism.

Conclusion

This chapter has been concerned with the relationship between tourism and societies, societies which both generate tourists and receive tourists. On the one hand, the way in which tourists behave, their motivations, expectations, perceptions, attitudes, and the type of tourism they participate in, is to a great extent determined or influenced by a variety of social factors. Therefore, from an industry point of view, it is important to recognise and understand how the demand for tourism is influenced by these factors in order to be able to both better satisfy the needs of tourists and to respond to changes in those needs. On the other hand, tourism and tourists bring about both positive and negative impacts upon destination societies and, thus, the challenge for tourism planners and managers is to balance these so that, overall, host communities benefit from the development of tourism. One way of achieving this balance is through the development of what is widely referred to as sustainable tourism, an approach which seeks to optimise the developmental benefits of tourism and the experience of tourists themselves whilst minimising the negative consequences of tourism on destination environments and communities (for example, see Inskeep 1991). However, the viability of sustainable tourism development remains the subject of intense debate, in particular with respect to tourist motivation and behaviour (McKercher 1993; Sharpley 2000).

Importantly, however, the two tourism-society relationships outlined in this chapter are not mutually exclusive. That is, the factors which influence tourists' behaviour also effect the nature of tourist-host encounters which, in turn, play a role in determining the extent of the socio-cultural consequences of tourism. This points to the inevitability of tourism's socio-cultural impacts and the conclusion that, if destinations are to be benefit from tourism development, then certain costs (including negative socio-cultural consequences) must be absorbed. The issue then becomes the degree of impact or change that is acceptable; the responsibility for that decision lies not with tourists or the tourism industry, but with the governments of destination societies.

Discussion questions

1. *Evaluate the contribution of tourist typologies to the understanding and prediction of tourist behaviour.*

2. *Is work the principal extrinsic factor influencing the motivation for tourism?*

3. *How important do you consider it to be for a touist to experience 'authenticity'?*

4. *Using different destinations as examples, explain the factors that determine the extent to which tourism development brings about social and cultural impacts.*

Further reading

Apostolopoulos, Y. *et al.* (eds.) (1996), *The Sociology of Tourism: Theoretical and Empirical Investigations*, London: Routledge.

Bossevain, J. (ed) (1996), *Coping with Tourists*, Oxford: Berghahn Books.

Cooper, C. et al. (1998), *Tourism: Principles and Practice, 2nd Edition*, Harlow: Longman – Part 2.

Holloway, J.C. (1998), *The Business of Tourism, 5th Edition*, Harlow: Longman – Chapter 17.

Mathieson, A. and Wall, G. (1982), *Tourism: Economic, Physical and Social Impacts*, Harloww: Longman.

Sharpley, R. (1999), *Tourism, Tourists & Society, 2nd Edition*, Huntingdon: Elm Publications.

References

Belisle, F. and Hoy, D. (1980), The perceived impact of tourism by residents: a case study of Santa Marta, Colombia, *Annals of Tourism Research* 7(1): 83-101.

Boorstin, D. (1964), *The Image: A Guide to Pseudo-Events in America*, New York: Harper & Row.

Butler, R. (1980), The concept of a tourism area cycle of evolution, *Canadian Geographer* 24: 5-12.

Clarke, J. and Critcher, C. (1985), *The Devil Makes Work: Leisure in Capitalist Britain*, Basingstoke: Macmillan.

Cohen, E. (1972), Towards a sociology of international tourism, *Social Research* 39(1): 64-81.

Cohen, E. (1979), A phenomenology of tourist experiences, *Sociology* 13: 179-201.

Dann, G. (1977), Anomie, ego-enhancement and tourism, *Annals of Tourism Research* 4(4): 184-194.

Dann, G. (1981), Tourist motivation: an appraisal, *Annals of Tourism Research* 8(2): 187-219.

de Kadt, E. (1979), *Tourism: Passport to Development?* New York: OUP.

Eco, U. (1995), *Faith in Fakes: Travels in Hyperreality*, London: Minerva.

Gilbert, D. (1991), An examination of the consumer behaviour process related to tourism, in C. Cooper (ed.) *Progress in Tourism, Recreation and Hospitality Management Vol III*, London: Bellhaven Press: 78-105.

Goodall, B. (1991), Understanding holiday choice, in C. Cooper (ed) *Progress in Tourism, Recreation and Hospitality Management Vol III*, London: Bellhaven Press: 58-77.

Harvey, D. (1990), *The Condition of Postmodernity*, Oxford: Blackwell.

Inskeep, E. (1991), *Tourism Planning: An Integrated and Sustainable Development Approach*, New York: Van Nostrand Reinhold.

Krippendorf, J. (1986), Tourism in the system of industrial society, *Annals of Tourism Research* 13(4): 517-532.

Lowyck, E., Van Langenhove, L. and Bollaert, L. (1992), Typologies of tourist roles, in P. Johnson and B. Thomas (eds.) *Choice and Demand in Tourism*, London: Mansell: 13-32.

MacCannell, D. (1989), *The Tourist: A New Theory of the Leisure Class, 2nd Edition*, New York: Schocken Books.

Mathieson, A. and Wall, G. (1982), *Tourism: Economic, Physical and Social Impacts*, Harlow: Longman.

Mc.Kercher, B. (1993), Some fundamental truths about tourism: understanding tourism's social and environmental impacts, *Journal of Sustainable Tourism* 1(1): 6-16.

Moutinho, L. (1987), Consumer behaviour in tourism, *European Journal of Marketing* 21(10): 5-44.

Parrinello, G. (1993), Motivation and anticipation in post-industrial tourism, *Annals of Tourism Research* 20(2): 233-249.

Pretes, M. (1995), Postmodern tourism: the Santa Claus industry, *Annals of Tourism Research* 22(1): 1-15.

Sharpley, R. (1999), *Tourism, Tourists & Society, 2nd Edition*, Huntingdon: Elm Publications.

Sharpley, R. (2000), Tourism and sustainable development: exploring the theoretical divide, *Journal of Sustainable Tourism* 8(1): 1-19.

Silver, I. (1993), Marketing authenticity in Third World countries, *Annals of Tourism Research* 20: 302-318.

Turner, L. and Ash J. (1975), *The Golden Hordes: International Tourism and the Pleasure Periphery*, London: Constable.

Urry, J. (1990a), The consumption of tourism, *Sociology* 24(1): 23-35.

Urry, J. (1990b), *The Tourist Gaze*, London: Sage Publications.

Walter, J. (1982), Social limits to tourism, *Leisure Studies* 1: 295-304.

Wood, K. and House, S. (1991), *The Good Tourist: A Worldwide Guide for the Green Traveller*, London: Mandarin.

World Tourism Organisation (1980), *Manila Declaration on World Tourism*, Madrid: World Tourism Organisation.

World Tourism Organisation (1981), *The Social and Cultural Dimension of Tourism*, Madrid: World Tourism Organisation.

Young, Sir G. (1973), *Tourism: Blessing or Blight?*, Harmondsworth: Penguin.

Index